William Edward Brown

A History of
18th Century
Russian Literature

ARDIS / / / ANN ARBOR

Library of Congress Cataloging in Publication Data

Brown, William Edward, 1904-
    A history of eighteenth-century Russian literature.

    Bibliography: p.
    Includes index.
    1. Russian literature—18th century—History and criticism.
I. Title.
PG3007.B7   891.7'09'002   79-21986
ISBN 0-88233-341-0

Published by Ardis,
2901 Heatherway,
Ann Arbor, Michigan, 48104

Manufactured by Lakeland Press, Dexter, Michigan

For Jeannie

FOREWORD

A new book on any subject needs to be justified. Does it add enough new information or enjoyment, or both, to the world to compensate for the trees that had to be sacrificed to make its paper? Probably a book on such a relatively obscure subject as the present one needs more justification than most, for it is certainly caviar to the general. The head of the English Department of a very reputable New England college said to me in surprise when I told him that I was writing on eighteenth-century Russian literature: "Why, is there any?" His attitude is not unusual. Every literate person knows the great prose of Russia's nineteenth century, and a good many know something of the Golden Age, even of the Silver Age poetry—"But didn't everything really start with Pushkin?" So as far as new information is concerned, the present book will certainly be providing an American reader with a good deal of it. Enjoyment is another matter, but I hope that whatever the interpreter's faults, the literature itself, even at second hand and in such straightforward translations as I have provided may afford enjoyment—at least to a reader sensitive to literature.

Over many years of teaching comparative literature courses to undergraduates I have become ever more firmly convinced that all European literatures are one, and that no national literature should be studied in isolation; and that, viewing the same truth from the other side, anyone who has a taste for, let us say, the poetry of Shelley and Keats, will enjoy Hölderlin and Leopardi and Oehlenschläger and Baratynsky. Language is the only barrier—but too much can be made of this barrier. It is a translucent screen, not an opaque wall. Someone who can go inside it can interpret what he finds—and second-best though such an approach may be, it is better than the alternative, which is to let an immense body of humanly created beauty go unappreciated. Ideally one might hope that such a study as mine would fire some of its readers to learn Russian, approach the literature as I have and either see what I have seen or confute me as a humbug. If it has such an effect in even one case, I shall be overjoyed; but what I more modestly hope for is that it may acquaint the open-minded literate reader with a fascinating new area of enjoyment, "seen through a glass darkly," but still rewarding.

It is for the lover of literature in general that this book is chiefly intended, and it is for him that I have provided copious bits of translation by way of illustration. But I have in mind also the needs of the student of Russian who knows the language and the more familiar literature of the nineteenth and twentieth centuries, but is baffled by the seemingly remote and alien style of the eighteenth. It is for him that I have expatiated on linguistic matters, on prosody, on technical poetic devices and the like, which the more general reader may find unintelligible or uninteresting. I have thought it better to be over-inclusive rather than to scant either class of reader of what is needed. It is easy enough, after all, to skip what seems superfluous or irrelevant.

This is a work of interpretation, not of academic scholarship. The reader will find in it an extensive bibliography of books and periodical articles in English on all aspects of eighteenth-century Russian literature. This is for the student or non-Russian-reading scholar, and I trust they will find it useful for investigation of special topics. There are not, however, many references to it in the notes to my text, for a very good reason: there are very few items in this list that I have used for this study. I have preferred to emphasize the original works themselves, in the context of world literature of this period.

In this connection let me make one more disclaimer. I am not and have never been a devotee of any particular school of literary criticism, whether biographical, sociological, political, psychological, mythological, or what have you. I have always regarded it as the interpreter's prime duty to treat his text with respect and say what he sees in it clearly and precisely, and not make it a pretext for displays of his own cleverness or fashionable critical jargon. In saying this I shall no doubt have alienated a whole group of the reading public who guages the quality of a critical work by its unintelligibility. I hope, in compensation, to win the approval of those who share my belief that standard literate English is adequate to express whatever a critic needs to express.

Russian eighteenth-century literature is very spottily represented in English translation, and a good deal of what exists is outmoded, inexact or downright wrong. Rather than undertake the labor of sorting out the good from the unusable, I have preferred to make almost all the translations in this book myself; whatever their faults, they have at least the virtue of uniformity.

I have had the encouragement of many friends and well-wishers while I worked, which I acknowledge with deep gratitude. Numerous former students will be relieved to see something tangible born at last from my labors —and I hope it may not prove to be Horace's "ridiculous mouse." For the assistance of Clyde Haselden, Robert Gennett, Daniel Evans and others of the David Bishop Skillman library of Lafayette College I am most grateful. Stimulating conversations with my friends Dr. Jean-Pierre Cap and Dr. Bronius Vaskelis of the Lafayette College Department of Languages have made an intangible but real contribution to this book, which I am happy to record. And without the devoted assistance of my sister, Mrs. George Winston, the whole project would have been impossible.

The kind permission of Harvard University Press to quote from Mr. Roderick Page Thaler's edition of the Leo Wiener translation of Radishchev's *Journey from St. Petersburg to Moscow* is herewith gratefully acknowledged.

Grafton, Vermont   *William Edward Brown*
August 1979

CONTENTS

NOTES / BIBLIOGRAPHY / INDEX

A History of
18th Century
Russian Literature

PART I

LITERATURE DURING THE REIGNS OF PETER I
AND HIS IMMEDIATE SUCCESSORS

Peter the Great, circa 1720, by Ivan Nikitin

CHAPTER I

INTRODUCTION AND GENERALITIES

Russian literature of the eighteenth century represents in so many ways a sharp break with the traditions and practices of the past that the impression has not unnaturally been given that here is a literature of entirely foreign derivation, artificially imposed on an unwilling Russian people, like the fashions of beardless chins and powdered wigs, by an all-powerful autocrat. Medieval Russian literature is, with very few exceptions, created by churchmen and for churchmen; the literature of the eighteenth century is entirely secular, created just as exclusively by and for a non-clerical population. The dominant genres of medieval literature—chronicle, saint's life, homily, compilation of edifying stories—are pushed into the background in the eighteenth century and almost, if not quite, disappear. And most striking of all: the literature of medieval Russia is exclusively in prose, verse being a form unheard-of; the eighteenth century is an age predominantly of verse—and of drama, again a genre which had no literary existence in the Middle Ages, although non-literary oral forms of mimetic representation undoubtedly existed.

The impression of what a geologist would call a "non-conformity" between the eighteenth and earlier centuries is, however, a false one. A close look at the immediately preceding period reveals in all cases a continuity between the eighteenth century and the past. To be sure, a foreign—i.e., western —model is always to be found, but there is also a native foundation on which to build. Thus, for example, in the sudden emergence and dominance of verse: medieval Russia was not ignorant of verse—only this was of an oral, unwritten, kind. When the foreign model was introduced—the Polish mode of syllable-counting—it dominated for a time in spite of its patently unsuitable character, but was ultimately discarded in favor of a new system—the syllabo-tonic—based on a compromise between the foreign principle of verse based on the *syllable* count and the native one, based on *accent* count. Similarly with other types of literature. The medieval chronicle lingers on during the eighteenth century (e.g., Tatishchev and Shcherbatov), but merges insensibly with western models of genuine history until by the first decade of the nineteenth century Karamzin's great *History of the Russian State* appears. The various sorts of plot-oriented narrative prose which appear in the seventeenth century—the exemplary tale, the historical romance, the chivalric adventure story, the *picaresca*, etc.—merge again with western models to create the complex phenomenon of the modern novel; thus there is a continuity between such an "exemplary tale" as "Savva Grudtsyn" and Karamzin's "Poor Liza," between the quasi-picaresque "Frol Skobeev" and Chulkov's "The Comely Cook," between the "Tale of the Founding of the Page's Monastery of Tver" and such a historical romance as Kheraskov's "Numa Pompilius," or between the extravagances of "Bova Korolevich" and "Uruslan Lazarevich" and Emin's "Adventures of Miramond." Everywhere we see the seventeenth century—chaotic and literarily immature as it is in Russia—as the era of transition. Even in the only literary genre which demonstrably has no native Russian roots, the tragedy, the seventeenth century provides models for the eighteenth—from Simeon Polotsky's "Parable of the Prodigal Son" to Feofan Prokopovich's "Tragicomedy of St. Vladimir."

The eighteenth century in Russian literature is thus by no means separated from the native traditions of form by a sharp discontinuity. There is, however, a fundamental separation of a much more significant sort. The ecclesiastical, "other-worldly" orientation of the Middle Ages, while it does not of course suddenly disappear without trace in and after the era of Peter the Great, does become an anachronism and is replaced for the most part by a "this-worldly" outlook which may run the gamut from the grossest kind of vulgar hedonism to the lofty civic morality represented by Nikolai Novikov in his earlier works, and by Alexander Radishchev at the end of the century. Here too, the western influence—the theories of Hobbes and Locke, Diderot and Rousseau—plays a large part in the emancipation; but without native roots this influence could scarcely have so easily overthrown the world-view of many centuries. In one important respect here too, however, we see a continuity: the concept of literature as existing primarily for instructional purposes, the suspicion of any kind of writing aimed primarily at affording entertainment—these feelings permeate eighteenth-century literature just as fully as they did the writing of the Middle Ages, only now the instructional goal is "enlightenment," not Christian morality as such. One of the most popular verse genres of the century is the "fable"; and the fable is always provided with a "moral"; its existence is conditioned by its didactic purpose. The teaching, however, is not specifically Christian, but is an endeavor to inculcate moral conduct unsupported by other-worldly sanctions. Even more strikingly: the comedy, a genre which one might suppose to be entertainment literature pure and simple, is given literary justification only by the obligation of showing "vices" in a bad light, and "virtue" triumphant in the last act. The satire, another favored eighteenth-century genre, must also, at least ostensibly, have the betterment of public morals as its object. Catherine the Great's favorite Horatian motto defines the object of satire as *"ridendo castigat mores."* The chief reproaches levelled at eighteenth-century satirists were that they sometimes tended to such indignant vituperation that the

4

ridendo was forgotten, and their purpose of "correcting morals" vitiated by the indignation which their attacks aroused.

The literature of the Russian Middle Ages was one marked by great homogeneity. Its creators were churchmen, largely because the clergy was the only literate class of the population. Its audience, in so far as the literature was to be read by individuals, was of necessity also one of churchmen; but of course such literature, through being read aloud, was accessible to secular audiences also. In any case, medieval literature was not socially differentiated. Boyar and commoner were both illiterate, and both at least nominally Christian. Literature does not usually show evidences of being directed at any particular social class, but at "Orthodox Christians" in general. The seventeenth century sees for the first time a social differentiation emerging in literature. Certain genres, such as the chivalric tale of adventure or the satirical parody (e.g., "Ersh Ershovich") are obviously created by and for a lower class, just emerging into literacy, while such genres as the congratulatory poem or the verse tragedy just as obviously belong to the upper class, or more specifically, to the court of the monarch. In the eighteenth century this stratification becomes ever more prominent. Most of the major poets of the first half of the century, even when they are not themselves noblemen (e.g., Lomonosov) create for nobility and the court. At the same time, plebeian writers such as Chulkov or Emin direct their productions toward their own class; and it is only seldom that the two audiences overlap (perhaps with Fonvizin?). In a rather general way, verse in the eighteenth century tends to fall into the upper-class purview, while prose is the medium of the lower classes. Tragedy, an exotic form as has been mentioned, is exclusively an upper-class commodity, but comedy, at least of the genuinely funny varieties, belongs just as much to the plebs. As the "lower classes," that is, chiefly the urban bourgeoisie, become more literate and better educated, and as there grows up a large and influential class of non-noble *chinovniki*, or government officials, the literary differentiation becomes less noticeable, and begins to disappear by the nineteenth century.

When the eighteenth century comes to mind, the word "classicism" is likely to accompany it. Just what is the meaning of this association, and what precisely *is* classicism? A generation or more ago the term would have borne the derogatory prefix "pseudo," or at least the neutral "neo." Some kind of explanation seems in order, for the terms "classicism" and "classical" will be encountered frequently in this study.

In the first place, the entity we are dealing with is one of what D. S. Likhachev terms "period styles," that is, pervasive artistic uniformities affecting many different areas of creativity--in this case, not only literature, but architecture, painting, sculpture, music, even, as Likhachev remarks, "the art of gardens." Such a uniformity must obviously be based upon a universally accepted philosophical and aesthetic premise of some sort. Such a premise is to be found here in what is known as the doctrine of imitation and the

5

canonization of a set of models to be imitated. Eighteenth-century theorists, far from respecting originality as a virtue in the creative arts, derogated it: true art consists in the faithful following of the best models in each kind. Such models are the "classics," and hence the terms "classical" applied to the age. The theory of course implies a curious historical pessimism: the best in every kind has already been created, and can only be approached, perhaps equalled, but never superseded, by subsequent efforts. The models—the "classics"—are not, however, exclusively the great works of Greece and Rome. This is a misconception which the "pseudo-" prefix enshrines, and which would imply that eighteenth-century imitation is a "false" copy of something real, presumably the Greek and Latin originals, which must be the sole "classics." The eighteenth century does accept most of the Greek and Roman monuments as classics, that is, as models to be copied, but not these exclusively. Other great literary ages have also created such classics, as, for example, the Renaissance and the France of Louis XIV. Greek and Latin models for drama, for example, have been equalled by the great tragic and comic poets of France—Corneille, Racine, Molière and Voltaire—and these in turn have assumed the role of classics. In Russia the classically oriented generation that followed Sumarokov regarded *him* as a classic, just as he regarded Racine and Molière.

The theory of imitation was closely associated with the theory of "kinds." Greek and Roman literature was believed to be compartmentalized into a certain number of pigeon-holes bearing such labels as: epic, tragedy, epigram, pastoral, and the like. In each of these compartments would be found a few "classical" models: e.g., Homer, Virgil and Voltaire in that of the epic. Any aspirant in one of these fields must imitate the models of that *kind*: to imitate a pastoral while writing an epic would of course be absurd, for the compartments allowed no interpenetration. That Tasso, for example, did exactly this in his *Jerusalem Delivered,* accounts incidentally for his neglect as a model: it is not until the romantic period that his and Ariosto's great epics attain full recognition.

There is no point at this time in attempting an exhaustive definition of classicism, which can better be appreciated in the concrete examples which we shall encounter in the course of this study. What has been said will suffice to clarify what is meant by "the classics" and hence by "classicism"—an ideology based on veneration of supreme models—as a term applied to the age. But the question then arises: to what extent is this term really applicable to the eighteenth century?

It is customary in Russian literary studies to label Alexander Sumarokov the "classicist par excellence." One critic, somewhat cynically, has opined that he is indeed the only one! Certainly not all his contemporaries can be so labelled without qualification. Lomonosov, with whom Sumarokov was most violently at odds on literary—and not only on literary—matters, has evident traits of the "Baroque" style, which in the West had become

6

obsolete as a period style by the end of the preceding century. The Baroque in Russia belongs to the seventeenth century—e.g., Andrei Belobotsky or Silvester Medvedev—but dominates at least the first third of the eighteenth century as well—witness Kantemir and Trediakovsky, as well as Lomonosov. Full classicism certainly begins with Sumarokov. But again: when we say that Lomonosov, Kantemir and Trediakovsky belong to the Baroque, the statement is too crude and unqualified. There are "classical" traits in all of them. "Period styles" do not change with such abruptness that a line can be drawn between two contemporaries, leaving one on one side, a "classical," and one on the other, a "Baroque" writer. And the same phenomenon can be seen at the other end of the century as well. By the time we reach Dmitriev and Karamzin, we are aware of a strongly anti-classical tendency: the rigidly compartmentalized genres begin to break down and interpenetrate; the "classical" models begin to give way to new models, from the Celtic and Northern lands· ("Ossian" and the Norse *Edda*, etc.); and most fundamentally, originality begins to take precedence over faithful imitation. The movement which these tendencies represent is usually called "sentimentalism," from another typical anti-classical reaction, the dethronement of the "reason" as the central human quality in favor of the emotions or "sentiments." In Germany this movement is quite commonly called *Irrationalismus*, but the connotations of "irrationalism" in English are too negative to permit its use in this context. Whatever it is called, this anti-classical tendency is recognizably a prelude to the next great "period style," romanticism, which in Russian begins early in the nineteenth century with poets such as Zhukovsky and Batiushkov. Indeed, "sentimentalism" and "pre-romanticism" are almost interchangeable as labels. But does "sentimentalism" appear at any time *before* it comes belligerently into the open with Dmitriev and Karamzin? Yes, it certainly does, with the "Lvov Circle," especially Kapnist, and most prominently, with the century's greatest poet, Derzhavin. And again as with Lomonosov: here is a poet who marks a transition, whose work shows traits of two different "period styles." Derzhavin in most respects is anti-classical—but by no means in all, as we shall see. There are aspects of his style which link him with the classicism of the past. Derzhavin's poetical career begins in the 1770s, and from there to the end of the century "sentimentalism," in varying degrees with various writers, shares the literary scene with waning "classicism."

It appears, then, that for Russia at least, "classicism" by no means dominates the entire eighteenth century. Beginning with, let us say, about 1747 (Sumarokov's first tragedy) and extending through the early 1770s, it begins to give ground to pre-romantic trends, quite seriously about 1780. It can thus be considered the dominant style in Russia for a period of only about thirty years—a generation—from c. 1750 to c. 1780. Even so, it is well to remember that even in the full flood of romanticism, in the heyday of Zhukovsky, Batiushkov, Delvig and the young Pushkin, such important poets as Krylov, Katenin, Griboedov and Küchelbecker still represent many of the

7

ideals of classicism. It cannot be emphasized too strongly that all boundary lines, all labels in literary history, are arbitrary.

These are some of the general features of the era which this study is intended to illuminate. Inadequate as they are, it may be hoped that they will serve to mark out some of the more prominent features of the *terra incognita* about to be entered.

CHAPTER II

LITERATURE IN THE REIGN OF PETER THE GREAT

A. The Political Background of the Eighteenth Century

If the first two decades of the seventeenth century were a "time of troubles" for Russia, with famine, civil war, social upheaval and foreign invasion, the first quarter of the eighteenth century was almost equally troubled, but with a greater promise for the future. The long-lasting "Great Northern War" (1700-1721) followed a shorter war with Turkey (1694-1700) and was followed by a shorter war with Persia (1722-23); and during all of Peter's personal reign (1694-1725) the entire social, economic, administrative, religious and cultural life of the country were being drastically and painfully overhauled. There were desperate revolts provoked by Peter's ruthlessness, such as that of the *streltsy* (1698) and of many peasants during the war with Sweden. The introduction (1718) of the "soul tax" *(podushnaia podat')* eliminated the last distinction between a "free" serf and a slave.

It is not therefore surprising that the age of Peter the Great has been called by Russian scholars "the most unliterary period in Russian history." Peter neither knew nor cared anything about such a civilized refinement as literature; his interests were intensely practical. If there was a vast increase during his reign of the amount of printed material available in the empire, this was largely made up of hurried translations from West-European languages of works on mathematics, navigation, fortification, medicine, and the like. And in so far as there was literary composition during the reign, it was backward-looking and old-fashioned, and in no way in keeping with the "westernizing" character of other aspects of Peter's reign.

The reign of the "great transformer," as Russian historians are fond of calling Peter I, was unquestionably in most respects successful in its purpose and beneficial to the country as a whole, however painful at the time. Perhaps its least successful aspect was the bungled problem of succession. Strong rulers in general are notorious for failure in this matter, and Peter's arrangements were little short of disastrous.

By his reluctant marriage, arranged by his mother, with the pious Princess Eudoxia, Peter had a son, who was named Alexei after his grandfather. Peter spent as little time as possible with his wife, and around her, and as he grew older, around his son Alexei the malcontents gathered. Even-

9

tually it became quite clear to the Tsar that when he died, his son would attempt to undo everything that he had accomplished and return the country to its "old Muscovite" tradition. The estrangement between father and son came to a head when the young Tsarevich, after having agreed under pressure to abide by his father's reforms, attempted to escape from the country in 1716. He was induced to return, made to renounce his rights to the throne, and jailed while inquiries were made into an alleged plot to overthrow Peter. Alexei was condemned to death, but cheated the executioner by dying in prison, presumably as a result of torture administered during the investigation. In the meantime, Peter had divorced Alexei's mother and married his long-time mistress, a Lithuanian commoner named Catherine. His several sons by Catherine all died in infancy, and the only male heir left was Alexei's child, Peter's grandson, also named Peter. Such a succession would obviously mean a regency, and this might prove as dangerous to the reforms as Alexei's reign would have been. Peter accordingly promulgated a decree (1722) which gave the ruling monarch the right to designate his successor without regard to the tradition of male primogeniture. No such designation was made, however, until on his death-bed the Emperor designated his wife Catherine, who had already received the imperial crown. Russia accordingly received her first Empress, Catherine I (1725-27).

Between the death of Peter the Great (1725) and the accession of Catherine the Great (1762) the Russian throne was occupied by a succession of incompetents—children and frivolous, pleasure-loving women—such as few countries have suffered from. At the death of Catherine I, the boy Peter II, then seventeen, received the crown. He died of smallpox in 1730, thus bringing to a close the male line from Peter I. A clique of noblemen, bent on emulating the oligarchic government of neighboring Poland, turned to the second Romanov line, that of Peter's brother, Tsar Ivan (V), who had not been too incompetent to found a family. His daughter Anna Ivanovna, Duchess of Courland, was offered the crown with the stipulation that she would let herself be ruled in effect by the noble clique who had called her. Backed by some of the lesser service nobility, including Feofan Prokopovich, Anna tore up the "conditions," and ruled as an autocrat from 1730 to 1740. At her death her German niece, Anna Leopoldovna, became regent for her eight-month-old son, on whom the meaningless title "Ivan VI" was bestowed. Anna's ten-year reign had been chiefly distinguished by the influx of Baltic and other Germans into influential positions—Biron, who became Anna's lover, General Münnich, foreign minister Ostermann, etc. Reaction against the Germans and the "Bironovshchina" led to a palace revolution which set aside the regent and her infant son in favor of Peter the Great's daughter Elizabeth (1741-1762). Elizabeth was good-hearted and well-meaning, but incapable of seriousness and an outrageous spendthrift. Her reign was punctuated by several European wars, most serious being the one with Frederick the Great of Prussia, known as the "Seven Years' War" (1756-63). Elizabeth's designated successor, who was a man of some thirty years at her death, was her nephew, the German Duke of Holstein-Gottorp, who took the title of Peter III. He had been married in 1745 to the German Princess of Anhalt-Zerbst, who received the name Catherine upon joining the Orthodox church. Peter III was of limited intelligence and unlimited passions, one of which was adulation of the King of Prussia. At the moment when Elizabeth died the Russian armies had reduced Frederick II to such despair that he was contemplating suicide; Peter abruptly reversed his aunt's foreign policy, made hasty peace and even alliance with Prussia, and thus saved his idol from ruin. After a few months of erratic and inept rule, Peter was removed from the throne, and shortly from life, by a coup d'état in favor of his wife Catherine (II), managed by her lover Alexei Orlov and his brothers. Thus in 1762 the throne of the Romanovs passed without much bloodshed into the hands of a German woman without a drop of Russian blood. Officially Catherine's position was considered to be that of regent for her (and presumably also Peter's) son Pavel (Paul), born in 1754. Actually she ruled as autocrat, and never relinquished any part of her power to the son she detested.

During this thirty-seven year period, despite the vagaries of its monarchs, Russia became a formidable European power. The army and navy that Peter the Great had created dealt successfully with Poland, Sweden and Prussia, and the economic power which he had founded by the opening of his "window on Europe" was rapidly making the motherland a rival of the more advanced western nations. But Russia was still basically an agricultural state, and the agricultural class, the *khrestiane,* were, since Peter's time, an enserfed population, bound to the soil and subject to the oppression and misrule of the landlords. The only significant public act of Peter III's short reign was his proclamation of the "liberation of the nobility," an act which his usurping wife did not abrogate, as she did so many others. Peter I had insisted on, and enforced, the regulation that the *pomeshchiki* (landowners), or holders of what were originally state lands, owed the government their lifelong service in return, either in one of the armed forces or in the civil service. His grandson's "liberation" meant that in effect the government relinquished all rights to the land held by the *pomeshchiki,* and at the same time permitted them to retain the forced service of the peasants attached to it. Since the peasant service had originally been justified by the leisure which it afforded the gentry to devote to service for the state, this was manifestly inequitable—but the peasants were unable to meet the situation with anything more effective than sporadic and bloody revolts, the killing of occasional exceptionally tyrannical landlords, and the burning of manor houses.

One of the noteworthy effects which the enserfment of the Russian peasant brought with it was a widening and soon unbridgeable gulf between the privileged and the servile classes. This gulf had of course been perceptible already in the reign of Peter's father, Alexei Mikhailovich; but it reached alarming proportions only with the soul tax. What happened in effect was the creation of two Russias: a privileged upper class, made up of landed gentry and career bureaucrats, educated in western fashion, often in western schools, and sometimes incapable even of speaking Russian correctly; and a vast, mostly illiterate, peasant population, brought up in the traditions of the Russian Middle Ages, passively hostile to all innovation, but deeply and emotionally attached to "Mother Russia." In the course of time it became almost literally impossible for the two classes to speak one another's language—and the feeling of uselessness and alienation on the part of the aristocracy was matched by the feeling of resentment and suspicion on the part of the peasantry. Out of this divided nation—made up, it should be emphasized, of an ethnically homogeneous stock—were to come most of the ideological currents of the eighteenth and nineteenth centuries. We shall see many traces of "Slavophiles" and "Westernizers" long before the words are invented. And the problem of serfdom, of glaring social injustice and national dichotomy, was to become the all-engrossing problem of the nineteenth and early twentieth centuries, the focus of all revolutionary activity, and for better or worse, in some circles the very touchstone of artistic and literary values. And this aspect of the matter too has its beginnings in the eighteenth century.

B. The Russian Language in the Petrine Period[1]

The literary language of medieval Russia was a varying composite of the actual spoken Russian of the period and the static, frozen, ecclesiastical language which is usually termed "Church Slavonic." Since with very few exceptions all medieval writers were churchmen, the use of the Slavonic came naturally. The proportions of the two dialects in the written language varied of course in accordance with the genre of the work (history, for example, would contain less, the saint's life more Slavonic), the background of the writer, the date of the work, and other factors. By the seventeenth century the first important break in this tradition may be seen: a new literate class comes into existence, unconnected with the church, and by and for this class are created such works as "The Tale of Frol Skobeev," the "Tales" of Bova Korolevich and of Uruslan Lazarevich, etc., in the language of which may be seen other components than the usual two—e.g., in "Frol" the language of the government chanceries, and in "Bova" and "Uruslan" the language of the illiterate popular story-teller. The same kind of linguistic mixture is observable even in such a remarkable masterpiece as Avvakum's "Autobiography," in which the conventional Church Slavonic and the vulgate of the common peasant with whom Avvakum usually chose to identify himself stand side by side. But it must be emphasized that the mixture of linguistic levels which the seventeenth-century exhibits is almost entirely still a mixture of Church Slavonic or of different variations of Russian. Foreign admixture is still uncommon (some Polish may occasionally be found with writers originating in Belorussia or the Ukraine).

The situation changes with the advent of Peter the Great. Peter's own sharp break with Muscovite tradition, by leaving the country on the so-called Great Embassy, and spending about two years in Germany, the Netherlands and England, initiated the influx of vast numbers of western technological innovations and the corresponding vocabulary, for which of course neither spoken Russian nor Church Slavonic had words. In the mere matter of navigation, for instance, an art unknown to ancient Muscovy, an entire vocabulary of terms meaning such things as "top-sail," "bowsprit," "tack," "shoal water," "midshipman," "cabin boy," etc. had to be imported into the landlubberly Russian tongue. The source for most of these terms was Dutch, German, or English, since Peter's own nautical education had been largely acquired where these languages were native. Peter's new administrative arrangements similarly required a new vocabulary, and it is worth noting the names of some of the new "colleges" which he set up: *Berg i Manufaktur-kollegia* (mining and manufacture), *Iustitskollegia* (department of justice), *Ratusha* (German *Rathaus,* the state accounting office), *Kommertskollegia* (department of commerce), *Admiralteiskaia Kollegia* (the Admiralty), etc. The new executive body created to take the Tsar's place during his absences from the capital was the *Senat,* and its chief officer was the *Ober-Prokurator,* and so forth. Almost every reform was necessarily accompanied by new vocabulary. Many of these strange, outlandish words never took root in the Russian language, and eventually dropped out of use; but many have become part and parcel of present-day Russian, and could hardly be dispensed with. Sometimes, when the foreign word did not represent a new object or concept, but merely doubled an existing native term, the native term eventually ousted its competitor, as for example the imported faddish words *viktoria, batalia,* or the like. The new western social life which Peter made obligatory for the upper classes of the capital also brought its own vocabulary, in this case quite naturally mostly from the French. The man and woman of fashion would attend an *assambleia (assemblée)* or make a *vizit (visite).* Their conduct would be dictated by *polites (politesse),* and they would be *punktualny* in

observance of it. From time to time voices would later be raised against this "corruption" of the native language—Admiral Shishkov's in the early nineteenth century is perhaps the most strident—but for the most part the innovations were accepted and naturalized. There remained nevertheless a

13

period during which the new element remained unassimilated, a foreign body in the language, and the written work of the time has a motley quality that nullifies all stylistic distinction.

C. Russian Prose Writing of the Petrine Period

Of literary prose there is not a great deal during the reign of Peter I, and what there is affords relatively little interest. Perhaps the most significant from all points of view is that of Feofan Prokopovich.[2] When Peter, victorious at Poltava over Charles XII and the Swedes, visited Kiev in 1709, Prokopovich, then professor of eloquence, greeted him with a pompous triumphal ode, the *Epinikion*. The personal contact thus happily made brought the author immediate and spectacular preferment. Brought to the capital and consecrated as Bishop of Pskov, Feofan exercised his episcopal duties by proxy and remained to be one of Peter's most valuable assistants and propagandists.His "Sermons" very often appear to a modern observer as very able promotional documents. A good example is the *Slovo,* or "Speech" "In Eulogy of the Russian Fleet and the Victory Won by Russian Galleys over the Swedish Ships on July 27 [1720]."[3] The "victory" thus celebrated was that of Grönhamn in the Aland Islands, which had as its decisive result Sweden's decision to open negotiations that were to lead to the final Peace of Nystedt in 1721.

The "Speech" was pronounced in Trinity Cathedral in September 1720, in the presence of Peter himself and his chief officials. It is composed in the usual florid ecclesiastical style, in the conventional Church Slavonic, but with an admixture of western vocabulary typical of the age—e.g., *viktoria, ammunitsiia, peregrinatsiia, aktsiia,* etc. It begins with an exposition of the providential nature of Peter's first interest in seafaring. It was obviously by the direct inspiration of the Almighty, concerned for the welfare of his Orthodox people, that the young Prince discovered an "old, decrepit, despised little boat," which first turned his thoughts to the sea. Prokopovich declares that some people are concerned to discover on Mount Ararat the remains of Noah's Ark—but they might discover the remains of this little boat and enshrine them as a national treasure. He then launches into an invective against the folly of those ancients who decried the art of navigation as a transgression of God's boundaries. On the contrary, God intentionally did not give all necessary things to all men, so that they might visit one another to obtain what each lacked—and the sea was given as the most convenient path for such communication. Finally he attributes again to God's providence the wisdom of Peter that created the Russian fleet, without which it would have been impossible not only to maintain possession of the coast which was wrested from the Swedes, but even to defend the inland towns, which would have been at the mercy of a naval power. "The approach of an enemy by land can be heard from afar, and is slow; there is time to prepare and forestall it. Not so an approach by sea: the tidings of voices do not fly before it, sounds are not heard, smoke and dust are not visible; the hour when you see it, the same hour expect its attack... Against an enemy striking so unexpectedly and quickly how could adequate defense be prepared? Only confusion *[konfusiia]*, only terror, trembling and riot. And what if someone did give information of its coming, how might one know to what shore it will sail? What town it will attack?" The "Speech" ends with a prayer for continued divine favor and protection to Russia and her "most pious sovereign, our Tsar, Thy faithful minister Peter the First and his most pious Tsaritsa, our sovereign lady Ekaterina Alexeevna."

Through the "Speeches" Feofan preaches the "gospel according to Peter," eulogizing the sovereign's innovations as necessary, useful and contributory to Russia's world position. Thus the "new army," as compared with its predecessor ("Speech on the Peace of Nystad")[4]: "How efficient the old army of *streltsy* was, is known by now to everyone. And it was a good thing that it was disbanded and cashiered, for it would have been a gangrene, hurting its own and not another's body." Thus the most suspect of Peter's innovations, foreign travel *[peregrinatsiia]* : "Above all, foreign travel marvelously illumines the reason for government, and is, I say boldly, the best and liveliest school of honorable politics. For it offers, not on paper but in very fact, not to the ear but to the very sight, the customs and behavior of peoples. If we hear the same things from tales or read them in books of history, there is much that the thought refuses to credit; for not a little is falsely related. But much also even of what is credible and genuine (I know not why) we do not recognize so clearly as when we have seen the very places where something happened... How much more clearly will all this be realized when, as travellers, we look on not merely the bare places of ancient actions, but see clearly the veritable deeds and actions of peoples, their purposes, counsels, judgments, manners, and modes of government.... In a word, foreign travel makes a man far wiser in a few years than the span of many years of age."

Occasionally the solemnity of Feofan's oratorical style, accentuated by numerous citations of Scripture or from the church fathers, is broken by an unexpected glimpse of real life, a satirical picture such as one might find in the *Caractères* of La Bruyère. In the "Speech of Praise on St. Catherine's Day,"[5] with the theme of "Love stronger than death," he contrasts genuine with hypocritical love, and deplores the difficulty of distinguishing one from the other:

However, there are even certain indications of this: even as in an affected love for God the proper character is a bootless vanity, so also in love for one's neighbor, unstable and false, there are the characters of a certain vain adulation. He [i.e., the hypocrite] praises whatsoever he sees in the one he feigns to love, even if it is undeserving even of mention, let alone praise. He praises both what is natural and what is accidental: 'what

15

an elegant carriage!' 'What a delightful gown!' He will find, I suppose, means for praising even his master's cough; and he praises with just the same intention as that fox of Aesop's had, when seeing a crow with a piece of meat in its mouth, he praised it for the beauty of its countenance, and asked for it to utter its sweetest of voices—that is, so that it might drop that morsel of food. He even pretends similarity of character and similarity of feeling on his own part: if he hears of some mischance to his lord, he contrives a misfortune of his own, and enters with a tale of this; if he hears of an illness, straightaway he is beforehand with a tale of his own aches and pains.

It is probably not accidental that just this same sort of lively thumb-nail sketch is characteristic, as we shall see, of the *Satires* of Antiokh Kantemir, a younger friend and admirer of Feofan Prokopovich.

Peter's age, as has been said, preferred practical writing to *belles-lettres*. Of all the recognized prose genres of bookish literature the most practical is certainly history—and the writing of history had been the chief glory of Byzantine prose literature, and was inherited by the converted Russians. As we have seen earlier, historical, or at least memoiristic, works had been composed under the stimulus of the Time of Troubles by such writers as Avraamii Palitsyn and Prince Katyrev-Rostovsky. These were, however, still in the medieval annalistic tradition and based most commonly on the authors' own experiences or on immediate eye-witness accounts. Very different is Russia's first "modern" history, the *Russian History (Istoriia Rossiiskaia)* of Vasily Nikitich Tatishchev (1686-1750).[6] Its author was a nobleman of ancient family, himself a product of Peter the Great's artillery and engineering school, and a cultured and enlightened gentleman. He served in central administration in the College of Mines, and later in eastern Russia in the direction of mining enterprises in Perm and Orenburg, and rose eventually to be Governor of Astrakhan. In his leisure he composed works on the utility of the sciences in education, on mercantilistic economics, and his major work, the *Russian History*. For the latter he followed an essentially scientific method, consulting, comparing and collating the ancient annalistic accounts and trying to arrive at a probable sequence of events by critical methods. Although knowledge of sources has been greatly augmented since the eighteenth century, Tatishchev's work still has great historical value, because the author was able to utilize some documents which have since disappeared. His style is not particularly distinguished; although not an ecclesiastic, he employs a conventional Slavonic vocabulary, partly no doubt under the influence of the ancient sources which he quotes.

Practical in its entirety and without pretensions to literary quality at all is the work of Ivan Tikhonovich Pososhkov (1652-1726),[7] a commoner who distinguished himself as an inventor, industrialist and entrepreneur. He was an ardent follower of Peter I, wrote several works on technical matters, the art of war, and the like, and in his masterpiece "On Poverty and Wealth" (1725) propagandized the leading eighteenth-century economic theory of

16

merchantilism. His Russian, naturally for an ex-peasant, is simple and direct, with no literary graces and relatively little Slavonic admixture. Pososhkov's radical views and admiration for Peter, as well as probably his invidious financial success, brought about his downfall and death within a few months of Peter's; he was jailed as a "dangerous person," probably tortured, and died in prison.

Of the scanty literary production of Peter's reign the most interesting and attractive is the anonymous popular adventure tale, usually designated in this age as a "history" [gistoriia].[8] The genre is a continuation of the popular *povest'* (tale) of the preceding generation, translated or original, but bears numerous marks of its later date; a new kind of hero emerges in these "histories," and a new kind of attitude toward life.

The best known of these productions, and universally regarded as typifying the age of Peter, is entitled "History of the Russian Sailor Vasily Koriotsky and the Beautiful Queen Iraklia of the Land of Florence" [Gistoriia o rossiiskom matrose Vasilii Koriotskom i o prekrasnoi korolevne Iraklii Florenskoi zemli].[9] Although probably the composition of a single author, this history falls into two quite distinct parts: the first, which narrates the decision of the young and impecunious nobleman Vasily Koriotsky to "enroll as a sailor" in St. Petersburg, his success in "learning the ropes," and his journey to Holland "to learn the arithmetical science and various languages"; and the second, which begins with the hero's shipwreck on his return voyage and ends with his marriage to the "beautiful Queen Iraklia" and accession as "King of Florence."

The first part is sober, factual, and reflects faithfully the actual conditions of Peter's age. Young Vasily obtains the permission of his beloved father to enroll as a sailor, with the intention of using his pay to help out his father's desperate financial situation. After mastering the art of navigation, which it must be remembered was an art unknown to the Russians before Peter, and which undoubtedly had much glamour for the more imaginative and energetic youth of the time, Vasily is sent abroad and takes up residence with a Dutch merchant who comes to regard him as a son. Despite this, Vasily feels drawn to return to Russia and visit his old father, to whom, incidentally, he has sent by "bill of exchange" some of his earnings—again, a feature of Peter's time, unknown before. On the return voyage Vasily's ship is wrecked, and he alone escapes to a desert island. It is at this point that the realistic success story is suddenly transposed to fairy land. Since the only water route from Russia to Holland lies through the North and Baltic Seas, one wonders where might lie the "desert island" to which Vasily makes his way, and which he finds inhabited only by a band of pirates. These extremely gullible buccaneers, who remind one of the highwaymen of *Two Gentlemen of Verona*, almost immediately choose Vasily as their "ataman." His protests are met with the alternative: either become their leader or die. Vasily prefers to live, but takes no

17

actual part in piratic activities. During the absence of the band on one foray, Vasily investigates a "store-room" which he has been warned under no circumstances to open, and discovers the ravishingly beautiful Queen Iraklia, who is being held for ransom by the pirates. The two young people of course immediately fall in love, Vasily eludes the pirates and escapes with Iraklia, and reaches the mainland, which he discovers to be the land of "Tsesariia." Again one wonders at the geography, for "Tsesariia" ("the land of Caesar") is evidently a shadowy reminiscence of Austria. Vasily and Iraklia, who have been living in Platonic chastity, are introduced to the Emperor ("Tsesar"), who is so taken by the intelligence and courage of the Russian sailor that he makes him his "sworn brother." From Tsesariia Vasily and Iraklia set out for her home in Florence, accompanying the "Admiral of Florence," whom Iraklia's father the king has sent out in search of his kidnapped daughter. Since the princess's hand and the succession to the kingdom have been promised to the man who rescues her, the Admiral has Vasily thrown into the sea and forces the princess under threat of death to swear that she will declare the Admiral to be her rescuer. This nefarious plot is of course unsuccessful: the sailors, whom Vasily has befriended, provide the castaway with a boat; he reaches Florence and makes himself known to Iraklia by means of singing an "aria" just in time to prevent her from becoming the unwilling bride of the perfidious Admiral. The lovers are united, the villain is punished, and Vasily Koriotsky "the Russian sailor" becomes successor to the King of Florence.

Scholars have conjectured that the second part of Vasily's "History" is a free reworking of a western tale, popular in Russia in translation, about "the Spanish Nobleman Doltorn." G. N. Moiseeva, in her edition of *Russian Tales of the First Third of the Eighteenth Century* (Moscow, 1965) calls this hypothesis into question and inclines to see elements of the popular fairytale (*skazka*) in the story. There are without question a considerable number of folklore themes and situations in it, but translated foreign models almost certainly have something to do with the development. Regardless, however, of the precise nature of the sources, the difference between the two parts of the "History" is blatant. One of the most curious anomalies concerns the geography of the story. In the first part the young man, who lives in what is quaintly called "The Russian Europes" *[v rossiiskikh Evropiakh]* —a mark of Peter's "Europeanizing" age; incidentally—voyages by sea to Holland in a perfectly normal fashion. In the second, as we have seen, he is wrecked on a piratic island, the location of which must be sought in either the North Sea or the Baltic, and from there arrives by sea on the coast of what must be Austria! From "Tsesariia," again, to "Florentsiia," which can scarcely be anywhere but Florence, the access is by sea—the Adriatic and Tyrrhenian? And since when has Florence been a sea port? One can only conclude that neither the author nor his expected readers knew or cared very much about the real map of Europe.

Another inconsistency in the work is the hero's character. To be sure, throughout Vasily Koriotsky is the energetic, bold, attractive young man who might well have been the ideal of Peter the Great's age. He excels in learning the art of navigation; he is a business success in Holland; he is clever and courageous and his personal charm wins even the "Tsesar" as a sworn friend. But in the first part Vasily is also a most devoted son; his voyage back to Russia is motivated by desire to revisit his father. After the shipwreck, however, this father is never heard of again, and Vasily apparently assumes his position as King of Florence without a further thought for the old man.

In contrast to the "Valiant Russian Cavalier Alexander," whose "history" we shall consider shortly, Vasily's sentimental involvement is simple and uncomplicated. Neither he nor Iraklia ever waver in their devotion to each other; and in spite of the obvious temptations which fate throws in their way, Iraklia remains "in all maidenly purity" until their marriage. The psychology of the hero and heroine concerns the author of the tale but little; his principal interests are patriotic—to show how a simple Russian sailor could become an emperor's sworn friend and a king's son-in-law; and social—the poor and humbly born is the equal of the most noble, if he possesses intelligence, energy and courage. Here again is an echo of Peter's time, when the self-conceited nobleman's sons were often passed over in favor of such a person as Menshikov, who was reputed to have hawked pies on the streets of Moscow!

The only other "history" of consequence from the age of Peter I has the full title "History of the Valiant Russian Cavalier Alexander and His Mistresses Tira and Eleonora."[10] The tale is undoubtedly, as critics have pointed out, an example of plot complication and variety of interest not to be matched elsewhere in the age; it is also an example of the most inept cobbling together of wildly disparate source material to be found in Russian literature. The unknown author has combined into one narrative three or more stories from popular western literature, creating a three-bodied monstrosity that strikes the bewildered reader much as the legendary chimaera might strike a naturalist—a most implausible combination, it may be recalled, of she-goat, lion, and snake! G. A. Gukovsky, in his *History of Russian Eighteenth-Century Literature* singles out the relatively sober first part of the story for treatment, consigning the rest to oblivion. His remarks are certainly pertinent: only the first part has any literary merit, and this part at the same time bears evident marks of the age of Peter the Great, closely paralleling those in the "History of Vasily Koriotsky." The second and third parts are very crudely stitched onto the first, with no continuity other than that provided by the hero's name. Any attempt, such as G. N. Moiseeva makes in her edition, to discover unity in this fantastic hodgepodge is time wasted.

A very brief summary of this history will make clear its character. Like the "History of Vasily Koriotsky," this begins in a sober and factual way. The young nobleman Alexander convinces his family that it is his duty to go abroad and "study the sciences"; his position as a nobleman depends on this. He goes, accordingly, to Paris, and from there, rather unexpectedly, to Lille,

19

where he takes up residence in a house not far from that of a "pastor." He sees there, and falls in love with, the pastor's beautiful daughter Eleonora. This entire episode is developed with considerable psychological skill, as the feelings of the shy, inexperienced lovers are described. The hero is prone to write sentimental love letters, which the author quotes in full, almost as though part of his purpose were to provide models for gallant declarations of love; Alexander also at times lapses into verse to give vent to his emotions, or plays the flute. Incidentally, the frequent intrusion of letters into the narrative constitutes one of the few links between the first and second parts. Vladimir, who first appears in Part II, is a more constant letter writer even than his friend Alexander. After winning Eleonora's love and swearing undying fidelity to her, the Russian cavalier forgets his purpose in visiting "foreign regions," and neglects his "study of the sciences" for three years. Perhaps, as Moiseeva suggests, the author's original conception may have been to make the tragic outcome of the first part a retribution for this civic defection. In any case, the couple's period of happiness is interrupted by another woman, a general's daughter named Hedwig Dorothea, who falls in love with the handsome Alexander, and contrives to seduce him and make him forget his first love. Eleonora finds out about his infidelity and dies of a broken heart.

The second part of the "History" introduces a new character, another Russian nobleman named Vladimir, who becomes Alexander's "sworn brother." Vladimir on two occasions—at their first encounter, and toward the end of the tale, when he is reunited with Alexander—tells stories of his amorous adventures, which form interpolations in the main narrative. Since Vladimir's adventures are usually comic and often ribald, these intruded episodes are apparently intended to furnish contrast with the tragic and heroic fortunes of Alexander. The first part of Alexander's "History," as we have seen, is realistic and factual. It takes place in a recognizable city (Lille) in a France not too remote from reality, and the triangular love plot is perfectly credible. The second part, as with the story of Vasily Koriotsky, belongs to the realm of late medieval chivalric adventure. Alexander falls in love with, and wins, the beautiful Tira, daughter of a French "Hofmarschal of the Court." Eloping with Tira, and accompanied by his friend Vladimir, Alexander encounters (about ten miles from Paris!) a band of highwaymen in a most impenetrable forest. The brigands are of course routed, but during the melee the three friends are separated. Tira wanders off and presently finds herself in Spain (!), where she becomes, temporarily, a shepherdess; Alexander, now a knight errant, roams the western half of Europe in search of her (he even visits Egypt, to see the pyramids!), while Vladimir undergoes numerous misadventures during his endless quest for feminine conquests. Alexander encounters a "Knight of Malta" named Tigranor, who becomes his "sworn brother." Each friend swears to avenge the death of the other if this should be necessary, and when they become separated each thinks the other has been killed, and there

20

begins a tiresomely repetitious series of episodes in which the two knights, masked as "The Cavalier of Vengeance" and "The Cavalier of Victory," chase up and down over Europe, frequently encountering each other without recognition, and doing each other as much harm as possible short of actual death. At long last the three are once more momentarily reunited, only to be shipwrecked and separated again. Tira is carried off to China, where Alexander and Tigranor rescue her rather tamely; the party return to France, and Tigranor departs, presumably for Malta, while the lovers abruptly decide to head for Russia. At this point Vladimir turns up again, and the third part begins, which is chiefly an account of some bawdy adventures of Vladimir, told in the first person, and a report in quasi-dramatic form, of a conversation on the subject of women which Vladimir has overheard. The conversation is carried on by three gentlemen, "The Prussian Baron Stark, the Danish Baron Forjar and the Saxon nobleman Silberstein." This unedifying discussion of the fair sex is so completely irrelevant to either part of the story of Alexander that it is likely to be a bungling later intrusion. When it is finished, the three principals of the main narrative resume their journey to Russia; but on the way Alexander and Vladimir attempt to bathe in the sea (their course this time is overland, along the coast), but a huge—and entirely unmotivated—wave carries them off, and Alexander is drowned. Vladimir reaches shore, Tira laments her lover in two pages of bad verse, and then falls on her sword (she has been masquerading as another knight errant under the ironic name "The Cavalier of Hope"), and Vladimir buries the bodies. As he continues his way alone, he abruptly meets Hedwig Dorothea, who has not been heard from since Part I; when she learns the fate of her beloved Alexander, she laments appropriately, and then throws herself down from the mountain top where the lovers have been buried, and "breaks her head." Vladimir adds her to his graveyard, and then makes his way to Russia, breaks the sad news to Alexander's parents, and is forthwith adopted by them in place of their dead son.

This absurd conglomeration of literary types and styles would not merit any consideration were it not for the pathetic attempt which the author is evidently making to produce a narrative that would combine exciting and exotic adventure (it must be remembered that the very concept of "chivalry" or "knight errantry" was as bewilderingly unfamiliar to a Russian reader of this age, as was the gallant western treatment of love) with psychological analysis and fashionable effusions in epistolary or poetical form, the whole spiced with a bit of bawdry. That the attempt is an artistic failure of catastrophic proportions is scarcely surprising; but that an author of the age of Peter the Great was aware of the problems and in order to meet them was willing to fly in the face of so many "old Muscovite" prejudices is most surprising. From such a medley as the "History of Alexander" such a genuine, if minor, work of art as Chulkov's "The Comely Cook" may have been pointed the way.

21

The reign of Peter I (1682-1725) is the most momentous reign in the entire course of Russian history. Its significance, however, is economic, social, political—but in no sense literary. In fact, it is no exaggeration for Professor Likhachev to call it "the most unliterary period in Russian history." The great Tsar-reformer was preoccupied with the material advancement of his backward country, and with a rather superficial "Westernization," symbolized by such things as the clipping of long Muscovite beards and the substitution of short Western-style coats for the ankle-length kaftans of Turkish origin. He had no interest in literature as such, and his only attention to literary matters consisted of favor extended to the drama, as a form of Western social background. We shall have a brief look at the results of this interest in another section of this study.

The chief, and indeed almost the only, verse writer of Peter's reign is the Archbishop of Novgorod, Vice-President of the Holy Synod, Feofan Prokopovich, whose contributions to the beginnings of Russian drama and to oratorical prose have already been discussed.[12] Prokopovich was a convinced and enthusiastic supporter of Peter's reforms; during the turbulent period between the Emperor's death and the accession of his niece Anna Ivanovna (1730) he was the object of determined attack by the conservative church element who were bent on reversing Peter's reforms. He managed to weather the storm, and when at the death of Peter II a move was made by a group of ambitious noblemen, the *verkhovniki,* or "top men," to put the monarchy under the dominance of a small oligarchy, in the Polish tradition, by extorting from the Empress Anna a number of "conditions" that would have seriously limited her autocratic power, Prokopovich and his friends the historian Tatishchev and the young satirist Kantemir thwarted the move and supported the Empress, who tore up the "conditions" she had signed. Prokopovich was the leader until his death in 1736 of a coterie of young intellectuals, most important of whom was Kantemir, which bore the unofficial title of the "learned band" *(uchennaia druzhina).* They were the "Westernizers" of their day.

His strenuous activities as ecclesiastical administrator and political leader of the reform group gave Prokopovich little time for purely literary activity. His sermons, which have already been discussed, were as much propaganda as literature, and aside from them his work consists of a couple dozen poems of various sorts, all written in syllabic form. The most pretentious of these is the *Epinikion,*[13] or "Victory Song," written in 1709 to celebrate Peter's great triumph at Poltava. It is a predecessor, under an older name, of the pompous triumphal odes of Trediakovsky, Lomonosov, and legions of later imitators. "Now, if ever, it befits us to wish for many mouths, since neither the golden rhyme-creating organ now suffices for our joy, nor does the utterance of eloquent mouths succeed in its task." So he starts off;

presently God himself intervenes, "from Heaven's height viewing His People, and not suffering that false heresy should fall upon the necks of His chosen ones." With a typical Baroque indifference to the mixture of classical and Christian, the poet then remarks: "Thus when God on high had settled the fates of both sides, forthwith cruel Mars began to spur on this side and that." The poem, after a properly mythologized description of the Battle of Poltava, ends with a prayer that the victorious Russian troops may behold the walls of the New Jerusalem.

It may be remembered that when Prokopovich composed his "Tragicomedy of St. Vladimir," he dedicated it to Ivan Mazeppa, Hetman of the Ukraine and patron of the Mogila Academy where the drama was presented. Mazeppa, however, made the fatal mistake of siding with the Swedish king during the Poltava campaign, and was forced after Peter's victory to seek refuge with Charles XII in Turkey. Before his death in 1709 (he poisoned himself), Mazeppa had with some success attempted to bring the Zaporozh Cossacks to rebel against Peter. On this occasion Feofan, himself a Ukrainian, wrote a short three-stanza poem in eight-syllable lines called "The Repentant Zaporozh Cossack."[14] The final strophe of this lyric runs thus:

> I have angered the autocrat [samoderavtsa]
> With heart unreasoning,
> Yet in this I have a firm assurance
> That God and the Tsar are merciful.
> The Sovereign will lay aside his wrath,
> And God will not desert me.

The most successful of Feofan's small lyric output is a piece written during the troubled five-year period between the death of Peter I and the accession of Anna Ivanovna, when the reforms of the first great "Westernizer" seemed likely to be reversed by ecclesiastical conservatism, and the poet himself faced possible disgrace or worse. The poem is called "The Shepherd Mourns in the Long-lasting Bad Weather" (Plachet pastushek v dolgom nenast'i).[15] The symbolism, obvious enough in view of Feofan's own position as "shepherd" of the Novgorod flock, marks the formal introduction into Russian literature of the familiar Western pastoral tradition:

> When may I expect cheerful weather
>   and beautiful days?
> When will the abundant grace appear
>   of bright skies?
> From no side is light visible—
>   all is foul weather,
> And there is no hope. O, wretched
>   is my fate!

Though it will show some small comfort
    and allure,
And as it were offer [my] flock alleviation,
    it will deceive.
I shiver beneath the oak; and the sheep waste away
    in extreme hunger
And already with the damp cold
    are disappearing.
The fifth day has passed, and of the rainy waters
    there is no surcease.
And also of tearful complaints and sorrow
    there is no end.
Hasten, O God, to deliver us
    from woe;
Our forefathers taught us
    to cry to Thee!

The "fifth day," of course, stands for the fifth year since Peter's death and marks 1730 as the poem's date. It was presently to be answered, in a more optimistic vein, by the Archbishop's young friend and admirer, Antiokh Kantemir. It should be noted that although in "The Shepherd's Complaint" Feofan continues to employ the harsh and awkward syllabic system of versification, he attempts to lighten it and give it variety by alternating 10-syllable and 4-syllable lines (as in other purely syllabic Russian poetry, the sequence of accented and unaccented syllable is random). Kantemir's reply uses the same form.

E. Eighteenth-Century Russian Drama before Sumarokov[16]

Written drama, like written verse, was unknown to the Russian Middle Ages. Its beginnings belong to the reign of Alexei Mikhailovich, and are entirely Western, although unwritten popular farces probably contributed something to the emergent genre of comedy. Two Western traditions converged to create seventeenth-century Russian drama: the ecclesiastical and didactic "school drama," fostered by the Jesuits and reaching Russia by way of the more or less Westernized and Polonized Ukraine; and the secular German tradition, with an ultimate, though remote, derivation from the Renaissance drama of England. The first, Jesuit, tradition, may be seen in such a piece as Simeon Polotsky's "Parable of the Prodigal Son"; the second in the plays written and produced for Tsar Alexei by the German pastor Johann Gottfried Gregory, such as "Judith." The "school plays" were generally composed in syllabic verse, the secular plays in prose. Both varieties employed almost exclusively Biblical subjects.

Johann Gregory died in 1674 and his royal patron in 1676; for a few years the public theater, like other innovations of Tsar Alexei, went into oblivion. The first few years of Tsar Peter's reign were too much occupied with a war against the Turks, the famous pilgrimage to the West, and the creation of Russia's first navy to allow much time for such a minor concern as the theater. As a Western, and presumably civilizing, institution, however, the theater could not fail sometime to attract Peter's attention. This it did in 1701, at the very beginning of what was to be a very long-lasting war with Sweden. In a fashion altogether typical of Peter, the new theater was created by decree: the bewildered clerks of the Foreign Office were directed to improvise an acting company from their number, and build on Red Square a permanent theater. A German named Johann Kunst was put in charge of the project, and the first performance was given in December 1702. Kunst died about a year later, and the management of the theater devolved on another German, Otto Fürst, who carried on the venture until 1706, when the Moscow public theater was closed as summarily as it had been created.

Various reasons have been alleged for the abandonment of the project: the Tsar's preoccupation after 1703 with the creation of his new capital on the Neva; the vicissitudes of the Swedish war; the expense of the theater, which for want of patronage never paid for itself, etc. Probably a more cogent reason was the dissatisfaction of both Tsar and public with the extremely mediocre repertory which Kunst and Fürst were able to offer.

By good fortune there has been preserved in the archives of the Foreign Office a list, dating from 1709, of the theater's repertory, which records fifteen plays. Of these six are extant, in part or entire; the subjects of the rest can be gathered from the titles. In contrast to the plays presented in Alexei's theater, which were almost exclusively on Biblical subjects, those in Peter's are exclusively secular—many of them on historical themes, such as the conquests of Alexander the Great and of Julius Caesar. Among the extant dramas—anonymous, like all of them—is one entitled "Scipio Africanus." This, despite its title, does not deal with the career of the conqueror of Carthage, but is actually a reworking of the tragedy *Sophonisbe* (1680) of the German Baroque dramatist Daniel Casper von Lohenstein. The subject, drawn from the history of Livy, was a favorite of European dramatists: the first Renaissance tragedy is Trissino's *Sofonisba*. Scipio Africanus enters the Russian version only at the end, to convince Massinissa, who has helped his beloved wife Sophonisba to commit suicide in order not to become an object of shame and derision in a Roman triumph, not to follow her example, but live in resigned obedience to the call of civic duty as King of Numidia. Kniazhnin was later to use this subject in his tragedy *Sophonisba.*

Two of the plays listed in the 1709 repertory are reworkings of Molière originals: "The Birth of Hercules, in Which Jupiter is the Leading Character" is none other than *Amphitryon;* and "A Doctor Perforce" is of course *Le Médecin malgré lui.* The play entitled "Comedy about Don Juan and Don

Petro," however, does not stem from Molière's *Don Juan,* but from an Italian version of the tale by one Giliberti. An Italian opera by a certain Cicognini is reputed to be the source of the bloody melodrama of adultery and marital vengeance: "The Honorable Betrayer, or Friderico von Poplei and Aloizia His Wife."

One of the characteristics of the German theatrical tradition, as was seen already in such an example as Gregory's "Judith," is the unclassical mingling of comic elements with serious or tragic. Such a mingling classical theory sanctions only in the hybrid genre, the "tragicomedy," of which Feofan Prokopovich's "St. Vladimir" is the earliest Russian example. Among the repertory of Peter's theater is a piece entitled "Prince Pickelhäring, or Jodelet. Himself His Own Jailer." This enigmatic title conceals an original by Thomas Corneille, *Le Geôlier de soi-même,* which in turn goes back to a Calderón *comedia.* The plot turns on the accidental discovery of a prince's arms and clothing by a buffoon (Pickelharing is the traditional German clown, closely related to Hanswurst), who puts it on and is thereupon taken for the authentic prince. The humor of the piece consists of the piquant contrast between the presumed high station of the "prince" and his extremely low discourse.

The plays of this earliest eighteenth-century Russian theater are all translations of West European originals. They were contrived by clerks of the Foreign Office, whose only qualification for the task was probably their knowledge of foreign languages. Even this, judging by the results, must not have been particularly remarkable, for the texts are filled with ludicrous literal translations of French or German idioms and the like. Typical is the translation of Molière's *Les Précieuses ridicules* as *Dragyia smeiania,* quite literally "the precious ridicules!" Apparently the Tsar, who had created the theater by fiat, was rather impatient of the results, which were a motley mixture of extravagant and unnatural rhetoric, *précieux* gallantry and coarse and vulgar farce. Peter, according to a contemporary, offered a prize to the actors if they would "give a pathetic piece without that love which they drag in everywhere—which bores the Tsar—and an amusing farce without buffonery." This was asking too much, quite evidently: the alternative was to close the theater.

Toward the end of his life Peter tried again, this time in his new capital. A travelling German troupe visited St. Petersburg in 1723-24, and the Tsar "directed the actors to play such a piece as would be in only three acts and without a love intrigue; not very sad and not very serious, and withal not [merely] funny." Peter died before any results could have been expected of such a revolutionary directive.[17]

Besides the public variety of theater which Tsar Peter attempted to foster, the so-called "school drama" and a private theater continued to exist, and indeed may be found even into the age of Sumarokov. The school-drama tradition had been transferred from the Mogila Academy of Kiev (where Feofan's "St. Vladimir" was played) to the Slavonic-Greek-Latin Academy of

Moscow, which in 1701 performed a piece in the tradition of Simeon Polotsky on the New Testament parable of Lazarus and the Rich Man. The Academy's next attempt was a most ambitious one: "The Fearful Representation of Our Lord's Second Coming on Earth,"—in other words, "The Last Judgment." Room was found in this apocalyptic pageant for some panegyrics of the Russian Tsar. Subsequently the Academy's offerings became largely propaganda pieces, lauding Peter's victories and utilizing for the purpose the entire Graeco-Roman pantheon of divinities, augmented by a large selection of personifications, such as Glory, Valor, Emulation, etc.

Another Muscovite school, of a rather unlikely sort, also became a center for amateur drama. This was one of Peter's foundations, the "School of Surgery." The Netherlander Dr. Bidloo, whom Peter had called to head this institution, happened to have an avid interest in the theater, which he apparently communicated to his students. In any case, the School of Surgery came to rival the Greek-Latin-Slavonic Academy in its sumptuous mythological and allegorical representations.

A curious reversion to the past in these years seems the dramatic activity of Peter's favorite sister, Natalia Alexeevna, who in 1707 took what was left of the Moscow public theater (closed the year before), in the way of properties and costumes, to the old Preobrazhenskoe location of her father's theater, and watched over the production of a series of mostly Biblical and ecclesiastical dramas, some of which she composed herself. Natalia and her troupe moved to St. Petersburg in 1707. Among the subjects represented in this private theater are recorded "comedies" on the Virgin, on the prophet Daniel, on the birth of Christ, the calling of St. Andrew, the martyrdom of St. Eudocia, etc. The story of Varlaam and Iosaphat, from Dmitri Rostovsky's *Reading Meneae,* is also mentioned. Another royal lady, Praskovia Fedorovna, widow of Peter's half-brother Tsar Ivan V, also opened a private theater in another Moscow suburb, Izmailovo.

Such private and academic acting groups were occasionally called upon for large public performances in celebration of the holidays of Christmas and Easter, or of great military victories and the like. For such occasions very elaborate spectacles were mounted, the subjects for which were mostly furnished by the extremely popular romances of the Petrine period. We know of pieces of this kind, such as the "Curious History of the Valiant Prince Eudo and the Beautiful Princess Bertha," "History of the Valiant and Glorious Knight Peter of the Golden Keys and the Beautiful Queen Magelona of Naples," "Comedy of the Beautiful Melusina," etc. Of particular interest among these works is the "Comedy about the Italian Marquis," which is a version of the famous story of "the patient Griselda," from Boccaccio's *Decameron* (Day X, novel 10), well known to English readers from Chaucer's "Clerk's Tale." Some of these pieces assumed gigantic proportions; "The Comedial Action [komedial'nyi akt] about Kaleandra, Princess of Greece, and the Valiant Neonild, Prince of Trebizond," performed in 1731, consists of some 8000 lines, occupying 400 pages of text! The performance took several days, and involved a vast number of actors, who represented not only the ordinary human persons of the story, but pagan gods (one scene took place on Olympus) and numerous personifications of moral abstractions. The drama itself is composed in verse, but every act has both a prologue and an epilogue, which are in prose. A foreign observer records one performance done in Dr. Bidloo's "hospital": "The subject of the piece was the history of Alexander the Great and Darius; it consisted of eighteen acts, of which nine were given at one time, the rest on another day. Interludes were inserted between as entr'actes."[18]

The subjects of most of these plays are love and adventure in remote and romantic places; they all come from the West, and have nothing whatever Russian about them. They do, however, like the tales from which so many of them come, afford an opportunity for glorifying the achievements and ideals of Peter's reforms.

The drama which was composed and played during the first third of the eighteenth century in Moscow, St. Petersburg and a few provincial towns offers little literary interest. It is entirely derivative, and its sources are not the great dramas of the Western tradition, such as the Renaissance produced in Spain and England and the seventeenth century in France. Rather, its derivation is from the static and allegorical tradition of the school drama, ponderously didactic, spectacle rather than action; and from the motley and formless German drama. Linguistically it represents all the worst features of the Russian of Peter's age: a jumble of Church Slavonic, of the officialese of the government bureaucracy, of the ordinary spoken language, and of numerous barbarisms imported from French and German. From such a medley a sense of style cannot be expected. Moreover, the deadly influence of school rhetoric is everywhere apparent: dialogue takes the form of alternating declamations, devised in accordance with what propriety demands in a given situation, but without regard for the character of the persons uttering the tirades. And finally, where the drama is composed in verse, the medium is that lumbering, pedestrian, prosy monstrosity, the syllabic verse, totally incapable by its very nature of anything approaching lightness or natural expression. All that can be said for this drama is that it did serve to keep alive the theatrical tradition until the reform of versification and acquaintance at last with the best Western models, a real drama in Russian finally became possible.

PART II

RUSSIAN LITERATURE BETWEEN
PETER I AND CATHERINE II (1725-1762)

Prince Antiokh Kantemir, Russian Imperial Ambassador to France.
An engraving in the 1762 edition of his satires.

CHAPTER III

ANTIOKH KANTEMIR AND THE SATIRE[1]

In 1709 the great Russian victory at Poltava ended forever Swedish hopes of driving Russia from the Baltic. Charles XII with some remnants of his army fled into Turkish territory and was given asylum. Peter, victorious over Sweden, turned now against his old enemy Turkey, and crossed the Pruth River into Moldavia, one of the principalities dependent on the Ottoman Empire. The Moldavians and Wallachians, who were Orthodox Christians, enjoyed a certain measure of self-government under the Empire, but chafed, of course, under the arbitrary and tyrannical rule of the foreign Muslims. The Hospodar of Moldavia at this time (1710) was Dimitry Kantemir, a very learned prince whose youth had been spent as a hostage in Constantinople. Here he had received a brilliant education, acquired an interest in philosophy, mathematics, architecture and music, learned numerous languages, and a great deal about the early history of the Turks. Newly seated as hospodar in 1710 after the death of his father Constantine, Dimitry Kantemir saw the campaign of the powerful Russian Tsar as a promise of liberation for Moldavia and supported Peter. His calculations were mistaken, however; the Pruth campaign failed, Peter was defeated and forced in the final settlement to return to Turkey even the Azov region which an earlier war had won him. He was able, however, to obtain in the negotiations the Sultan's acquiescence in the free migration to Russia of the Moldavian and Wallachian noblemen who had supported the Russian cause. It was thus that Dimitry Kantemir and his family—a wife, four sons and two daughters— in 1711 left Moldavia forever and took up residence in Russia, where Peter granted them estates and soon employed the former hospodar in diplomatic and administrative duties.

The youngest son of Dimitry Kantemir, by his Greek wife Kassandra Kantakuzena, was a boy of three at the time of the family migration. This son, Antiokh Dimitrievich Kantemir (1708-1744) is usually, and properly, regarded as the founder of modern Russian literature, although, as we shall see, his literary position is ambivalent, and in some respects he belongs as much to the past as to the modern period.

The elder Kantemir, as has been noted, was brilliantly educated, and a very respectable scholar. His *History of the Ottoman Empire*, written in

Latin, is still an indispensable source for any investigator of early Ottoman history. The family employed Italian in conversation, and the boy learned Greek from his mother and Russian from his new countrymen. Like most noblemen's sons of Peter's age, he also learned French. Antiokh apparently studied for a time at the Slavonic-Greek-Latin Academy in Moscow, although without taking a degree. In 1718 it is recorded that he delivered in Greek an oration in praise of his father's patron saint, Demetrios of Thessalonica.

In 1722 the elder Kantemir, accompanied by his youngest son, followed Peter the Great on his campaign against Persia. On the return trip, Dimitry Kantemir died (1723), leaving his children to be taken care of by the Emperor. But Peter I himself soon died (1725), the family estates went to the older sons, and young Antiokh was left to complete his education and make his way as best he might. He entered military service and simultaneously began to write and publish. His earliest literary efforts are translations: one of the Greek chronicle of Constantine Manasses (1725), one of a "Letter of a Sicilian to One of His Friends," with criticisms of Paris and the French; and a paraphrase of some of the Psalms. He also busied himself with a translation of Boileau's *Satires*. In these earliest of Kantemir's works may be observed a very swift evolution of the literary language: the first (the Manasses *Synopsis*) is couched in the conventional "Russo-Slavonic," with the obsolete syntax and vocabulary inherited from centuries of ecclesiastical use. But almost at once elements of ordinary spoken Russian, even of the vulgate (*prostorechie*) begin to appear, creating a rather curious mixture of linguistic levels. Later, as we shall see, Kantemir leans more and more toward the common, idiomatic language of everyday conversation and avoids the pompous and obsolete church language. This is of course the easier for him in that Kantemir is himself in no way whatsoever connected with the church: he is one of the earliest purely secular writers in Russian history.

The true beginnings of Kantemir's literary career can be dated to 1729, when he wrote his "First Satire: To My Mind." Because of its highly critical nature, this work could not, of course, be printed; indeed it was only in 1762 that Kantemir's satires were published in Russia in their original form— eighteen years after the poet's death. The satires, however, circulated widely in manuscript anonymously, in a manner that has been almost normal for "dangerous" Russian literature down to the present time. One of the copies of the piece came to the attention of the powerful Archbishop of Novgorod, Feofan Prokopovich, leader of what was unofficially known as "the learned band." In 1729 Prokopovich was waging a desperate battle against some of the more reactionary church leaders, such as Georgy Dashkov, in defense of Peter's reforms, and indeed in defense of his own life and liberty. The unexpected appearance of a vigorous blast against ignorance and obscurantism must have encouraged Prokopovich mightily. He at once wrote a poem, "To the Composer of the Satire":[2]

I do not know what you are, horned [i.e., powerful] prophet,
    [but] I know how much fame you deserve.
But wherefore conceal your name?
To be sure, the ways of powerful fools are frightening to you.
Spit on their threats! You are thriced blessed.
It is a blessing that God has given you a mind so sound.
What though the whole world be angry at you,
Even without fortune you are fortunate enough.

Great Apollo embraces you.
Everyone loves you, who is a spectator of his mysteries.
The choirs of Parnassus sing of you.
To all men of honor your virtue is sweet
And will be sweet even to future ages.
Even now I am your genuine admirer,
But let this be the summit of your fame—
That evil men hate you.

But do you, as you have begun, continue your glorious course,
On which literary giants have run,
And with bold pen smite evident vice
Against those who do not like the 'learned band.'
And break every vicious habit,
Wishing a good change among men,
Whereby will result more than one fruit of learning,
And the malice of fools will bite its tongue.

                                          (April, 1730)

Evidently the identity of the "composer of satires" soon became known, and young Kantemir became one of "the learned band."

    Tsar Peter II died unexpectedly in January 1730, and hectic intrigues began over the question of a successor. Since the male Romanov line had become extinct, the only heir had to be found on the female side, among the daughters of either Peter I or of his elder half-brother Ivan V. It was, as has been noted, the daughter of the latter, Anna, Duchess of Courland (her husband, the Duke was dead) who was picked. A group of ranking noblemen, whom contemporaries knew as the *verkhovniki*, or "top men," plotted to secure the real power for themselves and keep it in the hands of the chief magnates, as the example of neighboring Poland showed could be done. Anna, in Mitau, faced the alternative of agreeing to a limitation of autocratic power, or to being passed over in favor of one of Peter's daughters: she signed the "conditions." But to the rank and file nobility of Russia such an oligarchy as the "top men" envisaged was far worse than autocracy, and counter-measures were taken to defeat the move. Chief actor in this drama was Prokopovich, who contrived to get a secret letter to the Duchess assuring her of support against the "conditions"; and when Anna arrived in the capital, two proposals were read in the assembly of the gentry in Anna's presence, the first by the historian Tatishchev and the second by young Antiokh Kantemir, demanding the restoration of full autocratic power to the monarch. With this evidence of support, Anna tore up the "conditions" which she had previously signed, and the oligarchic plot collapsed.

Prokopovich's position was of course secure after this, and he died peacefully in 1736. It might be expected that Kantemir would at once attain a brilliant position at court; but Anna Ivanovna, a surly and stupid woman who found the cultured and intellectual Kantemir most uncongenial, was dominated by a horde of Baltic Germans who moved triumphantly in from Courland and occupied all the chief military and administrative posts—her lover Biron, General Münnich, Chancellor Ostermann, et al. The reward, accordingly, which Kantemir obtained for his part in Anna's accession was the post of Russian ambassador to England—a post of great responsibility, since England was at this time openly hostile to Russia, and engaged in undercover negotiations with Poland, Turkey and Sweden. Kantemir, however, was extraordinarily successful as diplomat; and in spite of the niggardly financial backing of the jealous Ostermann, managed to secure for Russia grudging English recognition of her new international position. During his residence in London Kantemir learned English and familiarized himself with English philosophy—Newton, Locke and Hobbes: and English literature—Milton, Pope, Swift, Addison and Steele. He found time also to do some writing—a translation (unpublished) of the "Odes of Anacreon," and a translation from the Latin of Justin's historical epitome. Kantemir remained at this post for six years (1732-1738). In the latter year he was transferred to a still more important diplomatic post, that of ambassador to France, where he continued to the end of his life, another six years (1738-1744), with the same outstanding success against the anti-Russian intrigue and lack of recognition or support from his home government. During this period Empress Anna died (1740) and after the brief regency of her niece, Peter's daughter Elizabeth ascended the throne (1741). These governmental changes did not affect Kantemir's position. In Paris he quickly became acquainted with the leading writers and philosophers, as he had in London with the English. He was on friendly terms with Montesquieu, became acquainted with Voltaire, and admired Nivelle de la Chaussée, the chief representative of the *comédie larmoyante* which classicists such as Voltaire and in Russia Sumarokov regarded with abhorrence. One of his Parisian friends was the philosopher Maupertuis, which perhaps accounts for Kantemir's reserved attitude toward Voltaire, one of Maupertuis' most acrimonious enemies. Kantemir during his Parisian residence also became very close to the Italian colony there, especially Luigi Riccoboni, whose dramatic theories parallel those of

Diderot and de La Chaussée, and envisage the stage as a vehicle for moral uplift.

In 1740 Kantemir, still a comparatively young man, began to suffer from some stomach malady, which worsened alarmingly. Convinced of an early death, he made a last attempt in 1743 to get his satires, of which there were by this time eight, published by the St. Petersburg Academy of Sciences. The attempt failed, and this discouragement, added to his physical condition, hastened his end. He died in April 1744, in the anomalous position of the most important Russian poet of his age, whose most important work was known only in manuscript copies and in prose translations into Russian from a French version published in Paris!

The *Satires* are not Kantemir's only poetical heritage. He translated, as has been noted, some of the so-called "Odes of Anacreon," four of Horace's "Epistles," four of Boileau's "Satires," and a few other small items; he wrote original "Epistles" on the Horatian model, seven "Fables" after Aesop, and a series of epigrams. There is an "Ode" to the Empress Anna on the occasion of her birthday (1731), and a number of other "occasional" poems, including one, mentioned earlier, in reply to Prokopovich's "Shepherd's Complaint." Like many other Baroque poets, Kantemir composed verse paraphrases of some Psalms (36 and 72), and a dozen or so epigrams. There are two poems in his "Complete Works" written in French: "Madrigal à la Duchesse d'Aiguillon" and "Vers sur la critique."[3] The latter—a four-line epigram—goes as follows:

> Cet art de dépriser, toujours si condamnable,
> Par ses propres succès est bien souvent trahi;
> Critique on est bientôt haï,
> Moqueur on devient méprisable.

In the mouth of such an inveterate "critic" of manners as Kantemir, such an utterance gives a strange impression.

Kantemir was, as has been said, a fervent admirer of Peter the Great, and was a youth of seventeen at the date of the Emperor's death. Five years later, in 1730, he composed the first book of what was to have been an epic poem. It is entitled: "*Petriada*, or a Poetical Description of the Death of Peter the Great, Emperor of all the Russias."[4] The conception of this work is highly original: the Almighty, annoyed by Russia's failure to appreciate its Tsar-Emperor, determines to deprive the ungrateful country of his presence, and commissions the Archangel Michael to empower the disease 'Stranguria' to take Peter's life—but only after the lapse of a year. The malady is introduced by the words: "Stranguria is the name the Romans once gave her; 'Blockage of Urine' the Russians have subsequently begun to call her." This singular *dea ex machina* was obviously intended to effect the dénouement, but for the main portion of the epic Peter would have been alive, though ailing, and there would have been ample opportunity for flashbacks to earlier episodes in his career. It is rather a pity that the poet gave up his project after one canto, although the loss to poetry is not likely to be very serious.

Kantemir's major literary contribution is the *Satires*. These were never published in his lifetime, although a prose French translation of one version was published abroad. There are two groups of these poems: the first, which number five, were composed in the years 1729-1731. Satires VI, VII and VIII were written during the poet's Paris residence. One isolated piece, which was not circulated in manuscript as were the first five, nor prepared, with the revised first group and the whole of the second group, for publication by the author (1739-42) is usually given the arbitrary number IX, although from the date "1738" which Kantemir's autograph manuscript gives for it, it belongs to his London period and should accordingly follow V chronologically.

When Kantemir had visions of getting his *Satires* at last published in their original language by the St. Petersburg Academy of Sciences, he prepared a fair copy, which exists, and provides evidence of a very major revision of the first five poems. In part this revision is motivated by the modifications in the syllabic system of versification which Kantemir advocates in his theoretical treatise: "Epistle of Khariton Makentin to a Friend on the Composition of Russian Verses," to which we shall return. In much larger part, however, the revision is evidently intended to bring the older five satires into stylistic conformity with the later three. Since the principles of French classicism dominate the later group, it is not surprising that the revision has the effect often of toning down the sharpness of the language and substituting a universalizing and generalizing approach for the concretely national one of the first version. Liveliness and vigor are thus often sacrificed in the revision; yet in their new form the *Satires* often reveal greater maturity and a more consistent philosophical position in the author than the youthful first version.

The theme of the First Satire[5] is defined by the words: "On Those Who Censure Learning." The further indication of address: "To My Mind" echoes Boileau's "A son esprit" (Satire IX); there is, however, no similarity of either theme or treatment between Kantemir's and Boileau's poems. "Those Who Censure Learning" are very plainly the opponents of Peter the Great's westernizing efforts; the portraits which he gives are vividly and recognizably Russian—a trait that marks them as unclassical, since genuinely classical theory repudiates national and temporal color in favor of a universalized abstractness.

Kantemir begins with an admonition "to his mind" to keep still, pass life quietly without literary effort. Thus the poet's days will be undisturbed; the public is hostile to learning and to any "empty" occupation that does not bring in profit. The first "character study" is so vividly personal that it could be, and was, recognized by contemporaries as that of Georgy Dashkov, Metropolitan of Rostov, one of the most reactionary churchmen of his time: In prose translation:

If you want to be a bishop, deck yourself in a cassock, and over this let a striped chasuble cover your body with pride; hang around your neck a chain of gold, cover your head with a cowl, your belly with a beard, bid the crozier be carried magnificently before you; puffed up in a carriage, while your heart is trembling with wrath, you must bless everyone to the right and the left. Beneath an appearance of humility envy is very deep, and a cruel lust for power blooms in your heart. By these signs everyone recognizes you as a clerical commander, and piously calls you "father." "What's in learning? What profit will come to the Church from it?"

After the ignorant churchman comes the fop who regrets the waste of paper used in printing books—it might be better used for curl-papers! Then the money-lender, whose sole preoccupation is getting "five altyns on the ruble" (about fifteen percent); then the envious man, bent on discrediting in others the learning that he does not himself possess. The envious man's monologue decries grammar as a waste of time because "nature teaches how to speak, without any rules." Metaphysical speculation is useless: "What need is there to know what God is like? It's enough to acknowledge Him." Medicine is all poppycock—"no one has ever seen inside a living body." Astronomy and geometry fare no better.

Next comes the bleary-eyed drunkard, intent on "leading life in merriment"—it's short enough as it is. The satirist then laments: "Pride, sloth, wealth have overcome wisdom; ignorance has taken the place of knowledge." "If one knows how to shuffle cards, knows the taste of various wines, can play three tunes on the pipes, has wit enough to gamble away in a single night what his father has taken pains to collect through a whole lifetime— he is quite skilled enough, he deserves to rank first after Apollo and Plato." The poet finally consoles his mind with the admonition: "If all-kindly wisdom has granted you to know something, gladden yourself in secret, arguing to yourself the value of learning."

In many ways the second version of the First Satire improves on the original; notable is the picture of the hypocritical obscurantist:

"Schisms and heresies are the children of learning. The more understanding one has been given, the more nonsense he talks. He comes to godlessness, who wastes away over a book," grumbles Criton with rosary in hand, and sighs, and begs the Holy Spirit with bitter tears to behold how injurious the seed of learning is among us. "Our children, who formerly used to walk in quietness and submission on the path of their forefathers, nimbly to the divine service, and listened in fear to what they did not themselves understand, have now, to the detriment of the Church, begun to read the Bible! They interpret, want to know the reason, the cause for everything, giving but little credit to the consecrated hierarchy [of the clergy]. They have lost good manners; they have forgotten how to drink kvas, and you couldn't drive them with a stick to eat salt meat. They no longer lay out candles, they don't know what fast-days are. They consider secular power in ecclesiastical hands superfluous, whispering that for those who have already left the secular life, estates and patrimonies are altogether unsuited."

Toward the end of the second version Kantemir adds an unflattering portrait of the ignorant judge, which is wanting in the earlier edition:

Do you want to become a judge? Put on a wig with ties, abuse the man who comes empty-handed with a petition; let your hard heart despise the tears of the poor; and sleep on the bench while the clerk is reading the testimony. If anyone reminds you of the civil law-code, or of the law of nature, or of the rights of peoples, spit in his mug; tell him he is talking utter humbug, in laying upon judges this intolerable burden. It is for scriveners to climb up mountains of paper—it is enough for the judge to know how to fix a sentence.

The Second Satire[6] is also highly relevant to contemporary conditions. As everyone knows, Peter the Great despised "ancient family" unless it was accompanied by personal merit; his chief assistants were many of them parvenus who reached the highest rank and influence solely through their own abilities, while the possessors of ancient names saw themselves passed over. Kantemir casts his second satire in the form of a dialogue— in the original version between "Aretophilus" ("Lover of Virtue") and an unnamed "Courtier"; in the 1738 revision between "Filaret" ("Lover of Virtue") and "Eugene" ("nobly born"). The "nobly born courtier" has only one fairly long speech in which to present his case for conventional "nobility"; the rest of the satire belongs to the "Lover of Virtue."

The original version of Satire II shows evidence of hasty and careless composition, but has in places a great deal more crude vigor than the revision. The latter has eliminated inconsistencies, elaborated some points, toned down others, and created a more artistic whole.

In both versions the "Lover of Virtue" (Kantemir's mouthpiece) accosts an acquaintance (the "Courtier" or "Eugene") with a query as to the reason for his downcast appearance. There seems no obvious reason for this—his mother and relatives are well and keep him plentifully supplied with money (in the first version Aretophilus says: "Your father, I know, is alive and your mother in good health"; and a few lines later the Courtier refers to his father as deceased—"that he was overcome by death"— after all his successes—"is no small marvel to me"!). Then the "Lover of virtue" guesses by himself the reason for "Eugene's" despondency: three men whom he names have recently received advancement in rank, while Eugene has been passed by.

This introduces the expostulation of the "Nobly Born" one: "A fellow from whose hands the calluses have not yet been all wiped away, who used to trade in bast shoes, who used to sell to the ragtag-and-bobtail, who wore down his shoulders miserably with a pot full of pies—who used to be a porter in Moscow, who used to pour tallow-candles—that fellow is honored, famous, wealthy, that fellow is resplendent in rank, while in me nobility groans and sighs. My ancestors for seven hundred and four years have borne an honored name [this would date the Courtier's earliest "noble" ancestor to the reign of Yaroslav the Wise, 1019-1054; the revision takes it back to the time of Olga, 945-962]." The reference to the "pie-seller" of course concerns Prince Menshikov, one of Peter's ablest assistants, whose enemies said he had sold pies in Moscow as a boy. In the first version of the satire the Courtier then goes on to enumerate at length the achievements of his ancestors: "My great-grandfather's great-great-grandfather was his own master; my great-grandfather's grandfather trampled down armies and won praise; his father governed a whole fleet on the sea." Kantemir has evidently forgotten that a nobleman six generations before 1729-30 could hardly have commanded a fleet, when Peter the Great had built the first one only some forty years before! The second version, of course, drops this absurdity. The Courtier then (Version I) enumerates the extraordinary merits of his father, and naively in doing so underlines his own worthlessness: "A hundred gold medals and chains were left by him, which I had recast into drinking cups so that they might not be wasted. In civil government, so help me, he was not the last—Richelieu and Mazarin were poor in deeds beside him. In learning he was very deep; he used to sit over books at night—from this he was stoop-shouldered and weak in the eyes. His library was most wonderful, and although not very large, was reputed to be perfect; various books had been collected on the best subjects. (I remember there was a good book among them on piquet). I would have liked to adorn my walls with them, but I was afraid of mice: [books] are fragile things, so I traded them for a pair of excellent horses, and had six dress coats for myself made from them. In a word, it would be hard to calculate which to praise the more in him—the sword or the pen! In both he was perfect; he adorned both, a man who deserved to live forever and be exempt from the grave." This paragon disappears from version II, to be replaced by a (probably more realistic) bigwig to whom everyone kowtows because he is a royal favorite. Eugene ends his speech with the words: "Judge then for yourself how lightly I must take it, having such glorious ancestors, to remain forgotten, to see myself the last, wherever I raise my eyes."

Aretophilus-Filaret (Kantemir) then launches into the principal matter of the satire, a vehement indictment of the parasitism and worthlessness of his interlocutor, and a defense of the Petrine system of advancement for merit regardless of birth. "Noble birth is bare, when devoid of good actions—a name vainly dreamed up for the indolent, who, adorning themselves with the actions of others, vaunt an honor which they did not earn themselves" (Version I). "A charter riddled by mold and worms is witness that we are the children of noblemen—but virtue alone declares *us* to be noble" (Version II). "Have *you*, despising rest, taken on yourself the toils of war? Have you chased before you the frightened enemy?.... Or, supposing

39

that your youth hasn't permitted this, can there be shown any will and capacity for this in the future?.... Yourself unenvying, kindly, upright, not quick to anger, free of malice, do you believe that every human being is like yourself? Then you can truly say you are noble. You can count yourself Hector's or Achilles' kinsman; Julius [Caesar] and Alexander and all men of glory can be your ancestors, if they're to your liking." (Version II). "There is a difference between being the descendant of noble ancestors and being noble. The same blood flows in freemen and in slaves, they have the same flesh, the same bones" (Version II). "But you, my friend, just consider whether there is the least thing in you to contribute to the beauty of your family name.... How to draw up an army, how to dig trenches, is as outlandish a thing to you as Chinese dances to us; when I mention sieges, entrenchment, attack, you think I'm talking Arabic!.... How could a fleet be entrusted to you? You haven't steered even a rowboat. You have avoided catching fish, because they live in the water. A ship seems to you a coffin, the tackle a winding-sheet, the sea a hell, the sail a shroud, a storm, life's recall; the compass, the rudder on ships are as familiar to you as marble buildings to the Siberian Votyaks.... Not only are you bare of knowledge, but you have as little liking for it, to put it bluntly, as the devil has for incense" (Version I).

Then the actual occupations and interests of the unworthy scion of energetic ancestors are mercilessly passed in review.

The cock would crow, the dawn come up, the sun's rays illumine the mountain-summits—then your ancestors would be leading their armies into the field, while, you, under a brocade coverlet, sunk, body and soul, in soft down, would be snoring thunderously until two parts of the day had fled. Yawning, you would open your eyes, sleep again to your heart's content, stretching out for another hour or two, luxuriating, as you waited for the drink which India sends or is imported from China [i.e., morning tea]. Then you make one jump from bed to mirror, and there, in concentration and profound labor, with a wrap thrown over your back that is fit for a woman's shoulders, you put yourself in order, hair by hair. A part will stand up majestically over the lustrous brow, a part, curled in ringlets, will play freely along the ruddy cheeks, and a part will go into a bag at the back of your head. The tribe of your ilk will admire this arrangement; you yourself, a new Narcissus, are greedily devouring yourself with your eyes. Your foot is duly squeezed into a tight shoe; sweat pours from the servant, and red blotches stand out on two of your corns. The floor is beaten, and a great deal of chalk rubbed under the shoe. Thereupon you don an entire village [i.e., your outer costume has been bought by selling a peasant village]. It did not cost as much to lay the decent foundations of the Roman people as for you to pick color and brocade and have a coat tailored to fit according to the rules of stylish foppery.

Peter the Great had opened the gates to European travel, for himself and others, in order to advance learning in his backward land. And what has "Eugene" learned from his visit to Europe? "From a long-extended journey to foreign parts, from expenditures and labors heavy and extensive, you have derived a marvelous profit. At the sacrifice of your revenue, you have learned

40

that coat-tails should be firm, not flowing [Kantemir's note: "When this satire was written, it was the fashion for coat-tails to stick out firmly, and not hang around the legs, for which purpose they used to be stuffed with cotton-wool."], a half-arshin long [i.e., fourteen inches] and lined with cotton; that when the coat is folded, they should not be covered by the waist [Kantemir's note: "That is, the waist should be shorter than the distance between the gores and the hem of the coat"], what the sleeve should be like, where to put in the gores, where the pocket should be, and how much to add in going around the chest; in summer or fall, in winter or spring, what sort of brocade should be lined with what; which, silver or gold, is more appropriate to stitch on [the coat]. Even Rex [a famous fashionable tailor] would have trouble in knowing more than you."

Is this effete nobleman fit to be a judge? "To judge the children of Adam over the red cloth, or correct them, only that man is fit who has a clean conscience, a heart inclined to pity, and whom neither persuasive money, nor fear, nor hope are strong enough to overcome. Before such a man the wise man and the fool, the rich man and the beggar with his scrip, the old woman's ugly mug and the bloom of a lovely face, the plowman and the grandee, are all equal in court, and one justice is supreme.... Are you able to promise any such thing to the people? The tears of the poor are poured out before you, while you mock maliciously at their poverty; stony-hearted, you beat a slave so as to draw blood because he waved his left hand instead of his right (blood-thirstiness is for beasts only; your servant's flesh is just the same as yours)" (Version II).

But, the nobleman may object, if I am not fit to be a general, a naval commander or a judge, am I any less deserving of ornamental court rank than say, Clitus? Clitus, though he seems to have no other merits, is at least an energetic and indefatigable courtier, and knows how to ingratiate himself. "Clitus is circumspect—he measures his words precisely, flatters everyone, trusts almost no one, does not blush to strike up a friendship with the slaves of new men; his real intentions are assiduously concealed in his actions. He does not regret his labors, as he goes stubbornly toward his goal. Fortune serves Clitus: he needs no other qualities, who has fortune as a friend. But Clitus, even without this, has something which that man must possess who has determined to pass his life in the Tsar's household.... a short tongue, a face fitted to express gladness and sorrow—most favorable to his own profit as it adapts itself to the faces of others." "In short, even vain concerns require a great deal of bother—and I do not see a single laudable quality in you." (Version II)

The peroration of the "Virtue-Lover's" speech comes when he returns to the parvenus—Damon, Tryphon, Tullius—who have just received rewards and advancement. Maybe their ancestors have not been "their own masters" for as long as yours; they are, by their own good qualities, founding their families, as one of your ancestors once did yours. "Your family has been known for seven hundred and four years—and yet, you know, even that wasn't the beginning of the world!.... Adam begot no princes, but one of his sons delved his garden, the other pastured his flock in the fields. All the people Noah saved with him in the ark were simple cultivators of the soil like himself—only they were dear to God. From these we all have our beginning—so what have we to be proud of?" (Version I). The diatribe ends, in Version I, with a classical analogy: "It is more glorious to adorn poverty of birth by good character than to cover up a bad way of life with a title. Baldness did not take away from the glory of Julius '[Caesar]: he covered it up with his laurels—and good character."

Kantemir's Third Satire,[7] in both versions, is addressed to Feofan Prokopovich, "Archbishop of Novgorod and Velikie Luki," with the rhetorical query: why do men, although all made of the same matter and endowed with the same soul, have such different passions? Thereupon follows a gallery of "character sketches," depicting these passions—greed, prodigality, loquacity, envy, gluttony, etc. The classical model is Horace's First Satire of Book I, addressed to Maecenas with the question: why is no one ever quite happy with his own lot, but envies that of another? But Kantemir's treatment and style owe little to Horace; rather, the vivid sketches seem to have their models in the *Characters* of Theophrastus, as translated by La Bruyère. Although presumably universal types, Kantemir's characters in detail are thoroughly Russian. Their names (which the poet in a note, rather gratuitously, assures us are fictitious!) are all drawn, as elsewhere in the *Satires*, from the classical world—Chrysippus, Criton, Menander, etc. The two versions do not show a great deal of difference, except in language; the first redaction is markedly more Slavonic than the second. Kantemir has evidently by 1738 come to the conclusion that the "high style" is inappropriate to the satire.

The gallery of character types starts, as does the Horatian model, with the miser, who is called Titius in the first, Chrysippus in the second version. "The dawn has not yet come, night with her darkness still covers the heavens; all are resting everywhere, all creation is boldly sleeping. But Titius is tossing on his bed; hastily he wipes the sleep from his eyes, lest the day find him in bed. He goes out—the cocks have not yet crowed. You would suppose that he hasn't any food for the morning, he hurries so, fasting, in order not to lose time. But not so! His coffers are already groaning beneath their weight, in his purses coins already corroded are wasting away with rust," etc. The difference in treatment between the two versions here is instructive. Titius (Version I) has a very concrete bit of business in hand when he gets up before dawn and hurries away without breakfast: "Today he has heard that a caravan has arrived from China, and in it has brought precious porcelain in quantity, and they are selling it for a small price; if one were to take it to Vienna, he would get a great profit." Chrysippus too (Version II) is concerned with "a caravan from China," but there are no

42

details about the precise "deal" that he hopes to carry off. This is of course in keeping with the classical demand for abstractness. Similar is the difference in the descriptions of the two men: Titius, "decrepit for he has already lived, a useless burden on the earth, for eighty-four and a half years, trembles all over," etc. Chrysippus is described in a single vigorous line as: "gray-haired, toothless, and already entirely decrepit." His precise age is not mentioned. His character, however, is identical with that of Titius: "Though there is mud up to one's ears, though the sky is bright with fire and is raining rivers, Chrysippus runs three times a day from one end of Moscow to the other." "Every evening Chrysippus is without candles, he is stiff all winter through saving firewood; he is often able to get along without a servant at home; he wears a shirt for two weeks, and the sheets are quite rotten on his bed. He has one coat, and on it the nap, already worn away, has left the thread bare, and even that is by now worn through; and if food is served to him on two plates, he cries: 'To what a point has prodigality come among men!' " Titius is imagined to justify his conduct with the remark of Horace's miser: "It's pleasant to take from a big pile." The satirist warns him, however, again with Horatian precedent, that the "big pile" which he will leave at his death will be rapidly dissipated by his heir, "either drunk up in the tavern, or gambled away at cards, or worn out in rich clothing, or driven away in carriages [adorned] with gold."

Naturally the next example is the spendthrift. The first version leaves him nameless: he is "Titius's neighbor." In the second version, where he is described in very nearly the same terms, he is called Clearchus. "He has a huge house in town, and a house outside of Moscow likewise, both adorned by a hand that is elegance itself; he has an extensive table, all the service on it like a king's, surrounded by a host of servants decked in gold; singers have free access to him, and vile pimps and whores, and the artful enterprises of all the passions, which he showers [with gold] in full handfuls... One would suppose him to be richer than Croesus, though his revenues are no more extensive than mine and will hardly last him for four days. All the rest is procured by debt."

"Damon is not a miser and not prodigal; he is moderate in luxury, [but] it is impossible to tell [him] anything. He is not to be trusted with a secret" (Version I). His name is changed in Version II, but not much else: "When Menander has gathered a plentiful supply of news, the new wine just poured into the cask seethes, hisses, bursts the hoops, blowing out the staves and blows its bung, fiercely flowing out of the mouth. If he meets you, he'll straightway whisper in your ears about two hundred tales—and he's heard these tales from reliable sources, and is communicating them to you out of his love for you, but begging you to keep them to yourself... When he has done telling, he flees from you as a cautious judge flees a petitioner whose pocket is empty; he still has many other people in town to bore."

The original version introduces next an unnamed "hunter after news."

His "passion" is evidently so similar to Menander's that Kantemir suppressed him in the revision, but he has some vivid lines: "He gets up at the crack of dawn, lowers his ears everywhere to listen to what people are saying in their houses and on the streets.... 'Haven't you heard,' says he, 'what they write from Paris? The army will be going to Italy; there will be war, I see. The Spaniard has come over, and their alliance is strong; at present everyone in Italy, I believe, is favorable. In the Senate a decree has been issued to all govenors to submit a list of tax arrears for past years. Yesterday there was a shift of ranks in the Guards. The price has already risen for both firewood and hay. The Synod is going to be enlarged according to Peter's code, the better to spread the glory of the Church. The general from Persia will be here shortly; he is already aboard, I believe, and has already put to sea.' " Here again one can see Kantemir's endeavor to eliminate concrete detail in the interests of classical abstractness.

The "hypocrite" (Fabius in Version I, Varlam in Version II) and the "talkative man" (Grunnius in Version I, Longinus in Version II) have exchanged places. Perhaps because the Latin name carries an irrelevant association with a pig, Longinus replaces it in Version II. Fortunately here the picturesque and realistic details of his loquacity have not been eliminated:

Beware, beware of having Longinus as your neighbor at dinner if you haven't breakfasted. He will direct to you a lengthy embassy from his wife and children, then express his dissatisfaction that you haven't been to see him in a long time, though you know that his daughter is sick with teething: the fourth tooth has already made its appearance on the right side. She cries all night and all day; yesterday the fever abated. His other daughter he is marrying off; the bridegroom is of a well-known family, rich, and only a year older than the bride. He will describe his daughter's dowry in detail, read you the whole settlement contract straight through, and interpret each individual article in it. His younger son, who has only lately learned his alphabet, is now reading syllables excellently. In his village he has begun to dig a new pond—and thereupon he either pulls out of his pocket a sketch of it all prepared, and sets it under your nose to look at, or arranges the knives and forks to represent it. He will reckon up how much land is in [the village], how much quit-rent it brings in, the date at which each of his vegetables gets ripe, and all the owners of the village exactly, one after another, from the very Flood, and how it has passed down intact from hand to hand to him, together with the judges' decrees that brought an end to debt and his quarrel with his uncle.

The first version adds a little to the picture by noting that "he has one ewe that produces two lambs a year; and his cabbage-heads weigh half a pood (i.e., 18 pounds): he loves to tell the truth with a little addition." The first version continues with a section that is omitted in the revision:

But if you aren't acquainted with him, he'll begin to ask questions (for it's impossible for him to keep quiet): What's your name and your father's name? Of what family? Who are you—Russian or foreign? Did you come here on your own, or were you invited? What's your rank? Are you married? Do you have any children? How much income do you have a year? How old are you?

44

After this flood of questions he begins to elaborate on his own affairs;
Version I has him detailing his military career: "On what year and day he
was taken into the service, at how many sieges, in how many wars he has
been boldly present, where his body has been pierced by bullets; he will
recite a whole calendar of the names of his commanders, he will recall who
was appointed in their regiment for latrine duty; he won't forget to recount
how much deprivation he suffered in the wars, in actions... and finally how
he obtained his latest rank." The second version merely says: "God is being
merciful to you, if he doesn't tack the siege of Azov directly on to this; he
rarely skips that, and a whole day is needed to listen to all that tale."

The sketch of the hypocrite (Fabius in Version I, Varlam in Version
II: there is perhaps significance in the fact that this is the only genuinely
Russian name in the whole group—is his vice perhaps a uniquely Russian
one?) comes next; it is decidedly the most savage part of the whole satire:

Varlam is humble, silent; when he enters a room, he will bow low to all, approach
everyone; then having retired into a corner, he will lower his eyes to the ground; you
can hardly hear what he says, hardly hear his steps when he walks. The rosary is constantly in his hands, and in that mouth at every word the terrible name of Christ is
ready. He is inclined to read prayers and set up candles without measure. Touchingly,
ten times an hour, he praises the faith of those who have exalted the Church's glory,
and founded a magnificent temple of God: their souls will assuredly enjoy eternal
bliss. Whither his talk tends, you can guess: he inclines to talk about the Church's
revenues. One who has given that with which it grows fat, he praises: no other act is
so pleasing to God; with this alone we are able to find an easy road to Heaven. When he
is a guest, at table meat is repugnant to him, and he won't drink wine; and this is no
wonder—at home he has eaten a whole capon, and on top of the fat and grease has
with difficulty drunk down a bottle of Hungarian wine. Pitiable to him are people who
have perished in their lusts: but his eye blazes greedily from under his brows at round
breasts, and I would never let my wife make his acquaintance. He is constantly advising
to refrain from anger and forget grievances—but he is trying to wipe his enemy in the
dust in secret, and will give him no rest until his death. And deceiving himself, the poor
wretch thinks: it is as easy to deceive God's all-seeing eye as men's.

The fame-seeker is dealt with shortly. "If he (Cato) publishes a book,
it's not to be a profit to the people, but in order that the name of his family
may be known, it gleams in big letters on the title-page." (Version I).

Narcissus isn't pleased with anything, everything is offensive to him. If someone is
courageous, that's nothing; if he is peaceable, that's not surprising; if someone has overcome powerful and important enemies—that's nothing great, he says, the deeds are
not significant; if one has rectified the law, or if one promises justice, if one is virtuous,
or has a sound judgment, if one is learned, if one has done the people a service, if one
has given [the people] dominion over fire or tame water—it's all something to spit on!
Before him even the whole human race is nothing. He is the only one out of all the
ages whom it is right for everyone to honor. According to his words, other people are
cattle.... Entirely full of himself, he thinks [only] of himself; he imagines that God
doesn't count all the rest in creation, and that everything that has intelligence, possesses

45

eyes and ears in order to admire him, and to listen to what he does and says, and that they wouldn't have any other function—they would be superfluous parts of the body. Though there are everywhere in the world plenty of people of stupidity, the world is crammed most of all with Narcissuses. (Version I).

It may be noted that for once Kantemir has chosen a "speaking name" for his character; but Narcissus becomes Glycon in Version II.

Clitus the drunkard (his name is the same in both versions) is treated with amused contempt:

Clitus is pitiable and ridiculous; in a word, he loves to tipple.... Wherever there is a banquet, wherever there is jollification—it is empty without him. He doesn't drink weak wine—he guzzles stout beer. His eyes are red, he is all swollen, in the rags of his coat one can read that it belongs to one of the sottish clan. When he reaches for anything, his hands tremble; and so do his legs, as a one-wheeled sulky trembles under a pot-bellied clerk. He is free of intoxication—until he wakes from sleep; he rarely lies down at night until he is drunk. All day long he philosophizes, demonstrating plainly that there is a vacuum in creation—whoever disputes it is talking twaddle [he is, of course, engaged in trying to "fill" this vacuum!].

Kantemir then adverts (via Juvenal) to the quaint gods of the ancient Egyptians—dog, cat, the sun, garlic—and presumes that Clitus would be a worshipper of wine. "He sees little of the sun, he knows a dead dog, a cat likewise, while garlic lingers vilely in his stomach. But how blissfully he lives, who gets drunk with wine; without passions, merry, he alone despises all misfortunes, all sorrows, and is quite content with himself!" (Version I).

After the drunkard comes the man of pride. "When he (Celadon in Version I) enters a house where there are a multitude of people, he shoulders everyone aside as a ship in full sail cuts the water.... If he is being seated anywhere at table, he will seize the first chair, he will drink the first glass.... He fancies that that substance which has given him flesh was not the same, but something that shone before all others; it was porcelain clay from which he was made, barnyard mud that made us." Celadon's name is Hyrcanus in Version II.

The revision of the satire contains several "types" who are not to be found in the original version. One of these is Sozimus the malicious backbiter, whose conversation runs in this fashion: " 'Soft Silvanus is successful with his golden bait with his neighbor's chaste wife. I came away hungry from Procopius' dinner. Nastia is red or white by her own efforts: her beauty lies in a cabinet under lock and key. Judge Clementius doesn't know how to behave himself, and dares not read anything without the clerk's spectacles...' " The poet declares: "I count that day unfortunate for me when I chance to meet with him, because I know that as soon as I'm out of his sight, just as malicious talk will be forthcoming about me."

Trophimus is the utterly shameless flatterer, from whom even Juvenal's "hungry Greekling" might learn something: " 'If Titus's wife had been known

46

to Paris,' he avers, 'Menelaus's wife [i.e., Helen of Troy] would still be spinning her wool at home.' he exalts to the clouds all Titus's doings; Titus even knows how to blow his crooked nose intelligently. And not Titus alone is outstanding for him, but he flatters everyone equally. Everything for him is wonderful and glorious, and he fancies that by this means he is making himself liked by everyone. In your piss-pot, in your night-stool he recognizes the odor of musk, and he will shamelessly asseverate this."

Finally comes Naevius, the man who is so morbidly suspicious that he will send one serf to make sure that a carrier doesn't abscond with his parcel, and then a second serf to watch the first; and the envious Zoilus.

At this point in the First Version the satirist admits that however vexatious his characters may be to others, they themselves enjoy the way they are; and it would be possible to look only on the better side, and merely call Titius rich instead of a miser, Clitus (the drunkard) "free of worries," etc.

Suddenly the poet pulls himself up with the words—"Whoa, my Muse! Why don't you know measure in your discourses? Have you forgotten to whom you are talking, whom you are pestering? And do you suppose that Feofan sits idle and hasn't got any other business than to read satire?" Reluctantly he runs over a few other "passions" which he hasn't had time to denounce, and winds up with the admission that everyone has his own foible: "As many heads, so many different notions and desires. Mine is, to write verses against unseemly actions and words; anyone who will correct mine (I too am not spotless)—he will be to me an honored friend."

Of Kantemir's *Satires* the first three are certainly the best, and the last two of the older group and all three (or four) of the newer may be treated more summarily. The Fourth[8] is an expostulation of the poet to his Muse: by inspiring him to write satire, she is getting him into trouble with people. Even though he is careful to use fictitious names, people recognize themselves in his portraits and take offense. Wouldn't it be better to try some other type of writing? How about eulogy? Tullius, for instance, is a sly man—you could praise him for intelligence. Or Silvander—he's a man of very few words, "and even if you know that he's silent out of stupidity, you can, if you choose, give powerful evidence that he is no simpleton, but bridles a sharp tongue intentionally." Or, if eulogy doesn't suit you, try the pastoral: "Sing of how shepherd Tirsis is inacceptable to Lucinda; how he weeps, as he leads his sheep to the streams of water; his wounds from love are deep; how, as he wanders in his grief from end to end in the woods, he often makes echo sing, as he exalts Lucinda." Or there is the elegy: "What is more to the purpose for us mortals than sorrow? We can grieve in good earnest, as we hour by hour draw nearer to death." At this point the quasi-dialogue with the Muse breaks off, and the poet, in his own person, refuses one after another the genres he has just been suggesting to the goddess: "I am unable in any way to eulogize what is deserving of censure"; "It's awkward, it seems to me, to drive a flock in the house, and to blow the sounding horn in the midst of Moscow; while sitting in a warm house, to curse the evil winds, and within walls to make echo sing the songs of the field." And what of elegy? "Wouldn't I be ridiculous if, without knowing love, I were to try to show myself sighing for Iris, who is imaginary—I never saw her in my life! Now to burn for her, now to drown myself in the water, and to keep saying at all times that here I am, dying—though I sleep, eat heartily, and drink off a bucket a day!" So there is nothing for it but to keep on writing satire—especially when I see such tempting examples of vice and folly before me.

The several genres and their conventional characteristics which Kantemir reviews—eulogy, pastoral and elegy—are of course among the most popular of the eighteenth century. It is interesting, however, to note that pastoral and elegy have not yet, in 1731, been naturalized in Russia. The content of these genres, as he pictures it, will be repeated *ad nauseam* by later eighteenth-century Russian poets; but as Kantemir presents it, he must be thinking of French or Italian models.

Satire V[9] underwent the most drastic revision of all. It began as a kind of paraphrase of Boileau's Satire VIII, "On Man," and had as its principal theme the inconsistencies of human desires: the merchant would be a judge, the peasant a soldier, etc., very much along the lines of the first satire of Horace's first book of *Sermones*. The original version took the form of a catalogue of types, rather like those in the Third Satire, but much more general, and without even fictitious names. Man alone suffers from such follies—the other animals are free from them. But, one may object, man's superiority to the animals is surely evidenced by his invention of laws. Not so, says the satirist, quite the contrary: animals do not need the constraint of law, but man does. What about human altruism? You might find ten examples in seven and more centuries. Then follows an enumeration of human folly—first of the youth, then of the mature man, and finally of the aged. "Man alone, endowed with the light of reason, goes all his life in darkness; assiduous out of season, he toils for what he doesn't need, and is idle in what is necessary." The first version cites Adam and Eve and the eating of the apple as typical of all the conduct of their descendants.

As rewritten this satire becomes inordinately long—748 lines as against 464 of the first version. In form it is now a dialogue. A human poet (perhaps Kantemir himself under the name of Perierg, i.e., "the inquisitive") sees a satyr, ridiculously attired in wig, knee-breeches, etc., busily disrobing. He accosts the creature, who at first rebuffs him—he has had enough of human beings!—but after a little relents and tells his story. It must be interjected here that for the eighteenth century the Greek "satyr," imagined as a partially human figure with goats' horns and feet, was made the eponym of the Latin "satira," through a fancied connection of the name. Kantemir's "satyr" is therefore "satire" embodied. The device of employing a non-human critic of man's follies was probably suggested to Kantemir by Boileau's Satire VIII, where an ass is imagined in the same role. It seems that

Pan, the "king" of the satyrs, loves to be amused, and so sends out some of his subjects every three years to live among men, and from the follies that he observes, gather material to amuse the king. But this satyr has had enough before the end of his term—he is going back to Pan at once, even if it means punishment. Even as it is, he is sure he has material sufficient, from his brief stay, to keep Pan in laughter.

This framework holds the revised version together. The satyr relates how he reluctantly put on human clothes, emerged from his woods and entered "your city" (no further designation), where he found all the streets full of drunkards, either lying inert on the ground, or walking about in a daze. A portly gentleman tells him the reason—it is customary to celebrate church festivals in this fashion, and this happens to be a day sacred to St. Nicholas. The gentleman takes the satyr into his service, which consists chiefly in bringing water from the river with which he dilutes wine and then sells it to the people. When the satyr makes some rather sharp comments on this practice, the wine merchant dismisses him as an ignoramus. The merchant's next-door neighbor is the trusted steward of a prominent nobleman; he takes on the satyr as a helper in his business, which seems to be chiefly the pilfering of his master's property, from which he has grown very rich. He is caught, however, disgraced, and with his family ends up begging his bread. The satyr then passes into the service of the "prominent nobleman," whose name is Chiron. Though Chiron is so stupid that he can scarcely speak an intelligible sentence, he imagines, because of his constant flatterers, that he is enormously clever, and so undertakes to increase his revenues by dipping into the royal treasury. He is of course detected, and follows his dishonest steward into penury. The satyr then takes service with Menander, one of Chiron's fair-weather friends, who has deserted him in adversity. When the satyr protests this kind of conduct, Menander contemptuously replies: "Chiron's bright days have already fled—there's nothing more to be expected from him. When we've sucked out all the juice, we're in the habit of throwing away a lemon." Chiron's twenty-year-old heir, Xenon, takes Chiron's place as Menander's friend, and the satyr is presented to him as his jester. Impatiently interrupted here by Perierg, the narrator passes over Xenon's fate and goes on to tell of his service with Milon, an apparently honest citizen of moderate means, "quiet and pious." Milon, however, proves to be "quiet and pious" only when among outsiders— he, his wife, and his three children fight all the time at home, and their brawls usually end up involving their unhappy servant. The climax comes when a most unseemly family altercation takes place in the midst of a mass which a priest is conducting in the house. The priest is mauled for attempting to quiet things, and the satyr thrown downstairs for his protests. A section of generalized moralizing then follows, in which the narrator departs from chronology and cites a series of typical "fools" without autobiographical reference. Most of these are drawn from Version I and ultimately from

49

Boileau. In a final paragraph the satyr observes to "the inquisitive one": "The sun has already begun to hide himself behind the mountain. I am undressed, [so] farewell. It's time for me to part from you. Conceal my discourse [and keep it] to yourself, if you think there is any profit in it. Don't try to use it to straighten people out: you and I have too little strength for that—we might more easily straighten out hunchbacks."

Satire IX[10], so-called, is actually, as we have noted, next in date after VI; it was written in London in 1738, but for some reason not revised for publication with the older group when Kantemir was preparing his satires for a printing that never materialized. It is addressed: "To the Sun. On the Make-up of This World." According to the author's note, the sun is invoked as the source of all light, i.e., enlightenment. An ignorant ex-peasant is supposed to be grumbling over modern "scientific" views on nature, ecclesiastical traditions, etc. "He babbles theological discourses to you: how many candles should be set up before the icons..... how it's a wonder to him that God tolerates the shaving of beards; and why do they issue the Bible in print, which is mighty sinful for Christians to know?" Another argues that it is contrary to church teaching to decry drunkenness. Superstitious beliefs about God are too numerous to list. And outward piety often conceals the worst of morals: "Just look: a merchant adorned to his waist with a beard.... upright, pious in everything: when he approaches the icons, he makes the whole floor shake with his genuflections! You would suppose that he was a person of dignity and altogether righteous. But just look tomorrow, where is he? Ensconced in jail. You ask: 'What is a holy, elderly man sitting there for?' He was smuggling in goods without paying a duty." A printed advertisement announces: "Tomorrow lofty instruction will begin: teachers from beyond the sea are being collected. Let everyone as speedily as possible take thought for himself, who has a desire to be taught." "A poor man, who desires with all his heart to be instructed, hurries there with all his might and speed. He arrives—he'll see a great deal of politeness *[komplimenty]*, but of lofty learning not a shadow." As for us, we "swear to God we will not offend the poor, but all in righteousness take thought for our souls, and not consider persons or silver. But when they bring presents, where gold glitters, all that notion flees a hundred versts away from us." "Where is fear of God or man? Farewell our souls, when the silver bell begins to tinkle in our ears." But instead of being offended by such conduct as this, our "village philosopher" inveighs against the immorality of smoking tobacco! "Truly, O Sun, I shall never cease marveling that you have been granted the will to keep on patiently shining on us poor wretches, who live so contrary to God."

Kantemir began writing satires apparently with the youthfully naive belief that they might actually serve to correct the vices and follies of mankind. He was deeply imbued with the enlightenment philosophy, which was essentially optimistic. Man, after all, was a rational creature, and only needed to have the folly of his ways clearly pointed out to him to change them. Kantemir had also counted on the rulers who succeeded his idol Peter to continue along the lines of the great reformer. When they did not do so, when his own signal services to Anna Ivanovna were dismissed almost unrewarded, when he saw that far from becoming an instrument for the improvement of morals, his satires could not even be printed—the poet became despondent and pessimistic. When after the lapse of several years (1731-1738) he began again to compose satires, these took a quite different form from the earlier group. The subjects of the final three (VI, VII and VIII) are all general, abstract, and their intention is plainly no longer to promote the "enlightenment" of mankind, but rather to create for the poet himself a quiet oasis in the midst of universal evil and folly. Significantly the first satire of the second group, VI[11], is entitled: "On Genuine Happiness." It begins with an echo of Horace's "Beatus ille qui—," but follows up with an elaboration of other Horatian maxims for contentment:

In this life that man alone is happy, who, content with a little, knows how to pass his life in quietness, free from vain fancies such as torment others, and treads the hopeful path of virtue to its inevitable conclusion. His house is small, built on land of his own, which produces what is necessary for a moderate desire; food not scanty and not excessive, and moderate entertainment—where, with another chosen friend I may in my own fashion in idle hours chase away the time of boredom, where I, remote from tumult, may pass all the rest of my time among the dead Greeks and Latins, pursuing actions and causes of all things, learning to know by the examples of others what is useful, what injurious in manners, what is disgusting, what attractive in them—this constitutes the summit of my desires.

The life of the ambitious man is laborious and at the best he attains his end when he is already old and feeble and no longer able to enjoy himself. Better to live unnoticed, in Epicurean retirement, and not to be prey to "the tooth of envy." "To be good is already no small reward in itself."

The Seventh Satire[12] begins rather bitterly with the poet's acknowledgement that his verse has little effect toward "correcting morals." "If I, seeing a person who never lets the breviary out of his hands, and goes to church five times a day, fasts, sets up candles, and doesn't sleep with his wife, though he takes from a poor man the one shirt that he possesses and makes him go naked—if I should say, seeing him, 'My friend, your mind is astray; by this path you won't get into heaven, and if you have a care to save your soul, give back that which you wrongly possess.' Flaring up, he will reward my zeal with this answer: 'In vain, you whipper-snapper, are you butting in with your advice.' "

If you ponder the reason why men should be so prone to follow wrong courses of action, the common man will say that it is because of "original sin"—men were born evil. And it is true that a piece of ground, neglected, will grow up to weeds. But there is one time of life when we have but little inclination to wrong—that is youth. And it is a bad education in youth that leads to vice in maturity.

To leave our children a rich heritage is our anxiety, and we sweat over this; but it rarely enters the mind of two or three [fathers] how their childhood is to be passed. And a man who spends more than one thousand on trifles, begrudges even the slightest expense on the upbringing of his children. But when his son comes to maturity and plays the rogue, the father is grieved and ashamed. In vain does he attempt to shake the blame from his own shoulders: he has heaped up riches for his son—but scorned to implant morality in his heart. His son will be rich, but will live his life without glory, little liked and despised by the world—if he does not, a complete rascal, run straight into the noose.

    The chief business of education consists in this, that the child's heart, expelling passions, should be confirmed in good morals, so that thereby your son may be useful to his fatherland, well liked among people, and always wanted—and to this end all the arts and sciences must lend a hand.

The maxims which Kantemir gives for a good education are sensible and enlightened, and the satire, which is one of the mildest and most moderate of the nine, is also one of the most mature. Ironically, it is also the one in which the poet seems most painfully aware of his own youth (his imaginary opponents call him *molokosos*—"milk-sucker," i.e., "whipper-snapper"), and of the inadequacy of his own qualifications for preaching on education— since he is himself unmarried and childless.

    The final one of the nine satires is number VIII[13], subtitled "On Shameless Impudence." It is the shortest (135 lines) and least consequential of the entire group; the poet begins with an ironical congratulation to the man who can compose verses rapidly and without much consideration; as for himself, he is always painfully aware of offending people, and of his own inadequacies. From here the satire goes on to contrast this modesty and discretion with the "shameless impudence" which is rife in the world, and is so tiresome and irritating.

    As Belinsky remarks in his article on Kantemir,[14] everyone agrees that modern Russian literature was created by Lomonosov, yet all histories of it begin with Kantemir. One reason why the latter, despite the genuine importance of his *Satires,* cannot be given credit for setting the new direction in Russian literature is the poet's mistaken attitude toward his own medium. In the matter of versification Kantemir belongs to the seventeenth, not the eighteenth century. He clings to the end to the awkward syllabic system of versification, so ill-suited to the Russian language, and this at a time when both Trediakovsky and Lomonosov had pointed the way toward a new and better system. He has been excused for this on the ground that all the latter part of his life was passed away from his native land, and among foreigners (the French), whose own system of versification was the basis for the syllabic method in Russian. This is undoubtedly a valid conclusion; but certainly more pertinent is Kantemir's own complete lack of a poetical sense. His verse is at its best forceful, pungent, even epigrammatic.; he learned in the course of composing his *Satires* to avoid the crabbed and antiquated Church Slavonic, with its inevitable ecclesiastical associations, and to write in plain, idiomatic Russian; but he had not the slightest glimmer of poetical feeling, and of beauty in his verse there is not a trace. The old-fashioned syllabic system satisfied him because he neither sought nor would have recognized euphony in a line of verse; as long as it said, clearly and unambiguously, what he meant, he was content. This attitude is of course in keeping with the eighteenth-century view of poetry as a kind of geometry, in which clarity is the highest virtue; but even the eighteenth-century poets are seldom as tone-deaf as Kantemir.

He encountered Trediakovsky's pioneer treatise, "A New and Short Method for Composing Russian Verse," which was published in 1735. Asked by his friend Nikita Yurievich Trubetskoy to comment on it, Kantemir wrote his "Epistle of Khariton Makentin [an anagram of Antiokh Kantemir] to a Friend on the Composition of Verses in Russian,"[15] which was published after the poet's death, in 1744, along with his translation of the *Epistles* of Horace. The "Epistle of Khariton Makentin" starts out with a wholly inadequate and unrealistic division of verse into three kinds: Greek and Latin quantitative verse (which Kantemir thinks could perfectly well be used in Russian also!); the verse which the Italians call "free," that is, unrhymed; and rhymed verse. He ignores entirely the essential division which Trediakovsky makes, between verse based on number of syllables and verse based on accent. In the course of the treatise, however, he makes the concession that the best verse will be the thirteen-syllable line (the so-called "heroic" line) in which there will be an obligatory accent not only, as always, on the syllable next to the last, but also on the fifth or seventh, just before the caesura. There is thus some intrusion of a syllabo-tonic system in the "Epistle," and the line which he uses as his example (the first of his own Satire VI) is actually, though accidentally, tonic: *tot lish' v zhizni sei blazhen/ / kto malym dovolen.* But in defining the "rules for the thirteen-syllable verse" he states unequivocally: "The syllables of the first hemistich up to and including the fourth can be either long or short, as the case may be; but it is absolutely essential that either the seventh or the fifth be long. And in the latter case [i.e., if the fifth is "long," i.e., accented] that the sixth and seventh be short." In other words, the actual word accent is completely disregarded in the first four syllables of the first hemistich; and the second hemistich must be terminated with a two-syllable, i.e., feminine, rhyme. As we shall see, Trediakovsky was also timidly conservative in the latter regard, and long maintained that a line of verse must have a trochaic rhythm and feminine rhyme. In conformity with the principles which his "Epistle" enunciates, Kantemir rewrote his earlier five Satires, which thus may be regarded as the last examples of the literary use of syllabic versification in Russian.

CHAPTER IV

VASILY TREDIAKOVSKY AND THE REFORM OF RUSSIAN VERSIFICATION

Vasily Kirillovich Trediakovsky (1703-1769)[1] was one of the most productive scholars of his century, an original poet and a theorist on language and versification who has left an indelible mark on the history of his country's literature. His contributions to Russian literary history are numerous and impressive: he was the first important writer to introduce the theme of love into Russian literature, a theme which ecclesiastical puritanism had before him kept at a distance; in his old age his verse translation of Fénelon's *Les Aventures de Télémaque* introduced the accentual dactylic hexameter into Russian verse; and his "New and Short Method of Composing Russian Verse" (1735) paved the way for the complete reform of Russian versification. In spite of these great services to his native language, Trediakovsky died an embittered and almost forgotten man, and only in quite recent times have scholars begun to do him justice.

The reasons for the indifference and contempt to which contemporaries subjected him are various, and largely unconnected with literary judgments. Trediakovsky was doubtless a quarrelsome, vindictive person, extremely vain and touchy about his own merits; he offended Elizabeth and Catherine the Great by his devotion to their predecessor Anna Ivanovna and by his critical attitude toward autocratic monarchy; he quarreled with the German professors of the Academy, who had tried—in his case unsuccessfully—to keep all Russian scholars out of that citadel of learning; he won the hatred of the conservative clergy by reputed atheism and by the "corruption of the youth" which his translation of the *Voyage à l'isle d'amour* of Paul Tallemant was supposed to have occasioned; and he made himself foolish and earned contempt by a bold and fruitless attempt to falsify the evidence that Lomonosov and not he was the real reformer of the Russian verse system. Most of these counts against Trediakovsky reflect on his character, rather than his literary achievements, and are irrelevant to a literary evaluation.

The man had a turbulent and most uncommon youth. The son of an Orthodox priest, born in Astrakhan, he was educated first in a Catholic school run by Capuchin monks and conducted entirely in Latin. At the age of twenty he ran away to Moscow, where he studied in the Greek-Latin-Slavonic Academy. In 1725 he fled from Russia, under circumstances not yet clear, to The Hague, and thence in 1727 to Paris, where he studied for three years at the Sorbonne. When he returned in 1730 to his native land, Trediakovsky was a master of four languages besides his own—Greek, Latin, French and Italian—was a competent mathematician and well versed in the natural science of his day, as well as in philosophy and theology. His knowledge of French was fluent and idiomatic, and he even composed some quite passable verses in that language. Almost at once after his return, Trediakovsky published (1730) his translation of a frivolous allegorical work, *Voyage à l'isle d'amour*, of the Abbé Paul Tallemant (1663). This was a typical product of French *préciosité*, partly in prose and partly in verse, recounting the adventures of Tirsis, his beloved Aminta and her rival Iris. The map of "The Isle of Love," like the "Carte du Tendre," is marked by towns called "Bon Accueil" and "Espérance," and peopled by such personifications as "Modestie," "Coquetterie," and the like. Honor, Shame and Pride attempt to divert Tirsis from his pursuit of Aminta, and at the end of the work Tirsis falls in love with Glory and abandons the Isle.

Trediakovsky's translation, *Ezda v ostrov liubvi*,[2] attracted immediate and generally favorable attention. It was significant for two reasons. In the first place, it was the first attempt to naturalize in conservative Muscovy the western attitude toward love. The *Voyage to the Isle of Love* is certainly not a licentious work by modern standards, but it does treat love as an exciting and absorbing pastime, rather than as a diabolical trap (as Muscovite tradition regarded it). In the sense that Trediakovsky's work made love seem like an innocent, natural and attractive diversion, it might have contributed to "corrupting the morals" of young Muscovites of both sexes. However, it had another and in the long run perhaps more significant effect. In his foreword to the translation, Trediakovsky explained his choice of language: he had eschewed the Church Slavonic, he said, for several reasons. First, it was an ecclesiastical language, and his work was decidedly secular; second, because Slavonic had become, to his generation, a "dark" and often unintelligible language, and the "Voyage," being about the universal passion of love, required an easy understanding; and lastly, because "the Slavonic language sounded too harsh to his ear." He endeavored therefore, as he said, to compose his translation "in the simplest Russian speech, that which we use in our daily intercourse." It must be admitted that in this last endeavor Trediakovsky was not altogether successful. His language is a rather crude mixture of the Russian vulgate, foreign borrowings, occasional Slavonicisms, and even neologisms of his own. But at least he was aware of the linguistic problem—the necessity of freeing Russian from the hampering ecclesiastical tradition of Slavonic—and of the writer's prime necessity of being intelligible. One wishes that he might have retained this youthful attitude toward language in his later days, but unhappily he fell back in most of his subsequent verse into the most extreme forms of traditionalism, and composed verse which a combination of Slavonic vocabulary and a perverse and unnatural word positioning makes almost unintelligible.

In June 1735, during the course of the so-called "War of Polish Succession," the forces of Empress Anna Ivanovna won a signal victory over the French at Dantzig (Polish Gdansk). The French fleet was routed from Baltic waters, and the 2000-man French landing force captured, after which the well-fortified port city surrendered to the Russian commander. Stanislaus Leszczynski, the Polish pretender supported by France, was obliged to flee from the city disguised as a peasant. This brilliant victory inspired Trediakovsky to the composition of a panegyric pompously entitled: "Triumphal Ode on the Capture of the City of Gdansk, Composed to the Great Glory of the Name of the Most Illustrious, Imperial Great Sovereign Anna Ivanovna, Empress and Autocrat of All Russia, by Vasily Trediakovsky, Secretary of the Imperial Academy of Sciences of St. Petersburg."[3] The poem consists of nineteen 10-line stanzas, each line of nine syllables, and rhymed *ababccdeed*, all the rhymes being feminine. The composition is syllabic, that is, the lines are measured by number of syllables, with no regard for the placing of the word accent; and the lines are without caesura. The effect of this kind of versification may be judged from the first strophe, with the natural accent marked:

> Кóе трéзвое мнé пиáнство
> Слóво даéт к слáвной причи́не?
> Чи́стое Парнáса убрáнство
> Мýзы! не вáс ли ви́жу ны́не?
> И звóн вáших стрýн сладкоглáсных,
> И силу ли́ков слы́шу крáсных;
> Всé чи́нит во мнé рéчь избрáнну.
> Нарóды! рáдостно внемли́те;
> Бурли́вые вéтры! молчи́те:
> Хрáбру прославя́ть хощý Áнну.

("What sober intoxication gives me words for the glorious occasion? Chaste ornament of Parnassus, O Muses! Is it not you whom I behold? And the sound of your sweet-voiced strings, and the power of beautiful choirs that I hear? Everything creates in me elegant speech. O peoples! Hearken with gladness! Tempestuous winds, be silent! I desire to glorify the valiant Anna!")

The genre which Trediakovsky's "Ode" thus formally introduces into Russian literature is one which of course had long been cultivated, under other names. The "Greetings" (*privetstva*), "Congratulations" (*pozdravleniia*) and similar occasional verses of Simeon Polotsky, Silvester Medvedev, Karion Istomin and their compeers are in fact very similar in content, if not in form; and the *Epinikion* of Feofan Prokopovich on the victory of Poltava is an "ode" in all but name. The name, however, is important here; although Prokopovich composed Latin "odes," he did not use the term, or the precise construction, in Russian. Trediakovsky's poem was, as he himself declares, directly modelled on the famous French composition of Boileau, "Ode sur la prise de Namur" (1694). The "triumphal ode" was not a genre much cultivated in the West, but Malherbe had introduced it, and Boileau's example had popularized it; the traditions governing it prescribe a strophic division, with a regular rhyme scheme, alternating masculine and feminine rhymes; short lines, usually octosyllabic; a lofty, poetic language, remote from ordinary speech; an inspired, prophetic manner, etc. All this is a heritage from the two ancient poets whose odes served as models, Pindar and Horace; and in his "Ode" Trediakovsky attempts to naturalize these characteristics of the genre in Russian. Metrically his "Ode" is a compromise between the western traditions and the exigencies of the syllabic system of versification; his language is strongly Slavonic and his syntax, as usual, Latinate.

The original composition of 1734 was still in "syllabic" verse, of which more presently; after his great discovery of the syllabo-tonic system, the poet rewrote his "Ode," following the new principles, and published the second version in the edition of his "Works" in 1752.[4] A comparison of the re-written first strophe with the original is revealing:

Ко́е стра́нное пиа́нство	What strange intoxication
К пе́нию мой гла́с бодри́т!	Emboldens my voice to song!
Вы́ парна́сское убра́нство	You, the adornment of Parnassus,
Му́зы! у́м не ва́с ли зри́т?	O Muses—is it you my mind be-
Стру́ны ва́ши сладкогла́сны,	holds?
Ме́ру, ли́ки слы́шу кра́сны;	Your sweet-voiced strings,
Пла́мень в мы́слях восстае́т.	Measures, lovely choirs I hear;
О! наро́ды, всё внемли́те;	A flame arises in my thoughts.
Бу́рны ве́тры! не шуми́те:	Oh, peoples, all hearken;
А́нну сти́х мой воспое́т.	Tempestuous winds, do not clamor;
	My verse will celebrate Anna.

Several features of the revision should be noted and borne in mind in connection with Trediakovsky's reform, to be presently discussed: first, the nine-syllable line has been shortened; second, the rhymes are alternately feminine and masculine, and the lines accordingly have either eight syllables (feminine) or seven (masculine); third, the lines are measured by feet, which are prevailingly trochaic, four to a line, i.e., trochaic tetrameter; and fourth, a certain "license" is allowed, whereby a foot of two unaccented syllables (a "Pyrrhichius" *[pirrixii]* in Trediakovsky's classical terminology) is substituted for a trochee (e.g., in the first line, which is scanned: *koe strannoe pianstvo*).

The original form of Trediakovsky's "Ode" was published in the year of the victory, 1734. Later in the same year he wrote his "New and Short Method of Composing Russian Verse,"[5] with its complete repudiation of the syllabic principle; and in 1739 Lomonosov, having appropriated Trediakovsky's "Method," composed and published his "Ode on the Capture of Khotin," which has been generally regarded, both in his own and in a later age, as a far more successful poem and representative of the genre than that of his rival, in either of the latter's versions. But it should not be forgotten that Trediakovsky was unquestionably the one responsible for introducing the form, which was to become almost the dominant verse genre throughout the first half of the eighteenth century.

The literary stir occasioned by Trediakovsky's *Voyage to the Isle of Love* brought him at once to government attention; in 1732 he was made an official translator for the Academy of Sciences, and in 1733 secretary of that learned body. The Academy of Sciences, which Peter the Great had planned, but which was opened only after his death, by his wife in 1725, was staffed entirely by Germans. During the pronounced "German tyranny" of the reign of Anna Ivanovna, this was not surprising, especially in view of the scarcity of fully trained Russian scholars. When in 1745 Trediakovsky and Lomonosov were made Professors of the Academy (Trediakovsky "Professor of Eloquence"), they were the first Russians actually to be admitted to equality with the German academicians.

The final stage in Trediakovsky's early, and short-lived, success came as a result of his most important and prestigious contribution to Russian literature. In 1734 he wrote, and published in the following year, his epoch-making treatise "A New and Short Method for Composing Russian Verse, Together with a Definition of the Names Appertaining Thereto."[5] For a full understanding of the importance and bearing of this treatise, it will be necessary to review briefly the state of Russian versification in 1734.

The verse system[6] which had prevailed in Muscovy for nearly a century and a half was, as has been noted before, a foreign importation, completely without native roots. It was, moreover, a system grotesquely unsuited to the nature of the Russian language. "Syllabic verse" had been introduced into Russian from Ukrainian and Belorussian centers, to which Polish influence had brought it. For Ukrainian and Belorussian it was just as unsuited as for Great Russian; but for Polish, with its fixed word accent (always on the penult), the system was natural and inevitable. Polish had taken it over, with some modifications, from French, a language in which a very peculiar evolution had brought to the virtual elimination of word accent.

The Romance languages, with the exception of French, and all the Teutonic languages, including English, as well as the ancient tongues of Greece and Rome, measure lines of verse by units called *feet*. Such feet in the ancient languages may be of two syllables, of three, of four, and even of five; but the two-and three-syllable feet predominate. Latin and Greek are

58

quantitative languages, and feet are defined by alternations of "long" and "short" syllables. Neither Romance, Teutonic, nor Slavic languages, however, possess quantity as a significant linguistic feature, and metrical "feet" are therefore defined not by alternations of "long" and "short" syllables, but by accentual alternation. An accented syllable takes the place in such a "tonic" system of a "long" syllable, and an unaccented of a "short" syllable. By the seventeenth century all west European languages had evolved a system of versification based on such alternation of "tonic" feet, except the French. The Teutonic languages, from their earliest beginnings, had been freer in this regard than the Romance. A completely "tonic" system takes account simply of the *number of accents* in a line, regardless of the number of syllables; but the Romance languages have generally observed a system of *feet*, and thus of a regularity of syllables, as well as accents. The French language, alone of west European tongues, having established its word accent uniformly on the final syllable and thus practically eliminated it, could not make use of the tonic principle in verse construction. French was therefore obliged to resort to a much less satisfactory, because less definite, means of defining a line of verse—the counting of syllables. Since such syllable-counting is difficult for the ear to apprehend without aid, the device of end-rhyme was adopted as an obligatory feature of French verse. The final rhyming word informs the ear that a certain number of syllables has been ticked off, and the line is ended. Another peculiar feature of the French language comes into play here—the "mute e." French has eliminated from ordinary pronunciation all original post-tonic syllables, but retains in writing the post-tonic "e," which is unpronounced, or "mute," except in solemn declamation. It is given syllabic value, however, in versification when it comes before a consonant or at the end of a line. Under the latter condition the end-rhyme is "feminine," that is, two-syllabled; and from at least the sixteenth century French poets have generally observed the rule that "feminine" and "masculine" (one-syllabled) rhymes should alternate.

Of course lines of French verse can have any desired number of syllables, and one thinks of such a nineteenth-century *tour de force* as Victor Hugo's *Les Djinns,* with lines running from two to thirteen syllables. By Malherbe's time, however, at the end of the sixteenth century, the "Alexandrine," of alternately 12 and 13 syllables, had come to be the standard line for verse drama, for narrative verse, and for much lyric verse. It was this line which the Poles chiefly utilized, and which from them passed into Russian use. Since Polish word accent is uniformly on the next to the last syllable of every word (except, of course, monosyllables!), it follows that "masculine" rhyme is impossible. The longer, 13-syllable, form of the "Alexandrine" accordingly became the standard Polish line, and it was this which Simeon Polotsky and the other "syllabic" poets imported into Russian.

The Russian language, however, although belonging to the same linguistic family as Polish, is radically different in the matter of accent. Russian retains the original Slavic "free accent,"—that is, the accent of a word may fall on *any* syllable at all, from the last to sometimes as many as seven or eight from the end; and there is, moreover, no such "secondary accent" as Teutonic languages have. When a language of such a sort is forced into the straight-jacket of a "syllabic" line, in which only two syllables at most out of the thirteen (the seventh and twelfth) have a fixed accent, the result is invincibly prosy. What results inevitably is a series of lumbering, heavy lines, distinguished from prose only by the monotonous feminine rhyme and the presence of a definite number of syllables. Syllabic verse is incapable of the grace of genuine poetry, and is at the same time not even good prose. The amazing thing about the situation is that such an ill-adapted medium survived for nearly a century and a half before anyone realized and pointed out its shortcomings.

Vasily Trediakovsky had some natural advantages for making the epoch-making discovery: he was well acquainted with Latin and Greek, and hence with the system of verse "feet"; he also knew Italian, which utilizes a syllabo-tonic system of versification. He did not know German, but he knew Germans, and very probably had come across some of the hybrid lyrics which various Teutons—Danes, Swedes and Germans—who were at home in Russian had written in their adopted language, but using the accentual principles of their native tongues. Some of these experiments have survived to our day, particularly those of the Swede Sparvenfeldt and the Germans Gluck and Paus. They are the earliest syllabo-tonic verses in Russian, but by themselves could of course have never effected the necessary reform. Trediakovsky's intimate association with the French and with French verse might be thought to have stood in the way of his taking a step that went directly counter to French tradition; but here, it would seem, another influence was at work which proved decisive. Trediakovsky's earliest Russian verse, published at the same time as his *Voyage to the Isle of Love,* consists of "songs." These are written, to be sure, according to the syllabic system, but in shorter lines than the standard "heroic" verse, and with a freer rhyme scheme; and in many cases the lines can be read accentually. The pieces are genuine songs, and were enthusiastically adopted as such and passed into a repertory that may well be termed "popular"; they often turn up in the hand-written song-books of the eighteenth century. As songs, they tend to maintain accent in rhythmic alternation, perhaps even unconsciously. Thus, for example, the four-stanza "Love Song," of which the first strophe reads:[7]

Красо́т уми́льна!	O beloved one of beauties,
Па́че всех си́льна!	Mighty beyond all [others]!
Уже́ склони́вши,	Already inclining,
Уж победи́вши,	Already victorious,
Изво́ль сотвори́ть	Deign to perform

Ми́лость, мя́ люби́ть:	A kindness, and love me:
Люблю́, драга́я,	I love, O precious one,
Тя́, са́м весь та́я.	Thee, myself all wasting away.

In composing these songs Trediakovsky was undoubtedly influenced by the songs of the common people, both lyric and narrative (the *byliny*); and in these native Russian productions he recognized the accentual system of versification, and correctly inferred that the original Slavic method of composition was accentual, and had nothing to do with syllable-counting.

Stender-Petersen[8] has suggested still another possible influence that may have pointed to Trediakovsky the advantages of the accentual system over the syllabic. Associated as he was with the Academy, he must have known many of the German professors there; and one of the routine duties of the Academicians was to turn out Russian verses in honor of royalty on certain state occasions. The normal method employed by the German professors for this purpose was to compose a poem *in German* and then translate it into Russian; and in this procedure the flexible and harmonious German accentual meter must have made a striking contrast with the stiff and prosy syllabic verse of the final product.

In any case, whatever stimulus or stimuli may have worked on him, Trediakovsky must have full credit for first formulating the principles of what he calls the "tonic" (i.e., accentual) method for composing Russian verse. In his brief introductory statement to the "New and Short Method" he mentions first the absurd and unworkable method of imposing classical quantity on the non-quantitative Slavonic languages, proposed by Maximov's grammar; and then, coming to the syllabic system, writes: "Others in composing our [i.e., Russian] verses have proceeded up to now more correctly, in setting a certain definite number of syllables in a verse, cutting it into two parts, and introducing a mutual concord of syllables together at the line ends. But even such verses seem so unsatisfactory that they may more appropriately be designated as prose that proceeds by a definite number [of syllables], but is absolutely devoid of feet and cadence, which make verse sing and distinguish it from prose, that is, non-verse." Trediakovsky insists, correctly, that syllabic verse is a foreign importation, and a method of versification entirely unsuited to the Russian language, the ancient and popular verse of which is accentual and without rhyme.

Unfortunately, however, the "New and Short Method" has a very limited scope. The only "feet" which Trediakovsky can see at this stage as suitable for Russian are those of two syllables—he uses the classical names, substituting an accented syllable for a "long"—spondee (two "longs"), trochee (long and short), iamb (short and long) and pyrrhichius (two shorts). Of these he insists that the trochee must be basic, as being more truly suited to the normal rhythm of Russian. He also eliminates from his "Method" any lines shorter than that of eleven syllables: all such short lines must still be composed by syllable-counting. The 13-syllable line ("heroic" verse) and the 11-syllable line must have caesuras, after the seventh and fifth syllable respectively; and these lines must have rhyme. By a most extraordinary aberration Trediakovsky at this point feels that what the French call "marriage des vers," that is, the uniform alternation in a long poem between feminine (2-syllable) and masculine (1-syllable) rhyme is an impossible monstrosity in Russian. Pushing the sexual metaphor to a grotesque extreme, he writes: "Such a combination of verses would be with us just as loathsome and disgusting as it would be if one should see the most attractive, tender, European beauty, aglow in the full flower of her youth, coupled with a decrepit ninety-year-old blackamoor!"[9] Masculine rhyme he considers fit only for satire or humorous verse. But the obligatory feminine rhyme of Russian syllabic verse is of course actually a mere carry-over from Polish usage, where the penultimate word accent makes it unavoidable, and has nothing to do with Russian conditions whatever. It is this combination of limitations and baseless prejudices that vitiated to a significant degree Trediakovsky's great reform, and made it possible for Lomonosov, who saw and realized his rival's inconsistencies, to claim credit for the reform as a whole. Several extremely vulnerable spots in Trediakovsky's "Method" may be summarized: he limited the system of accentual feet to long 11- and 13-syllable lines capable of supporting a caesura; he had an ineradicable dislike for iambic rhythm and for masculine rhyme; and he kept to the end an unreasoning fondness for what he calls the "heroic" verse, that is, the 13-syllable line of the old syllabic system, brought into conformity with his "tonic" principles, and defined by Trediakovsky as a "trochaic hexameter." Actually, some of the latest stages of syllabic verse, such as the second version of Kantemir's *Satires*, tend toward accentual alternation; and it is worth noting that the line which Trediakovsky uses and repeats several times as an example of his "tonic trochaic hexameter" (the only verse form to which his treatise devotes much attention) is the first line of Kantemir's First Satire: *um tol' slabyi plod trudov kratkiia nauki,* a line that the poet himself composed by syllabic principles. Still another of Trediakovsky's prejudices, rather hard to understand in view of his avowed interest in the verse of the common people, is that against metrical feet of three syllables—dactyls, anapests and amphibrachs—which are so commonly used in popular Russian verse.

We may anticipate here and remark that before the end of his life Trediakovsky had seen the inadequacy of his early "Short Method," and was writing iambics, alternating masculine and feminine rhymes, and even writing Russian dactylo-trochaic hexameters. It did nothing for his reputation, however, when in reissuing his early metrical treatise among the volumes of his complete "Works" (1752) he rewrote it in such a way as to make it appear that he had all along advocated the complete substitution of his syllabo-tonic system for the syllabic—which was actually the position of Lomonosov. Trediakovsky's attempted falsification of well-known facts led only to contempt and derision. None the less, his is unquestionably the priority in discovering the new system, even if he was too timid and conservative to carry it to its logical conclusion.

As a kind of appendix to his "New and Short Method" Trediakovsky gave the literate public some examples of western verse forms in Russian syllabo-tonic verse—a sonnet, rondeau, two elegies, an epistle, an "Ode in Praise of the Rose," etc. None of these pieces can be given very high rank as poetry, but some are "firsts" for Russian literature, as for example, the sonnet, written in the poet's "trochaic hexameter," in imitation of a French original in Alexandrines. The rhyme-scheme of the octet, exceptional for a sonnet, is *abababab*.

After an acrimonious controversy with Lomonosov over the respective merits of the trochaic and iambic meters, Trediakovsky composed and published in 1755 what has to be ranked as one of the most successful of all his critical endeavors, a treatise entitled: "On Russian Versification, Ancient, Middle, and Modern."[10] His account of the genesis of the Russian syllabic verse (his "middle" system) is remarkably clear, perceptive and even by modern standards essentially correct. In discussing the "new" (i.e., the syllabo-tonic) system he presupposes, without specifically mentioning them, Lomonosov's contributions to his own discoveries. He holds fast, however, to his essentially erroneous notion that the trochee is the foot best suited to Russian: "I was led to the trochee by the character of our language, because our periods more frequently and harmoniously end in a trochee; and our rhyme also, both in the middle [i.e., syllabic] verse system, and that which is at present called 'feminine,' is precisely this same trochee. Furthermore I had then in my hands a certain printed example [of verse] of the Illyrian [i.e., Yugoslav] peoples, composed in trochaic tetrameters [this was a dramatic poem on the Prodigal Son, composed by Ivan Gundulic (1589-1638)] ... So this threefold ground led me from the very beginning, that is, in 1735, to prefer the trochaic foot to all others. Many have been the attacks against me for this; I have endured them all patiently, and, enduring them, however much I pointed out the truth, that neither is the trochee tender nor the iamb noble by themselves, but that both the one foot and the other are noble and tender according to the words [of the poem], my demonstrations have been but little regarded..."[11] The last remarks refer to the polemics with Lomonosov, whose absurd contention it was that the iambic meter was inherently "noble," the trochaic inherently "tender." At the conclusion of his short history of Russian versification Trediakovsky again gives examples, this time not of poetical forms but of various syllabo-tonic meters, including the iambic, and even dactylic and anapestic three-syllable feet. Two stanza forms are also included, the Sapphic and the Alcaic ("Horatian"). The Sapphic, of course, had been quite commonly used by the syllabic poets, e.g., Simeon Polotsky, in its Polish form. Trediakovsky's Sapphic stanza, although still rhymed, is otherwise closer to the original; its metrical arrangement allows for the two unaccented syllables in the third foot (part of the Greek "cyclic dactyl") and in the adonic ('xx 'x) of the last line, which give the verse its peculiar lilting quality.

Trediakovsky's literary activity after the years of his first successes (1730-1735) is mostly connected with translation. Aside from hack work of a purely utilitarian nature (e.g., Saint-Rémy's "Artillery Handbook"), his translations are chiefly of history. In 1738 he began to translate the monumental works of Charles Rollin on ancient history, and with unremitting and at times discouraging labor (on one occasion several volumes of translation in manuscript were destroyed when his house burned, and had to be redone), by the year before his death he had completed the 30 volumes: 10 volumes of Rollin's *Histoire ancienne;* 16 volumes of Rollin's *Histoire romaine;* and four volumes of the *Histoire des empereurs romains* of Rollin's pupil Crévier. The Rollin work, highly regarded throughout Europe in its time, is extremely third-rate history, being nothing more than a smooth, entirely uncritical, retelling of the facts as narrated by the ancient sources, with all difficulties harmonized and smoothed over. As Gukovsky points out, however,[11] the scholarly moralist's glorification of the republican virtues of Sparta and Rome, and Crévier's generally black picture of the Roman emperors were very influential in France toward the "Roman masquerade" which marks the revolution of 1789, and through Trediakovsky's translation had their effect also on Russian intellectual opposition to monarchy, e.g., of the Decembrists.

Two of Trediakovsky's other translations require mention: John Barclay's *Argenis* (1751) and Fénelon's *Les Aventures de Télémaque* (1766). Both works are "translations" of such a highly original sort that the translator must be regarded as in fact a co-author. Barclay's *Argenis* (1621) is a Latin novel which is reputed to satirize the contemporary situation in France under the cloak of various fictional kings, queens and princes, whose adventures compose the novel's plot. Barclay, like his grandfather Alexander, was a convinced advocate of absolute monarchy, and the principal theme of his work is demonstration of all the ills that befall a kingdom through feudal anarchy and the benefits which a benevolent monarchy brings. Trediakovsky of course found this point of view congenial; but another aspect of the work doubtless intrigued him equally: in the person of the sage counsellor Nicopompus (Nikopomp), the author was able to give some "instruction to kings." Since the final great work of Trediakovsky was a very free translation of Fénelon's *Les Aventures de Télémaque* (the *Tilimakhida*), the entire substance of which is the education of young Telemachus for kingship, it is evident that this aspect of the poet's mission was of great concern to him.

Trediakovsky's original contribution and addition to Barclay's novel is in the form of inserted verses, mostly translations from Latin and Greek classical authors, with which he illustrates the extremely ample "Explanations of Mythological Passages in the *Argenis*," attached to each of the five parts of the novel. His translation is also accompanied by an extensive "Avant-propos" *(Preduvedomleniie)* in which he discusses among other things his priority in introducing the tonic system of versification, and his ideas on rhyme, of which he writes: "It [i.e., rhyme] is a toy invented during Gothic times [i.e., in the Middle Ages]," and claims that "Our original poetry was without rhyme and was accentual *[tonicheskaia]* ."[12]

In 1766, three years before his death, Trediakovsky finished his most ambitious translation, the *Tilimakhida*. It came at a time in Russia's history which was extremely inopportune, and the neglect and derision with which it was met embittered the poet's last years. It consists of some 16,000 verses into which Fénelon's original prose romance has been recast. These verses are most interesting. Stender-Petersen's characterization of the *Tilimakhida* as composed in "ungewöhnlich schlechte russische Hexameter"[13] is entirely unjust. The hexameters are not "uncommonly bad" on the whole (there are, of course, some individual verses to which the description applies); and they are, in any case, the *first* Russian hexameters, with the exception of a few translations in the notes of the *Argenida*. This fact is in itself remarkable, since as we have seen Trediakovsky in his first discussions of the "tonic" system of versification dismissed the notion of feet of three syllables as unsuited to Russian. The influence of the popular *Messias* of the German poet Klopstock (1748-51), which introduced the dactylo-trochaic hexameter into German, is certainly in part responsible for Trediakovsky's change of mind. More important, however, was the contact which his work necessitated with the Greek *Odyssey*. After all, the *Adventures of Telemachus* is, in a formal way, conceived as a sequel to Homer's epic of the adventures of Telemachus's father Ulysses. And Trediakovsky was a good Greek scholar and trained in the classics. Many of the accentual hexameters of his transla- tion are as good as those of Gnedich's *Iliad* (1829) or Zhukovsky's *Odyssey* (1849); and he has a perfectly correct understanding of the requirements of the verse: the accentual dactyls must be from time to time relieved by the insertion of an accentual trochee (substituting for the quantitative spon- dee of the Greek) to prevent monotony; and the verse must, of course, be unrhymed.

The bad reputation of Trediakovsky's *Tilimakhida* is due in large part to the attitude of Catherine II toward it. According to a nineteenth-century anecdotist:[14] "Under the Empress Catherine II a jocular penalty for a slight offense was established in the Hermitage: to drink a glass of cold water and read a page from the *Tilimakhida;* and for a more serious one, to learn by heart six lines from it." Catherine is also reputed to have recommended Trediakovsky's verses as a prime remedy for insomnia. But as A.S. Orlov[14a] has well pointed out, it was not so much Trediakovsky's verses which the Empress disliked, as his ideas. In his choice of Fénelon's romance for trans- lation he was exhibiting a disquieting predilection for instructing royalty— and Catherine could brook no such insolence. Moreover, one of the episodes

65

in the romance (that of King Pygmalion and Queen Astarveia) has a dangerous similarity to the lurid story of Catherine's own suppression of her husband Peter III and usurpation of the throne. Her answer to these indiscretions was to subject the poet to ridicule—perhaps the most painful kind of punishment.

Among Trediakovsky's original works, again neglected in his lifetime but of considerable interest to later times, is the tragedy *Deidamia*.[15] This was written at the express orders, as the poet announced to the Academy of Sciences, of the Empress Elizabeth, that "Professors Trediakovsky and Lomonosov should each write a tragedy." Lomonosov's answer to this challenge was *Tamira and Selim,* on a national Russian theme—the rout of Mamai. For his subject Trediakovsky chose a Greek legend, that of the youth of Achilles, who was concealed by his goddess mother Thetis among the daughters of the King of Scyrus in order to save him from having to go to war against Troy, where the goddess knew he must lose his life. The result of her maneuver was of course foreseeable: "Pyrrha," the transvested Achilles, fell in love with Deidamia, one of the king's daughters, and got her with child, and was discovered anyhow and taken to Troy through the wiles of Odysseus. In order to force this story into tragic form Trediakovsky had to invent a rival for Deidamia, Nauplia, and complicate the plot to a degree which was thought to make the tragedy unsuitable for staging. *Deidamia* is composed, again in defiance of Trediakovsky's early theories of versification, in a six-beat iambic verse with alternate masculine and feminine rhymes—the so-called "Russian Alexandrine." Portions are in other meters, as for example Deidamia's monologue over what she believes to be Achilles's faithlessness, which consists of twelve six-line stanzas in "Alexandrines" with the rhyme scheme *aaBccB* (the lower case letter representing a feminine, the upper case a masculine rhyme), and the constantly repeated refrain at the end of each strophe: *kogda liubeznyi moi vozmog tak izmenit'*— "Since my darling could so betray (me)!"

Trediakovsky's only other dramatic essay was never published in his lifetime (first in 1935, from a manuscript of 1752). It is entitled: "The Eunuch: A Comedy in five acts, from the Latin of Terence, purged by the verses of Vasily Trediakovsky of its foulest indecencies."[16] The meter of the translation is a six-beat trochaic line, with alternate masculine and feminine rhymes by single lines rather than by couplets, as in the tragedy. In the foreword to his translation Trediakovsky states that in conformity with ancient usage he wishes to present with his tragedy a "sister" comedy, and finding the task too difficult for his own powers, he has chosen "the best of Terence's six comedies" for translation. It happens that this "best" comedy is the only one of the Latin poet's works which is quite decidedly licentious in plot and even occasionally in expression; it requires accordingly a consierable "purgation" to eliminate its "foul indecencies" and make it suitable for the chaste ears of the court of Elizaveta Petrovna!

One of the most original of Trediakovsky's works, and certainly one of his most ambitious undertakings in verse is the six-book philosophical treatise called *Theoptia (Feoptiia),* the composition of which occupied the poet from 1750 to 1754. It was never published in his lifetime because of a combination of petty jealousies in the Academy of Sciences and of religious obscurantism in the Holy Synod. The manuscript was discovered by I.Z. Serman and published for the first time in the "Poet's Library" edition of Trediakovsky's *Selected Works* in 1963.[17] Its obvious inspiration is Alexander Pope's *Essay on Man,* known to Russia at this time through the rather free translation by Nikolai Nikitich Popovsky (1730-1760).[18] In substance the work is, as its title indicates, a "view of God" as revealed, not in scriptural, but in natural "miracles." It takes the form, as some of Pope's philosophical works also do, of "Epistles," six in number, addressed to a fictional "Eusebius" (i.e., "Reverent One"). The first epistle demonstrates the existence of God by ontological principles, by the familiar "argument from design" (i.e., such a complex and harmonious universe could not have arisen by accident) and by "universal consent" of all races of mankind. The second, designed, as the poet says, to be more intelligible to those who find metaphysics rather hard to comprehend, deals with the four elements—earth, air, fire and water—as evidences of a providential design for the good of man. This line of reasoning is continued in Epistle III, which is devoted to the "cattle, beasts, reptiles, fish, birds and insects" as creations of Providence. Epistle IV "demonstrates the wisdom and goodness of God in the construction of the human body." The fifth epistle attempts to deal with the relations of the human (and animal) soul with the body. "In the preceding five epistles the existence of God has been demonstrated, and in this sixth and last explanation is made of the qualities of God, which it is better for the Supreme Being to have than not to have."

The *Theoptia* is thus a kind of compendium of the scientific knowledge of the mid-eighteenth century, all directed toward a deistic explanation of the universe. Some of the views expressed were sufficiently radical to explain the refusal of the reactionary Synod to permit the work's publication. For example, the poet, in dealing with the heavenly bodies (Epistle III) hedges skillfully, but unsuccessfully, on the Copernican hypothesis:

> We behold the sun; it (how many million miles distant?)
> Is larger than the Earth, and by a community of laws
> Either moves or stands still at such a distance
> That it is in itself only a small circle. (lines 171-174)

Trediakovsky is, no more than Pope, a great original philosopher. His treatise, however, is competently developed and his attempt to fit science into the framework of a poem (for which Lucretius furnished him a model) is extremely interesting. There are moments when his subject kindles his imagination almost to the point of genuine poetry, but they are rare, and usually vitiated by a perverse syntax and vocabulary, of which we shall have more to say presently. As a fair example of the more intelligible portions of his treatise, the following passage (II, 145-154) may be cited:

> The Earth's inequalities are considered to be not of service,
> But are for her adornment, and necessary for our use.
> Where the crests of mountains go, there are just as many valleys,
> And in them most excellent herbage as food for cattle.
> Beyond them round about, the fields and furrows of the cornland
> are yellow,
> The ears of the rich harvests wave and are ripe.
> On the one side their region is flowery and grassy
> And fertile with trees, and healthful and pure of air;
> On the other, the mountains raise their summits to the clouds,
> Astonish us with their height, as they gladden our eyes.

Trediakovsky's finalistic interpretation of nature may be well observed in another passage from Epistle II (285-302):

> O Providence! Where intolerable cold rages,
> In those countries are seen more thick forests.
> Not only is the forest serviceable to us in this one way from the
> first,
> In that we may obtain in it wood for fuel,
> But the material of the forests, though hard and perishable,
> We make of it every sort of thing for our needs:
> We make ourselves a house as habitation out of wood,
> And we build likewise boats and ships.
> And the orchard beautiful to see, burdened with fruit,
> Is by this same [i.e., the fruit] bent down sufficiently low
> So that, as though intentionally, it may offer its fruit as a gift,
> While this is fresh and ripe and tasty, and not old.
> Meanwhile these fruits as they fall to the earth's surface
> And rot on the bosom of mother earth,
> From their seed revivify their race once more
> And multiply it for the succeeding year.
> Everything which earth receives, she thus preserves in herself,
> And while changing this, does not change herself!

Reading these quite transparent and intelligible passages of the *Theoptia*, one gets a one-sided impression, however; the whole poem is not such easy going. The murkiest parts are the First and the Fifth Epistle, which by their subjects—metaphysics and a sort of bastard psychology respectively—

are impenetrable enough; but to this have to be added the special difficulties contributed by Trediakovsky's peculiar style.

We shall reserve until a little later a general consideration of this style; but it may be observed here that the *Theoptia* offers an excellent illustration of a generalization of Professor G.A. Gukovsky[19] to the effect that when using iambics, and particularly Alexandrines, Trediakovsky tends to follow a more or less natural word order, in the manner of Lomonosov, who introduced these meters, while in writing trochaics, and particularly the "heroic verse" (his "trochaic tetrameter", the old 13-syllable line revamped) he follows the Latinate word order which he apparently learned in his earliest years and obstinately continued all his life to regard as elegant and beautiful. To convey any idea in another language of what this kind of word-juggling means is very difficult, but perhaps a small example can illustrate it. The *Theoptia*, which Gukovsky of course did not know, since it was discovered only after his death, is, as it happens, written in precisely the two kinds of meter which he mentions—the iambic Alexandrine and the trochaic "heroic" verse. Trediakovsky is "most himself," that is, most difficult and unintelligible, in Epistles I and VI, which are in his "trochaic hexameter," while Epistles II and III, in iambic Alexandrines, offer far less difficulty. The subject matter of IV, also in trochaics, helps lighten the stylistic gloom, while the subject matter of V, in Alexandrines, succeeds in counteracting the iambic ease. As an example of Trediakovsky's "trochaic style" the following may serve:

$$
\begin{matrix} 1 & 4 & 2 & 3 & 5 & 6 & 7 \end{matrix}
$$
Посему Бог если б правдой так определил,
$$
\begin{matrix} 8 & 10 & 11 & 9 & 12 & 14 & 15 & 13 \end{matrix}
$$
Чтоб в самых он людях ненавистных грех казнил,
$$
\begin{matrix} 16 & 17 & 20 & 19 & 18 & 22 & 21 & 23 \end{matrix}
$$
Уж давно б погибли мы самым точно делом,
Как душою в век веков, так и нашим телом,
Но что мы не гибнем, то ходатай некий есть,
Кой упрашивает божиея правды месть.
Кая ж тварь ту упросить может раздраженну?
Се ходатаю долг быть точно обоженну.

Wherefore if God determined thus in justice
That He should punish in men themselves [their] hateful sin,
We would in very deed have long since perished,
As much in soul forever more, as in our bodies.
But that we do not perish [is because] there is a certain Intercessor
Who begs off the vengeance of God's justice.
What creature, however, can beg off aggrieved [justice]?
The Intercessor must thus be of a divine nature.

(VI, 600-607)

As indicated by the numbers over the Russian words, the natural word order of the first three lines of this passage would be: *Posemu esli b Bog pravdoi tak opredelil, chtob on v samykh liudakh kaznil nenavistnyi grekh, uzh davno my pogibli tochno samym delom...* The exigencies of verse writing inevitably require a certain rearranging of a prose word order in any language—but Trediakovsky's juggling is not necessitated by the verse, it is systematic and deliberate.

Professor Gukovsky[20] discusses Trediakovsky's poetic style with great discernment and sympathy. "Early on, apparently, Trediakovsky had come to consider Latin syntax the ideal norm for any kind of syntactically ordered speech." This conviction accounts for the qualities of his style; his obscurity and difficulty are deliberate, and not the result of poetical incapacity, and in his literary controversies with Lomonosov and Sumarokov he is the defender of a dense, complex, Latinate style as against the relative simplicity of the styles of his rivals.

In English, French, and most other Romance languages we are accustomed to what we consider a "normal word order," which can be loosely defined as: subject with modifiers—verb with modifiers—object with modifiers. The position of the modifiers is of course not the same in all these languages, but they are normally either closely before or closely after the word modified; and the order of subject-predicate-object is fundamental. With Latin, however, and to a much lesser extent Greek, such an order is almost exceptional; and the Old Slavonic language shares the characteristics of the classical tongues. This is because of the highly developed system of substantive inflection in all these languages. If, for example, there is a distinctive ending for, let us say, a masculine dative singular adjective, there is no cogent reason why this adjective should be directly before or directly after the noun it modifies—the mind will unmistakably connect it with a masculine dative singular noun. If nominative and accusative cases are very clearly distinguished—and they are in most instances in these highly inflected languages—there is no necessity for placing the subject before and the object after the verb—the contrary order is just as intelligible, and may be recommended for purposes of emphasis. Latin poets made exceptionally large use of this freedom of word position, and *hyperbaton* (literally "a stepping across"), whereby adjective modifier and modified noun are often widely separated, or subject and verb, is one of the commonest rhetorical devices in Latin verse. Horace is particularly fond of hyperbaton, and the device contributes a great deal to the famous epigrammatic succinctness of that poet; note for example the first strophe of Ode I, 9:

> Vides (1) ut (2) alta (4) stet (7) nive (5) candidum (6)
> Soracte (3), nec (8) iam (9) sustineant (13) onus (12)
> Silvae (10) laborantes (11), geluque (16)
> Flumina (14) constiterint (15) acuto (17),

> You see how Mount Soracte, white with deep snow, stands
> out, and no longer do the toiling forests bear up their burden,
> and [how] the streams are standing still in the sharp cold.

where the "natural" Latin word order is indicated by the number sequence. It was this inheritance from his Latin-trained youth that Trediakovsky tried to impose on Russian. The effort was not entirely unwarranted, for Russian is as highly inflected, on the substantive side, as Latin; but even for Russian readers (and who can say that the same was not true for Latin readers as well!) constant hyperbaton, inversion, and other "licenses" of the sort (e.g., the postponement of a relative pronoun to nearly the end of its clause) has an irritating effect; the reader has to keep such constant watch for tricks of verbal order, that he may have to repeat a reading several times before the *sense* of what he has read becomes clear. He may even, as Gukovsky suggests, have to have the passage rewritten in "normal order" before it become intelligible. "Just because of constant inversions the verses of Trediakovsky often require translation into the ordinary construction; without translation they are unintelligible. Thus, for example, the beginning of such an important program piece as the 'Epistle to Apollo' is not at once intelligible:

> Девяти Парнасских сестр купно Геликона
> О начальник Аполлин и Пермесска звона!
> Посылаю ти сию, росска поэзия,
> Кланяяся до земли, должно что, самыя.

> ("O Apollo, commander of the nine Parnassian sisters, also of
> Helicon and the sound [i.e., music] of Permessus! I, Russian
> poetry, am sending to you this [epistle], bowing down (in doing
> so), as is my duty, to the very ground.")

An added difficulty, of course, must also be taken into account: much of Trediakovsky's poetic vocabulary, especially in the solemn odes, is Slavonic and not Russian, sometimes even "hyper-Slavonic"—that is, forms invented by the poet himself by analogy, but never existing elsewhere in Slavonic usage. Gukovsky notes, for example,[22] that in the poem "Spring Warmth" Trediakovsky uses so many Slavonicisms that even the nightingale (Russian *solovei*) becomes a non-existent Slavonic *slavii!* But it is characteristic also of Trediakovsky's lexical usage that side by side with the extremes of Slavonicism are words and idioms from the most ordinary Russian vulgate. This painful juxtaposition of different linguistic levels is what, in Gukovsky's opinion, did the greatest damage to his reputation as a poet among his contemporaries.

His insensitivity to lexical mixture and his perverse fondness for rhetorical tricks such as inversion and hyperbaton are certainly serious flaws in Trediakovsky's poetical style. Nonetheless, it must be remembered that he is a transitional figure, and inevitably bears the marks of the age that precedes him; and that his latest verse, e.g., the hexameters of the *Tilimakhida*, are very often quite happily free of these mannerisms, as though something of Homeric simplicity and naturalness inhered in the Homeric meter. Note, for example, Athena's final address to Telemachus: [23]

В том наконец, Паллада сама изрекла, провеща:
"Сын Одиссеев! послушай меня, и сие уж впоследни.
Я никого не учила из смертных с радением большим,
Коль тебя. Я тебя вела сквозь бедства рукою,
По неизвестным странам, во бранех прекроволитных
И в злоключениях всяких, которы могут неложно
Сердце все испытать и то искусить в человече.

Whereat, finally, Pallas herself spoke in prophecy:
"Son of Odysseus! Hearken to me, and this now for the last time.
I have instructed no one of mortals with greater care
Than you. I have guided you by hand through troubles,
By unknown lands, in bloody battles,
And in all manner of misfortunes, which can try
Every true heart, and tempt it in a man."

(XXIV, 677-678)

Trediakovsky belongs to the Russian Baroque, and some of his characteristics are those of this fashion, e.g., his Latinate syntax, his inflated and ornate style, the preciosity of his early *Voyage to the Isle of Love,* and so forth. His steps along the new path he discovered were cautious and hesitant, and bolder spirits, such as Lomonosov, quickly passed him and made him seem antiquated and silly. But it is well to remember some of the pioneering services of Trediakovsky: besides the really epoch-making discovery of the syllabo-tonic system of versification, there is the first conscious and systematic repudiation of Slavonic in favor of spoken Russian as a medium for light secular verse; the first introduction into Russian of love as a literary theme; his are the first written lyrics that can be classified as "song" in Russian; his translations of Tallemant and Barclay introduce a western type of "novel" into serious Russian literature; his *Deidamia* is one of the first "regular" tragedies, his translation of Terence one of the first regular comedies in the language; his "fables," along with those of Kantemir, are the first of their kind; his *Theoptia* is one of Russia's first philosophical poems; his hexameters, in some illustrative verses in the *Argenida* notes, and in the *Tilimakhida,* are the first in the language, etc. These are not inconsiderable achievements. It was a personal misfortune for Vasily

Trediakovsky that his lifetime coincided with that of one of the most towering universal geniuses that Russia ever produced; but it should now be possible for scholars of a later generation to see more clearly than those of his own, and to discern beside the great Lomonosov the more modestly proportioned figure of a predecessor to whom even the giant owed much.

CHAPTER V

MIKHAIL LOMONOSOV AND THE SOLEMN ODE[1]

Modern Russian literature, as Belinsky correctly observed, has its beginning with Lomonosov—a figure so prestigious that he dominates the entire first half of the eighteenth century. His contribution to Russian life is enormous, and it has been a temptation, not always avoided by Russian writers, to dwell at length on many phases of it which belong to the histories of chemistry, technology, education et al., rather than to the history of literature. Yet even in the latter field he must be reckoned with in many areas—oratorical prose, drama, lyric poetry, satire, linguistics, and the theory of versification, to mention the most significant. To American readers Lomonosov has often been presented as "the Russian Ben Franklin," but this does him an injustice. In many aspects the two men's careers do offer parallels, especially in their enlightenment ideals and their devotion to science. But the author of "Franklin's Autobiography" and *Poor Richard's Almanac* can hardly be mentioned in the same breath with the inspired poet of the great "triumphal odes," who was at the same time the emancipator of Russian verse from the shackles of a foreign system of versification, and the molder of poetic style for the better part of a century.

Communist critics make much of the peasant origin of Lomonosov, and of his early bringing up in the far north of Russia (his father was a White Sea fisherman) where the "Tatar Yoke" had never reached and serfdom was unknown, where a great deal of the old Russian folk literature and custom survived. Mikhail was born in 1711 in a village in the Kholmogory district; he learned as a boy to idolize Peter the Great, who was a very popular figure in the far north, and in his voyages with his father came in contact with West Europeans to an extent unparalleled except perhaps by Peter's own contacts with the foreigners of the Nemetskaya Sloboda. Until the founding of St. Petersburg, of course, the Archangel area was the only gateway of Russia to the West. From his early background, then, Lomonosov derived a sturdy peasant independence—not to say truculence; a fervent nationalism which did not exclude deep respect for western culture; and a hero-worship of Peter I. These inheritances he never lost.

Because of disagreements with his father and an unsympathetic stepmother, the young man left his home at the age of nineteen and made his way, partly on foot, to Moscow. He had received some education in Khol-mogory: his textbooks were the Church Slavonic grammar of Melety Smo-tritsky, the "Arithmetic" of Magnitsky (printed at Peter's orders) and Simeon Polotsky's translation of the Psalter. Arrived in Moscow, Lomonosov was obliged to falsify his class status in order to be accepted as a student in the Slavonic-Greek-Latin Academy, to which only noblemen's sons were ad-mitted. He also had to endure, as he tells in an autobiographical letter, the jeers of the small boys who were his class-mates at "the blockhead, all of twenty years old, who has come to learn Latin!" He made his mark, however, finished three years work in one, learned Greek as well as Latin, and was sent a few years later by the school authorities to St. Petersburg, to the re-cently opened University. From there the government sent him in 1736, one of a very small number of picked students, to Germany for further study— in Lomonosov's case, of mining! One might suppose that a youth whose interests had seemed to be preeminently literary and historical (he had made a study of the old Russian chronicles) would find mining engineering little to his taste. But Lomonosov had an intensely active mind, a deep interest in science as well as what we call "the humanities," and an omni-vorous craving for knowledge of every kind. While dutifully studying mining, as he was commissioned to do, in several German universities, he likewise absorbed chemistry, such as the science then was, philosophy and philology. He returned to Russia in 1741 and was given a post as "adjunct" in the Aca-demy of Sciences. This institution had been founded by Peter the Great as part of a program for bringing learning to Russia; but since there were no Russian savants with whom to staff it, Peter's successors had imported Germans, who occupied all the professorships. Probably as part of the general reaction against things German which accompanied the governmental coup of 1741 and brought Elizaveta Petrovna to the throne, two Russians were in 1745 installed as "Academicians," Trediakovsky and Lomonosov. These two were not on good terms with each other, and Lomonosov at least was on the worst of terms with many members of the German staff of the Academy, who regarded their positions as sinecures and were jealously determined not to yield any part of their lucrative monopoly to "Russian barbarians." Lomo-nosov enjoyed, however, the patronage of the powerful Russian Maecenas, Ivan I. Shuvalov, Elizabeth's favorite, and in his endless battles with the Germans, frequently came out ahead. In 1755 one of his favorite aspirations was achieved with the help of Shuvalov, the founding of the University of Moscow, which now under Soviet rule bears his name. Circumstances for Lomonosov changed with the death of Empress Elizabeth in 1761; the last few years of his life were embittered by financial difficulties (the failure of his glass factory), the coldness of Empress Catherine II and the evident col-lapse of many grandiose enterprises which he had been passionately advo-cating for years. He died, still relatively young, in 1765.

Before considering Lomonosov's creative literary work we must take account of his theories of versification and style, which have marked almost all subsequent Russian verse.

When the young man traveled to Germany in 1736, he carried with him a copy (bought, as his note in the book indicates, on November 24 of that year) of Trediakovsky's epoch-making treatise, "A New and Short Method for Composing Russian Verses," published in 1735. Lomonosov's copy of this work is filled with hand-written annotations, in Latin, German, and Russian, indicating the areas of his disagreement with Trediakovsky. In 1738 Lomonosov was called upon by the St. Petersburg University authorities to give an account of the progress of his studies abroad, which he did in great detail, partly in German and partly in Latin, and appended to his report his verse translation, side by side with the original for purposes of comparison, of the "Ode à l'abbé de Langeron" of François Salignac de la Mothe Fénelon, the famous author of *Les Aventures de Télémaque*. Fénelon's ode is written in lines of seven and eight syllables, with masculine and feminine rhymes. Lomonosov's translation follows closely the pattern of the original, with lines likewise of seven and eight syllables. His verse, however, is *tonic*, not syllabic, and the rhythm is trochaic*; strophe one of original and translation will serve for comparison:

Montagnes de qui l'audace	Горы, толь что дерзновенно
Va porter jusques aux cieux	Взносите верхи к звездам,
Un front d'éternelle glace	Льдом покрыты беспременно,
Soutien du séjour des dieux;	Нерушим столп небесам:
Dessus vos têtes chenues	Вашими под сединами
Je cueille au-dessus des nues	Рву цветы над облаками,
Toutes les fleurs du printemps.	Чем пестрит вас взор весны;
A mes pieds, contre la terre,	Тучи подо мной гремящи
J'entends gronder le tonnerre	Слышу, и дожди шумящи,
Et tomber mille torrens. 2	Как ручьев падучих тьмы.

In this early essay may be seen Lomonosov's first, still somewhat tentative, approach to verse reform. He has fully accepted Trediakovsky's fundamental principle, that accentual (tonic) versification, and not syllabic, is natural and proper for the Russian language. He has also, in this experiment, accepted Trediakovsky's pronouncements in favor of trochaic as

---

* French prosody, of course, is not based on metrical feet, and hence does not recognize "iambic" or "trochaic" rhythm as such. None the less, a foreigner hearing French verse declaimed will very often feel that the movement is iambic or trochaic, depending on the number of syllables in the line, as the German classicist Gottsched notes: "Z.E. die erste Zeile aus des Boileau Ode auf die Eroberung Namurs: 'Quelle docte et sainte ivresse!' wird von allen Franzosen als eine trochaische von vier Füssen ausgesprochen." [*Versuch einer Kritischen Dichtkunst*, 1742]. Fénelon's ode uses the same scheme as Boileau's.

76

against iambic meter: but it should be noted that the French line which he is translating is one which any non-Frenchman will feel as trochaic. It is also noteworthy that in spite of Trediakovsky's violent aversion for the combination of masculine and feminine rhymes (his absurd figure of the sweet white maiden coupled with a decrepit blackamoor will be remembered!), Lomonosov has followed his French original in this regard exactly.

Evidently the insufficiencies of Trediakovsky's reform continued to trouble Lomonosov. In 1739 the Russian armies captured the Turkish fortress of Khotin, causing a considerable European sensation, and Lomonosov, in a burst of patriotism, wrote his "Ode on the Victory over the Turks and Tatars and the Capture of Khotin, 1739."[3] When he sent this original ode to the St. Petersburg Academy of Sciences, he dispatched with it a "Letter on the Rules for Russian Verse Composition."[4] In this letter Lomonosov for the first time goes to the logical limit of the theory of "syllabo-tonic" versification. The chief points of disagreement with Trediakovsky are these: (1) he feels that the iambic meter has an inherent nobility that makes it more suitable for the solemn ode than the more lyrical trochaic; (2) he rejects the idea that an iambic or trochaic verse can exceptionally allow the substitution of the opposite foot, or of a "pyrrhic" (two unaccented syllables): this would, in his opinion, lead to anarchy and reduce a line to prose. Later, however, Lomonosov came to realize that such a limitation must inevitably exclude from binary verse all words of more than three syllables, and hence revised his theory to permit the pyrrhic to substitute frequently for either iamb or trochee. (3) He rejects totally the idea that ternary or trisyllabic feet (dactyls and anapests: he says nothing about amphibrachs) are unsuitable to Russian; (4) he rejects as absurd the idea, which he says is based on Polish practice, that only feminine rhyme is permissible; this is, as he puts it, as much as to say that a man with two healthy legs must get around by hopping on one foot! He even admits the dactylic (three-syllable) rhyme. (5) He insists that the accentual principle of versification must be applied not only, as Trediakovsky had done, to the long 13- and 11-syllable lines, but to short lines as well.

The "Letter on the Rules for Russian Verse Composition" was directed to the "Russian Assembly," a subdivision of the Academy of Sciences concerned specifically with matters pertaining to the Russian language. Trediakovsky was a member of this group (his "New and Short Method" had also been directed to it), and he felt personally attacked by Lomonosov's letter, to which he made an apparently rather intemperate rejoinder, which has not survived. Relations between the two men were never thereafter very cordial. It was probably due to Trediakovsky's opposition that Lomonosov's ode and the accompanying letter were not published; they were, however, widely circulated in manuscript, and the prosodic reforms they embodied were almost immediately accepted everywhere. By 1752, when Trediakovsky's *Collected Works* were published, he wrote a second treatise on versification, in which he revised some of his earlier positions; and in his essay "On the Ancient, Middle and New Russian Versification" (1755)[5] he accepted almost all of Lomonosov's revisions of his syllabo-tonic theory, even trying to convey the impression that they had been his ideas all along!

Lomonosov's importance, then, in the area of Russian versification is very great indeed, for until the most recent times all verse-writing in the language has followed his principles. Not as long lasting, but very significant for at least a century was his contribution to Russian stylistics. Here the crucial work is an essay which he prefixed as preface to the first volume of his *Collected Works* (1757), and rather strangely entitled: "Foreword on the Utility of Ecclesiastical Books in the Russian Language."[6]

Basic to this essay are two considerations: first, the peculiar dual nature of the Russian literary language; and second, the eighteenth-century theory of synonyms. From the moment of Russia's Christianization the East Slavic dialect spoken by the people of the Kievan principality began to be penetrated by the basically South Slavic literary language in which translations of the Bible, liturgical works and Greek patristic writings had been made. Since during the Middle Ages very nearly all literary composition in Russia was done by churchmen, it was quite natural for the ecclesiastical language to be employed—a Russian heavily intermingled with "Church Slavonic" vocabulary, morphology, and even syntax. This was the easier in that in the earlier centuries the two dialects had not grown as far apart as they eventually did. By the seventeenth century, however, certain writers made their appearance who were not churchmen, and who accordingly used a language much closer to the normal spoken Russian. The reign of Peter the Great had the effect linguistically, as we have seen, of flooding the language with a multitude of western borrowings, as well as of accentuating the secular type of composition. By 1757, when Lomonosov's essay was published, the literary language had begun to crystallize, but the relationship between the Slavonic and the Russian elements in the vocabulary had never been clarified and formalized.

The second aspect of the matter relates to the eighteenth-century attitude toward synonyms.

A basic concern of European Enlightenment thinking in the middle of the eighteenth century on questions of poetical word usage (poetical style) was directed toward stripping the word of elements of the irrational, of the logically inaccessible, of the unintelligible from the point of view of common sense and good taste, of what is not reducible to rationalistic logic, and in the final analysis, to grammar.

Behind the style of Sumarokov and Kheraskov (up to and including the *Rossiad*) stands the idea of unshakeable and objectively existing categories, genuinely, logically conceived by poetic speech. The word in the style of the *Rossiad* is flat, terminological, univocal, exact. It signifies in the measure of its own exactly defined logical meaning. The very principle of the loftiness of Slavonic usage does not appear as a mark of an emotional aureole around a given word (as it does in part with Lomonosov), but as a result of the detailed classification of exact phenomena.[7]

From the conception of the word thus defined it follows as a matter of course that there should be no such thing as a genuine synonym. "In the last analysis the existence of synonyms, linguistic (Slavonicism-Russism) or stylistic, was excluded; no wonder that Fonvizin, both in *The Minor* and in his special work 'Attempt at a Russian Thesaurus' concerned himself with such interest in sharpening the differentiation of meaning of synonyms.... The whole world was divided into a multiplicity of concepts, and each of these required a conventional sign—a word. The atomism of the world concept was reflected in an atomism of style."[8]

Many of the critics of Lomonosov's verse, both in his own times and in the early decades of the nineteenth century, aim their attacks at his "inexactitude" in the use of words. The sum of the matter is, however, that the prevalent classicist concept of the word as a colorless and quasi-algebraic sign for a precise and narrow concept was not acceptable to Lomonosov, because he approached the question from another point of view. What this point of view is he quite clearly explained in the "Foreword on the Utility of Ecclesiastical Books." It is the theory of the "three styles."

The theory itself is not a discovery of Lomonosov's. Rhetorical treatises had long recognized a threefold division of style—high, middle and low[9]—whereby a kind of hierarchy of genres was established. What Lomonosov did with this theory was to apply it consistently to the discrimination of synonyms in the two component dialects that made up the literary Russian of the eighteenth century. There are in existence lists of synonyms in Lomonosov's handwriting, evidently graded in accordance with this theory. Thus, for example, words all meaning "way, path, road": *stezia, put', doroga, sled, prokhod, khod.* Of these the first, *stezia,* is the Church Slavonic word, not found in Russian; the next four are all ordinary Russian, but also found in Church Slavonic, while the last two belong to the vulgate, or language of the common people. As he formulates the hierarchies in his "Foreword," there are five, one of which he rejects for modern literary use. They are: (1) "Unused and extremely obsolete words" of the Church Slavonic dialect, which are to be entirely excluded; (2) words which are Church Slavonic, never used in common speech, but still intelligible to educated Russians; (3) words common to both dialects; (4) words in good usage in Russian, but not found in Church Slavonic; and (5) "mean words, which it is not appropriate to use in any style, save in vulgar comedies." Of the first four categories he gives examples, but not of "mean words." On the basis of this division the lexical characteristics of the "three styles" are defined: the "high style," in which should be composed "heroic poems, odes, and prose orations on important matters," should use words of the second and third classes as arranged above—that is, they should practically exclude "words which do not exist in the remains of the Slavonic language." "The middle style should consist of words used for the most part in the Russian language, to which may be added certain Slavonic words used in the high style, but with great care so

79

that the style may not appear inflated." "In this style should be written all theatrical productions.... friendly epistles in verse, satires, eclogues and elegies should hold chiefly to this style. In prose it is proper to compose in it descriptions of memorable events [i.e., histories] and noble instructions." The third style will use words of the third class, that is, those common to both dialects, and also of the fourth, that is, words found only in Russian. It will be used in "comedies, humorous epigrams, songs, and in prose letters to friends and descriptions of ordinary doings." As already noted, the vulgate, of "low and colloquial words" can be used in these at discretion.

Since the "ecclesiastical books" of earlier ages in Russian were composed with large use of the Church Slavonic, and familiarity with these books is the only means by which the Russian can obtain familiarity with that "dead" language, which is never used in speech, it follows that reading the ecclesiastical books has the greatest utility. Not only does the Russian learn by this to place the numerous synonyms of his language in their proper categories, but he will also be able to avoid the barbarisms which Peter's reform had brought into Russian: "By such an assiduous and careful use of the basic Slavonic language, akin to our own, together with the Russian, are avoided wild and strange absurdities of expression which intrude upon us from foreign languages... These improprieties, through neglect to read ecclesiastical books, are even now stealing unawares upon us, spoiling the proper beauty of our language, subverting it by continual change, and pushing it to a decline."

Abstract and mechanical as this theory may at first sight appear, the essence of it is profoundly poetical, since it takes cognizance, as the orthodox rationalistic theories of the Enlightenment utterly fail to do, of the connotations, the colors of words, the emotional charge that a certain word may have through the associations in which it has usually been encountered. There is nothing in the English language strictly comparable, but we can perhaps appreciate a little of the effect of this discreet and sparing use of Slavonic vocabulary if we think of the King James Bible and the Book of Common Prayer, and the emotional coloration which from association with such a content inheres in certain seldom used English words and phrases. For example, when we read in "Travels in Arabia Deserta" the sentence: "These townsmen's heartless levity and shrewish looseness of tongue is noted by the *comely* Beduw," the adjective "comely," which would never be used in ordinary speech and very seldom even in written English, is rendered even more remote and impressive by its very unusual figurative meaning, which however carries with it memories of its context in the Psalter: "Rejoice in the Lord, O ye righteous; praise is *comely* for the upright" (Psalm XXXIII, i). Whether this precise passage was in Doughty's mind is of course immaterial; the coloration of the word is the effect of its very removal from the erosion of common speech and its distinctly solemn and religious associations. If we can imagine, not a few isolated and still English words of this

80

sort, but a whole related dialect, in part very close to our normal language and yet still distinct, we gain some idea of the effect of the Slavonic element in Lomonosov's "high style."

The doctrine of the "three styles," as it was concisely presented in Lomonosov's "Foreword," became canonical in Russian poetry for the rest of the eighteenth century until Derzhavin, and echoes of it may still be heard in the nineteenth, as when Pushkin's *Ruslan and Liudmila* was criticized for failing to conform to it.

It may be noted, incidentally, that there were certain perils in the doctrine, resulting from insufficient familiarity with "the ecclesiastical books," or sometimes, with the "vulgar tongue." Thus Trediakovsky, in a devastating criticism of Sumarokov's first tragedy, *Khorev,* points to a line in the speech of Astrada in Act III, sc. ii: *protiv'sia tol'ko v tom poborno estestvu,* and exclaims: "What? Miss Astrada is bidding (Osnelda) 'opposè nature without opposition'! But what does this mean? Can anyone oppose nature and at the same time be unopposed to it?.... It would seem that the author took the word *poborno* for *protivno.*" Actually, Trediakovsky is the one in error here, for *poborno* means, and has always meant, "strenuously," not, as he appears to imagine, "without opposition." A more ludicrous example of the use of a word with an unfortunate connotation is cited by Serman in his book on Lomonosov's poetical style.[10] In Sumarokov's first tragedy Prince Kii, faced with apparent evidence of treason on the part of his younger brother, is so overcome with emotion that his legs give way, and he has to call to his attendants for a seat. His words are: "Let someone bring me a *sedalishche.*" Sumarokov probably was unconsciously recalling some such Biblical passage as the first verse of Psalm I: "Bazhen muzh, izhe ne ide na sovet nechestivykh, i na puti greshnykh ne sta, i na *sedalishchi* gupitelei ne sede" ("Blessed is the man that walketh not in the counsel of the ungodly, nor standeth in the way of sinners, nor sitteth in the seat of the scornful"). Trediakovsky's ironical comment is quoted by Serman: "The author knows that the word is Slavonic, and used in the Psalms for 'chair'; he doesn't know that the Russo-Slavonic language, in which the author writes all his [work], has coupled with this word at the present time a filthy idea, to wit, what we call in the written language *afedron* [a Greek word for "privy"!]." There are no extant records of titters from the audience at the first performance of *Khorev,* but there must have been some! The passage was of course revised when Sumarokov published his plays.

Although in many respects far in advance of his times, Lomonosov shared the deistic beliefs of many of the great thinkers of the Enlightenment. Marxist scholars have sometimes attempted to show that the belief in a Creator-God, which marks many of his odes, both religious and secular, is merely a sop to the authorities, that Lomonosov was really an atheist, but dared not express such a dangerous point of view. This interpretation is completely false, as may be inferred with certainty from the private notes which the poet made for his own eyes alone, and in which he expresses ideas identical with those in his public work. Like Voltaire, he believed in a Creator, because it was to him inconceivable that the orderly universe could have resulted from mere chance: "God is a necessary hypothesis." But also like Voltaire, Lomonosov was certain that this Creator, once having set the great clock-work in motion, had retired from activity and let His creation run of itself. There was no room in Lomonosov's thinking for arbitrary divine interference with the workings of Nature, that is, of His creation—for what the Church recognized as miracles. He recognized the study and understanding of Nature through science as the truest, perhaps the only, means of knowing God. "The Creator has given to the human race two books. In the one He has exhibited His greatness, in the other His will. The first book is this visible world which He has created; the second is Holy Scripture."[11] Lomonosov's attitude toward this "second book" is somewhat ambivalent; he evidently believes that it does indeed contain a revelation of God's will, but rejects it totally when it contains matter that contradicts the findings of science. "The mathematician is unsoundly minded, if he desires to measure God's will with a compass. Just so also is the theologian, if he thinks that astronomy and chemistry can be taught from the Psalter."[11] The Bible is apparently conceived of as the record of human beings inspired in certain areas—chiefly ethical—by God, but subject in other areas, such as explanations of the physical universe, to extremely human fallibility. On the other hand, the scientist, who studies the real nature of the physical universe from a purely secular point of view is in his own way a theologian. "The interpreters and explainers of the Holy Scriptures are the great teachers of the Church"; "but in that book of the construction of this visible world, the physicists, mathematicians, astronomers and other explainers of God's actions upon nature are just such as the prophets, apostles and church teachers in that other book."[11]

Needless to say, this point of view brought Lomonosov into constant conflict with the authorities of the Orthodox Church. Particularly repellent to the Holy Synod was the Copernican discovery that the earth revolves around the sun instead of the reverse; and the supposition that in the vastness of the universe there may be other inhabited worlds. It may be remembered that Kantemir was refused permission to print his translation of Fontenelle's dialogue *Sur la pluralité des mondes.* In 1756 the Synod submitted a petition to Empress Elizabeth to decree "that no one should in any way venture to write and print anything either about a plurality of worlds or about anything else contrary to the holy faith and not in accord with pure morals, under pain of the cruelest punishment for infraction."[12] Lomonosov, however, defied the authorities, did write both about a plurality of worlds, and a great deal else that contradicted what the Synod regarded as articles of "the holy faith," and through the powerful protection of Ivan Shuvalov escaped unscathed. One of the episodes in his struggle we shall return to in connection with his satirical "Hymn to the Beard."

Just as Marxists critics have tried to make Lomonosov an atheist, so have they tried to make him a "democrat" in his political outlook, equally erroneously. Basic in Lomonosov's political thinking is the concept of the "people" (narod), but as elsewhere in the Russian eighteenth-century this concept is distinctly not that of the nineteenth-century "populists" or twentieth-century Marxists. Narod is the Russian equivalent of the peuple of the French Enlightenment, as also of the république; it is an abstraction more or less coinciding with the English "commonweal." Least of all does it mean, as it often does in the nineteenth century, "the mass of the country's population," i.e., the serfs. As Lomonosov uses the word, its nearest English equivalent would probably be "nation." He is a "nationalist," but certainly not a "populist," even though his own origin was from the peasantry. His political ideal is the great reformer whom he remembered from childhood— and Peter the Great was hardly a democrat! The "enlightened monarch," an eighteenth century ideal not often encountered in actuality, seemed to Lomonosov to be embodied in Peter: a monarch who ruled with an iron hand, brooking no opposition to the reforms which he demanded for the good of the country; and yet wholly unselfish, never arbitrarily tyrannical, and totally self-sacrificing. Time and again, as we shall see, Lomonosov in his Odes calls on the worthless successors of Peter to follow his illustrious example, lay aside selfish considerations of personal enjoyment, and labor for the good of the nation. That such a program could be accomplished without autocracy never occurred to him.

Lomonosov's voice, as a poet of the "triumphal odes," is that of the Russian nation, as he conceives it. Believing fervently that he does indeed speak for the nation as a whole, and not just for the individual Mikhail Lomonosov, he dares to preach to tsars and tsaritsas, calling on them to carry out projects and take actions which Peter had initiated, or presumably would have initiated if his life had not been cut short. In some of his patriotism there is even an element of the chauvinistic; he glorifies the great heroes of the Russian nation, who are the equals of those of ancient Rome and Greece; he attributes to the Russian language all the excellencies of all the modern languages of Europe, as well as of Greek and Latin; he demands the education of the Russian commoner so as to end the hated dominance of arrogant foreigners in institutions of learning. He rejoices in the military victories of Russian armies over the Turks—e.g., the capture of Khotin— and over the Germans in the Seven Years War, e.g., at "Memel, Frankfurt and Küstrin, Schweidnitz, Königsberg and Berlin,"[13] but he is never a jingoist. War is to him a necessary evil, which should be waged not for aggrandizement, but to free the nation from obstacles that hamper its natural development. Such a war was the "Great Northern," by which Peter broke the Swedish grip on the Baltic that would have sentenced Russia to stagnation and isolation from the European centers of culture and enlightenment. But not every war was of such a kind, and Lomonosov did not hesitate to glorify to Empress Elizabeth the blessings of peace at the very moment when her advisors were pressing her into war, contrary to the country's real interests, as Lomonosov saw it.

From Lomonosov's leading ideas, which are pretty much those of his age, with certain individual emphases, we may pass to a consideration of his literary work, beginning with his prose. Most of this is of a sober, technical sort, on scientific or philosophical matters, and of no literary concern. He did, however, venture into the realm of historical writing, which following antique tradition, was regarded as part of literature (the Muse Clio presided over it!), and wrote a few solemn orations, of which the best example is the "Panegyric on Peter the Great," pronounced in 1755. As the "Foreword on the Utility of Ecclesiastical Books" makes explicit, "prose orations on important matters" should be composed in the "high style," and as his "Rhetoric" makes abundantly clear, with the use of all the classical Greek and Roman stylistic ornaments associated with the orations of Demosthenes and Cicero, and the sermons of St. John Chrysostom and St. Gregory Nazianzen. It would require a very lengthy and technical discussion to demonstrate all the characteristics of Lomonosov's eloquence; but a few extracts will suffice to show some of the classical features of word order and style, and the Slavonic admixture in the vocabulary:

In thee, O dearest fatherland, in thee we see examples enough of this. God, enraged by the internecine enmities of our ancestors, by injustices, rapines and fratricides, enslaved thee once to a foreign tongue; and upon thy body, stricken with deep wounds, He laid heavy chains.[14]

The second sentence of this passage reads in the literal Latinate word order: "By the internecine of ancestors—our enmities, by injustices, by rapines and fratricides enraged God enslaved thee once to a foreign tongue." The typical devices of locking possessive modifying phrases into a group between adjective and noun, and of preceding a passive participle by a whole series of instrumentals mark this sentence. The only distinct Slavonicisms are the use of the word *iazyk*, "tongue" in the sense of "Gentiles, pagan peoples," and the adjective *tiazhkii*, "heavy" and the similar *chuzhii*, "foreign" for the common Russian doublets *tiazhelyi* and *chuzhdyi*.

A good example of the complicated "periodic sentence," imitating Ciceronian usage, is afforded by the following, translated in the literal word order:

Of this for the protection of the fatherland, for the security of subjects and for the unencumbered carrying out within the realm of important undertakings, of this necessary institution of a regular army, such a great—had the great monarch—solicitude, such a strenuous zeal, such a careful—of all means, of all ways—searching out—to all this when to marvel enough we are not able, shall we be able to represent it in words?[15]

The periodic structure of the sentence is obvious; note should be taken also of the common classical figure of successive cola introduced by the same words, e.g., *o sem.... o sem; kol'.... kol'*; of the repetition in close sequence of the same word in different forms: *velikoie... velikii* ("great ... great"); and the careful juxtaposition of two tenses of the same verb: *mozhem... vozmozhem* ("are able.... shall be able").

A final example will make a little clearer the difference of vocabulary between the solemn oration and ordinary speech:

Contrary to the general expectation (*pache ... chaianiia:* Slavonic), against the unbelief (*neveroiatiia:* Slavonic) of those who had abandoned hope, and above the hindering attempts and wounding murmurs of envy itself, suddenly thundered Peter's new regiments, and in loyal Russians (*rossiianakh:* Slavonic) awakened hope, in enemies fear, in both amazement. The impossible had been made possible by extraordinary solicitude (*racheniie:* Slavonic) and above (*pache:* Slavonic) all by an unheard-of example.[16]

Of course the mere labeling of distinctly Slavonic words does not tell the whole story, for the "high style" just as frequently employs words which, although "common to both languages," as Lomonosov defines them, are in ordinary literate speech or writing of the "middle style" passed over in favor of common synonyms.

Although he did not attempt with the ambition of his contemporary and rival Sumarokov to present Russian models in virtually all recognized genres, Lomonosov did try his hand at several. Most of these fall within the bounds of what he defined as the "high style": "solemn odes," composed for various royal anniversaries and other important occasions; five so-called "spiritual odes"; paraphrases of the Psalms; the first two cantos of an epic poem, "Peter the Great"; and two tragedies, "Tamira and Selim" and "Demophon." In the high style are also composed the so-called "inscriptions" (*nadpisi*), a genre which coincides with the Greek "epideictic epigram": short, lapidary poems such as might have been (but of course seldom really were) "inscribed" on monuments or engravings. To the "middle style" belong a number of miscellaneous poems, including the famous "Conversation with Anacreon," and a very popular "Anacreontic" imitation ("Nochnoiu temnotoiu..."), and the "idyll" Polidor. The "Hymn to the Beard" and the various epigrams which served him as bludgeons in his war with the Synod are examples of the "low style." One quite remarkable didactic poem, "Epistle on the Usefulness of Glass," seems to fall in the no-man's land between "middle" and "low."

The themes which Lomonosov treats in his major work (excluding the polemics of the epigrams and the "Hymn to the Beard") are those dictated by his world-view: the glorification of Russia; the glorification of the "hero," the ideal monarch, often embodied in the figure of Peter I; the meaning of peace and war for the country's well-being; the glorification of science and learning; and the celebration of the glory of the Creator-God as revealed in nature.

In one of his first poems, "Conversation with Anacreon,"[17] two of these themes are prominent. The piece is ingeniously constructed: the poet translated four of the Greek "Anacreontics," which his age accepted as genuine work of the sixth century poet; and after each he offers his own criticism or rectification. Thus, beginning with the famous one (I) in which the Greek poet complains that no matter what his efforts, he is unable to make his lyre sing of anything but love, Lomonosov turns the figure around, and claims that though he tries to celebrate love, "My strings sound willy-nilly the tumult of heroes." "Though I am not devoid of tenderness of heart in love, I am more entranced by the everlasting glory of heroes." The last of the four Anacreontics (XXVIII) presents the poet commissioning a painter to create a likeness of his love, whose beauties he eloquently describes. Lomonosov's reply calls upon the painter to put on canvas the image of a majestic woman, his beloved—"mother Russia." "Clothe her, clothe her in purple, give her a scepter, set a crown upon her; she needs but give laws to the world, and decree an end to strife. O how like is the image, beautiful, lovable, noble. Speak out, great Mother, and bid wars cease."

In many of the odes the conventional, obligatory eulogy of the monarch who happens to be temporarily occupying the Russian throne passes rapidly into the celebration of the greatness of the country; thus the poem may begin with the announcement that the day which is dawning ushers in the anniversary of Empress Elizabeth's accession to her father's throne, and all over the broad empire loyal Russians are celebrating the happy occasion. Then follows a vast, panoramic picture of the Russian land.

The first of Lomonosov's "replies" to Anacreon introduces the theme of the hero. In that poem there is no further elaboration, but elsewhere the theme is greatly expanded and often becomes very concrete. Thus, in the "Ode on the Capture of Khotin," Lomonosov's first original ode, two apparitions appear in the clouds to encourage the Russians and affright the Turks. "With sword bathed in blood, driving the foe, the Hero appears. Is it not he who by the streams of the Don scattered the walls injurious to the men of Rus?" (stanzas 9 and 10). The allusion is of course to the capture of the Turkish town of Azov by Peter the Great. Side by side with Peter is another great shade: "Who is it that with him gazes so terribly (grozno) toward the south, clothed round about with dreadful (strashnym) thunder? Is it not the pacifier of the lands of Kazan?" (stanza 11). If the deliberate use of the adverb grozno, "terribly," has not already made clear the identity of this second wraith, the reference to Kazan points unmistakably to Ivan IV "the Terrible" (Groznyi), who destroyed the Muslim khanates of Kazan and Astrakhan.

Peter is of course Lomonosov's hero par excellence, and there is scarcely an ode in which he does not appear. The monarch (Peter III, Elizabeth) or probable heir (Pavel Petrovich) who is actually descended from the great "transformer," as the Russians like to call him, usually gives a pretext for Lomonosov to expand on the glories of his reign, the great benefits which it brought to Russia, and to call upon his successor to follow in his footsteps and finish the great work which their ancestor began. It is particularly easy to pass from the celebration of Peter's own daughter to that of her glorious father, and the formula which the poet uses in his prose "Panegyric of Peter the Great," "In praising Peter, we are praising Elizabeth," if not usually so explicitly stated, serves him many times. Of course it was far easier to find material for glorification in Peter's action-filled reign than in the lax and shabby tenure of his daughter. In one ode ("On the Anniversary of the Accession of Elizabeth, 1761") a whole gallery of Russian heroes is passed in review: Sviatoslav, Vladimir "the Saint," Vladimir Monomakh, Dmitry Donskoy, Alexei Mikhailovich—and then: "What a son he begot!"—Peter the Great again.

Naturally, since so much of his verse is "public,"—the eulogies of reigning monarchs, the glorification of Peter (the epic "Peter the Great") or of Russia's liberation from the Tatar yoke (the tragedy "Tamira and Selim," with its background of Kulikovo Pole and the defeat of Mamay)—the theme of "war and peace" takes a large place in it. Lomonosov's attitude is ambivalent. Certain wars he regards as fully justified, e.g., Peter's long struggle with Sweden or Dmitry Donskoy's courageous defiance of the Tatars, and these he celebrates wholeheartedly. When he is obliged, however, to make some mention of Elizabeth's wars with Sweden and with Frederick II of Prussia (the "Seven Years War"), it is the perfidious breaking of treaties and attack on allies that he invokes as justification, rather lamely, for involvement in the horrors of war. In general, far from glorifying war and military heroism, Lomonosov programmatically eulogizes peace, sometimes (e.g., the Ode of 1747) at the very moment when the monarch is on the point of being drawn into war. During the height of the Seven Years War (1759)[18] he contrasts the situations "there" (Prussia) and "here" (Russia):

O how contradictory the reveries that embrace my mind at once! Here I see marvelous blessings! There—flame, cries, and wailing and tumult! Here the noonday and summer of mercy, society warmed by generosity; there, Hell has thrown open the gulf of death! (st. 3).

This remarkable ode ends with the strophe (24) addressed to "God, O God of peace":

Are we born less mortal, that we must double our mortality? Have we become too little wearied by the weight of life's burdens? Look upon the wails of the orphaned, look upon the tears of the aged, look upon the blood of thy slaves. To thee, love and joy of the world, Elizabeth calls this day! Wipe out strife from the ends of the world!

On the occasion of the marriage of Peter Fedorovich (later Peter III) and Ekaterina Alexeevna (later Catherine II), the poet calls for an end to war:

In the east, the west and the south, in all the wide circle of the world Russian regiments are feared; lay aside swords and helmets, and today take into your valiant hands green boughs and flowers. Allied kingdoms, maintain peace without your boundaries; and you, tempestuous winds, do not now venture to set the deep in motion. (st. 3)[19]

The Ode of 1747 on the anniversary of Elizabeth's coronation begins:

O delight of kings and earthly kingdoms, beloved peace, the blessedness of villages, bulwark of cities, how beautiful and helpful thou art! Around thee flowers show their hues, and the corn-ears are yellow in the fields; ships filled with treasures venture after thee upon the sea; with generous hand thou showerest thy riches over the earth (st. 1).[20]

Scientist and poet cannot be readily dissociated in Lomonosov: they interpenetrate. The theme of "science" (*nauka*) is one of the commonest in his poetry. Significantly, the "sciences" sometimes carry the epithet that emphasizes Lomonosov's concept of them as keys to an understanding of the Creator: "Then the *divine* sciences, over mountains, rivers and seas stretched out their hands to Russia, saying to this monarch [Peter I] : 'We are ready with utmost solicitude to give amid the Russian folk new fruits of purest intellect.' " ("Anniversary Ode of 1747," st. 9)[21] Toward the end of the same ode the poet foresees "that the Russian land can bring to birth its own Platos and Newtons, swift of reason " (st. 23). Usually in their appearance in the odes, the sciences are abstract and general, in keeping with the classical striving for universality. Once, however, Lomonosov even calls them individually by name and function ("Ode of 1750," st. 19-22):[21]

Colossi carved from the mountains, O Mechanics, raise up in honor of monarchs by whose hands Russians have been exalted with glory beneath the sun; fill the waters with ships, unite the seas with rivers and drain swamps with ditches, lighten military burdens, the cities founded by Peter complete beneath his daughter's scepter.

Penetrate, O Chemistry, into the recesses of the earth with keenness of vision, and discover the precious treasure which Russia contains within it; hasten to increase the glory of the Fatherland and to strengthen the realm more greatly, in the wake of wise nature, clothing thyself in seemly flowers, and what is beautiful only in summer, do thou with master craft make eternal.

Urania [i.e., Astronomy], exalt into the circles of the heavens amid the sun's rays the merits of Elizabeth, so that there to her eternal glory may shine a new planet. Having gathered the vastness of the Russian world into tiny outlines, display the cities saved by her [i.e., Elizabeth] and the villages blessed by her, O Geography.

Science of the light phenomena of air [i.e., Meteorology], forecast the changes of the heavens, and announce beforehand by trustworthy signs the stormy tumult of atmospheric quarrels: so that the cultivator may choose the time when to entrust the seed to the earth and when to give the furrows rest; and so that, not fearing the weather, far-off people may come with their riches to Elizabeth's shores.

The sciences are "divine" because they are the key to the great "book of Nature" which reveals the greatness of Nature's Creator. The glorification of God in this way, through man's increasing insight into His handiwork, is a final leading theme. This is most eloquently seen in the "spiritual odes," which are paraphrases of several Psalms, and in one exceptionally magnificent case, of portions of the Book of Job. Significantly, the main theme of the Book of Job—the incommensurability of man's concepts of justice and God's inscrutable ways—is completely ignored; the portions of the book which Lomonosov chooses to paraphrase are the great poetical passages in which Jehovah demands of Job: "Where wert thou when I—?" etc.—in other words, the sections of the book which exalt the Creator through exaltation of the beauty and might of His creation.

Who restrained the sea with shores and set bounds to the abyss, and bade it strive no further with its furious waves? The void that was hidden in darkness, was it not I, who with mighty hand disclosed it and dispelled the mist and separated Ocean from dry land?

Hast *thou* been able even once to bid the morning be earlier; hast thou been able on a day of wearying thirst to give the grain fields to drink of a refreshing rain, to direct a favoring wind to the mariner, to shake the heaviness of earth and hurl the godless down with it?

Hast thou passed through the deep of the sea with the precipices of divers paths? And counted the herds of multiform monsters, that walk upon the bottom? Have the gates of death, covered with darkness everlasting, been thrown open before thee with terror? Hast thou pushed back the mouth of Hell?

Canst thou hide the sun, pressing together with tempest the murky cloud, and make thick the transparent air, and engender the lightning in the rain, and suddenly with swift-flowing flash, and with a crash that shakes the hearts of the mountains, rock the ends of the universe, and proclaim thy wrath to mortals? (st. 4-7)[22]

Of course the classical example of Lomonosov's attitude toward God is that most anthologized of all his poetry, "Evening Meditation on the Greatness of God on the Occasion of a Great Display of Northern Lights,"[23] which ends with the significant strophe, addressed to the astronomers: "Full of doubts is your answer about what is around [even] near-by places. Then say, how vast is the world? And what is beyond the smallest stars? Is the end of creation unknown to you? Then say, how great is the Creator?"

Most of the examples we have cited of Lomonosov's themes have been drawn from his odes—and this is not surprising, since of all his poetry they are recognized as the best and most significant in the history of Russian verse.

It is time now to consider briefly the nature of the genre and the background of Lomonosov's use of it.

The Greek word *ode* signifies no more than "song," and was not among the Greeks the designation of a specific genre, but simply served to differentiate poetry that was "sung" from poetry that was "recited" (epic) or chanted to flute accompaniment (elegy). Poetry that was sung was of two types—the solo song, exemplified by the verses of the Aeolian poets Alcaeus and Sappho, or by the Ionian Anacreon; and the choral song, exemplified chiefly by the Boeotian Pindar. The Pindaric song was composed usually in "triads" of strophe, antistrophe and epode, in very complicated and difficult meters, the nature of which was totally obscure to later ages. The solo songs were composed either in stanzas (of Sappho and Alcaeus), usually of four lines each, or in continuous metrical units of a monotonous sing-song rhythm, occasionally broken by a shorter line (Anacreon).

The Roman Horace (Rome's only genuine lyric poet) evidently considered Pindar too difficult to naturalize in the stiff Latin language, and for some reason ignored Anacreon. His models were the Aeolic poets exclusively. From Horace the Latin poets of the Renaissance drew their inspiration. In the sixteenth century French poets (Du Bellay, Ronsard and others) tried to naturalize classical forms in their native language. Ronsard tried his hand on "Pindaric odes," with quite unfortunate results. He and others did much better with imitations of Horace, using four-line stanzas; and in his later life Ronsard became acquainted with what were then supposed to be the "Odes of Anacreon," and which are now known to be very late imitations of the verse of the sixth-century poet. A considerable vogue for these Epicurean celebrations of "wine, women and song" was initiated.

The odes of the Pléiade poets seemed to the next generation wordy, irregular, lacking in clarity and indeed almost barbaric. The pedantic lawgiver of French verse, Malherbe, set out to give his language true "odes" of proper classical form, as he believed. He took as his models not only Horace, but the Greeks. Most of Pindar's poetry which survived the dark ages fell into the four great collections of "Epinician Odes," i.e., poems written to the order of individual or city to celebrate the victory of an athlete in one of Greece's panegyric games. Malherbe took the theme of celebration and transposed it from athlete to monarch or general. He also rejected the complex Pindaric metrical form, the symmetry and regularity of which totally escaped him and his age, and prescribed a stanza form, which was then repeated without change throughout a poem. The stanza was a sort of compromise between the quatrains of Horace and the lengthy strophes of Pindar. The exact stanza form might be allowed some latitude: odes, however, should use a combination of masculine and feminine rhymes, and lines of generally either 7/8 or 8/9 syllables (the longer line reflecting the feminine ending). The stanza which Malherbe uses, for example, in his *Ode à la Reine mère du roi, sur sa bienvenue en France*,[24] has ten lines, of 8/9 syllables and the rhyme scheme *aBaBccDeeD*, the upper-case letters representing masculine, the lower-case feminine rhymes. This rhyme scheme is employed also by Boileau, in his only "triumphal ode," *Ode sur la prise de Namur;* in this, however, the lines are one syllabe shorter, 7/8.[25] This was the ode which, as we have seen, Trediakovsky imitated twice, first in syllabic verse, and then in his reformed syllabotonic prosody. The first version (1734) of his "Triumphal Ode on the Capture of the City of Dantzig" maintains lines of 9 syllables each, and an all-feminine rhyme scheme, *ababccdeed*. The revision (1752) of the ode keeps the original French length of line, 7/8, and alternation of rhymes, *aBaBccDeeD*. Of course, when the syllabic versification was superseded by the syllabo-tonic, a definite rhythm, only hinted at in French, was created. Since French verse dispenses with the foot as a unit, neither trochaic nor iambic movement is recognized. The hint, however, is there, and Russian poets took it. An instructive example is afforded by a comparison of the translations made by Lomonosov and Sumarokov of the well-known ode of J.-B. Rousseau *A la Fortune:*[26]

J.-B. Rousseau, strophe 1	*Сумароков, ст. 1*
Fortune, dont la main couronne	Ты, Фортуна, украшаешь
Les forfaits les plus inouis,	Злодеяния людей
Du faux éclat qui t'environne	И мечтание мешаешь
Serons-nous toujours éblouis?	Рассмотрети жизни сей.
Jusques à quand, trompeuse idole,	Долго ль нам повиноваться
D'un culte honteux et frivole	И доколе поклоняться
Honorerons-nous tes autels?	Нам обману твоему?
Verra-t-on toujours tes caprices	Все тобою побежденны:
Consacrés par les sacrifices	Все ли смертные рожденны
Et par l'hommage des mortels?	Супротивиться уму?

Ломоносов, ст. 1

Доколе, Счастье, ты венцами
Злодеев будешь украшать?
Доколе ложными лучами
Нам разум хочешь ослеплять?
Доколе, истукан прелестной,
Мы станем жертвой нам бесчестной
Твой тщетной почитать олтарь?
Доколе будем строить храмы,
Твои чтить замыслы упрямы,
Прельщенная словесна тварь?

It will be seen that both poets keep the ten-line stanza and the rhyme scheme of the original. Sumarokov, however, uses lines of 7/8 syllables, Lomonosov of 8/9 syllables, like the original. Sumarokov's lines are trochaic, Lomonosov's iambic. Which gives a closer approximation to the original French? Unquestionably Lomonosov's, because the French lines convey an iambic rhythm to anyone with an ear attuned to syllabo-tonic verse. In just the same way, as we have seen, the shorter line of Boileau's ode ("Quelle docte et sainte ivresse") inevitably sounds trochaic, and was reproduced in trochaic meter by Lomonosov, as was the Fénelon ode in identical form.

The genre of the ode came to Russia from France, and it was the practice of the French classical poets Malherbe, Boileau, J.-B. Rousseau, Pompignan et al. which determined that of Lomonosov, Sumarokov and their followers. Some of the remarks of Boileau in his short *Discours sur l'ode* came to be accepted as normative. Thus Boileau, who claims to be imitating Pindar, writes:

J'ai cru que je ne pouvais mieux justifier ce grand poète qu'en tâchant de faire une ode en français à sa manière, c'est-à-dire pleine de môuvements et de transports, où l'esprit parût plûtot entrainé du démon de la poésie, que guidé par la raison... J'ai pris pour sujet la prise de Namur, comme la plus grande action de guerre qui se soit fait de nos jours, et comme la matière la plus propre a échauffer l'imagination d'un poète. J'y ai jeté, autant qu j'ai pu, la magnificence des mots; et, à l'exemple des anciens poètes dithyrambiques, j'y ai employé les figures les plus audacieuses.[27]

Thus the solemn or triumphal ode in Russian, as in French, should be marked by what came to be known as "poetic disorder," which was supposed to show uncontrollable transports of inspiration; by "magnificence of words," which after Lomonosov meant the "high style," with plenty of Slavonicisms; and by bold and striking figures of speech. The subject should be some important occasion, such as a military victory, the negotiation of a peace, or the like; but very soon most odes came to be written on such occasions as royal birthdays, anniversaries, and the like. One French restriction in the practice of ode-writing the Russian poets never accepted—the prohibition against *enjambement,* or run-on lines, where the syntactic unit spills over from one line to the next.

Most histories of Russian literature, parroting each other tiresomely, assert that Lomonosov's model for the ode was not French, but German, and cite not only a specific poet, Johann Christian Günther (1695-1723), but a specific poem (Günther's only ode in the classical form: *Auf den zwischen Ihro Römischen Kaiserlichen Mäjestat und der Pforte 1718 geschlossenen Frieden)*[28] This 500-line piece follows most of the classical prescriptions for the ode: the occasion is the conclusion of what we know as the Peace of Passarowitz, after the great victories of Prince Eugene of Savoy over the Turks; the ode is filled with patriotic fervor, engendered by admiration of Prince Eugene and the courageous Austrian soldier; the form is the standard 10-line stanza, with iambic lines of 8/9 syllables and the rhyme scheme *AbAbCCdEEd.* Günther's poetry, which was first collected and published in

1735, was certainly known to Lomonosov. The great bulk of it consists of tender love poems addressed to his sweetheart Leonore, and of boisterous student drinking-songs. In the last years of his short life Günther wrote some very moving religious poetry. He is probably the best and most original German poet of his age, and his verses were great favorites among the university students at the very time when Lomonosov was studying at Marburg and Freiburg. It would be strange indeed if the "Ode on the Peace of 1718" was not known to the Russian poet. But did it influence him as much as the critics claim? I think this is very doubtful. From the aspect of form (the ten-line stanza, iambic rhythm, rhyme-scheme, etc.) it could have, for Lomonosov's first triumphal ode, "On the Capture of Khotin," employs exactly the same form—but so do any number of French odes which he must also have known: it must be remembered that it was a *French* ode (J.-B. Rousseau's *à la Fortune*) that he translated as his first experiment in syllabo-tonic iambics. From the point of view of style, however, Lomonosov's and Günther's verse have almost nothing in common, while the Russian poet's style is quite comparable to that of Malherbe, Boileau et al.

One of the leading principles of Lomonosov's odic style is that of abstraction. When landscape is introduced into the odes, it takes such an idealized form as the following("Ode of 1745," st. 6)[29]:"Crystal mountains are round about, cool streams glide by the flower-strewn meadow. Fruit, mottled with red, and branches watered with honey(!) exhibit spring at once with summer. Rapture captivates all feelings." Description of actual features of the northern landscape is totally absent from the odes. And as for the "persons" who move through them, they are either mythological figures— nymphs, goddesses, or the like—monarchs, e.g., Elizabeth, idealized so as to have no individual features whatever; or the shades of dead "heroes," e.g., Peter the Great, likewise unrecognizably transformed. Every effort is expended to universalize the scenes which the odes present. When battle is depicted, the scene may be described in terms of mythological allegory. For example:

Is it not brass glowing red in the maw of Etna, and boiling, seething with brimstone? Is it not Hell breaking its heavy bonds and striving to open its jaws? It is the race of the cast-off bond-maid [i.e., Hagar, legendary ancestress of the Muslims] ; having filled trenches with fire in the hills, they are hurling metal and flame down the slope to where our people, picked for the task, amid the foe, amid the swamps, are venturing across the swift stream to the fire. ("Ode on the Capture of Khotin," st. 5)[30]

Later the Russian forces are described, advancing "over hills where the blazing void belches smoke, ashes, flame and death"; "to them waters, woods, hills, precipices, the desert steppes are a level path. Where only the winds are able to blow, there the eagle regiments make their way."

This is as specific in description as Lomonosov ever becomes in the odes. One senses that Khotin must have been on a hill, and that the Turks employed fire in some fashion to keep back the attackers, but that is about all. Contrast with this procedure a few strophes from Günther's ode: "The battlefield is still wet and warm and stinks of Turks, shame and corpses; who can help seeing the Sava [river] choked with carrion, dragging along lazily and with difficulty?" (st. 2). Lomonosov ("Khotin Ode," st. 13) speaks of the fugitive Turks, affrighted by a falling leaf as by "the fierce whistle of balls [iadr] swiftly flying through the air." But mention of cannon and mortars he does not make; and such "low" ideas as are conveyed by the German stinkt and Äsern, however inseparable from a real battlefield, are excluded from the lofty ode. Günther addresses the approaching Turkish army (st. 8): "You are coming with horse, camel and wagons: so you are kindly bringing us the equipment with you, the more conveniently to carry off the spoils!" The crier appears in a German town to announce the peace treaty (st. 18): "The herald of peace blows his horn and rides in, and is questioned by great and small. The old man drops his stick and his feebleness; youth plays, childhood sings, and what is still drinking at the breast declares itself with a charming prattle." Then come some genre scenes which would be inconceivable with Lomonosov:

Here comes a young cavalier, and finds in the next garden, which has a view of all the streets, his lovely child [i.e., bride] painfully waiting. Then there begins a scene of tenderness [Zärtlichkeiten], the kissing gives the mouth no rest; the trembling "welcome" breaks off; then, with all the caresses possible, it is as though a second wedding were at hand.

There a full table pricks up its ears and listens to how neighbor Hans tells his tale. Hans eats and cuts double portions, and now and then wets his whistle. "Then," says he, "friends, just look here: suppose this were the Danube (here he makes a mark with beer); there we were moving, there stood the army, there things went sharper than one would think. God punish [me] ! You believe me without any oaths."

There a widow's bold son must provide his mother with new comfort; and if the father were not already sleeping, he would certainly now die of joy. The good woman is joyful, and runs and at once changes her will, and curses the false death certificate, and thinks: "Now I have a staff, and know who will one day weep at my grave with pure and loyal heart." (st. 19-21)

Günther's poem, to be sure, employs many of the same devices that Lomonosov uses. There are rhetorical questions, the addresses to the personnel of the ode—Prince Eugene, the Turks, etc.—there are the mythological allegories—Muses, nymphs, et al., there are the polite and conventional compliments to the reigning monarch (Charles VI). But these things are the stock in trade of all eighteenth-century ode-writers, and Lomonosov could have found them anywhere. What he could not have found anywhere else is Günther's bold realism—and it is precisely this which Lomonosov does not appropriate. It was this quality which occasioned Günther's catastrophic failure. His great ode was considered coarse and vulgar, and the ode on the same subject by the poetaster Johann Valentin Pietsch received applause and the author state remuneration. It may be noted, incidentally, that Pietsch was declared by that German arbiter Gottsched to be "the greatest poet of his age." Gottsched also thought very highly of Lomonosov's poetry, which he read in translation.

A good deal has been said already in the preceding discussion about the qualities of Lomonosov's style in the odes. These qualities are best described as "Baroque," for Lomonosov occupies a rather ambivalent position in Russian poetry. His world outlook is, as we have seen, that of the Enlightenment; but his literary practice is that of the late Baroque period. It is precisely the deviation of his verse from the norms accepted by classicism that brought on such an embittered literary feud between him and Sumarokov. The classicist Sumarokov found fault with Lomonosov's verse as inflated, exaggerated, and lacking in precision and clarity—all Baroque characteristics.

As was noted above, one of the qualities which, following Boileau, was expected of the triumphal ode was the supposedly Pindaric "poetic disorder." The force of inspiration (allegorized as "the Muse") is conceived to possess the poet so devastatingly that logic, clarity, sometimes even grammar, are sacrificed. This is Lomonosov's *vostorg*—"transport" or "rapture." It usually carries the poet to a great height above the earth, from which he sees an enormous panorama:

A sudden transport has taken my mind captive, and is leading me to the summit of a lofty mountain, where the wind has forgotten to sough in the forests; in the deep vale there is peace... Do I not behold Pindus beneath my feet? I hear the music of the pure sisters (i.e., the Muses)! I burn with the fire of Permessus, I haste to their choir. Healing water they give me: "Drink, and forget all toils; bathe with Castalian dew thine eyes, over plain and mountains spread thy gaze, and fix thy spirit on those lands where day is rising after dark night" ("Ode on the Capture of Khotin," st. 1-2)

What rapture is this I feel? Whither am I now rapt? The food of heaven I taste, borne aloft to Olympus's summit! ("Ode of 1750," st. 1).

To the beautiful summit of Parnassus' mountains strives the eye of the mind, to where pure waters flow and refresh the Muses' assembly. ("Ode of 1746," st. 1)[31]

When he is writing an anniversary ode, he usually begins it with the description of dawn, that is to usher in the happy day. Sometimes dawn is the classical goddess, with her classical function: "The Dawn with red hand is bringing up out of the peaceful morning waters, with the sun behind her, a new year of thy realm" (Ode of 1748, st. 1).[32] In connection with this allegory or one like it, incidentally, Prince Peter Vyazemsky once grumbled that the Dawn "with red hand from the peaceful morning waters" made him think of a Moscow washerwoman in December! The "red hand" of dawn (Lomonosov's equivalent of Homer's *rhododaktylos Eos!*) appears a number of times, e.g., in the "Ode of 1746," st. 2, where she is a door-opener

"And lo, now with red hand the dawn has thrown open the gates upon the world," etc. Such mythological allegories of natural events are exactly in keeping with Boileau's prescriptions for the ode:

> *L'ode, avec plus d'éclat, et non moins d'energie,*
> *Elevant jusqu'au ciel son vol ambitieux,*
> *Entretient dans ses vers commerce avec les dieux.*[33]

But it is not only the pagan gods with whom Lomonosov's odes hold converse; it happens from time to time that the poet overhears the Christian God addressing admonitory words to the saints in heaven! Thus, in his 1759 ode on Empress Elizabeth's name-day, celebrating "her glorious victory over the Prussian King," Lomonosov writes (st. 4): "Ether, earth and Hell await with terror the Creator! I see the Lord's Son taking the heavenly judgment. Almighty in His dominion, He proclaims on high to Moses: 'In wrath I shall harden Egypt's heart, puffed up; Israel I shall arm invincibly with illustrious strength.' "[34] Here, of course, the allegory, and even the words, are Biblical. "Egypt" stands for Frederick's Prussia, while Elizabeth's Russians, it hardly needs to be said, are the "chosen people."

Again, in his last ode (1761) to Empress Elizabeth, the poet has another vision of Paradise:

Be bold, my spirit, gaze, comprehend! Through the smoke the heavenly ray shines bright! There God stretches forth His right hand, and entrusts to Peter [III] on earth the solidity of measureless strength: "Overthrow cunning with valor, pacify wars with wars, clothe the realm with new weapons, bring new life to the northern lands." (st. 18)[35]

Lomonosov's most impressive encounter with the Almighty comes, not surprisingly, at the happy moment when in 1742 the daughter of his idol Peter the Great ascends her father's throne. Here, in typical Baroque fashion, classical and Biblical phraseology intermingle:

A holy horror grips my mind! Almighty Olympus has thrown open its door. All creation attends with great terror, beholding the daughter of great monarchs, chosen by all loyal hearts, crowned by the hand of the Most High, standing before His face; having abundantly glorified her in His world, He looks upon her, confirms His covenant and comforts her:

"Blessed be thou eternally," proclaims to her the Ancient of Days, "And all thy people with thee, whom I have entrusted to thy dominion. Thy lovable goodness calls forth my generosity to thee. To the Russians I have been the Creator in wrath, but now I am once more their Father: the power of thy most gentle soul has turned my wrath to gentleness" (st. 5-6)[36]

Of the "bold figures" which Boileau recommends for the ode, surely the boldest is that of exalting earthly doings with quotations from the Almighty! Audacious as this may seem to a later age, it was a practice already, since the Renaissance, commonly employed by epic writers, whom tradition required to make use of the miraculous. We have seen Kantemir's use of the same device in his unfinished *Petriad*.

The eighteenth century was prone to regard poetry as constituting a branch of rhetoric, and the oratorical element generally predominates— e.g., the verse of Voltaire or of Alexander Pope. We have seen in Lomonosov the prevalence of rhetorical questions, e.g., "Is it not Pindus I see beneath my feet?," and of impassioned exclamations, e.g., "Russia, how fortunate art thou beneath Anna's mighty protection!" ("Ode on the Capture of Khotin," st. 25). It would be tiresome to attempt a listing of all the rhetorical figures which Lomonosov employs in the Odes; anyone interested may consult his own *Rhetoric*, where he very frequently uses quotations from his odes as examples.[37] One such figure, however, is so pervasive and so typical that it may perhaps be safely said that it must have come naturally to Lomonosov, and did not need to be learned. This is the figure of hyperbole. Examples are legion; a few will suffice. Peter the Great's first war fleet is launched, and—("Ode of 1742," st. 23): "The proud deep retires, groaning under the ships' weight." Later in the same ode (st. 30): "On the Baltic's sounding shores there is more joy than water!" Later still (st. 42) the exaltation of Elizabeth to the rank of a goddess, which she thereafter predictably holds, is announced in these words: "If ancient ages had known thy generosity, coupled with beauty, they would have honored thy lovely image with sacrifices in temples."

The spectacle of the tender conjugal love of Peter Fedorovich and his bride Catherine (Lomonosov *must* have had tongue in cheek!) inspires even the trees to the same passion: "The trees wave their leaves, embrace one another with their branches; in inanimate things I behold the passion of love!" (Ode of 1745, st. 7).[38]

Commonest of all the figures of rhetoric in the Odes are similes and metaphors. An interesting combination of the two appears in the "Ode of 1742," st. 22-23; first the wind is metaphorically a mighty giant, and then the boisterous impetuosity of the Russian fleet is likened to his:

The stormy giant races on his way with great joy across the hills, steps on the stern summits, scorning the deep bottom of the valleys, and twists the air in a whirlwind behind him; beneath his mighty heel the flinty hillocks crash, and the trees lie prostrate in his wake, which have been standing for a multitude of lifetimes, and scorned the fury of the storms. Thus the Russian fleet ventures upon the deep, thus plows the surface of the waves.[39]

In the "Ode of 1748" the loyalty of Elizabeth's subjects is pictured in a vivid simile:

Into meadows strewn with flowers, the queen of the laborious bees, buzzing with flash-

97

ing wings, flies amid the cool hamlets; abandoning the roses and the juice-filled vines, the swarm gathers from everywhere with diligence, surrounds its queen and the formation, fixed by zeal, flies closely in her train. Fired by such heat, the Russian folk has gathered here [etc.] (st. 7-8).[40]

Often it is the world of antique mythology rather than that of nature that furnishes the object of comparison. For example:

Because, belching smoke and ashes, Enceladus darkened the universe, he now sobs and roars under Etna, and crams Hades with his body; transfixed by Zeus's blow, he shakes his yoke in despair, unable to raise the weight, covered up by the great mountain, bootlessly stirs beneath it, and vainly tries to stand. Thus barbarism lies, laid low by thy thunderbolt. ("Ode of 1750," st. 16-17).[41]

The extravagant and atmospheric use of metaphor, characteristic of Lomonosov's verse and a feature of the Baroque style, was one of the principal targets for the criticism of the classicists. Mention has already been made of Prince Vyazemsky's reflections on the Dawn's "red hand." A similar phrase, used several times by Lomonosov (e.g., "Ode of 1742," st. 17; "Ode of 1750," st. 11) is that of "stormy feet" (or "legs"—*nogi* means both) of horses; in the earliest use the phrase refers to the scene of the battle of Poltava ("Ode of 1742," st. 17):[42]

The horses with stormy feet whirl up the thick dust to heaven; there death, raging, runs amid the Gothic [i.e., Swedish] troops, from rank to rank, and opens his greedy jaws, and stretches out his cold hands, wresting away their haughty spirit.[42]

In this context, accompanied by the grim personification of Death, the metaphor seems entirely natural to us. Not so to the classicist. Lomonosov, as Gukovsky notes,[43] chooses his words "on the principle of their emotional aureole, sometimes more significant than their objective sense, because in that dazzling world of the ideals of monarchical greatness into which Lomonosov transports the reader, he is able to rise above the, for him, flat logic of the ordinary.... Sumarokov will later carp at such expressions of Lomonosov; for the classicist's rationalistically logical concept of language, the legs of a horse can be slender, well-shaped, can be swift, but not by any means 'stormy.' But Lomonosov means not to define the horses' legs logically, but to express that storm of the elements, that grandiose shock which in the inflamed imagination and in the excitement of civic enthusiasm makes all parts of the picture which he is sketching particularly significant—and the verse itself becomes stormy." We find Sumarokov's criticisms later having a chastening effect on Lomonosov's exuberance; in several instances he revises poems which seem too extravagantly worded.

It may be useful, as a final conspectus of Lomonosov's odic style, as this appeared to a critical contemporary, to cite two parodies by Sumarokov—the so-called "Nonsense Odes." In these quite clever travesties most of

Lomonosov's favorite stylistic devices may be seen in caricature:

First Nonsense Ode

Above the stars, the moon and sun I now soar in transport *[vostorg]*; from the regions on high I gaze upon the midnight [i.e., northern] ocean. Waves are there battling with waves, there whirlwinds are fighting it out with whirlwinds, and whipping the sea in foam to the clouds; the eternal ice is straining to the storm-clouds, and tearing their hugeness in its measureless fury.

The ship is raised to the heavens by tumultuous mountains; there thunders smite upon thunders, and do not kiss peace [or "quiet": *tishiny*]; the mouths of the lightnings bursting there do not get drunk on dew, and inflame the whole azure; Boreas with frozen hands hauls whales out of the deep and maliciously dashes them on the dry land.

Rise up, O lyre, raise yourself up, thunder to all the ends of the earth, and with magniloquent song increase my glory! Aeolus, set the winds at liberty, and put my thoughts upon their tempest-bearing wings! I shall dash through all space, I shall penetrate air, sky, sea, and I shall disquiet the whole ether.

I am not sleeping, but in a cheerful drowse, and awake I am seeing a terrible dream. Neptune is emerging from the gulfs, waves are flowing from his hair, and while touching the skies with his head, he tramples the abyss of the pyramids; wherever he treads, there is a hole. Under his heavy heel the ravening *[svirepy]* waves divide, and the sea-monsters scuttle to the bottom.

"If I am deserving of this, tell me, O Saturn's son! Why have you left your halls and the depths of the roaring waters?" The sea's governor opened his mouth—the storm became a hundred times worse, and the ocean began to tremble; woods and mountains began to crash, and the shores of the sea began to quake, and Zeus himself had a scare.

"To delight myself with your lyre I have come up out of the depths of the abyss; set up the walls of Thebes [like Amphion!] on the frosty northern shores; your songs are magniloquent like the songs of Amphion; do not tarry, build a new city and sumptuoulsy adorn a temple to the Muses with mosaic, glass beads, and gold." He spoke, and disappeared in the abyss of waters.[44]

The sea-god's final line would be unintelligible without the note that Lomonosov's non-poetical interests included a passion for mosaics and an (unsuccessful) factory for making colored glass!

The second "Nonsense Ode" is shorter, and if anything, a little wilder:

Thunder, lightning and eternal glaciers, seas and lakes are noisy, Vesuvius hurls from his midst burning hell into the subsolar region. From the eternal east smoke ascends, brings up terrible clouds, and covers the horizon with darkness. Ephesus is burning, Damascus is ablaze, Cerberus is baying with his three throats, and setting the Mediterranean afire.

Persepolis falls headlong, just like Phaethon; Neptune leaves his realm, and overturns his throne in the deep; the giants raise their arms, destroy the gods' dwelling-place, strike with mountains on the firmament of heaven; Boreas, annoyed, roars and groans, Japan sinks in the abyss, and Hercules fights it out with the Hydra.

With one ponderous foot the violent Titan treads on Pico [a mountain in the Azores], and, slipping with the other, in the terrible icy ocean. With his feet he is hardly in the world, and he conceals his head in the ether, touching the heavens with it. I have my whole mouth open, Muses, and I am chanting so ingeniously *[khitro]* that I myself don't understand my song.

In one respect, if not in many, Sumarokov's malicious parodies do his greater rival a cruel injustice. Whenever (almost) in the triumphal odes the poet uses the first person, he does so as the solemn, composite voice of the Russian people; almost never does he betray any hint of the individual Mikhail Lomonosov (once in the 1761 ode he refers to his "declining age"). Certainly in the odes he never claims immortality for his verses, although in a free translation of Horace (Odes III, 30) he declares: "I have reared myself a monument of immortality, higher than the Pyramids and stronger than brass" [Horace: *Exegi monumentum aere perennius, Regalique situ pyramidum altius*].[45] This poem, in fact, may serve as an example of the means which eighteenth-century poets often took to reveal their personal feelings—translation. When Lomonosov picks Horace's famous vaunt for translation (as Derzhavin was later to do, and Pushkin after him), he is unquestionably applying the verses to himself; yet if taken to task, he could always justify his apparent flaunting of self as a faithful rendering of the original.

The commonest instrument for this kind of oblique personal comment in the seventeenth and eighteenth centuries was the Psalms of David. As Boileau's *Discours sur l'ode* makes clear, these ancient Hebrew poems were regarded in the age of classicism as "odes" on a par with those of the Greeks and Romans, with the added authority of divine inspiration.[46] Few poets of the age could have read them in the Hebrew; but from the received translations (the Vulgate, the King James, or in Russia the Church Slavonic text) they could work out "paraphrases" (Rus. *prelozheniia*) in verse. Malherbe gave a model for such paraphrases, e.g., one on Psalm 145, with its stern warning that kings are only men, and mortal like all others.[47] This Psalm was also a favorite of the Russian poets, paraphrased by both Lomonosov and Sumarokov. It can be readily seen how such a sacred text might provide cover for a poet who would not venture on his own to call the attention of the mighty to the uncomfortable fact of man's general mortality. Lomonosov made poetical versions of eight of the Psalms (1, 14, 26, 34, 70, 103, 143, 145). Many other contemporary and later poets followed his example; perhaps the most striking of all *prelozheniia* is Derzhavin's of Psalm 81, "To Sovereigns and Judges" *(Vlastiteliam i sudiiam).*[48]

The poet of the original Psalms speaks to God forthrightly in his own person, pleading for help against his enemies, against the "wicked," or pouring out his thanks for aid received. He also, in a less personal tone, glorifies the great works of the Lord and the impossibility of their comprehension by frail mankind. Themes such as these lent themselves very readily to Lomonosov's use; and complaint and invective that convention forbade a poet's uttering in his own person could be safely indulged in behind the mask of the royal Psalmist. Thus, in paraphrasing Psalm 26 (27 in the English version) Lomonosov can assert his assurance of aid from above: "The Lord is my savior and light: of whom shall I be afraid? The Lord himself preserves my life: whom shall I fear?" and in strophes 10-13 pray for continued protection:

> My father abandoned me, and my mother while [I was] still in babyhood; but the Creator took me up and gave me to live in well-being. Set me, O Lord, upon the path with Thy holy law, that [my] enemy may not shake [me], who am strong therein.
> Do not deliver me in this life to the souls of godless men; with Thy right hand protect [me] from false slanders.[49]

The King James version of the original, not substantially different here from Lomonosov's Old Slavonic text, reads as follows:

> When my father and my mother forsake me, then the Lord will take me up. Teach me thy way, O Lord, and lead me in a plain path because of mine enemies.
> Deliver me not over unto the will of mine enemies: for false witnesses are risen up against me, and such as breathe out cruelty. (10-12)

One of the most magnificent pieces of poetry in the Bible is Psalm 103 (104), with its panoramic view of creation:

> Bless the Lord, O my soul. O Lord my God, thou art very great, thou art clothed with
>   honor and majesty;
> Who coverest thyself with light as with a garment; who stretchest out the heavens like
>   a curtain;
> Who layeth the beams of his chambers in the waters; who maketh the clouds his chariot;
>   who walketh upon the wings of the wind;
> Who maketh his angels spirits; his ministers a flaming fire;
> Who laid the foundations of the earth, that it should not be removed for ever;
>
> ———
>
> He sendeth the springs into the valley, which run among the hills.
> They give drink to every beast of the field; the wild asses quench their thirst.
> By them shall the fowls of the heaven have their habitation, which sing among the
>   branches." (Verses 1-5; 10-12)
>
> ———

A literal translation of the above passage of the Psalm in Lomonosov's paraphrase goes as follows:

> Let my spirit and tongue praise the kingdom of the Almighty Creator, His greatness and glory. O my God, how great thou art! Clothed with wondrous beauty, with the dawn of light divine, thou hast spread out the stars without number, like a tent before thee.
> [The word which the King James translation rendered as "curtain" is in Old Slavonic *kozhu*, "a skin," which Lomonosov construed as meaning "tent"]

Having covered the high places with waters, thou risest on the light clouds, thou makest a tumult with the wings of whirlwinds, when thou fliest upon them.

[Again there is a textual difference from the English; verse 3 reads in Old Slavonic: "Having covered with waters thy high places," etc.]

And the emissaries of thy will, like aerial emanations, obedient to the Almighty's beck, run, burn, knowing no darkness.

[Here there is no essential difference in the texts; but Lomonosov has "translated" the Biblical phraseology into "scientific" terms.]

Thou hast founded the earth firmly, and for secure strengthening, laid down rivets, and given immovability forever.

———

From the mountains thou pourest the springs into the valleys, and givest refreshment therewith from the heat; they gurgle for sweet sleep as they flow among the mountains. And they give drink to all beasts that nourish themselves among the fields; the wild asses, when they languish in thirst, await comfort from thy hand. The birds, flocking together into the shade there raise their song and whistling; they dwell in rocky dens, and therewith pass the hot day.[50]

[Where the King James translators have the birds, true to English custom, "sing among the branches," the Old Slavonic version, which Lomonosov tries to explain rationalistically, reads: "from the midst of the *rocks* they shall give [their] voice," following the Greek Septuagint.[51]]

Lomonosov's paraphrase breaks off with verse 16 of the Psalm, less than half of the original.

Quite similar in theme to Psalm 103, but original creations of Lomonosov, are the two "Meditations": "Morning Meditation on the Greatness of God"; and "Evening Meditation on the Greatness of God, on the Occasion of a Great Display of Northern Lights." The *Aurora Borealis*, literally "northern dawn," induces the poet to exclaim: "But where, O Nature, is thy law? From regions of the north the dawn arises! Is not the sun setting up his throne there? Are not the icy seas shooting out fire? Lo, a cold flame has covered us! Lo, in the night day has trodden upon the earth!" (3-4)[52] These contradictions bring him to consider various proposed scientific explanations, e.g., "Is it, like lightening without thunderclouds, straining from earth to the zenith?" (6), or "There thick darkness is contending with water; or the sun's rays are shining, refracted to us through the thick atmosphere; or the summits of cloudy mountains are afire; or the west wind has ceased to blow on the sea, and the smooth waves are reflecting in the ether." (7) All this, however, is so unsatisfactory that he rejects it, and ends with his challenge to the scientists: "Is the end of creation unknown to you? Then say, how great is the Creator?"

The paraphrases of the Psalms, the paraphrase of portions of Job, and

102

the two original meditations are classified as "religious" (or "spiritual") odes. It is a recognized eighteenth-century genre, but subject to less prescription than the secular ode. French examples usually make use of the long and dignified Alexandrine line, interspersed with regularly placed shorter lines. In this regard the Russian, like the English poets, proved independent. In an effort to match their paraphrases to the Biblical verses, they preferred quatrains of short lines; Lomonosov uses for Psalm 26 a quatrain of alternate four-beat iambic lines with masculine rhyme and three-beat iambic lines with feminine rhyme. For Psalm 103 the quatrain consists of four four-beat iambic lines with the rhyme scheme *AbbA*. The "Ode Selected from Job, Chapters 38, 39, 40 and 41," which is far more independent of the original than the Psalm paraphrases, employs a strophe of eight four-beat iambic lines, rhyming *aBaBccDD*. The "Morning Meditation" uses a six-line stanza, of four-beat iambic lines, rhyming *aBaBCC*. Exceptionally for Lomonosov's verse the "Evening Meditation" uses masculine rhymes throughout, in a six-line stanza: *ABABCC*, an arrangement which conveys a particularly strong and energetic effect.

Another metrical feature of the "Evening Meditation" deserves brief comment. The poem, according to Lomonosov's own words in the *Rhetoric*, where he quotes it, was composed in 1743.[53] At this early date the poet was still attempting to write "pure" iambics, that is, lines unmarred by what he regarded as the "license" of an occasional "pyrrhic" foot of two unaccented syllables. In this connection, of course, it must be borne in mind that Russian does not, like English, recognize a "secondary accent" in polysyllabic words. Naturally, a verse of pure iambic structure must accordingly exclude all words of more than three syllables. How closely Lomonosov followed his own rule at this date may be seen from the first strophe of the "Evening Meditation":

Лице́ свое́ скрыва́ет де́нь;
Поля́ покры́ла мра́чна но́чь;
Взошла́ на го́ры че́рна те́нь;

Лучи́ от на́с склони́лись про́чь;
Откры́лась бе́здна звезд полна́;
Звезда́м числа́ нет, бе́здне дна́.

Day conceals his face;
dark night has hidden the fields;
a black shadow has ascended the hills;
the sun's rays are diverted from us.
the abyss full of stars is revealed;
the stars without number, the abyss without bottom.

According to the records of the Academy of Sciences, under date of September 29, 1750, Count Razumovsky announced to the Academicians that by an express command of Empress Elizabeth herself, "Professors Lomonosov and Trediakovsky were to write each a tragedy." On Lomonosov's manuscript of *Tamira i Selim* is the annotation: "Begun on September 29, 1750, after dinner."[54] He wasted no time in obeying orders! The manuscript was delivered to the printers on November 1 of the same year, and the tragedy was performed in the Court Theater by cadets on January 9, 1751. Trediakovsky's tragedy, *Deidameia*, lagged far behind. The author announced in November that the first act was finished, and the whole would be ready in the following year.[55] When the tragedy was finally completed it had reached the monumental proportions of 2718 lines; Lomonosov's *Tamira i Selim* has 1564. *Deidameia* was never produced, and not even printed in its author's lifetime. After a moderate success with his first attempt, Lomonosov, this time without imperial prodding, wrote a second tragedy, *Demiphon*. Perhaps the subject, drawn from Greek legendary history with considerable dependence upon Racine's *Andromaque*, alienated readers; the play was not produced, and the triumph of Sumarokov's third tragedy, *Semira*, in 1751 signalized Lomonosov's discomfiture. He never returned to the writing of drama, but from that period a kind of delimitation of "spheres of influence" was tacitly arranged between him and Sumarokov: the latter should preside over tragedy, while the former made the ode his province. Neither trespassed on the other's realm.

Tamira and Selim[56] is a good example of the classical tragedy, the rules of which it follows quite meticulously. It is, of course, in five acts, is composed in Russian Alexandrine verse, observes the three unities without undue strain, and is couched in a lofty style marked by numerous Slavonicisms. The treatment of the verse form is slightly irregular: whereas the Alexandrines of Trediakovsky and Sumarokov follow the French rhyme scheme of alternating couplets, masculine and feminine, Lomonosov uses alternating *lines,* masculine and feminine.

The subject is an imaginary one, linked, according to classical precept, to a historical action for verisimilitude. Tamira, daughter of the Tsar of the Crimea, Mumet, is sought in marriage by two suitors: Selim, prince of Baghdad, and the Tatar khan Mamay. Mumet has reason to suppose Mamay's power the greater, and promises his daughter to him; her love, however, is already given to the handsome Selim, and she resists and even tries to escape to her lover. In the meanwhile Mamay has appeared on the scene, unaccompanied by his army; he has actually just been disastrously defeated by the Muscovite army under Dmitry Donskoy at Kulikovo Pole, but craftily conceals this knowledge in order to win Tamira and therewith her father's support. The dénouement is effected by the timely return of Tamira's brother Narsim, who has been serving as a reluctant auxiliary under Mamay, and has barely escaped a perfidious ambush laid by the latter. The despairing Tamira is prevented at the last moment from stabbing herself, when she hears false news that Selim is dead; the lovers are united, and Narsim gives a vivid account of the crucial defeat of Mamay by the Russians. Mamay himself, his treachery discovered, has been dispatched off-stage.

External circumstances evidently play a greater part in this drama than psychological conflicts, and in this regard the influence of Corneille would seem to be more powerful than that of Racine. Tamira, at the moment (end of Act III) when she is contemplating flight to Selim's ships, utters a soliloquy in which she teeters, in the approved classical fashion, between filial loyalty and love for Selim; but the outcome is such a foregone conclusion that her vacillation has only a ritual appearance. The real complication of the plot—the necessary obstacle to the consummation of true love—is Mamay's defeat and his treacherous concealment of it, which he communicates to the audience in a soliloquy at the beginning of Act III. From then on there is the assurance that his perfidy will be discovered in time, and thwarted, as the convention of *bonnes moeurs* demands. Evil must be punished, on the stage, and virtue rewarded.

In addition to the principals, Mumet, Tamira, Narsim, Selim and Mamay, there are three subordinate figures, whose functions are largely conventional. Cleona is Tamira's nurse, who lends a sympathetic ear to her mistress in Act I as the latter discloses her love for Selim. Zaisan is Mumet's vizier, who listens to the Khan's confidences; and this function he shares with Nadir, Mumet's brother. There is some originality in the rivalry of these two confidants: Zaisan is the advocate of Mamay's cause, Nadir, very cautiously, of Selim's. There is even a faint touch of humor when Zaisan complacently remarks to Nadir: "I think I have the better in our argument" when Mumet decides in Mamay's favor; and then, after the unmasking of Mamay's treachery, Nadir rejoins: "In our argument I think the upper hand is mine." This undercurrent of irony, bordering on humor (of course actual comedy is excluded from a classical tragedy) reaches its climax when, moved by his niece's pleas, old Nadir prepares to rush out and revenge the supposed death of Selim (Act V, scene iii).

One of the characteristic features of Russian classical tragedy is the use of what were called "allusions," that is, situations and remarks from the stage that could be interpreted to refer to the current political scene. Thus Sumarokov's *Hamlet* contained in its basic situation (Claudius's usurpation of the Danish throne) what was, probably mistakenly, believed to be an "allusion" to Catherine's murder of her husband and usurpation of the Russian throne. Lomonosov steers clear of such "allusions," but the tragedies are liberally sprinkled with what are called in Roman parlance *sententiae*— aphorisms designed to pound home to an obtuse audience the moral implications of a situation. Nadir, as an old man whose role is almost wholly passive, is the largest contributor of such maxims. Thus, in the midst of his first debate with Zaisan (Act II, scene v) he remarks: "A dominion of violence cannot long stand. He who persecutes one, threatens everyone." (lines 608-09). At the end of the scene he moralizes: "The magnanimous lion at once allays his heat, as soon as he sees his foe prostrate; but the rapacious wolf tears his opponent as long as the last blood seethes in him" (lines 624-627). The longest and most tedious of Nadir's moral discourses takes the form of a soliloquy (Act IV, scene ii, lines 1004-1039) on "insatiable greed for property and power," presumably inspired by his brother's heartless sacrifice of his daughter's happiness for the advantages of Tatar favor; the pertinence of this sermon, however, is extremely questionable. One of the most remarkable of Nadir's aphorisms is uttered later in the same act (scene iii) when Cleona announces the rumor in town that Mamay has been defeated: "The voice of the whole people is always the voice of God; by their mouth, the Most High speaks" (*Vox populi, vox Dei!*).

The tragedy is skillfully constructed and well written. Even when read, it conveys a sense of excitement, which is climaxed by Narsim's lengthy "messenger's speech" recounting the great battle of the Snipes' Field. But it cannot be said that Lomonosov has succeeded in creating any very credible or living characters in it. Mamay is a bloodthirsty and tyrannical villain, distinguished from others of his kind only by a greater degree of craft; Mumet is the usual heartless father, and the lovers are entirely conventional types. The only glimmers of original characterization are, oddly enough, in the minor figures—Cleona, with her surprising loyalty to Tamira in the face of Mamay's tempting promises; Nadir and Zaisan, and even Narsim, in his short part (he appears first in Act V). But this criticism does not apply to Lomonosov's play alone: his successful rival Sumarokov peoples his tragedies with exactly the same stereotypes. The very dramatic theory of classicism, with its insistence on universality and elimination of everything individual and distinctive results almost inevitably in such lay-figures.

Tragedy, epic, and ode—such are the genres requiring the "high style." Lomonosov, except in prose, rarely descended from these heights. Two of his most interesting works, however, belong to the middle, and even the low, style. To the low style must also be consigned his polemical epigrams, which are distinguished by their crude violence and pointlessness. Far better, both as verse and as polemic, is the "Hymn to the Beard." This Lomonosov composed probably in 1756 or 1757, during his struggle with the church authorities. The poem was circulated in manuscript, a copy of which fell into the hands of the Holy Synod. The poet was summoned for interrogation, and boldly and defiantly acknowledged his authorship. Evidently he was confident of the protection of Shuvalov and through him, of the Empress. The Holy Synod was constrained to vent its fury on him not, as it had wished, by excommunication and imprisonment, but more tamely by stupid and harmless pasquinades.

The "Hymn to the Beard" begins: "Not to lecherous Venus, not to the monstrous Chimaera do I offer sacrifice in hymns: I sing a song of eulogy to the hair that is respected by all, that spreads out over the breast, that in the evening of our years gives weight to our counsel."[57] Then follows a four-line refrain, which is repeated after each of the ten strophes: "O beard most precious! It's pity that you haven't been christened, and that the shameful part of the body is in this respect preferred before you." (Since baptism was performed in infancy, the beard was of course unbaptized!) The eulogy continues with references to the "nether beard" "through which we make our way into the world"; then passes to the fiscal possibilities of the beard, which Peter the Great subjected to a tax; thence to the superstition of the Old Ritualists, who clung to their beards, "fearing not the threat of death." In stanza 5 he adverts to the custom of swearing by one's beard, which secures the eyesight of "fools, tongue-waggers and rascals,"—were it not for the beard's protection, everyone would spit in their eyes! Then comes the forbidden subject—"plurality of worlds!" "If it is true that the planets are worlds like ours, in them of course, the wise men, and most of all the priests there will asseverate by their beards that we here do not exist at all. If anyone shall say we really are here—they'll burn him there on a pyre" (st. 6). The seventh strophe returns to this no less imperfect planet, where the weakling in body and mind will have respect and high office by virtue of his beard—an obvious hit at the bearded clergy. "O golden adornment, O precious adornment, mother of respectability and wits, mother of revenues and ranks, root of impossible actions, O curtain of false opinions! With what can I do you honor, with what repay your services?" (st. 8). The final two strophes show the poet planning to adorn his beard with all kinds of ribbons, etc., in fashionable style; but alas, because of the number of these decorations "the beard didn't grow." "I'll imitate the peasants and manure you like a field. Good-bye, now, beard, and grow in rich dampness" (st. 10).

While hardly subtle, the satire is vigorous. The wording, appropriately to the genre, is colloquial, even provincial.

The "Epistle on the Usefulness of Glass,"[58] addressed in 1752 to Lomonosov's patron Shuvalov, occupies stylistically a middle position. It is written in a simple, but not vulgar, Russian, with very few Slavonicisms, and with almost scientific precision and clarity. For all its genuinely serious purpose, the Epistle assumes a rather bantering tone, as it enumerates the "usefulness of glass" to the ladies—mirrors for the city belle and glass beads for her country cousin! But the mention of glass beads leads directly into an excursus on the European treatment of the savages of America, who were simpleminded enough to exchange their silver for such baubles, and were cruelly and heartlessly exploited.

The Epistle has the form normally taken by a classical didactic poem—heroic, that is, Alexandrine, verse, rhyming in couplets, alternately masculine and feminine. In its small way it copies the method of Lucretius in the *De Rerum Natura:* "Glass" is first given a mythological geneology. It is the child of Nature by Fire, and was born on Mount Etna—a reference to volcanic natural glass, or obsidian. Later, in connection with the prosaic use of the burning glass for lighting the tobacco in one's pipe, comes Lomonosov's interpretation of the myth of Prometheus—he stole fire from heaven—by the use of the burning glass!

Most of the poem is devoted to just what its title suggests—the uses of glass: for vials to contain medicines, for the glaze on porcelain, for faience and mosaic, for window-panes in houses and conservatories, for ladies' mirrors and peasant girls' beads; for spectacles to help the feeble sight of old age—"A great grief to the heart to be deprived of reading books; more vexatious than eternal darkness, heavier than chains!" For telescopes and microscopes, and—in the climactic final position—for lightning rods!

But the prosaic and utilitarian discourse on glass is certainly only a screen for the real purpose—battle with what Voltaire called "L'Infame"—ecclesiastical bigotry. This first becomes evident when the mention of the telescope brings up the Copernican theory and ancient persecution of heliocentrism. Following out the interpretation of Prometheus as a primitive scientist·, the poet exclaims:

Did not the horde of furious fools, enraged at him, subject his noble inventions to untrue gossip? Was he not then observing the stars through the telescope, which the toil of fortunate Europe has now resurrected? Did he not know by Glass [i.e., the burning glass] to bring down fire from heaven, and did he not bring ruin on himself from the barbarians, who gave him over to execution, charging him with sorcery? How many such examples we have, that envy, hiding beneath the cover of holiness, and crude bigotry [revnost'] with it, laying plots against truth, from very antiquity have been waging incessant war, whereby much knowledge has perished irretrievably! How exactly we would have known the heavenly regions, the movement of the planets, the course of the moon, if Aristarchus [the Greek proponent of heliocentrism] had not been called in judgment by envious Cleanthes a 'furious Giant,' for venturing to shake the whole earth from its firm foundation, to draw it around its center, around the sun; for venturing to teach that all the household gods undergo the labor of eternal traveling; Neptune spins around, and Diana, and Pluto, and they suffer the same punishment as bold Ixion; and the immovable goddess of the earth, Vesta, can find no place for rest. Under the false appearance of respect for these gods the world of the stars was closed through a multitude of ages. Fearing the fall of that untrue belief, the hypocrites [litsemery] waged constant war with science: so that it might not, by disclosing the greatness of the heavens and the admirable variety of unknown wonders, show to all that the unapproachable might of a single Creator had created all this world, that Mars, Neptune, Zeus, all the host of gods, are not worth the fat sacrifices, not even the wood under the sacrifices! That it is the priests who eat the lambs and bulls, to no advantage. This one thing, this seemed dangerous to them. That was the reason they all considered the earth the center.

All his life the astronomer was engaged in fruitless labor, entangled in cycles, until Copernicus arose, scorner of envy and adversary of barbarism. In the midst of all the planets he placed the sun, he disclosed the earth's dual motion: with one it completes its daily path about the center, with the other it makes a year by its course around the sun. By the real System he smashed the 'cycles' and proved the truth by exactitude of phenomena.[59]

Taking a cue perhaps from Bayle, who under cover of denouncing ancient oracles as frauds, attacked contemporary belief in miracles, Lomonosov has made use of the intolerance of the Stoic Cleanthes, who according to Plutarch charged Aristarchus with blasphemy for daring "to put the hearth of the universe [i.e., the earth] in motion." Blandly assuming the entire truth of the Copernican theory as not even subject to question—"What Copernicus taught there is no doubt of"—he hints that it is only the selfish interests of priests that attempt to suppress the truth, and that a more exalted concept of God's power and glory is fostered by true science than by religious super-stition.

He goes on to subject the "western" St. Augustine to criticism for "measuring the universe without mathematics"—i.e., for accepting the literal truth of the primitive Biblical picture of the world, which excluded America and denied the possibility of the Antipodes! The falsity of Augustine's beliefs Columbus and Magellan have demonstrated. Turning to contemporary bigots directly, Lomonosov exclaims warningly: "Take this example, you Cleantheses, comprehending clearly how much Augustine was in error in this opinion; he utilized God's word to no purpose" (lines 308-309). It is worth noting that from the numerous church fathers whose erroneous notions of the earth's sphericity could have been cited, Lomonosov chooses Augustine, and pointedly calls him "western" [vechernii]; to have charged an Orthodox saint, such as St. John Chrysostom or St. Gregory Nazianzen, with preach-ing falsehood would have been considerably more dangerous. After an en-thusiastic eulogy of the services of the astronomers in broadening the picture of the universe, the poet, with certainly a touch of irony, queries: "In our blessed and enlightened age, what may not man attain in following them?" (lines 331-332)

There follows a brief discourse on the microscope (since the church had never thought to deny the existence of "animalculae," he had no need here for polemics!), and then on the barometer. Admitting that he is still far from the end of Glass's praiseworthiness, for which he would need a whole year, Lomonosov then turns to his particular interest, electricity, and the identi-fication of lightning as a celestial manifestation of it. Here again he waxes eloquent as he inveighs against the ignorance of those who consider it blas-phemous to "look upon the scourge with which the Father threatens us in His wrath." As a final example of the "Usefulness of Glass" he cites the lightning-rod, not yet quite perfected: "Europe has now bent all its thought upon this, and already constructed reliable machines." At this point he bids his subject adieu: "Following her [i.e., Europe's] example, I now descend from the Parnassian mountains, and apply all my labor to Glass for the while." The poem ends with some fulsome eulogy of Elizabeth and her Maecenas, I.I. Shuvalov, to whom it is addressed.

Lomonosov's career was so varied that it is hard to assess it wholly from a literary point of view. In certain areas, however, it was absolutely decisive, and without it Russian literature would not have been the same. Most significant, surely is his contribution to the theory of versification, though it is certain that if he had not turned Russian practice toward the syllabo-tonic system, someone else would have. Important also is his codification of stylistic norms, which remained unchallenged at least until Derzhavin and Karamzin. In his creative work he can be discounted as a dramatist and as an epic poet; neither his tragedies nor his aborted epic contain anything genuinely original, and Sumarokov in the one area and Kheraskov in the other are more significant.[60] In the minor fields of the satire and the didactic Lomonosov is indeed highly original and creative, but remained without a following. It is the ode primarily that brought him contemporary fame, and the ode remains his most serious literary accomplishment. His odes casts those of the classicist Sumarokov completely in the shade, and the grandiose oratorical style which he created for them served as model for the genre until the revolutionary odes of Derzhavin. The court poet Vasily Petrov delighted in being called the "new Lomonosov," and even such an avowed follower of Sumarokov as Vasily Maikov, in his odes attempted the thunderous majesty of Lomonosov with almost ludicrous servility. If these formal, dithyrambic effusions leave our age rather cold, as they did Pushkin, this means little more than that fashions in poetry, as in everything else, change, and that our age has a different criterion of poetic beauty than had the eighteenth century.

CHAPTER VI

ALEXANDER SUMAROKOV AND RUSSIAN CLASSICISM[1]

French classicism is usually conceded to have begun toward the middle of the seventeenth century. The dramatist Corneille is a transitional figure—a few of his tragedies exhibit the characteristic features of the new style (*Le Cid, Horace* et al.), but for the most part he belongs to the Baroque. Racine and Molière, La Fontaine and Boileau are the purest representatives of classicism. By the end of the seventeenth century a new phase begins, which we generally characterize as "the Enlightenment," with Voltaire its great legislator and exemplar; but by the date of his death (1778) the epoch-making writings of Rousseau and Diderot have already initiated in France the pre-Romantic movement which is often designated as "sentimentalism." Thus the course of French "classicism" can be fixed to the approximate dates of 1636-1778, or roughly 150 years. From France the mode won acceptance in Spain, England, Italy and Germany. Johann Christoph Gottsched (1700-1766) in Germany, a narrow, opinionated and rather pedestrian poet, was the principal spokesman (*Versuch einer kritischen Dichtkunst:* 1732) for classicism.

In Russia, as in Germany, the literary ideals of the Baroque dominate the first third of the eighteenth century. Antiokh Kantemir, Vasily Trediakovsky and above all Mikhail Lomonosov, dissimilar as they may be in views and in style, all represent the same general literary trend and react with little sympathy or understanding to the ideals that are embodied in the work of their younger competitor, Alexander Petrovich Sumarokov (1717-1777).

The legislator of French classicism, Nicholas Boileau-Despréaux, set forth the principles of the system in a fashion that remained authoritative throughout the century and a half of its dominance and was widely copied elsewhere (e.g., by Gottsched and Sumarokov). The classical literary mode has been characterized (by G.A. Gukovsky[2]) as: "anti-individualist, abstract, and rationalistic." A fundamental principle is the unquestioned axiom that "nature" (i.e., human nature) is identical in all places and all times, and consequently will express itself in identical ways, regardless of the accidents of geographical milieu or temporal distance. It follows from this axiom that the poet's endeavor must be to abstract this "nature" from all such accidental circumstances as nationality or historical conditions impose, and to view it

111

as it were *sub specie aeternitatis*. Another fundamental axiom is the optimistic notion that human nature is basically rational. The reason will always dominate unless "the passions," which constitute a baser stratum of the personality, are allowed free rein. Virtuous conduct, accordingly, is rational, while vicious conduct—that dominated by the unruly passions—is irrational. Any human activity, including literary creation, must also, to be excellent, submit to the rule of reason. The critic's primary duty is to deduce and set forth in entirely perspicuous language the applications of the rule of reason to the concepts of his art.

Marxist critics make a convincing case for the thought connection between the political ideas of the "age of absolutism" and the respect for authority which is one of the earmarks of classicism. The great writers of antiquity have once and for all established certain rationally derived forms or "kinds" and the conditions for their use, and it remains for the modern writer to "imitate" these. Such "imitation" does not, however, mean servility: latitude is permitted in details, as long as the basic principles are not jeopardized. One of these basic principles is that of "purity of genre"; each literary "kind" has a compartment of its own, and trespass of one upon the territory of another is impermissible. For each genre there is established a social and linguistic evaluation which parallels the actual hierarchy of social castes. Thus, the highest position in the hierarchy belongs to the epic poem, tragedy, and ode; the social analogue of this group would be nobility and royalty, and a corresponding loftiness of language is demanded. A second group consists of comedy, elegy, eclogue, oratory, history, etc., and a language appropriate to the middle class or bourgeoisie suits this; the lowest social grouping—the "common people"—and their vulgar tongue belong to the "low" genres of fable, farce and satire.

The first major writers of the Russian eighteenth century—Kantemir, Trediakovsky and Lomonosov—occupy a transitional position in literary history. In some important respects they belong to the Enlightenment and Classicism. Thus all three share a seriousness of purpose that is directed toward the improvement and "enlightenment" of their fellow-citizens, and view literature as primarily an instrument toward this end; they accept without question the classical theory of sharply differentiated genres; Lomonosov preaches the classical doctrine of the "three styles," etc. They are at the same time, however, also marked by certain tendencies that are usually associated in the West with the "Baroque" style—note in particular Lomonosov's hyperbolic, exaggerated and metaphorical language in his odes and unfinished epic, and the pre-classical or anti-classical tendencies of all three to an affective use of language antithetical to the abstract and algebraic ideal of classicism. It is not until the advent of Sumarokov that Russian literature can properly be said to enter the classical period. It would, however, be an unwarranted exaggeration to regard Sumarokov, as some scholars have done, as the perfect and indeed almost the solitary model of Russian classicism. In him too there are lingering traces of the more exuberant Baroque and even premonitions of sentimentalism. But since Sumarokov attempted in his own work to be Russia's Racine, Molière, La Fontaine and Boileau, all in one, and the models of tragedy, comedy, fable and satire that he created in this attempt remained authoritative throughout the rest of the century, it is inevitable that he should be given the principal place in any discussion of Russian classicism. This is the more so, in view of his Boileau-inspired codification of the classical "rules."

Sumarokov was a member of the Russian landed gentry, educated, like many of his class, for service to the state in either the army or the civil service. It must be borne in mind that until 1762 such service was still a legal obligation of his class, although under Peter the Great's lax and incompetent successors it was becoming more and more easy to evade it. Sumarokov throughout his life retained a very high conception of civic duty and idealized the position which he believed the Russian gentry *(dvorianstvo)* had been divinely appointed to hold as advisers and coadjutors of monarchs. Sumarokov's lofty concept of the functions of his class and his stubborn and often tactless insistence upon these are the sources of his embroilment and disgrace with the autocratic Catherine the Great. Sumarokov was perhaps unduly confident in the high quality of his own genius; he certainly quite naively over-estimated Catherine's sham liberalism. His life was a long series of disappointments and disillusions, and he ended it embittered and poverty-stricken. He was, nevertheless, the most influential representative of classicism in Russia during his age, and the revered master of such other classicists as Yakov Borisovich Kniazhnin (1742-1791), Mikhail Matveevich Kheraskov (1733-1807) and Vasily Maikov (1728-1778).

Sumarokov's philosophical and political views are in general those of a typical "enlightened" gentleman of the eighteenth century. He is a materialist, a follower of the epistemological theories of John Locke. All matter, in his view, consists of associations of particles: "The foundations of matter are hidden from us, but they must be infinitely numerous."[3] His theory seems closer to Anaxagoras's *pammixia* than to Democritus's atomism: "I also hold this, that all particles are intermingled and that they cannot by any means be completely separated, and that accordingly in every smallest particle there is something of all the kinds, and that they form by differences of quantity the substances of different kinds" (ibid.). He regards the world of living things as forming a hierarchy—the "great chain of being": "The growing kind" (i.e., the vegetable world), "the crawling kind" (reptiles and insects), the "swimming kind" (fish), "the winged kind" (birds) and "quadrupeds." "If man is not a quadruped, then to what class should he be attached?" Sumarokov is a little wary, however, of carrying this logic to its conclusion, and says, after citing one analogy: "I do not say this of man, because Holy Scripture contradicts it." However, he finds that man's natural condition should be that of a quadruped, the arms being only "forelegs" with

113

a different function.

It has often been erroneously stated that classicism, both in France and elsewhere, is as it were a literary corollary of Cartesianism. On the contrary, the philosophical system which most truly parallels and supports classicism is that evolved by the English philosophers Hobbes and Locke. Against the notion of "innate ideas" which is the center of Descartes' epistemology, Sumarokov writes in the same "Letter to a Friend": "Almost all of Cartesian philosophy is an unadorned romance." The foundations of all knowledge are sense perceptions, not "innate ideas." "All that we do not understand is explained to the reason by the senses."[4] "The reason is nothing more than merely the activities of the mind put into motion by the senses." "If reason were innate, of what use would the sciences be? The blind man would have no need of eyes, nor the deaf man of ears. Reason would have done everything, and the senses would have been unnecessary. Reason does nothing: it only preserves that with which the senses have enriched it. In short: there is no innate concept." (ibid.) Conscience also is not innate. "If conscience were innate, all men would live honorably, all would obey a single law. But what is honorable among one people should be honorable also among another; there would be neither wars nor quarrels, because there would be no divergent opinions on justice" (ibid.).

In his social philosophy Sumarokov held the typically eighteenth-century view that the aristocracy should be an honored and responsible partner with the monarch in the form of government: only thus is its existence justified. The hierarchy of which the serf class forms the lowest stratum is natural and defensible so that the nobleman may have the opulence and leisure to perform his function. This view, incidentally, is that of Peter the Great, embodied in his legislation. The serf, however, is not a slave, not a piece of property to be disposed of at will. In his notes on the *Nakaz* ("Legislative Instruction") of Catherine II Sumarokov writes: "People must not be sold like cattle." "Between serf and slave there is a difference: the former is attached to the soil, the latter to the owner."[5] His ideas on this matter are most fully set forth in his article "On Household Management": "The good of the state, or rather, of society, is the increase of abundance for all, not for one. Why then call these greedy landowners 'good managers' *[ekonomy]*, who either for their own aggrandizement or for the accumulation of gold and silver in their coffers flay the very skin from their peasants, and whose manufactures and other fancies burden the peasants and take all their time from them for [the landowners'] profit, rendering [the peasants] innocent convicts at forced labor, feeding and giving them drink like so many draft horses, in contravention of moral and political right, offending God and man solely for the sake of their own imagined abundance....

The landowner who enriches himself through the excessive labors of his subjects vainly bears the honored name of 'household manager' *[domos-troitel'*—the Russian equivalent of the Greek *oikonomos*] and should be called 'household destroyer *[domorazoritel']*. Such a monster of nature, an ignoramus both in natural history and in all the sciences, an illiterate creature, without regard for either God or man, repenting by habit and by the same habit returning to his evil-doing, compelling his peasants to fast, destroying the happiness of the people entrusted to him—is a hundred times more injurious to society than a bandit. And shall I be gladdened, I who have a good heart and a clean conscience, when such a monster shows me his gardens, his orangeries, his horses, cattle, fowl, handicrafts, and the like? But with such 'household managers' I shall have no converse, and food watered with tears I shall not eat. He will leave much to his children; but his peasants too have children. At such a feast the food is human flesh, the drink their tears and their blood. Let him eat this himself with his children!"[6] Sumarokov, as Marxists are always quick to point out, was not (alas!) a revolutionary; but such views as this indignant passage expresses are exactly those of Radishchev, who *was* perhaps a revolutionary, and were certainly not welcome in the age of Catherine II. It is worth noting also, in this connection, that the entire sentiment is one typical of the "sentimentalist" period that dominates the end of the century.

Sumarokov's social and political views and his lofty conception of the poet's function as a teacher and corrector of society permeate his works in the "lofty style"—odes and tragedies. The ideal human being can attain personal happiness only by the victory of his "reason" over his "passions." These passions are the source also of every social ill, and the poet, as moral preceptor, must make every effort to combat them. Chief among those that introduce injustice and chaos into the social order are the inordinate cravings for wealth and arbitrary power. Sumarokov is in perfect accord with the great western representatives of classicism in seeing the poet's function as primarily didactic: he must, in the most telling and appropriate fashion, inculcate the principles of private and public morality for the "common good."

Turning next to Sumarokov's vast literary heritage and its importance in the history of Russian classicism and of Russian letters in general, let us first consider a genre which perhaps best of all typifies Russian classicism— the ode. The earliest of Sumarokov's published works belong to this genre: an ode addressed to Anna Ivanovna (1740) and another to her successor Elizaveta Petrovna (1743).[7]

The genre "ode" was, as we have noted, one of the classical forms for which a "lofty style" was prescribed. In his first efforts Sumarokov obediently followed the system recommended by Trediakovsky, whose "Ode on the Capture of Dantzig" is the pioneer in this genre. In the same year (1740), however, as Sumarokov's first ode appeared, the first of Lomonosov's also were published. Lomonosov, a far greater poet and more able theorist of verse than Trediakovsky, made a great impression on Sumarokov, and until the end of the 1740s, when their poetical ways parted, the latter attempted to emulate the Lomonosov style. In 1744 the two poets together entered the lists against Trediakovsky on a purely technical controversy—whether iambic or trochaic verse is more suited to the Russian language, and has a greater emotional content. All three poets composed, as examples, versions of the 143rd Psalm. A few years later, in 1747, Sumarokov, in imitation of Boileau, issued two "Epistles": "On the Russian Tongue" and "On Verse-Writing."[8] In these he still advocates a Slavonic vocabulary, drawn from the Bible and other ecclesiastical writings, and the elaborate, solemn and sonorous style of Lomonosov. Unlike Lomonosov, however, he includes such "light" genres as the song, the eclogue and the comic poem along with the solemn ode and the tragedy as subjects for the poet of the "high style."

Sumarokov's two epistles (1747) and his first two tragedies (*Khorev,* 1747 and *Hamlet,* 1748) brought him into a position of literary prominence as leading ideologue of the gentry class and coryphaeus of a school of young admirers and imitators. This success no doubt had something to do also with his breach with Lomonosov which occurred soon after, and the literary occasion for which was Sumarokov's definitive rejection of the pompous and semi-Slavonic "high style" of his rival in favor of a simple diction, much closer to ordinary speech.

Lomonosov's "solemn odes" are mostly addressed to Empress Elizabeth, daughter of his idol, Peter the Great. The occasions which evoke them are imperial birthdays, anniversaries of accession, and the like. Speaking almost as though he were the incarnate voice of Russia, and sometimes even putting solemn warnings into the mouth of God Almighty, the poet lays down the lines of political, social and economic policies which he conceives Peter to have initiated, and which it is his daughter's duty to continue. His language is exalted, and sometimes lacks the cool logical quality which came to be the classical ideal. A famous example is the phrase, in one of his battle odes, "horses, with stormy legs"; Sumarokov grumbled that horses can have thin legs, or thick legs, or swift legs—but not "stormy." Sumarokov's mature style is quiet, persuasive and graceful, where Lomonosov's is passionate and grandiose. But Sumarokov too uses his verse as a medium for "giving lessons to monarchs." Thus, in his "Ode to the Sovereign Empress Catherine II on the Day of Her Birth, April 21, 1768" he writes:

Thus reasons the throne [i.e., the Empress] about glory: "Unto me has an extensive country been entrusted by heaven for the rectification of the law. And in the days of my reign I seek no other enjoyment than the happiness of my people. Everything possible I correct in them; with my diadem I inculcate in them what is good and honorable for them.

Ocean's waves are raised higher than mountains by the wind; thoughts, full of the common good are the stay of our loftiness. The scepter is no great matter, if the monarch makes its glitter alone his good. The royal name is frightening; if it does not com-

116

fort, vain is the applause of the people.

"My delight is in toil; this applause I desire to receive, that all in Russia are my children, and that to all in Russia I am a mother. O my beloved children! This flatters me to possess: that you all love me. In that which is good for you, in this I take pride; and I love you also equally, fulfilling a mother's duty."[9]

Doubtless Catherine did herself foster the mother image, and pride herself on her unremitting labors; but it may reasonably be doubted if even she would have declared: "I seek no other enjoyment but the happiness of my people!" Sumarokov, in typical classicist fashion, is picturing the ideal of the "enlightened despot" as the reality.

On June 29, 1771 Sumarokov presented Catherine's son, then seventeen and expected at that date to assume the imperial title, with a solemn "Ode to the Sovereign Prince Paul Petrovich on His Name Day." Along with some rather tactless intimations that his expected reign will correct some of his mother's mistakes, Prince Paul, hailed as a "Russian Achilles" and a "Socrates on the throne," is admonished with the reminder that:

Not by this does the monarch distinguish his rank, that he is permitted to slay and imprison, that all stand before him in fear and trembling, that he has power over man as over dust, and that he is able to take life.

When the monarch exercises violence, he is an enemy of the people, not a Tsar. The tiger and the lion too take life, and the lowliest of creatures. The serpent does not lessen contempt, when, crawling, he stings someone—rather the said serpent increases it. Thus this great soul [i.e., Paul's] reckons about the wearers of crowns, whom he considers as a gift of God.

And that those raised to thrones are not [thus raised] for themselves alone. Although born for themselves, they are also for their subjects. A disordered Tsar is an abominable idol, and an untrained pilot on the sea; his epitaph is: "He was poison." His reign comes to an end, his glory too comes to an end. Flattery disappears, his soul is in Hell.

Tsars never wear the splendor of their crowns into the grave. The splendor of the Tsar's person is the name "Father of his subjects." Eternally noisy streams will pass away, deeds will remain forever, and raise honor to the sun. The swift-flowing years will pass away, but the souls in us, to be sure, are eternal, as God's righteous judgment is eternal.

Do not alter this reflection, and thus you will be our shield and our protection...[10]

But Sumarokov is not always so overtly didactic in his odes. Perhaps a more typical vein is that of humble adulation, such as may be seen in his first ode to Catherine the Great: "Ode to the Sovereign Empress Catherine the Second on Her Name Day, November 24, 1762," of which the first strophe reads: "Upon all the vast dominions unto the sons of Catherine, gaze from [thy] burning chariot, gaze from the heavens, O sun, on us; be witness of our gladness, and of what virtue now adorns the Russian throne;

behold the likeness of a lily of Paradise, the beauty of empires, the beauty of crowns, the sage Catherine."[11] It may be noted incidentally that the rhyme which Sumarokov in this ode hit upon for the name "Catherine" (here Ekaterinu), that is, "Paradisal lily" (*raisku krinu*), he complacently repeats several times in later poems, and his imitators after him, until it becomes an object of mockery to a younger generation. In the light of what later ages have come to know about Catherine the Great, the notion of her as a "lily of Paradise," or as incarnate virtue on the throne, seems a little grotesque—but again, it is the ideal, not the reality, that is celebrated.

In 1747, the year that saw the appearance of Sumarokov's first tragedy, the poet issued his two related "Epistles," in which are gathered most of the regulations which classicism imposed upon the poetic art. These "Epistles" were read in the Academy of Sciences in 1747, and issued by the Academy Press in the following year. Since any consideration of Sumarokov's drama, or indeed of his poetical work in general, must rely to a considerable extent on the theory presented in these, it will be well to review their content here. In 1771 an abbreviated and somewhat modified conflation of the two poems was issued under the title: "Admonition for those desiring to be writers."[12]

The genre "Epistle" originated with Horace, as a poetical vehicle closely related to the "satire," in which the poet presents his opinions in a relatively free and unconstrained fashion in the form of a personal letter. The most famous of Horace's "Epistles" is that addressed to two Roman gentlemen, father and son, "the Pisos," who were attempting in the first century B.C. the hopeless task of reviving classical (Greek) drama. This accounts for the large part in the epistle devoted to a discussion of the drama; but other genres also come in for remark. Since it seemed to the Renaissance that Horace's poem constituted a sort of epitome of ancient practice in the area, it was given the title *Ars Poetica*. Boileau's *Art poétique* was modeled upon Horace's Epistle, and Sumarokov's largely upon Boileau's, although, as we shall see, with considerable independence of treatment.

The first of the Russian poet's original epistles,[13] which deals with the Russian language, has of course no parallel in the French. In it Sumarokov begins with the consideration of the advantages which the possession of language gives to man over the other animals—but at once comes the limiting remark: "but of no use are such languages as the Mordvins and Votyaks speak"; rather the classical tongues of Greece and Rome, the present language of Rome and Italy, and the French language, as it was brought to perfection by the seventeenth century—these are the languages of literature. Such can also be the Russian language, which ignorant writers abuse by introducing words and turns of phrase from France and Germany, thus obscuring its native beauties, or which they sometimes even declare to be incapable of expressing lofty thoughts. It is, of course, an essential theory of classicism that the writer must imitate the best models, and the worst thing that can be said of Russian is that there are too few such models. However, the aspiring poet is advised to clarify his thoughts most fully and to set them forth in the most appropriate language. He must not be led astray by the misdirected admiration of readers who "marvel at him, and think there must be a mystery there, and who, hiding their reason and reading in darkness, take the writer's incomprehensible style as beauty." Simple types of writing should use simple words, but "discourses which are presented to society, whether they are offered by pen or tongue, ought to be far more splendidly composed, and rhetorical beauties included in them, which are unusual in simple discourses, but appropriate and necessary for the dignity of speeches, for the explication of reason and the passions, so as to enter into hearts and attract people." Translation is a laudable undertaking, but it must be done with good sense: a literal translation may turn out meaningless gibberish. "Though you have before you a lexicon weighing three poods [about a hundred pounds!], don't imagine that it will give you great help, if you set down the words and phrases without the proper order, and your translation becomes a sort of riddle, which no one is going to unriddle for all time." Despite the admiration of illiterate officials for such old-fashioned tales as "Bova" and "Peter of the Golden Keys," the would-be writer must avoid their style. He must imitate the "laborious bee," which "gathers for itself something from everywhere, whatever is needed for its sweet honey." Though the ignoramus may complain: "If there are no Russian books, whose footsteps are we to follow?" Sumarokov declares decisively: "We do have, moreover, plenty of spiritual books; who is then to blame for your not having reached the Psalter, but, running over it like a boat on a heavy sea, you dash from one end of it a hundred times irrationally." Some of the expressions in these "spiritual books," i.e., ecclesiastical works written in what we call Old Slavonic, are obsolete, and it is useless to try to reintroduce them into the current language. But the language in which these books are written, Sumarokov declares, is still Russian (modern philology, of course—and Lomonosov—know that he is wrong). "It is one and the same; if it were different, as you suppose, just because you don't understand it, then what would be left of the Russian language?" These views of Sumarokov's first epistle closely parallel those of Lomonosov, as he presented them later in his treatise "On the Utility of Ecclesiastical Books in the Russian Tongue." Sumarokov's breach with Lomonosov and his increasing fondness for classical clarity and simplicity brought him subsequently to modify his attitude toward the Old Church Slavonic.

Like Boileau's original, which he follows closely enough in some places to seem to be merely adapting it, Sumarokov's second epistle[14] is an attempt to codify the rules governing classical verse-writing. This second epistle is considerably longer than the first, and deals in part with the major genres accepted by classicism. The poet begins by warning against attempting to "climb Parnassus without being summoned by Apollo," that is, against trying to write poetry without inspiration. Such poetasters were Pradon and

119

Chapelain in the great age of Corneille, Racine, Boileau, Molière and La Fontaine. Such in Russian literature were the satirist Kantemir and Feofan Prokopovich! Writing verse is not as easy as some think. The great models to follow are the Greek and Roman classics—and he enumerates twenty-two of them, including Menander, who was known in his time only for a selection of aphorisms, and Cornelius Gallus, who was then as now nothing but a name. A select few moderns follow: Malherbe, J.-B. Rousseau, Quinault, Milton, Shakespeare ("even though he is unenlightened!"), Tasso, Ariosto, Camoes, Pope. "Let us follow such great writers." If you have talent ("a gift of nature"), endeavor to increase it by art. "Do not irritate the Muses with your bad success—Thalia (i.e., Comedy) with tears and Melpomene (i.e., Tragedy) with laughter." (Sumarokov, it may be noted here, was stoutly opposed to that late eighteenth century "sentimentalist" innovation, the *comédie larmoyante* and its companion, Diderot's *drame* or domestic tragedy; he even wrote to Voltaire for a pronouncement on the question of the authenticity of these new, mixed, genres, and received a rather non-commital reply which he cherished). He then begins his consideration of genres with the pastoral, which must be simple and natural in style as befits the shepherds and shepherdesses who people it. The pastoral swain must use neither the coarse language of the peasant nor the over-refined diction of the courtier. An ideal springtime landscape must be the background for the pastoral. Sumarokov next treats the ode in a scant fourteen lines; it must utilize mythological and heroic subjects. "The creator of such verses casts his glance everywhere; he soars to the heavens, he descends into hell, and swiftly darting into all regions of the universe, he has gates and paths opened to him everywhere." The epic, a similarly lofty genre, follows. In this the classical divinities must figure as allegorical representatives of intangible ideas or natural events. "Minerva is wisdom, Diana purity, Cupid is love and Venus beauty in it." A thunder-storm is Zeus enraged, a storm at sea is angry Neptune, etc.

Next comes a fairly lengthy discussion of drama in general. "The poet finds a way to move the mind of his audience through action." "If you want tears, then move me to pity; for laughter, present before me some worldly rascality." The three unities then follow: "Do not present two actions, to the confusion of my thoughts; the spectator directs his mind to one alone" (unity of action). "Don't attempt to deceive eyes and ears, and put the events of three years into three hours," but try to make the action on the stage come as close as possible to the actual time that passes in the theater, "so that your action may not seem a play, but the very event itself then taking place" (unity of time). "Don't make difficulties for me with your place, so that your scene, which as I see, is in Rome, may not fly off to Moscow and from Moscow to Peking" (unity of place). He then separates tragedy from comedy (the unities, of course, belong to both genres), and after the general declaration, "tragedy presents us with mourning and sorrow," he proceeds to cite as illustrations six plays of Racine (*Phèdre, Andromaque, Iphigénie,*

Britannicus, Mithridate and *Athalie*) and two of Voltaire (*Mérope* and *Alzire*). It is significant that none of Corneille's dramas is cited, nor Racine's *Bajazet*— probably because they all in some fashion depart from the classical rules. In comedy the models cited are Molière (*Le Misanthrope* and *Tartuffe*) and Destouches (*Le Philosophe marié* and *Le Glorieux*). The function of comedy is "by mockery to correct manners; to amuse and be helpful are its direct law." He then goes on to cite various type characters appropriate to comedy.

Satire, related to comedy, follows: "In satires we must censure vices, turn pompous witlessness to ridicule, mock at passions and follies." Examples follow. Five lines then dispose of the epigram: "They live, rich in their beauty, when they are composed sharp and rather malicious." We are then introduced to the fable, with La Fontaine, of course, as the model. A considerable space (twenty-six lines) is next devoted to the burlesque poem or parody epic, a genre which Boileau condemns. There are two kinds, that in which noble heroes and their actions are mocked by being described in low terms (Dido is a common wench, Aeneas a stevedore, etc.), and that in which low characters are dignified by pompous epic treatment ("A peasant woman spanks a baby—it is Juno in wrath"; "a puddle of rain-water is the ocean"). Four lines next take care of the epistle and eighty more of the imported and unnaturalized lyric varieties of the sonnet, rondeau and ballade. Sumarokov, determined to try every literary form, composed several undistinguished sonnets, a rondeau and a couple of ballades; in the last named he abandoned, however, the classical French eight-line stanza form, the obligatory refrain line, and the *envoi!* In other words, his "ballades" have only the name in common with the French original.[15]

He goes on next to the genre of the song, which Boileau ignores, and devotes to it a fairly lengthy treatment. Since Sumarokov's own songs are among his best and most original work, this proportion is not unnatural. He recommends for the song simplicity above all—"The style of the song should be pleasant, simple and clear; no floweriness is in order—it is beautiful in itself." He gives two interesting variants of a lover's farewell, one "florid"— "Farewell now, my Venus; though all the goddesses were gathered together, there is none more beautiful than you!"—and one natural and simple. He comments: "No one speaks ornately in sorrow; when the lover is parting from his beloved, then Venus does not enter his thoughts." After emphatically rejecting certain stylistic niceties as inappropriate to lyric "thought," the poet suddenly checks himself. "But what am I saying, 'to thought'? Why, in such a fine little song, there is no thought at all!"

After the "song," the poet is admonished in four lines: "If you are soft of heart and born full of pity, and if moreover you are overcome by love, then write elegies, then sing of the bonds of love with the pitiful voice of the mourning [Countess] de La Suze." After this brief and rather contemptuous dismissal of the elegy, follows the concluding portion of the epistle, devoted to a cursory list of models for various genres—Boileau,

121

Molière, Pindar, Lomonosov (for the ode), Homer, etc. The work concludes: though the Romans Virgil, Ovid and Horace worked in different genres, all three distinguished themselves. "Everything is praiseworthy—drama, eclogue or ode. Compose whatever your nature disposes you to. Only, writer, give your mind enlightenment. Our beautiful language is capable of everything."

Of all the genres it recognized the tragedy is that which classicism most favored and with which it succeeded best. Antiquity had handed down to the contemporary world the great dramas of Aeschylus, Sophocles and Euripides, and of their Roman imitator Seneca. Aristotle, greatest of ancient critics, and Horace in his *Ars Poetica,* had prescribed regulations for the drama, especially the tragedy; and the tragedy of the age of Louis XIV, in the unsurpassed masterpieces of Jean Racine, had triumphantly established the ability of modern "imitators" of antiquity to approach, if not to outdo, the ancient masters. It is not therefore surprising that it was in the realm of the tragedy that the zealous apostles of classicism chose first and chiefly to operate. Gottsched in the year before the appearance of his theoretical treatise (the *Kritische Dichtkunst*) had presented his "regular" tragedy *Der sterbende Cato* (1731); Sumarokov's *Khorev* (1747) and *Hamlet* (1748) accompanied or followed closely upon his "Epistles."

Rationalism had, according to the classicist theory, dictated certain "rules" for tragedy, aimed partly at achieving "verisimilitude"—the rules of "unity of time" and "unity of place"—and partly at concentration and singleness of effect—"unity of action," "purity of genre" and propriety of language. The attention of the audience must be fixed exclusively upon one line of story, while the tragic tone must not be broken by the intrusion of effects proper to comedy, nor by the employ of words inappropriate to the "high style."

With the advent of Voltaire, whom French critics venerated as a worthy third in the classical trinity of tragic poets after Corneille and Racine, two new elements make their appearance in the classical drama. Voltaire's years of exile in England had made him acquainted with the drama of Shakespeare, and despite his contempt for what he regarded as the "Gothic barbarism" of the English genius, Voltaire did not scruple to borrow a good deal of the element of spectacle which earlier French tragedy had entirely neglected. Voltaire's tragedies can scarcely be said to present much "local color," yet their exotic scenes—the Near East during the Crusades, the Peru of the Conquistadores, China under the Mongols, etc.—mitigate a little the habitual abstractness of French drama. More importantly, the psychological drama of Racine gives place in the tragedies of Voltaire to a "drama of ideas," and to a sharply polemical tone and a prevailing preoccupation with public and political issues (e.g., *Mahomet, Brutus, La Mort de César,* etc.). Tragedy, at first only unobtrusively didactic in the general sense of exemplifying the nobility of the life of reason and the lamentable effects of the passions, becomes with Voltaire a vehicle for propaganda against the tyranny of irresponsible power and ecclesiastical superstition. It is not surprising, in view of the overpowering authority of the "sage of Ferney" that it was his kind of tragedy rather than the subtler and less superficially brilliant drama of Racine, that Russian classicists first sought to imitate.

The theater as an institution in Russia was almost contemporary with Sumarokov. Peter the Great had made some small attempt at introducing this, among his other western innovations, but the effort was abandoned after his death. Various German, French and Italian companies, playing all sorts of dramatic material, from opera to puppet farces, enjoyed some success in the capitals; but the only native dramatic efforts were those presented in the aristocratic schools by the pupils. It was in this way that Sumarokov's first tragedy, *Khorev*, was first staged by the pupils of the *Shliaketskii Kadetskii Korpus* ("Gentlemen's Cadet Corps"), of which the author was a former cadet. In this production the female parts were of course taken by boys. A later production in improved form was given at court, and the poet's name became famous.

At almost the same time in the provincial town of Iaroslavl a very talented young man of the merchant class, Fedor Grigorievich Volkov, instituted an amateur theater, in which most of the actors and actresses were members of his own family or friends. The fame of this enterprise spread so rapidly that in 1751 Elizaveta Petrovna ordered the troop to the capital. A few years later, in 1756, a permanent theater was established in St. Petersburg, with Sumarokov as director and Volkov as first actor. Volkov died in 1763, and in his place succeeded Ivan Afanasievich Dmitrievsky, who became a most famous actor and a very cultured and enlightened gentleman, friend of many poets and writers. Sumarokov soon became embroiled in some painful altercations with officious and stupid civil authorities, and in a pique retired in 1761 from the theater. A few years later, however, in 1769, he settled in Moscow and became interested in the theater there; it was for this that he wrote his last tragedies, *Dmitry the Pretender* (1771) and *Mstislav* (1774).

Sumarokov's nine tragedies are the best Russian examples of the classical tragic genre. Although it is Racine to whom he likes most to compare himself, it seems to be rather Corneille and Voltaire whom he used as models. In any case the Cornelian system of founding the principal conflict on the clash between love and honor, with the outcome more commonly in the triumph of the latter—that is, of "reason" over the "passions"—and the consequent inevitable utilization of Corneille's boasted addition of "admiration" to the Aristotelian "pity and fear" as springs of tragic emotion, is the pattern which Sumarokov most often uses. Of his nine tragedies only two (*Khorev*, 1747 and *Sinav and Truvor*, 1750) end with the deaths of their heroes. By this means the triumph of reason and the resulting happy outcome presumably serve as moral lessons to the audience.

The subjects of classical tragedies are most often taken from classical antiquity, either Greek legend or Roman history. Most of Corneille's dramas derive from the latter source, of Racine's from the former. Voltaire, of course, ranged widely over the whole course of history known to him to cull subjects—medieval, Islamic, Chinese, American Indian, etc. Very rarely, however, does French classical tragedy utilize French national subjects (Voltaire's *Adélaide Du Guesclin* is an exception). In this respect Sumarokov is out of line with his models, for with the two exceptions of *Hamlet* (laid in Denmark) and *Aristona* (laid in Persia) all his tragedies have ostensibly Russian subjects, remotely derived from the chronicles. The matter of subject, however, is of least consequence for classical tragedy, for in keeping with the assumption that human reason and passion are universal and unchanging with the changes of time and place, the classical dramatist schematizes his action in the highest degree. Neither scene nor costume nor language bear the slightest trace of "local color," nor are the character traits or details of action in any way historical. The poet, as Corneille says, can best make his drama *vraisemblable* by employing an occurrence that is attested by history—but he is at liberty to alter this occurrence beyond all recognizability, as Corneille himself does for instance with his *Heraclius.* The only element of national color in Sumarokov's tragedies is to be found in the names of the characters, of which some are actually attested by the chronicles (e.g., Kii in *Khorev,* Sinav and Truvor in their play, Mstislav in his) and some are invented by the poet so as to have what he imagines to be a Slavic sound, e.g., Stalverkh and Velkar in *Khorev,* Vitozar and Izbrana in *Semira,* etc. On one occasion only Sumarokov boldly chose an event in actual Russian history as the subject for a tragedy which was removed from his time by no more than a century and a half. This is the tragedy *Dmitry the Pretender.* The manner of his treatment is noteworthy. The career of the "First False Dmitry" was indeed a colorful and tragic one, full of dramatic incidents, which the great Pushkin utilized to the fullest in constructing his *Boris Godunov.* Sumarokov, however, chooses to involve his two historical characters, Dmitry and Vasily Shuisky, in a completely fabricated and conventional love intrigue, ignoring every aspect of the historical realities. Shuisky is made the father of a non-existent daughter Xenia (named, presumably, from the actual daughter of Boris Godunov whom the Pretender took as a mistress after the overthrow of her father). Xenia is the faithful fiancee of Prince George (also non-existent), whom the Pretender condemns to death in order to possess himself of Xenia. The crime is prevented by the double-dealing of Dmitry's confidant Parmen (non-existent), who under cover of faithful cooperation with his master actually plots a popular uprising which overthrows the tyrant. Nothing in the drama but the names of Shuisky and Dmitry belongs to history.

Sumarokov's classical tragedies follow all the rules and conventions of their French models, chief of which is the rule of the "three unities"—

of time: what is represented on the stage is a critical point in the plot, such as can be plausibly concentrated into a period of about twelve hours, or at the most, twenty-four; of place: only one, vaguely defined, place is used for all scenes of the drama—usually some part of the royal palace; and of action: the single main story line must not be confused with subordinate plots or irrelevant episodes. What takes place on the stage is conversation or declamation, never action. If any action is involved in the plot—e.g., a battle, duel, suicide, or the like—it will be reported in greater or less detail: thus the battle between the forces of Khorev and of Zavlokh in *Khorev* is reported by Velkar in a "messenger's speech" a page and a half long, and the death of Osnelda in the same play by an unnamed messenger in about fifteen lines. Hamlet in the last act of his play describes at length to Ophelia the popular uprising that destroys the usurper Claudius. The principal characters in the plays engage in discussions, disputes and the like, and not infrequently soliloquize rather briefly. Their motives and traits of character are revealed either in these discussions with each other, or more frequently in conversations with their "confidants," secondary persons whose sole function in most cases is to listen to the inmost thoughts and intentions of the principals and make brief comment on them. Occasionally one of Sumarokov's "confidants," e.g., Parmen in *Dmitry the Pretender* or Stalverkh in *Khorev,* have a major part in the plot development—a situation not common in French tragedy.

The pattern of a Sumarokov tragedy is almost invariable: the first act of the five is largely devoted to exposition and the setting forth of the conflict; the second sharpens the conflict; the third represents the culmination of the dramatic content of the play; the fourth prepares the denouement, which is always short, and occurs in the fifth act. Thus in *Khorev*[16] the audience learns in the first act of the love between Khorev, younger brother of the elderly Prince Kii, and Osnelda, daughter of Zavlokh, one-time Prince of Kiev, and of the conflict in each of the principals between love and loyalty (of Osnelda toward her ousted father, of Khorev toward his brother). The final act brings the denouement: Khorev, falsely suspected of treason to his brother through the officious machinations of Stalverkh, returns triumphant from an encounter with the army of Zavlokh, who has come to recover his daughter from her captivity; at the moment of triumph he discovers that Osnelda has been administered poison by Kii, and commits suicide. In *Hamlet*[17] the first act reveals the Danish Prince's suspicions of his usurping uncle Claudius, strengthened by a dream he has had of his dead father (Sumarokov's *Hamlet* has no ghost!), and the plot proceeds with his confrontation with Gertrude and her confession. The conflict develops around the plot of the scheming Polonius, who has abetted Claudius in murdering the previous king, to poison Gertrude so as to allow the King to marry his daughter Ophelia, Hamlet's fiancée. In the final act Ophelia, resolutely refusing her father's order to marry Claudius, is condemned by him in a fury to death, but rescued at the last moment by Hamlet's opportune arrival at the head of a popular mutiny to overthrow Claudius. Ophelia's ardent plea to her lover to spare her wicked father's life succeeds, but Polonius eliminates possible embarrassment by defiantly taking his own life.[18]

As in the Greek tragedies upon which the classical tragedy is ultimately based, characters are fixed and invariable. The limitation upon time in the classical tragedy of course precludes the possibility of character development. In any case, classical psychology conceives of "character" (literally, the "stamp" or "die" of a coin) as something existing from birth and incapable of change. Thus Voltaire lays down the law in his "General Rules of the Theater": "The persons who take part in the action must always preserve their qualities... Art consists in showing every trait and all the qualities of a person in the action as these make him speak, and not by having the person in the action speak of himself." Sumarokov often violates the second part of this prescription: his characters are quite prone to define their own qualities. Thus Dmitry the Pretender[19] in his very first words to his confidant Parmen announces: "An evil fury gnaws my afflicted heart within me; my wicked soul is unable to be at rest." A little later he replies to Parmen's accusations that he is a tyrant with the words: "I acknowledge that I am a pitiless spectator of evil, and the doer in this world of all shameless deeds." Dmitry is perfectly consistent in the character which he thus establishes for himself from the outset; after several self-revealing soliloquies in which he admits his iniquity but excuses it as an unchangeable part of him, he is faced at the end with overthrow and death, and reacts thus:

> Away to Hell, my soul, and be forever damned!
> (*He strikes himself in the breast with the dagger and falls expiring into the arms of the guards*)
> Ah, if only the whole universe might perish with me!

One feature of French classical drama, drawn rather from Seneca than from the Greek tragic poets, is the prevalence of *sententiae,* or succinct aphoristic expressions, "winged words" (what the French call *vers à retenir*). These abound in Sumarokov. Thus in *Mstislav* (Act III, sc. vi) we read: "Monsters sometimes rise to splendid thrones;/ The honored man is honored even without a crown." Oskold in *Semira* declaims: "Nothing affrights him who fears not death." Later in the same play he declares: "When heroes lose dominion through force of arms,/ Through force of arms they also recover dominion." The hero of *Vysheslav* (Act V, scene ii) announces: "In reigning, I desire to be more than man." In *Dmitry the Pretender* there is a regular set political debate between the tyrant Dmitry and Prince George.[20] The latter voices the opinion: "Unhappy that land, where there is a multitude of magnates;/ truth there is silent, and the lie holds sway." In this debate Dmitry represents the ultimate claim of autocracy, that the monarch possesses his subjects, soul and body. To this George opposes his view that:

> But God gave freedom to even the least of His creatures;
> Then can sovereigns lawfully take this away?
> They have authority to change the laws,
> But is even their power able to excuse injustice?

Such utterances from the stage are taken by Soviet critics to be evidences of oppositional tendencies on Sumarokov's part; that Elizabeth or Catherine let them pass indicates only that to have suppressed them would have called public attention to the tyranny of their regimes. This view is probably correct, although Sumarokov can certainly not be considered in any proper sense as a *frondeur*.

Sumarokov's success with the comedy even in his own time was only mediocre. Curiously enough, this ardent classicist and avowed admirer of Molière and Destouches is entirely unclassical in his comedies. In his "Second Epistle" (1747), when he comes to set forth the rules for writing comedy, he declares:

For people with knowledge you must not write *igrishcha* [i.e., popular farces] ; to amuse without reason is the talent of a common soul. Do not present that which may please me for a moment, but let the action be retained by me for a long time. The function of comedy is by mockery to correct morals; to amuse and profit are its fundamental law.[21]

Then he runs through a list of vicious types whom the comic poet should present on the stage for mockery: "the soulless pettifogger," the judge ignorant of the law, the dandy who thinks only of his coiffure and dreams of female conquests, the pedant, the proud man "puffed up like (Aesop's) frog," and the gambler, ready to hazard his all on a single card. These are, of course, all familiar types, mocked by satire as well as comedy.

But when we come to look at Sumarokov's practice, what do we find? In the first place, not one of his twelve comedies is in verse, as classical practice demanded; and most of them are in only one act. To be sure, a good many of the types presented on the stage are such as he enumerates in his epistle—e.g., the French-speaking fop Diulizh of his *Quarrel Between Husband and Wife*,[22] the rapacious Chuzhekhvat (his name implies that he "grabs what doesn't belong to him") in *The Guardian*, the usurer Kashchei in *The Usurer*, the "Narcissus" of the play by that name, etc. But his entire procedure in the construction of his pieces is unclassical in the extreme— indeed, from the structural point of view they are all mere strings of amusing scenes, virtually plotless, and seemingly devised only with the object of demonstrating character. The presentation of such a character as for example Chuzhekhvat is doubtless intended "by mockery to correct morals," but it is needlessly detailed for the purposes of the flimsy plot.

Furthermore, whatever he may say about the vulgarity of amusement "without reason," that is, of amusement for its own sake, unjustified by a high moral purpose, this is exactly what his comedies are. They resemble nothing so much as the kind of "popular farces" which he decries, and their real intent is entertainment pure and simple, except in so far as the portrayals of certain characters (e.g., Tressotinus or Kashchei) give the poet the relished opportunity of hitting at personal enemies. This unclassical attitude toward the comedy was observed even by Sumarokov's contemporaries, and made an object of criticism. The comic writer Lukin, whose notions of "corrective" art differed radically from Sumarokov's (he favored the "tearful comedy," which Sumarokov abhorred), wrote in a polemical foreword to his play *Constancy Rewarded* (1765):[23]

There are many such comedies as produce nothing but laughter, and not even a little of profit, although the precise intent of comic writers from the beginning of the genre was founded upon this, and although this it is which all persons who are endowed with reason follow even now. But when the audience want only to laugh, our *igrishcha* can divert them equally well, and with this additional gain, moreover, that the audience will see in them Russian characters and hear words which may be completely unknown to them [i.e., the common, peasant, vernacular], but useful for all that to convey to them the strength, spaciousness, and sometimes even the beauty, of our native language.

Here Lukin is hitting at another very vulnerable mark in Sumarokov's comedies—their superficially un-Russian character. Elsewhere Lukin inveighs against the absurd conventional names, straight from Molière or the Italian *commedia dell' arte*, which Sumarokov uses—Oronte, Valère, Clitandre, Sostrata, Harlequin, Pasquin, and the like—and makes a particular point of the incongruity of having a "notary" come in "to draw up a marriage contract"—neither officer nor document being Russian, but imported straight from France. But Lukin's criticism is shallow and external: the names, especially of the upper-class characters, and some of the types, e.g., the pert maid and the clever valet, may be foreign importations, going back ultimately to Greek and Latin originals, but the characters themselves, certainly at least those of the more "negative" sort, are genuinely Russian, and speak a quite natural, idiomatic, Russian language. A good example is the stupid country bumpkin who is one of Delamida's suitors in the early version of *An Empty Quarrel (Quarrel Between Husband and Wife)*. What though this oaf bears a name never borne (one hopes!) by any man in real life, French, Danish or Russian—"Fatiui" (probably intended to remind one of the French *fat*): yet he is a genuine Russian product, a country squire who almost dies of thirst at an expensive dinner in town where only wine is served, when he wants beer or kvas, and who diverts himself in his leisure moments by playing *svaika* with his serfs (more or less the equivalent of pitching horseshoes). He is so obtuse that he doesn't even get the point when Salmina, Oronte's wife, replies to his naive remark: "Fools don't always have fools for children; if, according to what you say, Mr. Oronte is stupid, then is Miss Delamida also stupid?" with the sharp query: "And who ever told you that she's his daughter?"[22]

The rascal Chuzhekhvat could doubtless be French or German or Italian—grabbers of other's property are certainly not a Russian monopoly!—but the language he speaks and the choice proverbs he is constantly quoting are unquestionably those of his native land and people. Note his first speech in the play (*The Guardian*, scene 4),[24] when his servant Paskvin claims that fellow-servants have stolen the gold cross that he wore around his neck:

That they steal isn't the point; let 'em steal, as long as they don't touch what's the master's or belongs to their own kind. In that way the household will gradually be added to. But to steal from one of their own, that's nothing but shifting from one pocket to another, and causing a hullabaloo and disturbing my rest. Let 'em steal; who's without sin, and who isn't a woman's grandson? But if out of weakness one should take on the sly from his comrades, then he ought to cover up his tracks so that no one would suppose one of his own people had taken anything. I teach them this, but you can teach a fool for a lifetime, and not be finished.

In response to a pointed remark of Nisa's, about "empty-headed people," Chuzhekhvat expatiates (scene 6):

But with me, not only is my head not empty, but neither is my purse, even if it isn't fancy on the outside and is made of only hempen cloth. Outside it isn't prettified in the French fashion, but it's fine inside, as the proverb says: "A house isn't beautiful for corners, it's beautiful for pies." And this pie isn't stuffed with buckwheat, but with gold and silver. Copper coins aren't to my mind.

Chuzhekhvat reveals his character most fully in what must have seemed a remarkably bold, almost blasphemous, scene (scene 11). He soliloquizes:

The knout I'm not afraid of, but I am afraid of eternal torment, and it looks as if I can't avoid it. Great God! It would be fine, living in this world, if you didn't exist. We'd never give anyone account of anything in the matter of secret doings; but as it is, it's impossible to hide from you in any way. Why such strictness in the law—"Don't take what belongs to another." Why, even if I do appropriate what is another's, I won't be taking what is another's out of your world. So isn't it all the same, whether it's in this man's or another man's coffers? "The earth is the Lord's and the fullness thereof." (*he gets down on his knees*). Great God! Enter not into judgment with thy servant. I repent before you with all my heart and with the sincerity of my soul. Forgive me my sins, but don't ask me to give back what I've appropriated illegally—for that's beyond human nature! I know, O Lord, that I be a rascal and a self-seeker, and have not the least love for you or my neighbor. However, fixing my hope on your love of mankind, I cry unto thee: "Remember me, O Lord, in Thy kingdom." Save me, God, whether I will or no! For if thou savest me for my deeds, there's no grace nor gift in that, but duty rather. For if thou savest a righteous man, that's nothing great, and if thou hast mercy on a pure soul, that's nothing wonderful—they're deserving of your mercy; show the wonder of your mercy on me, a rascal!

It is impossible to convey fully in a translation the effect of the mixture in this speech of common, though not illiterate, Russian (Chuzhekhvat is, after all, a nobleman!) and sanctimonious Church Slavonic, of ill-digested quotations from Scripture, and a rascal's vernacular.

Sumarokov's negative characters all seem to be drawn from nature, and Russian nature. Indeed they probably are: the title character of the play Tressotinus (a name Latinized from the French *tres sot,* "very stupid") is supposed to have been modeled on Trediakovsky, while the usurer Kashchei *(The Usurer)* is the poet's own despised brother-in-law A.I. Buturlin, portrayed deliberately with enough realism to render the victim recognizable both to himself and others!

Of the twelve comedies, the masterpiece (if one can use so grandiose a word for so slight a work) is the three-act *Imaginary Cuckold* of 1772.[25] It should be noted incidentally that, beyond the similarity of the titles, this piece has nothing in common with Molière's *Sganarelle, ou le cocu imaginaire.* The plot contrivance which holds the play together is as follows: an elderly couple, Vikul and Khavronia, provincial landowners, stupid, ignorant and quite uncivilized, have living with them a beautiful young ward name Floriza, who of course has no dowry. Count Cassandre, while hunting, happens into the establishment and falls in love with Floriza. Old Vikul, unable to comprehend the situation, supposes that it is his Khavronia whom the Count is courting, and that his beloved wife is cuckolding him! Everything is of course explained at length, Vikul's suspicions are dispelled, and the young pair are married. It is the portrait of the old couple which may be considered the first entirely realistic picture of Russian life in comedy, with touches that lead directly to *The Brigadier.* For all the absurdity of the plot, old Vikul and Khavronia are quite touching in their devotion to one another, and their language is vigorously, racily colloquial—as comedy seldom permits except with low-class servants. When Vikul divulges his suspicions to his wife, a delicious dialogue ensues (Act I, scene 13):

Khav. Fie, sir! Have you no fear of God? What ideas have got into your head in your old age! If you tell this to people, they'll laugh out loud! Maybe you didn't think of that.
Vik. How can I help being afraid of what goes on with other people?
Khav. I'm no longer a young woman, so what have you got to be afraid of?
Vik. There's a proverb, that the thunder doesn't always thunder from a cloud in the sky, but sometimes from a pile of dung.
Khav. A pimple on your tongue! What sort of pile of dung am I?

Floriza overhears this altercation, and breaks in with the question: "What's this all about, ma'am?" and Vikul, who doesn't want his suspicions broadcast, answers hastily:

Vik. Wife, keep this to yourself.
Khav. Why to myself? Is this a shame and a disgrace?

Vik. Don't babble, my treasure, my little diamond.
Khav. But this isn't good, my little cherry.
Vik. Stop it, wife.
Khav. Kiss me, my big, strong bogatyr.
Vik. Let's kiss, my little star under the sun.
Khav. So be cheerier, and as shining as the new moon, and don't be jealous.
Vik. Wife, who's talking about jealousy?
Khav. How that [word] just burst out! But enough—a horse has four legs, and even he stumbles; I'm an illiterate woman—how can I help making slips?
Vik. But it wasn't in the word you made the slip, but in deed.
Khav. I'm country-born, and I don't know what's word, what's deed.

To imagine that Sumarokov, whatever he may have held ideally about the social mission of comedy for improving morals, intended these poor old lovers to be a horrendous example for the audience, is an absurdity beyond belief. Perhaps, pressed hard, he might have said: *"The Imaginary Cuckold was designed to show the folly of jealousy."* Well and good; there is just enough of the didactic in the play to give this interpretation some color. But Vikul and Khavronia are pictured in too much detail, they are too individual, too lovingly ridiculous, to be meant as moral lessons. One is inevitably reminded, certainly not, as some Soviet critics have obtusely said, of the Prostakovs, but of Gogol's wonderful "Old World Landowners" (1835). The comedy itself is, like all Sumarokov's comedies, a mere rudimentary sketch; but the characters are credible human beings, ignorant, naive, narrow-minded, but attractive for all that, and far more alive than any of the puppets who inhabit the poet's tragedies.

Sumarokov endeavored assiduously to prove the truth of the concluding lines of his "Second Epistle": "Our beautiful language is capable of everything," by composing in most of the genres which the epistle discusses, and several more. Many of these efforts are mere curiosities and can be passed over quickly. Thus, for example, a single page is extant (probably the only part ever written) of what was evidently intended to be an epic poem, the *Demetriad,* on the exploits of Dmitry Donskoy.[26] It begins, in classical fashion: *Poiu oruzhie i khrabrogo geroia,* "I sing of arms and the valiant hero," etc. Besides the quite numerous epigrams which he composed according to the rules laid down in his epistle, the poet left also a few "epitaphs" and some *nadpisi,* or "inscriptions"—both in classical Greek usage varieties of the epigram. In the epistolary genre we have, besides the three works previously discussed, a few others, including one addressed to Prince Paul Petrovich on his birthday in 1761. His experimental "sonnets, rondeau and ballades" mentioned in the Epistle, have been discussed; in addition to these exotic lyric varieties, Sumarokov also essayed some madrigals in the Italian style, and some "stanzas," one of which is addressed to the city of Simbirsk against the rebel Pugachev. In his odes Sumarokov employed not only the French form standardized by Malherbe (believed to be "Pindaric"), but attempted to use both the Alcaic and Sapphic strophes (accentual, of course) of Horace, and the monotonous trochaic tetrameter and iambic trimeter which were supposed to represent the "Anacreontic ode"[27] A curiosity is a pair of "Heroides"—"Osnelda to Zavlokh" and "Zavlokh to Osnelda"—supplementing the tragedy *Khorev.*[28] The genre was created by Ovid, and consisted of letters written by classical heroines to various men—husbands, lovers, fathers, brothers, etc. In a few cases Ovid's *Heroides* are paired with replies from the man. Sumarokov's examples may be considered as the letters, which are only reported on in the tragedy itself, addressed by the heroine to her father and reporting her passion for Khorev, her family's hereditary enemy, and the father's stern reply, denouncing this love and calling on his daughter to give it up.

A few other genres not treated in the epistle are represented in Sumarokov's poetical work: a few parody pieces—the "nonsense odes" quoted above, sonnets, dithyrambs, etc.; some choruses, most noteworthy those written for an allegorized court pageant called "The Topsy-Turvy World";[29] and two "Tales" (*skazki*), modeled on the *Contes* of La Fontaine which the epistle mentions briefly in connection with the *Fables.*[30]

Sumarokov's Epistle begins its treatment of genres with the pastoral, recommending for it simplicity of style, a bright, attractive natural background, and the like. Four eclogues are printed in his *Selected Works,*[31] three of which are revisions of earlier versions. Their model is obviously Virgil, and the situations, "characterizations," etc., are quite conventional. Notable, however, and rather out of line with the usually rather proper morality of the pastoral genre, is the free-and-easy sexual conduct of Sumarokov's shepherds and shepherdesses. In *Doriza* the love-lorn Damon takes refuge from a frightful nocturnal thunder-storm in the cottage of his coy lady-love Doriza, who wakes from a pleasant dream that Damon is kissing her, to find that he is indeed! The eclogue ends with the lines: "The moon parted from the amorous night, and she [i.e., Doriza] parted from her amorous shepherd." In *Klarisa* the shepherdess thus named relates to her inexperienced girl-friend Miliza the passionate encounter she has had with the enamored Palemon. "Her girl-friend's love fires Miliza, and within five days she imitates Klarisa." In *Kalista* the shepherd Atis laments his unhappy love for Kalista, and is overheard by the shepherdess Alfiza, who generously offers herself as a substitute. Atis, however, remains faithful, Kalista learns of this and is touched, and "having found him loyal, gave herself to him." In *Melita* the love-sick Agenor sees his mistress Melita bathing in the nude, and is so fired by this that he persuades her to undress before him in private, in her own cottage at night! "The shepherdess is angered, but she fulfills the request, and with Agenor she then experiences that which she had not promised him." Apparently in the never-never land of pastoral Arcadia, in the legendary "Golden Age," conduct was permitted which in the age of Elizabeth and Catherine II would have received at least public reprobation!

Classified separately from the *Eclogues* are four *Idylls*,[32] which appear to form a separate pastoral sub-genre. In form these differ from the *Eclogues*, which utilize the conventional Alexandrine line; three of the *Idylls* are in the *vers libre* which Sumarokov uses elsewhere only for his *Pritchi*, or "Fables." The fourth employs a six-line stanza in trochaic tetrameter. The content of these *Idylls* is in all cases a lover's lament, presented directly, without any introductory stage-setting. Phyllis figures in two of them, Klarisa in one; the obdurate beauty who torments the first lover is unnamed.

Sumarokov's *Elegies*[33] differ from the classical genre of Tibullus, Propertius and Ovid, which is primarily a vehicle for recording the ups and downs of a turbulent love affair. Several are laments for the deaths of persons either dear to the poet (the first is for that of his sister, E.P. Buturlina, 1759) or to his friends (e.g., to Dmitrievsky on the death of his fellow-actor F.G. Volkov, 1763; to Ushakov, governor of St. Petersburg, on the death of Count Alexei Razumovsky; and to Dmitrievsky again on the passing of Tatiana Troepolskaya, leading lady of the Imperial Court Theater). Several elegies, however, are quite originally composed as personal complaints of the poet over the vexations and injustices which he has experienced. Thus in 1768, exasperated by a succession of theatrical tribulations and by the Empress's coldness, the poet writes:[34]

Suffer, sorrowful spirit! Be lacerated, my breast! More miserable than all men in the world am I! I did not flatter myself with seeking a splendid fortune, and from my birth I have not bothered myself with this; with peace of mind alone I soothed myself. Not gold, not silver, but the Muses alone I sought. Without guidance I made my way to the Muses, and broke my path through the deep forest to Parnassus. I overcame the toil, I caught a glimpse of Helicon; like Paradise it presented itself to my eyes. Eden I named the bright garden—but now I name you, Parnassus, a gloomy Hell. You are the torment of the Furies to me, not the pastime of the Muses. O misfortune-bringing, hostile mount, support of my cruel lot, source and cause of all my wretchedness, lamentable sight to my eyes and to my heart, which has brought with it countless bitternesses! Unhappy was that day, most unhappy the minute, when by the sternness and wrath of a cruel fate, flattering myself with [thoughts of] comfort and glory, I first set foot upon me. The winged steed was at that time a little stubborn to me, but later Pegasus was harnessed and subdued. Erato [Muse of lyric verse] first fired my blood, and I sang of tender love and the contagion of [bright] eyes. Charming glances multiplied this flame for me, my eyes raced to those eyes, and verses raced to me. Then I began to sing of streams, banks, herds and shepherds, and clean meadows. To Melpomene [Tragedy] I finally turned, and receiving the dagger from her, I made my way to the theater, and, to my misfortune, falling in love with that best of the Muses, I plunged the dagger, alas! into myself, I made an end of living with my former entertainments, contenting myself with future fame alone—which I shall never hear. Having lived a lifetime in the world, I am ever mourning, since I have lost beautiful Melpomene and have begun to seek changes of verse: de La Fontaine and Aesop became the goal of my mind. Farewell, Racine, Sophocles, and Euripides; let your Monime sob pitifully, Racine [heroine of *Mithridate*]—her tender love touches me no more. Let Orestes' sister [Electra] curse the barbarian—there is not the least movement, Sophocles, in me. Let Alcestis part weeping from her husband—do not seek, Euripides, for a place in my heart. Aristophanes and Plautus, Terence, and Molière, favorites of Thalia [Comedy] and models for the comic poet, hardly caught a glimpse of me in the flowers of Parnassus. I shall not write dramas, I shall not weave fables, and everything which is on Parnassus is hateful to me. I shall not write! But—O unhappy lot! Is my will in this undertaking? Against my desire the Muses will allure me, and will pronounce for me another decision. I desire to leave the Muses and I am saying farewell to the Muses—and in saying farewell to the Muses I am even returning to the Muses. Thus the lover irritated by his beloved, who for many days has been her victim, who is minded to leave her forever, at that very moment inclines toward her with all his heart! Most harmful to me, O Muses! is your sway! O profitless and fateful passion, which taught me to write verses! You have deprived me forever of peace of mind; but though my verses bring me contempt, and though the Muses suck my blood like Furies, let [my] proud, thunderous odes be praised, and let Europe and posterity wreathe me with eulogy.

Stripping this piece of its conventional allegory, we find that Sumarokov prides himself on having, unguided, created a literature for Russia ("I broke my path through the deep forest to Parnassus"). His first literary essays were songs; he then turned to the pastoral, and finally to "the best of the Muses," Melpomene, i.e., tragedy. Hostile events, which he does not specify (they were actually cabals of envious rivals, Catherine's indifference or actual hostility, etc.) have forced him to say farewell to tragedy. As we know, he did in fact compose nothing in this genre from 1756 to 1770. During this time he occupied himself largely with *pritchi* (literally, "parables," i.e., fables). He considers his comedy rather a slight performance—the great comic masters barely caught sight of him on Parnassus! But despite his resolution to write no more, he is fatally attracted to poetry, and counts on the applause at least of posterity. How far all this is from the accepted content of the classical elegy hardly needs to be pointed out.

    Sumarokov does not mention among his labors on Mount Parnassus the writing of satire—perhaps because the satiric genre belonged to the "low style" and can claim no Muse as patron! Most of his satires, however, were composed at a period later than the elegy. The subjects in this case are more conventional and follow quite closely the models furnished by Horace and Boileau. The first, entitled *Krivoi tolk*,[35] or "Crooked Talk," begins in a typically Horatian fashion with the statement: "We never see our own weaknesses, and everything appears good to us which we see in ourselves." From here he goes on to illustrate his theme with numerous examples—the dandy, the miser, the glutton, the swindler, etc. At the end of the piece pride in noble birth is ridiculed—a vice to which he later devotes an entire satire. "The Poet and His Friend,"[36] composed between 1770 and 1774 and intended as the program piece of the set, proceeds from the dialogue between Horace and his friend Trebatius on the dangers of writing satire (*Sermones* II, 1). The "Friend," conjecturing from the Poet's inspired expression that he is writing tragedy, is told that he is mistaken. "Then an eclogue?" "Shepherds, meadows, flowers, zephyrs are as distant from me; I mean to write satires." The friend remarks: "By writing satires you may be vexatious, and by this vexation do yourself an injury." The poet is defiant: "Ignorance and rascality I do not fear, as long as I keep the esteem of honorable people." "Idleness," objects the Friend, "will double its poison against you." People do not like to have their faults brought to light. "Tell the composer of the most clumsy ode to throw it, without printing it, into the stove—and he will be readier to set fire to you." And all sorts of illogical excuses can be found for wrong conduct, for "Among us even the name of logic is known to but few; so hard it is to show what is dishonorable and what is honorable." "Still harder is it," rejoins the Poet, "seeing vice, to endure, and with a clear view of everything, to keep quiet and seethe. Until I fade away, through feebleness or death, I shall not cease to write against vice." Such is the Poet's spirited last word. The whole satire, of course, is pretty much a paraphrase of Juvenal's *First*, with a good deal of Kantemir's *Fourth*.

The third satire, "On Nobility," contains some of Sumarokov's most caustic remarks on the absurd pride of birth exhibited by the "noblemen" of his time, as well as on the callous inhumanity of their conduct toward their unfortunate serfs. Of what worth, he queries, is a splendid ancestry, if its present representative is an idle ignoramus and parasite?

> This satire, nobles, I indite to you!
> Our fatherland's first members in my view;
> Nobles know well their duty without me,
> Yet many one sole thing are prone to see,
> Remembering but this, their own 'nobility';
> Unmindful that whatever has perception,
> Whether of peasant wives' or high-born dames' conception,
> Has Adam for a sire without exception.
> Is our nobility that men should toil
> That of their labor we may them despoil?
> Peasant and lord, are they of different birth?
> Each one is but a clod of breathing earth,
> And if the lord have not a clearer mind
> Than has his serf, no difference I find.
> The peasant drinks and eats, is born and dies;
> The lord, though fed more sweetly, does likewise;
> Though of his gentle birth he often boast
> That lets him stake at cards a peasant host!
> Oh, is it right that cattle men should own,
> And sell to other cattle? Yet 'tis done.[37]

High birth does not necessarily qualify a man for every kind of task. "Praiseworthy is the man who does not seek a task in which he can never succeed. He seeks out precisely that for which he is fitted; not born a poet, he does not smear paper. If you have a brainless head, go dig the earth and chop

135

wood; separate yourself no longer from 'low' folk, and puff yourself up no more with your ancestors' titles." "I am deserving, if I myself have won respect; but if I am fit for no duty, my ancestor may have been a gentleman, but I am not noble."

Though the theme itself is hackneyed and banal—Russia's first satirist, Kantemir, had used it (most vigorously in his Second Satire), and it goes back at least to Horace, and probably to Lucilius—yet in Sumarokov's time, in the reign which historians commonly refer to as "the golden age of the nobility," it took courage to write as he did, and he paid for his daring by earning the Empress's dislike.

The subjects of his other satires are more literary and less touchy. "On the French Language"[38] makes fun of the young nobleman who parades his Parisian language and manners and cannot express himself properly in Russian—a subject which Denis Fonvizin was soon to dramatize in *The Brigadier.* "In all lands great intellects are born, but everywhere stupidities flourish even more, and the fashion of foreign countries is not the law for Russia." "Neither fur hat nor cap nor chapeau nor turban is able to multiply the wit that is given us. The brunette equally with the blonde, if she is intelligent, she is intelligent; if she is stupid, she is a fool." There is, of course, a use for knowing a foreign language: "Foreign tongues are useful for us, so that we may read in them—in Russian there is nothing to read! It is well-known that as yet there are very few Russian books... Our tongue is beautiful for its antiquity alone, but, through the stupidity of writers, it has now become otherwise." The satire, which pretends to be addressed to the parents of a promising boy, ends rather brutally: "Previously your son was noisy in Russian; now, having mastered French, he has become quite witless." The following piece, entitled "On Honor,"[39] is one of the weakest of the set; its theme, of course, is the deformation of the concept of honor, which is invoked to justify duels, selling peasants to pay gambling debts, and the like. The positive recommendations of the satire are noble, but unoriginal: "But real honor is giving comfort to the unfortunate, without expecting any reward for this; loving one's neighbor, being grateful to the Creator, and what is in one's thoughts, saying this only. And if it is imposssible to speak the truth openly, to keep silent at need, though hard, is not discreditable." Winding up his sermon, the poet exclaims:

Be slow to enmity, to friendship be ready! When anyone repents, forgive him without revenge; do not weave blandishments and flatteries for anyone; don't crawl before anyone, and do not be arrogant; do not be an attacker and do not be cowardly; do not be immodest, and do not be hypocritical; be the son of your fatherland and faithful to your monarch.

The satirist finds only forty lines in which to pillory the vice in "On Slander,"[40] and nothing that he says is particularly significant. On the other hand the satire entitled "Exhortation to a Son"[41] is one of the most original and caustic of the group. In form this is somewhat unusual, in that the Alexandrine lines are irregularly interrupted by short lines of two or three iambs with variable rhyme scheme, almost as in the *pritchi*. The content is no less unusual: the satire begins: "Thus a certain person gave directions, seeing his own tearful end, to his only-begotten beloved heir." The rest of the poem, down to the final four lines, is the father's dying instructions to his son. There is no indication at first that the admonition is meant ironically; it begins quite straightforwardly:

My son, beloved son! Now I am already old; my mind is growing dull, my fire is disappearing. I am preparing myself for judgment. I shall soon go into eternity and into the infinity prescribed for us mortals; and so I shall now tell you how you are to live, I shall show you the path of your happiness. My end is near, and you will be going on a path which is very slippery.

Abruptly the tone changes:

Though everything in the world is vanity, should one despise the happiness of the belly?" [The word *zhivot* is of course ambiguous, probably intentionally; its modern meaning is "belly," but in older and more formal usage it means "life." The more vulgar meaning seems indicated here by what follows]. "So we must bend our every thought toward this, and always strive for what we require. Forget that chimera which is known as 'honor'; what is it good for, when we don't have what we need to eat?

Then follows a series of straight-faced directions for a life of the most consummate rascality: "Increase your income in every fashion every year"; "honor the rich so as to receive gain from them"; "if a powerful lord abuses anyone, you too, with the nobility, abuse him!" "What a big-wig says, know that this is a sacred word"; "continue to be an honorable man for yourself, sincerely loving yourself alone!" "Honor yourself with your heart, honor others with your mouth!" "I permit you to play at cards, if you know how to pick up [winnings] at these games.... but this, my son, do not forget: while playing don't ever be honorable in the game!" "Give bribes yourself, and take them in turn yourself; if there are no witnesses, thieve, play the rascal as much as possible—but with witnesses, be circumspectly dishonest!" "Hate the learned and despise the ignorant, having but one thought—of your own fresh profit!" "Confuse and break the ties of kinship, friendship, marriage; in muddy water, you know, it is easier to catch crabs!" "For your own profit bring your friends to misfortune. This, they prate, is dishonorable, but this is not apparent. Duty bids me love only myself. It is no harm to me, if need bids me ruin a friend. It is against nature not to love oneself. Let misery take up its abode in my fatherland; let [my fatherland] quite sink through the earth, let everything that is another's be destroyed, so that I have repose." The father ends his exhortations with the words: "Live, my son, as your parent has lived." Not content to let his horrendous picture speak for itself,

137

the poet then, with relish, announces: "When he had pronounced this, he was struck by a thunderbolt, and parted from his child and his house; and his soul, that had sowed poison for so long, departed from his body and plunged into Hell."

After this really Juvenalian satire, the last comes anticlimactically—"On Bad Rhymesters."[42] "Is only that which is sinful in the world, bad?" the poet queries, and answers his own question: "That too is not good, which is mingled with stupidity." "The poet, who does not comfort us with his verse, is a contemptible fellow, even though not a sinner!" But poetry, like any art, requires learning. Indignantly the satirist exclaims: "But a cook sometimes, if he knows how to cook, makes more income than a professor. Is poetry alone in having such regulations that it has need of a learned head?" "In any other science [nauka] taste is worth nothing, but in poetry there is no possibility without it." "Not all men are born for this science: are there Racines and Molières in all ages?" No, the poet answers: only four times have such geniuses flourished—an interesting observation, and typically classicist: the Golden Age of Greece; Augustus's Rome; the Renaissance ("When after the grievous loss of poetry, Europe heard Tasso and Malherbe"); and the age of French classicism. After a few invidious comparisons between masterpieces and examples of hack work, the poet gets off on one of his critical hobbies—the comédie larmoyante. "Taste has coupled Thalia [Comedy] with Melpomene [Tragedy], but it has become the foe of both Thalia and Melpomene. Neither the one nor the other can dominate the theater, if one must guffaw and immediately after, sob. To anyone who commends this, I shall say: 'It is false!' " Then comes the inevitable reference to the authority of Voltaire, and his "reply" (almost, it seems, an imperial "rescript"!) to Sumarokov's questions about the legitimacy of the "tearful comedy." At this point the satire trails off into a diffuse and irrelevant eulogy of the great achievements of Catherine's reign to the lining of the Neva banks with granite and the building of St. Isaac's!

Sumarokov's satires, then, show a curious mingling of the quite conventional and hackneyed with a few examples of extraordinary vigor and originality. Much the same is the picture, as we shall see, in that other more or less satiric genre, the *pritcha* (parable or fable), which may for convenience be considered next.[43]

In his autobiographical elegy, quoted above, Sumarokov refers to his writing of "Fables," inspired by Aesop and La Fontaine. To these "classical" models have to be added, for the later period at least, the German fabulist Christian Fürchtegott Gellert, and of course the Latin Phaedrus. The actual name which Sumarokov uses for the genre, however, is somewhat inexactly translated "Fables." *Pritcha* is the word used in the New Testament to translate the Greek *parabole* (English "parable," as for example the story of "The Prodigal Son"); *Pritchi Solomonovye* is the name of the Old Testament book which in English is called "Proverbs." Here it translates the Hebrew *mashal*,

138

which means literally "similitude," and this is the basic meaning of the Slavonic word. This meaning belongs to the original purpose of the genre. The Aesopic *mythos* is a "similitude," often, but not necessarily, using animals, birds, even inanimate objects as persons, but *always* told as a "likeness" of human life and conduct, and hence as a *lesson*. This didactic purpose is the genesis of the genre, and it is only late in the eighteenth century, just before the genre itself disappears from use, that the "moral" of the fable retires into the background, and the fabulist's chief preoccupation becomes that of telling an original story in an elegant and entertaining way. For English readers the term "fable" usually connotes such an "animal anecdote" as that of "The Fox and the Crow" or "The Wolf and the Lamb"; but *pritcha* is a much broader term than "fable" (Russian *basnia*), and among the *pritchi* of Sumarokov many are simply short poems retelling well-known anecdotes, usually from antiquity, e.g., "Alexander and Parmenion," "Simonides and the Dioscuri," "Midas" ("King Midas has Asses' Ears!"), or "The Distraught Widow," which is a very tame version of "The Widow of Ephesus" story, first told in Petronius's *Satiricon*.

At first sight Sumarokov's fables are somewhat disappointing, largely because a modern reader approaches them inevitably with prior knowledge of their elegantly beautiful models, La Fontaine's *Fables*, or of their vigorously colloquial and sharply pointed successors, Krylov's *Basni*. Seen against this background, Sumarokov's versions give an impression often of tameness and flabbiness. They were, however, admired by the poet's contemporaries more than almost any of his works, and viewed in their proper perspective they certainly deserve this admiration. In form they follow the usage established by La Fontaine, of the so-called *vers libre,* iambic lines of varying lengths irregularly placed, and with irregularly recurring rhymes. It should be noted that while in his Alexandrines Sumarokov often uses the most banal of rhymes, in the fables he strives for originality, and very often achieves it, with quite novel and startling rhymes.

Sumarokov composed fables during most of his literary life, and published several collections, which enjoyed great popularity. Some were not printed in his lifetime, but collected after his death and published in the first "Collected Works" by the poet's editor Nikolai Novikov. In all, his fables number 374, with dates of composition covering more than twenty years, from 1752 to his death. Some of the pieces, like his epigrams, satires, and comedies, lampoon personal or literary enemies, or refer to contemporary political events. These in most cases seem particularly vapid, the immediacy of the situation having disappeared. Thus the very early "Beetles and Bees" (probably 1752), which is directed against Trediakovsky:[44]

I shall compose a witticism and tell a tale. Ignorant Beetles sneaked into learning, and began to teach the Bees how to make honey. The Bees weren't quiet for long, because they were bothered, and a great noise began in the hive. Apollo descended from Parnassus to them, and drove all the Beetles away, saying: "My friends, be off to the dung-heaps. They are working, and you are devouring their labor, and you are spoiling their honey with your outrageousness!

Similarly, "The War of the Eagles" [Voina orlov], between 1762 and 1765:[45]

The Eagles were fighting, and were very angry. Why? This no one knows. They fought under the very skies; they did not fight on earth, but above the clouds—so, consequently, [it seems] that there are plenty of fools even there. Of course, we too fight, not knowing ourselves for what. Enough, that the Eagles want to go to war, and the feathers flutter down. They fight in earnest, and without pretence. The Eagles quarreled—eagle-feathers for arrows.

This would be quite unintelligible without the historical gloss that the "eagles" ["orly"] referred to (the title Voina orlov makes this even clearer) are the three Orlov brothers, who quarreled over the position of chief lover of Catherine the Great! But even with this gloss, it is pretty pointless.

Fortunately, such feeble efforts are an exception. Many of the fables, even on well-worn Aesopic themes, are brisk, pointed, and vigorous. Of course a great deal of the effectiveness is contributed by the rhymes, and is lost in translation. "The Snake and the Saw" is a good example:[46]

Don't exert yourself to criticize one whom it is a teeny bit hard to undermine: all your preparations and contrived nonsense will not do him the least harm, but will bring you a very great deal of shame.
  A Snake found a Saw. The creature eyed it. The Snake thinks seriously of no one, and is not stingy about wasting its poison. It bites the Saw and licks it with its tongue. The more it coils in its fury around the Saw, the more blood flows, and, as it pours blood in streams from itself, while trying to destroy the Saw, it takes its own for the other's blood, and melts with blood, saws the Saw, hurts its tongue, lacerates its lips" [i krov'iu taet, Pilu pilit, Iazyk bolit, Istrekalis' guby]." "The Snake saw, after it had knocked out its teeth, that it was hit, and not the Saw" [Uvidela Zmeia, Perelo-mavshi zuby, chto tronuta ona byla, A ne Pila].

Sumarokov's fables are usually provided, as this is, with a "moral." Here the moral is a general statement at the beginning of the poem, which the fable then follows as an exemplification. Often, however, the moral, or some generalization taking its place, is appended to the fable, as most commonly in Aesop. Thus, for example, the little apologue of the clay pot and the iron pot which went walking together is followed by the two-line moral: "Submitting to your fate, have association only with your own kind." Sometimes there is no overt moral at all, except as an interpolated parenthesis, e.g., in "The Raven and the Fox," where in the midst of the Fox's flattering speech the poet inserts his own comment: " 'Your feathers,' says the Fox, 'are a hundred times more beautiful than the peacock's.' Praises from flattery free we find it agreeable to endure," is the fabulist's ironical comment.

Many of Sumarokov's fables, as has already been mentioned, are no more than small anecdotes in verse. Such, for example, is "The Empty-Headed Girl" [shalunia], which has as its point the poet's familiar aversion to French affectations:[47]

A certain empty-headed girl in conversation at a solemn dinner could not keep up her ravings without a word or two of French, although of this language she knew nothing, not a single word. She wanted, however, to shine with her learning, and put in French words any old way. She said, among other things, 'I'm going to make a cure' [Ia edu delat' kur, i.e., a literal translation of the French Je vais faire une cure, "take a cure," at a watering-place or the like]. Her astonished neighbors said, when they heard this: "What nonsense she's talking! Brood-hens make chicks!" [delaiut kur: the point lies in the confusion between the French cure, in an inexact Russian pronunciation, and the native word for "chicks."]

Another such anecdote is: "The Ass as Ambassador":[48]

In Venice a certain fop [shalun] was ambassador. He was arrogant and he offended many a great deal. The Venetians were fired with vexation against him, and wrote to the court from which he was ambassador about the matter. There they already knew about the ambassador's tricks, and replied: "Forgive him, he's a fool. A man doesn't quarrel with a jackass." To this [the Venetians] responded: "We too have no dearth of jackasses here; we don't, however, make ambassadors of them."

A few of the anecdotal fables have subjects taken from early Russian history; the "point" of these is usually directed against the egotism of the nobility, e.g., "The Boyar Council," called to consider defense measures against the Tatars, and terminated by the profound advice of one old councillor:[49]

The Tatar isn't burning me, nor doing me any damage on yon side of the Moscow river. Do as you please, but my advice is this: my house isn't across the Moscow.

Among the hardest-hitting of Sumarokov's fables are those that in content coincide perfectly with his *Satires,* but differ only in their form and greater brevity. Such, for example, is "Lack of Time"[50]:

Having lived a life of idleness, a young and stupid lord did not for even a single day exercise himself at a task. Qualities, it seems, are pretty scant, where there are no services, even small, to one's fatherland. For what is a man born, when he spends his life as a parasite? Is he a member of society? My own reply to this question is recorded in the minutes: he is not a *member,* but a wart of the body! He is not a tree in the forest, but a dried-up stump; he is not a man, but a bullock which hasn't been roasted—and God knows why he is made a nobleman. It seems to me there is no reason for such as he to have privileges and rank. Am I able to respect a monster, which nature produced an ass? I don't know why the thunder spares such fellows. Even in thought such a one doesn't come near a task; he is a friend to idleness alone—but he lays the blame on Time. He only says: "Today I'm not at leisure." He lays the blame on Time that tasks are a burden to him in his parasite's existence, as he babbles that he has no Time for a task.

Time comes to him at ten o'clock; he is sleeping, snoring. Time finds no welcome and departs. At eleven o'clock he has tea, smokes tobacco, and says nothing. So his appropriate hour is unknown to Time. At twelve o'clock he is carousing at dinner, then he sleeps, and snores again. Toward evening, he sits up, the blockhead—and puts in order, not his thoughts, but his hair; he rides off to a public assembly, the scum, and then plays at cards and loses. Unhappy the city where almost every day there is a club and a masquerade.

As a final example of Sumarokov's satirical vigor, humor, and genuine sympathy with human suffering, may be quoted the fable titled "The Legless Soldier." Incidentally, Sumarokov's technique of introducing himself here in an unflattering light as a presumably typical hard-hearted idler, is remarkably like that of Derzhavin in *Felitsa*[51]:

A soldier, whose legs had been blown off in war, was sent to a monastery to be fed. But the servants were too strict for this poor fellow; the unfortunate was unable to pamper himself with food, and so, unhappy with his life, the legless soldier left the monastery. He had no legs, so he crawled, and began to drag himself about the world.

I had some very important business, and I didn't want anyone at that time to make a noise; all my brain, as much as I have in my body, was engaged in this business, and my head was empty. The soldier, crawling along with an empty basket, bawled before [my] window: "Someone give me alms, for Christ's sake, for God's sake give. All day long I have not eaten, and night is approaching." I became angry and yelled: 'Crawl away, you good-for-nothing, wherever your road lies. It was long since time for you to die, you legless one! Crawl away, and don't disturb my chess game!'

The soldier still bawled, but no longer in front of me, but in front of a merchant's widow's [house]. I glanced out the window, and began to laugh at what I had at first been angry at, and I was amused, as I looked, by the legless man. It was then the time to go to the all-night service. The merchant's widow was already old, and she was very pious. She was widowed, and well provided with money; she and her departed husband had salted away a pile at contracts. She was going on foot to pray—not out of poverty, however; but she lived as piously as ever she could. All days were for her Friday and Wednesday [i.e., fast-days], she hadn't eaten meat for ten years, it was already three days since she had had a drink of vodka; and to top it all, she was always telling her beads. The soldier bothered her too about food, and bawled the same thing. His bawling tickled her ear, and this pious old woman pitied the soldier, as he begged her to give a poor man a penny. The widow burst into tears—and hurried to church.

A workman had been digging all day at the beds in a garden, and when he encountered that unfortunate, he gave him everything he had earned. This workman is witness with the crawling warrior, in what disregard genuine virtue is.

The last genre of Sumarokov's extensive work which we need consider is probably the first that he actually cultivated, the song.[52] As we have seen, in his autobiographical elegy the first Muse he served was Erato, and while she presided over the Ode as well as the Song, it was the latter which won Sumarokov his earliest literary fame. His songs, however, were not published in his lifetime, and doubtless many have perished, or perhaps exist as anonymous productions, the composer's name having been lost. His first

142

editor, Nikolai Novikov, collected as many of the songs *(pesni)* as he could identify as Sumarokov's, and published them in the *Collected Works* of 1787. About 130 songs are known.

In his songs, as elsewhere, Sumarokov is a classicist. The songs are almost all expressions of love—not, however, the poet's own personal love for this or that particular lady; rather they are the generalized experiences of the generalized lover or lady—because the songs are often put in the lady's mouth as well as the lover's. They are devoid of any individualizing traits: if the lady has been deserted, she mourns her loss without any reference to the reasons for the lover's faithlessness; if the lover parts from his lady, all we learn of the circumstances is that he is obliged for some reason to leave for distant parts—but neither the locale he is leaving, nor his objective, nor the reason for the parting is specified. Everything is idealized, generalized.

Most of Sumarokov's verse is composed in the Russian Alexandrine meter, itself a close imitation, allowing for the accentual rather than the syllabic basis, of the French original. As we have seen, the fables are composed in a Russian form derived from La Fontaine's *vers libre,* without a fixed stanza form or rhyme scheme. The odes, of course (except those imitating "Anacreon") employ fixed stanza form, but exclusively iambic meter and ten-line strophes. The songs, on the other hand, seem to be without a French background; they have mostly strophic form, but the strophes are freely composed, with varying number of lines, of syllables to the line, of meter, and of rhyme scheme. Their form is much closer to that of German verse than to French or Italian; and the fact that Sumarokov admired and translated some seventeenth-century German verse, e.g., of Paul Fleming (1609-1640) during the '50s, when many of his "songs" were written, makes German influence probable.

The language of the songs is, for the eighteenth century, exceptionally simple, light and flexible. Slavonicisms are not entirely absent (*zhizn' dragaia* instead of *dorogaia,* or *khladnu krov'* rather than *kholodnuiu*), but are not obtrusive, and the poetical inversions, so common in the fables, are kept to a minimum. The easy simplicity of the songs, which doubtless accounts for their popularity when they were composed, certainly makes them the most accessible today of all Sumarokov's work. As a fairly short example, typical in many respects, may be quoted the twelve-line song, composed in 1755, beginning *Uzhe voskhodit solntse, stada idut v luga.* The movement of the verse is worth noting: each line is divided into hemistichs, with three beats each, in iambic meter; the first hemistich of each line ends in a downbeat, the second alternately in an up-beat and a down-beat. The scheme would thus be: x'x'x'x/ x'x'x'(x). The rhyme scheme is very simple: in each four-line stanza *AAbb.* In a line-for-line translation the poem goes as follows:[53]

Already the sun is rising, the flocks are going to the meadows,
The currents in the stream are splashing against the steep banks.
The amorous shepherdess has already driven her sheep,
And invited me to the woods on the eve of this day.

O dusky groves, the refuge of wantonness!
In your delightful shade there is none of the world's sorrow;
Nature has introduced lovely glades in you
As though on purpose, that love might live there.

This evening await me beneath your shade,
And in you I shall be seeing my amorous one.
Beneath your leafage I was once happy,
And gave countless kisses to my faithful shepherdess.

Pass on, pass on quickly, day hateful to me,
Your light is unwelcome, let the shade of night cover [me].
Hasten, most precious evening, and fly, O Time!
And do you, dear one, forbid me nothing.

A less happy lover laments in another song, of 1759, the first stanza of which reads[54]:

Vanished are those hours when you sought me out,
And all my solace you have taken away.
I see that you have now become faithless to me,
And toward me you have now become altogether different.
　　My groaning and cruel pangs
　　Imagine to yourself,
　　And recollect those moments
　　When I was dear to you.

Here the form is more complicated: each stanza consists of two parts, of four lines each. The first four lines have a six-beat iambic scheme: x'x'x'/ x'x'x'(x), with alternate rhymes, feminine and masculine, i.e., *bAbA*. The second four lines have only half as many beats, i.e., x'x'x'(x), with the same alternate rhyme scheme, *bAbA*.

Among the songs are a few in which, quite unexpectedly, Sumarokov attempts to utilize a popular form. Thus, for example, the song celebrating the capture of the Turkish fortress of Bender by Count Peter Panin in 1770, which is composed in four-beat trochaic lines with dactylic unrhymed endings[55]:

　　O ty, krepkii, krepkii Bender-grad,
　　O razumnyi, khrabryi Panin-graf, etc.

144

Even more remarkable is the "maiden song," of thirty couplet-rhyming lines,[56] after every one of which is intruded the popular refrain line: *Kalina li moia, malina li moia* (literally "my guelder-rose, or my raspberry!"). The first four lines set the scene: *V roshche devki guliali (Kalina li moia, malina li moia), I vesnu proslavliali (Kalina* etc.) *Devku gorest' morila (Kalina* etc.) *Devka tut govorila (Kalina* etc.): "In the woods the maidens were walking.... and celebrating the spring-time.... Sorrow plagued a maiden.... the maiden said." The rest of the song presents the maiden's plaint. While the imitation of genuinely popular anonymous verse is not exact—the rhymes are too careful and regular—the poet has most astonishingly caught the atmosphere, and not until Pushkin and Koltsov will one find a more successful attempt to naturalize the popular musical idiom.

In brief summary, Alexander Sumarokov's place in Russian literature is that of a most astonishingly versatile innovator. He is the initiator of nearly all the classical genres that his successors in Russia cultivated, and while certainly not a master in each of them, which would be too much to expect, left some truly notable achievements in the tragedy, the fable, the satire, and the song. Even in the genres in which his success is less significant, such as the elegy, the pastoral, and the comedy, he pointed the way for more inspired successors. He may thus be rightfully considered the true founder of Russian classicism.

Nevsky Prospect.
Detail of a 1753 engraving
by Ya. Vasiliev, from a M. Makhaev drawing.

Видъ новаго ИМПЕРАТОРСКАГО Зимняго Дворца
и Эрмитажа на берегу большой Невы Р.
въ Санктпетербургѣ 1770 г.

Façade du Palais IMPERIAL d´ hyver et
de l´Hermitage sur la Neva
a S. Peterbourg 1770

The Winter Palace and the Hermitage.
A 1770 engraving by N. Chelkanov, from a drawing by Makhaev.

Ships by the Stock Exchange. Detail of a 1753 engraving by I. P. Ilyakov.

Lomonosov

Alexander Sumarokov

ПРИТЧИ

АЛЕКСАНДРА СУМАРОКОВА.

Title-page of the 1762 editor
of Sumarokov's fables.

КНИГА ПЕРВАЯ.

ВЪ САНКТПЕТЕРБУРГѢ
1762.

A wax figure (based on a work by C. Rastrelli) of Peter the Great, 1725.
It conveys well his unusual height – 6 feet 7 inches.

Elizaveta Petrovna, 1745.
Portrait by L. Karavakk.

Petersburg. The Palace
bankment in the 1790s.
nting by Fyodor Alexeev.

ЕЛИСЕЙ

или

раздраженный

ВАКХЪ

ПОЕМА.

ВЪ САНКТПЕТЕРБУРГѢ.

Title-page of Maikov's "Elisei," published anonymously 1775?

ЯБЕДА,

КОМЕДІЯ

ВЪ ПЯТИ ДѢЙСТВІЯХЪ.

Съ дозволенія Санктпетербургской Цензуры.

Въ Санктпетербургѣ, 1798.
Печатано въ Императорской Типографіи.
Иждивеніемъ Г. Крутицкого.

Title-page of Kapnist's "Iabeda," St. Petersburg, 1798. It is called "A Comedy in Five Acts," and it is noted that it was published "With the permission of the St. Petersburg Censorship."

Maikov

Lvov

Kapnist

Kheraskov

Bartolommeo Rastrelli, the brilliant Italian architect, c. 1762.

Rastrelli's Catherine Palace at Tsarskoe Selo.

PART III

PROSE LITERATURE IN THE FIRST HALF
OF THE REIGN OF CATHERINE II

Catherine the Great, 1745.
Portrait by L. Karavakk.

CHAPTER VII

PROSE LITERATURE IN THE FIRST HALF OF THE REIGN OF CATHERINE II

A. The Political and Social Scene

The coup d'etat by which the German Catherine took possession of the throne of the Romanovs appeared quite similar to several other "palace revolutions" of the eighteenth century; as a matter of fact, however, both its background and its results were of a quite different order. Ostensibly Catherine's position could be only that of a regent for her son Paul, then eight years old; her accession manifesto emphasized the necessity of protecting the heir from his father's murderous intentions as justification for her usurpation. Actually she relied on the support of the landed gentry (*dvorianstvo*) and intended to rule with their support in her own name. In order to assure herself of the gentry's cooperation she made them very large concessions, beginning with the reaffirmation of her late husband's proclamation that established what became known as "the freedom of the gentry." By this act the gentry were freed from the condition that had originally justified their existence—the obligation of life-time service to the state in the military or naval forces or the administrative bureaucracy. The gentleman might now settle down on his estates, or in the capital if he preferred, and continue to be supported in unproductive idleness by his estate peasantry. The restrictions binding the peasant to his landlord's estate became, under Catherine, ever more harsh; the Empress's numerous lovers and other favorites were given lavish grants of land, together with the attached peasants, from state reserves; serfdom was extended into the once free Ukraine, which had never known it; the practice became general of selling individual peasants or even whole families away from the land; and in general the position of the "serf" became identical with that of the "slave." The age of Catherine II has become rightly known in history as "the golden age of the gentry." The landlord was allowed to exercise virtually untrammeled authority on his estates, and by an early decree of Catherine's the peasant was forbidden the right of making any complaint against his authority. It was a tacitly understood agreement between the Empress and the gentry that she would do nothing to restrict their activity, in return for their support of her usurped position.

At the same time Russia's nascent middle class of traders, artisans and intellectuals outside the gentry (e,g., the sons of priests) had begun to flourish in the larger cities as a result of the country's economic rise, and the western culture, rather superficially introduced by Peter I, began to seep down from the gentry to the *meshchane*. More and more sons of the middle group managed, by one means or another, to acquire an education and to take positions in the ranks of the bureaucracy--the beginnings of the *raznochintsy* so important in the intellectual life of the next century. If they succeeded in reaching high enough rank in the hierarchies established by Peter's "Table of Ranks," they were automatically enrolled in the landed gentry, a body which was thus continually being recruited by fresh blood from beneath.

Catherine might have had greater difficulty in maintaining her position if she had not succeeded with such outward brilliance in the field of foreign affairs. As it was, a series of wars and diplomatic triumphs established Russia in a position of unparalleled and imposing European strength. Intervention in anarchic neighboring Poland in collusion with Prussian Frederich II led by 1775 to large annexations of Polish territory and a virtual protectorate over the monarchy itself. Involvement with Poland led to hostilities with Turkey, and in the war of 1768-1774 Russian land forces and navy won spectacular victories over the declining Ottoman Empire, as a result of which the Crimea (a Turkish possession) became "independent," that is, Russian-dominated, and the whole area of Podolia, formerly Turkish, was annexed outright.

An ominous development, however, clouded these resounding successes and had the effect of rendering Catherine's rule more tyrannical and repressive in the second part of her reign. The tightening of the landlord's control over the peasants led to repeated minor outbreaks, which culminated in a full-scale war (1773-75) between the government and an army of insurgent peasants in the lower Volga region, led by the Cossack Emelian Pugachev. Though Pugachev was captured and executed (1775), the country had been thoroughly terrified, Catherine's prestige shaken, and her resolution to tolerate no "dangerous ideas," such as might foster a repetition of the Pugachevshchina, hardened into a mania.

In 1772 Pavel Petrovich, Catherine's son by Peter III, reached his majority, the age of eighteen (born in 1754). Catherine's position was seemingly precarious, with a son now officially of age, and a great many of the gentry gathered around the young prince and his more or less liberal tutor, Count Nikita Panin, with the intention of forcing Catherine's abdication. She was able, however, to seize the initiative and forestall such action; Nikita Panin was retired, his brother Peter, a general, removed from a dangerous command, and Paul himself disposed of at least temporarily by a hasty marriage to a German princess, whom he detested and who presently took one of the prince's closest friends as her lover. By her energetic actions Catherine so overawed Paul's supporters that they tamely acquiesced in her continued rule. By 1775 Catherine's position was more than ever secure; she ruled autocratically in her own name, relegated her son to his country estate at Gatchina and kept him completely out of state affairs, while she and her succession of lovers, such as Grigory Orlov and Grigory Potemkin, continued to receive the support and adulation of the gentry of her own country and the long-distance homage of Europe's intellectual arbiter, Voltaire.

B. Enlightenment and the Masonic Movement[1]

The eighteenth century as a whole is often designated the "age of reason." Quite aside from the question of the propriety of so designating any century in the history of irrational man, the applicability of this tag to the whole century is dubious. "Enlightenment" begins as a French phenomenon, and scarcely reaches major proportions until the second third of the century. Its chief focus is the famous *Encyclopedia*, under publication by Denis Diderot and his associates from 1751 to 1780. 1789 and the beginning of the French Revolution marks in effect the end of the Enlightenment as well as of the *ancien regime*. The movement can really therefore be restricted to the period from about 1735 to 1789. This approximately fifty years is also the period of the intellectual dominance of Voltaire (1694-1778), whose name is not infrequently also used to qualify the whole century, as a sort of synonym of "age of reason."

What actually is meant by "age of reason"? Broadly it means that a fairly small, but brilliant and extremely vocal intellectual elite emancipated itself from the age-old domination of the Church, and instead of accepting Biblical text or ecclesiastical doctrine as the ultimate truth, insisted on subjecting everything to the test of reason. If, for example, the Bible related that Joshua had "made the sun stand still," whereas Copernicus had demonstrated that it is the earth, not the sun, that moves, and in either case reason repudiated the possibility of such a breach of natural law, then it followed that the Bible was doubly wrong. In similar fashion the supernatural sanction of legal systems, of the absolute monarchy, and of the system of social castes were all subjected to rational scrutiny, and rejected. Rousseau found violence, "the will of the stronger," the foundation of social inequality; Montesquieu derived the laws of a people, not from God, but from climatic and geographical conditions; and the *philosophes* generally imagined, with Rousseau, a "social contract" between a people and its sovereign, which bound the latter to rule in his nation's interest, not his own.

"The Enlightenment" is a blanket term, and obscures many differences in application of the fundamental rationalism that distinguishes the age. Actually, two quite distinct periods may be made out, with the chronological line running between the 1740s and the 1750s. The earlier, dominated by

Voltaire and Montesquieu, while rejecting the traditional Christian Church, retains belief in a deity—Voltaire's famous "clock-maker God." The admirable order and regularity of the universe, as it seemed to the deist, required belief in a Creator; but once having set the mechanism in motion, they believed, God had retired and left it to function of itself. Science, in this view, afforded the surest, indeed the only, means of knowing anything about this remote and impersonal God. In regard to earthly matters, the earlier phase of the Enlightenment cherished the ideal of the monarch who should indeed govern in his people's interest, and concern himself above all with raising their intellectual and moral level. "Enlightened absolutism" was conceived to be the best means to the end of a people's betterment; a model in actual history for such an enlightened reign was admittedly hard to find. Voltaire chose that of Henri IV for his epic, *La Henriade*; in Russia the ideal lay closer to hand, for Peter the Great approached it more nearly than any other monarch in the country's history.

The second period of the Enlightenment is dominated in France by such intellectuals as Diderot, Helvétius, Baron d'Holbach and La Mettrie. With these more radical *philosophes* atheism and materialism are the fundamental philosophical positions. Voltaire's "God is a necessary hypothesis" has ceased to be convincing: the universe can be explained, including the origin of life and of man, without resort to the hypothesis, as for example, by Diderot. As to the political question, the later *philosophes* tend more and more to republicanism: the people can best govern themselves.

Both groups of "enlighteners" are at one in basing ethical conduct as well as the functioning of the world machine on rational principle. Altruism is an "enlightened self-interest," and the mandate to "do unto others as you would that they do unto you" should be followed not because it is an injunction of Jesus Christ, but because it can be logically demonstrated as the best course. To better the lot of one's fellow man is inevitably to better one's own.

The ideas of the Enlightenment were first formulated and defended in France, which since the age of Louis XIV had been the recognized intellectual center of Europe. They spread rapidly to the rest of Europe, and were received with particular ease in England, where indeed some of them (the "sensualism" of Hobbes and Locke et al.) had originated. Russia, with its strongly French-oriented upper class, was affected by the Enlightenment almost as soon as the rest of Europe. Intimates of the new outlook on life can be seen in the thoroughly Europeanized Kantemir; the philosopher and scientist Lomonosov exhibits them to the fullest degree, although in his poetic practice he is still dominated by the Baroque tradition. Sumarokov, with little originality in either philosophical or poetic outlook, is rightly regarded as the chief Russian exemplar of "classicism" in literature and rationalism in philosophy.

160

A movement closely connected in its origins with the rationalism of the Enlightenment is that of Free Masonry. Originating in England in 1717, this movement made very rapid progress throughout Europe and America, and by the middle of the century had branches in almost all European states, including Russia. Founded on principles of anticlerical rationalism, its teachings embodied belief in a deistic "clock-maker" God, in a universe of orderly laws exempt from divine interference, and in a universal brotherhood of man. Masonry was at the outset egalitarian and anti-aristocratic; men of all faiths, even Jews, were admitted, and the highest ranks in the hierarchy were accessible to men of all classes. Very soon after its initial spread, however, Free Masonry lost most of its Enlightenment character, and by the period when we encounter it in Russia, it has become conservative and even reactionary. It lost its egalitarianism; the upper ranks of the order were regularly filled by noblemen, and commoners were even excluded from membership. A distinctly Christian belief replaced deism, and with the spread of Rosicrucianism, mystical and occult ideas began to dominate. In France such ideas are associated with the name of St. Martin, who vigorously denounced the atheism and materialism of the later *philosophes;* his works had wide currency in Russia, especially his 1775 treatise: "On Errors and the Truth." The Voltairean belief that scientific comprehension of the workings of Nature provided the only means of understanding God was displaced by the mystical pretensions of direct intuitional communion with the deity. The works of many European mystics, not directly connected with the Masonic movement—Thomas à Kempis, Jacob Boehme, Angelus Silesius, etc.—became appropriated by the order. The philanthropic character of the movement remained, but the preoccupation with improving the lot of mankind, which was one of its enduring ideals, now took the form of a program of personal self-improvement, on the assumption that the best way to better the condition of the race is for each individual to reach the highest possible degree of moral perfection.

Free Masonry reached Russia by the middle of the century, and was embraced by some very important persons in both governmental and literary circles. Among others, Count Nikita Panin was a Mason, and his charge, Prince Pavel Petrovich, the heir apparent of the Russian throne, was, if not actually a member, which is uncertain, at least a very sympathetic outsider. This certainly accounts in part for Catherine's active opposition to the order, since she suspected it of harboring the secret design of putting her son on the throne in her place. Of course, the secret character of the organization and its international ties helped to make it suspect. Paul's connection with the order certainly throws some light on his strange involvement after his accession with the Knights of St. John of Malta, which came close to plunging Russia into a premature war with Napoleon.

Of the principal literary figures of the age, Sumarokov became a Mason about 1756, and many of the writers of his "school" imitated his example.

161

Chief of these was M.M. Kheraskov, whose later literary production shows evident marks of Masonic views. The historian M. M. Shcherbatov belonged to the "Urania" lodge of St. Petersburg. The prose writer and dramatist V.I. Lukin was a Mason, as was the poet Vasily Maikov. The revolutionary poet Alexander Radishchev was a member in his student days, and N.M. Karamzin had close connections with the order in his youth. Above all, the very influential journalist, publisher and philanthropist N.I. Novikov must be mentioned, whose own writing of the '80s and '90s is the most important of specifically Masonic literature. Novikov founded and edited a number of Masonic periodicals, among which may be mentioned "Morning Light" and "The Laborer at Rest."

The order of Free Masons was regarded with considerable suspicion in Russia, and not alone by the government. Sumarokov felt it necesary to write a verse apology, which, while scarcely great poetry, clearly indicates the bases for popular mistrust:

> He who finds fault with the Free Masons
> For their secret code,
> That they do not respect the laws [*zakonov*—i.e., laws of the
> > state]
>
> [But] hold to their own [ideas of] right [*prav*—i.e., fundamental
> > moral laws] :
>
> If you were asked
> How loyal a Free Mason is,
> He also keeps the law *[zakon]*
> In which he was born....
> ... To love a fellow man as is one's duty,
> And to help the poor,
> And wherever possible
> To divert misfortune from them.
> To put it to you in a word,
> He is an honorable man;
> But to get to learn their secret
> Is impossible for you forever.[2]

C. Journalism: Catherine II, Nikolai Novikov et al.

On June 28, 1762 the Tsar of Russia, Peter III, was quietly dethroned by the ambitious German princess who was his wife, and a few days later met an inglorious end during a drunken brawl in the place of his confinement at the hands of one of his wife's favorite guardsmen. He had allowed himself, as Frederick the Great said scornfully, "to be deposed as a baby is sent to bed." Thus began the "enlightened" reign of Catherine II, the "Semiramis of the North," as her friend Voltaire delighted in calling her.

Catherine was a woman of enormous vitality, inordinate ambition, and very considerable intelligence. She had had a sketchy but rather impressive education, and reportedly had at an early age read through the entire *Dictionnaire philosophique* of Pierre Bayle (1695-97), a monument of what might be called the "pre-enlightenment." It was a formidable task, for Bayle's style is anything but perspicuous. Catherine had been married young to the heir to the Russian throne, whom she despised as a boor and a fool; according to her own account, she had from the beginning cherished the expectation that some day she would herself be sole and autocratic ruler of her adopted land. She had not a drop of Russian blood, but took pains to make herself more Russian than her silly husband, who was by birth only half German, yet ostentatiously despised all things Russian. Catherine was determined, having once attained the power which she coveted, to rule as a model of "enlightened despotism." Russia, she discovered, was still in 1762 being governed under an antique code of laws promulgated in 1648 (the *Ulozhenie* of Alexei Mikhailovich). She determined to remedy this situation, and in a fashion that would exhibit her "enlightenment" to all of Europe. A Legislative Commission, with representatives from all classes except the manorial peasants (the bulk of Russia's population) was convoked, to deliberate on a new law code. To this Commission was submitted the Empress's own "Instruction" *(Nakaz)*—a compilation of glittering generalities, largely pilfered from Montesquieu and Beccaria, and totally without relevance to the peculiar social conditions of Russia. In this document Catherine proclaimed that Russia was a European country, and must of course have a European government; but the size and traditions of the country demanded that this government be autocratic, the only kind that could function in such a country.

Catherine was revolted by many of the aspects of Russian society. The landed gentry, who were the privileged class and her own political support, were crude, ignorant and conservative. Their manners were atrocious, they were superstitious and fanatical, and the younger set, who lived idle lives in the capital, as a result of her own decree of "freedom for the gentry," were empty-headed and useless creatures, who had picked up some of the superficial qualities of their European counterparts, without any of the breeding which went with these. Of course the entire class of gentry lived their parasitic existence through the toil of the millions of enslaved peasants, whose life was hardly above the animal level. This fact, however, Catherine chose to ignore. Serfdom was an essential fact, like autocracy, in the Russian tradition, and must be maintained. She carefully blinded herself to the realities of the peasant situation, but was unpleasantly surprised when her Legislative Commission, instead of remaining, as her Instruction presupposed, on the safely abstract level that she had set, began to discuss such dangerously concrete subjects as peasant destitution, the tyranny of landlords, and even the legality of the serf system as a whole. Obviously the Legislative Commission had been a bad blunder, and Catherine waited only until the outbreak of her first war with Turkey afforded a plausible pretext for suspending its activity. It was adjourned *sine die,* and of course never reconvened.

To combat some of the evils of ignorance and bad manners which she observed in the Russian society around her Catherine determined to employ the offices of satire. The eighteenth century had seen the rebirth of this form of classical literature, chiefly in the prose sketches published in England in the periodicals *The Tatler* (1709-11), *The Spectator* (1711-14) and *The Guardian* (1713) by Joseph Addison and Sir Richard Steele. Catherine was familiar with this literature, and approved of the genial, good-tempered tone of it. Something of the kind, she thought, would have a salutary effect on the crudities of Russian social life.

Among the numerous and diversified talents which Catherine com-placently imagined herself to possess was that of a writer. Her *Instruction* of 1767 was much more of a literary essay than a working "instruction" for a legislative body, and she had in her spare time translated (doubtless with some anonymous help) a French novel that the Sorbonne had condemned for its free-thinking. When the project of a satirical journal along the lines of *The Spectator* took form in her mind, Catherine quite naturally determined to take the leading part in it herself. In this way she hoped to be able to mold public opinion and undo some of the damage which the fiasco of the Legislative Commission had done. Thus in the early part of 1769 she created Russia's first important literary periodical, under the nominal editorship of G.V. Kozitsky, Catherine's private secretary. It was innocently entitled *Vsiakaia Vsiachina, All Kinds of Things,* and its avowed purpose was to follow the Horatian motto "Ridendo castigat mores," "It corrects manners by laughing [at them]." She attached great importance, as we shall see, to the "ridendo." How much of the actual writing of the journal was done by Catherine herself is uncertain, but probably a great deal of it. Since her own command of Russian, despite assiduous effort, remained inadequate, she certainly employed here, as later in her comedies, the services of one or more discreet editors. With surprising unawareness of possible consequences she allowed herself in the first issue of her periodical to throw out a general invitation to other journalists to follow her lead: "I see in the future, I see an endless tribe of *All Kinds of Things.* I see that she will be followed by children, both legitimate and illegitimate."[3] Actually, for some golden months in 1769 the eternal Russian press censorship was lifted and a host of journalistic children and grandchildren of Catherine's periodical made their appearance. Most of these were extremely ephemeral and of little importance. M.D. Chulkov, better known for his Defoeish novel *The Comely Cook, or The Adventures of a Debauched Woman,* to which we shall return, began a weekly *This and That.* His rival V.G. Ruban issued a short-lived parody entitled *Neither This nor That, in Prose and Verse. The Medley (Smes'),* a weekly, and *Hell's Post,* a monthly, were handled with great legerdemain by Fedor A. Emin, an adventurer and extremely prolific (and extremely bad) novelist. In early May of 1769 came out what proved to be the most important of the brood, Novikov's *The Drone (Truten')*. Both of Emin's journals cavalierly disregarded Catherine's predilection for a gently smiling satire, and inveighed against "gentlemen of the nobility," "whose tribe is like the leech, which fattens by sucking the bloody sweat of the poor people."[4] His *Hell's Post,* which has the subtitle "Correspondence of a Lame Devil with a Crooked One," employs a device purloined from Lesage's *Le Diable boiteux,* with some hints from Montesquieu's *Lettres persanes:* one of the diabolic correspondents regales the other with intimate glimpses he has had of the life of the nobility when he has, unknown to the occupants, temporarily unroofed their houses!

Emin's boldness in calling attention to the iniquities of the serf system is symptomatic of Catherine's general failure to hold in line the numerous periodicals which her initial invitation had so incautiously called into being. The benevolent tone of *All Kinds of Things*, the self-styled "grandmother" of this brood, began to be replaced by a certain asperity, especially in articles directed toward Novikov's *Drone,* which more than any other offended against Catherine's demand that satire should be gentle and entirely general in nature. Addison and Steele in the English model had been careful to keep their social criticism on a purely abstract level, relying for their effect on the elegant wit of their style: "In the English *Spectator*," wrote Catherine (or her editor), "there is no want of wit, and *All Kinds of Things* follows after this." Such a program would exclude any ill-tempered attacks, either on individuals or classes; instead of an indignant tongue-lashing, a gentle ribbing should suffice. In practice, however, Catherine's "satire" was rendered even more innocuous by being in large part mere translation or adaptation from French or English models, and completely alien to the realities of Russian life.[5]

Catherine's chief antagonist proved to be Nikolai Ivanovich Novikov (1744-1818), editor of *The Drone*. Novikov was a member of the gentry by birth, with estates in the neighborhood of Moscow. He studied in the gymnasium attached to Moscow University, while, according to the custom of the time, being at the same time on the roster of one of the Guards Regiments. His regiment took part in the uprising of 1762 which set Catherine on the throne, and he received a promotion from the grateful Empress. A few years later he became involved in book publishing, an enterprise which he continued with the greatest success until his final incarceration in 1792. It is said that a third of the books published in Catherine's reign issued from Novikov's presses. From this congenial occupation Novikov was temporarily removed by Catherine's invitation to participate in the deliberations of the Legislative Commission (1767). The deliberations came to nothing, but undoubtedly contributed a great deal to opening the eyes of a sensitive person such as Novikov to the horrors of serfdom. Thenceforth he determined to devote his efforts to combatting this iniquity. The perfect opportunity was afforded him by Catherine's invitation to follow her lead into the field of satirical journalism.

To Novikov Catherine's ladylike and kid-glove handling of social questions was both futile and hypocritical. His *The Drone,* founded a few months after Catherine's ancestral periodical, aimed from the beginning to give more vigorous treatment. The very name was a patent reference to the useless and parasitic gentry, living on the labor of the workers of the hive. As an epigraph for his journal Novikov took a line from one of Sumarokov's fables: "They labor, and you eat up their toil." Sumarokov was also in an indirect way, responsible for the journal's title, for *The Drone* was obviously a companion to the older man's *Trudoliubivaia Pchela, The Labor-loving Bee* (1759), Russia's earliest private periodical. Indeed, it was often thought at the time that the illustrious dramatist himself had some part in the writing of *The Drone,* although this is probably not the case. Novikov certainly had collaborators, among them such important names as Ablesimov, the opera-librettist; the indefatigable Emin, the caustic playwright Denis Fonvizin, and Alexander Radishchev. Some of these men, like Novikov himself, were destined in Catherine's later and more tyrannical years to suffer for their outspokenness. Fonvizin was refused permission ever to have any of his writings. printed, after he had published some impudent "Questions" addressed to Catherine on some rather touchy subjects; Novikov spent the period from 1792 until Catherine's death in 1796 in the Petropavlovsk prison; and Radishchev was at first condemned to death for the attack made on the institution of serfdom in his *Journey from St. Petersburg to Moscow.* The sentence was "graciously" commuted to banishment to Siberia in 1790. Like Novikov, the poet was released from Catherine's benevolent chastisement only by her death and the general annulling of her acts by her vindictive son. But these were the reactions of a later and more arbitrary Catherine, alarmed to the point of mania by the French Revolution. Twenty years before 1789 she was still willing to play—under her own rules, to be sure—at liberalism.

Novikov's preferred target in *The Drone* was the parasitic nobility.[6] He devised several seemingly harmless ways of reaching them; thus, in the guise of "news items" from various parts of the country anecdotes concerning foolish or vicious "gentlemen" were recounted, as for example in issue 29 an encounter with a young nobleman just back from study at a German university, who professed to have majored in philosophy. "And what is philosophy?" his interlocutor asked. "Philosophy is nothing but foolishness," was the reply. "Aha!" said the other, "Then I see that you have spent your time very profitably, since you are evidently a perfect philosopher."[7] Another, and particularly effective device, which led in 1770 to a direct reprimand from the Empress, was that of publishing what were allegedly extracts from actual letters, e.g., from estate stewards to their masters, with detailed and specific figures on the burdens of quit-rent, *bar-shchina,* and other landlord exactions imposed on the peasants. Sometimes there would be "advertisements," such as the following: "In a certain law-court there is need of ten poods of justice; anyone desiring to contract to supply this, can apply at the said place."[8] One of the early devices employed was that of "health hints" ostensibly addressed by a physician to a corre-spondent. Thus, in issue 24, "Mr. Unreason" ["Gospodin Bezrasud"] receives this prescription for his complaint:

UNREASON is sick with the idea that peasants aren't human beings, but peasants; as to what peasants are, he knows of this only because they are his enserfed slaves. This is exactly how he behaves with them, collecting from them a heavy tribute, called the quit-rent [obrok]. With them he not only never exchanges a word, but never even acknowledges them with an inclination of the head, when they in Oriental fashion prostrate themselves to the ground before him. Then he thinks: 'I'm the master, they're my slaves. They were created in order to endure every kind of deprivation, to work day and night and carry out my will by punctual payment of the quit-rent. Remem-bering my and their conditions, they must tremble before my sight.' As a supplement to this he adds that "In the sweat of thy brow shalt thou eat bread," was said pre-cisely about the peasants. The poor peasants do not venture to love him like a father, but seeing in him their tyrant, tremble before him. They work day and night, but for all this barely have the wherewithal to meet their daily needs, for the reason that they must of necessity pay their lord's taxes. They say: 'This doesn't belong to me, but to God and the master.' The Most High blesses their work and rewards them, but UN-REASON plunders them. Unreasoning one! Can it be that you have forgotten that you were created a man? Can it be that you are disdaining yourself in the form of the pea-sants, your slaves? I suppose you don't realize that between your slaves and men there is a greater likeness than between you and a man? Imagine the condition of your slaves: it is hard, even without aggravation; but when you disdain those who, for the satis-faction of your passions toil almost without respite, do not dare even think they are human beings, but regard themselves as condemned for the sins of their fathers, since they see other brothers of their enjoying their coveted quiet with landowners who are fathers to them, and who do not envy the happiness of anyone on earth because they are fortunate in their own calling—consider this, how real human beings must disdain you—men who are masters, masters who are fathers of children, and not, like you, masters of slaves. They *do* disdain you as a monster of mankind, one who converts a necessary subordination into the intolerable yoke of slavery. But UNREASON is always asserting: 'I'm the master, they're my slaves, I'm a man, they're peasants.' For this deadly disease:

THE PRESCRIPTION

UNREASON must twice every day inspect the bones of masters and the bones of pea-sants until such time as he finds a difference between the bones of masters and those of peasants."[9]

This was decidedly not the kind of tone which Catherine had expected of Russia's "Spectators" and "Tatlers," and *All Kinds of Things* forthwith began to call her unruly "children and grandchildren" back into line. After the appearance of the first issue of *The Drone,* which already gave signs of a greater asperity than she cared for, Catherine's journal published what purported to be an answer to a very harsh letter (not published) from a "Mr. A." (Issue 52, May 1).[10] Mr. A. is ironically advised to hold his letter until "a lexicon has been compiled of all human weaknesses and of all the inadequacies of the various governments in the world." "Love of humanity and gentleness" are missing from such satire as Mr. A's, and Catherine points out: "It seems to us that his [i.e., Mr. A's] love for his neighbor aims at correction rather than at indulgence and love for humanity; but he who sees only vices without having love is incapable of giving admonitions to another." The article ends with the announcement that the editor "does not like melancholy letters," and hence will not print Mr. A's communication. Shortly after this *All Kinds of Things* published a letter from a certain Athenogenes Perochinov (his last name means "Pen-Whittler"), whose sentiments on satire's function as a purveyor of "innocent merriment" and no more are obviously those of Catherine herself.[11] The author of the letter begins with the declaration: "Dear Sir: I am of a very merry disposition and laugh a great deal." He goes on to recount an occasion when "he laughed at a man until his sides ached from it." The person who occasioned this Homeric outburst was a young fellow who seemed to find everything wrong with the world. "Everywhere he would see crimes, where others, not having such motives as his, could see at most weaknesses—and weaknesses are extremely common to mankind." Finally one of the company had enough of this, and silenced the critic with this sally: "My dear sir, you have extreme hatred for your neighbor. The tyrant Caligula in his madness used to say that he was sorry that the whole human race did not have one single head, so that it could be cut off at once. Are you not of the same opinion?" "Scribbler" ends his epistle with a set of "rules" which he and the rest of the group agreed upon after the new Caligula had departed: "First: never to call weaknesses vices; second: to maintain a philanthropic spirit in all cases; third: not to imagine that perfect men can ever be found, and therefore: fourth: to beg God to give us a spirit of meekness and humility." Later, after thinking the matter over in private, "Scribbler" adds two more rules of his own: "Fifth: that henceforth no one should judge someone for something that he does not understand; and sixth: that no one should imagine that he alone is able to set the whole world right."

Reasonable and indeed admirable as these rules might seem on the surface, they were obviously designed to prevent the airing of unpalatable truths about the relations of landlords and peasants. Novikov was not to be satisfied with such inoffensive generalities. Under date of May 9, 1769 (issue 5) *The Drone* published a letter purporting to be from one "Pravduliubov" ["Truth-Lover"] [12]:

Mr. Drone!
    Your second issue was not written in accord with your granny's (i.e., *All Kinds*

of Things) [the title of the journal has a feminine surname ending in Russian] rules. I myself am of the opinion that human weaknesses are deserving of pity—not, however, of praise; and I shall never think that your granny was not at that time distorting her thought and spirit in giving it out on her page 140, issue 52, that it is more praiseworthy to have indulgence for vices than to try to correct them. Many people of weak conscience never mention the name of vice without adding love of humanity to it. They say that weaknesses are common to men and must be covered by love of humanity. Thus they have stitched a cloak for vices out of love for humanity; such peoples' love of humanity might better be called love of vice. In my opinion the man shows more love of humanity who tries to correct vices than the man who shows indulgence to them, or (to put it in Russian) winks at them; and if they dare to write that a teacher who does not have love for weaknesses will be unable to correct them, then I can say with the best foundation that one who *does* have love for vices will never correct them. I also did not like the afore-mentioned lady's first rule, to wit, that weaknesses should not by any means be called vices—as though Ioann and Ivan were not one and the same. About the weakness of the human body we shall not try to judge, for I am not a physician, and she is not a midwife; but a weak and supple soul can be bent in any direction. Indeed, I do not know what in that lady's estimation is meant by "weakness." Nowadays it is generally called a "weakness" to whisper love in someone's ear—that is, the ear of someone else's wife or daughter. From this supposed "weakness" come these results: we corrupt the house into which we come, and make husband quarrel with wife and father with daughter—and I suppose this isn't a crime? Whoever judges more strictly about this than I, and in accord with the merits of the case, will rightfully call it even a breach of the law. Love of money is the same kind of "weakness"; why is it excusable for a weak man to take bribes and enrich himself with pilfering? Drunkenness is also a weakness, or by now, even a habit; but a drunken man can beat his wife and children half to death and come to blows with his own loyal friend. In a word, neither in weakness nor in vice can I see either anything good, or any distinction. Weakness and vice are in my opinion all one; and breach of the law is another matter.

At the end of her issue your granny praises those writers who only try to gratify everyone; but *you* didn't afford this rule any very large gratification in not denouncing crooked bureaucrats and a procurator who exercises his cleverness out of season. I don't mean to urge you on, as the rest are doing, to the continuation of this labor, or to sing your praises; the beast is known by its claws. I will only say this, that of your granny's entire brood, you are the first to whom I have written a letter. Maybe the gentlemen my critics will say that for me, a drone, it is extremely fitting to have dealings with *The Drone;* but for me it is more reasonable and far more praiseworthy to be a drone, doing damage to the foolish labors of others, than such a bee as flits over all places without being able to collect or find anything. I should have liked to send this letter to Madam your granny; but she doesn't like to read melancholy letters, and in this letter, I presume, she will find nothing of such a kind that her sides should ache for three days with laughing at it.

Your obedient servant,
Pravduliubov

May 9, 1769.

Catherine's imperial feathers were ruffled by Mr. Pravduliubov's impertinent letter, and her reply, written without any of the usual humorous pseudonyms, lashes out at "the scoldings printed in *The Drone* under its fifth issue, to which we do not mean to reply, since we annihilate them." The sense of this curious phrase is not altogether clear; perhaps Catherine really did not know Russian well enough, and simply used a very bad choice of words, as Novikov maliciously suggested in his answer. She went on to suggest that her "melancholy" opponent, Mr. Pravduliubov, might do well to take a cure. It might have been expected that Novikov, seeing his adversary so patently losing her temper, and realizing as he did without a question, her identity, might have taken alarm and withdrawn from the fray. Instead he was only emboldened to a new attack, in which he most impudently assailed the Empress in some rather sensitive places. Since the title of her journal was feminine, and had even labeled itself at the outset as the metaphorical "grandmother" of all the other journals, Novikov continued to refer to his adversary in the feminine gender, and even, no doubt particularly gallingly, as "an elderly lady." Catherine's foreign origin, moreover, and her incomplete mastery of Russian also receive due attention. In the June 16th issue of *The Drone* appeared the following letter from Mr. Pravduliubov:[13]

Mr. Editor:

Madam *All Kinds of Things* has become indignant with us, and refers to our ethical judgments as "scoldings." But here I see that she is less at fault than I supposed. Her entire fault consists in her not knowing how to express herself in Russian, and in her inability entirely to understand writing in Russian; this fault is peculiar to many of our writers.

From the words which she employs in Number 52 a Russian can conclude nothing else but that Mr. A. is right and that Madam *All Kinds of Things* criticized him improperly.

In the fifth issue of *The Drone* nothing was written, as Madam *All Kinds of Things* imagines, either against mercy or against indulgence; and the public, to which I appeal, is able to judge of this. If I wrote that the man who corrects vices is a greater lover of humanity than the one who winks at them, do I not know how by such an explanation I have been able to move mercy? It is evident that Madam *All Kinds of Things* has been so spoiled by praises that she now considers it a crime if anyone does not praise her.

I don't know for what reason she designates my letter as "scolding." Scolding is abuse, expressed in low words; but in my previous letter, which so grated on the heart of this elderly lady, there is nothing of knouts or gallows, or other expressions revolting to the ear, such as are found in *her* journal.

Madam *All Kinds of Things* has written that she is annihilating the fifth issue of *The Drone*. This too is not a Russian expression. To annihilate, i.e., 'to reduce to nothing,' is a word proper to autocracy; but such trifles as her issues are have no kind of authority. Supreme authority annihilates any kind of right belonging to others. But with Madam *All Kinds of Things* it would have been enough to have written that she despises, not "annihilates," my criticism. The majority of these issues is carried around from hand to hand, and so it is impossible for her to "annihilate" them all.

She asserts that I have a bad heart, because, in her belief, I exclude by my judgments both indulgence and mercy. I supposed I had written clearly that human weaknesses are deserving of pity, but that they require correction, not connivance; accordingly, I supposed that this explanation of mine, for anyone who knows the Russian language and the truth, could not seem contrary to either justice or mercy. As to her advice to me, to take a cure, I don't know whether it would be more appropriate for me or that lady to do so. After saying that she did not mean to reply to the fifth issue of *The Drone*, she did reply to it, with all her heart and mind, and in this letter all her gall was apparent. When she forgets herself, and has such a rheum that she often spits where she doesn't intend, it seems that to purify her thoughts and her interior it would not be unprofitable for her to take a cure!

This lady has designated my intent as stupid, because she did not understand its moral principles. To this I reply: my eyes too do not see what does not exist. I am quite content that Madam *All Kinds of Things* has delivered me to the judgment of the public. The public will see from our future letters which of us is right.

Your obedient servant,
Pravduliubov

June 6, 1769.

Perhaps Novikov had some misgivings about possible "annihilation" if his adversary should become thoroughly aroused, for he managed to protect himself in an audacious and quite ingenious fashion. In the following issue of *The Drone* appeared another "letter to the editor," from a certain Chistoserdov ["Open-Hearted"],[14] ostensibly complaining of the indecent liberties which the all too tolerant government (i.e., Catherine herself) was permitting the satirists. Referring to the editor of *The Drone,* Chistoserdov cites the feelings of the aggrieved gentry, who say: "This author isn't sitting in his own sleigh. He is beginning to write satires against people of the court, eminent noblemen, ladies, well-known judges—everybody. Such boldness is nothing else but audacity.... In olden times they would have sent him off to labor for the profit of the government, and describe the manners of any realm you please among the Russian possessions. But now they have given him liberty to write and make fun of eminent people, and they do not punish such satires." Thus, while belaboring Catherine in her masquerade, the satirist succeeded at the same time in complimenting her for her tolerance in letting him do so!

The battle over the proper scope and tone of satire, thus begun by the chief contestants, was presently joined by others of *All Kinds of Things* ephemeral progeny. Chulkov in *This and That* came gallantly (and scarcely disinterestedly) to the Empress's assistance, while the redoubtable Emin in *The Medley* rallied strongly to the defense of the *The Drone.* In the face of the not inconsiderable tempest she had conjured up, the "grandmotherly" Catherine thought it politic to retire, and toward the end of 1769 was inveighing in a stern and by no means indulgent tone against corrupt judges and bribe-taking bureaucrats, urging them to "repent while there is yet time," before an aggrieved government should take steps against them. *The Drone* had apparently won, even to the point of bringing his opponent around to the same stern and censorious position as his own. A very concrete indication of this can be seen in the comparative figures of printings. The first number of *All Kinds of Things* was printed, rather optimistically, in 1500 copies; by the thirteenth number, this had been reduced to 1000, and by the end of the year to a mere 500. During the same period *The Drone,* which had begun with 600 copies, rose to 800 with its ninth number, and with its thirteenth, at the end of the year, to 1200. Of course Catherine's livelihood was not dependent on the sales figures, but the trend may have caused her some pique.

The last word, however, still lay with the "supreme authority" which Novikov had so adroitly and audaciously challenged. Apparently the censor began his interrupted work with the beginning of 1770, for all the rest of the journals disappeared, leaving only the "grandmother" herself and *The Drone*. As for the latter, its continued existence had clearly been bought at the price of complete capitulation. The editor announced sadly at the beginning of the year: "I beg to inform Mr. Pravduliubov that henceforth I shall not print any more such letters as his." With the usual journalistic ventriloquism, Novikov under mask of one of his readers, expostulates against the innocuous nature of the new *Drone*[15]: "Mr. Drone! What the devil! What has happened to you? You have become entirely different, as though you had grown tired of having us all praise you, and had taken a notion to hear how we would all begin to find fault with you.... Please tell me for what reason you have altered last year's plan, of publishing satirical articles." The "reader" concludes his attack with the ominous observation that his bookseller has informed him that the new year's issues are not selling half as well as those of the previous year, and admonishes the editor: "Please listen to me, and to many others with me. If you don't, then good-bye *Drone*." Good-bye it was, for even with the emasculated journal of 1770 the censor's office had its way, and on April 27 the editor sadly informed his readers of *The Drone's* demise. Catherine herself had suspended publication of *All Kinds of Things* at about the same date.

Despite this sharp set-back, Novikov started another journal in the same year, 1770. The new venture was a monthly called *The Twaddler [Pustomelia]*, under the nominal editorship of a broker named Foka, since Catherine's closure of *The Drone* made it impossible for Novikov himself to reappear at once in the lime-light. *The Twaddler,* however, lasted for only two months, its end being hastened by a combination of circumstances. Novikov's hand in it was probably soon recognized; and an article in the second number, entitled "Testament of the Chinese Khan Yundzhin to His Son," the substance of which consisted of fatherly advice from the dying Khan to his heir apparent, touched closely enough on the Russian situation, as Pavel Petrovich was approaching his sixteenth birthday, to alarm Catherine. *The Twaddler* had no third issue.[16]

Even with this Novikov did not give up. His third venture *The Portrait-Painter [Zhivopisets]* began in April 1772 and lasted until June, 1773. Again Novikov's interest in the periodical (a weekly) was concealed by a "front man" as editor. The new journal had a curious beginning. In 1772 Catherine's literary ambitions found a new outlet, and a prose comedy entitled *O vremia* (Cicero's "O the Times!") was printed and presented on the stage. The piece was produced anonymously, but was actually written by the imperial authoress herself. It was, to be sure, freely "adapted" from a German original of Christian Furchtegott Gellert called *The Devout Lady (Die Betschwester)*, and its relevance to Russian life was not entirely obvious. It depicted the usual comic situation of young love thwarted but eventually triumphant. The heroine's grandmother is in this case the obstacle in the path, and the principal character of the play; her name, Khanzhakina ("Mrs. Hypocrite") suffices to characterize her, and she is abetted by two elderly cronies, Viestnikova ("Mrs. Gossip") and Chudikina ("Mrs. Miracle"). The satire is directed against the endless devotions of Khanzhakina, which she utilizes so effectively as an excuse for evading unwanted callers, particularly creditors. Although amusing in a mild way, it can scarcely be said to contribute a great deal to either Russian literature or Catherine's reputation.

Novikov, silent since the end of *The Drone*, seized the opportunity afforded by the appearance of *O Vremia* to begin publication of a new journal. Knowing perfectly well who was the author of the new comedy, the satirist disingenuously dedicated his weekly "To the unknown gentleman who is the author of the comedy 'O the Times!'," and whose pen, he proclaimed, was "worthy of rivalry with that of Molière." In his introductory article Novikov,[17] without of course revealing himself as in any way connected with the defunct *Drone*, states that hitherto he has been too shy to bring any of his own satirical views before the public, but that now, emboldened by the heroic example of "the unknown gentleman," he has determined to do so. It is really, of course, perfectly safe, for "such noble daring [as that of the unknown gentleman] has no reason to fear any persecution at the time when the wise Catherine rules over us, to the benefaction of the whole human race." In a final bit of audacity, the editor of *The Portrait-Painter* implored "the unknown gentleman" to deign to be a contributor to his journal! Catherine, always susceptible to flattery, even as gross as this, was entirely taken in, and wrote a gracious letter to the editor of *The Portrait-Painter*, whom of course she did not suspect of being the same as her former rival of *The Drone*, that she would be delighted to contribute to subsequent issues. Thus began Novikov's third journalistic venture, which was terminated in the middle of July, 1773, during the general repression which was Catherine's answer to the Pugachev uprising.

During the period of somewhat over a year of its existence, *The Portrait-Painter* printed some noteworthy satirical articles. The tone was at first very mild and conciliatory, but as early as the fifth number (May 10, 1772) appeared an anonymous contribution headed "Fragment from a Journey to—by I.... T...."[18] It has been very plausibly conjectured that the author of this piece is no other than Alexander Radishchev; the similarities with Radishchev's later famous *Journey from St. Petersburg to Moscow* are obvious. A few extracts will show the vigor of the piece; the "Fragment," which a note at the end of the first installment identifies as submitted by "Mr. I.T.," purports to be "Chapter XIV" of what must be supposed to be a fairly lengthy novelistic piece along the lines of Laurence Sterne's *Sentimental Journey Through France and Italy* (1768). The first installment (May 10, issue 5) was followed by the second and final one in issue 14 (July 12, 1772). The author is apparently visiting various sections of Russia and noting the conditions of the peasantry. In the course of his journey he encounters "Ruination Village" ("Razorennaia derevnia"):

"Ruination Village" is situated in the lowest and swampiest region. About twenty households, crowded one beside another, are fenced with dried wattle and covered from one end to the other with nothing but straw. What a hapless sacrifice, dedicated by their masters' carelessness, to the cruelty of the flame! The cottages, or better, the poor, tumble-down huts, present the appearance to the eye of a settlement abandoned by men. The street is covered with mud, slime, and filth of every sort, which dries up only in the winter season. Upon my entrance into this abode of lamentation, I saw not a single human being. The day was hot; I was traveling in an open calash; the dust and heat so incommoded me on the road that I hastened to one of these tumble-down huts to rest a little. My driver stopped at the gate of one poor little building, saying that this was the best in the whole hamlet and that its owner was better off than all the rest, because he owned a cow. We knocked a long time at the gate, but it was not opened to us. A dog, chained in the yard, seemed by his subdued and husky barking to be letting us know that he had nothing to guard. The driver got out in impatience, climbed over the gate and opened it. My calash was driven into a muddy courtyard, floored with straw (if it is possible to floor a muddy, marshy place), and I entered the cottage by the half-opened door. A miasmic breath of every kind of filth, and extraordinary heat, and the buzzing of a countless multitude of flies drove me away, but the wailing of three abandoned babies kept me there. I hurried to give assistance to these hapless creatures. I approached the baskets, attached with cords to poles, in which the abandoned infants lay without any supervision, and saw that one had let fall his bottle with milk; I set it right, and he became quiet. The second I found turned over with his face to a pillow of the coarsest canvas, stuffed with straw. I immediately turned him over and saw that without this timely aid he would certainly have died, for he was not merely blue in the face, but had turned quite black and was in the very hands of death. Soon he too became quiet. Approaching the third, I saw that he had become unswaddled, a multitude of flies was covering his face and body, and mercilessly tormenting the baby. The straw on which he was lying also pricked him, and he was putting up a piercing scream. I gave my service to this one too, chased away the flies, swaddled him with another—dirty, but at least dry—diaper, which was hanging in the cottage, straightened out the straw, which he in his tossing around had stirred up with his feet; he too became silent. Looking on these infants, and considering the poverty of these peoples' existence, I exclaimed: "O hard-hearted tyrant, who takes from the peasants their daily bread and their last repose! Behold, what do these infants require! One is bound hand and foot; will he make complaint of this? No, he looks quietly at his own chains. What does he require? The only absolute necessity is nourishment. Another puts up a wail only that he should not be deprived of his life. The third was wailing to humanity not to torment him. Scream, poor creatures," said I, shedding tears, "Make your complaints! Enjoy this last satisfaction in babyhood; when you are men, you will be deprived of even this consolation. O sun, who illuminest this hamlet with the rays of thine abundance, look down on these unfortunates!"

The extract continues with the discovery of one peasant lad, hidden in the village, who reports that the rest of the inhabitants have fled on seeing the author's calash approaching, in the belief that it must be "their squire," whom they all fear as a heartless tyrant. Finally a few children are lured to come near the calash, but retreat screaming when they see the author's red caftan: "Yes! What were we afraid of... you've deceived us... This squire has on a red caftan... It must be our squire... He'll whip us." At this the visitor bursts out: "Behold the fruits of cruelty and terror, O you evil-hearted and cruel masters! You have come to such a degree of wretchedness that men of your own kind fear you as they would wild beasts!" The children are presently pacified with the present of a penny apiece and some small pastries.

The second installment begins with an ironical description of the coming of evening, which "summons all from labor to rest. Meanwhile the wealthy favorites of Plutus, having spent their whole day in gaiety and banquetting, were preparing themselves for new diversions." The various ignoble categories of townspeople are passed in review: "the wicked judge and worthless shyster," "jealous husbands and lovers," "aged coquettes," etc. "Gamblers were gathering for their all-night vigil over the card tables and there, losing honor, conscience and love for their neighbor, were preparing to cheat and ruin rich simpletons with all manner of inadmissible means. Other gamblers were carrying in their pockets the labors and sweat of their peasants for a whole year, and making ready to stake these on a card." "And the peasants, my hosts, were returning from the fields in dust and sweat, exhausted and happy that for the caprice of one man they had all done a great deal of work during the past day." In the ensuing conversation with these peasants, the author learns that although the next day is Sunday, they will not be able to rest, for then is the only opportunity they have of getting in their own grain—all the rest of the week they must harvest the fields of their master. The "Journey," according to the final paragraph, is to be resumed the next day with a visit to "Fortunate" village. If such a chapter was ever written, *The Portrait-Painter* did not publish it.

There are a number of points in "Mr. I.T.'s Journey to—" that should be noted. One, of course, is the merciless realism of the piece—a feature most uncommon in eighteenth century writing, which usually occupies an exalted realm far above such ugly realities as mud, stench, flies, and screaming babies. The second is the symbolic use to which the author puts these unfortunate babies. It is, perhaps, hardly to be expected of even the prolific Russian peasant that one hut will hold *three* infants; but these three, in their various unhappy predicaments, are utilized as symbols for the plight of the peasant class in general: the one is unable to get the food he needs for existence; the second, bound hand and foot, is unable without help even to save his life; (in this regard, it should be said in explanation that these babies, according to a custom that was universal throughout Europe at the time, are "swaddled," that is, wrapped like cocoons in yards of cloth that immobilize both arms and legs; it was not until the publication of Rousseau's influential didactic novel *Emile* (1762) that this barbaric custom began to be given up. Russian peasants, however, were not readers of Jean-Jacques!). The third child is not in danger of death from starvation or imprisonment, but finds his life a torment from the flies and straw. And of course, as the author exclaims in his pathetic apostrophe to the three, they may even protest against the horrible conditions of their existence only while they are infants—as grown men even protest is a comfort denied them.

Whether or not the "Fragment" is actually the work of Radishchev (and certainty on this matter is unlikely ever to be reached), there is no doubt that the author is a writer of very great power and ability, and it is a great pity that the "Fragment" has to remain that. The piece is not merely a most effective bit of satirical propaganda; it is also a monument of Russian narrative prose.

A second and even bolder blast against serfdom followed hard on the heels of the second installment of the "Fragment." In number 15 (July 19, 1772) of *The Portrait-Painter* appeared the following[19]:

Mr. Portrait-Painter!
  Please find room in your pages for the following letter, if possible; its content, it seems, deserves that you fulfil the request of

Your Obedient Servant,
P*** R***

The initials P*** R*** are usually interpreted as standing for the words *Pisatel' Russkij* i.e., "Russian Writer." Who this "Russian writer" may have been remains as mysterious as the identity of the author I.T. of the Fragment." Novikov himself may have composed the four letters which were published in issues 15, 23 and 24 of *The Portrait-Painter;* but there is also a possibility that these may have been the work of the dramatist Denis Fonvizin, who is known to have been a collaborator of Novikov. Certainly there is a striking similarity between the unlovely "gentlemen's nest" depicted in the "Letters to Falalei" and the Prostakov household which is the setting of Fonvizin's famous comedy *The Minor (Nedorosl').*

The first letter which P*** R*** submits to the editor of *The Portrait-Painter,* purports to be "From a Provincial Gentleman to His Son." The son's name is Falalei, and he appears to be a minor member of the St. Petersburg bureaucracy. His father, Trifon Pankratievich, writes him an admonitory letter, the chief point of which is to get the young man to chuck the service and come home to an idle life in the country. In the course of the letter the write naively reveals a great deal about his narrow and amoral outlook on life. In connection with a wonder-working icon which Falalei's grandfather had bought for considerable farm produce from an extortionate priest, Trifon writes: "Don't hold this against the deceased, my light! He never used to give anything that was his for nothing; your grandfather's sins, my light, cost him pretty dear. If he, the deceased, had had less truck with the priests there would have been more left for us." There follow some grumblings about the newly instituted government monopoly on distilled spirits, and then remarks about the "freedom of the gentry" originally proclaimed by Peter III ten years before. "Whatever you say, the lives of us gentlemen at the present time are pretty hard. They say the gentry have been given freedom; the devil take it (forgive me, Lord!), what kind of freedom? They've given us freedom, but one can't do anything the way he wants to—you can't even take land away from your neighbor!" Things were better in the old days, when all you had to do was keep on the right side of the local judge, and you could do whatever you pleased. If you wanted to be released from compulsory state service, "even if one weren't free to leave it then, there were always the doctors. You'd take him a lamb wrapped in paper, and the judge another, and they'd retire you for disability. And it used to be, as soon as you got back to your country place, you'd make up for what you'd lost—provided you had your wits about you, knew the ways of the law, and didn't make a peep against the neighbors. That was life! You don't remember this, Falaleiushka."

Presently comes mention of Falalei's sister Varya, who is having to "learn grammar" with the local priest, because otherwise she won't be permitted to marry (a law of Peter the Great made it obligatory for members of the gentry class to be able to read and write before they could marry; it is this burdensome law that keeps Fonvizin's great booby Mitrofan still a "minor"!). Trifon, it seems, has heard terrible rumors about things in St. Petersburg—they're even thinking of building a bell-tower higher than Ivan the Great! "It's all the doings of those damned heathens! There's no living with the Germans! If we keep on associating with them the way we're doing, then we'll end up in hell with them." "Nowadays it isn't even forbidden to go overseas—but in the *Book of Canon Law [Kormchaia Kniga]* there is laid down an anathema for this... Only you mustn't take bribes, or charge interest above a stated amount... And yet there isn't a thing written about this in the Canon Law Book." Mention of money leads the writer on to the landowner's usual means of enrichment: "You can skin the hide off your peasants, and you won't be much the gainer.... Five days a week they work for you—and how much can they get done in five days? I flog them unmercifully, but still there's no profit in it. Every year the peasants get poorer and poorer; the Lord must be angry with us." Then the subject changes, and Trifon mentions that an apparently literate neighbor reports about some "Portrait-Painter" who has been publishing dreadful things in the capital: "What sort of 'Portrait-Painter' is this who has appeared among you? Some kind of German—no Orthodox Christian would ever have written so. He says the landowners torture the peasants, and he calls them tyrants! Doesn't the damned fool know that 'tyrants' lived in olden times and tortured the saints?.... Certainly our muzhiks aren't saints, so how can we be 'tyrants'?" "They work for us, and we flog them if they get lazy—and so we're even. What are they peasants for? It's a peasant's business to work

177

without a let-up."

In what is apparently an attempt to conciliate Catherine in spite of his frank exposure of the conditions in rural Russia, the unknown author then has Trifon contrast the shockingly lax treatment of his peasants by Grigory Orlov, one of Catherine's lovers, with the way they should be treated: "Do you know how much apiece he gets from them? [i.e., in quit-rent] . It's a shame to say it—a ruble and a half a soul.... And how rich his muzhiks are! They live as they please, without a care, richer than the said nobleman.... If that village were mine, I'd get thirty rubles apiece from them; and I wouldn't let them go freely out into the world." Then comes some more sighing over the "good old days": "Yes, sir! Our old great barons have died out! Those were real men; they used to flay the hide not only off their own, but off other people's peasants. They used to live and be kings; they got along like cheese in butter. Whether a thing belonged to the Tsar, or the gentry, or the merchants—it was all theirs. They grabbed things from everyone but God, and they came close to taking from Him too." The letter ends with the plea to Falalei to retire from the service and come home; his favorite hunting-dog Naletka is still around, although she nearly got bitten by a mad dog. "Your [mother] Sidorovna almost took the hide off everyone; she's a card! That's what I love about her—when she makes up her mind to do a flogging, she finishes the job!"

Issue number 23[20] of *The Portrait-Painter* contained a short letter from "Falalei," explaining that he was at first angry at seeing his father's letter aired in public, but then, enraged by the threats contained in the old man's second letter, he had decided to give the editor the whole corre-spondence. This consists of a second letter from Trifon Pankratievich, Fala-lei's father; one from his mother Akulina Sidorovna, and one from his uncle Ermolai Terentievich.

The father's letter begins with denunciations for publishing his previous letter, and making him a laughing stock to his neighbors. "I wrote to you, damn you, in admonition, and you give this letter to be printed! You've destroyed my life, you Satan! I could go out of my mind!" Falalei is re-minded that his father is still legally authorized to administer corporal punish-ment, and even more: "I have a right over even your life, which you've evi-dently forgotten. I think I've told you many times that if a father or mother beat their son even to death, for this only ecclesiastical penance is laid down.... Lent isn't far away, you know, and it wouldn't be hard for me to do a bit of fasting." After this warning, Trifon relents—"at your mother's request—but if it hadn't been for her, I'd have given you something to re-member me by. I wouldn't have listened even to her, if it weren't that she is sick unto death." Then follows a renewed plea to retire from the service and return home—there's always the possibility, that, with a war on (the Turkish war, presumably) the young man may be sent off with the army—"one has a hand shot off, another his legs, another his head; is it so pleasant for fathers

178

to look on their sons mutilated?" And if Falalei does come home, his father has provided a bride for him: "The girl isn't poor, she knows how to read and write, and more than that, she's a good manager.... I almost forgot to tell you that your affianced bride is the niece of our governor. Now this, you know, is no joke, my dear: all our disputes will be judged in our favor, and you and I will cut away those neighbors' lands right up to their very threshing-floors! That's what I call pleasant! They won't have enough left to let their hens run loose in." Uncle Ermolai agrees that Falalei should leave the service: "He and I have talked it over a good deal, sitting under that favorite oak of yours, where you used to entertain yourself when you were a youngster. You used to hang the dogs from the branches when they were bad at chasing hares, and flog the huntsmen when their dogs ran ahead of yours. What a card you were when you were a lad! It used to be, when you took to flog people, there would go up such a screaming and cracking as it might have been the torture room in the Police Court; we used to burst our bellies laughing!" The last paragraph of Trifon's letter returns to his wife's mortal illness; this, it appears, has been occasioned by over-exertion. Sidorovna had flogged some peasants so enthusiastically because of an accident that had through their fault happened to Falalei's favorite hunting-dog Naletka, that she caught a fever. The old man seems quite distressed at losing his wife: "It's sickening, Falaleiushka, to part with a wife; I had already got used to her. Thirty years we lived together.... She had a good many beatings from me.... Even if she and I did use to fight, nevertheless we lived together; and now, really, I'm sorry to lose her."

The mother's letter to her darling boy begins with alarmed concern over what may happen to Falaleiushka if he persists in irritating his father: "If you, my poor dear, should fall into his hands, you know he would trounce you beyond God's mercy. Certain it is, Falaleiushka, he has (Lord pardon me!) the devil's own temper." She counsels a little diplomacy: "Write a little soothingly to him, even a little lie—that's no such terrible sin, you won't be deceiving someone else's father, only your own; and all sons are not sinless—how can they help lying to their fathers?" Rather pathetically the old woman pleads with her boy to come home while she is still alive; she is sending him a hundred rubles which she has salted away without her husband's knowledge, and with which she urges him to "have a good time—there will come a time when even joy will not be to your mind." The dying woman ends her letter with: "Farewell, my darling, farewell, my light. I, your mother, Akulina Sidorovna, send you my blessing, and my humblest greetings, my light. Farewell, my darling, do not forget me."

The third of the packet of letters is from Falalei's uncle Ermolai Terentievich, and is largely taken up with a rather heartless description of poor Akulina Sidorovna's final moments and death. She has, it seems, bequeathed her icons to her son and Ermolai, who is presumably her brother: "She blessed you in your absence with your Angel and the Mother of God of

Farsul, and me with the Mother of God of the Burning Bush. Well, friend nephew, your mother didn't become any more generous even in the presence of death! She left for the remembrance of her soul [i.e., for saying masses] such an icon as you wouldn't get a ruble and a half for.... And that 'Burning Bush' certainly doesn't do any burning—the setting is all tarnished, God be with her!" Then, after a description of the last rites, the abrupt announcement: "Well, Falaleiushka, you know your mother has passed on; you've seen the last of her. I just received word of this. Your father, they say, is bawling like a cow. That's the way it always is with us: whatever cow dies, is always the one that was good at milking. When Sidorovna was alive, your father used to beat her like a sow; now she's dead, he's crying as though over his favorite horse." Then, like all the other letters, the uncle's ends with a fervent plea to Falalei to leave St. Petersburg and come home, where he can certainly get a lucrative job in some local administrative office, and feather his nest in short order. To make this prospect more alluring, Ermolai cites the example of a neighbor: "Avdul Eremeevich, our friend, although he didn't live for a very long time in charge of the monastery peasants [i.e., in a position in the Economic Administration, in charge of secularized monastery estates], has already married off all his daughters. As a dowry with one, I hear, he gave a clean ten thousand, and a village worth some five thousand. And he hasn't completely ruined himself, God be with him—he still has plenty left. And if they hadn't replaced him, he would have feathered his nest in plenty in the matter of the present recruitment [A peasant family that could afford to do so would of course try to buy an exemption for a son threatened with conscription]. You may be sure that their prayers reached God, those that got the job at that time! Their's was not a life, but a carnival!" It all depends, as Uncle Ermolai finally points out, on being able to keep "the ends in water"—a familiar expression equivalent to "covering one's tracks." Evidently there is no harm in this, for—"sin and misfortune who can avoid?"

Less literary in tone than the "Fragment of a Journey," the "Letters to Falalei" are most effective satire. Their effectiveness is very largely due to two devices: the earthy, colloquial language, full of proverbial sayings, oaths, endearments and the like, which has all the flavor of real speech; and the artless naivety of the correspondents, who indict themselves by their own words of callous cruelty, dishonesty, superstition, bigotry, and all the rest. At the same time one can hardly read Akulina Sidorovna's epistle without some feeling of compassion for the doting mother, however unpleasant her character may have been. And this perhaps almost unintentional glimpse of another side to her character is the mark of a great dramatist; Akulina is not one-dimensional: a monster of cruelty to her peasants, she loves her son unselfishly, if foolishly, and would be willing, as she says, to sacrifice her life for him. This picture is so akin to that of Prostakova, in *The Minor*, that

180

if Fonvizin is not the author of "Letters to Falalei," he most surely must have patterned the characterization of his tyrant-mother after the "portrait" painted ten years earlier by *The Portrait-Painter* .

After *The Portrait-Painter* Nikolai Novikov tried one more periodical, *The Purse (Koshelek),* which ran from July 8 to September 2, 1774. When this too was closed, the satirist became discouraged and turned to other avenues for bettering ailing society. He was converted to Free Masonry in 1774, and thenceforth for several years edited various Masonic periodicals: *Morning Light,* Sept. 1777-April 1779; *Moscow Monthly,* 1781; *Evening Light,* 1782; and *The Laborer at Rest,* 1784-85. In these journals he assiduously followed the Masonic principles for "philanthropy" (love of humankind). The highest duty of man is to attain individual goodness, and to help other men to do the same; direct combat of inhuman abuses such as serfdom is a mistake; improvement will come gradually, when enough human beings have earnestly set themselves to programs of self-perfection.

Novikov carried on his labors with the Masonic periodicals and with his enormous and highly influential publishing venture, by which he sought to place "enlightenment" within the reach of any literate Russian, without molestation from the government, until 1789. The outbreak of the French Revolution, and especially the news of the execution of Louis XVI and Marie Antoinette, frightened Catherine II into a frenzy of repression. Novikov was arrested, tried for sedition, and incarcerated in the Petropavlovsk Fortress in 1792; Radishchev had already (1790) been sentenced to ten years of Siberian exile. At his accession one of Emperor Paul's first acts was to release Novikov; the story is that Paul begged the venerable man with tears to forgive his mother's cruel act. Novikov retired to his estates, where he lived on until 1818, a broken and decrepit man.

The whole episode of the journalistic clash between Catherine and Nikolai Novikov affords a perfect example of the contradictions inherent in the activity of "the northern Semiramis." Brought up in the tradition of rationalism, and basking in the adulation of her philosopher friends, one part of her nature urged her to bring "enlightenment" into the medieval darkness of Russia. But another, and as it proved, much stronger part of her nature loved autocratic power for its own sake, was intolerant of all opposition, and drove her into an arbitrariness entirely at variance with the enlightened liberalism which she enjoyed displaying to her foreign admirers. Thus we see her espousing a mild program for improving the lot of the serfs in her "Instruction" for the Legislative Commission, and then letting her conservative advisers cut this out of the version published at home. Thus also we see her writing flippantly to Voltaire that the Russian peasants are so well off that they can have chicken to eat every Sunday, but that "latterly they have preferred turkey to chicken," and at almost the same time savagely repressing the massive peasant revolt of Emelian Pugachev. Catherine's liberalism was entirely verbal, and any attempt to lead her words in the direction of action disturbed and enraged her. So it was with the satirical journalism which she had imprudently called into being in 1769: to her it was a game, a mere ornamental concomitant of the enlightened despotism on the western model which she envisaged for Russia. She smiled benevolently on it as long as it remained a game; but when people like Emin and Novikov threatened to take it seriously, the spell was broken, and the traditional Russian deterrents to "dangerous thinking"—censorship, relegation, and outright banishment—resumed once more their never long suspended operation.

D . Fedor Emin, Journalist and Novelist

The designation of Catherine's reign as "the Golden Age of the Aristocracy" is no less apt for the literary than for the social and political aspects of the period. The great literary figures of the age—Novikov, Kheraskov, Kniazhnin, Fonvizin, Derzhavin et al.—are noblemen, and their favored literary genres—tragedy, satire, the philosophical novel, the ode, etc.—are those which reflected most clearly the gentry ideals of life and conduct. Classicism, as a period style, bears the mark of upper class ideology, with its emphasis on restraint, the rule of reason over the emotions, the unquestioned acceptance of hierarchic distinctions in art as in social life, the transcendence of civic duty, and the rest. But even in "the age of classicism" all was not classical. The Russian "middle class" in the eighteenth century was small numerically and politically powerless; it was poorly educated, but literate, and it had its own literary tastes, which were not those of its social betters. It is probably not surprising that these tastes were largely manifested in two types of writing which had least of all felt the impact of classicism— the comedy and the novel. The comedy was, to be sure, one of the accepted classical genres, but even in western Europe it had, by the middle of the century, taken a turn that went counter to the theories of the great legislators, such as Boileau and La Harpe, and brought it much closer to the realities of everyday life. The novel, unlike the comedy, had never, strictly speaking, been subject to classical regulation. In antiquity it had been so far beneath the attention of critics that it lacked even a name, and this lofty contempt was carried over into the neo-classicism of the eighteenth century. Certain forms of the novel gained acceptance—the pastoral version, which had been cultivated in the Renaissance; the pseudo-historical and didactic variety, of which the most prestigious example was Fénelon's *Télémaque ;* and the philosophical novel, exemplified in the eighteenth century chiefly by Voltaire's *Candide, Zadig, Micromégas,* etc. A new-comer from Spain, the *picaresca,* obtained grudging acceptance in France and England (Lesage's *Gil Blas,* Fielding's *Joseph Andrews,* etc.). Finally, in 1741, Richardson's great novel *Pamela* broke ground for an entirely new development in the novel, which may perhaps best be called the "psychological." Shortly after, in 1761, Rousseau's *La Nouvelle Héloise* brought the new trend into the very citadel of classicism, France, and marked the triumphant advance of "sentimentalism." Both *Pamela* and *La Nouvelle Héloise* were "epistolary novels": the heroes' and heroines' feelings, even the most intimate, could be plausibly confided to personal letters without the intervention of an "omniscient author."

In Russia remnants of another novelistic tradition survived into the eighteenth century—one which had mostly died out in the west. This was the adventure story, of ultimate Byzantine and Oriental origin, such as had flourished in the late seventeenth century—*Eruslan Lazarevich, Peter of the Golden Keys,* etc. This "escape literature" had generally circulated in manuscript copies, and among the lower classes with less sophisticated literary tastes. Its appeal was primarily that of plot, of a lively and ever-moving series of adventures, no matter how far-fetched and implausible. It is not surprising that the first examples of the popular novel in the eighteenth century in Russia owe a great deal to this artless story-telling of past generations.

The first popular novels in eighteenth century Russia are the work of a most curious figure, Fedor Alexandrovich Emin.[21] The origins, even the birth date, of Emin are wholly mysterious. He appeared in 1758 before the Russian minister to the Court of St. James in London and requested to be baptized into the Orthodox Church; in this Prince A.M. Golitsyn was happy to oblige him. According to the account which Emin gave at this time, he was born in Turkey of Orthodox parents, but was himself a Mohammedan (he gave his name as Mehmet Emin). He was given a Russian passport in 1761 and arrived in St. Petersburg, where he shortly obtained a post as translator in the Foreign Office. In the passport his birth date is given as 1735. Subsequently he disseminated at least three other versions of his background, all of them highly romantic in color. It is now thought probable that he was born in the Ukraine. He knew a number of foreign languages, but the extraordinary speed with which he acquired a fluency in Russian—he began publishing Russian novels in 1763, two years after his arrival in a country which purportedly he had never seen!—make it likely that he had known the language before 1761. He had certainly done a good deal of travel in Europe and was familiar with some modern literary trends, particularly in France and England.

Emin in 1763 poured from the presses three original novels—*The Vineyard of Love, or the Invincible Constancy of Kamber and Arisena; Inconstant Fortune, or the Voyage of Miramond; The Adventures of Themistocles;*—and a translation from the Italian of a popular romance, *Unfortunate Floridor.* In 1764 appeared: *Constancy Rewarded, or the Adventures of Lizark and*

Sarmanda; The Sad Love of the Marquis of Toledo, Translated from the Spanish; and *Moral Fables.* In 1766 Emin published his four-volume novel *The Letters of Ernest and Doravra.* His later works, while ostensibly histories, are no less fictional than his novels: *Polish History,* from the French of Salignac (1766) and *A Russian History of the Lives of All the Ancient Monarchs from the very Beginning of Russia* (1768-69). In 1769, during the journalistic flurry inaugurated by Catherine's *All Kinds of Things,* Emin ran single-handed two journals, *The Medley,* a weekly, and the monthly *Hell's Post.* His swan song was a religious tract, *Path to Salvation,* published in the year of his death, 1770.

It goes without saying that such a prodigious literary feat as this represents could have been accomplished, even by a person of Emin's energy and restlessness, only by dint of shameless borrowing. His "histories" are particularly glaring examples of this: he makes no use of such sober—and difficult—predecessors as Tatishchev, who was most painstaking in the matter of sources, but pilfered, without acknowledgement, worthless French compilations. Not content with this, he even invented non-existent "Annalistic Chronicles," cited imaginary authors, misread the old Russian word for "friend" into a proper name, confused the Volga Bulgars with their kinsmen on the Danube, etc. etc. The "Russian History" is a perfectly worthless tissue of fables.

His original novels, with one exception, are not much better. All the clichés of Byzantine romance are employed *ad nauseam*—shipwreck, abduction by pirates, separations of lovers, recognitions, temptations by enterprising seductors, and triumphant maintenance of chastity in spite of overwhelming odds, etc. etc. Heroes and heroines race wildly across the map of Europe, and the author takes the occasion wherever possible to deliver lectures on the geography and political conditions of European states unfamiliar to Russians. Characters often voice their transports of joy or sorrow in rhetorical set speeches, and there is a rudimentary effort to depict the psychology of love, a malady to which all the novel's cast is subject. Structurally a similarity may be noted with *The Tale of the Russian Cavalier Alexander;* as in that novel the hero's story is intertwined with that of his friend Vladimir, so here Miramond's idealized adventures contrast with the more realistic ones of his friend Feridat.

The Adventures of Themistocles is an evident attempt to capitalize on the fame of Fénelon's great didactic and political novel. The Athenian statesman and his son Neocles, after the father's banishment, undergo experiences vaguely laid in Asia, where the historical Themistocles did in fact become a pensioner of the King of Persia. The novel consists of continual conversation between father and son, with verbose lectures on social and political matters. Here one may find Emin's most famous utterance, evidently directed toward a solid segment of his audience: "The merchant class is the soul of the state and it is very necessary to preserve this so that the body may not sicken."

184

While in theory advocating an aristocratic government, he is contemptuous of the Russian landed gentry; in one of his journalistic pieces he writes: "Who is more useful to society, a simple townsman who has about 200 people working for him, who receive money for this and therewith take care of their needs—or His Excellency Sir Arrogance ["Nadmen"], all of whose merits consist in his having in his lifetime shot six wild ducks and coursed 120 hares?"[22] One may wonder, incidentally, if both parts of this picture are not taken from English rather than Russian life.

Emin's masterpiece, if such a word is applicable to any of his works, is *The Letters of Ernest and Doravra*. Here the model is obviously Rousseau's *La Nouvelle Héloise*, published only five years before and not translated into Russian until 1769. *The Letters* is Russia's first epistolary novel, and it is also the first appearance of the sentimental trend, usually associated with Karamzin's "Poor Liza," almost a generation later. Ernest is a poor young man of noble birth who falls madly in love with Doravra, a wealthy young woman of the same class. The barrier to happiness for this pair thus is not, as with St. Preux and Julie, a difference of social standing, but an entirely external circumstance. Ernest obtains a diplomatic post in Paris, and he and Doravra appear about to be happily united, when Ernest's former wife, whom he had supposed dead, suddenly turns up. Doravra's father induces her to marry a wealthy man; Ernest's wife dies and Doravra's husband dies—but Emin, as he naively confesses, cannot bring his romance to an unrealistically happy conclusion! So Doravra admits to her lover that she has lost interest in him; she marries again, and Ernest remains inconsolable.

Emin's contact with his great model was enough to have faintly infected him with some of Rousseau's virtues. To be sure, his substitution of a prior marriage for Rousseau's class barrier deprives his novel of any sort of social significance; and his relatively tame ending contrasts unfavorably with Julie's heroic and somewhat melodramatic death. But his hero, like St. Preux, communes sentimentally with nature and reads in the natural moods of tempest, awakening spring, winter desolation, etc., reflections of his own emotional states. The natural descriptions, though conventionalized, are not much more so than Karamzin's. Thus, for example, Ernest's friend Ippolit invites him for a visit:

Here nature in her tender colors and green leafage manifests her gaiety and liveliness; here the roses, seeing us admiring them, blush as though ashamed; and the pleasant lilies, which do not have such a pleasant aspect as the roses, seeing their natural shamefastness, manifest as it were in their own tender color a pleasant smile.

Emin's style is execrable; here one may note the extreme poverty of vocabulary: "tender" ["nezhnyi"] repeated twice; "manifest" ["iavliaet, iavliaiut"] repeated twice; and "pleasant" ["priiatnyi"] repeated three times—all in a single sentence!

Ernest and Doravra spend many tedious pages analyzing their own feelings for each other's benefit, but for all this the impression which they make on the reader is entirely artificial and unconvincing. Emin evidently felt constrained to apologize in a way for the length of his hero's letters in Part III: "Living in solitude, it was natural for him to write long letters, for he had nothing else to do!" These lengthy bouts of self-analysis are reminiscent of the classical tragedy, e.g., of Sumarokov; but Emin is outspokenly hostile to the classicist Sumarokov, and Ernest, who spends most of his time in France and England (there is no Russian color in the novel) writes disparagingly of French classical tragedy, to which he prefers the English, i.e., Shakespeare—another mark of pre-romanticism long before Karamzin.

As in all his novels, Emin salts his *Letters of Ernest and Doravra* with disquisitions on political inequality, the arrogance and worthlessness of the aristocracy, the corruption of justice, etc.; but these remain to a large extent mere interpolations, since they are without relevance to the actual plot. In one respect, however, there is an immediate pertinence in some of these remarks. Ernest becomes a writer, and his satires are so scathing that he is threatened with imprisonment and even exile. His friend Ippolit admonishes him to curb his attacks, which he directs pointedly at individual sinners, and confine himself to attacking the abstract vice; but this kind of innocuous and denatured satire is not to Ernest's taste—he will direct his shafts "not at the vice but at the vicious person." This controversy prefigures that of a few years later (1769) between Novikov's *Drone* and Catherine's *All Kinds of Things* on the same subject, where Catherine's ideal of "smiling satire" is vehemently rejected by Novikov. It may be remembered that Emin's periodicals, especially *Hell's Post,* came boldly to Novikov's defense in this dispute.

As Gukovsky remarks, *The Letters of Ernest and Doravra* are more a caricature than an imitation of *La Nouvelle Héloise.* Emin either missed the main points of Rousseau's novel, or was too unskillful to reproduce them. It has already been pointed out that the entire "third estate" theme of social equality, so passionately argued by Rousseau, is nullified by having Ernest and Doravra both belong to the noble class; even the difference in wealth plays no major part, since the real obstacle, Ernest's first wife, appears before Doravra's father learns of the contemplated marriage. Lip-service is paid to the Rousseau theme that virtue depends more on a tender heart than a tough mind; one of the lovers exclaims: "Oh, what a misfortune it is to have a sensitive soul!" But when it comes to the point of putting passion ahead of reason in practice, Emin balks. Rousseau's Julie, like the original Héloise, lets passion for her tutor overcome her maidenly scruples and filial "duty"; Doravra, it seems, is quite willing to do the same, but is dissuaded from the fateful step by the more conventional Ernest!

In spite of all the very numerous faults that may be found with Emin's novel, it still has to be reckoned with in the history of the Russian eighteenth century literature. It is only a faint reflection of Rousseau, but it is a reflection none the less, and the distorted and ill-assimilated version of sentimentalism which it introduced to the Russian reader is a quarter of a century in advance of the movement's final acceptance. If Emin were not such a wretched writer, his bulky heritage would undoubtedly be regarded as something of a landmark of the age.

E The Novels and Verses of Mikhail Chulkov[24] (1734?-1792)

Perhaps a year older than Emin, Chulkov's literary career falls in the same period, although he survived his rival by more than twenty years. The productions of his later years, when he held a bureaucratic position with the Senate, are outside of the literary province: *Juridical Dictionary* (1781-1788); *Historical Description of Russian Commerce* (1781-88); *Economic Notes* and *Rural Doctor's Book*. He edited the journal *This and That* in 1769-70 during the brief heyday of St. Petersburg journalism.

Chulkov was a *raznochinets*, although after years of service with the Senate he was rewarded in 1789 with personal ennoblement and a small estate. He obtained what we would call a secondary school education in the gymnasium attached to Moscow University, where the Fonvizin brothers were students at the same time. He was an actor in the court theater from 1761 to 1765.

Two novels, a number of journalistic pieces and some verse constitute Chulkov's literary heritage. The first novel, *The Mocker, or Slavonic Folk-Tales (Peresmeshnik, ili slavenskie skazki)* was published in four parts in 1766-68, with a fifth part added in 1789. It is a fantastic conglomeration of wild adventure by sea and land in the tradition of the medieval "chivalric romance," with magic castles, enchanted islands, battles with terrible monsters, transformations into—and out of—animals, trees, etc. The geography is "Slavonic," with Novgorod, Staraia Russ and other ancient Russian cities cheek by jowl with a wholly imaginary "Vineta," purportedly on the site of later St. Petersburg! The action is supposed to take place in pagan times, and allegedly Slavonic deities, mingled with some from classical antiquity, adorn the action. In the traditions of its kind, the principal line of story is frequently interrupted by interpolated secondary stories, told by or about subsidiary characters. Some of these secondary stories, oddly enough, are almost realistic accounts of the serf's bitter lot, ostensibly thrown back into the ninth century, and of the idleness and frivolity of the pagan Slavonic nobility.

The second of Chulkov's novels is the first Russian example of the kind of tale which is usually called picaresque. Characteristic of this genre is a first person narrative, usually covering a good deal of the narrator's life history, and often interspersed with moralistic reflections on past sins. There is usually no central plot, but merely a series of episodes strung toge-

187

ther and unified only by the person of the central character; and the tale is ordinarily set in a low-life milieu and with a good deal of often satirical and always realistic description of society from the point of view of the plebeian narrator. The narrator is not always a "rogue," as Elizabethan English usually renders the Spanish *picaro,* but he or she is generally, at least at the outset, on the periphery of society, and constrained to meet the elementary needs of life by means that a more secure and more squeamish upper class could regard as ignoble. The picaresque genre originated in Spain with the anonymous *Lazarillo de Tormes* (1554) and rapidly spread throughout Europe; Lesage's *Gil Blas de Santillane* (1715-1735) became particularly popular and influential. Whether Chulkov could have had any knowledge of Defoe's *Moll Flanders* (1722), which in many respects resembles the Russian tale, is uncertain.

In 1770 appeared *The Comely Cook [Prigozhaia povarikha], or the Adventures of a Depraved Woman: Part I.*[25] Part II was never published, and perhaps never written—at least no trace of it has ever been discovered. The tale is told in the first person by Martona (a non-Russian name, like all of the names used in the novel, but suggesting the familiar Matryona), and consists of the narrator's adventures from the moment when she is left a widow after her young husband's death at the battle of Poltava, up to a point a number of years later when she visits the dying Akhal, one of her former lovers, whose death is the result of remorse for the supposed killing in a duel of his friend Svidal, Martona's current lover. In the interim Martona has lived with a considerable number of men—once ostensibly as a cook, hence the title—and passed through several abrupt reversals of fortune. She has been the unscrupulous plunderer of some of her lovers, and the victim of one—Akhal—who has plundered her. She has had experience of several levels of Russian life, the most vividly described being that which she has enjoyed as mistress of an elderly ex-colonel in Moscow.

The narrative gives a convincing picture of Martona as a quite amoral young woman who finds it perfectly natural to trade her charms for hard cash, and looks on most of her liaisons as simple business deals. "Virtue was to me a thing unknown from way back," she says on one occasion, "and so in two words, my lover and I agree to squander his master's fortune." Early on, after being set on her mercenary course by a friendly older woman, Martona remarks: "I didn't know there was any such thing as gratitude in the world, nor ever heard of it from anyone, and I supposed one could make his way in the world without it." Of one of her early affairs she writes: "He was a gentleman ["gospodin"], and not the last of his kind. This first rendezvous of ours was a deal ["torgom"], and we talked about nothing but about how to conclude a contract: he bid for my charms, and I turned them over to him for a fair price, and we bound ourselves thereupon with signed papers.... The gentleman proposed to visit me often, and I promised to receive him every time, and with this we parted." Martona's affections are not

188

aroused by any of her affairs until she meets the handsome and self-centered Akhal, who absconds with her property and leaves her stranded (like Phillis abandoned by Demophon, she unexpectedly notes). By the end of the story, however, she has fallen genuinely in love with the noble and honorable Svidal, and apparently formed a quite permanent attachment to him. How the "second part" might have developed is hard to guess; but perhaps a clue may be found in the story's subtitle: "The Adventures of a Depraved, Woman." Martona gives no evidence of repentance in the first part; but perhaps she might have come to view her past as "depraved" if Chulkov had continued her story.

The style of the novel is somewhat uneven. The narrative portions are plain and straightforward, adorned however by a considerable wealth of mythological allusions, rather out of character for such an uneducated girl as Martona is supposed to be. Side by side with these literary clichés are numerous popular sayings of a proverbial character. Martona is very fond of illuminating her situation with pithy bits of folk wisdom. Thus, when her fortunes have taken a sudden turn for the better, she writes: "Heretofore Makar used to dig in the garden, but now Makar has got to be a governor" ["Doseleva Makar griadu kopal, a nyne Makar v voevody popal"], with the jingle "kopal—popal" typical of the "raek"; or on an occasion when her designs have been thwarted, she says philosophically: "It isn't always Shrovetide for the tom-cat—there's also Lent." "The ewe hankers after salt, the goat after freedom, and a fickle woman after a new lover"; with these words she preludes one of her numerous infidelities.

Sometimes the simple and rather pedestrian style is interrupted by bits of preciosity, usually in quoted love letters or amorous verbal declarations. Thus, Akhal's first note to Martona[26]:

My lady!
    To fall in love with someone is something outside our control. Everything beautiful in the world draws to it our feelings and reason. You are beautiful, and therefore you took my heart captive at the very moment when I saw you first in church; it seemed to me then that your beautiful eyes were speaking to me in your heart's stead. And so, be assured of this, I have been so bold as to declare myself to you, in the confident hope that even if you have not come to love me, yet perhaps you do not altogether hate me.

The adorer of your beauty,
Akhal

When Martona returns disconsolate to her decrepit ex-colonel after her abortive elopement with Akhal, the old man addresses her in flowery language that reminds one forcibly of the set speech with which Goncharov's Ivan Savvich Podzhabrin preludes his seductions: "Is it not slumber that flatters me with this delightful dream? Is it not a delusive hope that deceives my reason? Beautiful Martona! Is it you whom I hold in my embraces, is it your mouth that I now kiss, your charms that I now behold, is it you before me? Speak, answer, beautiful one—or am I bereft of you forever?"[27]

The Comely Cook is something of a landmark in the history of the Russian novel. It marks the first appearance of a realistic depiction of Russian society in a literary narrative, and bridges the gap between such an artless popular tale as that of "Frol Skobeev" and the nineteenth century precursors of realism, such as Narezhny.

One curious piece of verse of Chulkov's deserves mention for its critical polemics, if for little else. It appeared in three numbers (16, 17, 18) of the periodical *This and That* in 1769. Its title "Stikhi na kacheli," can perhaps best be rendered as "Verses at the Merry-go-round."[28] Reference is made in the poem itself to a popular jollification at Easter time in which a contrivance called a *kruglye kacheli* figures, and from the description this would appear to have been a species of Ferris wheel which was set up at a street crossing in town, and probably powered by the young men who treated their girls to rides on it. There is also a *priamaia kachel*, where the girl sits on a lion—presumably a regular carrousel.

Chulkov addresses his verses to an ill-defined "kuma" ("gossip"—a feminine "pal"), who is probably to be envisioned as the composite feminine reader of *This and That*. She is a lady of taste, and appreciates good verse. The author begins with a mock-epic invocation to the Muse:

> Tell me, O Muse, how should one begin,
> When a writer is minded to tell lies about something,
> So that he may be able to pass off fable as truth,
> And all at once make an old widow into a young maiden.
> We like gold better than silver,
> But if there isn't any gold, then [silver] is all right;
> If one can't get a razor anywhere, then even an awl does the
>   shaving (!),
> And necessity never knows laws.

The "people's poet" then proceeds to make fun of Emin and his novels, which he puts on a par with the anonymous popular romances of the preceding century. These latter, he says, he is going to turn into verse—presumably epic. Probably Sumarokov and the classical genre system are being mocked in the following lines as well as Emin:

> I myself am now an author, and I know A and B;
> There's no reason for me to go to Egypt for knowledge [as Emin
>   claimed to have done!]
> I understand everything, I'll kill off all prose
> And turn valiant "Bova" into a poem.

190

The tale of "Peter of the Golden Keys" is clumsy,
But with rhymes I'll put it nicely into verse;
"Evdon [and] Bertha" I'll fit into poetry
And tell their tale in dactyls or iambics, etc.

————

I'll translate all the bogatyrs into verse,
And interweave "the vineyards of love" [Emin's novel] with dog-
                                                        gerel—
Fashioned as they were without the knowledge of Pallas [i.e.,
                                            without technical skill] .'

After this round with epic verse, the poet turns to his "gossip" and asks her:

Have you ever read in a description of the world
That the earth is clothed with the abyss [i.e., the sea] as with
                                                    a garment;
The ocean serves her as a foundation does a house.
And the rivers as trimming, like a fashionable border,
The woods as embroidery, while the mountains are buttons....
Once I reached such an altitude as this,
And, I presume, I lost my wits then, went mad,
My mind could not hold back my passion,
And suddenly your "kum" took the notion to be a poet.

Of course all this high-flown cosmological description is a mockery of the
fustian of the ode, and presently he even more pointedly parodies some of
Lomonosov's and Sumarokov's. After the ode comes the turn of the mock-
epic, such as Maikov's *Elisei,* and a tedious vulgarization of Olympus follows,
in which, for example:

I heard Minerva's voice on the threshing-floor,
Ceres was in the garden pulling nettles for *shchi,*
Jupiter was in the yard splitting wood for fire, etc.

Then, says Chulkov, "abandoning the trumpet, I betook myself to the pipes,"
and became a love poet. After some more vapid fun with the Olympians,
in which he seems to be satirizing Satire, the poet describes his misadventures
with the pastoral. At last—"And with a hundred various fancies I already
have too much; first of all, in the course of this week I shall begin to look
with respect on the 'circular swings' [i.e., Ferris-wheels] ; and in order the
better to gaze on them, I shall endeavor for this purpose to fly up to Olympus; there I shall seek out the Castalian spring, wash myself from it, and I
shall gaze straight at all those squares below where there is the terrifying
revolution [i.e., of the "swing"] , and where our unpowdered folk revolve."

The rest of the poem follows the program thus announced, and is devoted to a description of the merry-making around the merry-go-round:

> The earth groans from the trampling of the tipsy,
> And every townsman drowns in wine and beer.
> Red tulips blossom on their faces,
> And faded roses grow on mouths.
> There reign games, diversions and laughter.
> Roasted walnuts are the beginning of their love,
> Adonis throws them down from the swing
> [And] says with a smile: 'Miss, bend over!'
> And she answers him with a pleasant look,
> And when he has asserted his love with talk,
> Then he will hire a pavilion for the whole day,
> To swing his beauty, and he will take the prize.

But this idyllic picture is shortly interrupted by a rowdy free-for-all precipitated by a drunk whose rudeness to the women calls forth verbal vengeance; some reckless young drivers ("Phaethons") spread havoc through the crowds, and the poem ends with a monumental fist-fight, worthy of the verses, the poet suggests, of classical writers of epic:

> I've heard there was a certain wise man named Homer,
> And likewise Virgil has much renown,
> And they praise Malherbe and Pindar as well.
> Great, they say, great were these men;
> Oh, you poor thing, my darling [i.e., his "Muse"],
> That you don't know them and have missed your chance...
> But the world is wide, one can't sail over all of it.
> And not every monk can be an abbot.

With this consoling reflection he decides to do the best he can, which he does, with copious references to Homeric heroes and the Olympic pantheon.

The concluding lines of the poem return to the gossip who has presumably inspired it:

> With all respect I offer this to you,
> And if it pleases others too, I beg them
> To accept my verses, a production without rules.
> The reason for this is that I did not establish them,
> As many people among us have long since become accustomed to
> writing without intelligence, and sending [their words] into
>   the world,
> Once they have merely provided their compositions with rhymes;

192

But I have great hesitation toward this,
And I shall exert all my efforts toward this only,
To write as well and regularly as I can.
I pledge myself to the service of society,
And I consider it a great good fortune
If I have in even some small way given pleasure to the people.
In service to my "gossip" I shall have served society.

It is perhaps difficult to discern in just what way this rambling and desultory pamphlet may have been "of service to society," but the critical point is clear enough—overt hostility to the "aristocratic" genres of verse—the epic, the mock-epic, the satire, the ode, the elegy, the pastoral, etc.—and in their place an earthy, sympathetic pictrue of the naive and hearty pleasures of the common people of St. Petersburg.

In the latter part of his life Chulkov busied himself with some works of compilation which, though not in themselves literature, have had a considerable impact on literature. As early as 1767 he had put together a *Short Mythological Lexicon,* in which he attempted to systematize Slavonic mythology—sometimes with entirely fictional additions of his own—on the pattern of the classical. In 1770-1771 he published a rich collection of Russian folksongs, which had a great influence on the course of Romantic poetry. In his second journalistic venture, *The Parnassian Curio Shop [Parnasskii shchepetil'nik]* he amassed a collection of popular riddles; and finally, in 1782 published a *Dictionary of Russian Superstitions.* He was thus a pioneer in the study of Russian folk-lore, and even though his contributions cannot always be trusted, they still have great value in the field.

F. Vasily Alexeevich Levshin (1746-1826) and the Folk-Tale[29]

Some ten years after Chulkov's *The Mocker,* discussed above, a collection of Russian folk stories was published in Moscow (1780-83), entitled in full: *Russian Folk-Tales [Skazki],* Containing the Most Ancient Narratives of the Famous Bogatyrs, Folk-Tales of the People et cetera, Adventures Which Have Remained in the Memory Through Retelling. The author of this collection was an industrious writer from the outskirts of literature proper, Vasily Alexeevich Levshin. Levshin also translated for Russian readers a volume of German folk-stories, and in his Russian collection there is clear evidence of his intent to mold the Slavic material into conformity with west European models.

These models were the chivalric romances, and Levshin rightly saw the Russian bogatyrs as the Slavic equivalents of the western "knights errant." He went directly to the popular *byliny* for his versions of the adventures of

Dobrinia, Alesha Popovich and the rest, and in that he was the first to do so for literary purposes, his artless retellings of the old ballads deserve consideration. Unfortunately he was very much inclined to stylize his bogatyrs along western lines, thus quite falsifying their real character. Thus, he makes Prince Vladimir of Kiev the founder of a "knightly order" analogous to that of King Arthur's "Round Table" or Charlemagne's "Twelve Peers," and he does not scruple to adorn the adventures of the bogatyrs with episodes drawn directly from foreign sources. But in his prose "tales after the *byliny*" Levshin often employs the very language of the old popular ballads. It was undoubtedly his *Skazki* that inspired many writers of far greater talent than his to turn to the *byliny* for material—among others, Karamzin and Derzhavin. It is even possible that some of the episodes in Pushkin's *Ruslan and Liudmila*, e.g., the adventure of Ruslan with the gigantic severed head, may have been suggested by this collection.

The *Skazki* contain two varieties of tales—the knightly and the homely-satirical. Professor Blagoi[30] suggests that, for example, the story "A Vexatious Awakening" ("Dosadnoe probuzhdenie"), which, incidentally, is an invention of Levshin himself, may have served as the beginning of a line of nineteenth century stories about "the little man." A drunken petty official named Elagin has a lovely dream that he is being married to the goddess Fortuna. Actually he is wallowing in a street puddle, and holding fast to a pig's leg, which he takes for the goddess! Poor Elagin, then, may be an ancestor of those other petty officials of greater renown, Pushkin's "Station Master" and Gogol's Akaky Akakievich, of "The Overcoat." An attractive conjecture, but rather far-fetched.

CHAPTER VIII

COMEDY AND THE COMIC OPERA IN THE FIRST HALF OF CATHERINE'S REIGN

A *The Comic Opera*[1]

Catherine II appears to be responsible for introducing the comic opera to Russia. In 1764 a French troupe, at her invitation, presented a piece called *The Blacksmith (Le Maréchal ferrant)* in St. Petersburg. Typically, the scene of such pieces is laid in a village, and the actors are peasants. The plot inevitably consists of the tribulations of a pair of young lovers whose marriage is hindered by some obstacle, which is of course triumphantly overcome in the last act. The dialogue is mostly spoken, but songs are introduced from time to time. The opera usually begins with an overture, but the songs are either unaccompanied, or only by a harpsichord.

The most famous French example of the genre, and one which, from the fame of its author, had considerable impact in Russia, is J.-J. Rousseau's *Le Devin du village* (1752)[2] The plot of this little piece is the height of simplicity. Colette mourns the defection of her lover Colin (these are of course both conventional rustic names) and resorts to "the village soothsayer" to learn whether he will return to her. The soothsayer reports that Colin is now the lover of "La dame de ces lieux," but still loves Colette; he appears to be less interested in the great lady herself than in the fine raiment she gives him. The soothsayer instructs Colette to pretend that she herself has another lover, when Colin returns, as he will. Colin in his turn interviews the soothsayer, and learns that Colette now prefers to him "un beau monsieur de la ville." At Colin's despair the soothsayer does a little hocus-pocus and announces Colette's return. The two lovers are hesitant about approaching each other, but finally do so; Colette pretends indifference until Colin is about to leave, disconsolate; then she breaks down, and there is a happy reconciliation. In gratitude to the arts of the soothsayer, both lovers give him presents, and there follows a village jollification, with dancing and a mimed allegory of a pair of village lovers and an interfering "monsieur de la ville."

The influence of Rousseau's miniature opera upon the Russian genre can be seen in two ways; in the first place, certain comic devices in it were directly imitated, as we shall see—but much more importantly, the underlying, quite serious, theme of hostility between village and city, aristocrat and peasant, became a quite common feature of the Russian comic opera. Thus, in Popov's *Anyuta,* Filat, Anyuta's rustic lover, threatens violence against the nobleman Victor. But under the tense social conditions of the period of Pugachev's uprising in Russia, this theme had to be played down, and some writers chose to ignore it altogether, e.g., Ablesimov, while others shifted the conflict between peasant and landowner to that between peasant and bailiff: after all, the bailiff was himself a peasant, but as the master's agent in a peasant village, capable of playing the petty tyrant without the master's knowledge.

1. Mikhail Ivanovich Popov (1742-1790)[3]

The first Russian experiment in the imported genre of the comic opera was made by a merchant's son, educated in Moscow University, who had collaborated with N.I. Novikov on his *Drone,* and served for several years on a subcommittee of Catherine II's abortive Legislative Commission (1767-1769). This was Mikhail Ivanovich Popov. As a young man he had been an actor in the court theater in St. Petersburg, and throughout his life he retained a great fondness for the theater. He translated two comedies in 1765— *The Distrustful Man* of Johann Friedrich von Cronegk (1731-58) and *Deucalion and Pyrrha* of Saint-Foix. After the great success of his *Anyuta* (1772), he translated the didactic poem of Claude Joseph Dorat (1734-1780), *La Déclamation théâtrale;* and in 1782 Beaumarchais' *Le Barbier de Seville.* He was active also in other literary areas: he collaborated with Chulkov in the latter's work of codifying Slavonic mythology, translated from the French *The Thousand and One Nights,* and made a very valuable collection of Russian songs, which was published posthumously in 1792.

In this connection must be mentioned Popov's own volume of *Songs*[4] (1765), one of the first—and best—of its kind in Russia. His most important predecessor in this area was of course Sumarokov, and Popov's songs are quite similar in style to those of the older poet. Thematically they are rather close to the tradition of elegy: in most cases the words are given to one or the other of a pair of lovers, whose situation, like that of a hero of elegy, is exposed in the most general terms—infidelity, separation, etc. In some instances there is a framing narrative, into which the lover's words are fitted. In two songs of a later period (1772) Popov makes an attempt to imitate the unrhymed and irregular verse form of actual popular song. The metrical structure of most of Popov's songs is considerably simpler than Sumarokov's; the commonest length of strophe is eight lines, with iambic and trochaic rhythms about equally represented. There is even one experiment in dactyls— rather a novelty at this period. The simple, harmonious lines are eminently singable. A good example is the following[5]:

> In parting from me
> Grieve for me if but for an hour;
> It may be I am already speaking
> To you for the last time.
> Fate decrees that I must lose you,
> However hard this may be to bear,
> And loving you, that I must sorrow,
> Weep, saying: "Farewell!"
> Weep for me in the same way, you too,
> Grief is my due....
> No! Do not torment my spirit so cruelly
> With your anguish for me:
> A drop of your tears is more to me
> Than the stream of my blood!
> Continue in a lot without sorrow,
> Let me suffer alone.
> If fate, relenting at my anguish,
> Shall bid me continue my life,
> I shall see you once more.
> I shall be happy once again;
> But if sorrow shall end my life,
> Do not torment yourself too greatly:
> Weeping will not return us to life;
> Be happy, and live.

The work with which Popov made his fame, and which continues to live in Russian literature, is the comic opera *Anyuta* (1772).[6] Structurally this follows the tradition inherited from French models: the verse dialogue (recitative) is interrupted from time to time by solo songs; the two lovers sing a duet; the four principals sing a lively line-for-line dialogue; and at the end there is an ensemble in which a "chorus" takes part, presumably of villagers. The author provides the piece with indications of the setting: "The action is in the field, near Victor's village." The first scene is thus described: "The theater represents a field and a village, surrounded by a forest," and this continues unchanged. Stage directions are also indicated, e.g., in the first scene, after the name "Miron," the note: "alone, is chopping wood, and accompanying his strokes with the tune."

As in Rousseau's *Village Soothsayer*, the plot is extremely simple. The peasant Miron has brought up Anyuta as his daughter, but she had actually been brought to him as a baby by an unknown servant-girl together with 100 rubles; this exposition is conveyed in Miron's first song. Miron has destined the girl to be the wife of his hired man ["batrak"], Filat, but

Anyuta herself has fallen in love with a young nobleman Victor, who is equally in lover with her, and she disdains Filat and indignantly refuses to be his wife. Filat accidentally observes her at a rendezvous with Victor, and sees the latter kissing her hand; he threatens Victor, and a violent altercation ensues. Filat reports Anyuta's conduct to her "father" Milon, and both men descend on Anyuta with threats and vituperation. In the meanwhile Victor has left briefly to procure money with which he hopes to bribe Filat and Milon to let him marry Anyuta. He returns in the nick of time, with the unexpected news that Anyuta is not a peasant girl at all, but "the daughter of Colonel Tsvetkov and a noblewoman." He then explains this, and distributes money to both Milon and Filat, and the play ends with general rejoicing: Victor can marry Anyuta without hindrance, since she really belongs to his social level.

For so slight a piece as this is, the characterization is surprisingly sharp. Victor is the most conventional, but shows himself in a rather unpleasant light in his quarrel with Filat as the overbearing "gentleman" contemptuous of a serf. Milon's first song, in which he laments over the hard fate of his kind: "Alack, alack, peasants, why aren't you gentlemen?" sets his character from the beginning; he is tyrannical with his "daughter," in his determination to marry her to the man who will help him in his work, as Filat promises to do—but of course the revelation of Anyuta's noble birth changes everything, and he accepts the purse from Victor with effusive gratitude, remarking:

> Be merciful, heavenly powers,
> My gracious lord,
> And may the King of Heaven grant you
>   To marry her
> And get children and be happy with them.
> But don't ever send them to us,
> For if you do, you know, sometimes
> With us peasants even a nobleman's children
>   Will be like those of peasants.

Filat is pictured closest to life; he tells Anyuta that he is to be her husband, and she bursts out: "You! My husband! Such an impudent fool and monster!" After a little more of this, Filat resorts to the typical peasant argument:

> Well, so be it. All right! For now I'll be silent,
> But tomorrow, perhaps, I'll have a word to say,
> And turn things
> As I wish;
> And perhaps get after

Your sides with a club:
Then you won't be calling me any swine!

The sight of a gentleman kissing his bride infuriates Filat, and he threatens both the lovers. To Victor's indignant: "You rascal! Do you dare threaten me?" he replies: "Well, indeed! Threaten? It could be you'll regret this, if you don't stop messing with other men's brides!" Yet even this spunky peasant backs down in quite tame fashion when Anyuta turns out to be a colonel's daughter—and Victor appeases him with a full purse:

Oh! My gracious and honest lord,
You're a straight-dealing gentleman!

In the finale Filat sings: "I haven't any reason to be sorry if I don't have a wife from the gentry; for thirty rubles I could buy two peasant wives!"

Anyuta, the heroine, has more color than most of her kind, who are usually rather pallid. She is contemptuous of Filat, romantically devoted to Victor, and declares to her "father" that she would rather die than submit to marriage with her peasant suitor; her father scorns this romantic talk of "dying," but offers her another alternative:

Don't worry, you won't die; marriage won't kill you,
But will teach you to stay at home.
And don't you get this into your head.
But choose which you please of two things—
A husband or a beating.

The unexpected news of her noble parentage is greeted by Anyuta with remarkable aplomb; after her first exclamation: "What do I hear!" she says to Victor: "Tell me how I have suddenly become so fortunate; never in my life did I expect such good fortune."

The play is written in verse, as has been noted, and except for Victor's speeches and songs, is in various degrees of north Russian peasant dialect— Anyuta's language being only slightly flavored with this, while Filat's is so colloquial as to be at times unintelligible. Eighteenth century peasant dialect is often mysterious, even to Russians. That this was so even for contemporaries is evidenced by the appraisal of the opera contained in an anonymous review[7]:

As regards his [i.e., Popov's] comic opera *Anyuta,* over and above its fine arrangement and pleasantness of style, the honor of primacy in this genre of composition in our language belongs to it. Justice, however, compels us to say that the heroine of his piece, Anyuta, throughout the whole opera speaks and thinks in a more noble fashion and more pleasingly, and in a more correct dialect, than her peasant upbringing would have allowed; moreover it seems to us that the peasants in the entire opera speak, though in this correct dialect and one which is used in remote provinces, yet for an opera this dialect seems to us rather uncouth. Poets, though obliged in such cases to imitate nature, yet have the liberty of choosing a better [natural model], and Russian peasants do not all talk in the same dialect. There are provinces in which they employ a dialect which would not in any theatrical piece be offensive to the tender ears of the audience.

It is worth noting that Popov's example was not followed in this regard by other comic opera writers: peasants are always represented as speaking dialect, but it is never again so extreme, and is probably quite conventionalized.

2 Nikolai Petrovich Nikolev: Rozana and Liubim[8]

In the years of the Pugachev insurrection and immediately after, when Catherine II's government became extremely repressive, and any expression of sympathy with the peasants was likely to be construed as treasonable, the comic opera, with its obligatory rustic setting, was considerably prettified and falsified. Of such a sort is the trifling two-act piece of Vasily Maikov, *Village Holiday, or Virtue Crowned* (1777), in which, in defiance of reality, the idyllic delights of country life are contrasted with the depravity of the town! Similar is Kheraskov's *Good Soldiers.* In 1777, however, the dramatist Nikolai Petrovich Nikolev (1758-1815), whose serious work we shall consider later, submitted his four-act "drama with voices" *Rozana and Liubim* to the St. Petersburg theater; it was produced, after some hesitation, in the following year. The plot of this piece is conveniently summarized by Professor A. Kokorev:[9]

An enserfed peasant, a former soldier [Izlet], has two daughters—Rozana and Milena. Rozana and the young peasant [fisherman] Liubim are in love with one another. However the landowner Shchedrov has seen Rozana, taken a fancy to her, and determined to possess her. The voluptuary landowner orders the arrest of Liubim, carries Rozana off by force to his manor-house, and tries to seduce her with sumptuous presents, but she rejects all his efforts. Rozana's father Izlet hurries to the manor-house, whither also Liubim flees, having broken loose from the landowner's dog-keepers who have been holding him. The pleas of Izlet and Liubim touch the landowner's heart; he repents, allows Liubim and Rozana to get married, and sets them free with a generous gift.

The summary ignores the very interesting and well-drawn character of the "forester" Semen, who had connived at the abduction of Rozana, and rather heartlessly jokes with the desperate father when Izlet determines to confront the landowner. The Forester is finally, despite his fears of the gentry, induced by Rozana's sister Milena to go along with her to attempt her sister's rescue, at the end of Act III.

The picture of the relations between landowner and peasants in this "comic" opera is anything but idyllic, and the "happy ending" is so patently improbable and absurd that the whole piece gives a very somber impression. The characterizations of the gallant old soldier Izlet and of the Forester are excellent. When the Forester first discloses the whereabouts of the abducted girl, her father exclaims:

Shchedrov!... that neighbor, [the most] honorable and laudable in the whole vicinity? So that's what the virtues of noblemen amount to; if they aren't plundering their neighbors, they are carrying off maidens; they don't count it a sin to dishonor a poor man, as long as they fling him some money! He isn't a Christian! He doesn't know that honor is as dear to us [as it is to him]. Oh, is this an easy thing for a father! *(he weeps)*...
The Forester: Enough of your snivelling—she hasn't croaked yet, has she?
Izlet: Oh! it would be easier for me to see her in her grave, than in shame.

Later in the next scene, as Izlet is about to set off to the manor-house, the Forester stops him: "Hold on, hold on, you! Really, brother, I guess you've gone off your rocker! Where are you thinking of going? Why, they'll give you such a drubbing that you won't forget it till your dying day. Is it for us peasant swine to tangle with noblemen?—and Shchedrov is a gentleman not to be trifled with!" Izlet replies: "And what if he is a gentleman? I've seen sovereigns; I've shed my blood for them. I've served myself under their very eyes. I know what our tears mean to them—so I'll find judgment even against a gentleman... Maybe even a gentleman will tremble, to stand with such a case before the judgment of the earthly god [i.e., the Tsar]."

3. Yakov Borisovich Kniazhnin: Misfortune from a Carriage

Considerably less dramatic, as well as less sharply characterized, is the two-act comic opera of the dramatist Yakov Borisovich Kniazhnin, one of the leading tragic writers of the age, *Misfortune from a Carriage* (1779)[10] In this version of conflict between nobleman and peasant the nobleman's bailiff is made the villain, and the nobleman himself appears only as a fool. The plot, in brief, is as follows: the peasant girl Anyuta and her lover Lukian are just about to be happily married, when Anyuta's father Trofim enters sadly with the announcement that the bailiff Klementy has appeared, angry, and ordered a stop to the wedding. Presently the bailiff himself appears, and reads the peasants a letter from their landlord Firiulin, the tenor of which is that he absolutely must have a new carriage from Paris, or be eternally disgraced. Since he is short of money, a peasant must be sold to the army and the bailiff has decided that Lukian is the choice. As for Anyuta, the bailiff himself will take her! This is the state of affairs when Firiulin's jester Afanasy appears. Learning the situation, he agrees to try to persuade the master to rescind his orders. In the second act Afanasy has to report failure to Lukian, Anyuta, and Trofim, but when he learns by chance that Anyuta and Lukian had been brought up as children by the "old master" in the town, and know a few words of French, he sees a way out. Firiulin and his wife enter, and Afanasy points to Lukian in chains and says: "Look, what a fine young fellow—and he knows French besides." At this magic word the Gallomaniac Firiulin at once orders Lukian released; Anyuta joins her lover and they plead in unison, one to Firiulin and one to his wife, with the words: "Monseigneur... Madame... have pity on us—intercede for us." Directly the wicked bailiff is reprimanded, the happy couple united, the jester rewarded, and all ends happily. The Jester and the peasant chorus sing, echoed by Trofim, Lukian and Anyuta: "A trifle [i.e., the carriage] ruined us, but a trifle [i.e., knowledge of French] also saved us."

It would be idle to speak of characterization in such a light-weight piece as this. The only development is that of Firiulin, and his portrait is a caricature. In his letter he says to his bailiff: "Imagine, Monsieur Clément, what a disgrace, not only to me, but to all of you, if your master doesn't ride in this beautiful carriage, and your mistress doesn't buy herself those beautiful head-dresses which have also been imported directly from Paris. From such shame an honorable man should hang himself!" At his first appearance on the stage, Firiulin says to his wife: "Barbarous nation! Savage region! What ignorance! What crude names! How the *délicatesse* of my hearing is offended!" His wife feels the same way: "I'm amazed, my dear! Our village is so close to the capital, and yet no one here knows French! But in France, a hundred versts from the capital, everybody speaks French!" To the Jester's plea to have pity on his servants, Firiulin exclaims: "Pity for Russians? You're out of your mind, Buffon. My pity was left behind in Paris—and now I can't hold back my tears, when I remember.... Oh, Paris!" "That's fine! Weep because you aren't there, but pitilessly torment your servants—and what for? To buy a French carriage!" exclaims the Jester. Firiulin: "Stop, don't talk of that! For us unfortunates who have returned from France to this savage region, only one consolation is left: that for Russian rubbish, making an honest exchange, it is possible to get something French. And now they want to deprive us of even that satisfaction!"

On the surface *Misfortune from a Carriage* has to be reckoned with such other attacks against Gallomania as Elagin's *Russian Frenchman* and Fonvizin's *The Brigadier.* The fundamental impact of the play, however, is directed against the tyranny and arbitrariness of the nobility, and the frivolity motivating their actions—"A trifle ruined us, and a trifle saved us."

4. *Alexander Anisimovich Ablesimov* (1742-1783)[11]

In the same year (1779) as *Misfortune from a Carriage,* appeared the piece which certainly has the honor of being the most popular of all Russian comic operas. Ablesimov's *Miller—Wizard, Cheat and Marriage-Broker* had 27 successive performances in St. Petersburg at its opening, which constitutes a record for that time. Although the author tried his hand several times later in the same genre—*Good Fortune by Lot* (1779), and *Expedition from Permanent Quarters* (on military life), he was never again successful.

Ablesimov was an impecunious nobleman by birth, who spent most of his earlier life as a soldier. After the Seven Years War he returned to Russia, became a friend of Mikhail Popov, Vasily Maikov and Nikolai I. Novikov, and with the latter served on Catherine's Legislative Commission. He participated with Novikov in 1769 on *The Drone,* and soon after this journal was closed, went back to military service because he found himself unable in any other way to make a living. Retired as a captain, he settled in Moscow, where he entered the civil service; it was at this time that his *Miller* was produced, first in Moscow, and then in the capital. The subsequent literary career of Ablesimov is of no interest, although he edited, with Novikov's assistance, another journal, *The Teller of Amusing Tales* (1781).

Miller—Wizard, Cheat and Marriage-Broker[12] *[Mel'nik— koldun, obmanshchik i svat]* employs the peasant-nobleman opposition not as a tragic, but a comic device. The bashful young Filemon approaches the miller Faddei, who is reputed in the village to be a wizard, with request for his supernatural assistance. At first Filemon claims to be looking for some lost horses, but later confesses that he is in love with a girl, but his suit is thwarted by the dissension of her parents: her mother, Fetinia, who is of gentle birth and has been married to a peasant against her will, insists that her daughter must marry a gentleman, while her father, Ankudin, insists equally on having a peasant as son-in-law. For the promise of "a quarter of good rye" the Miller undertakes to solve the dilemma. After a charming scene of very naive and bashful love-making between Filemon and Anyuta, the Miller comes on the pair and thus learns the girl's identity. He next encounters Fetinia, and gets himself invited to her house for a drink. Thus fortified, he goes through some impressive conjuring tricks, and shows first the girl her future husband's face in a mirror (with Filemon's cooperation, of course), and then to Fetinia her future son-in-law's, with the same cooperation. He hints to Fetinia that the youth is a nobleman, but gives only the name of his village. After the two women have retired, satisfied, Ankudin appears, driving a very slow and balky mare. The Miller accosts him directly, and in the quality now of a *svat* or "marriage-broker," proposes his client, still unnamed, as a proper, hard-working, prosperous husband for Anyuta. The agreement is made, and Ankudin leaves. In the next scene husband and wife have a wordy battle, carried on partly in song, over Anyuta's husband-to-be: peasant or nobleman? The third and final act opens with preparations for the wedding and a continuation of the dispute, which is interrupted by the Miller with a balalaika; reproached as a cheat by both Ankudin and Fetinia, he declares that he can satisfy both their desires, and after proposing his solution as a riddle (in song), he finally discloses the truth: Filemon is at the same time "a landowner and a peasant, a serf and a gentleman, he plows and he tills, and he collects quit-rent from the peasants." He is, in short, an *odnodvorets,* a free man, that is, but the owner of very few peasants—the old English word would be "franklin." Both parents are satisifed, Anyuta and Filemon are duly united, and amid the general rejoicing the Miller gets presents from all sides.

Although the once-held view that the opera is merely a Russian elaboration of Rousseau's *Le Devin du village* is untenable, it is certain that the French model suggested certain episodes and comic devices. Thus the scene in which Filemon and Anyuta timidly and hesitantly approach each other in the dusk is very similar to the meeting of Colette and Colin in *Le Devin;* and the terror which the wizard's conjuring instills in the superstitious peasants, as well as the description of the conjuring antics themselves, are very much alike in the two plays. At the end of both the theme, so dear to Rousseau's heart, of the superiority of the village, with its unspoiled innocence, to the decadent town, is voiced in the chorus:

> *A là ville on fait bien plus de fracas;*
> *Mais sont-ils aussi gais dans leurs ébats?*
> *Toujours contents,*
> *Toujours chantants,*
> *Beauté sans fard,*
> *Plaisir sans art;*
> *Tous leurs concerts valent-ils nos musettes?*

Ablesimov's villagers similarly boast of their happy country life:

> Let us gather here and be joyful,
> We're afraid of no one...
> Nature rejoices us,
> Beautifies, enriches,
> And simplicity gives us repose....
> We're happier than they [i.e., the city people] a hundred times.
> In the city there's a mountain of whims.
> There selfishness, deceit, vexation
> Oppress the thoughts of the inhabitants.

There is a certain similarity in the characterization of the Miller too, although of course Rousseau's opera is so slight that only hints can be given. In both he is represented as sympathetic to the young lovers, but still determined to make a little profit from his services. The French wizard responds to the gratitude of Colin and Colette at the end with the words: "Je suis assez payé si vous êtes heureux"—but he makes this remark, according to the stage direction, "recevant des deux mains." Ablesimov's Miller is more straightforward; to Filemon's first request that he "read the future" ["ugadat' "], he sings:

> Read the future—don't get tired—but when the case is rather
> desperate, then one pays rather generously.

At this hint Filemon promises a reward, but the Miller insists on cash down. Later, in Act II, when Fetinia says to the Miller: "Tell her fortune ["povorozhi-to"] : will she [i.e., Anyuta] have success?" the latter replies, holding out his hand: "Tell her fortune! One doesn't tell fortunes for free!"

Not a great deal of characterization can be expected from a comic opera, and certainly in this one Anyuta is pallid and conventional. Surprisingly, the rest of the principals have quite distinctive personalities. Filemon is marked by bashfulness and timidity, both toward the object of his affections (he has to be prodded into showing his reflection in Anyuta's mirror) and toward the Miller's *diablerie*. Fetinia is obstinate and inflexible in her determination that Anyuta shall have a nobleman for husband, and she is rather abusive of her husband, who holds the contrary view; yet she is quite easily mollified at the end, and accedes to the compromise—Filemon is at least half a nobleman!—without struggle. She is also quite considerate and kind toward her daughter, and there seems to be no hostility between the two. Ankudin, too, has his own character, and is not a mere peasant cliché. He is, for instance, remarkably considerate of his old gray mare (Act II, scene ii):

Ankudin (*drives his horse, and she stops*): Now, now! Gray!.... There she is, she's
    stopped... What shall I do? (*He helps her*). Now, now! Drag on just a little more...
    No, the devil take her, she won't pull.... Well, all right, take a rest, Gray! You and
    I won't budge.

When he and the Miller have concluded their arrangement for Anyuta's marriage, Ankudin says to his horse: "Well, now, Gray, have you had your rest?... Now, now! Get going, now, right home..."

The Miller is of course the center of the play, and his character is the best drawn. He is himself a skeptic, and notifies the audience at the very beginning that his supernatural powers are hokum—but his reputation is profitable:

Really, it's laughable, it seems to me; people say that a mill can't stand without a wizard, and any miller is no simple fellow: why, they are supposed to be on good terms with the house-spirits ["domovymi"], and the house-spirits turn things in the mill like very devils.... ha, ha, ha! What nonsense they grind out! I, I think, am a miller to the core; I was born, grew up, and have grown old in the mill, but never a house-spirit have I seen since I was born. But to tell the mother-truth, anyone who is inclined to a bit of cheating—that's all the wizardry there is—Let them talk all the nonsense they please, we'll earn our grub by this art.

He sympathizes with the young couple, but has his eye on hard cash; he quite evidently enjoys the fright which his dreadful conjuring instills in the timid Filemon. Apparently one of the most appreciated of his "fringe benefits" is a good drink now and then from his clients; he fondles his "little brown jug," a gift of Fetinia, with loving solicitude, and makes use of it to prepare himself for the mirror trick that reveals Anyuta's husband-to-be. With Ankudin, evidently more hard-headed than his wife or daughter, the Miller drops all references to wizardry and behaves in a perfectly business-like fashion. In his final appearance, drunk, with his balalaika, the Miller occupies the center of the stage, and with his adroit solution of the marital problem, he is quite smug over his cleverness:

> And so, my friends, it wasn't for nothing
> That I came to you;
> I've arranged the wedding for you,
> And done you all a service, all of you.

A word must be said about the musical aspect of the Russian comic operas. In most cases the actual musical arrangements have not been preserved, and although composers are named for some, and the librettist may himself also have been in some instances the composer as well, it is evident that the actual tunes utilized for the songs were almost always the tunes of well-known popular songs, and the new words were fitted to these anonymous melodies. This conclusion results from the notes that frequently accompany the beginning of a song in the opera, e.g., in Act II of the *Miller:* Anyuta's song is annotated: "She sings the beginning on the tune: 'If I had known, if I had realized, my darling.' " At the end of Act I the Miller's duet with Filemon has the note: "On the tune: 'You little brooks, little brooks.' "

One of the reasons for the great popularity of the comic opera house genre at the end of the eighteenth century in Russia was precisely the popular element which it contained, of which the use of popular tunes is one aspect. We have seen this same interest in other areas, e.g., the collections of folk-stories by Verevkin, Levshin, et al., the collections of popular sayings, riddles, etc. No recognized dramatic form except the comic opera gave an opportunity to exhibit this popular material. Of course peasant dialect, usually of a very conventional and artifical sort, appears occasionally in comedy proper, but the plot of a true comedy is never laid among peasants. Even when Fonvizin in his *Nedorosl'* introduces real peasants speaking real peasant dialect, the main action still takes place among the "upper class" characters. But the comic opera, as one of its conventions, was always laid in a rustic, or at least, lower class environment, and this characteristic apparently exerted the attraction of novelty on upper class audiences.

5. Mikhail Alexeevich Matinsky: The St. Petersburg Fair[13]

Although less an "opera" than most of its kind (most of the songs are in the second act), and with satire rather than sentiment as its attraction, the three-act piece by M.A. Matinsky called *Sankt-Peterburgsky gostinyi dvor* has to be considered here; it is on the border-line between the older comic opera tradition and the realistic comedy of the next century. The play's title, which is very hard to render conveniently in English, refers to the great shed-like building on Nevsky Prospekt in Saint Petersburg in which the shops of a large number of small independent merchants were located. A wide aisle led down the center of the building, and shoppers would saunter down the aisle while the shop-keepers on each side tried to attract their attention by advertising bargains. The title might almost be translated as *The Saint Petersburg Shopping Center*, except for the incongruous modern connotation; probably *The St. Petersburg Merchants' Mart* might serve. The play was written by Mikhail Alexeevich Matinsky (1750–?), a liberated serf who became a teacher of mathematics in the Smolny Institute, Catherine's "finishing school for young ladies." Matinsky was a musician, and himself wrote the music for the opera. Judging by the play, the author must have had great familiarity with the merchant class of the capital, and a very observant eye and ear.

There is, properly speaking, no central plot in the play, which is rather a series of slightly connected scenes. The musical numbers are short and fewer than in other operas, and in other respects too the *Merchants' Mart* is exceptional: the cast of characters numbers 21, not including a considerable number of mute extras; and the entire second act is the wedding ceremony by which the daughter of the play's principal rascal, Skvalygin, is united with the runner-up in rascality, Kriuchkodei. The ethnographical interest of the lower-class wedding was very considerable for the audience of 1779 and later, and is not without interest even to a modern reader; but the second act is without dramatic content and totally unrelated to the plot or theme of the play.

The opera opens picturesquely: as various potential buyers wander down the central aisle of the *gostinyi dvor*, four merchants sing jingles advertising their wares. Two ladies are shopping, and prove disdainful of all the finery that is shown them. Then comes a scene that introduces the rascal Skvalygin (the name means "cheat") at his tricks: the officer Priamikov ("straight-shooter") has deposited some money with Skvalygin, which he has now come to request. Skvalygin claims to have repaid it already. Presently the two ladies reenter, and accost Skvalygin: Shchepetkova ("stylish") has given him a bill of exchange which she wants to buy back—he claims that he has had to sell it to someone else. Krepyshkina ("miserly") has lent him some money on interest: Skvalygin claims to be unable to return it because of some great financial losses. Disappointed, the two ladies retire and meet

Priamikov, and the three compare notes. Krepyshkina has given her note for collection to lawyer Kriuchkodei (something like "dirty-dealer")—but Priamikov tells her that the lawyer is the son-in-law to be of Skvalygin! The three leave to try to find some means of recovering their money. Skvalygin's wife Salamonida appears, squabbles with her husband; then Kriuchkodei enters, hauling in a poor peasant, whom he accuses of almost running him down with his wagon. The peasant claims, obviously with reason, that "you deliberately fell under the wagon." Kriuchkodei is for suing the peasant not only for damages from the accident, but for insulting him, an upper class official, with improper language when warning him to get out of the way! The peasant finally buys his way out of the situation by giving up all the money he has; he goes away muttering at "robbery in broad daylight!"

The second act, as mentioned, is devoted to the wedding of Kriuchkodei and Khavronia. In the third there are some more instances of Skvalygin's heartlessness and villainy: when a poor widow, to whom he has lent money—at 24 percent interest, or four times the legal limit!—protests the seizure of her household gear for non-payment, he refuses her curtly. The widow's nine-year-old son says: "Please, tell them to give me back my jacket, shoes and stockings." Skvalygin's reply is: "Likely! Run in your shirt and go barefoot." The eight-year-old daughter then pleads: "At least order them to give us back our bed." Skvalygin: "Roll on the floor."

Next Skvalygin and Kriuchkodei operate on Shchepetkova's and Krepyshkina's bills of exchange. Kriuchkodei, who has obviously had experience at this sort of thing, says: "Now, just see here. Cut the validation [poruchitel'stvo] (the signature of the lender attesting his receipt of a pledge) off the note, as though you hadn't had the pledge; and I'll scrape Krepyshkina's note on the back, and so all the devils are in the water, and (only) bubbles above." At this inspired bit of rascality Salamonida observes: "It's a treasure, not a son-in-law God has given us!" But of course, since a comedy cannot end with villainy triumphant, The Merchants' Mart rather improbably shows Priamikov bringing the evil-doers to justice, and—most improbably— Kriuchkodei and Skvalygin repentant. This play, incidentally, may well have given some hints to Vasily Kapnist, for his Iabeda (Chicane) exhibits some of the same themes, e.g., nefarious collusion of father-in-law and son-in-law, unscrupulous and domineering wife, etc.

The sharpness of Matinsky's satire gives The Merchants' Mart a completely different character from other eighteenth century "comic" operas. Except for the occasional musical numbers, the piece could well be one of Ostrovsky's—Svoi liudi—pochtemsia—or a close relative of Gogol's Revizor.

B. Lukin and the "Tearful Comedy"[14]

Russian comedy developed in the second half of the eighteenth century at the same time as the novel, and in part under the same social conditions.

Comedy, although a classical genre (unlike the comic opera), was less rigorously regulated than tragedy—for example prose might be used instead of verse; three acts, or even one, might be substituted for five, etc. Molière's and Holberg's examples sanctioned many such exceptions. In one major respect, however, classical theory was inflexible: comedy, like all literature, had a didactic purpose. It was justified by its mission of exhibiting vice or folly on the stage as a warning lesson to the audience. Necessarily, for such a warning to be effective, the vice or folly must be represented unattractively, and properly punished at the play's end. Unfortunately for the theorists, however, comic writers sometimes got carried away by what the moralist regarded as the quite secondary purpose of purveying amusement and evoking laughter. Serious writers in France had, by the middle of the century, evolved a kind of comedy which would avoid this pitfall, and keep the audience's attention fixed on the main issue of having its morals improved. This new type of drama, however, involved a distinct break with another sacrosanct classical canon—the strict separation of genres. As Sumarokov laid down the law, Melpomene ("Tragedy") must never trespass on the domain of Thalia ("Comedy"). Such trespass, however, was precisely the nature of the comedies composed by such poets as Nivelle de la Chaussée (1692-1754) and Philippe Destouches (1680-1754). Later in the century Denis Diderot demonstrated, both in theory, and in two plays of his own, that there could be such a thing as a "serious comedy." In the actual plays of this new genre the element of entertainment was so far pushed into the background that the audience was not expected to laugh at the human frailties depicted on the stage, but to shed sympathetic tears over innocence victimized or nobility exhibited, especially by a person of low estate. Thus arose a new drama of pathetic situations and noble "sensibilities." This *comédie larmoyante*, a bugbear to the classicist, is one of the first symptoms of the new bourgeois values of the age—for it appealed primarily to the middle class, who were less concerned than the aristocracy with classical canons—and of the style in art and literature known as "sentimentalism," of which we shall see more in the latter half of the century.

The establishment of permanent theaters in the capitals for the benefit of the general public led to a considerable amount of dramatic writing. We have seen how Sumarokov won his sobriquet of "the Russian Racine" by his nine tragedies; and other writers of his following, e.g., Vasily Maikov, continued his work. Comedy, however, was quite understandably more popular with middle-class audiences than tragedy; and since the audiences in Moscow and St. Petersburg were in large part made up of non-noble burghers, a writer would ignore their preferences at his peril.

Native Russian fare, however, was in short supply at the beginning of Catherine's reign, and even the early comedies of Sumarokov, who had aimed at being "the Russian Molière" as well as "the Russian Racine," were in some respects so closely modeled on French practice that they might as well have been translated. Thus, the tricky man-servant and the saucy soubrette, traditional in French comedy, had no possible counterparts in Russian life; and even some of the traditional plot devices of classical comedy were based on usages unknown to Russia. Lukin mentions, in one of his prefaces, the alienation felt by a Russian spectator when he sees a character appear on the stage, "looking for Mr. Oronte," and claiming to be a notary summoned to draw up a marriage contract! Russian betrothals were church affairs and involved no legal papers, and the name Oronte had never been borne by any Russian—nor, for the matter of that, by any Frenchman either! Oronte, Geronte, Dorante, etc., are the never-never names of classical comedy, vaguely Greek in flavor, but employed precisely because they do *not* suggest any actual person.

This situation troubled certain lovers of the theater, and the line of development which comedy took after 1760 was in the direction of a closer approximation to genuine Russian life. The final step in this development is represented by Denis Fonvizin's *The Minor;* but a less definitive stage may be observed in the work of Vladimir Ignatievich Lukin and of a circle of government bureaucrats with which he was associated, and to which Fonvizin also belonged for a time.

The leader of this circle was a prominent nobleman, Ivan Perfilevich Elagin (1725-1796), vice-president of the Court Chancery from 1762 to 1768, and thereafter a state secretary and theater director. Elagin himself was a dilettantish writer, and author of a comedy, after Holberg, called *The Russian Frenchman* . Another member of the group was B.E. Elchaninov, author of *The Feather-Brain Punished* (1767). V.I. Lukin, a young man in the civil service who became one of Elagin's secretaries, was a third member.

Lukin was by birth a *dvorianin*, but poor, and not noble. He was employed in the service as a translator, and completed the Russian version, begun by Elagin, of Abbé Prévost's sentimental novel *Mémoires et aventures d'un homme de qualité qui s'est retiré du monde*, of which the famous *Manon Lescaut* is a part. Elagin's preoccupation with the drama was conveyed to his secretary, and after 1763 Lukin himself began writing for the stage, at first as translator of French originals, and later on his own. In 1763 *The Menaechmi*, translated from Regnard, was played; in 1764, *The Jealous Man Delivered of His Delusions*, of Campistron; and in 1765 three more or less original comedies: *The Twaddler [Pustomel']* ; *The Curio Shop [Shchepetil'nik]* ; and *The Prodigal Reformed by Love.* A later translation, *Father-in law and Son-in-law*, from the French of Collé, was played in 1769.

The Elagin circle had a preference for the French sentimental comedy with didactic overtones. Classical theory, of course, insisted that the purpose of comedy was the "correction of morals," and not mere amusement. But if the scene on the stage is not recognizably true to life, the moral effect of the comedy is likely to be lost. A Russian audience, seeing an obviously French comedy, would be likely to dissociate itself from both the vice and its punishment, with the smug observation that "only heathen Frenchmen would behave so." The task, accordingly, which engaged Elagin and his friends was to bring comedy closer to the actual Russian world. Their efforts were timid and resulted in no very great successes, for they seemed to believe that the construction of a proper comedy plot was quite beyond Russian capability, and the best that could be done was to borrow a ready-made plot, French or Danish, and "bend it to Russian manners," that is, rename persons and places, cut out obviously alien elements and introduce some "local color." Still hesitant to employ actual Russian names for persons, they generally resorted to "speaking names," such as "Chistoserdov" ("pure heart"), "Samokhvalov" ("self-praiser") and the like. Of such a kind as this are the two comedies of Lukin which most nearly deserve to be called original, *The Curio Shop* and *The Prodigal Reformed by Love*, both of 1765.[15]

The Curio Shop has a curious history; Lukin took it from an anonymous French piece called *La Boutique de bijoutier,* which was in turn an adaptation of a dramatic satire by the English publisher Robert Dodsley, *The Toy Shop* (1753). Since the French version is unidentifiable, it is hard to say how much of Lukin's comedy is original. The scene of the uncle and nephew and of the two workmen Miron and Vasily, which begin the piece, are certainly additions to the English, as is a good deal else, but to what extent they may reproduce the French is impossible to say. The piece is not actually a comedy at all (Dodsley calls it "a dramatic satire"), but a strung-together series of scenes without any plot. The setting is defined as the *Vol'-nyi Maskarad* ("Free," i.e., "open" to all comers "Masquerade"). Dodsley's original is simply, as his title indicates, a "toy shop." The Russian "Masquerade" appears to have been held in a large hall, provided with dance music, where anyone who chose might come in domino to enjoy an evening of dancing. The hall itself, however, is not the scene, but an adjoining gallery with chairs and tables, and a long bench on which the wares of the curio shop are displayed. These wares are of a mixed sort, partly jewelry—rings, bracelets, snuff-boxes, etc.—partly curios—stones, antique artifacts, etc.— and partly small toilet articles, lorgnettes, telescopes and the like. The original "Toy shop" has the same kind of inventory. Since no single modern English term covers all this ground, it is simpler to use the Russian *Shchepetil'nik* without attempting a translation; the word, however, it should be noted, means not the shop itself, but its owner. Lukin, in his prose preface, points out that he might have called his play *Galantereishchik,* but preferred the obsolescent *Shchepetil'nik* because it was genuine Russian, and not a Gallic borrowing.

The scene begins with the arrival of two Russian gentlemen, Chisto-serdov ("pure heart," i.e., "candid") and his nephew, who has recently arrived from the provinces. It is Major Chistoserdov's purpose to display to the unsophisticated young man a cross section of the capital's so-called "fashionable society," and since the masquerade draws all types, and many

211

of them come to buy from the *shchepetil'nik,* this is a strategic observation point. Two workmen, one, as he remarks, only "twenty weeks" away from his native Galich, and speaking very heavy peasant dialect, appear to set up the display table and lay out the wares. Chistoserdov tells his nephew that the proprietor, the *shchepetil'nik,* is actually a man of good birth and education; he charges outrageous prices for his goods, which the fops usually pay, and gives a third of his earnings to the poor. When he sells his goods, he accompanies them with a satirical "spiel" in which he extols their virtues and mocks and insults the buyer. When the *shchepetil'nik* himself comes on the scene, he is introduced to the nephew, whom he recognizes as a different sort from his usual customers; uncle and nephew take seats, and the file of purchasers begins. Two feather-brained ladies, Nimfodora and Mariemiana, escorted by the fop Polidor, are the first. He is sold a small mirror in which he can see all his vices when he looks at it, and a tiny snuff-box, quite large enough to hold all his virtues, etc. Then come the turns of Pritvorov ("dis-. sembler"), a former courtier; Vzdoroliubov ("rubbish lover"), a collector of curios who buys for an enormous price an assortment of antiques, including a snuff-box made of Diogenes's tub, the invisible chains that Vulcan used to catch his wife in bed with Mars, and three rare stones from the island of "Nowhere—Nohow"; the dandy Legkomyslov ("light thought"); judge Obiralov ("snatcher"); the lady-killer Verkhogliadov ("superficial"); the senile lover Starosvetov ("old world") and the quarrelsome poet Samokh-valov ("self-praiser"), who can see no good in anyone's verses but his own. He is supposed to have been meant as a caricature of Sumarokov. One of the most extended scenes is that between the *shchepetil'nik* and Verkhogliadov, who talks a most bizarre mixture of Russian and partially digested French. A sample of his style is the following speech:

No sound reason! O, *mon ami,* how badly you *jugez* about us! The devil take me! You have *formulé* ideas *désavantageux* about us. Listen to me, and I'll show you that better than all the people in the world we *possédons* sound reason! It [i.e., sound reason] is pleasant, just, *gentil,* amusing... truthful, *léger,* entertaining—*commode....* and—Uf! I'm almost choked! However, to put it to you *tout court, mon cher....* I'm ashamed to be a pedant and *définir* this word. But you've seen, that if I wanted to, I could show you once for all! I am *capable de contredire* you in everything, and I am *capable* also of not doing so. In me, *excepté cela,* there are many *mérites.* I drink *à la sante du beau sexe,* speaking the wittiest *équivoques;* I can *moquer* staid people and the clergy, dis-regard every kind of law and make a fool and an ass of *tout-le-sérieux moralistes,* such as you; and that, *entre nous,* is what is called "sound reason."

This scene has some significance as one item in the campaign waged by the Elagin circle against the modish affectation of French and the contempt for Russian (Verkhogliadov remarks: "Our language is the most beastly, and if we didn't *orné* it with foreign words, it would be impossible for decent people to *discourir* in it without *horreur!"*). Other items in this same cam-paign are Elagin's own comedy, *A Russian Frenchman,* and, as we shall see,

Fonvizin's *Brigadier.*

Lukin's second, full-length comedy of 1765, although its title echoes that of a play of Destouches *(Le Dissipateur)* is, as the author points out at length in his preface, an independent work. It is a good example of the *comédie larmoyante;* it is a comedy only by virtue of ending with young love triumphant and vice punished. There is not a trace of humor in it. Virtue has numerous opportunities to shine, and presumably evoke tearful admiration from the audience; e.g., when the merchant Pravdoliubov ("truth lover"), in contrast to the other of the hero's creditors, tears up the note which he holds and announces his trust in his debtor's pledged word; when the hero's servant Vasily, despite distrust and ill treatment from his master, remains faithful to him and refuses his freedom until the "happy ending"; when the magnanimous younger brother of the hero sways their dying uncle's favor to his scapegrace brother, to his own personal detriment, etc. The elder Dobroserdov brother ("good heart": the hero) indignantly rejects the shady devices which the shyster Prolazin ("old fox") proposes for evading his debts; Vasily denounces the rascally creditor Bezotviazny ("importunate"); Kleopatra, at the cost of her own love and happiness, refuses the proposal of her lover to flee from her aunt's house, etc.

The plot of *The Prodigal Reformed by Love* is in general rather well engineered, but has the defect of a *deus ex machina* solution. Zloradov ("happy in evil") is an implausibly complete villain, and Lukin is not content with letting his villainy speak for itself, but must give Zloradov a number of soliloquies in which he exposes his own perfidy, his disbelief in heaven and hell or divine retribution, his principle that "it is proper to do good—for myself, not others," etc. Zloradov at least remains a villain to the end, and leaves the stage gnashing his teeth and vowing vengeance on the "virtuous," who have triumphed.

In brief, the plot is the following. The elder Dobroserdov has inherited a fortune from his hard-working merchant father, and squandered it, largely through the prompting of his false "friend" Zloradov. The audience learns this from a soliloquy of his servant Vasily and a conversation with Stepanida at the beginning of the first act. But Dobroserdov even before the play begins has been "corrected by love"—for the beautiful Kleopatra, niece of "The Princess." In order to gain access to his love, Dobroserdov has taken lodgings with "the Princess," for whom he pretends love and to whom he has promised marriage. But he is beset by creditors, e.g., Dokukin ("nuisance"), whom he has to fob off by the pretense that he is going to make a rich marriage with the Princess. In the meantime he has arranged with his faithful servant Vasily, with the help of Stepanida (she is Kleopatra's maid) a plot to escape from town to his brother's country estate with Kleopatra—if he can induce her to go. In spite of the protests of Vasily, who hates and suspects Zloradov, Dobroserdov confides his plot to his "friend," who of course offers his help, but actually betrays the whole scheme to the

Princess. In any case, the virtuous Kleopatra refuses to elope, out of duty to her aunt, and she and Dobroserdov are surprised together in his apartment while he is trying to persuade her, by the Princess, as a result of Zloradov's treachery. The Princess in a rage threatens to send her niece to a nunnery at once, and packs her off in the charge of Stepanida. Naturally she also repudiates Dobroserdov, orders him out of her house, and to complete his discomfiture, promises her hand to Zloradov, whose double-dealing is at length realized by the hero. In the final act the dénouement comes as an official from the "magistrat" (town administration) arrives with Dobroserdov's creditors to take him to debtor's prison; at the crucial moment the younger brother of the hero arrives with the news that their uncle has died and left half of his immense fortune (1000 souls and 50,000 rubles) to the profligate older brother. The tables are turned: it is Zloradov whom the creditors now seize; the Princess is overwhelmed with remorse; Stepanida, to whom Kleopatra has been entrusted for incarceration in the nunnery, has brought the girl instead to her lover's brother—and of course Vasily and Stepanida are liberated and permitted to marry. Everything ends happily except for Zloradov, and the audience has, it may be hoped, been taught a sound lesson about not heeding the advice of such rascals as he and not getting into debt over their ears.

The characterization in the play is, of course, highly conventional. Zloradov has the most originality. He is, by his own admission, completely devoid of conscience; he pretends friendship to his victim, pretends love to the Princess, and when at length he reveals his perfidy to Dobroserdov, he takes a high moral tone—he has disclosed his "friend's" plot to the Princess in order to prevent such a crime from being successful. Dobroserdov is gullible beyond all belief, and distinguished otherwise chiefly by helplessness and resourcelessness. He reveals his "good heart" by asides in which he laments the necessity he is under of lying to his creditors; he gives his last 300 rubles to a poor widow to whose husband he owed about 450; he meditates suicide (not very seriously) if he loses Kleopatra; he is overcome with remorse at the thought that his conduct may have hastened his uncle's death; he is effusively repentant to Vasily when the Servant proves to have been right about Zloradov's character, etc. As for Kleopatra, she is the soul of propriety and completely colorless. She doesn't even appear on the stage until the play is more than half over, and it is only through Stepanida's reports and Dobroserdov's soliloquies that the audience comes to know anything about her. She is horrified at the thought of disobedience to her aunt, and refuses to elope with her lover; and she even apologizes to the Princess when Stepanida brings her back home instead of depositing her in the nunnery! No doubt this kind of picture would conform to the bourgeois audience's ideal of a well-brought-up young lady; but it does not do much for dramatic tension.

Lukin's language in his comedies is rather drab and undistinguished, for the most part conventional, somewhat awkward, middle-class Russian. The peasant helpers of the *shchepetil'nik,* however, speak in what is probably a fair approximation of actual peasant speech (Vasily's idiom is marked by *tsokanie,* i.e., the pronunciation of the "ch" sound as "ts"), even though Lukin, in his preface to the play, apologizes for unfamiliarity with peasant language: not being a land-owner, he has never had much contact with peasants. Some of Dobroserdov's creditors in "The Prodigal" are given a modified and diluted version of the merchant dialect.

Lukin's comedies have no important place in Russian literature, but mark a transition between the rather un-Russian early attempts of Sumarokov and the quite genuinely Russian comedies of Fonvizin. *The Prodigal* has also some interest as one of the most successful examples of that strange and unlovely literary hybrid, the "tearful comedy." Faulty as it may be, it would probably be far more tolerable on the stage than his rival Fonvizin's verse "comedy," *Korion,* produced the year before (1764).

C. Catherine II as a Dramatist[16]

The Empress of all the Russias plumed herself on being not only a most enlightened monarch, but also a talented writer. Her pretensions were as ill-founded in the one case as in the other. Quantitatively, indeed, her literary production is impressive—twelve volumes in her *Collected Works.* Her journalistic ventures have already been considered; she carried on an extremely active correspondence, mostly in French and with such *illuminati* as Voltaire, Diderot and Melchior Grimm; she wrote what she considered to be contributions to Russian history—actually no more than ill-organized excerpts from chronicles; she composed, for her grandsons Alexander and Constantine two rather charming children's fairy tales, one of which gave Derzhavin the hint for his ode "Felitsa"; and she wrote no less than 25 complete dramas, which are the only part of this extensive literary heritage that deserve much attention. Most of these dramas are comedies, but in the second period of her literary activity (1785-86) she tried her hand at Shakespearian chronicle plays.

Catherine's native language was German, and French was almost a second language. She never quite mastered Russian, however, especially Russian spelling, and the many works in that language which she published had to be carefully gone over by her private secretaries (Grigory Kozitsky and Alexander Khrapovitsky, both themselves writers) to correct her grammar and spelling. Writing Russian verse was entirely beyond her—all her dramas are in prose. Nevertheless it must be conceded that she had considerable dramatic skill, and her early comedies are light and witty—qualities not prominent in Russian dramaturgy of any period. In another aspect too she

215

is exceptional: with her very close contacts with the intellectual leaders of western Europe, especially France, she was more quickly touched than any of her Russian contemporaries by the new currents of literary style and taste. Her comedies, indeed, may be taken as almost a record of the changing concepts of the genre from 1769 to 1786.

In her comedies Catherine adheres strictly to the classical concept of character as a static datum, universal and unchanging. Moreover, in the construction of her plots character plays very little part. Neither is character revealed through action, as is, for example, Molière's model hypocrite through what the audience sees him doing; nor is the plot complicated by the peculiarities of character, as is, for example, the plot of *Le Malade imaginaire* by Argan's hypochondria. Catherine's persons usually reveal their character through soliloquies, or are wittily described by other persons, usually the servants. Catherine assured Voltaire that she "knew her Russian people"— but of course the "people" for her were the upper class; and it is true that in her comedies she does make an effort to depict persons of this stratum with lifelike traits. This is in fact the most successful aspect of her comedies— the old hypocrite noblewoman in *Oh, the Times!* (1769), or the peevish heroine of *Mrs. Grumpy's Name-Day* (1772), or the inveterate gossip in *Mrs. Tale-Bearer and her Family.* But where her plots and characterization are particularly unsatisfactory is in the treatment of the "lower class" characters. Following French usage blindly (she liked to consider herself the Russian Molière), Catherine gives to the valet and the soubrette in most cases the chief part in working out the intrigue. Her maid-servants are pert and saucy, extremely clever, and possessed of great initiative—qualities totally alien to the brow-beaten Russian serfs of real life.

As the titles of the early comedies reveal, Catherine's targets are very minor social vices—the satire is of the "smiling" variety which she defended in *All Kinds of Things.* The old-fashioned, "unenlightened" life of the backward gentry is mocked with tolerance and good humor. Catherine apparently thought that her admonitions from the stage and the journal would bring about a reform of Russian manners. But political motives are not wanting in some of these plays; she makes the critics of "the government" (which was of course *her* government) as ridiculous as possible, by giving them perfectly preposterous ideas, and thus implying that all such visionary schemes for the country's betterment are similar. Thus, in *Mrs. Grumpy's Name-Day (Imeniny gospozhi Vorchalinoi)* the bankrupt merchant Nekopeikov ("Penniless") conceives a scheme for catching rats on a large scale and making cordage for the Russian fleet of their tails!

After 1772 the series of "smiling comedies" was interrupted, and for the next few years Catherine's literary talents were exerted in other fields. In 1783-84 a periodical began publication under the nominal editorship of Princess E.R. Dashkova, entitled: *Conversational Journal of Lovers of the Russian Word (Sobesednik liubitelei russkogo slova).* A feature of this journal was an anonymous "column" in each issue headed: "Fact and Fable" ("byli i nebylitsy"). Catherine's authorship of this was an open secret. In it she clumsily attempts to imitate the style of Laurence Sterne's *Tristram Shandy,* with its planned illogicality, its whimsical breaking of continuity, etc. "Fact and Fable" has no literary value, but does give evidence of Catherine's remarkable receptivity to new literary fashions. We shall presently see some of the political aspects of this journalistic venture in connection with Fonvizin.

In 1785 another series of Catherine's comedies begins, but these are now no longer "smiling." Embittered by the covert antagonism of the Russian intelligentsia, Catherine takes vengeance in her later "comedies" on what seems to her one of the most vulnerable sides of progressive Russian thought, the Masonic movement. As has been mentioned earlier, Masonry became a very powerful movement in Russia in the late eighteenth century. Ignoring the immense good which the Order accomplished in the neglected areas of education and social welfare, the great publishing enterprise of Novikov, the many schools and hospitals founded by the Masons, etc., Catherine hit at the childish mummery of the Masonic initiation ceremony, the religious mysticism of its later orientation, and especially the secrecy that surrounded it. These aspects of Masonry she savagely attacks in the comic trilogy: *The Deceiver (Obmanshchik), The Seduced (Obol'shchennyi)* and *The Siberian Medicine-Man (Shaman sibirskii).* In these bitter and humorless "comedies" she equates noble and philanthropic Russian Masons, such as Novikov, Schwarz, Kheraskov et al., with the notorious impostor Cagliostro and the alchemists!

As has already been noted, Catherine underwent a "Shakespearean" inoculation. Even though Voltaire had labeled the English poet a barbarian, he still recognized his genius, and himself felt his influence. By way of Voltaire the first Shakespearean drama became imperfectly known to Russia through Sumarokov's amazing *Hamlet.* Of course, for Voltaire—and Sumarokov—one of the chief marks of Shakespeare's "barbarism" was his ignorance of the "rules" of classical drama. This, however, was precisely one of the things that Catherine found attractive in his dramas—and in this she was considerably ahead of her age. She also liked the Shakespearean use of prose in many of his plays, since she was unable to write verse. Catherine, it may be noted, began as a perfectly consistent classicist, but became less and less classical as time went on, until in her latest plays she is already anticipating some of the revolutionary innovations of the early romantics.

Shakespeare in the original was of course inaccessible to Catherine II; her knowledge of the plays came from the German translation by J.J. Eschenburg, published in Switzerland in the mid '70s. Eschenburg's version was entirely in prose. She probably also knew the Le Tourneur translation into French, which appeared in Paris at about the same time.

Inspired by this second-hand contact with the great English poet,

Catherine issued in 1786 what the title-page apologetically described as "A free, but weak paraphrase from Shakespeare, the comedy "This is what it is to have a basket full of laundry." *The Merry Wives of Windsor* may not be at once apparent as the original of this paraphrase; actually the title is a Russian attempt to render Ford's exclamation (Act III, scene v): "This 'tis to have linen and buck-baskets!" Shakespearean chronicle plays also inspired the would-be historian of Russia's monarchs, and in the same year 1786 was published: *A Shakespearean Imitation, a historical perspective without observation of the usual rules of the theater, from the life of Riurik.* In this drama the first Varangian monarch of Novgorod is represented as the benevolent ruler who brings peace and order to a faction-ridden city, and frees it from the revolutionary Vadim. When, a few years later (1793) Kniazhnin's *Vadim of Novgorod* was posthumously published, Catherine was enraged to find herself and her concept of the history of Russian monarchy sharply controverted. Still in 1786 a second Shakespearean "imitation" saw the light: *The Beginning of the Reign of Oleg.* A fourth Shakespearean venture was never completed: *Timon of Athens,* rather interestingly adapted to Russian manners and places.

The theatrical output of Catherine II is of interest chiefly for the light it sheds on the literary fashions which reached Russia from western Europe in the last two decades of the eighteenth century. Her contribution to the literature of her adopted country was far less than she imagined and advertised it to be. She was, however, an excellent barometer.

CHAPTER IX

DENIS FONVIZIN AND THE COMEDY (1745-1792)[1]

The man who revolutionized Russian comedy and can more truly than any other be regarded as the eighteenth-century forerunner of realism was probably better known in his own age as a translator and influential government official. Indeed it was a matter of the greatest difficulty for his own age to know Fonvizin's works at all completely, for most of them were published, if at all, anonymously, and a great deal of what has since become known was either not written for publication or was suppressed by the censors. It is only in the twentieth century that anything approaching a complete edition of Fonvizin's works has been published; and even in this completeness has been achieved only with the original work—the translations are represented in selections.

Denis Ivanovich Fonvizin was born in 1745 and died in 1792. His active life falls thus almost entirely within the long reign of Catherine II. His father was a nobleman of small means, descendant of a Baltic German named Von Wiesen who, taken prisoner by Ivan the Terrible in the Livonian wars, settled in Russia and became thoroughly Russianized. Young Denis was sent with his brother Pavel at the age of ten to Moscow, where he was enrolled in the Gymnasium attached to the newly formed University of Moscow. After finishing the Gymnasium course he continued into the University, and distinguished himself in learning foreign languages—Latin, French and German—to the extent that even while still a student, and at the age of sixteen, he published a translation (from the German) of the *Fables* of the Danish classicist Ludvig Holberg. The translation is in prose, and is partial—about three quarters of the *Moral Fables* of the great comic poet. Holberg's *Moralske Fabler* (1751) are certainly the poorest of his work, and Fonvizin's translations are tame and tedious. One wonders what could have attracted anyone to this wretched stuff, and concludes that in Fonvizin's case it must have been juvenile adulation: the boy had had his first experience with the professional theater, during a visit to St. Petersburg, when he had seen a performance of Holberg's *Henrik and Pernille*—the beginning of his lifelong infatuation with the stage.

The Fonvizin brothers distinguished themselves early by their literary interests and attracted the attention of that academic factotum, Mikhail

Kheraskov, who was at that time in charge of the library, theater, and printing-press of Moscow University. Pavel Ivanovich (1744-1802) contributed a considerable amount of material, both translations and original verses, to Kheraskov's journals; Denis is represented by one mediocre translation ("Jupiter as Judge"), printed in *Profitable Diversion*.

In conformity with a wide-spread custom of the times, the Fonvizin brothers had been enrolled in one of the Guards Regiments at the time of their matriculation; they were considered to be on "detached service" during their student years, and were promoted to the rank of sergeant before graduation, as a reward for good grades. The military service, however, did not appeal to Denis. It apparently did to Pavel, who continued in it and eventually reached the rank of brigadier before he transferred to civil service. Denis left the University in 1762, the year of the *coup d'état* which seated Catherine II on the Russian throne; he was presently picked by the new government for the Foreign Office on the basis of his proficiency in foreign languages.

The exact dating of many of Fonvizin's early translations is uncertain, but it appears that he had already begun a version in Russian Alexandrines of Voltaire's popular tragedy *Alzire;* and he worked at the same time on a prose translation of a political didactic "novel" by Abbé Terrasson, *Séthos* (1731). The first part of this long work was published in 1762, the fourth and the last in 1768. The full title of the Russian version is: *Heroic Virtue, or the Life of Seth, King of Egypt.*[2] The work, which has no literary merit, is one of the popular imitations, numerous in the age, of Fénelon's *Télémaque*—the portrayal of an "ideal enlightened monarch" in a safely remote age. Other translations, which may have been begun as early as 1762, but were completed later, may be mentioned here: one of Ovid's *Metamorphoses*, which is lost; a florid and sentimental version of the Biblical story, translated from the *Joseph* of Paul Bitaubé (1732-1808),[3] which was published in 1766; and a translation from the French of François-Thomas de Baculard d'Arnaud (1718-1805) of a cloyingly sentimental tale of altruistic friendship entitled *Sidney and Silli, or Benefaction and Gratitude.*[4] This last was not published until 1769. According to the dedication, Fonvizin was inspired to undertake this unrewarding work by the desires of his mistress, a circumstance that may perhaps excuse him.

A translation of quite another sort, published in 1766, was probably also begun while Fonvizin was still connected with the Foreign Office. This is a treatise on political economy by Abbé Gabriel-François Couaille entitled *The Gentry in Commerce, as Opposed to a Military Gentry, or Two Discussions on Whether the Well-Being of a State is Served by the Gentry's Entering into Commerce?*[5] Needless to say the liberal author concludes that a commercial aristocracy does subserve the interest of the state. (It may be noted incidentally that Silli, in the Arnaud tale, overcomes his aristocratic prejudices and in order to support his family, engages in trade.) Another political treatise, published anonymously (and apparently also surreptitiously) is partially a translation (from the German political theorist Johann Gottlob von Justi : 1705-1779) and partially original: *A Brief Explanation of the Freedom of the French Nobility, and of the Advantage of the Third Estate.*[6] Fonvizin's conclusions are summed up in the succinct concluding paragraph: "In a word, there should be in Russia: 1) a nobility entirely free; 2) a third estate, entirely liberated; and 3) a populace occupied with agriculture, although not entirely free, yet having at least the hope of being so." Fonvizin's political views are of course irrelevant to a consideration of his place in literature, but since they permeate so much of his artistic writing, it may be well to emphasize here that this paragraph hardly needs elaboration—it presents them in a nutshell. Fonvizin was a nobleman, of ancient family, and believed very strongly in both the privileges and responsibilities of the nobleman. The justification of the privileges is to be found in the gentleman's sense of honor, which forbids—or should forbid—a lazy parasitic existence, and demands lifelong and self-sacrificing service to the native land, whether in the armed forces or the civil service. Such a nobility must also be a partner in the government, advisory and auxiliary to the monarch. A healthy state must also have a "third estate," which can be recruited only from below, that is, from the agricultural peasantry, which must have opportunities afforded for education and for mobility in the social hierarchy. The total and immediate abolition of serfdom, however, forms no part of Fonvizin's ideal program.

As has been mentioned before, the theater always exercised a fascination upon Fonvizin, and one of his early translations was a version of Voltaire's *Alzire*. The ideas of the "Sage of Ferney" were very popular in court circles of this period—Catherine herself, of course, carried on a correspondence with the master and flattered herself that she was indeed the "Semiramis of the North," as he called her. Fonvizin became attached to a circle of young intellectuals headed by F.A. Koslovsky, whose philosophical position was anti-clerical and "free-thinking," and who were close to the monarch. It was probably through this association that Fonvizin was transferred from his post with the Foreign Office to one with the cabinet minister I.P. Elagin, who was presently to be put in charge of the court theater. Elagin was a vain but astute magnate and himself a literary dilettante; to his office was also attached at this time the comic writer Vladimir I. Lukin. From 1763 until 1769, with a half-year's leave of absence in 1768, Fonvizin remained with Elagin; from this period date his first genuinely literary efforts.

The first of these are two satires in verse, *The Fox as Panegyrist*[7] *(Lisitsa-koznodei)* was not published until 1787, but circulated widely in manuscript and was familiar to the literary world long before. It is an "Aesopic" fable obviously inspired by the obsequies of Empress Elizabeth in 1762. The "Lion," king of beasts, has died, and the Fox has taken the podium to deliver an eloquent eulogy of the deceased monarch. "O fate! O cruel fate! Of whom is the world bereft!" he begins. "Smitten by the demise of your gentle sovereign, wail and sob, O honored assemblage of beasts! This emperor, wisest of all the beasts of the forest, deserving of eternal tears, deserving of altars, father of his slaves, dangerous to his enemies, is stretched out before us, senseless and voiceless!'' The panegyric proceeds in this key. " 'O basest flattery!' whispered the mole to the dog. 'I had a brief acquaintance with the Lion: he was a perfect ass, malicious and senseless, and by the power of his supreme sovereignty he did nothing but sate his tyrannical passions. The throne of this gentle emperor, deserving of altars, was cobbled with the bones of beasts torn to pieces!' " At the end of the Mole's angry denunciation the Dog replies: " 'Why are you surprised, when a distinguished fool is flattered by base fools? If this amazes you so much, that low creatures prefer greed to everything, and make their way toward fortune by contemptible means—then it's evident that you have never lived among people.' "

The second of Fonvizin's verse satires is much longer and of a quite different sort. It is inappropriately entitled: *Epistle to My Servants Shumilov, Vanka and Petrushka.*[8] It is not an epistle at all, but rather a conversation between the master and his old "uncle" (i.e., a serf with the functions of a Greek *paidagogos*—the guardian and instructor of a boy of the gentry class), his coachman Vanka and his house-serf Petrushka. These, incidentally, were real people of Fonvizin's household. The satire opens with the master's question, addressed to his old tutor: "Tell me, Shumilov, for what purpose was the world created? And how should I live in it—answer me this." The old man's honest answer is: "I don't know.... But I do know that we must be servants all our lives, and work all our lives with hands and feet... But why this world was created, be pleased to ask Vanka." "To you I now direct my words, broad-shoulders, big-head—spacious capital of minuscule wit! In your province are horses and chariots, and it has finally pleased heaven that both my driver and I myself listen to you. Daily you look upon worldly vanity, and mounted in the rear (of the carriage) you traverse Petropolis. Prepare yourself to give a wise answer to my question. Tell me, great man, for what purpose was the world created?" Vanka angrily replies: "To all your whims not even those who know their letters can answer—and am I to judge about this, when my eyes can't tell A from Z?" Vanka volunteers, however, his opinion of the fashionable world that he sees from his coachman's box: "I've seen cowards and I've seen dare-devils; I've seen simple lords, and I've seen generals; but not to get into a vain squabble with you, know this that I count the whole world as just nonsense... Driver, horses, carriage, horse-collars and everything, it seems to me, in the world is vanity. Here I see prodigality and there I see stinginess; wherever I turn, everywhere I see stupidity.... The priests try to deceive the people, servants the major-domo, major-domos the master, masters each other, and noble boyars often want to deceive the sovereign; and everyone, in order to stuff his pockets a little more thickly, has determined to try his hand at deception for gain.

222

Burghers are greedy for money, and gentry-folk, judges, lawyers, soldiers and peasants. The humble shepherds of our souls and hearts are pleased to collect quit-rent from their sheep. The sheep marry, are fruitful, die, and the shepherds line their pockets accordingly. They forgive every kind of sin for pure cash, and for cash they promise a multitude of diversions in heaven. But if one may speak the truth in this world, I shall tell you my honest opinion: both shepherds and sheep are ready, for money, to deceive the Most High Creator Himself!" When Vanka has had his say, he turns the question over to the lackey Petrushka, whose opinion of the world is no more optimistic—"The whole world, it seems to me, is a child's game. It is only necessary to know most solidly how best, while you're alive, to play this game." "What matter, if afterward the devils take your soul, so long as you have succeeded in living as best possible until your death!" Petrushka's notions of "playing the game" are entirely cynical: "Play, even though your neighbor will weep from the game; pilfer his treasury—your own will be the gainer." "The Creator of the whole creation, for His own praise, sent us forth in the world, like puppets on a table. Some sport, laugh, dance and leap, others scowl, mourn, grieve, weep. That's the way the world turns! But as to why it is so, no one knows that, whether wise or foolish." Finally, turning the tables on their master, with his foolish questions, the three serfs propose that he, who is so wise, let them in on the secret! To this the poet replies: "My friends, comprehend my answer: I myself don't know for what purpose this world was created!"

From the point of view of its open rejection of church ideology this satire is remarkable (it was, of course, not printed until 1769, and then in company with the innocuous *Sidney and Silli* story); but even more remarkable is the power of characterization revealed in the relatively short piece. Although in a different medium, here is the evidence of a brilliant dramatic talent. The three serfs come through as individuals, sharply distinguished— the kindly, conventional, devoted Shumilov, the brawny, taciturn, somewhat morose Vanka, and the worldly-wise Petrushka. The master himself is a paler figure—patriarchally patronizing and yet self-ironical.

The bureau chief under whom Fonvizin worked for some six years, I.P. Elagin, was himself a dramatist, and intensely interested in the theater. As we have seen, his subordinate Lukin was also a writer of comedies. The atmosphere of the office was evidently conducive to dramatic occupations. Comedy was at this time a serious deficiency of the Russian stage. Outside of two or three comedies of Sumarokov, themselves very imitative of French models, there existed no Russian comedy, and the repertoires of the acting companies had, of necessity, to be filled by translations of foreign works, such as those of Ludvig Holberg or Molière. The Elagin circle was inspired to remedy this situation. They were outspokenly critical of Sumarokov and his classical comedies, which they found very remote from actual Russian life (of course such a small masterpiece as *The Imaginary Cuckold* was not written until 1772). The classical theory of comedy justified the genre as a means of "correcting the vices" of society by laughter; but since the situations presented in Sumarokov's comedies were French, in so far as they could be related to any actual society, how could Russian vices be corrected by them? The obvious conclusion from this observation, it would seem, would be to write original comedies on Russian subjects. This, however, would involve departure from the classical canon of generalization, of universality. The Elagin compromise was to utilize successful French plays and rework the plots in such a fashion that Russian names of persons and places and Russian manners would be substituted for those of the original. Thus Elagin's own comedy *The Russian Frenchman* was a translation or adaptation of Holberg's play *Jean de France,* and Lukin's *Shchepetil'nik,* as we have seen, of a French translation of Dodsley's *The Toy Shop.* It should be noted that one of the leading vices of Russian society which Elagin, Lukin and their group were minded to correct by ridicule was the servile adulation of everything French and the denigration of everything Russian. This is, of course, the theme of the Holberg play, for Danish society too had been infected by Francomania. Fonvizin's first successful comedy, *The Brigadier,* as we shall see, makes use of this theme, but with an original plot and far greater fidelity to actual Russian manners than Elagin's classicism approved of.

One of the trends of French comedy in the middle of the eighteenth century was toward that peculiar genre called *comédie larmoyante*—a genre which Voltaire deplored and which his Russian follower Sumarokov inveighed against bitterly. The mixture of comedy and tragedy, Sumarokov declared, was as nauseous as "cabbage soup with sugar or coffee with garlic!" The ugly hybrid made its way, however, and the comedies of Destouches and La Chaussée became very popular. Since the serious side of the *comédie larmoyante* was almost invariably highly didactic, it might be considered as a proper weapon for the correction of social vices—not, indeed, by "laughter," since seldom are such comedies in any degree amusing. The Elagin circle adopted the new trend, however, and Lukin, as we have seen, produced in 1765 his original comedy, with a non-original title, *The Prodigal Reformed by Love.*

A year before Lukin's comedy was presented Denis Fonvizin, at the time nineteen years old, gave the Russian stage its first *verse* comedy, entitled *Korion* (1764).[9] This is a typical example both of the serious comedy and of the procedure of adapting foreign plots to Russian manners. The original which furnished the plot is *Sidney,* a "drame morale" (1745) by Jean-Baptiste Louis Gresset (1709-1777). The hero, renamed in Fonvizin's version, is Korion, his friend is Menander and his sweetheart is Zenovia— the only Russian name encountered in the play is that of the servant Andrei. The scene, vaguely conceived, is a country estate in the neighborhood of Moscow. One character, introduced by Fonvizin and without a French counterpart, is an unnamed peasant, who describes quite realistically the miseries of peasant life, the oppression of the landlords, the burdensome taxes, etc. This peasant, in startling contrast to the conventional upper-class Russian of the other characters, speaks a stylized dialect, with the *-sta, -sto* suffixes suposed to characterize peasant language; his speech is also marked by *tsokanie*, that is, the substitution of the "ts" for the "ch" sound. Modest as these Russian elements are, they mark at least a beginning; and it is indeed amazing to see how from this very timid start Fonvizin within five years comes to the remarkable lifelikeness of the characterization and language in *The Brigadier*.

In his introduction to the two-volume edition of Fonvizin's works the critic G.P. Makogonenko remarks, apropos of *Korion*: "First of all Gresset's sentimental drama has been turned by Fonvizin into a light comedy."[10] A more obtuse piece of criticism would be hard to find. "Light" is an adjective scarcely applicable to a play whose hero, through three acts, avows at every turn his utter disgust with life and fixed determination to end it, and who actually does, in intent at least, commit suicide at the beginning of the third and last act. That his intention is thwarted by the substitution of a harmless glass of water for the fatal poison does not alter the tone of the whole. Sombre, sentimental and lachrymose, the work is a *drame* in the French taste, unredeemed by even a vestige of humor. The irony and satire against fashionable sentimentalism, which Makogonenko claims to find in it, are simply not there. It is a well-nigh perfect example of the "tearful comedy," with the only flaw in the relatively subordinate role which didacticism plays in it. Korion's infidelity to his mistress Zenovia, which motivates his pathological repentance, is too far in the past and outside the action of the play to convey much of a moral lesson to the audience; and since the hero's obstinate and completely callous determination on suicide, despite all the affectionate protests of faithful servant and devoted friend, is not punished, but almost rewarded by the unexpectedly happy outcome, the conventional demands of *bonnes moeurs* are flouted.

The singularly static plot can be thus summarized: Korion has retired to his country estate without the knowledge of his friends and with the intention, which he reveals in a letter addressed to his friend Menander, of leaving all his possessions to his mistress Zenovia, whom he has betrayed, and then committing suicide. He tries to send his servant Andrei to Moscow with the letter, but Andrei, fearful for his master's life, refuses to go and entrusts the letter to "the peasant." The latter opportunely meets Menander already on his way to visit Korion. When his friend arrives, the hero is obliged to acknowledge his intentions, and the second act is largely taken up with debates in which Korion discloses his world-weariness and misanthropy and Menander upholds the claims of patriotic and social duty. Andrei reassures Menander that he has removed Korion's sword and pistols to prevent the planned suicide. At the beginning of the final act Korion in a soliloquy discloses that he has taken a fatal draught which will put an end to his life during the coming night. At this point Zenovia appears; she has also retired from the city after Korion's betrayal, and her presence on a near-by estate has been hinted at as early as the first act in the words of the peasant about an unnamed lady of the neighborhood who, like Korion, is continually moping and weeping and calling for death. She has now come to have a final confrontation with her former lover. She first meets Menander and learns from him that Korion still loves her and is bent on suicide, which his friends are thwarting. When Zenovia and Korion meet it is quickly discovered that they are still in love with each other and that Zenovia is ready to forgive Korion's infidelity—but alas, he has taken poison! At the last moment Andrei enters, and reassures his master: seeing the glass by Korion's bedside, he has taken the liberty of pouring out the poison and substituting a glass of water! Everything accordingly can now end happily.

The drama is presumably a psychological study of Korion's character. This is a most disagreeable one, and it is very hard to see from the play itself how such a person could have inspired the devoted loyalty of Andrei, the affection of Menander and the love of Zenovia. He is morbidly self-centered, obstinate, and completely unfeeling in his relations toward Andrei and Menander. Even in his despairing colloquy with Zenovia, while he believes himself condemned to a self-inflicted death, it is not her feelings that concern him so much as the frustration of his own last-minute chance for happiness. Such a character is not necessarily unlifelike; but inevitably a reader, or presumably an audience, must react with little sympathy toward it. To "empathize," in the modern term, with Korion, is singularly difficult.

As for the other characters, Menander is a preachy mannikin, the scarcely personalized embodiment of friendship and patriotic sentiments. Zenovia, who appears only in the last act, is so slightly sketched that nothing can be said of her character except that it appears to be a very pallid reflection of Korion's. Like him, she has retired to the country to mope and contemplate suicide. Unlike him, however, she brightens up at once and flies into raptures when she learns that Korion is still faithful and that there is a good chance that all may end well. Korion is so devoted to his somber hopelessness that he exhibits a reluctance amounting almost to impatience at the very notion that happiness might be possible.

The only real character in the play is Andrei. He has some resemblance to a genuine human being; he soliloquizes at the beginning of the first act over the boredom of country life after the bustle of Moscow, where he was born. It appears that he has a wife in Moscow, and would dearly like an opportunity to return to find out if she is still faithful to him—but when Korion tries to send him to Moscow with the letter to Menander, Andrei refuses point-blank to go, even if this may mean punishment, because he suspects his master is planning suicide. All the action of the play, in so far as it is not the result of chance (Menander's opportune arrival and Zenovia's visit) is the result of Andrei's efforts; and appropriately he ends the drama, as

226

he began it: his final four lines are by way of a "moral": "We must never have repugnance for the world; we see, what a thing it is to try to take leave of the world. Even though in life it be our chance to suffer much grief, nevertheless we like to live on a little longer."

Korion was neither a literary nor a stage success, nor were the other experimental comedies of the circle—Elagin's *Russian Frenchman,* and Elchaninov's *Virtue Rewarded*—which were presented in the same year (1764) any more successful. As Lukin ruefully remarks in the preface to his *Prodigal Reformed by Love:* "One, and a very small, part of the parterre likes [comedies] that evoke pity and are filled with noble thoughts; the other, and principal part, [likes] those that are amusing." Lukin avers that in his *Prodigal* he attempts to please both parties—the small elite with a plot that evokes pity and characters that are full of noble sentiments, and the rest with secondary comic characters and scenes—the creditors of Chistoserdov.

Fonvizin's genuine adhesion to the dramatic principles of Lukin and Elagin at any time is more than questionable; and in any case a few years of living in the intimacy of the group, which was riddled with petty intrigue, must have sickened him. Particularly the jealousy of Lukin, with whom he had to work, irritated him, and he sought means to get himself transferred to another branch of the civil service. The opportunity did not come until 1769, after a leave of absence spent with his family during which he worked on his new comedy, *The Brigadier.* To this we shall return presently.

In 1933 G. Korovin published a fragment of a comedy from a manuscript in the Leningrad Library which he claimed, and which has been generally accepted to be, an early version of the later comedy *The Minor (Nedorosl').*[11] There are three acts, in prose, and the action terminates without conclusion—the play is obviously unfinished. Makogonenko attributes it to the year 1764—in other words, it is contemporary with *Korion.* A greater contrast would be hard to find. The theme of the fragment is "education," and the products of two contrasting systems are juxtaposed; there is no plot—in a later age the piece would be called a "sketch." How the comedy would have ended if Fonvizin had finished it is indeed hard to say; there must certainly have been a confrontation in Act IV of the two young hopefuls Ivanushka and Milovid, but it is hard to imagine from what we have how a properly dramatic or comic finale might have been arranged. Perhaps this is the reason why the fragment was abandoned.

None of the characters in this early version have the names that they bear in the final play, and there is nothing to correspond to the conventional love story of the mature *Minor,* nor to the moralizing of the "positive characters" Pravdin and Starodum. In this embryonic *Minor* the central character is a twenty-year-old booby named Ivanushka. He is discovered as the scene opens laboring, under the tender care of his indulgent mother Ulita Abakumova, at the formidable task of learning the alphabet! To fortify

227

him in his task a dish of *blini* and a pot of melted butter rest on the table beside him, into which he dips from time to time. His father Aksen Mikheich, a retired captain of dragoons, grumbles from the other side of the room over his son's slow progress and the mother's indulgence. During the course of the scene Ivanushka never gets beyond the letter "p"—his mother sends him off at that point to play! In spite of his verbal menaces, Aksen is just as easy-going as his wife, and Ivanushka is allowed to get away with the most outrageous conduct. He gets into a scuffle with his father in the course of which the old man is knocked down and hurts his leg, and at his final departure from the torments of the school-room Ivanushka stuffs his mouth with *blini* and then, with a loud belch, spews them out into his parents' faces, and then runs off, hooting with laughter. In the ensuing conversation between husband and wife Ulita defends her darling on the grounds that he is still a "baby" ("rebenok"); Aksen, however, points out that until he learns to read and write, there can be no question of his being accepted into service (presumably military). The old serf Fedul, evidently a long-time retainer of the family, tries to have a serious talk with Ivanushka: he is getting older all the while, and still doesn't know his letters—what will become of him? Ivanushka makes him the derisive "sign of the fig" for his pains, and runs away. "You might as well throw peas at a wall," sighs the old man. At the end of Act II Ulita, contemplating the horrible possibility of her darling's having to enter the service, soliloquizes: "Oh, the service, the Sovereign's service! *(she wails).* How can you get used, lovey, to a strange, far-away land? Darling of my heart, who will fondle you? Oh, my darling baby, who will give you *blini* and *pirozhki?* You won't have either daddy or mummy or kith or kin on whom to lay your poor little wild head! Oh, oh, oh! *(she weeps).* I'll send nanny Afagia with you, lovey—she'll sometimes bake *blini* for you!" Ridiculous as this lamentation is, one may see in it faint intimations of that marvelously complex characterization of both Akulina Timofeevna (the "Brigadirsha") and Prostakova in the final *Minor.* Absurd and almost revolting in her maternal indulgence, Ulita is still a little touching.

The final act, as far as preserved, introduces guests into the household of Aksen and Ulita. The neighboring nobleman Dobromyslov ("good thought") and his son Milovid ("dear look") have come for a call. It is all too apparent that Dobromyslov's sole purpose is to show off his model son, who has newly arrived from school. There is a great flurry at the unexpected visit: the furniture is rearranged, old Fedul sent off to put on his "livery," which turns out to be both ancient and a very bad fit, and Ulita and Aksen express some trepidation and the not unnatural but badly based hope that young Milovid will prove to be a bigger ignoramus than their own son. In this they are badly disappointed. From a conversation with Dobromyslov Aksen learns that the boy, although only 17—three years younger than Ivanushka— has been tutored by French teachers, and knows French, German and Italian, as well as a formidable list of other subjects: "arithmetic, geometry, trigonometry, fortification, architecture, history, geography, how to dance, how to handle a horse, and how to fence with rapiers." He even knows how to play various musical instruments. What is more, he has been in the (military) service for four years (as Fonvizin himself had been, during his gymnasium course) and has already attained the rank of a *kapitan-poruchik* (a grade intermediate between lieutenant and captain). Aksen is appalled—it has taken him forty-two years to reach a captaincy! At this point Ulita makes a formal entrance and is introduced; she begins a polite conversation with young Milovid, by asking him how he found life in St. Petersburg and what there was to do there. The boy mentions balls, masquerades, and clubs ("kloby"). Never having heard this fashionable term, Ulita thinks he is talking about "klopy" ("bedbugs"), and an amusing misunderstanding arises:

Ulita: And what do you do with the "klopy" ("bedbugs")?
Boy: We have a good time, we play concerts and then dance, and afterward we have supper with the whole company.
Ulita: Oh! *(she spits)*. Pfui, pfui—you eat them? What don't those damned Germans and Frenchmen think up! And how do they dance? I suppose by some possession of the devil? We have a lot of them too, and we have no rest with the accursed things, but *our* bedbugs don't do anything more than crawl on the walls and at nights bite unbearably—that's all.

After the boy's father has straightened out this misunderstanding, Aksen and Ulita begin to ask questions about religious practices in the capital: is it true that people there don't keep the fasts? Those damned Germans have spread their heresies everywhere! And does young Milovid know all the church responses by heart? When told that he does not, but can of course read them, Ivanushka's parents begin to boast about *their* darling, who knows the Book of Hours by heart; what good is all Milovid's learning, if he doesn't have this precious knowledge? At the point when Fedul is sent off to find and bring Ivanushka to join the company, the fragment breaks off.

The characterizations in the sketch are exaggerated, but lifelike. Ulita's solicitude for her "baby" and Aksen's easy-going good nature, masked by meaningless bluster, are evidently the factors which have resulted in the deplorable kind of training that Ivanushka exhibits. The narrow-minded provincial outlook of the "minor's" family, with its emphasis on trivial church practices is mocked—but it can hardly be said that Dobromyslov is a compensatingly attractive character: he is too smug and patronizing, and Milovid, very faintly characterized, is rather a prig.

There are a number of discrepancies between this early version and the finished *Minor*. Of course the absence of the love story leaves the sketch plotless, as has been noted; and there is not much place for the obtrusive moralizing that Starodum and the other "positive" characters contribute to the later play, although Dobromyslov, as his name would suggest, does have some sound ideas on a citizen's duties to his native land. The chief difference, however, lies in the intents of the two dramas. The theme of this sketch is "education," and nothing more; the theme of the final comedy is a general exposé of the crass ignorance, boorishness and inhumanity of the Russian "nobility," with chief emphasis on the treatment of the serfs. Here, outside of a few harsh words when Ulita is knocked about by the bustle attending the arrival of Dobromyslov, the serfs are neither mistreated nor threatened with serious mistreatment. Fedul is sympathetically pictured as the faithful old retainer, pathetically anxious that his young master get along in the world; Mitka is a contemptible toady, who lets Ivanushka out-wrestle him when the boy boasts of his strength. To be sure, Ivanushka is rude and derisive to Fedul—but no more so than to his parents. It is plain that the relation of master to serfs, which is such an important element in the final *Minor,* has not yet emerged as a theme with the nineteen-year-old Fonvizin.

The exact date of composition of Fonvizin's *The Brigadier*[12] is uncertain; some put it as early as 1766, others as late as 1769. The most probable date is 1768, during the period when the author was enjoying a half-year's release from active duty. In any case, the comedy became known in 1769, at which time it was circulated in manuscript, and read by the author at numerous private gatherings, including one before Catherine II at Peterhof. It was not published until very much later, the date here also being disputed—from 1783 to 1790.

Among those who invited Fonvizin to give a reading of his comedy in their private houses was Count Nikita I. Panin, Catherine's foreign minister. The association begun by this encounter was to last until Panin's death in 1783, and to have a decisive effect on the author's entire subsequent life. Panin was the most brilliant statesman whom Russia produced during the eighteenth century. He headed a considerable group of liberal noblemen who envisioned the possibility of reforming Russia's Byzantine autocracy along the lines of a constitutional monarchy. In 1762 the group supported Catherine against her husband, with the thought that she could be more readily induced to allow a limitation of the power which she had not yet enjoyed. When this hope proved delusive, the liberals next concentrated their efforts on manipulating the deliberations of the Legislative Commission, convoked in 1768 at Catherine's orders, to draw up a new code of laws. The meetings of the Commission did in fact begin to turn in the direction of reform, and Catherine accordingly dismissed it, on the pretext of the outbreak of the first war with Turkey. A third opportunity seemed to be opened by the prospect of another change of sovereign; since Catherine was a usurper, it might be hoped that the legitimate heir to the throne, Pavel Petrovich (1754-1801), once seated, might make the desired concessions; and this was the more likely in that Nikita Panin had been Pavel's tutor and enjoyed his love and respect. Pavel reached the age of eighteen in 1772, and there was an abortive movement to place him on the throne, which Catherine and her unofficial consort Potemkin were able to frustrate. It may be noted in this connection that the heir suffered a serious illness (designated officially as a recurrent fever) in 1771, which led to wide-spread rumors that his mother was poisoning him. Fonvizin, programmatically defining his opposition to Catherine's tyranny, wrote a florid prose "Speech on the Recovery of Prince Paul Petrovich"[13] in 1771. He was by that time secretary and close friend of Nikita Panin. Panin retained his post as foreign minister, despite Catherine's suspicion and dislike, until 1782, at which time he was removed and went into retirement. He suffered a paralytic stroke soon after, and died in the following year. His biography was written by Fonvizin and published in 1784, ostensibly in London (a second edition in Paris), but in all probability by an illicit press in St. Petersburg.[14]

The friendship of Panin enabled Denis Fonvizin to leave the service of Elagin, which petty jealousies had made unbearable, and return to the Foreign Office, which had been his first department. As Panin's personal secretary he was entrusted with many very important confidential matters, and played a considerable part in the diplomatic history of the next decades. He made his second European journey in 1777-1778 (the first had been in 1762-63) and wrote some very penetrating letters, to Panin and others, on the pre-revolutionary situation in France.[15] Throughout the latter period of his life Fonvizin remained a courageous champion of liberalism against the arbitrary rule of Catherine and Potemkin, and more than once risked disgrace and probably worse by his outspoken opposition.

From a literary point of view Fonvizin's involvement in the absorbing business of foreign affairs is a misfortune, since it allowed him little time for writing. *The Brigadier* had been finished before his shift to Panin's service, and the only comedy to be written subsequently was *The Minor* (1782). *Choosing a Tutor,*[16] although sketched out, remains a fragment of no real significance. As for non-dramatic work of the period, the most important is the prose *Eulogy of Marcus Aurelius,*[17] published in 1777, in which the noble life and rule of the great philosopher-emperor is implicitly contrasted with the base and egotistic tyranny of Catherine. The *Letters to Falalei* we shall consider presently.

The Brigadier is dramatically a great step in advance of either *Korion* or the early *Minor* sketch. It has a plot, rudimentary and improbable, to be sure, but constructed in proper comedy fashion from character; and the characterization is brilliant, realistic, and genuinely Russian. Ostensibly the theme is ridicule of fashionable Francomania (cf. Elagin's *Russian Frenchman*), but beneath this surface motif is the most biting criticism of the corruption and oafishness of current Russian society. The characters are schematically represented—the Brigadier is a narrow-minded soldier, his son Ivan is a feather-brained fop, the Councillor is a combination of shady lawyer and religious hypocrite, and his wife an idle, extravagant society dame. Only the Brigadier's wife, Akulina Timofeevna, seems not to be typical of anything

231

but herself—monumentally stupid, penurious, brow-beaten, but somehow genuinely human and likeable. The two "positive" characters, the Councillor's daughter Sofia and her lover Dobroliubov ("lover of good") are, as usual, totally colorless and insignificant.

The plot is built up entirely from the given peculiarities of character: the Brigadier has made arrangements with the Councillor for the marriage of his son Ivanushka to the latter's daughter Sofia. Neither party to this match cares for the idea; Sofia is in love with Dobroliubov, and Ivanushka is disdainful of any female who, like Sofia, doesn't know French and hasn't seen Paris. The Councillor's wife, Avdotia Potapovna, although she hasn't been to Paris, knows some French and is just such a simpering flirt as Ivanushka himself, so she attracts him and is quite willing to pay off her despised husband by having an affair with the young man who is supposed to marry her step-daughter. Akulina Timofeevna, the Brigadirsha, manages all her husband's financial affairs and is a model of frugality, so that the penurious Councillor is attracted to her good qualities. Contemptuous of his wife's invincible stupidity and serenely confident that no sane man would ever want her, the Brigadier himself is not above some philandering, and casts his eyes on the Councillor's wife—thus putting himself in the position of becoming his own son's rival. The situation thus presented in the first act is developed by a series of "declarations": Ivanushka makes his to the Councillor's wife in a ridiculous half-French jargon, full of clichés from fashionable novels; the Councillor makes his to the Brigadier's wife, in spite of the prospect of hell fire which his terrified conscience keeps reminding him of; he is met by the most frustrating incomprehension—Akulina doesn't even know what he is talking about! The Brigadier interrupts his son's scene with the Councillor's wife and sends him about his business, and then proceeds to make his own declaration in a forthright soldierly fashion, comparing Avdotiia to a fortress which he is about to storm. The only element of external chance in the plot is Dobroliubov's abrupt announcement to the Councillor that he has just won a law-suit as a result of which he is now the owner of a considerable estate; this, of course, leads the Councillor to second thoughts about the marriage alliance with Ivanushka. The denouement comes when one after another these scandalous "declarations" are made public property; the Brigadier informs the Councillor that his son has been making love to his prospective mother-in-law, and the Councillor rages against both his wife and Ivanushka; Ivanushka, who has walked in on the Councillor's abortive overtures to Akulina Timofeevna, reveals them to the Councillor's wife, in order to give her a stick with which to beat her husband; and the Councillor's wife, in order to protect her lover Ivan from his father's wrath, herself reveals the Brigadier's propositions to her. As a result of all this, the projected marriage is of course broken off, the Brigadier, his wife and son leave the Councillor's house, and Sofia and Dobroliubov are duly betrothed.

This flimsy and implausible plot, it may be noted, is more in line with the farces of Sumarokov than with the seriousness of *Korion* or the didacticism of Lukin's *Prodigal Reformed by Love*. It is evident that Fonvizin's rupture with the Elagin circle extended beyond merely his official service. Although we shall see plenty, and more than plenty, of moral preaching in *The Minor*, this is external to the plot and placed entirely in the mouths of Starodum and Pravdin. The "moral lessons" which *The Brigadier* and *The Minor* are contrived to present depend on the power and fidelity of the characterization, as they never do in a Lukin comedy. Starodum's sermons could be pruned away entirely, and the effect of *The Minor* would be as great—perhaps greater. In *The Brigadier*, fortunately, Fonvizin has not provided a raisonneur.

The *Brigadier* plot, as has been mentioned, follows classical precept in being evolved out of character; but the plot is so silly that the character inevitably stands out as the play's principal interest. And in the depiction of character Fonvizin has taken a remarkable step, which justifies the claim that *The Brigadier* is Russia's first "realistic" comedy. Classical "character comedy," as for example Molière's *L'Avare*, or *Le Malade imaginaire*, or *Tartuffe*, is a picture of a monomaniac, a one-sided, univocal character dominated by a single personality trait: Harpagon is a miser and nothing else; Argan is a hypochondriac and all the thoughts which Molière gives him relate to his own health; Tartuffe's lechery and treachery are merely parts of his all-embracing hypocrisy. To be sure, even Molière on occasion defies the classical conventions, as in *Le Misanthrope*: Alceste is an uncomfortably honest man, but he is also not a little ridiculous. There are germs in Molière's comedies of character complication. But Fonvizin in *The Brigadier* presents us for the first time with characters who are not mere moral abstractions, but social types; without explicitly telling us as much, he makes us see, in the Brigadier himself, for instance, the product of a limited, spit-and-polish military training, for whom it is not unnatural to suppose that the only use for literacy must be ability to read the military statutes and drill manuals! The Councillor is similar; his "character" is that of the shifty, devious, grasping shyster—a product of Russian social conditions and inexplicable without them. And Ivanushka, of course, is an older version of the Ivanushka of the *Minor* sketch, who has had the advantage (!) of a stay in Paris. He is patently the result of the same kind of parental indulgence as that of Ulita and Aksen; his father is gruffer and there is probably more likelihood of his threats being meant seriously—but unquestionably Ivanushka's present character is not something "stamped on" him at birth, according to the classical conception, but something imposed on him by a thoroughly bad system of education, in which not only his parents, but the whole of his and their society have to share the guilt. As for Akulina Timofeevna, the relations exhibited on the stage between her and her husband make clear the origins of her character. The Brigadier seldom addresses her without reference to her stupidity, and is prone to call her "my sow," when talking, in her presence, with the Councillor and his wife. The poor woman, in one most revealing speech to Sofia, gives us a vivid glimpse of the life she has led as a poor officer's wife without much money—and even so, she says, her lot has been far better than that of a captain's wife of her acquaintance, whose husband beat her, especially when drunk! And once, she relates, the Brigadier, just as a joke, hit her so hard in the chest that the breath was knocked out of her and she nearly passed on to the other world—and he stood there and laughed! There can be no doubt of the realism of such a description; but it has the effect of fixing the reader' sympathy on this pathetic old creature, however unlovely some of her qualities may be. And undoubtedly her utter stupidity has something of the same effect—we are prone to feel indulgent toward the unredeemable blockhead out of a sense of our own intellectual superiority. When the absurd love-making of the Councillor meets with nothing but complete bewilderment on Akulina's part, we inevitably begin to have an affection for her. Ivanushka (Act II, scene iv) breaks in and finds the Councillor on his knees before Akulina:

Ivan. Bravissimo! Bravissimo!
Akul. What are you jumping around for, Ivanushka? We were talking about business. You've interrupted Artamon Vlasich; he wanted to ask me something, I don't know what.
Ivan. Why, mother, he is making you a *déclaration en forme!*
Councillor. Judge not, and thou shalt not be judged. *(He departs, blushing)*
Akul. Ivanushka! Please interpret what you just said to me?
Ivan. Mother, he's making love to you! Don't you at least understand that?
Akul. He, making love! My dear, what has got into your mind!
Ivan. The devil take me, if that isn't the truth.
Akul. Cross yourself! What an oath you're swearing—recollect yourself! You can't joke with the Devil, you know. Now take your little hand, Ivanushka, and cross yourself nicely.
Ivan. Mother, I see you don't believe me. But why was he on his knees?
Akul. I know why, Ivanushka. Surely it wasn't for making love? Oh, this damned son of mine! What won't he think of!

Fonvizin's "negative" characters in *The Brigadier* are thus palpably creations of their social environment and their kinds of education—and these kinds of education are, for better or worse, those of eighteenth century Russia specifically, and not those of some abstract "anywhere, any time," as the canons of classical comedy demanded. The same, however, cannot be said for the "positive" characters. Sofia and her lover are completely colorless and might as well belong to Denmark or France as Russia. Fonvizin never succeeded in creating a really plausible and convincing "positive" character.

During the period immediately after the writing of *The Brigadier*, Fonvizin evidently became acquainted with the journalist Novikov. In 1770 Novikov published in his short-lived periodical *The Twaddler (Pustomel'ia)* Fonvizin's satire "Epistle to my Servants," which had of course been written

234

some while earlier and circulated in manuscript. In 1772, in the periodical *The Portrait-Painter (Zhivopisets)* appeared the famous *Letters to Falalei*,[18] signed only with the initials "R.P.," which have usually been interpreted as meaning "Russkii Pisatel'," i.e., "Russian Writer." There is no certainty, of course, as to the authorship of these letters, which we have considered in detail earlier; but the vivid and realistic portrayal of a rustic "gentleman's nest," marked by stupidity, corruption and heartless cruelty to the serf population is so remarkably like that which we see in Fonvizin's *The Minor*, and so unlike anything else which we know by Novikov himself, that it is almost inevitable to conclude that Fonvizin was indeed the "Russian Writer" in question. Particularly great is the similarity in the portrayal of Falalei's mother with the multi-dimensional women of Fonvizin's comedies, Akulina Timofeevna and Prostakova. Sidorovna is depicted, in the letters of her husband and brother, as tyrannical and cruel to her serfs, in the manner of Prostakova; but in her own letter to Falalei she reveals such a touching affection for her absent son that an entirely different light is cast on her personality, just as the final heart-rending utterance of Prostakova: "I have no son any longer!" almost makes that ugly monster a tragic figure. It is worth noting too, in this connection, that Sidorovna's brother makes the typical remark apropos of the grief of Falalei's father for his dead wife: "He is mourning for her as if he had lost his favorite cow!" The comparison of a wife to "skot" ("cattle") of some kind is a favorite device of Fonvizin—note that Prostakova is a Skotinina by birth, that Akulina is usually qualified by her loving husband as "a sow," and the like. There will probably never be any means of attaining certainty on the authorship of the *Letters to Falalei*, but stylistically the evidence is overwhelming.

During the period of the 1770s Fonvizin's time was largely taken up with his diplomatic labors in the service of Nikita Panin, and there was little leisure for purely literary activity. In 1777 he published a translation of a *Panegyric Oration on Marcus Aurelius*, by the director of the Paris Academy of Sciences Antoine-Leonard Thomas (1732-1785).[17] In the same year Fonvizin and his wife (he was married in 1774) traveled overland to France and spent some nine months in the country, visiting various places in the south as well as Paris. His letters from France, addressed to his sister and to various friends, including N.I. Panin, are often brilliant and show a very observant mind. During his stay in France he became acquainted with several of the leading *philosophes*, among them Voltaire. To his great regret Rousseau, whom he greatly admired, died before he had an opportunity of meeting him.

Upon his return to Russia Fonvizin continued in the service, and published nothing of consequence. In 1781 Catherine suddenly removed N.I. Panin from his post as Foreign Minister and replaced him with Baron Ostermann. Panin retired to his estates and suffered a stroke from which he never recovered; he died in 1782. Fonvizin was briefly installed in the department of the post, but resigned in 1782 from the government service.

During the last illness of his friend Panin, Fonvizin cooperated in writing a very important secret document which Panin intended to be submitted to his former ward, Prince Pavel Petrovich, as a sort of guide to the latter's conduct when he should succeed to. the throne. This document, entitled *Discourse on the Indispensable Laws of the State*,[19] was largely drafted by Fonvizin, doubtless after conversation with the half-paralyzed Panin. The discourse did actually reach Tsar Paul after his accession, but was not acted upon, but safely stowed away among secret papers where it was not discovered until 1831 by his son Nikolai I, who was so horrified by its contents that he ordered it locked away where its revolutionary poison might not corrupt anyone.

The *Discourse,* while not overtly addressed to the monarch, is actually a kind of general admonition to a prince, dwelling on the evils of an autocracy, the viciousness of a regime of "favorites," the necessity of inalterable laws (a "constitution") which even the monarch may not suspend, etc. Toward the end there is an eloquently rhetorical passage pointing out the anomalies of Russia's situation among the states of the world—the largest in size, but with only two cities worthy of the name, etc. There is no advocacy in the document of immediate liberation of the serfs, but an indication that the welfare of the country depends on restraints laid by the government on the arbitrary power of the landlords. As for the autocracy itself, the monarch is warned more than once that his power is granted only for the good of his country, and that if he should employ it for selfish ends and contrary to Russia's interests, the people would be justified in taking it away. Copies of the *Discourse,* apparently provided by a nephew of Fonvizin who had access to his uncle's papers, found their way into the hands of the Decembrists, and some were confiscated when the investigating commission interrogated the conspirators. It was qualified by one of the police officials as "one of the most outrageous works of its age, when the revolutionary torches were burning in France and French free-thinkers were striving from these to kindle a spark in our beloved country likewise."

Shortly after his return from France Fonvizin returned to a work which had evidently been in his mind for many years—the comedy *The Minor.*[20] As we have seen, a first sketch with this name was carried through three acts as early as 1764. The final version was completed by 1779, and as with *The Brigadier,* read to select groups of friends by the author himself, who was gifted with a most remarkable acting ability. The acclaim which the comedy excited at these readings lead to the hope that it might be put on the stage; but difficulties with the censors thwarted all efforts until 1782, when permission was finally obtained (some think through a personal appeal to Potemkin) to produce *The Minor* in the capital city with the company of the "Free Theater." In the following year it was also produced in Moscow. The public success was enormous and the piece was at once acclaimed as "the first real

Russian comedy."

The title, *Nedorosl'* in Russian, has been variously rendered in English; *The Minor* is perhaps the least unsatisfactory translation, but requires explanation. By a law of Peter the Great a nobleman's son remained a *nedorosl'* until such time as he could pass a literacy examination in the capital city; until this examination was passed he could not enter the obligatory government service nor marry. Ivanushka, in the early sketch, had not progressed, by the age of twenty, to the point of even knowing the alphabet, although he could recite church responses by heart. Mitrofanushka, in the final version, is somewhat farther advanced, to be sure, and his accomplishments are not painfully juxtaposed with those of a brighter competitor; but when he makes the word "door" an adjective because the door "depends" on its jamb, and explains his liking for history because of the "stories" ("istorii") which the milkmaid tells him, it is fairly evident that he is still a legal minor even at the age of twenty.

In the final version of the comedy almost everything but the name has been changed. The theme of the sketch was, as we have seen, education, and there was an absurd, but not particularly significant picture of a backward rural family of "noblemen." The theme of the final comedy is quite different, and the characterization has been changed accordingly. Ivanushka's family, backward and stupid though they were, were not depicted as particularly harsh toward their serfs, since the focus of the sketch was elsewhere. The Prostakovs, on the other hand, are pictured as tyrannical and overbearing in their relations with their underlings, just as they are subservient and ingratiating toward their superiors. Education remains a very significant theme in the final comedy, but it is depicted as something linked indissolubly to the entire social evil of serfdom, and the principal theme is unquestionably the larger one of serfdom itself.

The structure of the play in its final form adheres externally to the canons of classical comedy. It has five acts; a room in the house of the Prostakovs is the only scene; and the time falls easily within the twelve-hour limit; it has no sub-plot to dissipate audience attention. In other words, the three unities are strictly observed. At the end of the comedy the young lovers are happily united and villainy is properly punished, as comic propriety demands. It may be noted, however, that when Pravdin suddenly produces an official authorization for sequestering the Prostakov estates and putting them into trusteeship because of the owners' abuses, the effect is just as artificial and implausible as the ending of *Tartuffe:* the Russian audience must certainly have realized that no such dénouement would have been possible in real life, and that even if Mrs. Prostakov had been thwarted in her designs on Sofia, she would certainly have met with no hindrance in carrying out her dire threats against the serfs who had not prevented Sofia's escape. Both Molière and Fonvizin were indulging in "wishful thinking" in contriving the endings of their comedies and the grim realities in both cases must have been clearly apparent behind the flimsy conclusions.

The plot of *The Minor,* however, does not, as the plots of most classical comedies do, serve to create suspense. Most of the formal plot is worked out in the first two acts, and a great deal of what remains is, from a formal point of view, mere padding, in which the characterizations of Mrs. Prostakov, of Skotinin and of Mitrofanushka are elaborated and Starodum and Pravdin have an opportunity of expounding their noble sentiments. In the first act we discover that the virtuous young lady Sofia, orphaned during the absence of her uncle, has been taken in by distant relatives, the Prostakovs, who have appropriated her property and mean to marry her off to Mrs. Prostakov's boorish brother, Taras Skotinin, in order to cover up their tracks. Sofia, of course, is in love with a young officer whom she has met in St. Petersburg, Milon, who opportunely comes on the scene as commander of a detachment which has been quartered in the Prostakov village. Sofia receives a letter from her uncle Starodum, announcing his return from a gold-mining enterprise in Siberia; he has amassed a fortune and is now about to claim his niece. Mrs. Prostakov now changes her mind: Sofia as an heiress should now be married not to Skotinin, but to the Prostakovs' twenty-year-old "minor" son, Mitrofanushka.

A gentleman with the declarative name of Pravdin ("pravda"—"truth" or "justice") appears at the beginning of Act II, and in a conversation with his old friend Milon reveals that the provincial governor has empowered him to investigate the abuse of serfs by landlords in the province, and at his discretion deprive them of the use of their estates. From what he has heard of the Prostakovs, they are likely subjects for such action, and he is accordingly only waiting for an overt act. It is thus, by the end of the second act, a foregone conclusion that: Sofia and Milon will be happily married through the intervention of her uncle Starodum ("Old Thought"), whose imminent arrival is announced as early as Act I, and who is on the scene at the beginning of Act III; and that Mrs. Prostakov will commit some outrageous act in order to bring off the marriage of her oafish son and Sofia, and that Pravdin will exercise his authority to punish her and her hen-pecked husband. The only possible element of suspense left is the exact manner in which Mrs. Prostakov's desperation will be expressed. In the meanwhile, the rest of the play is filled out with amusing scenes in which uncle Skotinin and nephew Mitrofan are pitted against one another as rivals for Sofia's hand; and in which Mitrofanushka's education is sketched as he suffers at the hands of his three tutors, the seminary student Kuteikin, the ex-sergeant Tsyfirkin, who tries to teach him arithmetic, and the German Vralman ("vral' "—"liar"), who lets him do much as he pleases and gets handsomely paid for doing so. The moment Starodum appears on the scene, the comedy takes another turn, and in long and tedious scenes with his niece and with his friend Pravdin Mr. "Old Thought" holds forth on the duties of a citizen, on moral conduct in domestic life, on the degeneracy of contemporary life, and much else. Action halts almost completely until at the end of Act IV we learn of Mrs. Prostakov's plot to kidnap Sofia and marry her off forcibly to Mitrofanushka. The attempt is of course thwarted and Pravdin employs his authority to punish the Prostakovs. The effect of this peculiar structure is to make the "positive" characters mere ironical bystanders and observers of the base and ridiculous antics of the "negative" characters through four-fifths of the play. That in spite of this complete failure of suspense the comedy remains interesting is entirely the result of the characterization—and this only of the "negative" characters.

The very first scenes of the play sketch the main characters unforget-tably: Mr. Prostakov, a shallow, foolish ("prostoi"—"simple"), compliant hus-band, who, when his wife snaps at him: "And I suppose you yourself are blind?" replies submissively: "In the presence of your eyes, mine see nothing." Mrs. Prostakov, the genuine "heroine" of the comedy, shrewish, loud-mouthed, tyrannical, and also sly and mealy-mouthed when it serves her purposes, with an almost touching animal love for her lout of a son; Mitrofan himself, an over-fed, spoiled brat, contemptuous of his father, confident of his ability to get anything he wants from his mother, and utter-ly callous toward the serfs. And finally Taras Skotinin, whose name is ap-propriately derived from the word "skot," "a domestic animal of any kind," and whose almost sole interest in life is pigs, which on his estate are obviously better housed and cared for than his miserable peasants. A few minor char-acters are also quite sharply characterized: the peasant tailor Trishka, whose new coat made for Mitrofan is the object of such acid criticism in the first scene; Eremeevna, Mitrofan's old nurse, who stands up to Skotinin with talons bared when Mitrofanushka, like a frightened child, runs to her for protection from his uncle's threats; and the three ridiculous tutors, whose squabble at the end of Act III is a concession to the popular farce. As for the "positive" characters, they are obviously less lifelike and less interest-ing. Sofia has no individuality at all, nor has Milon (his name is derived from "milyi," "dear, beloved"). Pravdin is little more than a lay-figure, whose edi-fying discourse is mostly a mere supplement to that of Starodum. The latter is of course the principal positive character, and the bearer of Fonvizin's own ideas. From the similarity between the characterization of Starodum in *The Minor* and the picture which Fonvizin gives of his father in his auto-biographical *Candid Confession of My Acts and Thoughts*[21] it is apparent that the model for Starodum was Ivan Andreevich Fonvizin. The elder Fonvizin was evidently an admirable character, strictly honest, patriotic, self-sacrificing, a man of old-fashioned morality. So is Starodum. He is also an unconscionable bore on the stage. Contemporary accounts tell of wild bursts of applause for some of the long monologues of Starodum; and the author was so certain that the success of his play was due to "Mr. Old Thought," that he envisaged a periodical to be called by his name and sub-titled "Friend of Honorable People," which would have consisted in large part of discourses in the form of edifying letters from Starodum. It can only be said that eighteenth century audiences must have been far less conscious of dramatic appropriateness and far more receptive to moral preaching than those of our day. Of course Fonvizin was not an innovator here: Diderot's *père de famille* is just such another long-winded moralizer—and he has many French, and some English, competitors. But the fact remains that however high-minded and edifying a stage person's sentiments may be, he is a dramatic dead weight unless his character is manifested for us in action—and this truth is just as much true for an eighteenth century comedy as for a Greek tragedy or a play of Shakespeare. Diderot's theory of drama as a school of morals, inculcated by precept from the stage and not by action, was wrong, and Fonvizin was wrong in following this mistaken principle.

The living portion of *The Minor*, therefore, is the portrayal of the Prostakovs and Skotinin. This is properly developed by self-revelation in word and act. Prostakova's attitude toward education is revealed in her naive words in the first page; the tailor Trishka, abused for making Mitrofan's coat too tight, objects: "But, ma'am, you see I learned my trade self-taught. And I kept telling you at the very time: 'Well, be so good as to give it to a tailor.' " Prostakova: "And so I suppose you have to be a tailor in order to know how to sew a coat properly! What stupid reasoning." So far as Prostakova is concerned learning of any kind is a waste of time, mere ornament. When the tutors appear at the end of Act II, she says to her darling boy: "You won't have to study all your life, dearie, not all your life. You already know so much that you yourself could bring up youngsters." She contrives a scene in Act III to put her child on display before Starodum as a model student: "While he's resting [i.e., Starodum], my dear, you study, just for show, so that it may get to his ears how hard you work, Mitrofanushka." Her attitude toward the tutors, except for the oily German, is contemptuous. When the ex-sergeant Tsyfirkin ("tsyfir"—"cipher") notes that his charge is always calling him names (here it is "garrison rat!"), Prostkova says in a huff: "Oh, Lord my God! Now the child can't dare call Paphnutych names! Now he's angry!" Tsyfirkin, as Mitrofan demands, begins his lesson with review problems—indeed, he never gets beyond them—but grumbles that with only review problems one doesn't get forward very fast. Prostakova: "That's not your business, Paphnutych. I like it very much, that Mitrofanushka doesn't care to get ahead. With his mind, he might fly far away, and then God help him!" Incidentally, the arithmetic lesson serves to illuminate Prostakova's attitude toward money as well. The problem set is: suppose that you and two other people find on the road a treasure of 300 rubles. How would you divide it? Mitrofanushka begins laboriously: "One times three is three, one times zero is zero, one times zero is zero." His mother interrupts to find out what he is doing, and upon being told, says decisively: "He's talking nonsense, my darling! You found the money, don't divide it with anyone. Keep it all for yourself, Mitrofanushka. Don't study this fool's science!" One of the tutors at least has his revenge in a sly way: when the "fool's science" of arithmetic is abandoned, the ex-seminarist Kuteikin opens the Book of Hours and sets his pupil to reciting by rote the following ostensibly Biblical passage, couched in Old Church Slavonic: " 'Lo, I am a worm.... a worm,' that is an animal, a beast; that is: 'I am a beast.... and not a man.... the derision of men.... and a humi—' " At this point Vralman breaks in and the religious lesson finds its end as had the lesson in simple division.

In some respects the characterization of Skotinin is the most successful part of the comedy. He has come, at his sister's invitation, to marry Sofia—but no one has seen fit to inform the bride of her good fortune! When she first appears, she holds in her hands a letter from her uncle informing her of his return. Prostakova is indignant: Starodum can't return, for he's dead! He must be dead, because she has duly had requiem masses said for his soul! The letter must be a fraud of Sofia's. She hands it to her brother to read; outraged, he cries: "I? I haven't read anything since I was a lad, sister! God has saved me from any such vexation." At the end of Act I Skotinin is alone on the empty stage; he muses: "They've all left me to myself. I might as well go have a turn in the cattle yard." Skotinin's fondness for—and resemblance to—"the beasts of the field" is made the object of a subtle joke when (Act IV, scene vii) he tries to explain to Starodum the antiquity of his family: "I'm Taras Skotinin, and not the last in my family. The Skotinin family is great and ancient. You won't find our forefather in any Book of Heraldry." Pravdin (laughing): "So you'll make us believe that he was older than Adam." Skotinin: "And what do you suppose? Only just a little—" Starodum (laughing): "That is, your forefather was created on the sixth day, and so a little before Adam?" The Book of Genesis, of course, places the creation of the animals on the sixth day, and Skotinin is unwittingly classifying himself with them. Skotinin's last speech, when in Act V he has learned that Sofia has been definitively betrothed to another, differs in different texts of the play. In the Makogonenko edition he replies to Pravdin's stern warning not to lay hands on his serfs, and to admonish his neighbors to similar moderation, with the cringing words: "How should I not look after my friends! I'll inform them that.... they're not to lay hands on people." But in the version which I find in an old 1869 anthology[22] Pravdin says: "Yes, go back to your pigsties. However, I advise you to watch yourself. I've heard that you behave with pigs immeasurably better than with people." Skotinin replies: "Merciful sir! How could I have any taste for people? People show off their brains in front of me, but with pigs I myself am the brightest of all."

As with *The Brigadier*, Fonvizin's characterizations in *The Minor* depict people not as individuals in a vacuum, but as part of an entire social milieu—and here the milieu includes the serfs as well as the "noble" landlords. Prostakova is the unscrupulous tyrant that she is and Mitrofanushka is the lazy good-for-nothing that he is because of a social system that relieves them from any necessity of working and delivers a servile population body and soul into their hands. Mrs. Prostakov's habitual attitude toward any serf is contemptuous and threatening. Eremeevna, Mitrofan's old nurse, rushes at her "baby's" call for help, to defy the enraged Skotinin, which she most effectually does; but all the thanks she receives from Prostakova is: "You bitch, you stood like a block of wood, you didn't latch on to my brother's mug, you didn't tear his snout back to his ears!" The most telling scene comes in Act V when her plot to kidnap Sofia is forestalled and she falls in fake repentance at Starodum's feet and pleads for forgiveness. When Starodum says: "I desire no one's ruin. I forgive her," Prostakova cries: "He has forgiven! Oh, sir.... Well! Now I'll give those scoundrelly people of mine a going over! Now I'll take them all, one by one! Now I'll find out who let her slip out of their hands. No, you rascals! No, you thieves! As long as I live I won't forgive, I won't forgive this insult!" Pravdin: "And for what are you intending to punish your people?" Prostakova: "What sort of question is this, sir? I suppose I haven't authority over my people?" Pravdin: "And do you suppose that you have a right to flog them whenever you take a notion?" Skotinin breaks in indignantly: "Doesn't a gentleman have the liberty to beat up a servant when he wants to, I'd like to know?" Pravdin replies: "No one is at liberty to be a tyrant." Prostakova: "Not at liberty! A gentleman, when he wants to, and not at liberty to flog his servants! Then for what were we given the decree on the liberty of the gentry?" Prostakova' query is of course well taken, for except under the ideal conditions envisaged by Fonvizin in his comedy, the 1762 decree that "liberated the gentry" from obligatory state service also in effect set them free to treat their serfs as chattels devoid of rights.

The dehumanizing effect of the serf system may be seen most repulsively in Mitrofanushka, who has been brought up to think of his servants as so many animals. Except when the menacing sight of his uncle Skotinin bearing down on him makes him scream in infantile terror for the protection of his "mamushka," his attitude toward the serfs is copied from his mother's and is expressed by "old witch," "garrison rat," and the like. But, more ominously, this contempt for beings of a "lower" class extends with him even to his family. He reports in Act I on a disturbing dream he has had (as a result of over-eating): "It seemed to me, mummy, that you were pleased to be beating daddy." Mr. Prostakov confides in an aside to the audience: "The dream, more's the pity, is all too real!" and Mitrofanushka continues: "And so I felt sorry!" Mrs. Prostakov (vexed): "For whom, Mitrofanushka?" Mitrofanushka: "For you, mummy; you got so tired clobbering daddy!" But real affection for "mummy" is an emotion unknown to this self-centered lout. The scene at the end of the play, when Prostakova is totally crushed, her scheme for marrying her son to a rich heiress thwarted and her liberty to abuse her servants unaccountably taken from her, she most unexpectedly becomes suddenly almost pitiable as she embraces her darling child with the words: "You're all that's left to me, my heart's darling, Mitrofanushka!" The boy replies petulantly: "Oh, leave me alone, mummy! How you've latched on to me!" Prostakova: "You too! You too have deserted me! Oh, ungrateful!" (she falls in a faint). When Prostakova comes out of her swoon she sums up her whole plight in the despairing cry: "I'm ruined altogether! My power is taken from me! I can never show my face again for shame! I have no son any more!" Starodum ends the "comedy" with a word to the audience, as he gestures toward the broken woman: "Here are the deserved fruits of vicious ways!"

The Minor is Fonvizin's masterpiece, for all its faults. He never approached it in any of his later work. After his partial paralysis he worked on a comedy which he entitled *Choosing a Tutor,*[23] and of which three acts were written in a very hurried and sketchy fashion. Interestingly enough, this is again a treatment of the theme of education, which preoccupied him so lastingly. But even if it had been completed, this work would never have made much mark. Prince and Princess Slaboumov ("weak mind") discuss together the choice of a tutor for their son Vasily. The local Marshal of the Nobility, Seum, recommends a gentleman of the neighborhood, Nelstetsov ("non-flatterer"); but the Princess's friend, Countess Samodurova ("household tyrant") produces the accomplished Frenchman Pelikan, who always addresses nobility as "Votre altesse," and is an expert at paring corns! Even though the Marshal recognizes Pelikan as an impostor totally without education or morals, his qualifications are obviously superior to those of the honorable Nelstetsov, and he is accordingly employed. There are a few good bits of characterization, but as a whole the sketch is a failure.

The last years of Fonvizin's life were very gloomy; during a journey to France and Italy in 1784-85 he suffered a stroke which resulted in the paralysis of his right side and the partial loss of speech. He recovered sufficiently to be able, on his return to Russia, to think once more of literature; but the suspicion and dislike of Catherine closed all avenues of publication to him. He projected a sort of one-man journal to be called *The Friend of Honorable Men, or Starodum,* and composed several pieces which were to fill the first issues—but the censors refused permission for the publication.[24] Some of the pieces are in the form of letters to and from characters of *The Minor.* We learn, for instance, from a letter of Sofia to her uncle that her husband Milon has succumbed to the charms of a society lady, and Sofia is in despair. Starodum's reply is the eminently sensible one: Pay no attention to his infidelity; he'll get tired of his new flame and return to you. Skotinin writes to his sister about the mortal blow he has suffered by the death of his favorite sow, etc. Part of the material was a short parody entitled: "General Court Grammar," in the form of question and answer. Thus, for example, to the first question: "What is Court Grammar?" we find the reply: "Court Grammar is the Science of being cleverly false with tongue and pen." To the question: "What is court lying?" the reply is: "It is the expression of a base soul before an arrogant soul. It consists of shameless eulogies to a great lord for services which he has not done and for merits which he does not possess."

During these years Fonvizin was able, anonymously, to contribute some material to a periodical which Catherine herself sponsored, *Conversational Journal of Lovers of the Russian Word (Sobesednik liubitelei rossiiskogo slova)*. One of the best of these contributions is what purports to be a copy of the sermon delivered by Father Vasily in an unnamed village to his peasant flock on Whit Monday.[25] It is perhaps a parody, but has all the earmarks of authenticity, as the good priest enumerates by name and upbraids one after another of his bleary-eyed parisioners, and sternly asks where and how they have been celebrating the previous day's festival of Whit Sunday. The sermon is mainly directed against drunkenness, and ends with the citation of two contrasting lives: Iakov Lysoy, whom drunkenness has reduced to beggary, and Iakov Alexeev, who is present in the church, surrounded by a blooming family of thirty-five sons, grandsons and great-grandsons! It is evident that Fonvizin has not yet lost his sense of humor or his powers of observation. In the same periodical, *Sobesednik*, he also engaged in a masked battle with the Empress that is reminiscent of Novikov's encounters with the imperial editor of *All Kinds of Things.* Catherine, anonymously of course, ran what we would call a "column" in the journal under the caption of "Fact and Fable" ("Byli i nebylitsy"). Fonvizin, also anonymously, addressed in 1783 a series of very pointed and embarrassing "Questions" to "The Editor of 'Fact and Fable.' "[26] Catherine was under the impression that the vexatious questioner was the prominent magnate I.I. Shuvalov, so she felt constrained to publish answers. These are usually rather lame and often hint at the Empress's impatience and irritation. The episode is interesting, but of no great literary significance. There is even less to be said for the story "Callisthenes," [27] published (again anonymously) in 1786, and purporting to be a biography of the Athenian philosopher, nephew of Aristotle, who accompanied Alexander the Great on his eastern expedition and was executed for complicity in a plot to assassinate the King. Callisthenes is made the spokesman for Fonvizin's detestation of autocracy and the victim of an irresponsible tyrant.

The most important of Fonvizin's later works are autobiographical. Under the influence of Rousseau's *Confessions* he undertook to give an account of his life, and probably actually finished this, in spite of the handicap of his paralysis; the extant portion, however, breaks off in the middle of the third chapter (or "book") with the end of the 1760s. The autobiography is entitled *Candid Admission of My Acts and Thoughts.*[21] There is evidence in it of Fonvizin's return to religion, which occurred after his paralysis (he interpreted this as divine punishment for his "free-thinking"); he writes with apparent regret of the "blasphemies" of his *Epistle to My Servants,* and of the "sins" of his youth. None the less, his repentance is not sufficient to dull his wit or blunt the sharp and lifelike characterizations of people he has encountered. We find, for example, that his first love affair was with a very stupid girl with whom he shared his theoretical knowledge (derived, it would seem, from some erotic engravings) of the more intimate facts of life; the couple were deterred from putting theory into practice only by the fact that the doors in the girl's house were all typically Russian—so badly made that they wouldn't close properly! The girl's mother, from whom the daughter inherited her invincible stupidity, served as the life model for the engaging portrait of Akulina Timofeevna, the Brigardirsha! It is a very great pity that the remainder of the *Candid Admission* has been lost; it is certainly the best of the author's later work.

Fonvizin's death on December 1, 1792 terminated the career of Russia's most talented satirist and dramatist of the eighteenth century. The importance of his work was well appreciated by some of his younger contemporaries, e.g., the poet Dmitriev, and in the early nineteenth century most notably by Pushkin, who wrote at the age of 17 a poem called "The Shade of Fonvizin," and who retained throughout the rest of his life a great admiration for the author of *The Minor*. Mediocre imitators attempted to exploit Fonvizin's characters in epigonal comedies, but the real "school" of Fonvizin as a dramatist extends for a hundred years through the great comedies *Woe from Wit (Gore ot uma)* of Griboedov, *The Inspector General (Revizor)* of Gogol, to Ostrovsky's *Svoi liudi—sochtemsia (The Bankrupt,* as it was originally called). Fonvizin belongs still to the age of classicism, but the realistic elements in his two comedies *The Brigadier* and *The Minor*, and in a few other sketches, give evidence of the beginning of a new trend. Belinsky's evaluation of him as author of "Russia's first realistic comedy" is probably not exaggerated.

CHAPTER X

MIKHAIL KHERASKOV AND THE NATIONAL EPIC

If Alexander Sumarokov had been the acknowledged arbiter of Russian classicism during the 1750s and 1760s, his position was rivalled in the 1770s by his younger follower Kheraskov, and after Sumarokov's death it was the latter who dominated Russian literature for the rest of the century. So exalted a position did Kheraskov hold, in fact, after the publication of his epic *The Rossiad*, that he was regarded with an all but religious awe, and few were the voices raised in criticism of anything that he wrote. All the more surprising is the rapidity of his fall; by the middle of the nineteenth century Kheraskov was a synonym for the quaintly old-fashioned and dull, and most people who read him at all would have agreed fully with Belinsky's patronizing comment that he was "for his time a distinguished versifier, but decidedly not a poet." Of all his enormous literary heritage—and he wrote as much, if not more, than Sumarokov—the *Rossiad* is the only thing ever read, and that only in anthologized excerpts, in the twentieth century; it is even a matter of some difficulty to gain access to his prose romances and long narrative poems, which have never been reedited since their first publication.

Kheraskov[1] was born in 1733, and died in 1807 at the age of seventy-four; he had at that time been actively engaged in literature for over fifty years. Like Sumarokov, he tried his hand at nearly all genres which classicism recognized—in Gukovsky's enumeration:[2] "odes of all sorts, elegies, stanzas, epigrams, epistles, fables, satirical and moralizing articles, idylls, sonnets, madrigals, meditations in verse, eclogues, fairy tales in verse, psalms, cantatas.... tragedies, dramas, comedies, comic operas.... didactic poems, epic poems, fairy tale poems.... and philosophical and didactive novels." He also edited, and very largely contributed to, several literary journals. One would think that this would have left but little time for other activity, but he was for a large part of his life also a very active official of Moscow University.

Kheraskov's family descended from a Wallachian émigré named Kheresko who, like Kantemir's father, abandoned his native land to follow Peter the Great after the failure of the Pruth campaign. His father died when the boy was young, and he was brought up in the company of two stepbrothers, by his mother's second husband, the cultured and literarily inclined

Nikita Yurievich Trubetskoy, who was a friend of Kantemir, Sumarokov and Lomonosov. Young Kheraskov was educated in a military school in St. Petersburg with a surprisingly humanistic curriculum, and was graduated as an officer; his interests, however, led him toward literature, and he very shortly resigned his commission, and when Moscow University was opened in 1755, took up an official position with it. In this capacity he managed the University's library, theater, and press!

Apparently about 1760 he became involved with Masonic activity, and began the publication of a journal that was obviously inspired by Masonic ideas—*Profitable Diversion* (1760-62). The journal was caught in the political events of these years: at the death of Elizabeth it hailed the accession of Peter III rather too enthusiastically, and when in a few months Peter's wife ascended the throne over her husband's body, Kheraskov thought it discreet to bring the journal to a close. He shortly inaugurated a new one called *Free Hours* (1763), which was followed by *Innocent Exercise* (1763) and *Good Intentions* (1764). A good deal of the material which these periodicals printed was by the editor—in the first year of the existence of *Profitable Diversion* Kheraskov contributed 86 pieces, of prose and poetry.

Masonic activity was regarded with suspicion by Catherine II, as has been noted before, and perhaps in an effort to deprive the Moscow center of its leader and bring him more directly under her eye, she abruptly transferred Kheraskov from his congenial post with Moscow University to the vice-presidency of the *Berg-Collegium*—that is, of the government's Department of Mining! The shift naturally involved Kheraskov's migration to St. Petersburg, but it did not mean any lessening of his Masonic activity; and in spite of some outstanding literary successes during the early 1770s, Catherine in 1775 dismissed him from his post and forced his retirement from the capital. It was during the leisure thus afforded that he finished work on *The Rossiad*. The publication of this, Russia's first epic poem of classical style, mollified the Empress, and she presently reinstated its author in his former post with Moscow University, where he continued for the rest of his life, most of the time in the very high position of "Procurator," corresponding to that of "Rector" in a German university. Immediately after his return to Moscow Kheraskov, again in charge of the University press, rented this out to his fellow Mason Nikolai Novikov for the latter's great printing enterprise, referred to earlier.

During his residence in the capital Kheraskov surrounded himself with a coterie of earnest young men, mostly Masons, whose sincere belief it was that the deplorable frivolity and immorality of St. Petersburg society could be corrected by attractively presented "moral lessons." These they attempted to provide in a publication (1772-73) entitled *Evenings*. Among the leading figures in this circle were Kheraskov's protégé Bogdanovich, later author of the beloved *Dushenka;* Vasily Maikov, who had by 1769 composed his mock epic *Elisei, or Bacchus Enraged* (it was not published until 1772);

and A.A. Rzhevsky, a talented and facile poet who later defected, to Kheraskov's chagrin, and was drawn into official life. Kheraskov's circle was avowedly hostile to the favorite diversions of the capital high society—card playing and gossip—and the *Evenings* were inspired by the idea of providing something more solid in the way of entertainment. In the article which introduced the new journal Kheraskov wrote:[3] "We have determined to find out whether it is possible for a person of the nobility, for one evening a week, not to play either whist or ombre, and for five hours together to exercise himself in literary sciences." To his great disappointment, social life showed no marked improvement, even after a year of his efforts! But it was perhaps the implied criticism of her own way of life that, added to the Masonic bugbear, caused Catherine to lose patience in the end and rusticate the moralist.

Kheraskov's earliest efforts belong to the period while he was still in the "Gentlemen's Infantry Corps": in the taste of the 50s, they are "solemn odes": "Ode in Memory of the Victory of Peter the Great Over the Swedes" (1751), and "Ode to the Empress Elizaveta Petrovna on the Anniversary of Her Ascension to the Throne" (1753). The exalted and emotional Lomonosov style was uncongenial to Kheraskov, who was from the beginning imbued with the ideals of classicism which Sumarokov represented. Accordingly the "solemn ode" plays a rather small part in his production, and he presently worked out another kind of ode; in the meanwhile, he tried his hand at the drama. Surprisingly enough, in view of his classical leanings "The Venetian Nun" (1758)[4] violates nearly all the canons of the Sumarokov tragedy. The characters are neither royalty nor nobility, but commoners; the medium is verse, but there are only three instead of five acts; the first act takes place at night, and the scene is only fitfully illuminated by torches; the unities of time and of action are faithfully preserved, but that of place is tacitly violated: the divided scene of Act I: "part of the convent of St. Justina and part of the residence of the European ambassadors" can hardly be imagined as functioning later as Mirozi's tribunal! The action is supposed to take place in a contemporary Venice; and the heroine, Zaneta, appears in the final act, like King Oedipus, with blood streaming down her face from her self-inflicted blinding—a ghastly spectacle that the classical dramatist would have spared an audience. Some of these features belong to the kind of *bürgerliches Trauerspiel* which German and English dramatists were at about the same period experimenting with (e.g., Lessing's *Miss Sara Sampson,* 1755 or George Lillo's *The London Merchant,* 1732). A direct influence from either Lessing or Lillo is not provable; but it must be remembered that Kheraskov was closely associated with the Masonic movement, and that this was international in its connections; moreover that Masonry was from the beginning imbued with the kind of sentimentalist and mildly anti-clerical views which mark "The Venetian Nun."

The tragedy is more boldly experimental than any of Kheraskov's other plays, but the experiment cannot be considered dramatically successful. It is possible, although doubtful, that the Republic of Venice at some period suffered from such morbid xenophobia that a citizen might expect the death penalty from a mere visit to the "residence of the foreign ambassadors," which Kheraskov makes contiguous to the "Convent of St. Justina." But even if this improbable datum is accepted, the "voluntary suspension of disbelief" in regard to other matters will hardly be achieved. It is probably not too surprising that a young man of Orthodox faith should know little about the ways of Catholic nuns—but one might have expected a little elementary research if a tragedy was to be written involving them! Such research might have revealed that (1) Catholic nuns are never permitted to venture outside their convent walls except in *pairs;* (2) that once vows have been taken, nothing but a papal dispensation can set them aside; and (3) that convents are ordinarily inhabited by more than one nun! as it is, Zaneta appears to wander about with perfect freedom and all by herself at even some rather questionable night hours, totally without supervision or any indication that any rules other than her own sense of propriety are being infringed; Mirozi, father of her young lover Korans, seems to believe that if he appeals to the "people" of Venice in his son's behalf, they can readily release Zaneta from her vows and order the marriage of the two young lovers! And finally, as far as one can tell, the Convent of St. Justina is untenanted except by Zaneta—at least no other nun ever appears, or is even referred to, and even when the self-blinded penitent appears in the third act, she is led on by soldiers, not by fellow nuns!

Kheraskov's basic theme is doubtless protest against the life-denying asceticism that turns Zaneta's and Korans's innocent love into tragedy. The young hero, and later his father, are given some rather powerful protests against the selfish egotism of cloister life and the piety that allows family wishes (here, of Zaneta's parents and brother) to condemn a daughter to a life of celibacy. But the characterization is crude and schematic; Zaneta is convincing neither when she glibly mouths the conventional church responses to her lover's protests, nor when, after she learns of his imminent execution she turns hysterical and condemns herself. On the whole, not much can be said for "The Venetian Nun" in regard to plausibility of plot or characterization. Least of all is it possible to condone the lurid melodrama of the finale. The ending of the tragedy, as Kheraskov outlines his "original" story, with Korans's premature execution, and posthumous rehabilitation, would have been far better than the self-blinding episode and Korans's suicide.

Later in his life Kheraskov wrote a considerable number of tragedies, comedies and "dramas," or serious plays on bourgeois subjects. Of this dramatic production only the patriotic *Moscow Delivered* (1798) deserves consideration, and remains in any degree readable.[5] It will be considered later.

Literary historians usually accord Kheraskov's two comedies only slight mention. It would probably be kinder to ignore them altogether; they are, however, in their way typical both of the humorless author himself and of the low estate of Russian comedy before Fonvizin. A brief description of one will suffice for both. *The Envious Man (Nenavistnik)* "a comedy in three acts,"[6] was, according to the information under the title in Kheraskov's *Works* (Volume 5), "composed in 1770, and first presented at the Imperial Russian Court Theater in 1779...." The work is written in the conventional Russian Alexandrine verse.

The central character, Zmeiad ("snake poison"), eager to improve his financial condition by a rich marriage, has "set his nets" for the daughter, Priiata, of the gullible country squire, Zdorust, who is dazzled by the probably counterfeit nobility of Zmeiad. Priiata, while unchaperoned in the country, has met and fallen in love with a young neighbor, Milat; the young man, however, has gone to the city on unspecified business, and not been heard from. Zdorust and his daughter, on a visit to the city, are put up at Zmeiad's house, which is the scene of the play; and Zmeiad's wiles have been so effective on Zdorust that the latter has promised his daughter to his host, and Priiata, the consummate model of filial obedience, has tamely consented, despite her continued love for Milat. This exposition is given in the first act, partly by Zmeiad's servant, the boorish Grublon, and partly by Milat himself in a conversation with Razved. Milat, in an effort to learn whether rumor is correct in reporting Priiata's coming marriage to Zmeiad, has entered Zmeiad's service under the assumed name of Stovid; Razved, a young writer, is also in Zmeiad's service. The duties of the two, it seems, are to frequent social gatherings anywhere in town, and whenever any person is praised for any quality whatever, to break in with a slanderous rebuttal—for Zmeiad considers praise of anyone else to be implied censure of himself! The first act of the play shows Zmeiad issuing commissions of this sort to his henchmen and lecturing them on the usefulness of calumny as a weapon against his "enemies," as he considers all decent people to be! Milat-Stovid is assigned a special task—to embroil the family of his employer's bride-to-be so thoroughly against each other that father, uncle (Dobrov) and daughter will have nothing further to do with each other, and Zmeiad will be unencumbered with "in-laws" after his marriage. On the plea of a bad memory, Milat-Stovid gets this commission set down in writing in Zemiad's own hand.

The plot moves sluggishly ahead in Act II, as Priiata and her father discuss her coming marriage, and she and her sympathetic uncle, who is somewhat more intelligent than her fatuous father, discuss her sad plight, which Dobrov undertakes to try to relieve. Finally Priiata meets Milat (as Stovid), and finding him employed by Zmeiad and apparently his friend, abruptly assumes that he must be as bad as his employer, and throws him over forever. At the end of the act the discomfited lover is summoned by Grublon to accompany Zmeiad to a performance of a "comedy."

In the final act Milat plays his trump card by showing Zdorust, Priiata and Dobrov Zmeiad's written orders to foment a family quarrel among them. Unconvinced even by this evidence, Zdorust is induced to hide with his brother and daughter while "Stovid" lures Zmeiad into giving oral confirmation of his perfidy. Zmeiad enters, in a rage over the "comedy," which was apparently written by Razved, and was pointedly aimed at himself! He obligingly repeats his instructions regarding "Stovid's" mission to promote a family quarrel, and the hidden eavesdroppers burst in. Zmeiad is, however, quick-witted enough to claim that he knew they were there all the while, and was just playing a joke on them. Zdorust is completely taken in, and insists more strongly than ever that this admirable man must be his son-in-law; Priiata and Milat are in despair, and Dobrov is disgusted. At this moment a "Sergeant of Police" is announced, who reads a short writ according to which Zmeiad, as an "enemy of society" is stripped of his rank and ordered to leave town within twenty-four hours. Zdorust says: "Well, I don't dare tangle with the police, so my daughter won't marry Zmeiad, but will now be given to Milat."[7] This *deus ex machina* solution of a play's conflict is one of the most abrupt on record, but even so can hardly be said to do much damage to the play's verisimilitude!

Presumably Kheraskov's intention in composing this sorry piece was to show the audience what a dreadful thing jealousy and envy are; but one may doubt that an audience would have detected enough similarity between the stage puppets and human beings to make this lesson effective. All the "characters" are artificial contrivances, animated by strings arbitrarily pulled by the poet. Priiata is perfectly ready to face a life of torment with a man she loathes in order not to prove disobedient to her father; Zdorust is fatuous and gullible beyond any human comprehension; and as for the title character, one may have reasonable doubts that any human being, even one named "Snake-poison," would employ a whole staff of henchmen for the sole purpose of calumniating his "enemies" and singing his own praises. It is rare indeed to encounter a "comedy" inhabited by no recognizable human beings, marked by not the slightest trace of constructional skill, enlivened by not a single spark of wit or humor. Such, however, is *The Envious Man;* Kheraskov was indeed well advised to abandon "comedy" with this second try (his *Atheist,* which is no better, was composed in 1761). His "dramas" *The Friend of the Unfortunate* (1774), *The Persecuted* (1775), *Milana* (1786), *The School of Virtue* (1796) and *Excusable Jealousy* (1796) are the usual didactic tracts in dialogue form, neither better nor worse than other examples, both French and Russian, of their kind.

During his first Moscow period, while *Profitable Diversion, Free Hours,* etc., were his outlet, Kheraskov composed a good many poems to which he gave the title "odes." Since they differ radically from what has been previously understood by that designation, it will be necessary to consider these differences. A collection was gathered together and published in 1762 as a

251

separate volume under the title *New Odes.* The model from antiquity which the poet elected to use was Anacreon—but the content is grotesquely inappropriate to the form. As has been noted before, the poets of the pseudo-Anacreon collection evolved a genre in Greek which is marked chiefly by a light-hearted Epicurean devotion to love-making and drinking, with frequent admonitions to enjoy both while there is still time. The language of the Anacreontea is of course forthright and simple, with none of the pomposity that marks for example the odes of Pindar. It was this feature which appealed to Kheraskov. He took the Anacreontic meter—iambic trimeter or tetrameter unrhymed, with dissylabic endings—and filled it with moral platitudes. Some of the titles are revealing: "On the Power of Reason"; "On the Harm That Comes from Reason"; "On Vain Desires"; "On the Power of Virtue," etc. A good example of the type is "Genuine Happiness":[8]

That man leads a pleasant life and is immeasurably happy who has earned a great deal of gold; he passes his minutes in an abundant life; with pleasant orchards and sweet fruit he delights his heart. Very fortunate is the one whom Fortune guides to high ranks. At ease and happy is he to whom fate has given a beautiful wife. Happy in the world is he who extends his fame over the whole universe.... And that one too is happy who knows a great deal; but happier than all is he who knows how to overcome his passions and desires for wealth, for honor, for fame. Contend with me, Fortune, deprive me of ease—I overcome you. And even if I shall grow weary of opposing you, I shall never make myself your plaything. Though my shield be shattered, my spear grow blunt, even in this misfortune I shall be happy.

Not all the Odes of this collection are moralizing, however; some are devoted to literary themes, and set forth very clearly the poet's ideals, which parallel those of such contemporary "sentimentalist" writers as Edward Young (*Night Thoughts,* 1742-45), or Salomon Gessner (*Idyllen,* 1756). Kheraskov's allegiance to the relative simplicity of Sumarokov's style and his hostility to the Lomonosov tradition are readily seen in the program poem "To My Lyre," which begins the *New Odes,* and in the lyric: "To You More Pleasing—" ("Tebe priiazny bole—"):[9]

Prepare yourself now, O lyre, in your simple attire to stand before the eyes of the intelligent Russian woman. That you are in a new attire, do not feel ashamed: sing and be joyful. With your simplicity you will delight her more than with thunderous strings and bombastic words. Your simple feelings, unsubtle singing, are close to her heart. She hates, you know, the worldly splendor of a magnificent life. When she sees you, she will be content with you. And you, to whom I now dedicate my verses! Hearkening to their dissonance, do not on that account be angry. Even the Muses in their songs make mistakes not infrequently. I am composing verses without rhymes, but this does not deprive them of attractiveness and force, provided there be justice in them. There are no other rules in the world for tuning verses and lyres than only to sing intelligibly and harmoniously, mingling general profit with entertainment. To be a famous creator in the world costs great labors, and there is little profit in it. I do not strive to rise to the summits of Parnassus and there with Homer tune the lyre divine, or drink the sweet nectar with Ovidius Naso. The songs of Anacreon, and simplicity and sweetness put me in rapture. I do not flatter myself, however, that I can compare with him in singing; I am content with this only, if I am able with a simple style to sing on the lyre, if I am able to call myself if but the echo of his pipes; I shall be even more content if my playing shall be pleasing to you; the work of idle hours, of hours not many, my un-serious endeavor will receive all its reward, its crown and glory, if you will read these songs, read them, and say that you are content with them.

In this connection it is worth noting that Kheraskov envisages his ideal reader as "the intelligent Russian woman," just as Karamzin will later attempt to model his new prose style on the conversational usage of the upper class Russian lady. There are many lines of kinship between Kheraskov and Karamzin.

To you more pleasing are the songs of the thunderous lyre, and the tumult of Boreas in verses delights you; a pleasing disorder, fragments, amazement, magniloquent style and ravishing thoughts put you in raptures. Be captivated as you please with a magniloquent style and with the sonorous strings of the thundering lyre; be captivated as you please as you marvel at soaring thoughts; praise the dignity of the word, praise the greatness of the spirit, which as with thunder, pierce the heart in verses, and like a soaring eagle, fly up to the clouds. To me the quiet sighing of moaning doves is dear; to me the quiet streams, to me the groves, to me the dales are more pleasant than the lyre're voice. The shepherdess adorned with lovely flowers when in a circle of shepherdesses she sings, she sings and dances, is dearer than a thundering chorus. When the writer sighs in amorous verses, when he proclaims that which the heart enflamed must proclaim in passion— he puts me in tears and forces me to listen to these feelings in [his] tender heart, which are suitable for men in the world. O Muses! If my spirit is able to possess your gift, then grant me a gift like that with which you formerly rewarded Anacreon, or with which now the delightful Sumarokov is adorned. But if these things are not possible, I ask nothing else.[10]

Kheraskov's program seems to favor the smaller genres of elegy and pastoral over the "thunderous" ode; but as a matter of fact, his emphasis is not so much on the content of these as on their simplicity of style, and above all on their didactic purpose—the union of "general profit" with "entertainment" (Horace's *miscuit utile dulci*). Incidentally, despite Kheraskov's apparent admiration for Sumarokov, he decisively rejects one of the most important aspects of the older poet's genius—his satirical bent. Satire has no place in Kheraskov's literary world; he sees it as counter-productive—instead of wheedling the sinner into correcting himself the satirist will irritate him into a stiff-necked obstinacy. The columns of *Profitable Diversion* and the other Kheraskov journals are rife with invectives against satire.

In 1764 Kheraskov published a volume entitled *Moral Fables,* and in 1769 another under the title of *Moral Odes.* In these works the author's didactic bent is more than ever apparent. The fables are written in the traditional "free iambic" form popularized by La Fontaine; they are inordinately dull. The following, "Camel and Elephant," is a fair sample:[11]

The Camel was proud. Of what? Of his humped back? By no means; he was proud of his size, and imagined that he could amaze the world with his lofty stature; he calls small animals dwarfs. The Elephant chanced to encounter him, and the Camel dropped his ears, as such base spirits always do, which almost deify themselves until they see a better one than themselves before them.

That the Camel is a dwarf before the Elephant—in this there's nothing surprising. Everything is small or great by comparison.

The *Moral Odes* do not differ in content very markedly from the *New Odes,* but Kheraskov in them has abandoned his use of the Anacreontic form. The *Moral Odes* are rhymed, and the meters are short, four- and three-beat measures, obviously inspired by Anacreon, but more freely. One of these, which is in form an "epistle" rather than properly speaking an ode, is addressed "To A[lexei] A[ndreevich] R[zhevsky]."[13] As was mentioned above, Rzhevsky was a prolific contributor to some of Kheraskov's journals, but later became involved in bureaucratic duties connected with the Academy of Sciences and the College of Medicine. As a result of these new duties, the one-time poet altogether ceased to write. As far as one can gather from the quite extensive collection of Rzhevsky's verse reprinted in the first volume of the "Poet's Library" edition of *Poets of the Eighteenth Century,*[12] he was an extremely facile versifier who could turn out elegies, fables, epistles, epigrams, etc., of the utmost technical perfection, and as cold and impersonal as though they had been composed by a computer. Nevertheless the defection of this auxiliary of *Profitable Diversion* was keenly felt by Kheraskov, who addresses the apostate as follows:

You and I once used to play on the pipes and were then captivated with sweet games. Then, amid diversion, amid fields, meadows, you, seeing the simple manners, desired simple verses. There the dryads of the countryside used to dance around you; you used to feel no vexations, loving the rustic life. You were not diverted by the vanities of the world—at that time the beauties of nature entranced you. At that time you left luxury to the worldly circle; at that time you declared all your thoughts to me, as to a friend. Now the dryads have already hidden themselves in the forests, the places have been changed, and you are no longer the same. My verses will not find you on the wild plain where shepherdesses play and sing at liberty. Now the bright streams do not murmur around you, but loud-voiced choirs thunder from all sides. There are luxurious magnates, there are deceitful friends, flatterers are everywhere to be heard.... Is your life reposeful? Of the two lives in the world, which will you magnify to me? You are modest in this answer, so you might better be silent.

What we know of Rzhevsky's life in the capital does not seem to fit Kheraskov's bitter picture of luxury and sophistication; Derzhavin even dedicated to him and his second wife an admiring poem: "A Happy Family." But the patriarchal simplicity of country life always attracted Kheraskov, who looked askance at the ostentation of capital society. In this connection may be quoted the rather naive ode, "Wealth":[14]

Hearken, you beggars and poor people! to what the Muses think and sing! Silver and sumptuous palaces do not give the heart repose. In the spring the shepherd in his poor hut plays on his pipe; the rich man gathers money, having a spirit without repose. The rich man, tasting sweet food, is revolted by it; bread and water are pleasant to the beggar, when he is filled with them. When the seething waves roar, the rich man trembles on the land, fearing that perhaps, full of treasures, his ships may perish on the sea. The poor man has no anxiety, so long as he has nothing to lose. He dares to look at thunder and foul weather with a passionless eye. The rich man loses his life more than once; he counts gold above life; on its account he dies hourly and sees in death a ravager. Although all things on earth moulder, yet we have this comfort in life: the poor have pity for the poor, but wish death for the wealthy. However, is it possible for man to live in the world without money? It is not possible, I will say in reply, and it is for this reason that our age is burdensome.

For a writer of such a pronounced didactic turn of mind as Kheraskov the possibilities of the moralizing novel could hardly be overlooked. In 1768 appeared the short tale entitled: "Numa Pompilius, or Rome in Its Bloom".[15] The work is patently inspired by Fénelon's *Les Aventures de Télémaque,* and by the more recent "political novel" of Marmontel, *Bélisaire* (1766). It is composed in a pompous, semi-poetical prose style that sometimes comes very close to actual verse rhythm. The subject is furnished by Roman legendary history: the second kind of Rome, Romulus's successor, was supposedly the legislator Numa Pompilius, whose contributions to the life of his city were those of the peaceful consolidator, not the conqueror. The civic institutions and religious practices of early Rome are attributed by legend to Numa, who was inspired in his legislation by the advice of a divine monitor, the nymph Egeria. Kheraskov's "novel" consists for the most part of conversations between the king and the nymph, and the picture which emerges of Numa's legislative activity is that of a moderate "constitutional" monarchy, in which the senatorial aristocracy plays a large and beneficent part and the king is always willing to listen to its temperate and well-intentioned advice. Needless to say, such a Utopian state of affairs as the novel envisages was as remote from Roman history of any period as from the contemporary realities of Catherine's Russia.

A second excursion into narrative prose is the novel *Cadmus and Harmonia* (1786).[16] Here the "plot" is furnished by the ancient Greek legend of the Phoenician prince who journeys to Greece, and on the site of later Thebes kills a dragon, sows its teeth, reaps a harvest of armed men, and ultimately becomes king of the region and husband of Harmonia, daughter of Ares and Aphrodite. The work is a novel of a quest, with rather strong Masonic overtones. Cadmus, it is emphasized, is—like every man—a free agent: his course is not laid out for him by the gods. He goes astray, not seriously indeed, but enough to postpone the fulfillment of his destiny. But by submission to the will of the gods and by virtuous conduct he succeeds at last in attaining his kingship. The moralist author ends his "novel" with the words: "The mortal who masters his feelings, who reins in the turbulence of his passions, who regulates according to the rules of reason his spiritual qualities, is a mighty king on earth. Many wearers of crowns have not merited this title."[17]

Polydore, Son of Cadmus and Harmonia (1794)[18] is a sequel of the second novel, and a curious medley of the philosophical and the adventure tale. Its construction is considerably more complicated than that of its predecessors, as subsidiary figures appear and disappear, narrate their own stories, and sometimes are themselves interrupted by still other episodic narratives. Polydore visits numerous allegorical lands, each with marked characteristics that set it apart from other places, and each, of course, contributes political and moral instruction to the wanderer. The most sriking of these episodes is Polydore's visit to the floating island of Terzit, whose inhabitants have abolished kingship, and live in a frenetic anarchy which they call "liberty." The allegory is patently an unflattering picture of the French revolution, which Kheraskov, like most conservative Russians, viewed as the ultimate political disaster. Polydore by the end of the novel reaches his goal, the "tsarstvo Mudrosti," or "Kingdom of Wisdom," presided over by a benevolent nymph who reveals that ages hence she will inspire a great empress of the north, whose realm will approximate the "Kingdom of Wisdom" itself.

The work of Kheraskov which more than all the rest caught the fancy of his age and inspired his contemporaries to dub him "The Russian Homer" was of course *The Rossiad* (1779).[19] This, however, was not his first essay in the epic genre. As early as 1761 he had dedicated to Prince Pavel a didactic poem called "The Fruits of Learning."[20] This, interestingly enough in view of Kheraskov's rejection of the tradition of the "solemn ode," is inspired by Lomonosov's "Epistle on the Usefulness of Glass," and is couched in the simple, unadorned "middle style" of that work. The poem passes the sciences in review and points out their contributions to human life. Underlying the whole project is Kheraskov's indignant repudiation of the thesis of J.-J. Rousseau, in his *First Discourse,* that "the rebirth of the arts and sciences has not contributed to the improvement of morals." Rousseau's name is not mentioned, but there is no doubt of the object of the polemics.

A second, and more strictly "epic" poem is *The Battle of Chesme* (1771).[21] On June 25, 1770, in the course of Catherine's first war with Turkey, the Russian fleet, which was expected to arouse by its very presence in Aegean waters a widespread revolt among the Greek and other Orthodox populations, encountered the Turkish fleet in the strait between the island of Chios and the mainland of Turkey. The Russians, under the general command of Alexei Orlov, caused the Turkish fleet enough damage so that it retreated into the bay of Chesme, where it was supposedly protected by shore batteries. Here, however, Orlov and his British commander Admiral Greig, attacked during the night; a Russian fire-ship, steered by Lieutenant Ilyin, sailed among the closely packed Turkish ships and set one afire. Presently the entire fleet was ablaze, and the day ended with the complete destruction of the Turkish fleet of 15 ships of the line, 6 frigates and several smaller vessels. The Turkish crews, except such as were picked up from the water by the victors, were totally lost. It was a most spectacular victory, and there is no exaggeration in the medal which Catherine II struck in honor of the Battle of Chesme, and which depicts the Turkish fleet on one side, with the single word on the reverse: "byl"—"it was."

Like many poets whom the tremendous news electrified, Kheraskov rushed to turn the battle into a great patriotic poem. He collected the "facts" from newspaper accounts of the battle, and in some cases from participants whom he interviewed. In the prose note attached to his poem he writes: "It must be said once for my whole composition that everything written in it is the living truth, excluding the verse embellishments which every benevolent reader will easily be able to distinguish. All the remainder is disposed according to exact information received from the most trustworthy hands, and according to the very words which the writer had the good fortune of hearing from the heroes whom he is celebrating." Actually, the "verse embellishments" are very few and very modest—mostly the use, especially in metaphors and similes, of the names of classical Greek and Roman mythological figures. The events of the battle are indeed given with almost chronological exactitude in the five cantos of The Battle of Chesme. First, the background: Greece, oppressed by the Muslim Turks and dreaming of liberation; then the Russian intervention, and the first stage of the battle on the 25th of June. The central dramatic episode comes in Canto III, as the youngest brother of Alexei Orlov, Feodor, in his ship the "Evstafia," engages the Turkish flag-ship, and catches fire and explodes. The anxiety of Alexei for his brother, his grim determination to avenge his death, and the destruction of the Turkish fleet are described, and it is not until Canto IV that the welcome "messenger" comes to inform Alexei of his brother's rescue, from a small boat lowered from the "Evstafia" before the explosion. The final canto is devoted to the magnanimous efforts of the victorious Russians to pick up the survivors of the Turkish crews, and to Kheraskov's somewhat premature prophecies of the complete crumbling of the Turkish power and the Russian liberation of Constantinople.

The Battle of Chesme is one of the most impressive things we have from Kheraskov's pen, and is an extraordinary experiment—an "epic" poem composed within a few months of the very events it describes. It is full of the actual names of ships and of Russian heroes, e.g., Lieutenant Ilyin, who sacrificed his life to set the Turks afire. It is permeated everywhere with the most fervent patriotism:[22]

> Life is not so dear
> As the honor of the fatherland and their own glory.
> Such are your children, O Russian realm.

257

It is remarkable that in spite of all the temptations to portray the enemy as godless, perfidious infidels, Kheraskov is able to see heroism even on their side:[23]

> I must count as a hero even an evil-doer ("zlodeia"):
> Such we beheld Hassan-bey in the battle;
> Like lightning he flew everywhere with his sword;
> It seemed that he was bringing thunder at us from his hands;
> To give the laurel to him we would be constrained,
> If we had not been born into the world as Russians!

There are some curious linguistic features in the poem, which militate against a completely harmonious whole. Kheraskov is unable to break away altogether from some of the eighteenth century conventions of battle description. Bombs are described, explosions, obviously of gunpowder, occur, and artillery fire sets ships aflame. But when it comes to personal combat, the poet balks. His heroes not infrequently "launch the thunder"— one might think of Zeus on Olympus! and the "benevolent reader," presumably, will interpret this figure in the prosaic terms of musket fire. More commonly, they seem to be armed only with swords. Sabres are specifically mentioned, and as boarding weapons are undoubtedly appropriate—but sometimes the Russian marines pour over the sides of their vessels onto Turkish decks armed with sword and spear! A less useful piece of equipment for such an encounter than a spear would be hard to imagine—but it is a classical and hence "poetical" adjunct of battle, so we have to have it. And yet, suddenly, amid conventional battle scenes, comes this remarkable picture of the young Orlov:[24]

> Feodor, seeing the decisive moments of the battle,
> With his dishevelled hair over his forehead,
> Wiping the sweat from his face, the imprint of his toils,
> Hurries to the terrible engagement as to a banquet.

It was a bold poet indeed in the middle of the eighteenth century who, in a "lofty" epic poem would use the word "sweat"!

The Battle of Chesme was a great popular success, one measure of which is the fact that it was almost immediately translated into both French and German, at a time when Russian poetry was almost ignored outside the country.

Kheraskov's major work in the epic genre, the *Rossiada*,[25] was published in 1779, after eight years of labor. This was the poet's chief bid for literary immortality, and at once established him as the paramount figure on his country's Parnassus. The eighteenth century regarded the epic poem as the very culmination of literature: the Greeks had the *Iliad* and the *Odyssey*, the Romans the *Aeneid*, Italy the *Jerusalem Delivered*, Portugal *The Lusiads*, France Voltaire's *Henriade*. Until Russia could show a similar heroic poem on a great national theme, Russian literature was still incomplete and immature. Lomonosov had tried his hand, as had Kantemir, on a poem glorifying the exploits of Peter the Great; both these poets had abandoned the projects. Sumarokov's *Dmitriada* never got beyond the first page. When Kheraskov, therefore, triumphantly carried his *Rossiad* to the classical length of twelve books (like the *Aeneid*), and in every other way followed out all the classical precepts for the epic genre, there was great jubilation: at last Russia could join the great civilized nations of the world with the highest kind of poetical composition. Kheraskov was promptly dubbed "the Russian Homer."

An epic poem, according to classical theory, must have as its subject a historical incident which played a crucial part in the history of a nation— the Trojan War, the Trojan settlement in Italy, Vasco da Gama's voyage to India, etc. Kheraskov took for his theme the capture of Kazan by Ivan IV in 1555. Undoubtedly the Russian liberation from Tatar domination was indeed the crucial moment in the history of the Russians—but when precisely did this happen? The famous "shaking off of the Tatar yoke" accomplished by Ivan III was anything but an heroic event, and could never have been given epic dignity; Dmitry Donskoy's defeat of the Tatars at Kulikovo Pole was heroic indeed, but not decisive, since the defeated enemy raided Moscow itself two years later. Kheraskov chose the first successful Muscovite operation in the reverse direction—Russian incorporation of Tatar territory. It was in many ways a successful choice, for the capture of Kazan was followed almost immediately by the fall of Astrakhan and the Russian domination of the entire Volga, from source to the Caspian Sea. After this the Tatar world—the Crimea and the Siberian khanates and the small Nogay principalities—was put on the defensive, and the final phase of its liquidation (the annexation of the Crimea) could be anticipated with confidence by the epic poet of Catherine the Great (Russia obtained the Crimea only a few years after the *Rossiada* was published, in 1786).

The events of Ivan IV's war with Kazan were of course more than two hundred years behind Kheraskov, and he could not proceed as he had with *The Battle of Chesme*. For sources he took an anonymous chronicle of the fall of Kazan, and the history of the reign of Ivan IV, composed by Prince Andrei Kurbsky, who had in his youth been a rather important participant in the campaign. But a proper epic poem has to have more than merely prosaic military details, and one of Kheraskov's principal models was Tasso's *Jersualem Delivered*, whose narrative of the First Crusade is enlivened by a good deal of sorcery, by the romantic episode of the "warrior maiden" Clorinda and her tragic fate, and by the erotic history of the witch Armida and her lover the hero Rinaldo—embellishments for which the "histories" of the Crusades provide no hints. Kheraskov found in the actual chronicle of the last days of Kazan the figure of the princess Sumbeka (her real name was Siuiumbeka), widow of Khan Safa-Girey and mother of the two-year-old "khan," Utemysh-Girey. Sumbeka then becomes the heroine of a love story that involves another historical figure, Shakh-Ali (or Shig-Alei), a Russian puppet ruler briefly put on the throne of Kazan in 1551. When Shig-Alei is ousted by the Khan of Astrakhan, Yediger, supported by the Crimean Tatars and their Turkish suzerains, he retires to the Russian advance base of Sviyazhk, and is followed by the enamored Sumbeka and her infant son, who are all then baptized. In this development, incidentally, Kheraskov rejected the local tradition of Kazan, which made Siuiumbeka hurl herself from a still-existing tower in the city when Ivan's forces captured it.

A certain degree of historicity can be claimed for the Sumbeka-Shig-Alei episode, although Kheraskov greatly alters and romanticizes it. Another bit of "love interest," however, is fabricated in full. This is the story of the beautiful Persian "warrior maiden," Ramida, and her trio of princely lovers, Gidromir, Mirsed and Brazin, who follow her to Kazan to defend Islam against the Christian threat. A good deal of Book XI is devoted to the account of the battle among Ramida's suitors which ends with Gidromir's victory, and of Ramida's despair at the death of her favorite Mirsed, her killing of Gidromir and her own suicide. It should be noted that all of this, even to the name of the princess (Ra-mida, Ar-mida) bears a great resemblance to some of the incidents of Tasso's epic.

Ramida's father, Nigrin, is a sorcerer, and the final victory of the Russian forces in Book XII is briefly held up by his journey in a dragon chariot to the Caucasus, where he obtains the assistance of Winter against the Christians. The unseasonable cold and frost can be dispelled only by a solemn procession in which a sacred banner, in the staff of which is embedded a splinter from the True Cross, counteracts the pagan sorcery. This episode, incidentally, has chronicle backing: Prince Kurbsky's account refers to the Muslim spells which conjured up torrential rains to hamper the Christian advance, and which were similarly routed. Kazan, it may be mentioned, was captured at the end of September, 1552.

The choice of Ivan IV as an epic hero was a dangerous one, and Kheraskov did his best to obviate the inconveniences. Every literate Russian knew the Tsar's later bloody reputation as "Ivan the Terrible," and the story of the famous quarrel between the autocrat and his once loyal assistant Prince Andrei Kurbsky must have been perfectly familiar. Moreover, even if the hideous butchery of Ivan's later years could be somehow put out of sight for epic purposes, there remained the uncompromising authoritarianism of his reign, which could only have been deeply repugnant to Kheraskov. Accordingly, taking some hints from Kurbsky's picture of Ivan's early years, the poet depicts young Ivan as at first sunk in indolence and luxury, fostered by evil self-seeking counsellors. From such an ignoble sloth he is roused by the dream apparition of St. Alexander Nevsky, and his wise human counsellor Adashev helps confirm his resolution to take arms against the perfidious Tatars and relieve the sufferings of his Russian subjects. In Book II the meeting of the "chosen council," Ivan's boyar "senate," dramatizes the opposing forces: Prince Glinsky and the aged and ease-loving Prince Kubinsky try to dissuade the young Tsar from undertaking the possibly very dangerous war against the Tatars, while Adashev, Metropolitan Daniel and Prince Kurbsky argue in favor of the undertaking and win the day. Ivan is thus shown not as the later imperious autocrat, riding rough-shod over all opposition, but as the moderate and prudent ruler, conscious of his own youth and inexperience, and willing to listen calmly to both sides and choose the better.

From this point Prince Kurbsky, quite unhistorically, takes the center of the stage and becomes in some ways the poem's genuine hero. Thus, in Canto VI, it is he who intercepts the diversionary expedition of the Crimean Khan at Tula and even in a chivalric battle with the Tatar kills his enemy and causes the rout of his army. Again, in Canto X, Kurbsky and three other (historical) Russian noblemen fight off the desperate night sortie of the Tatars, and Kurbsky administers a disabling wound to the "warrior maiden" Ramida. Finally, it is Kurbsky—this time in agreement with that Prince's own account—who after the wall has been breached by the famous mining operation, storms the city and chiefly contributes to its fall. Kurbsky thus emerges as Christendom's chief champion and Ivan's stoutest helper toward the inevitable victory.

The actual military history of the siege of Kazan is short and not particularly impressive. Operations began in the spring of 1552, but the town was fully invested only in August, and the final act took place at the end of September. It was therefore necessary for purposes of epic treatment to pad the account considerably. This Kheraskov does by dwelling at length on the maneuvers surrounding Queen Sumbeka, who is at first enamored of Osman, a Crimean prince, who plays her false; she then, warned by her husband's ghost, chooses Shig-Alei for her consort, only to be again deceived by Osman. All this material takes up almost half of the poem (Cantos III-V, IX, X). Other intrusive material is piled around the figure of Ivan: he is warned (Canto VII) by an awesome gray-haired stranger of the terrible sufferings he and his army must encounter at Kazan, and is given an enchanted shield by the stranger; and in a terrible vision of the night (Canto VIII) he sees personified Islam as his formidable enemy. The mysterious stranger, who turns out to be the hermit Vassian, interprets his dream and leads him to the "mount of Virtue," from the summit of which he shows him God's temple in the sky and opens a book for him in which he reads the future. In these ways the somewhat banal siege and capture of Kazan are invested with a universal, indeed cosmic, significance. The devices of celestial apparitions, prophetic dreams, and visions of the future, are of course also almost obligatory features of the classical epic poem, from Virgil's *Aeneid* on.

Contemporary critics, like some modern ones, found Kheraskov's attention to the romantic element of his epic story excessive. A.F. Merzliakov, in a review in *Amfion*, 1815, queried:[26] "To whom is the *Rossiad* now devoted? Ivan or Sumbeka?" He angrily denounces the "three entire cantos, unworthily devoted to the intrigues of a flighty woman and her maid!" and adds: "I can't understand how the patriotic heart of the esteemed Kheraskov could have thus debased the triumphs of Ivan!" Modern critics have found some justification for this imbalance, perhaps over-subtly, in reading into the story of Sumbeka and her lovers a discreet reference to that most exasperating feature of the reigns of Anna Ivanovna, Elizabeth and Catherine II, the "rule of favorites."If this topical allusion was indeed intentional on Kheraskov's part, the poem would then embody a properly didactic contrast between the irresponsible and disastrous regime of favorites and the beneficent cooperation for the good of the fatherland between a prudent Tsar and his patriotic counsellors. But it must be remembered that Kheraskov's models, especially *Jerusalem Delivered*, had been constructed with just as much weight given to the romantic component, and with no such *arrière-pensée* as he is credited with.

Most epic poets have been content with one such effort, but not Kheraskov. In 1785 he presented the Russian public with the epic *Vladimir*, in eighteen cantos and about 10,000 lines. The ostensible subject is of course the Christianization of Russia—the subject of Feofan Prokopovich's tragicomedy. Kheraskov warns his potential reader not to expect the usual epic fare: "If anyone shall have the desire to read my *Vladimir*, I counsel him, particularly the youth, to read it not as the usual epic work, in which for the most part battles, knightly exploits and marvels are sung; but to read it as the pilgrimage of a remarkable person over the path of truth, on which he encounters worldly temptations, succumbs to many trials, falls into the darkness of doubt, struggles with his own inborn passions, finally overcomes himself, finds the path of truth, and having attained enlightenment, is reborn."[27] This summary gives an adequate notion of the nature of the poem, which is the account of an inner, not an external combat. The forces of evil, embodied as the pagan gods whom the converted Vladimir is abandoning, join forces to attempt to prevent the king from seeing the light; and for their purpose they find the best means in Vladimir's well-known propensity to lechery—the same means, incidentally, which they employ in Prokopovich's drama. Kheraskov is puritanically hostile to "the lusts of the flesh," but almost equally so to what he calls "umstvennost'," which may be rendered as "intellectualism," the sin, that is, of relying upon the intellect rather than upon divine grace. The incidents of the lengthy "epic" are thus almost entirely allegorical and symbolic, and in spite of a clear, readable style, the poem is from a modern point of view intolerable. The union of the "useful" with the "pleasant," Kheraskov's literary ideal, is here pretty much ignored:

the "useful," that is, the overtly tedious and preachy, dominates almost exclusively.

Worse, however, was to come. In 1790 appeared a three-canto poem entitled rather ambitiously *The Universe*. Following the lead of Milton in *Paradise Lost* and of Klopstock in *The Messiah*, Kheraskov narrates the Biblical story of the revolt of the angels, the creation and fall of man, and the redemption. The one possible interest of this dreary piece is the grotesque fashion in which Satan's revolt is patterned on the recent shattering events of the French Revolution! This poem is undoubtedly the nadir of Kheraskov's poetical work.

The basic ideals and assumptions of Kheraskov's literary endeavors do not change over his long life; he remains to the end faithful to the notion of "useful diversion," to the ideal of edifying, instructional composition. He does, however, show a surprising adaptability to new fashions and modes of accomplishing his basic purposes. Thus, in 1795, the five-canto poem *Pilgrims*, which is a didactic allegory of the human quest for happiness, shows the evident influence in its form of Bogdanovich's *Dushenka*, and in its general tone, of the sentimentalism of Karamzin. The poem is composed in the "free verse" which Bogdanovich used, and which originates with La Fontaine's *Fables*—that is, in iambic lines of varying lengths and with varying, often surprising, rhyme schemes. In a short introduction (in Alexandrines) to the poem, Kheraskov asserts his right to choose such a metrical form, and incidentally refers unequivocally to the influence of Karamzin:

> But I have a mind in my verse to be unfettered;
> Poets aren't forbidden a free course in their verses;
> Just as Columbus sought for new lands, sailing over the seas,
> So we seek new ideas, soaring everywhere;
> [Our] works are the true touchstone of our feelings;
> I have sung and shall continue to sing heroes and trifles.[28]

It may be remembered that Karamzin's volume of verse and stories published in 1794 was entitled *My Trifles (Moi Bezdelki)*. The appropriateness of "trifles" to Kheraskov's poem lies not in its quite serious content, but in the lightness of the chosen verse form, and in the half-playful tone which masks the didactic purpose of the "fairy tales" that make up the narrative of *Pilgrims*. Incidentally, the lightness of the verse form and the slightly bantering tone of the poem are curiously at variance with its extraordinarily erudite language. *Pilgrims* is so overloaded with classical names, mythological allusions and the like, that the poet felt obliged to provide it with a very extensive series of explanatory notes!

In 1793, after the death of the dramatist Kniazhnin (1791), his best tragedy, *Vadim of Novgorod*, was published. We have seen how this drama almost programmatically contradicted Empress Catherine's views on the beneficent and constructive place of autocracy in the history of the Russian people. The plot is based on the chronicle story of the attempted liberation of Novgorod (traditionally in A.D. 863) from the Varangian prince Riurik by the Novgorodian patriot Vadim. The attempt failed and Vadim killed himself. According to the not entirely reliable account of Kniazhnin's son, the tragedy had been composed before the outbreak of the French Revolution. It was, however, very obviously a revolutionary document, and there is nothing surprising in its having been withheld from publication until after the dramatist's death.

Kheraskov was, as we have seen, appalled by the "anarchy" of the French Revolution, and reacted against it, and against what he terms "the mad craving for equality" evinced by the revolutionaries in his "novel" *Polydore, Son of Cadmus and Harmonia* (1794) and in the poem *The Universe* (1790), where Satan and his rebel angels play the part of the French regicides. Apparently the Kniazhnin tragedy *Vadim of Novgorod,* which glorified tyrannicide, shocked him immeasurably, and he forthwith composed his counterblast, the poem *The Tsar, or Novgorod Saved* (1800). Novgorod, in this version of the legend, is "saved" from the anarchy and reign of terror initiated by the depraved and rebellious youth Ratmir (Vadim). The poem is reactionary in conception, but experimental in form, and shows surprising evidence of Ossianic influence, evidently mediated by Derzhavin.

At the age of seventy Kheraskov composed his last long poem, with the odd title of *Bakhariana* (1803).[29] In this work he shows himself closer to the new currents of Russian literature, represented by Karamzin and Derzhavin, than anyone would have imagined possible. *Bakhariana* is in most respects Kheraskov's most successful poem after the *Rossiad.*

The poem's name, as Kheraskov explains, is created from the obsolete Russian word "bakhar'," "a story-teller." It is subtitled "The Unknown One," and narrates in fourteen cantos the quest of the "unknown" hero for his abducted bride Felana, and for a magic mirror which will give him the power to change his father and his father's subjects back into human from bestial form. The substance of this tale is drawn from the chivalric romances of the Renaissance, such as Boiardo's and Ariosto's Orlando poems, and such imitations of these as Wieland's *Oberon.* There is, however, not merely in the title, an attempt to incorporate "popular" elements, although these are fairly conventional and not specifically Slavic. At the end of the poem it is revealed that the "Unknown" is Prince Orion, son of King Trigony. His wicked stepmother Zmiolana has expelled him from his father's kingdom for killing her hawk-lover, and turned Trigony into a bull and his subjects into flies, snakes and jackdaws. The "Unknown" is aided in his quest by a wise old man, Makrobios ("Long Life"); the entire fable is allegorical, and its import is explained by Kheraskov: the "Unknown" is Everyman, in search of his lost innocence (Felana), and aided by "Christian wisdom." The mirror which will accomplish the rehumanization of Trigony and his subjects is "pure conscience," which turns a brute into a man. Finishing his explanation of the poem's allegorical meaning, Kheraskov turns to the reader with the words:[30]

Know that this strange tale   (Znai, chto povest' strannaia siia,
Is, maybe, your own story.   mozhet byt', istoriia tvoia.)

The popular element in the *Bakhariana* is contained mostly in the metrical form. Eight of the poem's fourteen cantos are written in the so-called "Russian meter," that is, a four-beat unrhymed trochaic line with dactylic line endings. This line, regularized from the free line of the popular *byliny*, had been recently used by Karamzin for his experiment in the *bylina* form, *Ilya Muromets*, and had attained some currency. The rest of the poem, however, is written in rhymed verse, which Kheraskov admits he prefers: three cantos in four-beat rhymed trochees, and three in four-beat rhymed iambics. The latter is the verse which Pushkin employs in his first complete narrative poem, *Ruslan and Liudmila*, and there is some evidence that the *Bakhariana*, with its abducted bride, its malevolent witch, its benevolent sage, etc., served as one of the younger poet's models. Fortunately, Pushkin was content to let his delightful tale of witchcraft, knightly valor and senile lechery stand on its own feet, without any moralizing allegory.

As was noted earlier in this essay, Kheraskov continued throughout his life to write tragedies in the Sumarokov manner: *The Venetian Nun* remains an exception in its experimental form. Most of these tragedies are lifeless and afford no interest to a modern reader. *Borislav*, published in 1774 and written two years earlier, is in its extant version laid in "Bohemia," and the characters, including Borislav and his daughter Flavia, bear fictitious names. Kheraskov himself, however, indicates in a preface that the tragedy had originally been founded on historical reality, and that external circumstances (doubtless the Pugachev uprising) had induced him to rewrite it. The original plot, as can be readily inferred, had to do with the usurpation and "tyranny" of Boris Godunov. Borislav is represented, with some historical accuracy, as morbidly suspicious, but there seems to be no hint of his guilt in the murder of the legitimate heir, which becomes the key to Pushkin's great tragedy. *The Idolaters, or Goreslava* (1782) and *Plamena* (1786) are both laid, with either invented or very much distorted "historical" plots, in the reign of Vladimir the Saint. Probably quite contrary to the dramatist's intention, the "negative" characters Goreslava (Vladimir's Varangian wife Rogneda) in the one tragedy, and the stubborn pagan prince Prevyzd in the other attract the reader's sympathy and come close to achieving real tragic stature. The last tragedy, published posthumously in 1809, *Zareida and Rostislav*, is devoid of any interest whatsoever.

There remains the 1798 historical tragedy *Moscow Delivered*.[5] Here Kheraskov returns to the events of the "Time of Troubles," and this time without disguise. The liberation of the Russian capital from the Polish interventionists in 1612 gives the tragedy its title, and the actual events of that stirring period form the background: the gathering of the "Militia Army" ("Opolchanie") by the patriots Prince Pozharsky and Kozma Minin, the uneasy alliance of the patriot forces with the Cossack army under "Prince Dmitry" (Trubetskoy) and the dissensions that very nearly brought about the failure of the expedition, etc. But the "plot," in typical classical style, is fictitious in its entirety and involves a group of invented characters: Sofia, a sister of Prince Pozharsky, who is inside the besieged city of Moscow, and is in love with Vianko Zhelkovsky (i.e., Ziołkowski), son of the Polish commander. Sofia's attempts to induce her brother to betray the national cause in favor of her Polish lover are of course indignantly repudiated, and in the dénouement a duel between Vianko and Leon the (non-existent) son of Pozharsky results in the death of the Polish champion. Sofia stabs herself over her lover's body, and her stern brother, echoing Corneille's Roman Horace, cries:

> Thus let every Russian woman perish
> Who has been able to forget her fatherland![31]

There are undoubtedly merits in this drama, especially a quite genuine patriotism, but the classical tragic formula, with its obligatory "love interest," no matter how inappropriate, stultifies the real drama of Moscow's "deliverance" by substituting a personal and private crisis for the genuine public one. The effect is not quite as disastrous as that involved in Ozerov's *Dmitry Donskoy*, but comes uncomfortably close.

When Mikhail Kheraskov died in 1805 he had been industriously writing for about fifty years, and had dominated Russian literature to an unparalleled extent during much of that period. He had rather surprisingly shown himself receptive to many of the new and unclassical literary trends during that time—the "bourgeois tragedy" in *The Venetian Nun*, the sentimental current in *Pilgrims*, Ossianic influence in *The Tsar, or Novgorod Set Free*, pseudo-popular elements in the *Bakhariana*, etc.—but looked at as a whole his work shows how essentially superficial all these trends had been. Kheraskov never deviated from his fundamental adherence to the classical concept of literature as *teaching*. The method used in contriving the Horatian *dulce*—the sweetening of the cup of bitter but curative *utile*—might differ from one decade to another, but not the principle itself. The experiments which Kheraskov tried strike us as in any case timid and irresolute, but even they never go deep: they affect only the surface of his writing. Because the classical principle that art exists only to convey a lesson is one that was widely if not universally repudiated by the nineteenth and twentieth centuries, Kheraskov's work became dated very soon after his death. It is profoundly uncongenial, at first view, to a modern reader, and requires a considerable exercise of historical imagination to appreciate at all; nevertheless it is almost the most quintessentially classical of all the eighteenth century Russian production, and as such can never be ignored.

CHAPTER XI

MINOR VERSE WRITERS OF THE FIRST HALF
OF THE REIGN OF CATHERINE II

A. The School of Lomonosov

1. N. N. Popovsky

The age of classicism in Russia is also the age of verse; indeed the prose of the age, as we have seen, is very largely the work of *raznochintsy* like Chulkov and Emin, themselves alien and hostile to the prevailing gentry culture of which classicism is the literary reflex, and their writing mirrors this hostility. Verse writing, on the other hand, at least until Derzhavin, remains safely within the fold of classicism, although showing different trends within this general framework.

By the end of his life (1766) Lomonosov's poetic system was already archaic. In the embittered literary struggle between him and Sumarokov, the latter represented the ideals of classicism: clarity above all, logic, a light elegance, ready intelligibility. The rhetorical qualities of Lomonosov's verse, its inflated style, archaic vocabulary, its emotionalism—his characteristic "transport" ("vostorg")—were ridiculed and condemned by the classicists. Nevertheless Lomonosov's odes had been for a generation the acme of Russian poetry, and the style he had established did not at once yield to classical restraint. Several poetic imitators attempted to follow his lead, but without Lomonosov's genuine inspiration. Mimicking only his mannerisms, they succeeded in being ridiculous.

An actual pupil of Lomonosov was Nikolai Nikitich Popovsky (1730-1770),[1] who had studied verse composition under the master in the University attached to the Academy of Sciences. Most of his extant verse is translation; in 1752 he published translations of Horace's *Ars Poetica* ("Epistle to the Pisos") and of four odes, and in 1754 finished work on a translation (not from the original, but via a French version) of Alexander Pope's *Essay on Man.* This was published in 1757, and brought Popovsky considerable acclaim. Of original verse the most important are two odes, of 1754 and 1756, addressed to Empress Elizabeth, and an "Epistle" which Novikov published in 1772 in his *Portrait-Painter.* The "Epistle" is entitled in full: "Epistle on the Utility of the Sciences and on Education of the Youth Therein, Written by the Late Professor Popovsky to His Excellency Ivan Ivanovich Shuvalov at the Establishment of Moscow University in the Year 1756." The very subjects which Popovsky chose for his poetical efforts show the obvious influence of Lomonosov. So do the themes—Peter the Great, peace, enlightenment, science, etc. Often the very devices so characteristic of Lomonosov are lifted almost verbatim. Note, for example, the opening of Popovsky's 1754 ode to Elizaveta Petrovna:[2]

> From peaceful waters the Sun arises,
> Into Russia through the purple door
> Brings the beautiful day with him,
> [The day] on which we beheld Peter's daughter
> Ascending the throne;
> Hearts seethe with joy
> Remembering that most happy hour;
> Fields, forests and waters are tumultuous;
> To the clouds various peoples
> Raise their triumphant voice.
>
> [My] spirit is troubled with sudden care,
> The blood within me seethes in confusion,
> The Sun's beautiful light is darkened
> And thick night obscures the day;
> Through the gloom of sorrowful days [now] past,
> As though from distant frontiers
> A faint groan comes to my ears:
> Russia sobs piteously
> And stretches out her hands to heaven:
> "Where are rights," she cries, "where is law?" etc. (strophes 1-2)

Throughout the ode, and its companion of 1757, are scattered eulogies of Peter I (Ode of 1754, st. 3), classical figures ("1757," st. 1: Apollo, Helicon, Mount Olympus and the Vale of Tempe; st. 5: Zeus, Heracles, Achilles, Pegasus, the Chimaera, etc.), and personifications: thus, in a not very dignified plight, the Sciences plead with Elizabeth (Ode of 1757, st. 13):

> The infant sciences are speaking to you, O Empress;
> They are reaching out their hands to you
> And saying, stammeringly:
> "Our tongue is weak, our words unsure
> But thought and heart are already prepared
> To offer gratitude.

269

Wait until we have become stronger,
Then we shall endeavor with all zeal
To exalt you with praise."

The last quoted figure illustrates one of the great dangers of figurative language—what is called the "realization of metaphor." The sciences in Elizabeth's Russia are indeed newly established, and may hence be metaphorically called "infant"; but when the metaphor is "realized," that is, filled out logically, it becomes ridiculous. Infants either do not speak at all, or only haltingly—so Popovsky makes "the infant sciences stammer." And as if this were not bad enough, all they can promise, when they "grow up," is to be able adequately to sing the Empress's praises! Lomonosov's sciences "stretch out their hands to Russia"—to serve her and her people![2]

Popovsky was a good Latin scholar, and his translations of Horace are as good as any of his time; they do not attempt to follow the form of the original closely, but sometimes pad the concise Latin, turning four-line into six-line strophes. The translation of Pope's *Essay on Man* is another matter. Made from a French version by a certain Silhouette, it necessarily suffers from double dilution, and most of the brilliant epigrams of the original come out sadly dulled. Pope touches on a commonplace of eighteenth century satire, the folly of pride in ancestry:

Go! If your ancient but ignoble blood
Has crept thro' scoundrels ever since the flood,
Go! and pretend your family is young,
Nor own your fathers have been fools so long.

(Epistle IV, lines 211-214)

This becomes with Popovsky:

If your family shall be ancient, but inglorious,
Not virtuous, idle and vicious,
Then though it may have been living before the flood,
Yet it is better to hide in silence that it was all base,
And not let others know that through so long a time
Your tribe has exhibited no merits at all.

(IV, lines 367-372)

The translator has taken six lines to cover Pope's four (Book IV of the original has 398 lines; Popovsky's has 694!), and covered them in a most plodding fashion.

A comparison of the final lines of the poem will make Popovsky's merits as a translator still clearer:

That, urged by thee, I turn'd the tuneful art
From sounds to things, from fancy to the heart:
For Wit's false mirror held up Nature's light,
Show'd erring pride, *Whatever is, is right;*
That Reason, Passion, answer one great aim;
That true Self-love and Social are the same;
That Virtue only makes our bliss below,
And all our knowledge is, ourselves to know.

(Epistle IV, lines 391-398)

This beautifully succinct and lapidary compendium of Enlightenment philosophy emerges thus from its Russian translator:

That, incited by you, I abandoned the empty sound of words
And directed my mind to the experience of things;
From imaginings and merely empty ravings
I hastened to the realization of my rational powers,
That I exposed people in false opinions
And revealed to them the secrets of hidden nature,
And showed the proud that all the world is pretty good ("izriaden)
And that there is nothing bad in it at all;
That to one end both our reason and passions
Have been given by the supreme power that arranges everything;
That self-love must not be separated
From love for society, but counted as one;
That in the world only those are genuinely happy
Who live virtuously and discreetly,
And that we must all learn one thing,
That each be known to himself. (IV, lines 678-694)

2. *Vasily Petrovich Petrov* (1736-1799)[3]

One of the most hated and ridiculed poets of the century was Vasily Petrovich Petrov, who liked to be called "The new Lomonosov." Petrov was a *raznochinets* (his father was a priest) who, by the use of his very considerable talent and consummate powers of servility, succeeded in making himself Catherine's favorite writer of verse. The Empress used to call him her "pocket poet," a title in which Petrov took pride. His career of flattery began in 1766 with the "Ode on the Carousel," and continued for thirty years. When in 1796 Petrov received news of the death of his patroness, he was so affected that he suffered a stroke. He recovered sufficiently to be able to write a few more odes to her successor, but Paul, who hated everything and everybody that his mother had favored, treated her "pocket poet" very coldly, and Petrov died despised and forgotten.

Petrov's literary output consists chiefly of "triumphal odes" addressed to Catherine or to one of her favorites. Grigory Potemkin had been one of his school friends before Catherine's acquaintance with him, and the two remained on very good terms. One of Petrov's best pieces is his "Lamentation" of 1791 on the death of the favorite. Aside from offical odes, Petrov's principal work is his translation of Virgil's *Aeneid*. He also published (1777) a prose translation of three cantos of Milton's *Paradise Lost,* after a residence in England (1772-74) had familiarized him with the English language and literature.

Lomonosov's first original ode was in celebration of a great Russian military victory ("On the Capture of Khotin"). Petrov's was a glorification of one of Catherine's most grandiose entertainments, the "magnificent carousel" (1766). A "carousel" was a form of game in which knights competed in exhibiting their equestrian skills; Catherine's lover of the moment, Grigory Orlov, not unexpectedly, won the chief honors in this one. The participants were elaborately and fantastically costumed, in four divisions—Slavic, Roman, Indian, and Turkish, and in addition to the tournament proper, there were chariot races! Although he had been in Moscow at the time, and had to rely on newspaper accounts of the festivities, Petrov succeeded in composing an "ode" of such magnificence that Catherine rewarded him with the gift of a gold snuff-box and 200 rubles. This was the start of his official career.

The pompous and hyperbolic style which Petrov's first ode exhibits underwent few changes in the next thirty years. Lomonosov is the model, but instead of his genuine patriotic enthusiasm, which justifies his strained and exalted language, Petrov's inspiration seems to be sparked chiefly by imperial munificence. The kind of poetry which results can be judged from a translation of the second strophe of the "Ode on the Magnificent Carousel"[4] in its original version (it was extensively revised in 1782):

> I hear the strange roar of music!
> This soothes and emboldens my spirit;
> I behold the choirs of various peoples!
> This comforts and astonishes my gaze;
> In purple Rome, Istanbul, India
> And beneath the crown of glory, Russia
> Has disclosed a myriad delights to [my] thoughts!
> And envy, stopping afar, marvels
> That our age is rolling on so joyfully,
> And forgets to drink her serpents' poison.

The application of Lomonosov's devices of exclamatory excitement and personification in the above strophe to such a trivial subject as a court festival sounds thoroughly parodistic. Further and even more absurd lapses of taste may be seen later in the ode, for a description of which a paragraph from G.P. Makogonenko's preface to the "Poet's Library" edition of *Poets of the Eighteenth Century* may be used:[5]

Lomonosov, in hailing peace, "repose," needed for the development and establishment of Russia, exclaimed: "Be silent, flaming sounds!" The "Ode on the Carousel" also begins with an exclamation: "Be silent, noisy thunders of applause," after the poet has declared that he is going to sing—"the games and amusements" of the court. Lomonosov, glorifying the exploits of the Russian warriors, who under Peter's leadership had converted Russia into a mighty empire, compared them with the heroic Romans. Petrov employs this comparison in order to show "the Roman spirit"—in the Orlov brothers, who had distinguished themselves in the carousel. Lomonosov, in speaking of the heroism of "Russia's sons," wrote: "But to hold back the flight of eagles ("orlov") there are no obstacles on earth." Petrov, losing every kind of feeling for measure and tact, converts this figure into a pun, celebrating the "heroic spirit" of these same participants in the equestrian competition, the brothers Orlov:

> Thus speedily did Peter's warriors
> Ride on the fields of Mars,
> Such eagles' ("orlovy") hearts in them.

Petrov's contribution to Russian ode-writing was chiefly to discredit it and turn any serious poet to some other genre. He did, however, effect some technical changes in the form of the ode. The earlier examples are composed in the form consecrated by Lomonosov's practice: ten-line strophes of iambic tetrameter. Later, however, he began to experiment with other forms. Thus the "Ode to Grigory Orlov," of 1771, uses a strophe of six lines, the first four of iambic tetrameter, the last two of trimeter. The 1775 "Ode to the Illustrious Count Peter Alexandrovich Rumiantsev-Zadunaisky" even attempts to naturalize Pindar's triadic structure, of strophe-antistrophe-epode. Petrov's ode consists of three triads, each constructed of two identical units of fifteen iambic tetrameter lines, broken by two Alexandrines (11-12), and an "epode" of 22 Alexandrines with complex rhyme scheme. The "Lamentation and Consolation of Russia" of 1796 does not even use a strophic form, but is composed in the Russian equivalent of the French *vers libre*, that is, with lines of differing lengths and a non-repetitive rhyme scheme. Since this verse form had been used almost exclusively for fables (first by La Fontaine, and then in Russian by e.g., Sumarokov [1752], Maikov [1763], Rzhevsky [1761], etc., it contributes a rather bizarre effect to a solemn lamentation!

In 1770 Petrov published a translation, which he dedicated to Pavel Petrovich, of the first book of Virgil's *Aeneid*. The translation of the complete epic came out only in the years 1781-83. Petrov's version of *Aeneid I* pleased Catherine immensely, as it was no doubt meant to do; it may be recalled that the Latin poem celebrates in Book I the feat of the Phoenician

Queen Dido in founding the new city of Carthage, and her hospitality to the ship-wrecked Aeneas and his Trojans. As long as Dido's tragedy (Book IV) remained in the background, a flattering parallel could be implied between Catherine and the Carthaginian queen—"dux femina facti." The translation is in Russian Alexandrine verse, with couplet rhyme, and the language and style are the "highest of the high." Making the poem particularly difficult to read are the Latinate tricks of word order—inversions, hyperbata, etc.—and even such long obsolete syntax as the vocative case and the Slavonic "dative absolute." Needless to say, the vocabulary is equally archaic, and although the Latin is rendered accurately enough, Virgil is made, as one critic complained, to appear in periwig and knee-breeches! A parallel with Pope's version of Homer is immediately suggested. Virgil's opening lines:

> Arma virumque cano, Troiae qui primus ab oris
> Italiam fato profugus Laviniaque venit
> litora—

become:

> I sing the clash of arms and exploits of the hero
> Who first, when Troy had been laid in ashes by the Greeks,
> Hounded by fate, reached Italy's shores.

The inflated and archaic style of Petrov's *Enei*, as he called his *Aeneid*, led to immediate ridicule and parody. Vasily Maikov in 1772 published his "heroi-comic poem" *Elisei, or Bacchus Enraged,* which begins: "I sing the clash of cans, I sing that hero who, in his cups, wreaking dreadful woes," etc., and Novikov, according Petrov an entry in his *Dictionary of Russian Writers* (1772) writes:

In general it can be said of his works that he strains to follow in the footsteps of Russia's lyric poet [i.e., Lomonosov] ; and although certain ones even call him a second Lomonosov [as Catherine II did!] , for this comparison one must await some important work, and after that say conclusively whether he will be a second Lomonosov, or remain only Petrov, and have the honor of being known as a mimic of Lomonosov.[6]

Nettled by such criticism, the poet dispatched from London, where he was at the time, a verse epistle to an anonymous addressee, in which he lashes out at Maikov and Novikov. Of the latter he writes:[7]

The lexicographer [a reference to Novikov's "Essay at a Historical Lexicon of Russian Writers," 1772] knows everything—who has a profound intellect, and who a shallow; of reason and excellence he is the sure touchstone. Whoever has been in his crowd, has been a friend and brother to him, is not less in his calendar than Socrates.

It must be said that Petrov in his polemical verse is considerably more direct and perspicuous than in his odes!

On rare occasions even this coldly official versifier can write simply and from the heart. His elegy: "My Son's Death, March, 1793"[8] marks such an occasion. Nikolenka must have been a sickly child, who bore his sufferings stoically. His father writes:

> Great soul in little body,
> O how he bore cruel affliction,
> And defended by what protection
> Did he show such strength in battle with it?
>
> Not a single sigh came from him,
> He tried to lock the pain in his heart.
> Gray-haired father! Learn from your son
> How a *man* should die!
>
> ———
>
> Learn to be like him:
> Lock sorrow within your heart.
> Live like him, righteous, forgiving;
> Like him, die without trembling.

Little Nikolenka is pictured as an angel in heaven, where the weary father yearns to go, but fears he is unworthy: "But what? I am sinful, you are innocent; I a whirlwind, you sweet peace; I a boor, you a noble angel—shall our lot be equal?" But still he counts on the child as a heavenly intercessor:

> You know whereof I have need;
> Whither I have directed my desire.
> To you it has been granted by heaven to watch over
> Me, your mother, brothers and sisters.

In this poem one may see an interesting stylistic phenomenon. Written in the simplest kind of strophic form (four iambic tetrameter lines, with alternate rhyme), the word order is perfectly natural and direct, with none of the exasperating inversions that characterize the odes. At the same time the vocabulary and morphology are archaic and artificial. For example, in the third strophe the second line reads: "otets nesnosen tvoi sud'be"; the adjective "nesnosnyi" means, in normal Russian, then as now, "unbearable." But not here: the line has to be construed as "[your] father is *unable to bear* your fate." In the fifth strophe the Church Slavonic "zabralo," lit. "the visor of a helmet," is used in the sense of "protection." Later, in the third strophe from the end, two of the rhyme words "telesi" and "nebesi," are oblique cases (in Slavonic!) of the nouns "telo" and "nebo," "body" and "heaven." Petrov's fatal predilection for high-flown archaisms manifests itself even in this sincere and touching poem.

B. The School of Sumarokov

1. Vasily Ivanovich Maikov (1728-1778)[9]

It is customary to distinguish in the verse of the age of Catherine II two "schools," of Lomonosov and Sumarokov. This division is actually far too schematic, and although such a poet as Kheraskov can be counted among the Sumarokov followers in most of his work, he deviates, as we have seen, into sentimentalism, which Sumarokov loathed; and although Sumarokov can have had few more fervent admirers than Vasily Maikov, the odes which the latter turned out belong unmistakably to the Lomonosov tradition. Let us consider Maikov's heritage of odes first of his work, and in their Lomonosov connection.

Vasily Ivanovich Maikov was the son of a Yaroslav gentleman who had been educated under Peter the Great, and fought in several of Anna Ivanovna's wars. Young Maikov became an officer in one of the Guards Regiments, but never saw actual military service. He was returned at the age of 14 (1742) to his family home for "further education," but failed to acquire very much. Unlike almost all writers of his age, Vasily Maikov was completely ignorant of foreign languages—a fact which exposed him to the ridicule of both friends and foes. His education was in general of the sketchiest, and mostly self-acquired. From childhood he was attracted to the theater, and was acquainted, through his father, with the brilliant Yaroslav actor F.G. Volkov. Through such a connection apparently he came to know Sumarokov, who was in 1756 director of the St. Petersburg theater, to which Volkov had been called by Empress Elizabeth. To the same circle belonged also E.P. Elagin, an important official and minor writer who, like Sumarokov, was a Mason. Following the lead of these men, Maikov likewise joined the Order.

In 1761 the Empress Elizabeth fell gravely ill, and attention was turned to her expected successor, the future Peter III. Among Peter's unattractive traits (he had few of any other sort) was a fanatical military punctiliousness, and there were probably even in 1761 intimations that one of his first acts would be to start a Russian war with Denmark to recover from that kingdom the province of Holstein which had formed part of his father's duchy. Under such circumstances it seemed the part of prudence for Maikov to retire from the service, which he did with the rank of captain, and migrated to Moscow.

In Moscow he very soon became acquainted with Mikhail M. Kheraskov, then an official in the Moscow University and director of the University library and press. It was probably the Masonic membership of both men that brought them together. Kheraskov published a series of periodicals, using the University press, of Masonic inspiration: *Profitable Diversion* (1760-62), *Free Hours* (1763), *Innocent Exercise* (1763) and *Good Intentions* (1764). Maikov had by this time begun writing verse, and some of this was published in Kheraskov's journals. Since Kheraskov was by literary orientation a convinced classicist, at least at this time, and an admirer of Sumarokov, it it not surprising that Maikov's literary direction should follow the same lines.

In 1767, when Catherine II instituted the Legislative Commission that was to draw up a new code of laws, Maikov, who had attracted her attention by his early odes, was put into the responsible position of secretary to the Commission. In this post he remained until the sessions of the Commission were suspended, at which time he continued in St. Petersburg and presently found a post in the civil service. He spent the rest of his life in various governmental offices in the capital.

Maikov's first ode hails Catherine's *coup d'état* and accession to the throne, and copies, almost verbatim, the arguments by which she sought to justify her usurpation in the accession manifesto. The first strophe, with its exclamatory style, immediately proclaims its indebtedness to Lomonosov:[10]

Hasten, hasten, my spirit, boldly! Hasten, mount up to Parnassus. To sing so great a deed raise your loud voice, O lyre, pursue the joyful sound, sing now Peter's granddaughter [though Catherine had no Russian blood, she had been in a sense adopted by Elizabeth, and hence can be given this flattering genealogy!], who has ascended the Russian throne, and repeat the joyful shouts! Such great wonders has God wrought, putting an end to our groans. (strophe 1)

The second ode, "On the New Year 1763"[11] is even clearer evidence:

After the bright dawn's rising the sun is already coming into the world, from his gold-gleaming chariot the bright rays are shining in the ether. The moon grows pale, the stars have vanished, and to our gaze have been revealed meadows, hills, forests, seas, and the horses with stormy feet are carrying over the heavenly fields the planet of the beautiful king. (strophe 1)

The "stormy feet" of Lomonosov's cavalry at Poltava have now taken their place in a pseudo-classical allegory of the sunrise!

Maikov commemorated with odes most of the major public events of the first few years of Catherine's reign, down to the peace of Kuchuk Kainarii in 1775—with one significant exception: the victory over Pugachev and the rebellious peasants. Apparently like so many of the gentry class, Maikov was appalled by the revelation of the volcano beneath Catherine's glamorous empire, and turned away from public themes. More and more drawn into Masonic pietism, he turned out odes "To those seeking wisdom," "On Happiness," "On Hope," and "On the Immortality of the Soul,"—even "On the

Last Judgment."

Among the most notable of the earlier odes is the one simply entitled "War," composed during the Russo-Polish hostilities of 1768-69. It is most unusual among poems of the age on such a theme, which are numerous, in its evidently sincere horror of war, and its unabashed depiction of war's victims, as a few excerpts will show:

What dreadful wind has blown you, bloody war? Discord engendered you among mortals, and you were borne by Alecto [one of the Furies]. When you emerge from Hell, Comfort flees afar from all, and through the sulphur-thick clouds the bright light of the sun does not shine. (st. 1).

You pour your poison upon the earth, you bring forth dreadful fruit, you break the alliances of kingdoms, you torture and injure peoples: your counsels are all harmful, your deeds both wretched and fatal; your voice makes the whole firmament tremble, your gaze calls forth cruel death. (st. 2)

———

You part wives from husbands, you rob fathers of their children, you grieve true lovers, you separate friends from friends; you afflict all with sorrow unbearable, you do not pity those that are infants, nor beautiful maidens; you spare neither rank nor person. (st. 4)

———

Where you step, there everything blazes and is turned to ashes; there a myriad of the innocent dies; everywhere fear and despair, everywhere sobbing and tears; on captives, heavy irons; on the conquerors, their blood; there suffer friendship and love. (st. 6)

There unfortunate wives groan, robbed of their husbands forever; husbands, fighting for them, drown in streams of their own blood. Nature herself suffers there; every warrior is athirst for murder, and of these all order consists; there every murderer is a hero. (st. 7)

———

The earth, weighed down with corpses, cries out to heaven: "Is it for this, O God, that mortals were drawn by thee forth from the darkness, that all their feelings and minds might be thus cruelly treated, that they should pour out their blood in rivers, and become like wild beasts? Thou didst not, O God, create the world that it should be full of woes." (st. 17)[12]

Eighteenth century ode-writers usually depict the glories of war, the excitement of victory; it is not "men who have become like wild beasts" who range over the battle-fields, but Mars or Bellona, and the laurel wreath is more prominent than "mountains of corpses" and "rivers of blood." Maikov himself wrote such odes—e.g., "Ode to the Victorious Russian Arms," "Ode on the Capture of Bender," and "Ode on the Battle of Chesme." But in this one he sees war, for once in a way, as war really is, and the picture is grim.

In his ode of 1768 on the anniversary of Catherine's accession, Maikov, who has been busy with the Legislative Commission, calls on his "reposing lyre" to "rise and leave sweet sleep!" But, faced with the enormous task of celebrating his subject fitly, whom may he call on for aid? "Who is able to

278

direct them, who will give me riches of speech? Is it possible for my song to celebrate Russia's goddess? O thou, glorious singer of the Russ! O incomparable Lomonosov! Thy style of excellent beauty, thy enormous ("ogromna") and shapely song was worthy of the Empress, and thou wert worthy to sing her. I revere thy cold ashes—they are laid away in that city in which I am imitating thee, having been fired with thy flame; come, tune for me my feeble lyre, that I may to the wide world thunder forth with thy transport ("vostorg")." (st. 3-4).[13] For all his effort, Maikov's well-intentioned imitations were more often slumberous than thunderous, and Khemnitser's malicious epigram was not altogether unjustified:

> That M[aikov] in his writing never *fell*
> Is a perfectly exact observation of yours,
> And I have always held the same opinion;
> However much he wrote, he never *rose*.[14]

He succeeded in copying the externals of Lomonosov's style with an exactitude approaching servility, but he could never capture the master's genuine poetic fire.

One of Maikov's most interesting odes is the one written in 1776, "Ode on Taste, to Alexander Petrovich Sumarokov."[15] For all his reverence for Lomonosov, it was the Russian classicist who seemed to him the highest embodiment of "taste," and perhaps, in his rather naive way, Maikov was not quite aware of the inconsistency of this position. Sumarokov was, and in his "Reply to the Ode of Vasily Ivanovich Maikov" he utters some rather pointed warnings. The two poems say so much about the literary ideals of the age that they deserve to be cited entire; Maikov writes:

O thou, by the springs of Hippocrene, sweet singer of Parnassus, friend of Thalia [Muse of Comedy] and of Melpomene [Muse of Tragedy], father of the Russian theater, exposer of evil vice [reference to Sumarokov's satires], Sumarokov, the Racine of the North! The voice of thy charming pipe [reference to Sumarokov's pastorals], the voice of thy delightful lyre [reference to his lyric verse] have possessed my thoughts, revealing the paths to Parnassus: captivated by thy approbation, I too sing, my heart on fire.

And lo, lured on by thy delightful tones, and by my own heat, I became acquainted with Apollo and made myself known to the Muses; by now the path to Parnassus is well known to me; I am going toward it in thy footsteps.

And thus I am always flying after thee, as after a quiet zephyr; I am not minded to handle badly the lyre that thou hast tuned; always taste alone is delightful to me—taste which is dignified, pure and intelligible.

But it is impossible to celebrate the tastes of all, they are different with (different) people; Pradon, with his "Phedre" was falsely preferred to Racine; but what of that? Pradon's taste was brought to an end, Racine crowned with victory.

Not sumptuousness ("pyshnost' ") is charm in verses; charm in them is purity; not thunder ("grom"), but the riches of reason and dignified utterance is beauty. Style should be both pure and clear; this [kind of] taste is concordant with nature.

I shall always direct [my] style according to taste alone, and in this, copy nature, thee, and sound sense ("zdravomu umu"). Casual [kinds of] taste are all fragile, and will not go down to [our] descendants.

To this tribute the arbiter of *bon gout* replied:

Superfluous ornateness ("vitiistvo") is nature's worst enemy; avoid it as much as possible, Maikov; be circumspectly ornate! There remains for you but one more step to the summit of the mountain; you will indubitably be on the heights of Parnassus; pluck for yourself fragrant roses there, and with them alone adorn your poems! Without these flowers labors are vanity alone; sound sense ("zdravyi um") always loathes the dream ("mechtu"); if there is not in one's verse charming simplicity and clarity and purity, then those verses are devoid of beauty and full of emptiness.

If a pin shall prick an inflated bladder, all the sumptuousness of the bubble will disappear in one moment. All the air will go out of the bladder, to the bottom, and only the skin alone will remain.[16]

It is worth noting in Sumarokov's reply that he evidently sees some danger for Maikov from "ornateness" of style—which is precisely a Lomonosov characteristic. It is also worth noting now vehemently the classicist dismisses "dream": "sound sense always loathes the dream." "Mechta," as we shall see subsequently, is one of the most characteristic words of all the romantics' vocabulary, and "dream," that is, the freely imagined, private world of the romantic poet, is his inspiration, not "sound sense." It would be hard to find a sharper disagreement between the two world outlooks of romantic and classicist.

In his "Ode on Taste" Maikov touches allegorically on his master's principal fields of endeavor—lyric poetry, satire, pastoral, comedy and tragedy. He includes no mention of the fable, probably because this is a "low" genre, for which Parnassus provides no presiding Muse. He himself, however, followed Sumarokov's footsteps into this realm too, and in 1767 published a volume of *Didactic Fables.* These are mostly retellings of fables of Aesop, Phaedrus, the Indian Pilpai and the Dane Holberg—all, of course, available to Maikov in translation. There are a few also of Maikov's own invention. In them he uses the *vers libre* form consecrated by La Fontaine and Sumarokov, and in style approaches the colloquial, although not without occasional Slavonicisms. The situations are often given an external Russian coloring, and popular Russian proverbs and expressions are utilized. The chief quality of Maikov's fables, however, is their prolixity. The poet seems to have no "terminal facility," and runs on endlessly, with totally needless details. A relatively succinct example (only one page long!) may be compared with Krylov's famous one on the geese, with the same moral:

Two horses were sold; what ones, don't ask me. One of them was good, the other rather bad; so for the bad one it wasn't possible to give the same price as was given for the good one; the worse he was, so much less the price. They put the good horse in a stall, always gave him fodder and drink enough. The master was always fond of the horse. The horse, like a gentleman, drinks, eats, walks in the fields and holds up his nose. The other, always in servitude, carries on his back dirt, water, and dung. This becomes tiresome to the horse, that he and labor are inseparable; the smell of dung annoys him. The horse complains to his master: "Evidently you don't know my family, that you are always carrying dung and water on me. But if you knew my forefathers, of course you would give me priority over that horse that you recently bought with me. My birth, of course, is not on a par with his. In *me* you possess a horse that has Pegasus and Bucephalus for kindred; so can *that* horse be on an equality with me?" The master suddenly cut the horse's speech short with a club. Hitting him on the back, he said: "I have no concern with the noblest family; your price commands that you shall always carry water."[17]

In the precincts of Melpomene Maikov also pursued his master, and composed a tragedy, which was produced at the court theater in St. Petersburg in 1767. It is called *Agriopa*,[18] and was patently composed with Catherine's political situation in mind. In it Maikov grafted a plot apparently of his own invention upon a Greek legend of the Trojan War. The sequence of events is briefly as follows: the Greek hero Telephus has intervened when Achilles ravaged the land of Mysia, near Troy, and saved the life of King Teuthras. The latter in gratitude has betrothed his daughter Agriopa to Telephus, and promised him the Mysian throne as his son-in-law. Teuthras has died at the beginning of the play, and the time has come for Telephus to marry Agriopa, who is in love with him. Instead, he informs her that a divine portent has bidden him assume the Mysian crown, and then go help the Greeks at Troy. Actually, he is motivated by a sudden and uncontrollable passion for Polydora, daughter of the cunning nobleman Azor (Polydora does not appear on the stage at any time). Azor is ambitious and favors Telephus's project of becoming Mysia's king and getting rid of Agriopa. The heroine learns, through her indefatigable confidante Albina, of the plot, and forestalls it by calling upon her loyal warriors, led by an unnamed commander. In the final act Telephus is taken captive, magnanimously forgiven by Agriopa, who then attempts to stab herself, but is prevented by Albina and the "commander." When he learns that Polydora has been killed during the battle by a chance arrow, Telephus picks up the dagger which Agriopa has dropped, and successfully commits suicide. The dastardly Azor, of course, has already done so off-stage when his plot miscarried.

Not much can be said for *Agriopa* as a tragedy beyond the timeliness of the plot. Of course a detailed correspondence cannot be drawn between Catherine and Agriopa or Peter III and Telephus, but a certain similarity is hardly coincidental. The most striking aspect of this similarity lies in the impudent reversal of the parts: in the tragedy Telephus is the would-be usurper of Agriopa's throne; in real life the legitimate monarch was Peter, and Catherine was the usurper. The unnamed "commander" of Agriopa's warriors would have to be equated with Catherine's lover Grigory Orlov, who led the guard in the coup that ousted Peter. The project of Telephus to set aside his betrothed bride in favor of Azor's daughter also had its real life parallel: Peter was infatuated with Elizaveta Vorontsova, and if her father Roman Larionovich Vorontsov did not actively plot to put his daughter in Catherine's place, he certainly was acquiescent.

The characterization of the tragedy is pretty conventional and unexciting. The heroine is better developed than any of the other characters, as might be expected. The usual divided purpose, which after Racine seems to have been *de rigueur* for a tragic heroine, is only sketched: she says she is torn between continued love for the traitorous Telephus and a desire for vengeance—but revenge triumphs so easily that one doubts the love. Telephus's chief characteristic seems to be weak-willed vacillation: he is an antagonist who puts up too little fight to be interesting. Azor is indeed a thoroughly unscrupulous villain, but the one opportunity for some real drama is fumbled: Azor's duplicity in openly confessing Telephus's feelings for his daughter to Agriopa, and his profession of loyalty to his princess, which could have been utilized to complicate the action, is met so simply by her open disbelief that nothing comes of the plot. The psychology of classical tragedy is based, as we know, on the conflict between "reason" and "the passions," and it is indeed a rare genius who can depict this conflict convincingly without tipping the scales too obviously toward one direction or the other. When Corneille's Nicomède, for instance, faces such a conflict, he is so completely in command of himself that "the passions" have no chance at all, and interest tends to flag. The situation is the opposite with Telephus: he informs his confidant Ariston, who pallidly embodies the voice of reason: "It is quite in vain that one offers advice to him to whom it has been assigned by a cruel fate to be deprived of firmness, to have no control over himself." Having thus defined his own character, Telephus continues until the final moment to exemplify the correctness of his definition—and any possible tension disappears.

Maikov's only other tragedy, *Themistus and Hieronyma*,[19] was composed in 1772, accepted by the theater for production, but abandoned because of the death of the leading lady who was to have played the part of Hieronyma. The play is something of an anomaly among eighteenth century Russian tragedies. The subject was suggested and most of the names drawn from a French novel translated into Russian by a certain Shishkin, and again the timeliness of the plot was its chief recommendation. The scene was laid in Constantinople during the reign of Sultan Mehmet (Mahomet) II. In Maikov's entirely fictional plot a Greek prince, Themistus (Femist), son of Theodore Comnenus (the Comneni, except in Trebizond, had actually died out in the 13th century!) has disguised himself as a Turk under the name of Soliman, and succeeded in attaining the highest post in the empire, that of Grand Vizier. With his friend Klit (Cleitus?), masquerading under the Turkish name of Murat, Themistus tries to carry out a plot for overthrowing the Sultan, who has made himself unpopular with the Janissaries by his infatuation with the captive princess Hieronyma. In the third act Hieronyma is discovered to be Themistus' lost love, and to protect her from the Turk he precipitates the plot, which miscarries; Mahomet kills Hieronyma, and Themistus kills himself. The timeliness of this thriller in 1772 is obvious, when Russian navies were cruising the Aegean and Ionian Seas, and efforts were being made to rouse the Greeks to open rebellion against the Turks.

What makes the tragedy most unusual in its century is its complicated plot and the exciting turns that this takes. Plots of intrigue, the chief interest of which consists in uncertainty over what will happen next, are thoroughly unclassical. As A.V. Zapadov says, in his introduction to the *Selected Works* of Maikov:[20] "The new characters introduced by the dramatist lend attractiveness to the subject, by transforming the tragedy, to express ourselves in contemporary language, into a detective, 'spy' production—an amazing instance in eighteenth century dramaturgy!" Since, however, the play was never produced in Maikov's lifetime, and not published until 1775, this innovation had no sequel.

Before taking up the one genre in which Maikov produced a minor masterpiece, we may have a very brief glance at another in which he failed as badly as all his predecessors—the epic poem. It may be remembered that even Lomonosov, with a subject as dear to his heart as "Peter the Great," and a style that should have been ideally suited to the heroic poem, gave the attempt up after two cantos; and Sumarokov apparently wrote only a page of his projected *Dmitriad*—at least no more has survived. Maikov began a poem which remained in manuscript—*Moscow Liberated*.[21] The subject would have been, of course, the end of the Smuta and the accession of the Romanov dynasty in 1613. The attempt, however, never got off the ground: only 184 lines are contained in the manuscript, and presumably no more were written. Already in these Maikov has committed several serious historical boners. His language is appropriately "high," and he has been able to drag in one "divine intervention"—a dream sent directly by God to General Shein, under seige by the Poles in Pskov (historically, in Smolensk).

If the "heroic poem" of Russian classicism was denied to Maikov as to his masters and reserved for his friend Kheraskov, the "heroi-comic poem" belongs wholly to him. Some explanations of the genre are needed to put this feat in its place.

The first "heroi-comic poem" in western literature is the *Batrachomyiomachia*, traditionally ascribed to Homer, but actually a Hellenistic work. It is a parody of the *Iliad,* written in the traditional epic dialect and in dactylic hexameter, narrating the war between the frogs and mice. The war begins as the mice seek vengeance for one of their kin, drowned when a frog, on whose back he was fording a stream, dives at sight of a water-snake. The mice get the better in the engagement, and the frogs would have been exterminated but for Zeus's intervention; an army of crabs is sent against the victorious mice, which puts them to rout. This ancient example gave the "parody epic" a classical sanction, and the Renaissance saw a number of imitations. Lope de Vega wrote a *Gatomaquia*, or "Battle of the Cats," with a plot enlivened by a feline love story; and the Italian Alessandro Tassoni (1565-1635) composed a mock epic in twelve books, in octave stanzas (the Italian epic meter), *La secchia rapita*, "The Rape of the Bucket."

Classicism looked rather askance at the genre, which appears first in French verse (Rabelais' prose is another matter) with Paul Scarron (1610-1660). Scarron is the chief representative in France of what came to be called the "burlesque" poem, from the Italian "burla," "joke." Scarron's *Virgile travesti* (1648-1652) and his earlier and less familiar *Typhon ou la Gigantomachie* (1647) are the classical monuments of the genre. In *Virgil Travestied* the poet takes the plot of the *Aeneid* (only to the middle of Book VIII, however) and using the same incidents and characters, turns the entire "heroic" action into commonplace triviality. In the *Gigantomachy* the battle between the gods and giants begins when one of the giants, during a bowling contest, hurls a badly directed ball into Jupiter's dining-room and breaks some precious Venetian glass! The poems are written in a deliberately pompous style, with occasional vulgarisms for greater effect. Scarron, however, does not employ the canonical epic meter, which in French is of course the Alexandrine: *Virgile travesti* is written in octosyllabic verse with couplet rhyme—the form traditionally employed for the romances and *fabliaux*.

Boileau disapproved of Scarron's vulgarity; no mention is made in the *Art poétique* of the heroi-comic poem as a genre, but in Book I he warns his would-be poet: "Quoi que vous écriviez, évitez la bassesse," and goes on:

> *Au mépris du bon sens, le burlesque effronté*
> *Trompa les yeux d'abord, plut par sa nouveauté:*
> *On ne vit plus en vers que pointes triviales;*
> *Le Parnasse parla le langage des halles—*
> *Mais de ce style enfin la cour désabusée*
> *Dédaigna de ces vers l'extravagance aisée,*
> *Distingua le naif du plat et du bouffon,*
> *Et laissa la province admirer le Tryphon* [i.e., Scarron's *Gigantomachie*] .[22]

Boileau, of course, could find no classical precedent for such a work as *Virgil Travestied*—one in which a heroic action is made commonplace and trivial. Instead, he found the contrary procedure—that in which a small or

284

trivial action is treated in grandiloquent style. In an endeavor to correct French taste in this regard, he himself composed a heroi-comic poem, *Le Lutrin (The Lectern)*, in which a clerical brawl developing over the placing of a lectern in church becomes an epic battle; the first canto begins:[23]

> *Je chante les combats, et ce prélat terrible*
> *Qui, par ses longs travaux et sa force invincible*
> *Dans une illustre église exerçant son grand coeur,*
> *Fit placer à la fin un lutrin dans le choeur.*

Instead of a *Virgil Travestied,* we have Virgilian grandeur adapted to a ridiculous subject. In the eighteenth century a similar procedure gave English literature one of its chief monuments of the genre—Alexander Pope's *Rape of the Lock.*

When Alexander Sumarokov adapted Boileau's *Art poetique* to Russian purposes, he included a number of genres which Boileau had ignored. One of these is the heroi-comic poem. Broad-mindedly he recognizes *both* varieties as legitimate:

There is still the type of humorous heroic poem, and I would like to make some mention of this; it converts Dido into a common wench, or presents to us a bargeman as Aeneas, showing brawlers and bullies as knights. Thus the type of such humorous poems is twofold: in one the exploits of heroes are presented as scuffles, Paris gives the son of Thetis [i.e., Achilles] a cudgelling, Hector goes to a boxing-match, not war, and takes to the conflict with him not warriors, but fist-fighters. Zeus doesn't hurl lightning and thunder from heaven, he strikes fire with flint and steel, and he isn't trying to frighten the inhabitants of earth, but just wants to light a pine-splinter. Verses which deal with lofty actions in this type are written in very low words. In the other one of such poems his pen bids the skillful poet give a knightly spirit to a brawler. Some bullies get into a fight—it isn't a vulgar scuffle, but Achilles pursuing valiant Hector. In this type a soot-covered smith is Vulcan, and a rain-water puddle is no puddle, but an ocean. A woman spanking a baby is Juno in wrath, a fence around a threshing-floor is the wall of Ilion. In this type it is proper for the Muse to give lofty words for low actions.[24]

Vasily Maikov was inspired to write his first "parody epic" by a Spanish card game which had become the rage in Russian society of the 1760s; the poem is called *The Game of Ombre* (1763).[25] It belongs to the second of Sumarokov's two types of heroi-comic poems: the game, which involves three players, is described throughout in lofty terms as a kind of epic struggle. This is made the easier by the fact that the various face cards in the game have classical or Biblical names—David, Alexander, Judith, etc.; the three trumps—ace of spades, ace of clubs and the lowest card of the trump suit—are called "matadors" (i.e., "killers"), the ace of spades is called "shpadilia" (Spanish "espadilla," from "espada," "sword"), and the like. As an example of the style of the poem this passage from Canto I will serve:

Then from his hands David [king of spades] advances upon the table, whom a wicked jack of hearts smites; he leads him into captivity, plunging a spear into him. Leander sees this, but what to do? Aid is impossible. Then even Caesar himself [the king of diamonds] shows his stately face, and in pride snatches up the second trump, carries him off into captivity even as Pluto carried off Ceres' lovely daughter defenceless to Hades. And lo, how a tempestuous wind carries Judith [queen of hearts] into the fray: in pride she demands single combat. "Oh, is there," she cries, "such a hero among the cards? Let him enter with me, courageously, into deadly battle. I fear him not on this broad field." Then Charlemagne [king of hearts], moved by his hapless destiny, fell valiantly upon her and smote, and wrought due punishment upon Judith, who ere now had slain Holofernes, etc.[26]

Leander, the poem's "hero," loses heavily after an all-night game, and falls into a troubled sleep during which, in Canto III, he has a dream which is a quasi-Virgilian vision of Hades, where unfortunate gamblers are appropriately punished.

The immediate occasion that stirred Maikov to the writing of his second heroi-comic poem[27] was apparently a move of Catherine II to obtain the money needed for her extravagant court life and constant wars. This was the introduction of a state liquor monopoly and of the system of *otkupy* which went with it. The government would auction off to the highest bidder the right to sell spirits in a given town; the concessionaire ("otkupshchik") would then pay the government the sum which he had bid, and was thereafter at liberty to keep whatever amount in excess of this he might be able to extort. Immediately upon the introduction of this system, which did not begin fully until 1767, the price of spirits rose: a *vedro* of vodka (10 1/2 quarts) cost 2 rubles 23 1/2 copecks in 1762; by 1770 it cost 3 rubles. The "otkupshchiki" were also accused, probably with very good reason, of shamelessly diluting their products. Naturally it was the peasants who suffered chiefly from these developments, and there was widespread indignation, not at the government, but at the excisemen (this would be the nearest English equivalent of "otkupshchiki").

Maikov's initial thought, then, was embodied in the sub-title of his poem: *Bacchus Enraged.* His idea was to depict the pagan god of wine incensed at the excisemen because their evil practices interfered with intoxication, which was his particular province. In presenting Bacchus and the other denizens of Olympus he intended to follow the lead of Scarron, and reduce their majesty to everyday triviality. Early in the proem of *Bacchus—Enraged,* accordingly, he introduces the following invocation:

And you, darling, beloved Scarron! Leave the sumptuous throne of lecherous Priapus, leave the gang of blasphemous writers; come, tune for me my fiddle ["gudok"] or balalaika, so that I may be able to fiddle like you, to attire my heroes as bargemen ["burlakami"] ; so that my Zeus may be a windbag, Hermes a mischievous lad, Neptune the stupidest kind of animal ["skotina"] , and, in a word, that my little gods and goddesses may split the guts of all my readers (with laughter).[28]

286

G. P. Makogonenko conjectures[29] that because of the mention of Priapus, the person meant in this invocation is not Paul Scarron, author of *Virgil Travestied,* but the Russian poet I.S. Barkov, author of a considerable body of underground literature of such an obscene nature that the prudish Russian press has never published it; among his works, it is said, is an "Ode to Priapus." Since of Barkov's odes only the "Ode to a Fist-Fighter" has ever been printed, and this in an extremely bowdlerized form, it is impossible for one who has not access to the manuscript copies of the poems to make any valid judgment; but it does appear very likely that there is a connection between Maikov and Barkov. However that may be, the Scarronian treatment of the classical gods is certainly the one that Maikov followed.

Maikov had evidently conceived the idea of his *Bacchus Enraged* as early as 1768. In the next year occurred an event which caused him to make a radical change in this first idea. Vasily Petrov's translation of the first book of Virgil's *Aeneid* was circulated in manuscript, and published in 1770. At once all the more liberal *literati* of the capital fell upon the unfortunate translation, which was so stilted and archaic in style as to be an anachronism at its very birth. The thought of parodying Petrov's *Enei* was too good to pass up, so Maikov accordingly dubbed his peasant hero Elisei, and prefixed his name to the title *Bacchus Enraged.* He thereupon provided his hero with a Virgilian adventure or two, all inspired by Book I. Elisei is first introduced, in Canto I, entering a crowded bar and calling for a drink. Having tossed off his vodka, which one may assume was watered, he hurls his empty glass in the face of the hapless "chumak," or tapster, and a lively brawl ensues which is terminated by the arrival of a police officer, who carries Elisei off to jail. All this is prefaced by a description of Bacchus's rage at the excisemen and his journey to a St. Petersburg tavern, where the sight of Elisei, already "drunk before dinner," convinces him that here is his champion who will avenge him on the "otkupshchiki." Since there is nothing Virgilian in this episode, it may be supposed that it had been composed before the second idea occurred to Maikov. Bacchus, disappointed at the quick elimination of Elisei, goes to Olympus, where he finds Zeus dead drunk, but is able to get him to send Hermes, his messenger boy, to effect Elisei's release. Zeus also orders Hermes to summon all the gods to a full-dress assembly, for Ceres, goddess of agriculture, has a complaint against Bacchus for diverting so many peasants from their proper business. The assembly is scheduled for the following day, when Zeus sobers up.

In Canto II Hermes enters the malodorous prison disguised as a corporal of the guard, and finds Elisei, still drunk, in such a deep sleep that it is impossible to waken him. Hermes' solution is to undress the young man, and an equally drunken girl asleep beside him, and change their clothes. This done, he carries Elisei, still asleep, to a certain house located on the Fontanka, known as the "Kalinkin dom." This was, of course, well-known to Maikov's contemporaries as a "reformatory" for prostitutes; the girls were incarcerated there and obliged to occupy themselves with sewing, lace-making, and similar useful tasks, under the supervision of an old beldame with the title of "Superintendent." When Elisei awakes, he is puzzled to find himself wearing a woman's smock and in what he takes to be a nunnery! The Superintendent is equally puzzled to find a new "girl" in her establishment (Maikov explains that Elisei is only eighteen, good-looking, and beardless), but being a woman of the world, at once senses that here is more than meets the eye, and politely invites Elisei into her private room, where she asks him who he is and how he got there. Here begins the Virgilian part of the poem; just as Aeneas narrates to Dido the lamentable story of Troy's fall and his own escape and wanderings, Elisei regales the Superintendent with his story. He is a coachman, who lives presently in the Yamskaia district of St. Petersburg (the coachmen's quarter); but he was a native of the village of Zimogore—and at once he launches into the tale of the epic battle between his village and the villagers of Valdai over the boundary fields between the two places:

"Forgive these tears, that stream from my eyes," says the coachman;
"With them I proclaim to you well enough how much pity I feel even now when I recall my misfortunes; for there I lost mother, and brother and wife."

It appears, as the narrative proceeds, that this great family loss is not total: Elisei's mother did in fact die, after a violent attack of diarrhea brought on by terror during the battle. His brother, after performing prodigies of valor against the Valdaians, has his right ear bitten off; and when Elisei returns home with his defeated fellow-villagers, he finds his wife with her braids cut off!

The narrative continues in Canto III: Elisei leaves his village, goes to "Piter," and becomes a coachman. The Superintendent gives him some homework, locks him in her room, and arranges that he shall share her bed. Meanwhile on Olympus Zeus has slept off his drunk, and the divine assembly begins. Ceres pleads her case, and Bacchus his, which is to the effect that by his ministrations all classes are enabled to forget their troubles. Zeus promises a compromise that will satisfy both parties. In the Kalinkin house the Superintendent prettifies herself as much as possible, and gets into bed with Elisei; but their love-making has hardly begun when it is interrupted by another of the Superintendent's lovers—a forty-year-old captain of the guard who has come on an inspection tour. In spite of the Superintendent's story that she is sleeping with her niece who is on a visit, the captain hauls Elisei again off to jail, on suspicion. Once more Hermes intervenes, dressed now as a *petit-maitre*—a dandy—and Elisei is returned to the Kalinkin house. Again a Virgilian theme: after a period of happy inactivity with his Superintendent, Elisei is reminded that he has greater things to do—as Aeneas is warned by

Mercury of his mission to found Rome—and makes a hurried escape, leaving his pants and waistcoat behind! This time Hermes has thoughtfully provided him with a folk-lore piece of equipment, "the cap of darkness," which makes him invisible while wearing it. The Superintendent awakes, like Ariadne abandoned by Theseus, and finds only Elisei's pants and waistcoat left as mementos—and at this moment the Captain of the guard again inopportunely appears, and finds his suspicions confirmed. She wins him over with her blandishments, however, and later burns her precious mementos:

> His pants and waistcoat she burned in her stove, when she had got it heated for baking pies—and in this too she behaved like Dido—[who, it may be remembered, burned *herself* on a funeral pyre after Aeneas had left!]

The poem continues in Canto IV as Elisei, in his Tarnhelm, but without his pants, is wandering through the spring fields outside the city, where the singing birds turn his mind to his wife, whom he misses, even if she has lost her pig-tails. He takes a nap, and is awakened by a woman's screams: two men, with obviously evil intent, are running after a dishevelled young woman. Elisei, invisible, attacks, and the villains, each taking the other for his assailant, begin a battle with each other, during which the hero and the rescued damsel leave the scene. To his delight, Elisei finds the woman is his own wife! She tells her story, at the end of which Elisei sends her on to Yamskaia (no motivation is given for this curious dismissal, and the wife is never mentioned again), and he goes to town, where he invades the house of a liquor-concessionaire. The owner and his wife are steaming in the bath-house, where Elisei, still invisible, torments them; and when the couple retire for the night, he crawls under their bed. Awakened by a thunderstorm, the husband goes to say some prayers, and the unseen hero crawls in with the wife—to her considerable surprise and pleasure. The husband, on his return, observes some strange movements, and decides to send for an old woman to exorcise the devil that appears to inhabit the house.

In the final (fifth) canto, Elisei, not waiting to be exorcised, takes refuge in the cellar full of liquor in bottles and casks. After drinking his fill, he devastates the rest and leaves the place to continue his destructive career elsewhere. The old woman exorcist arrives, and boasts of her powers; among the marvelous cures she has effected are two outstanding ones—she can break a poet of the bad habit of versifying, and a drunkard of drinking. This is too much for the liquor-dealer—she could ruin him, so he sends her packing at once. Zeus gathers the gods at a "window in the zenith," warns them that a great battle is about to take place, but that they must be strictly neutral or they will feel his wrath, and they sit down meekly to watch. The battle that ensues is held at a bear-baiting pit called the "Ruka," where champions from Yamskaia and from the merchants' quarter have a free-for-all. Elisei enters the list for Yamskaia, and does great execution until someone knocks off his cap—whereupon he is pounced upon, carried off, and his head shaved:

Surely they aren't getting him ready directly for the service? Alas, it's true! The sentence has been passed: "Eliseika, as a runaway, and perhaps also a thief, who brought no payment from the commune [to buy him off from military duty], is inducted into the army and made a soldier."

Thus abruptly and unceremoniously Maikov dismisses his hero and the poem.

Elisei, or Bacchus Enraged is a curious medley. As a work of art it can hardly be called successful. The two leading ideas—Bacchus's vengeance on the liquor-dealers, and parody of Petrov's *Aeneid* translation—while not incompatible, are not easy to hold together; and still worse, both leading ideas get lost in the last two cantos. The episode of the recovery of Elisei's wife, and of the melee at the "Ruka" are totally irrelevant, and seem to have been added only as padding. The pranks in the liquor-dealer's bathhouse and bedroom, and the episode of the exorcism are connected with the first theme, but only remotely. Maikov dropped the piece after Canto V as though he were tired of it—but it is still too long. The prolixity which mars his *Fables* is evident here too. A poem based on parody, as this is, can be carried on for only a short while without becoming a bore; even Scarron had recognized this, and brought his *Travestied Virgil* to an end after only eight (out of twelve) cantos. Maikov could have finished all he needed to say in no more than four cantos, perhaps even three.

Of characterization there is of course not a trace: in such a work it could hardly be expected. His people, human or divine, are wooden marionettes, and their antics are most carelessly motivated, if at all. Why, for instance, is there such a battle as takes place at the "Ruka"? And what has it to do with either Bacchus or Virgil? The battle itself, moreover, is a not very exciting repetition or the already related one between Zimogore and Valdai. Repetitiveness is, with prolixity, Maikov's great weakness.

Something may be said for his originality, however, in using the heroicomic genre. *Elisei* belongs fully to neither one of Sumarokov's categories, but holds a middle ground: except for the Olympian scenes, there is none of the travesty element of the first type; but, unlike Boileau's *Lutrin* or Pope's *Rape of the Lock*, the trivial, naturalistic scenes—the tavern brawl, the village fight, the "Ruka" engagement, the scenes in Kalinkin house, etc.—are *not*, for the most part, narrated in lofty epic language, but in the commonest, most colloquial Russian. There are a few exceptions, such as Elisei's "forgive these tears" speech quoted above. Perhaps without quite realizing it, Maikov succeeded in *Elisei* in creating a third kind of heroi-comic poem, with a hint of realism.

The genre in Russian literature was born with Maikov, and very nearly died with him. A horrendously long and portentously dull full-scale parody of Virgil's *Aeneid* was created by a certain N.P. Osipov (1751-1799), and in Ukrainian a famous one by I.P. Kotliarevsky, which is said to be very amusing. Early in the nineteenth century Vasily Lvovich Pushkin, Alexander's uncle, wrote an entertaining short narrative poem with some elements of parody, *A Dangerous Neighbor,* which we shall consider in another place, and A.A. Shakhovskoy *The Ravished Fur-Coat.* But by the second decade of the century the heroi-comic poem had been given a completely new and far more attractive face by the genius of Alexander Sergeevich Pushkin, with *Ruslan and Liudmila.*

The literary affiliations of Poprovsky and Petrov, as we have seen, were with Lomonosov exclusively. Maikov occupies a somewhat ambivalent position: in his "odes" he follows the Lomonosov system, somewhat awkwardly and with little genuine inspiration, but in his *Fables,* his tragedies, and even in his heroi-comic poems it is Sumarokov who gives him his direction. What originality he can claim, in his tragedies, for instance, or in *Elisei,* seems almost to have emerged without his knowledge, or at any rate, without any conscious intention. Maikov was always a follower, never a leader.

During a period of his career he was rather strongly affected by the ideas of the Masons. Sumarokov, as has been mentioned, was a Mason, and Novikov, who encouraged Maikov's early efforts, was a Masonic leader. Although somewhat younger than Maikov, Mikhail Kheraskov, who remained throughout his life a convinced Mason, exerted considerable influence on him, and the literary associations which centered on Kheraskov's Moscow publications were strongly Masonic in orientation. One of the leading Enlightenment ideas espoused by the Masons was that of literature in all its branches as a form of teaching. The very name of Kheraskov's first journal, *Profitable Diversion,* embodies this ideal. The didactic element—the Horatian "utile" ("the useful") must dominate; but to make the useful palatable, the writer will have to give it an attractive form (the Horatian "dulce"). As we have seen, Kheraskov's entire literary production, in all its remarkable extent and variety, is dominated by this idea. Maikov's odes, fables, and tragedies belong without cavil to this tendency; but there may be a question as to his heroi-comic poems. Where is their didactic content? *The Game of Ombre* was perhaps generated by the bias of Kheraskov and his circle to which Maikov at that date belonged, against the frivolous social occupation of card-playing; and the poem's final canto, with its vision of lost gamblers in Hades, was probably seriously meant as a dreadful warning. In the same way, it is likely that *Elisei* was generated as a moral blast against drunkenness (Ceres' plea before Zeus would be a relic of this conception), but the humorous possibilities of the subject, both as travesty à la Scarron, and as parody (of Petrov) soon took over and the "diversion" aspect of the final poem almost smothered the didactic. Maikov, however, here also, probably was acting unconsciously. The first conscious, fully intentional revolt against and repudiation of the classical principle of literature as teaching was that of another of Kheraskov's friends and the intimates of his circle, Bogdanovich, with his masterpiece, the *Dushenka.* To this we shall return later.

2. A.A. Rzhevsky and the Elegy (1737-1804)[30]

In surveying the course of eighteenth century Russian poetry we have encountered in the work of the major writers most of the important genres recognized in the canons of classicism: the tragedy (Lomonosov, Sumarokov, Kheraskov); the ode (Lomonosov, Sumarokov, Maikov et al.), the satire (Kantemir, Sumarokov), the fable (Sumarokov, Maikov), and even such minor genres as the epigram and the "inscription" (Lomonosov, Sumarokov). The epic has appeared, after several false starts, triumphantly with Kheraskov, and the comedy, after a weak beginning with Sumarokov and Kheraskov, has been given a new direction by Lukin and carried to its acme by Fonvizin. The minor lyric genres, however, have been less adequately represented. Sumarokov's songs, and even those of Trediakovsky, are important contributions; and that same indefatigable polygraph, Sumarokov, tried his hand, as we have noted, with the pastoral poem. A few essays in the imported lyric forms of sonnet, madrigal, "stanza," and the like also belong to the great classical legislator. The elegy, however, in Sumarokov's work, occupies a very minor place, and the examples which he has left are most untypical of the eighteenth century elegy as a whole. In order therefore to give a more complete idea of that rather important minor literary kind, and therewith fill out the picture of eighteenth century poetry as a whole, it seems fitting to introduce at this point a quite minor poetic figure, Alexei Andreevich Rzhevsky. Very often, we find, a minor figure, even one of no literary merit whatever—and Rzhevsky is not of this class—typifies his age more truly in some ways than his more original contemporaries. Rzhevsky's poetic production almost seems to have been destined to fill out the gaps in the work of the greater poets: he specialized in the elegy, the sonnet, the madrigal, the epigram, the "stanza," and similar secondary lyric forms which his more ambitious colleagues usually ignored.

We may pause at this point to say a few words about the relation of the minor literary genres to the prevailing didactic bent of classicism. We have seen Kheraskov, the most consistently and persistently didactic of the poets of his age, adapting, not without violence, the Epicurean light verse of "Anacreon" to didactic themes. For the most part, however, it seems by a kind of tacit consent, the minor genres were exempt from the general rule that literature must teach. Particularly was this true of the elegy, which in its Graeco-Roman models was so strikingly unedifying, not to say openly immoral. The sexual frankness and sensuality of Ovid's elegies were discreetly ignored, but the elegy even so could never be brought around to teaching a moral lesson!

The elegy[31] is a genre with a long and contradictory history. The Greek name *elegeia* often seems to connote mourning; and yet the earliest examples of the genre are spirited war songs. With Mimnermus (6th century B.C.) the elegy for the first time—at least as far as we know—became associated with love. The Alexandrian poets (e.g., Callimachus) employed it as a vehicle for narrative (e.g., Callimachus's *Bath of Pallas* or the *Aitia*), and to convey all varieties of arcane erudition. The Roman poets (Gallus, Tibullus, Propertius and Ovid) employed it, for the most part, as a quasi-autobiographical medium, in which they might expound the joys and sorrows of their tumultuous love-affairs. The joys they celebrated were largely physical, and with Ovid especially were recounted in gloating and uninhibited detail. By and large, however, it would appear that sorrows predominated in the amours of the Roman elegists, and hence the element of lamentation or complaint came to be inseparable from the concept of the elegy. When the Renaissance poets, who were at least nominally Christian and hence debarred by public opinion from making open display of their amorous triumphs, inherited the elegy, they perforce chose the poem of lamentation for model; and it was this variety that the classicist elegists inherited. Boileau, thinking probably of such elegies as Propertius's lament over the death of Cynthia, or Ovid's on the death of Tibullus, stresses the dirge-like qualities of the genre, and then turns to its commoner use as a love poem:

> *D'un ton un peu plus haut, mais pourtant sans audace,*
> *La plaintive élégie, en longs habits de deuil,*
> *Sait, les cheveux épars, gémir sur un cercueil.*
> *Elle peint des amants la joie et la tristesse,*
> *Flatte, menace, irrite, apaise une maîtresse.*[32]

Sumarokov rather disdainfully says to his would-be poet:

> If you are soft of heart and plaintive born,
> And if to boot you are overcome by love,
> Write elegies, sing the bonds of love
> With the lamentable voice of the moaning De la Suze.[33]

For the eighteenth century writer of elegy the classical models were not numerous. The Greek elegists had been lost, and their scanty fragments recovered only in the nineteenth and twentieth centuries; of the Romans, Gallus is only a name, and Propertius, although known, was rather uncongenial. His style is too "baroque," obscure, allusive, difficult, and exasperatingly individual and personal, to fit in with the eighteenth century literary taste. Ovid, even in his own age, came close in his love elegies to the kind of generalized, non-personal approach to the elegy which the eighteenth century classi-

293

cist held as an ideal. Ovid's love affairs, which were doubtless real enough, did not affect him very deeply, and the picture of his erotic life which his *Amores* give is lacking in individual characteristics; it is quite evidently a "composite picture," in which all the sharp features are smoothed out. Tibullus, more personal than Ovid, exhibits a temperament wholly in keeping with the picture which Sumarokov gives of the typical elegist: he is gentle, melancholy and passive, very prone to pour forth his sorrows in plaintive lamentations. It was accordingly a combination of the generalized objectivity of Ovid, shorn of his sensuality, and the passive melancholy of Tibullus which we find the eighteenth century elegists attempting to imitate.

The neoclassical elegy, then, is most commonly a lover's complaint (usually, but not always, it is the male who voices it) over some mischance which has brought his bliss to an untimely end. The actual circumstances which have caused his distress are never specified, and often not even hinted at. When they are, it is usually the unfaithfulness of the other partner, or her unmotivated coldness. A more specific source of the lover's woe is separation: he may be faced with the ineluctable necessity of leaving his beloved, sometimes temporarily, or sometimes, presumably, forever. The reasons for such a separation are of course never specified—one may imagine a business trip, or military service, or even political exile, as possibilities, but mention of such base realities would mar the universality of the picture. Sometimes, however, the actualities of life enter at least to the extent that the lover's despair is the result of the decision of the hard-hearted parents of his beloved to marry her off to someone else. In such a case, of course, the rival remains an unnamed, shadowy figure, without qualities. Under such a system as this, character and situation in the elegy are so stereotyped that one often gets the impression that all classical elegies are written by one poet about a single affair! Only the poetic clothing changes; each poet does his best to say something a little more pointedly or a little more cleverly, or with somewhat less banal rhymes than his predecessors.

Let us turn now to Alexei Rzhevsky as a typical classical elegist. Rzhevsky was a poet, one may say, for no more than four years of his life (1760-1763), but in that short while piled up a formidable production—225 known pieces. As a contributor to Kheraskov's Moscow periodicals, and earlier to Sumarokov's *Labor-Loving Bee* he was, during his few years of productivity, one of the most respected of poets. He later, as we have noted in connection with his friend Kheraskov, accepted a governmental post that so thoroughly occupied his time that he abandoned literature. His last important effort, and the only one on a large scale, was the tragedy, composed about 1768, *The False Smerdis*, with a plot from Herodotus based on the historical facts of the dynastic change in the kingdom of Persia in the late sixth century B.C. Even after his own abandonment of literature, however, Rzhevsky performed an inestimable service to the Russian public in publishing in full, in 1783, the beautiful poem *Dushenka* of his friend Ippolit Fedorovich Bogdanovich, which we shall shortly consider. This alone would justify his inclusion in any history of the literature of the age.

Rzhevsky composed a considerable number of elegies—there are 17 among the 146 pieces reprinted in the "Poet's Library" edition, Volume I, of *Poets of the Eighteenth Century.* Among these three stand out for metrical peculiarities; the other fourteen are all in the conventional Alexandrine lines, with couplet rhyme, alternately masculine and feminine, which is the canonical elegiac form in Russian. Of the experiments, one (no. 186) is in the *vers libre* habitually used in fables; one (192) is in anapestic tetrameter, and one (191) in a short, jingling iambic measure, of alternately seven (feminine rhymes) and six (masculine rhymes) syllables. These three exceptions, incidentally, were all composed in 1763 (Rzhevsky's last poetic year), and differ somewhat in content and tone from the rest; one of them, at least, hints at the possibility of a happy outcome for the love affair!

It is a remarkable *tour de force,* or so it would seem, for a poet to write 17 love poems without once naming his beloved, or any concrete circumstance connected with his situation. Indeed, in the entire group, there is only one proper name—Moscow, the dear city which the lover in no. 172 must leave because of his sweetheart's coldness. But more than that: the only occupation, other than sighing and walking in the woods, which the elegist's *persona* ever mentions is, in a single case, committing his torments to paper! The situations are rarely particularized even to the extent usual with the elegy. Twice it is a successful rival who is the cause of the lover's woe; and once it is imminent separation (unmotivated, of course). More typically, an entire elegy is devoted to a description of amorous torments, but without a hint as to their reason; thus no. 115:[34]

> Torturous passion! Cease to torment me,
> Cease to image the beautiful one in my memory.
> Waking, I scarcely open my eyes—
> When I see the lovely vision before me.
> Formed in my imagination all the day thereafter,
> The charming shadow never leaves my memory.
> Whether in solitude, or whether I am amongst people,
> In all places in my mind I image my beloved.
> Passing thus the day, when I lie down to sleep,
> Then in vain I flatter myself with seeking peace through slumber:
> From my memory she-does not take flight,
> And appearing as a dream, she banishes slumber from my eyes.
> But even if slumber comes, peace does not come;
> I see even in my slumber my beloved before me.
> Just as much as when awake, slumber torments me,
> And slumber presents my misfortune to my imagination.

Cruel fate threatens me with woes,
I am tortured waking, I am tortured even in slumber.
Forthwith then I awake, I leave my bed;
But nowhere do I find alleviation.
My beloved comes to my imagination,
There comes to my imagination, how unfortunate I am.
Toward alleviation I flatter myself in vain.
I seek to have a meeting with my dear one;
Tortured by thoughts, I suffer and sorrow,
I sigh and seek for her in all places.
It is tiresome to me, where I do not find my dear one,
And I find it empty among people without her,
And if she is sometimes not with me,
The whole world then seems empty to me;
But if sometimes she and I meet,
I have no comfort of the meeting:
Longing more tormentingly begins to lacerate my spirit!
Surely, I shall not see joy forever!
She appears to me a hundred times more charming,
And my passion becomes a hundred times greater;
In feeling stronger within me my tender passion,
I feel my misfortune the more cruel:
I foresee that there will be no alleviation for me forever,
And I shall not see an end to my unbearable torment.
I know that I shall not wipe out my love forever:
And I realize that I shall not be happy forever:
A cruel fate lays down this bound,
And readies redoubled woes for me hereafter.
On what a hapless day did I come to know my dear one!
Ah, vainly did I consider you [i.e., the day] a fortunate one!
You are my torment! You are the beginning of my woes!
Because of you, luckless day, my heart is in chains.
In one hour I took the contagion into my breast,
But in this one hour I lost my freedom forever;
A single hour enflamed all my blood with love,
And the consequences of that hour even life does not wipe out.
Fate is to blame for my having come to know her,
She is to blame for my losing my liberty.
Ah, no! Why do I blame her, why?
Destiny is to blame, that I am tormented and suffer;
Fate has ordained for me to suffer until my death,
Until death to love, until death to see no joy;
However, even though I shall no longer see her,
Wherever I shall be living

Although it is forever impossible for me to be happy,
Yet I shall forever both sigh and love.

This elegy is couched, as so often, in the form of the lover's meditation; but probably even commoner is the form which purports to be, as Boileau defines the elegy, the lover's actual protest to his beloved. Such, for example, is Rzhevsky's no. 185:[35]

You forbid me, my light, to love you,
And by this you are striving to destroy my life.
I know that I love you in vain,
And vainly does my heart feel passion for you,
That for you to be mine is forbidden by fate,
That you and I are sundered by an obstacle.
But the passionate heart does not accept these laws,
Which only custom legislates.
Custom says: cease to be passionate.
But the heart says: it is impossible to forget her.
You flit through my memory at all times,
Your lovely face will not leave my thoughts;
The lovely glance of your eyes haunts my imagination,
I remember you every moment,
On you I feed my heart and my mind,
And I find for myself no other solace.
How is it possible to bid me not to love you?
Is it possible for the passionate heart not to languish?

***

Seek your own joy, I shall not disturb you:
I shall depart from hence and destroy myself.
To hide my weakness is impossible for me
And if you are going to carry this out [i.e., your order], then I
must depart.
I shall depart hence, so as not to see you,
But parting from you, I shall suffer forever.

One of Rzhevsky's last published poems (no. 212)[36] introduces a theme not often found in the elegy:

I don't know why my whole spirit is despondent
And intolerable longing tears my breast.
I don't know what it is that disturbs and disquiets me
And gives my heart no rest even for a moment.
Wherever I may go, nowhere do I see joy,
Whatever I look at, all is hateful.

I don't know why my soul is sad,
I only know that all the while I am
Longing, tormented, moaning, sorrowing, suffering, aching,
Sighing, in torture, that grief possesses me,
I am bored, I shed tears, I strive and endure.
I long, I exert myself, I seek.... Surely I'm not in love?
Oh, no!... Could this be? To love is very dangerous.
Love.... O feeling, pleasing and fatal!
Flee from me, and do not disturb my spirit,
And do not flatter my heart with joy,
That your delights may not hale in torments:
After joys in love always come sorrows....

Rzhevsky, as was mentioned, specialized in the small varieties of lyric. Many of his pieces are epigrams (often rather pointless!), riddles, etc. He liked to write clever little nothings that would show off his considerable technical skill, such as a sonnet (no. 95) which could be read in three ways— each line as an Alexandrine, straight across; or one half of each line (up to the caesura) on the left side, or the other half, from the caesura to the end, on the right side, read successively! A similar metrical feat is the little "idyll" (no. 166)[37] which follows: the speaker is a shepherd girl:

Upon the banks of flowing rivers ["rek"]
A shepherd lad thus said ["rek"] to me:
"I shall never see anything more charming than you,
Than your eyes, face, and eye-lids ["vek"].
Know, as long as my life ["vek"] is prolonged,
Truly, my light, believe me, I shall continue to love you."

My gaze beheld ["zrel"] his sighs.
My reason was not yet mature ["zrel"].
My thoughts consented to that flattering thought.
I said: "You shall be mine ["moi"];
Do not bathe ["moi"] your face in tears,
Only be true to me, if I am worth this."

Changing ["promenia"] passion now for deceit,
He does not even think about me ["pro menia"].
O faithless! Now you have become captivated by another.
You said to me: "Go away ["proch' "]
And pick ["proch' "] yourself another fellow."
How unbearably I now suffer, am tortured and ache!

It will be observed that in each six-line strophe of this piece, the third and

298

sixth lines are long, and rhyme together, while the first and second, fourth and fifth, are short, and rhyme as couplets, the rhyming words in each case being a pair of homonyms, e.g., "rek," "rivers," and "rek," "said."

The elegy, as was mentioned earlier, seems dispensed from the usual eighteenth century requirement of didacticism. So, of course, is the "song," a variety not represented in Rzhevsky's work. That in other minor genres he remained faithful to this rule may be seen, however, in such a sonnet as the following (no. 110):[38]

> Where are mortals to find happiness in this world?
> And in what fashion shall we live in quietness?
> Is there genuine well-being in magnitude of rank?
> Is wealth able to provide joys?
>
> In detailed knowledge of things shall we succeed
> in establishing perfection of given fortune?
> Or if equality among all were to come about,
> Then would griefs not afflict the spirit?
>
> Does one live in fame, glittering with light?
> In love, burned by charming eyes?
> On the fields of Mars or in crowns of laurel?
>
> In the society of town or in pleasant vanities?
> In solitude or in hearts without feeling?—
> It [i.e., happiness] is not there, but in souls, not made changeful
> though ease.

Final mention may be made of Rzhevsky's *stanzas;* this is a minor lyric genre, originating in Renaissance Italy, and consisting, as the name would imply, of a sequence of stanzas of a uniform metrical pattern (in Italian, usually tercets) not long enough to constitute a full-scale "poem," and not patterned in such a fixed form as e.g., the sonnet. The "stanza" lends itself admirably to hortatory and moralistic discourse, and is thus most commonly employed by Rzhevsky. A relatively short example, which might well be titled "Stanzas on Mutability," is no. 71:[39]

> We exert ourselves to bear misfortune with patience,
> And we keep flattering ourselves with hope:
> Shall a time of happiness for us never come?
> Or are we, in bitterness, to see no comfort?
>
> How can this be? Destiny changes everything here,
> Everything in it is always subject to change.

299

If something perishes here, another thing grows up there,
We never see eternity in anything.

Those mountains, whose summits smite the clouds,
And the gaze is unable to reach their crests,
Have been destroyed, and their places have now become channels,
And amidst their ruins the waters now flow.

Those rivers, which rushed with speed toward the plains,
Have become choked with sand, and trees have grown up there;
Where on the sea there was a path with depth for ships,
There, swelling, the bottom has heaved up spacious islands.

That which grows up in the morning, by midday is ripe,
And by evening has already quite fallen away;
There is hope even for us, if destiny does not prevent,
To expect a change for our woes: everything will pass with time.

[From non-being we came to birth, and having lived in the world,
                                                            we die;
It is enough to show our changes by this,
That this air is changeable, in which we dwell,
And this globe turns, on which we live.]

The fortunate man must await woes for himself at all times,
Because we in life always expect change.
Woes will pass, if one lives unhappily;
Thus we go toward happiness over woes.

[If everything here is created to be changed,
Then you and I must expect changes,
With such hope we shall keep feeding ourselves,
And thereby we shall suffer more lightly in sorrow.

We shall be the happy Phoenixes of love,
When after obstacles we shall attain freedom,
And feeling in our blood the flame of tender passion,
We shall mutually reward each other with faithfulness.]

The bracketed stanzas[40] were printed when the poem was first published, in Sumarokov's *Monthly Compositions,* in 1759; but omitted when the poem was republished in Kheraskov's *Profitable Diversion,* 1760, first issue. One may conjecture that stanza 6, with its reference to the rotation of the earth, was unpalatable to the censor, or might be thought to be; and the final two stanzas, which bring the theme of mutability to a quite personal level, were perhaps viewed by Kheraskov as too frivolous.

3. Ippolit Fedorovich Bogdanovich and Dushenka (1743-1803)[41]

Professor I.Z. Serman, writing his introductory article for the "Poet's Library" edition of Bogdanovich's poetry[42] remarks: "The biography of Ippolit Fedorovich Bogdanovich is scant in events and facts." Surely this matters less in his case than with most poets, for the masterpiece which alone of Bogdanovich's work is remembered and loved was spun out of a vivid imagination, and has few points of contact with the rather drab "real world" of the poet's experience.

Bogdanovich was by birth a Ukrainian, of a very poor gentry family; he was taken to Moscow at the age of ten, and obtained a post with the Justice Department as what we would probably call an office-boy. A few years later he attracted the attention of Mikhail Kheraskov, then director of the Moscow University theater, by his passion for acting. Kheraskov took the boy into his own household and got him appointed to a minor post in the University, which enabled him to acquire a rather scanty education. As a protégé of Kheraskov he became a Mason, a contributor to Kheraskov's Moscow journals and a collaborator with him and Rzhevsky on an ephemeral pageant to celebrate the visit of Catherine II to Moscow in 1762. The next year, however, Bogdanovich shifted allegiance from Kheraskov, and became associated with Princess Dashkova, under whose direction he edited the journal *Innocent Exercise* (1763). When this journal terminated its short existence, he passed into the service of the Panin brothers, first of General Peter Panin, and then of Nikita, head of the Foreign Office. During the years 1766-68 he resided in Dresden as secretary of the Russian legation there.

Bogdanovich, despite his rather sketchy education, showed a remarkable aptitude for languages, and readily mastered French. Among his early poetical efforts is a translation, published in *Innocent Exercise,* of Voltaire's famous poem on the "Destruction of Lisbon" in the earthquake of 1755.[43] Later he translated the French master's comedy *Nanine,* which he published in 1766.

As has been frequently noted before, the Panin brothers and Princess Dashkova were active until the critical year 1782 in upholding the claim of Pavel Petrovich to the throne which his mother was unlawfully usurping. We have seen that Kheraskov in 1761 dedicated his didactic poem "The Fruits of Learning" to Prince Pavel; not surprisingly Bogdanovich's first long poem, quaintly titled *Doubled Happiness (Suguboie Blazhenstvo)* was similarly dedicated. In its subsequent appearance, in a much abbreviated form in Bogdanovich's volume *Lyra* (1773) the poem bears the title "The Happiness of Nations."[44] The first version, in three books and 578 lines, is conceived as a polemic against both Kheraskov's picture of primitive society before "the fruits of learning" began to exercise their civilizing influence, and the doctrine of Jean-Jacques Rousseau, who had attributed to "learning" all the subsequent ills of mankind. The first book, which was largely retained in the shortened 1773 version, describes, in contrast to Kheraskov's dark picture of primitive savagery, a "golden age" before inequality, that source of all human misfortune, had come to be.

> No one then thought of amassing riches
> And no one caused his neighbor offense.
> But each was rich, though no one reckoned
> That house, land or fruits belonged to him.
> The earth was reckoned in that happy time
> To be the indivisible nourisher of all,
> And people did not feel the burden of poverty
> Amidst satisfaction, quietude and joys.[45]

But inequality, and the consequent rise of class distinctions, does not originate, according to Bogdanovich, from man's unfortunate creation of "The arts and sciences," as Rousseau's *First Discourse* had taught:

> Although the stern philosopher rejects the sciences
> And sets before us the subsequent harm,
> Is he right in faulting the advantages on this account,
> When the causes of these became the causes of sorrows?
> And if it is impossible to attain such good,
> Or for us to seek out so perfect a good fortune
> That in it there should be no bad consequences,
> Must we on this account despise good fortune?
> Man is to blame, [his] delusion is to blame,
> When from good causes we see an evil end;
> Unjust thought and abuse
> Always bring forth harm from an advantage begun.[46]

Bogdanovich does not have any explanation of his own for the rise of inequality: "man is to blame"—apparently as a result of his innate "passions"—a kind of "original sin."

The second chapter of the poem describes the degeneration of the happy state of the golden age; the third turns to the restoration—to the "doubled happiness" of the title—which he sees as resulting from enlightened monarchy. Seeing the miserable condition into which anarchy has brought them, men voluntarily consented to be governed, and chose wise and benevolent men to be their monarchs—a hint, of course, to Pavel Petrovich! Incidentally, it may be noted that again Bogdanovich is at variance with Kheraskov: the latter adheres to the more or less orthodox view of monarchy as of divine right—kings are God's appointees; Bogdanovich sees them as exercising their office through the consent and appointment of the governed.

Though *Redoubled Happiness* has no great merit either as a piece of poetry or as a contribution to political philosophy, it has considerable interest for the development of Bogdanovich's thought. He seems, from the beginning, to have been attracted to Utopias and to have viewed this flawed world of war, social inequality, poverty and human misery as something to flee from. One of his early translations was of the *Projet de paix perpétuelle* of the Abbé de Saint-Pierre (1713).[47] The picture which he paints in his poem of the blissful life of primitive man in a state of nature is a projection of his own longing to escape from the brutalities of the real world surrounding him. *Dushenka* in a very real way is his triumphant achievement of this escape, into a lovely, imaginary world of pure beauty and primitive innocence.

There is no reason for dwelling on the short poems which Bogdanovich published in various journals and finally collected and issued—anonymously—under the title *Lyra* in 1773. They are undistinguished, and belong to the less ambitious literary genres of fable, stanza, eclogue, song, etc. There are even some religious pieces in the collection, including a paraphrase of the Twenty-Third Psalm. Nor is it worth while to consider the similar pieces which appeared from time to time in subsequent years, during which Bogdanovich enjoyed considerable fame and the favor of the Empress as "the poet of Dushenka." His heart was never in the work he was obliged, as a semi-official poet of the court, to turn out, and this part of his production is well forgotten.

In the year 1778 appeared anonymously the "First Book" of a poem called *Dushenka's Adventures.*[48] Apparently at that time the complete poem was not yet ready. In 1783 Bogdanovich's old friend Rzhevsky published the poem in full, at his own expense;[49] Bogdanovich at the moment was without a position and practically penniless. In the preface to this edition Rzhevsky wrote:

The present poem was composed by Ippolit Fedorovich Bogdanovich. Being a friend of mine of long standing, he showed it to me during a chance conversation, as a work which he had once written for his own amusement in his idle hours, without the intention of publishing it. The unconstrained freedom of the style, the purity of the verses, the felicitous choice of words appropriate to the genre of this poem, and above all the abundance of poetical imagination pleased me so much that I begged the author to put his poem at my disposal, which he did through love and friendship to me; and I resolved to publish it, in order that it might afford the same satisfaction to others as it had to me. I believe that it will please many, not only because there are no verses of such a kind in our language, but because of the author's fortunate success [with it].[50]

It was not until the poem was reissued in 1794 by Bogdanovich himself that the short "Preface from the Author" introduced it.[51]

Dushenka is a retelling of the story of Cupid and Psyche, found first as an episode in the novel of Lucius Apuleius of Madaura (2nd century A.D.), *The Golden Ass,* and subsequently as one of the prose works of Jean de La Fontaine, *Les Amours de Psyché et de Cupidon* (1669). Other treatments of the story, e.g., by Francesco Bracciolini (1566-1645), Diamante Gabrielli (1649), and the opera written jointly by Pierre Corneille, Molière and Quinault (1671) seem not to have been known to Bogdanovich; at least he mentions only the first two as his sources.

As told by Apuleius (Books IV-VI of the *Golden Ass*) in a very florid and mannered Latin prose, the story is a curious combination of folk-tale, sophisticated mockery of anthropomorphic religion, and allegory. The first element is the most prominent; Psyche, for example, is the youngest of three sisters, of whom the two elder are wicked and envious while she is innocent and lovable (cf. *King Lear*); she is married to an invisible husband who is supposed to be a "monster" (cf. "Beauty and the Beast"); her husband is under a kind of taboo by which he is forced to leave his wife when the taboo is broken (cf. *Lohengrin*); Psyche is set three hopelessly impossible tasks to perform by her stern mistress Venus, which friendly natural powers carry out for her, etc. The very first line of the story, which in Apuleius's novel is told by an old woman to beguile the captivity of a kidnapped girl, reveals its folk-tale origin: "Erant in quadam civitate rex et regina" ("Once in a certain city there were a king and a queen"). The second element is confined to certain peripheral passages of the tale, e.g., the somewhat catty remarks of Ceres and Juno to Venus over the naturalness of Cupid's behavior—after all, he is only following his mother's example in indulging in love, and he *isn't* a child anymore, you know, even if he does carry his years well! *(aetatem bellule portrat).* Similar is Jupiter's summons of all the gods to assembly, under penalty of a 10,000 pound fine for non-attendance, his address to the assembly beginning with the words: *Dei conscripti,* and his promise to legalize the marriage of Cupid and Psyche in accordance with the civil law: *Iam faxo nuptias non impares sed legitimas et iuri civili congruas.* This is precisely the kind of reduction of the Graeco-Roman pantheon to all too human stature which Apuleius's contemporary Lucian of Samosata carried out in his *Dialogues of the Gods.* The third element is the least conspicuous of all, being apprehensible chiefly in the heroine's name (*Psyche* is the Greek word for "the soul") and in the announcement at the end of the tale that in due time the heroine was delivered of a daughter *quam Voluptatem nominamus* ("whom we name Pleasure"). Thus it would appear that the surface adventures of the loving couple are supposed to conceal the truth that Love (Amor) has a natural affinity for the Soul (Psyche), and that Pleasure is the fruit of their union. But the moralist will be hard put to it to explain in allegorical terms the place that Venus occupies in this plot, or the two envious sisters. Perhaps only the ill-starred curiosity of Psyche, which precipitates her misfortunes, and which is doubtless an inseparable quality of the human soul, can be comfortably fitted into the allegory.

Where Apuleius found the tale is unknown; perhaps he invented it. At any rate, it is not found in literature before him, though some representations in art have been interpreted as references to it. But it is important to point out very emphatically that it is *not,* as some hostile Russian critics of Bogdanovich have claimed, a "Neo-Platonic allegory" which Bogdanovich has reduced to frivolous triviality; and it is important also to realize that the folk-tale atmosphere inheres in the tale, and again, is not something incongruously imported into it by Bogdanovich. If he, for example, brings in the enchanter Koshchei the Deathless or "sytovaia voda, kiselny berega" (more or less "rivers of milk and honey" in Russian folk-tales), or the serpent Zmei Gorynych, he is doing the same thing that Apuleius had done, with the only difference that Bogdanovich's folk elements (none of them very essential to the story) are Slavic.

The second source which Bogdanovich cites for his tale is Jean de La Fontaine's long prose story, *Les Amours de Psyché et de Cupidon.* In this version of the legend (of course itself derived from Apuleius) the prose is occasionally interrupted by verse inserts—the oracles, for example, are given in verse, and some descriptions which the author evidently felt were too lofty in content for prose. The story itself is framed by an account of the meeting of four friends, who constitute a kind of informal "Academy," in a grotto in contemporary Versailles, where one of the four, Polyphile, who is patently La Fontaine himself, tells the story, with occasional interruptions and arguments from the others. The identity behind the Greek names of the friends is a matter of conjecture; it used to be thought that Acante represented Racine, Ariste Boileau, and Gelasime (Greek "gelasimos," "laughable") Molière, but this rather too pat identification is probably wrong. In any case, the story as La Fontaine tells it is basically that of Apuleius, with certain additions, one of which is a fairly long interpolated account (taken from Tasso's *Jerusalem Delivered*) of an old fisherman and his two daughters, with whom Psyche finds asylum for a time, and of his life and philosophy. None of this is to be found in the Latin original. The nature of the work is thus succinctly characterized by a recent editor of La Fontaine:[52] "Roman et poème à la fois, ou plutôt, comme le dit La Fontaine, oeuvre d'un genre intermédiaire, récit poétique où le ton galant tempère le ton 'héroique' approprié à la mythologie." It should be noted, however, that the delicate taste of the eighteenth century found even the style of the age of Louis XIV a little too robust. The Russian translator of La Fontaine's novel, F.I. Dmitriev-Mamonov,[53] complains of the great labor he was put to "because in the original the style, though nobler than [that of] his didactic fables, was extremely low for a heroic style." If Bogdanovich, then, quite simply eschews the heroic altogether and tells his story in the simplest Russian—Lomonosov's "middle style"—and in a bantering, whimsical tone, he is not departing essentially from his French model. Apuleius's Latin, of course, is another matter; it can hardly be called either "high" or "low": it is simply extravagant, *sui generis*—but in all likelihood is basically the rather archaic language of the author's native province of Africa.

The verse inserts in La Fontaine's novel are in various forms, but for the most part in standard Alexandrines. The *vers libre* which he uses with such beautiful effect in his *Fables* appears only twice, in short passages. This was the metrical form which Bogdanovich chose for his poem. It had been used since Sumarokov's *Pritchi* as the standard medium for fables, and was thus regularly associated with light verse, but it had never before in Russian been employed for a sustained poem of the length of *Dushenka* (three books, and 80 pages in the "Poet's Library" edition). Bogdanovich manages it with consummate ease, and it flows melodiously along, with so much intricate interweaving of rhymes and such swift changes of line length that there is never a hint of monotony. It is a meter almost ideally suited to the light, ironic, intimate tone of the poem—what German critics so aptly call the "Plauderstil."

This "chatty style," if one may so translate the term, is a characteristic, like the *vers libre,* of the genre of fable, in which the poet (e.g., Sumarokov) appears to be chattering away most unconstrainedly to an audience directly before him. It is never found in the eighteenth century, however, before Bogdanovich in a long narrative poem. He probably adapted it, like the meter, to his purposes from the fable; but it is not impossible that he may have had more remote models. The "Plauderstil" probably makes its first literary appearance in narrative poetry with the *Orlando Innamorato* of Matteo Maria Boiardo, from which it was carried to Ariosto's continuation of the Orlando epic, and thence to lesser imitators. Can it be entirely an accident that the tone of Bogdanovich's poem is so remarkably close to that of the *Orlando Furioso*—ironically wistful, with a hint of melancholy? Ariosto created a lovely, impossible world of chivalry and enchantment, and peopled it with heroes and heroines whose heroic stature is not cancelled by their often quite absurd and purely human characteristics. It is a dream world to which the poet happily escapes from the vexations of contemporary Ferrara, but which he realizes is only the creation of his own imagination, and which he is thus constrained to treat with a kind of tender irony. Just such is Bogdanovich's attitude toward the mythic world of *Dushenka*. Whether he knew the Italian romance epics or not we have no means of knowing; but the similarity is striking. Certainly Pushkin did, and when he employs the "chatty style" so masterfully in *Ruslan and Liudmila,* he is following not only his greatly admired *Dushenka,* but Boiardo and Ariosto as well.

One of the qualities of Bogdanovich's poem to first attract attention was the adroit manner in which elements of Russian folk-lore were grafted upon Greek myth. The very name of the poem's heroine is one example of this. As Bogdanovich explains, for those of his readers not familiar with Greek, the name Psyche means "soul," for which the Russian word is *dusha.* But in its simple form this noun is never used, and would be grotesque if used, for a person's name. But the diminutive form, *dushenka,* is a very common term of affection, with some of the overtones of "darling" or "sweetheart" in English. So the classical Psyche becomes the Russian "darling," and contributes by her name from the beginning to the intimate and Russified character of the story. When she appears (Book III) in Venus' temple as a supplicant and is mistaken by the priests for the goddess herself, she is wearing a peasant girl's *sarafan*—Venus in a *sarafan!* The first impossible task which Venus sets her is to bring back "within three hours some water living and dead" ["vody zhivoi i mertvoi"], a folk-lore item which in this case is guarded by "a large and fat snake" that reposes with its tail in its mouth, thus cutting off access to the water which it surrounds. Dushenka addresses this folk-lore snake appropriately with the words: "O zmei Gorynych Chudo-Iuda!" ("O snake Gorynych Chudo-Iuda!"). Her second mission takes her to the Greek "Isles of the Hesperides" to fetch the golden apples, which however are guarded now not by a dragon, as in Greek times, but by the Russian folk-tale enchanter Koshchei the Deathless! Admittedly these are only accessories incidental to the tale as a whole, and neither the snake Gorynych nor Koshchei is portrayed as Russian folk-lore sees them, but they contribute atmosphere, none the less.

La Fontaine in his novel, even though it is mostly in unheroic prose, does attempt to maintain at times a certain loftiness of style appropriate to Greek myth, and apparently feels somewhat on the defensive in regard to his medley of heroic and comic. In the conversation between Polyphile and his friends which interrupts the novel at the end of the first book, discussion centers on the appropriateness of this mixture of the laughable and the tragic—which Gelasime strongly approves, against the objections of the others. Bogdanovich makes no excuses for his unclassical mélange. His poem deliberately avoids the "lofty style" of epic or tragedy: the description of Dushenka's despair after Amor casts her off, and of her futile attempts at suicide, which in another treatment might have become genuinely tragic, are pathetic indeed, and moving, but too detached and ironic to evoke the tragic emotions of "pity and fear"; and the comic element is almost everywhere present. It is not a broad, farcical comedy, but the straight-faced introduction into the "heroic" world of commonplace "realistic" elements, akin to Ariosto's episode in which a knight, faced with an enchanted castle, but fortunately provided with a compendium of antidotes for spells, matter-of-factly refers to his book's index under the heading of "enchanted castles" to find the appropriate counter-spell! Thus, in Bogdanovich's first book, which is particularly full of this kind of ironic deflation of the tragic, when the pathetic cortege that is escorting Dushenka, in obedience to the oracle, to the grim mountain where she is to be delivered to her "monster" husband, the bride is accompanied by a number of homely items:

> They carried a crystal bed,
> On which Dushenka liked to repose;
> Sixteen men, having placed them on cushions,
> Carried the princess's embroidery-hoops and bobbins,
> Which the queen-mother herself had set up,
> Her travelling toilet kit, combs and pins,
> And all kinds of adjuncts to this.[54]

When Dushenka finds herself in an earthly paradise instead of the expected monster's den, she explores, and finds the palace adorned with countless statues and pictures of herself. Among these is one picturing Dushenka in the company of the Olympian deities:

> And there in front of her was Saturn, toothless, bald and gray,
> With a new crop of wrinkles on his ancient mug,
> Trying to forget that he was a grandfather of very long standing;
> He straightens up his ramshackle frame, wishes he were younger,
> Curls the locks of hair he has left,
> And in order to look at Dushenka, puts on spectacles.[55]

In this connection we may note the mischievous erotic allusions in Saturn's senile behavior, just as when an ancient hermit in Ariosto's *Orlando*, seemingly "of a scrupulous and squeamish conscience," at first sight of the ravishing Angelica "was moved—by pure charity—" to some rather unmonastic conduct. In Bogdanovich's poem, when the old fisherman hears Dushenka's despairing "Oh!" at the failure of her attempt to cremate herself in his campfire, he rows his boat hastily to shore and sees the princess, scantily clad:

> ... this grandfather, ancient in this world,
> Having cast a glance at the vicinity of his hut,
> Forgot the declivity of his advanced years,
> Let go the fishing-nets from his hands,
> Hopped out of the boat toward the firewood,
> And fell at the princess's feet.[56]

La Fontaine's description of the fisherman's age, incidentally, is far broader and less subtle: "La vieillesse en propre personne lui apparut, chargée de filets, et en habit de pêcheur.... Son front était plein de rides, dont la plus jeune était presque aussi ancienne que le déluge. Aussi Psyché le prit pour

Deucalion," etc. Bogdanovich says nothing about Deucalion, but does have Dushenka address the ancient as "O forefather of earthly generations, or son, surely, of the forefathers!"

One of the devices which Bogdanovich employs to achieve a comic effect is inseparable from his meter, and hence rather hard to illustrate; but note, from Book I, the lines in which he describes the horrendous fancies engendered by folk-stories, with which Dushenka's parents torment themselves at thought of the "monster" husband to which she is devoted:

> They imagined to themselves strings of wicked monsters,
> And the terror of cruel death
> Either in paws or in teeth,
> Where life would be cramped for her (!);
> From their nurses they had long since become familiar
> With the existence of such, both snakes and spirits,
> Which open their maws widely,
> And that besides they usually have ["I chto pritom u nikh by-
> vaiut"]
> Both seven heads, and seven horns ["I sem' golov, i sem' rogov,"]
> And seven or even more, tails.[57] ["I sem', il' bolee, khvostov."]

The triply repeated rhyme—"golov," "rogov," and "khvostov"—with its climax in the word "tails" in the final line, and the sly, matter-of-fact insertion of "or even more," have the effect of reducing the whole vision of horror to utter absurdity. A similar effect is obtained, later in the episode of Dushenka's actual arrival at the monster-haunted mountain, by the bizarre rhymes:

> To some there appeared there Furies, ["megery"]
> To some, flying dromedaries ["dromadery"]
> To some, dragons and Cerberuses, ["tserbery"]
> Which with roars, in various manners ["manery"]
> Deafened the ears, ["glushili slukh,"]
> Confounded the spirit.[58] ["mutili dukh"]

Bogdanovich's devices for obtaining comic effect are numerous, and could be the object of a special study. One more may be mentioned, which exactly parallels Apuleius's use of the formula "O conscript gods," quoted above, in Jupiter's address to his divine Senate. Dushenka, in Book III, finds posted on a pillar at a crossroad Venus's proclamation of her outlawry. It is couched in contemporary officialese:

> For as much as Dushenka has angered Venus,
> And Amor has praised Dushenka to Venus's shame;

And she, the said Dushenka, lowers the quality of rouge,
And darkness before her the merits of white paint,
And is an offense to every kind of beauty everywhere;
She, the said Dushenka, being of a slender build,
With alluring eyes and a pleasing smile,
Fails to honor the goddess of beauty and sets her at naught;
And the aforesaid with her glances makes hearts captive,
Attires herself as a goddess and wears a train three spans long—
For this or another reason
To all and sundry
Venus in due form
Gives information of her anger against her
And promises her favor to anyone
Who within a fixed time
Shall present Dushenka to Venus's person.
But should anyone give her aid and succor
Contrary to the import of these lines,
Or should conceal her anywhere
Or give her means for concealing herself,
That one will not in his lifetime wash away his guilt,
Even with his own lifeblood![59]

The center of Bogdanovich's *Dushenka*, occupying most of Book II, is
the description of Amor's aerial paradise, to which Zephyr conveys her,
and of the delights, esthetic and erotic, of that enchanted place. Again,
comparison with *Orlando Furioso* is almost inevitable. Ruggiero is wafted
through the air on his hippogriff to the magic realm of Alcina, which like
Amor's abode, is a sumptuous palace set in a natural park of superlative
beauty. In both cases the description of palace and park seems to owe a good
deal to certain earthly prototypes—in Bogdanovich's case to Catherine II's
palace at Tsarskoe Selo. Whether the similarity here is due to the poet's not
unnatural inclination to flatter the Empress, or simply to a quite understand-
able inability to visualize beauty totally outside of mortal experience, cannot
be decided. In any case, there can be no doubt of the whole-hearted ardor
with which he elaborates his description. Here is the world as he wishes it
were—a lovely, magic land, filled with peace and beauty, with painting,
sculpture, music, and a gentle, innocent sensuality. Karamzin, in his critical
article on Bogdanovich, written soon after the poet's death, describes the surroundings in which *Dushenka* was composed: a pleasant, rustic cottage in
the St. Petersburg suburbs, where Bogdanovich was surrounded by art objects, music, books, and in which he spent his time either in the company of
congenial friends or in solitude, spinning out of his imagination the delectable
scenes of his romance.[60]

And at this point we are faced with one more aspect of the poem, which is probably the most significant of all. Bogdanovich's one-time mentor, Mikhail Kheraskov, twelve years after *Dushenka* appeared in full, published his poem *Pilgrims,* which, as we have pointed out, utilizes the *vers libre* form of verse and in many other ways reveals the evident influence of *Dushenka.* But in one very major respect Kheraskov refused to follow his pupil: *Pilgrims* is a moral tale, however well disguised the didacticism may be by a light manner. But there is no didacticism in *Dushenka!* Bogdanovich in his poem has quite simply defied the accepted classical canon always so dear to Kheraskov's heart, that *art must teach. Dushenka* does not teach; the story is told for its own sake, and is justified by its own beauty, not by any considerations of moral effect. It is, if one may use an often abused modern term, "art for art's sake." One may say that since the poem belongs to no genre recognized by classicism (Rzhevsky remarked that "no poem of this kind exists in our literature"—he might have added, "or in any other literature of the age"), and is in form and tone more closely akin to the "fable" than to any other literary kind, it was easy to evade this mandate of didacticism. This is doubtless true—but the "fable" *is* didactic!

It may be objected that *Dushenka* does have a "moral": on the third of her missions the heroine returns from Hades with a sealed jar, which her fateful curiosity induces her to open; a thick black vapor issues from the jar and turns her face and breast coal-black! Much as she tries, she is unable to rid herself of this hue, and even though people still consider her "a beautiful African," she is so humiliated that she hides herself in a cave. But her husband Amor, with touching fidelity, seeks her out and proclaims to her and to the gods that it is Dushenka's inner beauty, which the blackness does not mar, and not her exterior that he loves. At this noble sentiment even Venus relents, forgives Dushenka, and washes her "white as snow." Jupiter decrees marriage for Amor and Dushenka, with the condition that Love "be always captivated by spiritual ["dushevnoi"] beauty." Here is didacticism with a vengeance! But the whole episode occupies only about four out of the poem's 80 pages, and gives the inevitable impression of an after-thought. It is, moreover, a part of La Fontaine's novel, which Bogdanovich would have had difficulty in altogether ignoring. But it would be the height of absurdity to imagine that the whole tale was conceived *in order to bring in* this quite extraneous and not very convincing "moral." As a matter of fact, as he approaches the end of his tale, Bogdanovich gives the impression that he is becoming bored and disinterested. The three missions are described quite perfunctorily: the riddles which Koshchei employs to discourage seekers after golden apples are not recorded—Dushenka, it seems, never disclosed them, and so her biographer is helpless! The episode of Dushenka's blackness, to which La Fontaine devotes pages, is quite summarily recounted, and the resolution of Venus's anger and Jupiter's decrees sanctioning the marriage of Amor and Dushenka are related with such an acceleration of tempo as compared with earlier episodes, that the impression is inevitably conveyed that the poet is in a hurry to be done with his tale—and this at the very point where, if he were really serious about his "moral," he might be expected to be most expansive. In just the same way, incidentally, Ariosto's episode of the loves of Alcina and Ruggiero comes to an end: Logistilla, an allegory of "reason" ("logos") empowers Ruggiero to see his seductress as the ugly witch she really is, and her whole enchantment vanishes—but only at the end, and quite evidently almost to Ariosto's regret. As an allegory of sin's ugliness masked by specious beauty the episode is a lamentable failure; both poet and reader feel only keen disappointment when "sin" is unmasked! The abbreviated, casual, and belated "lesson" of Bogdanovich's poem only emphasizes the real absence in its conception of any element of didacticism. In this he was ahead of his age; his example had no follower until a quarter of a century after his death a young poet of genius far greater than his created *Ruslan and Liudmila*.

C. I.S. Barkov and the Parody

A minor poet of a most uncommon sort is Ivan Semenovich Barkov (1732-1768),[61] whose published work consists almost entirely of quite scholarly translations of Horace, Phaedrus, and other Latin poets (he was an official translator of the Academy of Sciences), together with a few epistles and other original works of no particular interest. Barkov's contemporary fame, however—and he was extremely well known in his own time—rested on his unprintable poems, which were circulated in manuscript and read by everybody. Unhappily, modern readers no longer carry on this admirable tradition, and the existing manuscripts of Barkov's parody odes and similar productions are locked in library vaults where they will presumably not corrupt the few scholars who have access to them. One such scholar is G.P. Makogonenko, who in his introduction to the two-volume "Poet's Library" edition of *Poets of the Eighteenth Century* writes so glowingly of this material that scholars less fortunate than he can only be envious. "[Barkov's] original verses," writes Makogonenko,[62]

(written at the end of the 1750s and in the 1760s), which had a great influence on the development of Russian poetry, were never published, and presumably were never intended by their author for publication; but they received a wide dissemination and became well known to several generations of literary people, in numerous copies. It was these verses that the nineteenth century science of literary criticism contemptuously designated as "shameless," applying to them the label of "Barkovism" ["barkovshchina"]. But Barkov was writing not erotic verses, but parodies of all the genres which classicism sanctioned. His satiric poetry broke gaily and tumultuously into the temple of classicism that had been reared by the labors and exertions of Sumarokov. In this storming of the gentry culture the bold "Translator of the Academy of Sciences" showed an audacity and verve that amazed and delighted his contemporaries, a wealth of invention and a murderous ridicule.... His verses are coarse, they tell of pot-houses, of "factory fellows," of drunken brawls of bargemen with cabmen, but they are talented and clever....

What is the nature of the original production of this "most significant" poet, in Pushkin's words? There have come down to us only numerous copies of his works, most often in the form of a collection under the title of *Maidens' Plaything*. In it more than a hundred verse productions are contained. Barkov's collection bears witness that his struggle with the poetry of classicism, with the work of its leader Sumarokov, with his numerous imitators and epigones, had a conscious and strictly thought-out character. Barkov set himself the goal of parodying all the genres of classicism. In first place came odes, then tragedies, epistles, fables, satires, idylls, songs, elegies, epigrams, epitaphs, "billets"—as satiric distichs were called—(Sumarokov wrote them). Barkov even dared to write one parody of the verse paraphrase of the Psalms. The parody of each genre was founded on an exact correspondence with the Sumarokov model.

In giving a new face to odes and songs, elegies and tragedies, Barkov translated the conventional political or amorous passions of the heroes of classicism into the sphere of frank sensuality. The suffering heroes (of tragedy, elegy or song), in complete conformity with the genre, pronounced lofty words about their feelings: "Cruel misfortune has changed you" or "I have parted from you forever! Forever, alas, and you will never see me again," and the like. The comic and satiric effect arose from the fact that the speakers of Sumarokov's language were not heroes and heroines, but, to use Diderot's expression, their "indiscreet jewels." Sometimes the parodistic element in Barkov's verses retreated to the background, and the poet, turning to the objective world, began to sketch genuine and realistic pictures of Russian life. Such is the beginning of the tale *The Village Priest*....

Barkov wrote more than a dozen odes: "To Priapus," "Description of the Morning Light," "To a Monk," "To Bacchus," "To a Fist-Fighter," and others.

At this point Makogonenko sees fit to utter his regrets that Barkov was never able to raise himself sufficiently from the level at which realistic elements serve the purposes of parody to one in which they would stand by themselves—to genuine realism, in other words. As it was, "he was capable only of creating in the ode naturalistic and verisimilar scenes."

After arousing his readers' interest and curiosity about what must be an extraordinarily significant body of verse, Makogonenko most disappointingly includes in his anthology only one of Barkov's unpublished poems, and this in a form in which 34 complete lines out of a total of 240, besides a considerable number of individual words, are cut out. This bowdlerized poem is called "Ode to a Fist-Fighter."[63] Even in its mutilated form it shows "the wealth of invention and murderous ridicule" which the critic attributes to its author. The ode begins:

> I take the fiddle ["gudok"—a 3-stringed violin] , not the lyre,
> Entering the pot-house, not Parnassus;
> I yell and tear my gullet,
> Raising my voice with the bargemen:
> "Strike the tambourines, strike the drums,
> Stout, fine lads!
> [Strike] on plates, spoons and tumblers,

313

You famous factory singers!
Let's shake the damp earth with its mountains,
Let's shake the blue sea [with farts?].

Drunken mug, squabbler,
Universal brawler, rascal,
Champion, fighter I sing, beer-swiller,
Broad-shouldered bargeman!
Be silent, winds, do not rage!
Give ear, shapely heavens!
Cease, tempests, and do not blow!
I sing glorious marvels.
Amidst the fist-fight
I behold the hero of fist blows and kicks.

Little Homer with his balalaika,
And you, Virgilkin, with your pipe,
With the silly Trojan gang of Greeks
Squabbled, like hens under a wall.
Hide yourselves in a crack and don't say boo,
And stop your blithering nonsense—
You might better look this way!
Aren't there valiant heads here?
The beer-swiller would beat up Hector, if there were a fight,
Like a dog or a piece of carrion.

And you, Silenus, [your] son's [i.e., Bacchus'] confidant,
And bold, peppery, red-faced man:
Swine blown up with liquor,
Hero in drunkenness of thirsty souls,
You irrigate your belly with nectar,
Mixing for yourself honey-water with your wine,
You drink—but you forget me,
You don't give me any wine to drink.
Oh, be like Ganymede:
Give me some wine, some beer, some mead!

Strophe 7 of the "Ode" begins in Lomonosovian style: "I am seized by mighty transport, My head spins stormily." What follows, however, Mako-gonenko evidently considers unprintable, for the other eight lines of the strophe are indicated by the usual rows of dots. The poem's "hero," the cabman Alesha, makes his first appearance in Stanza 9:

314

Amidst drunken brows and flushed,
Amidst soldiers, amidst weavers,
Amidst picked or tipsy slaves,
Amidst dragoons, amidst kennel-keepers,
I see Alesha standing,
Having cast off his dark blue livery,
Threatening to smite his opponents.

In stanza 10 we have the usual epic comparison:

Zeus with angry fist
Smiting the brows of the smiths,
Never struck with such fury
As that with which he [i.e., Alesha] began to punish the boxers:
Having reddened the mask of one of them,
He knocked out a whole row of teeth,
Drew blood from another's lip,
And kicked him back into the crowd.

It is probably unnecessary to pursue the redoubtable fist-fighter through the rest of the ode, mutilated as it is; but one more strophe (no. 18) will show the poet's burlesque use of mythological trappings typical of the serious ode:

Upon the fallen hero the boozer
Hurled others like children.
His groans and howls cannot be heard,
Drifts of people lie over him.
Thus Zeus with thunderous [farts]
Smiting the giants, hurled them into Hades;
Having moved Aetna, he wiped out its damper;
Enceladus [one of the giants, buried under Aetna], rendered
                                            powerless,
Vainly gathers together his forces,
Shakes his shoulders, and shoves the weight.

One may hope that the day will come when the prudish Russian press will publish in full some, at least, of the hundred-odd poems of Ivan Barkov, so that the scholarly world at large may be given the opportunity of judging for itself the merits of what must be indeed a most remarkable and iconoclastic body of verse.

Detail from an obscene fresco in Catherine the Great's Gatchina Palace.

PART IV

LITERATURE IN THE SECOND HALF
OF THE REIGN OF CATHERINE II

Novikov

CHAPTER XII

DRAMA IN THE SECOND HALF
OF THE REIGN OF CATHERINE II

A. Political and Social Aspects of the Period

The years between the Treaty of Kuchuk Kainarji (1774) and Catherine's death (1796) are marked by an extraordinary territorial extension of the Russian Empire. The second war with Turkey (1787-91), although it did not result in the expulsion of the Turks from Constantinople and the reestablishment of the Greek Empire at Byzantium, as Catherine and Potemkin had dreamed, did add the Crimea and a good deal of the north coast of the Black Sea between the Dnieper and Dniester rivers to Catherine's realm—to the great disquiet, it may be added, of France, England and Prussia. Even Austria, which was an active Russian ally during the reign of Emperor Joseph II (1765-90), was not altogether happy with Russian gains in the direction of the Balkans. The first partition of Poland (1773-75) stirred that anarchic state to an extraordinary attempt at self-reform under the kingship of Stanislas Poniatowski, who was, however, unable to defend his diminished realm against the aggression of Russia and Prussia, and in 1793 a second partition reduced the Rzeczpospolita to a mere vestige. Even this was wiped out when the patriotic uprising under Kosciuszko in 1794 was crushed; Poland ceased to exist, and Russian territory was extended by the inclusion of all of Belorussia and most of what had once been Lithuania. Other Polish territories were incorporated into the Hapsburg Empire and Prussia. In the last year of her life Catherine, under the influence of her youthful lover Platon Zubov, embarked on a chimerical venture which was intended to create a zone of Russian control through Persia to the borders of India. Paul's first act was to recall the expedition.

An event of the greatest magnitude for all of Europe was the French Revolution which destroyed the Bourbon monarchy in 1789 and was followed by the radical government of Robespierre and the Jacobins. Russia was, under Catherine, a monarchy dominated by the interests of the gentry class, and economically based on an enormous and harshly exploited population of agricultural serfs. The dangers to the ruling class from a possible uprising of the serf population had been brought forcibly home to Catherine and the gentry by the Pugachev insurrection of 1773-75, and the French Revolution, although bourgeois and not popular in character, alarmed the

319

Empress and all upper-class Russia. The sympathizers with the French revolutionaries were very few in Russia, and confined to the small class of intelligentsia. Catherine herself is said to have been so appalled at events in France that she was actually taken ill at the news of the execution of Louis XVI. Naturally her government after 1793 became extremely repressive, and any suspicion of revolutionary sympathies usually meant incarceration or exile. We have seen this in the case of Nikolai I. Novikov, leader of the Russian Masons; and Denis Fonvizin was perhaps saved from a similar fate only by the stroke which rendered him helpless and obviously no political danger. Another of Catherine's victims, in her almost hysterical fear of revolution, was Alexander Radishchev, as we shall presently observe.

Catherine died in 1796 and the son whom she had kept from his father's throne for over thirty years was at last allowed to succeed. Pavel Petrovich—the Emperor Paul I—was by this date a man of 42. He had been systematically excluded all his life from any connection with the government, and had taken out his frustration by devoting himself with painful assiduity to military minutiae. He was quite evidently totally ignorant of the more important aspects of the science of war, but was an excellent drill sergeant. The relations between mother and son had always been hostile; Paul hated the woman who had usurped his throne, and Catherine hated the son who might pose a threat to her own autocratic control. As we have seen, there had been an abortive attempt to promote Paul's claims at the moment when he reached his majority, but Catherine and Potemkin were able to thwart it.

Paul was vindictive, and a great many of his early acts when he mounted the throne at last were designed to undo his mother's work. Particularly did her favorites suffer: Count Alexei Orlov was exiled and the Zubov brothers deemed it prudent to remove themselves from the scene voluntarily. There is no doubt that had he lived, Grigory Potemkin would have met an even worse fate. People like Radishchev and Novikov who had suffered harshly under Catherine were released or recalled—not because Paul was any less concerned than his mother with the danger of revolution, but simply because he hated all her acts.

It is very probable that the short reign of Pavel Petrovich has been unduly denigrated; he may not have been as bad a ruler as he is usually considered. After all, Catherine's policy had deliberately kept him in ignorance of the state of the realm and of the techniques of government; and in the five years during which he was autocrat he scarcely had time to learn all that he needed to know. After his murder, which his own son was accused of being privy to, there were few people to be found who would hazard saying anything good about him.

Paul's inexperience and indecisiveness are particularly visible in his foreign policy. Here was one area, however, where, at least at first, Catherine's lead was followed. After the fall of Robespierre, and especially after the Thermidorean reaction had taken its full course, France was clearly no longer an active revolutionary danger; under the Directoire, however (1795-99) a young Corsican general of genius, Napoleon Bonaparte had made it clear that there was still grave danger in French aggression, with or without a radical ideology. Napoleon's campaigns in northern Italy had almost erased Austrian control in that region; but after the Hapsburgs had been humbled at the Treaty of Campo Formio (1797), Napoleon returned to France, and presently, in pursuance of his audacious plan for striking at Great Britain by way of Egypt, embarked with his army for Egypt itself. In Italy were left only second-rate generals to hold Napoleon's conquests for France. Russia had maintained neutrality during the early years of the Directoire, but Russian sympathies were obviously with the *Ancien régime,* and Paul had given asylum to the Bourbon pretender, the later Louis XVIII, who obtained a palatial residence in Russian Courland. Oddly enough, it was Napoleon's seizure of the island of Malta in the Mediterranean in June 1798, as he was on his way to Egypt, that pushed Russia into an anti-French coalition. The Emperor Paul, it may be remembered, had always been sympathetic to Masons, and in 1797 had, most incongruously, accepted from the Maltese Order of the Knights of St. John of Jerusalem the title of "Protector" of that Order. After Napoleon's seizure of the Order's home island, the refugee Knights made the Orthodox Russian Emperor Grand Master of this Roman Catholic order of Crusaders! From this extraordinary involvement it came about that Russia adhered in 1799 to the anti-Napoleonic coalition with England, Austria and Turkey. Paul at once called out of retirement Russia's greatest military genius of all time, the then aged Alexander Suvorov, who had earlier on distinguished himself in wars with Turkey and Poland, but had offended Paul's military punctiliousness by his open contempt for "spit and polish." Suvorov was lent to Austria and made an Austrian field marshal. The campaign which he conducted in Italy was a brilliant success, but the jealousy of the Austrian commanders and the coolness of the Vienna government negated his efforts, and Paul, in a fit of pique with Francis II, recalled Suvorov in 1800.

Napoleon returned from the unsuccessful Egyptian campaign in 1799, and on 18 Brumaire (9 November) overthrew the Directoire and established himself as Consul for life. To Paul in Russia this meant a "legitimate," that is, monarchical, government in France, and with a lack of consistency in foreign policy that was entirely typical, he suddenly switched sides, ordered Louis XVIII out of Mitau, and allied himself with Napoleon. At once an expedition was improvised which would have been, if carried out, almost a repetition of the Zubov raid into Persia: a band of Cossacks was ordered to march through Persia to India and by seizing this rich and vital English possession paralyze Napoleon's chief enemy. By this time, however, sentiment among the Russian gentry had become thoroughly hostile to Paul, and a palace plot carried out in March 1801 assassinated the Emperor and set on the throne his eldest son, Alexander (I), whom Catherine had designated ever since his birth in 1777 as her successor.

During this rather perplexed period, roughly the last twenty years of the eighteenth century, Russia's position in the world of European politics had become truly prestigious. With Poland eliminated, Sweden chastised (in the brief war 1788-1790) and a large part of Turkey annexed, Russia had unquestioned dominance in eastern Europe; and, vacillating though it seemed, Russian policy toward France and England indicated that even in western Europe the Empire was a power to be reckoned with. At the same time, internal changes were taking place which were bound to lead sooner or later to the end of gentry dominance, and which had the effect of sapping the country's inner strength, although the full seriousness of this was not to be seen until the Crimean War. A middle class of merchants and manufacturers was rising, and even though still extremely small by comparison with western Europe, was beginning to make itself felt in government. The landowning gentry class, which still dominated the scene, tended to fall into two categories: one of these lived in idleness, extravagance and frivolity at the capital, and ran more and more hopelessly into debt. Estates were mortgaged and sold, and frequently, in order to save themselves from the financial pressures which their improvidence had brought on them, the estate owners imposed greater burdens in rent and services on an already oppressed peasantry. Not infrequently also the peasants were themselves sold, often with no regard for family ties, though this was strictly illegal. The second category of estate owners, while less financially reckless, were no less ruthless in dealings with the peasantry. This group realized the advantages of trading Russia's abundant grain for western money and manufactured products, mainly English, and stayed on their estates and ran them as profitably as possible. Inevitably this policy also meant greater and greater exploitation of the serfs, especially by way of "barshchina" ("corvée"), forced labor on the landlord's land— of course, to the detriment of the serf's own economy. By the beginning of the nineteenth century conditions among the peasantry were becoming intolerable, and there were constant alarming but uncoordinated outbreaks which continually raised the specter of another Pugachevshchina. At the same time, as we shall see, the small but very vocal Russian intelligentsia, which was still for the most part recruited from among the gentry, was becoming more and more aware of the inequities of the serf system and even timidly discussing the possibility of eliminating it. Genuine reform, however, was still a very long way in the future.

B. Late Classical Tragedy

The Russian archetype of classicism was, by common consent, Alexander Sumarokov. This position the poet himself consciously assumed, not only by virtue of his faithful and often pugnacious defense of all the canons of classicism as these had been evolved in the West, but by his forays into all the classical genres of literature. He aspired to be, and was by his admirers often regarded as, "the Russian Boileau," "the Russian Racine," and "the Russian Molière," all in one. He failed of being the Russian Homer, which must have been a humiliation, and had to yield that honor to Kheraskov. Sumarokov's merits were really numerous, and outmoded though they seem today, his voluminous works in all the recognized genres are no mean achievement. Personally, however, he was a disagreeable man, quarrelsome and overbearing, and insufferably egotistic. He was very much inclined to regard any branch of Russian literature in which he had had a hand—and that meant almost the whole gamut—as his private preserve and any other person who entered that field as an interloper. Particularly was this the case with the tragedy. His own nine tragedies filled the Russian stage and remained quite unrivalled by the few attempts, e.g., of Maikov or Kheraskov, to invade this realm.

The system of dramatic construction which Sumarokov evolved has been described earlier. It may be noted that despite his admiration for Racine, Sumarokov's own practice is more akin to that of Corneille. Racine's conflicts are inner battles in which an overmastering love plays the chief part—e.g., in *Phèdre, Andromaque* or *Mithridate*. Corneille's conflicts more commonly pit the reason against some instinctive passion (love in some instances, e.g., *Le Cid*), and their resolution is very commonly the triumph of reason. Moreover Corneille's subjects very frequently fall in the realm of what may be called "public" rather than "private" action—e.g., *Horace*, or *Cinna* or *Nicomède*. The concerns of the state and the "reasonable" motive of patriotism play parts in his drama larger than the individual passions, which predominate with Racine. Sumarokov did not excel—no more did Corneille—in depicting women, and his pictures of passionate love are conventional and unconvincing. But the larger, public, concern interests him strongly, and his best tragedies, e.g., *Dmitry the Pretender*, employ the obligatory love-intrigue, as Corneille himself usually does, only as a means of illuminating the public theme. Thus, the tyranny of the Pretender is exemplified through his lawless passion for Xenia and his attempt to kill Prince George in order to win her.

The career of Voltaire as a dramatist coincides roughly in time with that of Sumarokov. The Russian poet revered "the sage of Ferney" and deferred to his opinion as European arbiter of taste. We have seen how he wrote to the master for what amounted almost to an imperial rescript denouncing the "tearful comedy" as an anti-classical monstrosity. But Sumarokov's tragic system does not much rely on Voltairean practice. Voltaire's tragedy is preeminently a "tragedy of ideas." Typical is *Mahomet ou le Fanatisme*, where the very subtitle proclaims that this tragedy about Mohammed is constructed as a rational blast against the evil of fanaticism.

Voltaire's characters are for the most part mere puppets without individuality, whose stage existence is limited to the expression of certain ideas; the conflict inevitable in a tragedy is a battle not of human beings, but of ideas. In such battles the verbal texture of the tragedy becomes all important. The ideas must be crystal clear and sharply defined, in unforgettable, epigrammatic language. Voltaire, of course, was an unsurpassed master of precisely this kind of language, whether in prose or verse, and the overwhelming success which his tragedies enjoyed reflects to a great extent this scintillating, rapier-like verse, which serves to disguise the shallowness and conventionality of his characters. Compared with Voltaire's delicate weapon, Sumarokov's wit is of the order of a bludgeon, but he attempts to follow the French poet's example in tricking out his language with epigram to dazzle his audiences into thinking that his characters are profound.

1. Nikolai Petrovich Nikolev (1757-1815):[1] Sorena and Zamir

Sumarokov died in 1777. A few years later, in 1781, a young and well-educated nobleman, Nikolai Petrovich Nikolev, presented in Moscow a "character comedy" entitled The Self-Loving Poet.[2] The comedy had been written in 1775, when Nikolev was about 18, and it was a gross caricature of a dramatist named Nadmen ("Arrogance") who was generally, and probably correctly, supposed to represent Sumarokov. Characters and plot are flimsy and ridiculous, but the principal mechanism in the play's construction is Nadmen's insane egotism and his tendency to take mortal offense when anyone else presumes to compose a tragedy—a trait close enough to Sumarokov's character to lend color to the supposition that he was Nadmen's original. But if Sumarokov was in fact the object of the satire, it was as a man and not as a poet, for young Nikolev was one of the most ardent champions of Sumarokov's narrow classicism.

Nikolai Petrovich Nikolev was born in 1757 and was educated for a period in the home of his relative, Princess Dashkova, where he met the Panin brothers and other members of the circle of noblemen who dreamed of a constitutional monarchy in Russia. Some of their ideas doubtless appear in Nikolev's tragedy Sorena and Zamir. The young man, like so many gentry sons, was enrolled in a Guards Regiment, but at the age of twenty had to resign from the service as a result of a rapidly progressing blindness. He devoted himself accordingly for the rest of his life to literature. Under Emperor Paul he became a member of the Russian Academy; and he was, for a decade or so (the 1780s) rather commonly regarded as the leading figure in Russian literature. An admiring satirist, Gorchakov, called him "our leading dramatist." Nikolev's reputation, however, suffered a rapid decline, and by the time (1795-96) when he undertook to publish his complete works in ten volumes, the sales were so poor that the project was abandoned after Volume V.

Following Sumarokov not only in veneration for the conventions of classicism, but also in attempting to cover almost the whole recognized field of literature, Nikolev before his death in 1815 had created a truly impressive body of work. Some of this still remains in manuscript—the contents of the intended last five volumes of his collected edition—and of this material there are only vague rumors. Of the published works there are two five-act tragedies: *Palmira* (1781) and *Sorena i Zamir* (1784); three regular comedies: *Popytka ne shutka* (*Nothing Ventured, Nothing Gained*, 1774); *The Self-Loving Poet* (1775); and *Constancy Put to the Test*, (1775), in three acts, and one one-act comedy, *The Triumph of Innocence, or Love is Cleverer than Caution* (1815); and eight comic or fantastic operas, of which the best, *Rozana and Liubim* (1776) has been discussed earlier. Others are: *The Executor* (1777); *The Polisher* (1780); *Fenix* (1779); *Lover-Sorcerer* (1779); *Professor-Guardian, or Love is Cleverer than Eloquence* (1782). Aside from this dramatic production, Nikolev's work consists of a considerable body of lyric verse in all the eighteenth century genres: odes, both serious and parodistic; elegies; epistles; satires; epigrams; and fables.[3]

The satires mostly date to Nikolev's extreme youth—*Satire on the Depravity of Manners of the Present Age* and *Satire to the Muse* belong to his sixteenth year, and as literature are about what might be expected of that stage of maturity. The serious odes, e.g., "To Conscience" (1796), "Father of the Fatherland" (1796), "Flattery" (1796), "A Poet's Meditations" (1797), etc., are inflated, didactic pieces, of no particular originality, composed in the Lomonosovian 10-line strophe. The parody odes show somewhat greater originality. "Ode to the Wise Felitsa, by an Old Russian Poet from the Kingdom of the Dead" (1783 and 1787)[4] is constructed of dactylic quatrains with alternating feminine and masculine rhymes, and is conceived as a panegyric of Derzhavin's "Felitsa" (Catherine II) by the ghost of Trediakovsky! The parody of Trediakovsky's awkward and old-fashioned style is clever and convincing, and the conscious juxtaposition of the old and the new styles of panegyric is entertaining. When, however, Nikolev attempts to repeat his performance in an "Ode to the Russian Soldiers, on the Capture of the Fortress of Ochakov on the Sixth Day of December of the Year 1788, Composed by the Person of a Certain Ancient Russian Poet,"[5] the feat does not come off. The intent of seriously celebrating the valor of the Russian heroes is almost cancelled by the mockery of the style of the "Ancient Russian Poet"; and in any case making fun of Trediakovsky's way of writing twenty years after his death is certainly flogging a dead horse! Somewhat more successful is the second ode on the capture of Ochakov, described in the title as a "Fiddler's Song"[6] ("gudoshnaia pesn' "), that is, a song to be imagined as accompanied not by the solemn classical "lyre," but by the "fiddle" of the common street entertainer (as we have seen, this was the instrument which Barkov also imagined being used with his parodies). The ode, although in the classical 10-line strophe, rhyming *aBaBcc-Deed,* is in trochaic instead of iambic tetrameter, and hence has a much livelier and less solemn rhythm. The language, appropriately to the "fiddle" accompaniment, is quite popular. The ode begins:

Let him who will tune the thunderous lyre, to show himself in the heights; I shall present my song to the world, soldier-fashion, on the fiddle. Sumarokov in his *Epistles* is not the director of my will. Every family has its own character. What have I to do with Parnassus? Without any winged Pegasus I shall rise as far as the bench.

The pretentious classical allegory and mythology (the lyre, Parnassus, Pegasus, Pindus, Helicon, and the rest) lend themselves readily to mockery, and Nikolev's "ode" takes full advantage of the opportunities. But unhappily, before he brings it to a close, he has reverted to a thoroughly government-inspired and un-popular didacticism:

Freedom—the word is tempting; freedom—the reality frightens the mind. With the former, conscience does not reproach, while with the latter it destroys. Without command the people's liberty is killed. Reason is needed, and example. The point is that we must have ability ["umeli"], the officers must have understanding ["razumeli"] — and let reason ["razum"] be the officer.

There is little likelihood that "the heroes of Ochakov" reasoned in any such artificial and unnatural fashion, or would have understood the words Nikolev puts in their mouths.

The fables and tales which form part of Nikolev's non-dramatic production date mostly from the 1770s; they are often polemical in intent, directed against such rival poets as Dmitriev and Kapnist. The best of the lyric pieces, however, are the songs, which are sometimes close enough to genuinely popular thematic and vocabulary to pass for the real thing—e.g., the romance which begins "vecherkom rumaniu zoriu." The first three strophes of the fourteen are as follows; they are put in the mouth of an unhappy girl, suffering from a sorrow which of course, in true classical fashion, is never particularized, but left completely vague:[7]

In the evening I went out in sadness to have a look at the ruddy glow—but I always came back to my former sorrow, which bids me die.
    My sorrow lured me to the brook, [and] I sat down on the bank; my heart became yet more gloomy, [and] the pure current became turbid.
    Sighing, I said then: "Flow, little brook, like [my] tears!" And when I had said this, I showed my eyes full of tears.

Impossible to convey in translation is the quasi-popular use of diminutives—"vecherkom" ("in the evening"), "rechke" ("brook"), "berezhok" ("bank"), which lend the song a somewhat conventional air of genuine folk composition.

Nikolev's principal claim to contemporary fame was contained in his dramatic work. His comic and fantastic operas have been treated earlier, in connection with other examples of that genre, and his comedies will be considered shortly. Of his two published tragedies (there is said to be a *Sviatoslav* in manuscript) the earlier is *Palmira* (1781), a typical neo-classical piece constructed in the Cornelian fashion on the conflict between love and duty—in this instance between the filial duty of Palmira, daughter of Iroksers, tyrant of Tyre, and her passion for Zoleg, also called Omar, Prince of Sidon, who is her father's captive. The political aspect of the tragedy is completely eclipsed by the love intrigue, but even so the amorous passions of the hero and heroine are pallid and unconvincing. The play is thoroughly mediocre.

On the other hand, *Sorena and Zamir* (1784)[8] is a quite successful drama of its kind, and because of the abundance of anti-monarchic speeches in it, enjoyed great popularity both when it was first produced and subsequently. The plot of *Sorena and Zamir*, like that of *Palmira*, and following the example of Voltaire, is entirely fictional. It is obviously inspired by Voltaire's *Alzire* (1736)[9]—even to the name of the hero (Zamore in Voltaire, Zamir in Nikolev). The development of the plot, however, is quite unlike that of *Alzire*, and the emphasis is placed on a quite different element. Voltaire's tragedy turns on the contrast between the gentle, conciliatory, humane behavior of old Don Alvarez, former governor of Peru, and his genuine Christianity, with the tyranny and religious fanaticism of his son Don Gusman, the new governor. The love between the native Peruvian princess Alzire and prince Zamore is, as often with Voltaire, used simply as a mechanism for exhibiting Don Gusman's cruelty, tyranny and religious intolerance. The drama ends "happily," when Zamore succeeds in mortally wounding his rival and enemy Don Gusman, who in the face of imminent death abruptly becomes magnanimous, forgives his enemies and unites his own bride Alzire with her lover Zamore. His point made, that bigotry, intolerance and political represssion of a conquered people are counter-productive, Voltaire lets his lovers end up in each other's arms. Not so Nikolev, whose dramatic emphasis, despite the incidental anti-tyrannical declamations, lies entirely in the depiction of passionate love. He has no counterpart for Voltaire's Don Alvarez; his Mstislav, "Tsar of Russia" (a non-existent creation) is indeed incidentally a tyrant, but first and foremost an impassioned and convincing lover, unable, like a Racinian hero (e.g., Nero) to control a passion that he realizes is destructive and is leading him to act against conscience, religion and political wisdom. Nikolev's pagans, answering to Voltaire's "Americans" (i.e., Peruvian Indians) are Polovtsy: Zamir, their prince, and his wife Sorena, the object of Mstislav's volcanic passion. The tragedy's dénouement follows a different course from that of Voltaire: Sorena, undertaking reluctantly to commit murder in order to save her Zamir, seeks out the tyrant in the unlighted church attached to the palace, and stabs a man whom she takes for Mstislav, only to find that she has un-

327

wittingly killed her own husband. Of course she atones for this grave mistake by suicide, and Mstislav is left at the end completely crushed by the loss of the woman for whom he has let himself be led into folly and sin.

It is said that Catherine's chief censor denounced the play to her as dangerous because of its anti-tyrannical speeches, but the Empress assured him that since her own reign was "enlightened" and benevolent, Nikolev's blasts against tyranny did not concern her, and the tragedy could be performed. In this attitude Catherine was fully justified, although not entirely for the reasons alleged. *Sorena and Zamir* is not primarily a political tragedy, nor is it in any sense a "tragedy of ideas." It is a tragedy of passion, in which the emphasis is exactly the contrary of Voltaire's *Alzire:* the theme of "tyranny" is utilized primarily as a mechanism for developing the theme of uncontrollable passion. Mstislav is a tyrant incidentally, a lover first and foremost.

2. *Yakov Borisovich Kniazhnin* (1740-1791)[10]

Russia's foremost tragic poet of the late eighteenth century was a nobleman, son of the vice-governor of Pskov, whose early life was spent, like so many others of his kind, in the military service. His army career came to an ignominious end in 1773 when a military board of inquiry discovered that he had "borrowed"—and lost in some fashion, perhaps at cards—6000 rubles of regimental funds. He was actually sentenced to be hanged, but pardoned by the Empress. His lands, however, were confiscated and he was deprived for a time of his nobleman's rank. Lidia Kulakova, in her preface to the "Poet's Library" edition of Kniazhnin's *Selected Works*[11] conjectures that the exceptional severity of Kniazhnin's punishment may have been connected with his activity in the Panin circle which was endeavoring at this period to put Prince Paul on the throne in his mother's stead. The conjecture is plausible, but unconfirmed. In any case, Kniazhnin, deprived of income from either army position or estate, was obliged to support himself by a program of translating: Voltaire's *Henriade,* Corneille's *Le Cid, Cinna, La Mort de Pompée* and *Rodogune,* and a good deal else, from both French and Italian. During the period from 1778 to his death in 1791 Kniazhnin served as secretary under I.I. Betsky, who headed the educational institutions of the capital. Some mystery surrounds Kniazhnin's death; although in a short biography by his son and in a memoir by a friend his death is attributed to what would in modern times be diagnosed as pneumonia, a tradition, repeated by Pushkin,[12] held that he was "interrogated"—that is, put to torture—by Catherine's "household hangman" S.I. Sheshkovsky, and died as a result of this. Again, there is no confirmation of this; the last of Kniazhnin's tragedies, the anti-tyrannical *Vadim of Novgorod,* was not published until 1793, two years after the poet's death, and it was only after this that it came to the notice of the Empress, who of course ordered its immediate suppression and the punishment of all concerned in its publication. But it is not impossible that an article Kniazhnin is alleged to have written under the title of "Woe to My Fatherland" (not extant) may have led to Sheshkovsky's "interrogation" and the poet's death at the age of 51.

Kniazhnin is of course first and foremost a dramatist, the author of four full-length comedies in verse, eight comic operas, and eight verse tragedies. Like his contemporary Nikolev, however, he cultivated other genres of verse as well, with no outstanding success. Pompous eulogy apparently was not to his taste, for he wrote only one ode—on the marriage of Prince Paul; two serious poems of a philosophical sort, *Stanzas to God* and *Stanzas on Death* belong to the sentimentalist tradition, and a fictional epistle in verse given to the hero of a French novel which he translated, "The Unfortunate Lovers, or The True Adventures of Count Comminges, Filled with Pitiful Events Exceedingly Touching to Tender Hearts"[13] falls, needless to say, decidedly in the same tradition. Kniazhnin's most original and interesting non-dramatic verse efforts are a novella *Flor and Liza*,[14] which anticipates Karamzin's *Poor Liza,* and his satirical pieces, including some fables in Sumarokov's style. One of the most successful of his satires is *The Confession of Mme Affected (Ispovedeniie Zhemanikhi),* in which he makes merciless fun of the ridiculous modish jargon of upper class ladies. Of some literary interest also is his "Epistle from the Uncle of the Poet Rhyme-Squeak," aimed apparently at the inflated and pretentious style of the ode-writer V.P. Petrov. "Rhyme-Squeak" is eulogized as follows:

> Only low styles
> Are intelligible to everyone; but he who, like the gods,
> Speaking loftily, soars on pinions—
> That one need not even himself understand what he is saying.
> Is it any honor, if a poet is esteemed so little
> That everyone without distinction can read his verses?
> That everyone has free and easy access to him?
> That the mob with its understanding dishonors them [i.e., his
> verses]?[14]

Finally, mention may be made of his poem "The Parrot,"[15] which was published after Kniazhnin's death, although it evidently was known in manuscript before. It is a reworking of Gresset's well-known anticlerical poem *Vert-Vert* (1734). A pious old widow and her daughter acquire a parrot, which they teach to recite prayers and sing church responses. The old lady's sailor son, returned from long voyaging and stationed at Kronstadt near the capital, induces his mother to let him borrow Jacquot for a while, to enliven his and his fellow-sailors' boredom. The widow and her daughter are disconsolate without their pet, and greet him with rapture when he is returned—

329

but alas, during his sojourn with the navy he has unlearned all his ecclesiastical vocabulary and learned so much "salty" language that he can no longer be exhibited in polite company, but has to be kept in the rear of the house out of ear-shot.

In much of his non-dramatic verse Kniazhnin reveals himself as a rebel against the conventions of strict classicism, as interpreted by Sumarokov, even though that poet was his father-in-law. Kniazhnin's verse shows the unmistakable influence of Derzhavin, and leans toward sentimentalism. Typical is his apostrophe to "Sensibility" in *Stanzas to God*:[16]

> Sensibility! ["chuvstvitel'nost' "] O gift divine!
> Thou leadest us more directly to our end;
> And the triumphant flight of thy wings
> Carries our hearts aloft to the Creator.

As we shall see, even in his tragedies, that most classical of genres, he begins at least with a non-classical penchant for scenic effect (e.g., the burning of Carthage in *Dido*) and for the combination of music with drama (e.g., the chorus in *Vladisan*, etc.). But by the end of his life he returns in his masterpiece *Vadim of Novgorod* to both the political theme and the scenic simplicity characteristic of the strictest classicism.

Kniazhnin's dramatic career began with, typically, a "melodrama" (that is, a tragedy with music), *Orpheus* (1763), on a classical subject. His first genuine tragedy, however, *Dido* (1769),[17] is no longer accompanied by chorus or music. The subject comes, of course, from the Fourth Book of the *Aeneid*, but intermediaries are two earlier eighteenth century tragedies, *Didon* by Jean-Jacques Lefranc, marquis de Pompignan (1734) and *Didone abbandonata* by the Italian Metastasio (1724). Kniazhnin, however, even while appropriating a good deal from his western predecessors, remains surprisingly close to the spirit of the Latin original, and his work is in fact an excellent example of the classical tragedy of passion. It is totally remote from the Sumarokov tragic system, which generally uses Cornelian procedures—passion in conflict with duty—and gives the victory to duty or "reason"; Dido's concern for the welfare of her Carthaginian people does not so much overweigh her despair at Aeneas' abandonment of her as to restrain her from suicide. The tragedy has no political "message," and in this respect it follows the lead of Racine. The chief dramatic conflict which it depicts is the violent struggle in the breast of Aeneas between his passion for Dido and his divinely appointed mission to lead his Trojans to a new home in Italy. In dramatizing this conflict Kniazhnin makes his hero vacillate a great deal more than does Virgil's Aeneas. The first and second acts show Aeneas determined to leave Dido, following the divine admonition of a dream. In the third act Aeneas tries to explain himself to Dido, but overwhelmed by her reproaches and despair, changes his resolution and cries to Dido: "Live, dearest one! Your Aeneas will stay." But Act IV again reverses the situation, as Antenor, Aeneas's faithful friend, with eloquent reproaches at length persaudes his chief that he must leave Carthage and follow his destiny to Italy. To a degree this vacillation weakens the character of Aeneas, who is no longer the somber, destiny-haunted Stoic whose shoulders are weighted "with the fates and fortunes of his descendants." Undeniably, however, Kniazhnin's Aeneas is more human, more touching and more dramatic than Virgil's resigned lover. The picture of Dido, as the Russian dramatist portrays her, is strikingly Virgilian; her impassioned monologues to Aeneas are filled with verbal echoes of the Latin. Thus, her first speech in Act III to the Trojan as he confronts her:

I have heard that you were resolved on leaving unfortunate me, that you wanted to depart. Did you so desire or not? They assure me of this. I think that they have declared to me what is false. I do not believe it... O, tyrant! You bid me believe it! Your confusion and cruel silence are the terrible foreboding of my death. Here is the fruit of my love, here is the fire of our hearts! I burn for you, and I perish in the end. Look at me; why are you afraid to see the one whom you have brought yourself now to hate? Look, Aeneas; you will see no wrath in my face, you will see only the shadow of death upon it; look at me, understand my torment. Or are you afraid to enter into pity? Be a man, you are a hero: take away my life, and, oh, without fear, pierce this breast and passionate heart, where your image dwelling....[18]

Dramatically she changes roles when she finds Aeneas unbending, and from supplication turns to denunciation:

Go; I can beg no longer. I have enough of torment; I have poured forth my tears in multitudes, and for long been the lover in your presence. Now I shall be the queen. Be content with your heroism. Leave me, vagabond, like in character to the beasts. They tell me that in you flows the blood of the immortals. It is not true—the cruel tiger gave you to behold the light; you were begotten in the womb of a ravening lioness![19]

Her last soliloquy in Act V is the most touching, and reveals a Dido who, unlike Virgil's heroine, is able even in the midst of her own despair to understand and sympathize with the torments she knows her lover is suffering:

Has the host of woes then been fulfilled upon me, for which I was destined in this world? I am bereft of everything, and my lot is accomplished. I thank thee, inexorable Fate! Thou hast been so cruel to me, unhappy one, that thou hast no more severity to show! Thou hast exhausted thy power and art weak in thy cruelties. And you, Aeneas! Though you have destroyed the hapless one, the cause of all my woes—yet you are still dear to me. I loved you, when I entrusted my crown to you. I loved you happy, and I love you dying. I know, you are suffering in this hour, like me, and turning your gaze toward this lamentable land, you are imagining me moaning close to death, and in your thoughts you are washing out with tears my blood which I shall shed as a sacrifice to you; to give me life, you are giving your life, and perhaps in this hour wishing to return. O cruel one! Return, and Dido will revive.[20]

The dramatic mechanism of the tragedy involves a non-Virgilian episode, which is utilized by both Lefranc and Metastasio. Iarbas, king of Gaetulia, who is in the background in Virgil, appears in Kniazhnin's drama to complicate the action. He and a confidant enter in Act II in the disguise of ambassadors to sue for Dido's hand for their king, and are contemptuously refused. Iarbas plots revenge, and starts an uprising in Carthage in Act III which culminates in a battle in Act IV between Iarbas and Aeneas. Iarbas is taken captive by his rival, who, to his intense annoyance, returns his sword to him and sets him free. To wipe out this ignominy Iarbas gathers his army and storms the city after Aeneas's departure in Act V. Carthage is set afire, Dido's palace begins to burn, and Iarbas rushes in to offer her a last opportunity of saving herself by marrying him. Dido's answer is to plunge voluntarily into the flames of her burning palace. In this way, incidentally, Kniazhnin contrives a most dramatic spectacle for his dénouement, and returns to Virgil, whose Dido ends her life voluntarily on a funeral pyre. The more classical tragedies of Lefranc and Metastasio give her the traditional dagger for her suicide.

Kniazhnin's *Dido* is, for a first tragedy, a remarkable success. The characterization, especially of Dido and of the passionate young barbarian Iarbas, is excellent. Something has perhaps been learned from Voltaire, whose dramaturgy is marked by striking scenic effects, such as the fire of the final act; but unlike Voltaire's tragedies, *Dido* has no message, carries no political, social or religious propaganda, but appears to be more akin to Racine's "tragedy of passion" than to anything else, either Russian or western.

The date of Kniazhnin's tragedy *Olga,*[21] which was neither presented nor printed in his lifetime, is uncertain, but it appears to have been early, probably in the early 1770s. The author returned to it toward the end of his life, but apparently did not complete it to his satisfaction. Like most of Kniazhnin's tragedies, *Olga* is a reworking of a French original, in this case, of Voltaire's *Mérope* (1734).[22] Rather ingeniously the Greek legend which Voltaire took as his subject—utilized by Euripides in a lost tragedy—has been grafted on to Russian legend as recorded in the Primary Chronicle. This has indeed done considerable violence to the facts of history, but certainly no more than was habitual with Sumarokov, or even with Corneille. The Nestorian Chronicle relates that Igor, prince of Kiev, was killed by Mal, prince of the Drevlianians, when he made an ill-advised attempt to collect tribute a second time in the same year. Olga, Igor's widow, took a treacherous and cruel revenge on both Mal and his entire people. In Kniazhnin's version Igor has been killed fifteen years before the play begins, and his throne occupied by Mal; the "tyrant" has killed two of the sons of Olga and Igor (unknown to the Chronicle), but his mother has succeeded in saving her youngest, Sviatoslav, by sending him off with the faithful nobleman Volod to be reared to manhood in the forest until he can return and avenge his father's murder. In this cast of characters Olga is Voltaire's Mérope, Sviatoslav is Egisthe and Volod is Narbas. The complication is brought about when young Sviatoslav, unaware of his parentage and impatient of his rustic existence, runs away, turns up in Kiev where he gets into a quarrel with a man whom he kills, is apprehended and threatened with execution. His mother, without of course recognizing him, is attracted to him and takes his part until she learns that he has been apprehended with a sword which she recognizes as that of her husband which she had sent with Volod for her son when he should be grown. Perversely ignoring, for purposes of the drama, the possibility that Sviatoslav may *be* her son, Olga is convinced that the boy is her son's murderer, and resolves to be herself her son's avenger. She agrees to marry Mal, whom she detests, if she may have the privilege of herself killing the murderer. Thus is contrived Kniazhnin's version of the scene which is said to have so electrified the audience of Euripides's play, as mother raises sword against son. Of course Volod arrives in the nick of time to prevent the disaster. Mal learns that Sviatoslav has appeared and agrees to make the boy his heir, if Olga will marry him, which she promises to do, while privately planning to commit suicide instead. The final scene has the altar prepared for the marriage; Mal swears to make Sviatoslav his heir. Sviatoslav, called on in turn to swear, seizes a sacrificial axe and kills the king. The people assembled for the wedding ceremony make a slight commotion, but Mal's confidant Zlovred is quickly disarmed and the coup d'état is tamely accomplished.

The play is vastly inferior to *Dido;* in fact, it has very little merit at all. The characterization is crude and totally unconvincing, with the single exception of Mal, who has a surprisingly three-dimensional and lifelike look. He is not the typical tragic tyrant, but a calculating, cold, suspicious, yet in his own way, honorable ruler. He is disarming in his very first speech, long and tedious though it is, in which he admits that his desire to marry Olga is not based either on her great charms, which she no longer possesses, nor on his passion—he is too old for that—but purely on *raison d'état.*

The tragedy is one neither of passion, like *Dido,* nor of ideas, like Kniazhnin's later masterpieces *Rosslav* and *Vadim of Novgorod;* it is one of intrigue, with a quite complicated plot, which is awkwardly managed and thoroughly implausible. The large part which is played in it by Sviatoslav's murder of an unknown man who is never identified is a serious flaw; and Olga's obtuseness in refusing to recognize in Sviatoslav the son she has been impatiently awaiting for fifteen years is calculated to alienate the most sympathetic reader.

There is some historical interest in one aspect of the tragedy: Olga, in the first act, in response to the report that Mal wishes to marry her and thus make her again a queen, avows that she has no interest herself in occupying a throne—she desires it only for her son. In view of the situation of the Russian throne, which Catherine had usurped from her son Paul, this dramatic "allusion" could hardly be missed, and doubtless explains why Kniazhnin saw fit to leave the tragedy unpublished and unknown. If anything of its existence and nature could have reached the Empress, it might also explain why Kniazhnin's financial peccadillo earned him in 1773 the extraordinarily severe penalty which it did.

In 1772 the tragedy *Vladimir and Iaropolk*[23] was, according to Kniazhnin's friend and biographer Eugene Bolkhovitinov, "written but left unnoticed because of its many theatrical faults." Like *Olga* it is constructed as an awkward conflation·of Greek legend and Russian chronicle history. In this case Racine's *Andromaque* furnishes the classical model, and Prince Vladimir's murder of his brother Iaropolk the quasi-historical episode. The plot is complicated, but follows basically the French original, with the following equations: Iaropolk is Pyrrhus, murdered at the end of the play by his brother Vladimir, who is Racine's Oreste. Vladimir's act is motivated by his passion for Rogneda (Hermione), Iaropolk's jealous wife. The part of Andromaque is played by the minor character Kleomena, with whom Iaropolk is in love. Oreste's bosom friend Pylade is Vadim in the Russian version, and old Phoenix, tutor of Pyrrhus as of his father Achilles, is the nobleman Svadel. Unlike any of Kniazhnin's previous tragedies, *Vladimir and Iaropolk* contains, in the person of Svadel, a raisonneur of the author himself, and in so far as this character, who is extraneous to the intrigue, voices horror of the brothers' selfish internecine strife, and proud belief in the function of the nobility as councillors of royalty, the play can be called a "tragedy of ideas." It is, however, still an awkward and poorly constructed piece, and Svadel's noble and patriotic sentiments do not atone for "the many theatrical defects," not the least of which is the derivative and clichéd characterization. It may be noted incidentally that the depiction of "Saint" Vladimir as a love-maddened fratricide, even though this is before his "conversion," must have been offensive to many of the Orthodox.

Kniazhnin's trial and condemnation in 1773 was followed by several years during which he abandoned original writing and busied himself only with translations. The first important work composed after this period of disgrace was a drama which was quite patently intended to flatter the Empress and perhaps incline her to emulate the drama's hero—*The Clemency of Titus.*[24] This was apparently successful in at least winning Catherine's favor; it was presented in 1778 with sumptuous settings and music. The story told by both Kniazhnin's son in his biography and by Archbishop Eugene Bolkhovitinov in his memoir, that Catherine approached the poet in 1785 with hints that he should write a drama about the clemency of "the great Roman Emperor Titus" is false, although it has often been repeated.

The Clemency of Titus is unique among Kniazhnin's dramas for numerous reasons, not least of which is its systematic violation of all the conventions of classical tragedy. It is modeled, and in part even plagiarized from,

the opera *La Clemenza di Tito* of the Italian poet Metastasio (1698-1782) and
the tragedy *Titus* by Dormont de Belloy (1727-1775). Both the Italian and
the French dramatist had in turn utilized Corneille's *Cinna* for their pieces
by transferring from the history of Augustus Caesar the incident which
Seneca recounts of his clemency to the conspirator Cinna, to the life of the
emperor Titus, whose mildness was indeed proverbial, but of whom no particularly dramatic instance of clemency is recorded. The subject had in both
cases been chosen primarily to glorify the playwright's immediate royal
patron by adroit parallelism insinuated with the behavior of Titus: Metastasio's Titus reflects the Austrian Emperor Charles VI, De Belloy's Louis
XV, King of France.

Kniazhnin's *The Clemency of Titus* is Russia's first serious drama with
music; in form it approaches closer to the Italian *opera seria* than to the
classical tragedy. The drama is in three acts; it is written not in the Alexandrine verse of tragedy, but in iambic lines of unequal length—the so-called
"free verse" employed normally in fables and in such a verse tale as Bogdanovich's *Dushenka*, but known in French dramaturgy in such a "spectacle piece" as *Psyché*, that remarkable hybrid in which Molière, Pierre
Corneille and Quinault had each a hand. The convention of "unity of place"
is almost ostentatiously demolished: five times in three acts the scene
changes—the square in front of the Capitol, a walk planted with trees, the
Senate House, Titus' private study, and finally a great public square filled
with milling people. Mass effects play a large part in the spectacle—crowds of
Senators, lictors, guardsmen and "people." These are not given lines, but
"the people" constitute a chorus, which sings at beginning and end of the
drama, and occasionally elsewhere. Another unusual feature is the presence
of fairly elaborate stage directions and indications of scene, which are never
found in classical drama, where the scene is always a conventional "palace,"
and acting by facial expression, gesture, or the like, is entirely replaced by
declamation. Whatever the deficiencies of *The Clemency of Titus* as drama—
and it has few merits—it marks a milestone in the liberation of Russian
tragedy from the shackles of classicism. From it to Ozerov's dramatic innovations is but a step.

Kniazhnin's usual practice in both his tragedies, and, as we shall see,
his comedies, was to adapt a western (French or Italian) original. His first
break with this system is marked by the tragedy *Rosslav*,[25] written in 1784
and presented to enthusiastic audiences, but withdrawn from the stage at
Catherine's orders at the beginning of the French Revolution.

Rosslav is ostensibly a historical drama; the background is provided
by the history of Sweden, whose King Christian II, overthrown in 1520 by
Gustavus Vasa and the Dalecarlian revolt, is the original of the tyrant Khristiern. Little beyond this vague intimation, however, is historical. The play's
protagonist is a Russian general, Rosslav, who has been taken captive by

Khristiern, and has joined with the Swedes in saving Stockholm from capture by the "Sarmatians," i.e., Poles. Rosslav is in love with the princess Zafira, whom the dramatist describes as "last of the former line of Swedish kings" (Christian-Khristiern is of course a Dane), but hesitates, as a commoner, to confess his love for a princess. Kedar, Khristiern's commander-in-chief, who hypocritically professes friendship for Rosslav, is also in love with Zafira; and so also is Khristiern himself. To this private complication is added the principal, political one. A Russian ambassador, Liubomir, arrives in Stockholm to arrange for the liberation of Rosslav, who is a beloved friend of the Russian Tsar. This Tsar, unnamed, is ready to give up to Sweden all the territory which Rosslav and his armies have wrested from that country, as a price for his friend's release. In spite of Rosslav's indignant repudiation of such a shameful bargain, Liubomir proposes it to the Swedish king, who refuses it. He intimates, however, that Rosslav has it in his power himself to win his freedom: the Russian alone possesses a fateful secret which Khristiern must know at all costs—the whereabouts of the "rebel" Gustavus Vasa. If he will divulge this, he may have any reward he pleases. Rosslav of course refuses and is thrown into prison, from which he is brought in the third act for a dramatic confrontation with the king. In the meanwhile Rosslav's false friend Kedar and his true love Zafira (she has, in a most unconventional way, confessed her love to the astounded Rosslav) have been trying to influence the king each for his or her own ends. As Rosslav remains obdurate, he is again thrown into prison to face execution the next day. Zafira appears in this prison (Act IV), having with amazing ease bribed the guards; she will flee with Rosslav, renouncing her claim on the Swedish throne. Again Rosslav refuses; he will not like a coward run away from a glorious death! At this point, quite understandably, Zafira loses patience and heaps him with reproaches, finally threatening to kill herself with a dagger. Rosslav relents at this, but it is too late: Kedar has cut off his escape. Rosslav is led off to execution, but Zafira and Liubomir turn to their last recourse—a popular uprising. Opportunely, Gustavus is reported near at hand. The final act gives Rosslav the opportunity once more of refusing the king's mercy at the price of his and his country's honor; his execution is ordered, but a messenger rushes in with news of a popular uprising in Zafira's favor and the approach of Gustavus Vasa. Rosslav triumphs, Kedar is lynched by the populace, and Khristiern, after unsuccessful attempts to kill first Zafira and then Rosslav, succeeds finally in stabbing himself. The hero, united at last with his princess, announces: "I can still, I can serve my country; and my heart I devote to Zafira."

The intrigue is more complicated in appearance than in reality, largely through the presence of the double-dealing Kedar, whose self-seeking hypocrisy actually has no effect on the outcome of the tragedy. The drama resolves itself into a series of repetitions of an identical scene: Rosslav, tempted by promises of liberty, royal friendship, love and life itself as a reward for perfidy, resolutely refuses them all.

The tragedy is certainly one of Kniazhnin's best; in spite of its strongly rhetorical character, it is enthralling. Everything turns on the character of Rosslav—but in this very character lies the play's greatest defect. Kniazhnin's inspiration here was certainly the tragedy of Corneille; but in following the French master's use of his vaunted "third spring of tragedy," that is, "admiration," after Aristotle's "pity and fear," Kniazhnin falls into the same error as his model. A character of such inhuman firmness and constancy as Rosslav is in the long run undramatic. When the conflict between love and patriotic duty is so easily resolved every time by the triumph of the latter, the audience loses interest. Aristotle demanded in the ideal tragedy that the hero should be "of our kind," that is, a normal human being akin to the audience. Rosslav is certainly "beyond human kind," although perhaps no more so than Corneille's Polyeucte. He is particularly unconvincing in the fourth act, when Zafira offers him the opportunity of escape from prison, and her love, with no obvious compromise of his principles. Here his shrill denunciations of "cowardly flight" ring wholly false. He appears to be fanatically bent on martyrdom, and the audience, like Zafira, may well have doubts of the genuineness of his love for her.

This monomaniacal quality in Rosslav is certainly a dramatic defect; and yet, for an audience sated with heroes motivated by nothing but love, this change must have been a welcome novelty. And large as it bulks, Rosslav's character is not the only one in the tragedy. For a change, Zafira is something a great deal more than the usual colorless heroine. Her "unmaidenly" behavior in confessing her love to Rosslav, when it appears certain that his notions of duty and propriety will permanently inhibit him from making such a confession to her, is one evidence of spirit in the lady and of originality in the dramatist. The character of Kedar, too, is unusually full and convincing. The smooth-tongued hypocrite, playing a dangerous double game in which he hopes first to destroy Rosslav by means of Khristiern, and then Khristiern in turn by means of a revolution, is plausible enough, even though the audience has to learn of his perfidy in the conventional fashion, by means of his own admissions to his "confidant" Zlovred.

Rosslav is very highly regarded by Soviet critics for two reasons quite unconnected with its poetical or dramatic merits. In his colloquies with Khristiern the hero voices frequent and eloquent denunciations of "tyranny"; and his entire characterization is taken, perhaps correctly, as Kniazhnin's conception of the ideal "Russian character." Rosslav, in his loyalty to his Tsar and country, and his willingness—indeed, eagerness—to sacrifice his life and love to the welfare of his fatherland, becomes the great eighteenth century symbol of patriotism. That his characterization is almost grotesquely exaggerated and psychologically unconvincing is overlooked. A good example of the kind of dialogue which Russian patriotism finds so inspiring is this, from scene iii of Act III. Liubomir and Zafira have in turn been unsuccessful

337

in pleas to Rosslav to divulge the fateful secret to the king, and Khristiern himself now appears to confront the obstinate prisoner:

Khri. Has Zafira's compassion been successful in that in which hitherto the power of a king has had no success? Has the secret been revealed? Am I able, in learning it, not to be harsh?

Ross. Or am I no longer Rosslav?

Khri. Let us leave off cruelties; I am weary of them, and my wrath, just though it be, I shall moderate nevertheless, and from the throne incline myself toward generosity. My treasures are open for you. Tell me what I want to know, and you can have them all.

Ross. Keep your silver, that trap of tyrants for maintaining the crown upon their heads, but which can attract only base hearts. Be the possessor of thrones and of all your treasures; take even my life, but leave me virtue.

Khri. If you were a king, plunged into misfortune through captivity, I would not marvel at your boldness; I would respect the king in you, through esteem for myself. But you, though in captivity, are bold against me and, fearless of my wrath, do not tremble—who are you?

Ross. I am a Russian!

Khri. You insolent captive, you are my slave!

Ross. That man is free, who, fearless of death, does not comply with tyrants.

Khri. Understand! For the final time, I am willing to spare you, and for the final time I forgive your insolence.... I am willing to save you.... I see what troubles you, what will not let you disclose the vital secret to me—fear of earning ill-will from your prince. But be my subject, leave, leave him. Your fate hangs on your own will. What do you desire, say?

Ross. Not even a throne.

Khri. Die, villain! Exhausting my patience, on whom do you place your hope?

Ross. On myself.

This is lofty rhetoric, to be sure; one may detect Senecan influence in the abrupt, epigrammatic replies of Rosslav, e.g., *Ja Ross!* But it is humanly unconvincing.

The political implications of the tragedy are obvious, and it can occasion no surprise that Catherine kept it from the stage after the outbreak of the French Revolution. The spectacle of a monarch—even a "tyrant"—deposed by a popular uprising was decidedly unpalatable to her. She must also have been disturbed by many of Rosslav's bold pronouncements on the limitations of royal power. Thus, when Liubomir informs Rosslav that the Russian Tsar is surrendering the cities captured from Sweden, in return for Rosslav's freedom, the hero angrily declares: "He hasn't the right!" The Russian Tsar in 1520 was Vasily III, a historical fact which Kniazhnin diplomatically ignores by never naming him; it could hardly be imagined that that autocrat would dream of relinquishing an inch of conquered territory for even his favorite general's life. Nor can it be readily imagined that a sixteenth century Muscovite magnate would so boldly deny his monarch's "right" to do so. But such a "Jacobin" sentiment was hardly likely to appeal to Catherine II.

338

The tragedies of Kniazhnin seem to fall into two fairly distinct groups. One—*Vladimir and Iaropolk, Rosslav, Vadim of Novgorod*—is dominated by large political ideas in the tradition of Corneille and Sumarokov, and dispenses with striking scenic effects. The other—*Dido, The Clemency of Titus, Olga*—relies heavily on spectacle and much less on ideas. To the second group belongs the tragedy *Vladisan*,[26] written in 1784. Like so many of Kniazhnin's tragedies, this has a western plot adapted to Russian "history." Rather surprisingly, since the earlier *Olga* had already made use of this, Voltaire's *Mérope* is the source. The play has little to recommend it, but once more exhibits Kniazhnin's anti-classical side. Not as iconoclastic as *The Clemency of Titus,* it departs nevertheless from classical norms by having a chorus and making considerable use of spectacle (the chorus in the fourth act represents a crowd of "the people" armed with drawn swords) and an Ossianic atmosphere reminiscent of Ozerov's *Fingal.* The tomb of Plamira's supposedly murdered husband Vladisan is the most prominent feature of the scene; from it comes a deep groan at a climactic moment, and a "wanderer" emerges from behind it, who is Vladisan disguised, etc. There is also the very unusual feature, said to have appeared in only one Russian tragedy before this, of a small child on the stage—Vladisan's little son Velkar (Voltaire's Egisthe, but reduced from a youth to a child). Velkar is capable, despite his years, of some quite precocious declamation—he is similar in this to Mariamne's sons in Derzhavin's tragedy. The plot of the drama departs considerably from its Voltairean original: it is complicated by the fact that Vladisan has not really been killed by the tyrant Vitosar; and by the rivalry of the two monarchs for the love of Plamira (Voltaire's *Mérope*).

Another Voltairean tragedy served Kniazhnin as the model for his next drama, *Sophonisba* (c. 1787).[27] Here, of course, he had also the long series of other plays on this episode from Roman history, going back as far as Trissino in the sixteenth century (1515). *Sophonisba* is neither a spectacle play nor a play of ideas, that is, a vehicle for didactic political rhetoric, like *Rosslav.* As such, it is given rather scanty attention by Soviet scholars. It is, however, a much better tragedy than any of Kniazhnin's efforts since *Dido.* Like that earliest of his tragedies, *Sophonisba* is constructed on the most essential tragic situation, the conflict not of "right" and "wrong," or "reason" and "the passions," but of two rights. Just as in *Dido* Aeneas is "right" in obeying the divine behest to leave Dido and continue his mission to Italy, and equally Dido is "right" in her love for him and her demands that he stay with her; so in this play Scipio, the Roman general, loyal to his fatherland, is "right" in forbidding Sophonisba's marriage to Rome's ally Massinissa and demanding her as an ornament of a Roman triumph; Sophonisba is "right" in preferring to die rather than suffer such humiliation; and Massinissa is "right" in choosing to see his beloved dead rather than a Roman slave. The entire action of the play is on the private level, and Kniazhnin is very successful in his depiction of the emotional conflicts that develop.

Catherine II was, as has often been observed, her own "director of propaganda." When she was unable to find a compliant agent to inculcate in the public the ideas which she wished to see implanted, she took on the task herself. One of the ideas dearest to her was that Russia had always been throughout its history well and benevolently governed by its autocrats, and that whatever ills it had suffered had been the results of the selfish ambitions of its nobility. This idea she was particularly at pains to disseminate at a time when revolutionary disturbances in France seemed to threaten autocracy everywhere. In 1786 accordingly the St. Petersburg stage was honored by a production from the hand of the Empress herself, a drama in prose entitled *A Historical Presentation from the Life of Riurik.* The principal theme of this effort was the glorification of the traditional founder of Russia's autocratic form of government. The chronicles of Novgorod told of how that city was plagued by domestic dissensions until, in despair, the people sent abroad to the Varangians (Scandinavian Vikings) for a monarch to come and rule over them. Riurik answered the appeal, accepted the crown thus voluntarily proffered to him, restored order to Novgorod, and established the royal line that in theory continued in power until the usurpation of Boris Godunov. The chronicle told also, rather vaguely, of a citizen of Novgorod named Vadim who attempted to overthrow the foreign ruler, and was suppressed. In Catherine's *Presentation* Riurik is the benign despot, determined to promote the happiness of his adopted people who have confided their destinies to him, against whom an ambitious young kinsman, Vadim, raises a revolt with the object, not of restoring "liberty" to the city, but of himself taking over the power. Riurik's triumph over this selfish upstart is crowned by Vadim's repentance and voluntary submission.

Judging from Kniazhnin's dramatic works—and in this case, since his unpublished papers were all prudently destroyed after his death, there is no other way of judging—he had never been a republican by conviction or hostile to monarchy as such; the anti-tyrannical tirades put in the mouths of such characters as Svadel or Rosslav do not put in question the rights of a legitimate monarch, only the arbitrary abuse of monarchic power. It is possible that in his later life, perhaps under the influence of revolutionary ideas emanating from France, he may have come to a different view of things. It must, however, be remembered that it is a risky business to read into a dramatist's own mind ideas that his characters express in his plays. The good dramatist presents conflicts and their human consequences without taking sides; and he may indeed be objective enough to resolve such a conflict in a way quite contrary to his own private beliefs. Eighteenth century drama, however, was traditionally didactic (since Corneille), and in the hands of Voltaire had become little more than a vehicle for "enlightened" propaganda; and it is difficult to believe that in *Vadim of Novgorod,*[28] Kniazhnin was uttering sentiments entirely at variance with his own beliefs. That in doing so he was creating his own masterpiece but at the same time a drama which he must have been perfectly well aware could not under any conceivable circumstances be either published or staged, must argue in favor of the position that the tragedy does in fact represent Kniazhnin's own convictions. It would hardly otherwise have been written.

The play was composed in 1789, several years after Catherine's *Presentation from the Life of Riurik*. Kniazhnin died early in 1791; in 1793 the man who had been left as guardian of the poet's children discovered the manuscript among Kniazhnin's papers, and published the play among the *Complete Works*. One must marvel at the naivety of Chikhachev and of the publisher Glazunov, as well as at the laxity of Catherine's book censors on this occasion. The year was the very height of the French Revolution; Louis XVI had been executed, the guillotine was hard at work, and Catherine was in such a frenzy of horror at the developments that she was scarcely rational. The consequences could be readily foreseen. A copy of *Vadim* came into her hands; the play was not only, in her view, an impudent repudiation of her own carefully planned presentation of Novgorodian history, but even worse, a repudiation of the very principle of monarchy itself. The printed copies of the play were destroyed, and everyone concerned with its publication interrogated and punished. Kniazhnin himself was saved from a worse fate by his opportune death.

Vadim of Novgorod, like most of Kniazhnin's plays, has western models, although in this case for sentiment and wording rather than construction. Chief of these are Voltaire's *Brutus* and *La Mort de César;* the revolutionary drama *Spartacus* of Joseph Saurin (1706-1781) seems also to have contributed something.

Vadim is the most classical of Kniazhnin's tragedies—that is, it comes closest in its simple plot, political theme and lack of spectacle to the tragedies of Sumarokov. The two lines of development among Kniazhnin's tragedies have been noted; *Vadim* belongs with *Vladimir and Iaropojk* and *Rosslav*, but actually comes closer than either of them to the classical norm. A brief synopsis of the drama may clarify its position.

Act I. Two Novgorodian patriots, Prenest and Vigor discuss a secret meeting with Vadim, the Novgorodian general who has returned unannounced from a two-year campaign against the Swedes, during which time the city's turmoil has led to the "calling of the Varangians," and Riurik's acceptance, at the people's behest, of royal power. Vadim appears and with fiery speeches inspires the two young captains to undertake a plot to overthrow Riurik. Vadim promises his daughter Ramida to the one of the two who shall contribute most to the recovery of Novgorod's liberty. When Vigor leaves, Vadim assures Prenest that he is the more favored suitor.

Act II. Ramida discusses with her confidante Selena her love for Riurik and her coming happiness when Vadim returns and she can be married to the prince she loves. Selena warns her that Vadim is not likely to look with favor on his daughter's marrying a king, but Ramida believes his fatherly love will prevail. Riurik appears, and there is a tender love scene between the two. Riurik leaves to make preparations for the wedding. Vadim appears in disguise, and overwhelms his daughter with reproaches for her base love of a tyrant; she submits to his will, that she must give up her love, but demands death rather than marriage to a man whom she does not love and connivance in a plot against Riurik. Vadim's anger and contempt force her at length to swear obedience in everything. Prenest appears and is informed that Ramida is his; she merely says: "My duty is to be obedient to my father in everything." Vigor, unobserved, is witness of Vadim's words to Prenest, realizes that he is passed over in the competition for Ramida's hand, and vows vengeance.

Act III. Ramida mourns her sad fate with Selena; Riurik enters, and she turns away from him. He is astonished, and when she announces that all is over between them, Riurik believes that she loves another. His confidant, Izved, informs him that Prenest, who now enters, is the lucky rival. Riurik magnanimously congratulates Prenest on his good fortune, tells him that "everything is known"—that is, of course, about his engagement to Ramida. Prenest thinks from Riurik's words that the plot has been discovered, and inadvertently reveals that Vadim has returned and is hatching a plot. Riurik is thus forewarned, but refuses to take any action to arrest the plotters: he will meet their army in open battle. Prenest, left alone, ponders the means by which Riurik has learned of the plot—it must be that Vigor, his rival, has revealed it. At this moment Vigor appears, but when accused of treachery, indignantly denies it. He *is* Prenest's rival and enemy, and admits it; but only after Novgorod is freed will he yield to his private animosity and demand satisfaction.

Act IV. Riurik and Izved converse, and Riurik declares his determination to wipe the memory of Ramida from his heart. He will live for honor alone. Ramida enters, and in a conversation between them Riurik learns that she still loves him, but must obey her father's will. She proposes as the only solution to their dilemma that Riurik lay down the royal power—he may then be reconciled to Vadim. But this Riurik cannot do: he had reluctantly taken the power at the pleas of the strife-torn city, and it would be dishonorable to surrender it as though intimidated by Vadim's opposition. Ramida admits this: there is no way out of the dilemma. Izved summons Riurik to the battle; as he leaves, he begs Ramida, if he dies in the encounter, to shed tears for him. She replies: "When I have performed my cruel duties to my father, I shall shed for you not tears, but streams of blood!"

Act V. As Ramida soliloquizes, in suspense over the battle, Vadim is brought in, disarmed and a captive. He pleads with his daughter to procure him a sword with which to end his life and his shame. She refuses, but indicates that she is about to take her own life. Riurik enters, and magnanimously offers pardon and friendship, which Vadim indignantly refuses. Riurik then faces Vadim with his own services to Novgorod in having saved it from civil strife; he has been freely chosen by the people to rule over them, and has performed his duty scrupulously. He then takes off his crown, and appeals to "the people" who have assembled around the main characters: if it is their will, he will resign his power, and give the crown, if they wish, to Vadim. The latter refuses vehemently. "The people" show their will by kneeling in supplication to Riurik, and Vadim scornfully upbraids them as slaves. Riurik says to Vadim: "If you consider the power of a monarch deserving of punishment, see my justification in the hearts of the citizens. What answer have you for this?" Vadim's reply is: "Order my sword to be returned to me, and I shall answer!" The sword is returned, and Vadim then proclaims that he now has the means for reconcilement with his enemy: "you shall be satisfied, and the people, and my daughter, and I!" Strangely misinterpreting this announcement, Riurik seems to think that all is about to end happily. But Ramida, addressing herself to her father, who has begun again to doubt his daughter's fidelity, proclaims her obedience to his wishes and stabs herself. Vadim then plunges his sword into his own breast, and Riurik is left to mourn the loss of his love and this unjust reward for his own forbearance and virtuous conduct as ruler.

One may note that the tragedy observes the unities of place and time, and that the only hint of a sub-plot and a possible complication of intrigue, the jealous rivalry of Prenest and Vigor, is a dead end, and actually does not have any effect on the outcome of the drama. It is presumably introduced only in order to display the exemplary patriotism of the two rivals, who are able to put duty to their country above private concerns.

However it may be interpreted, *Vadim* is a tragedy in the most geniune sense, and the best of its kind in eighteenth century Russian literature. The influence of Corneille is very obvious, not surprisingly in a dramatist who translated four or five of that master's tragedies. Riurik's magnanimity is very reminiscent of that of Augustus in *Cinna,* though met with a different reception, and of Caesar in *La Mort de Pompée.* The uncompromising, fanatical passion of Vadim for Novgorodian liberty recalls the fierce Roman patriotism of the younger Horace in Corneille's tragedy of that name. It is notable that all the characters of *Vadim of Novgorod* are noble and magnanimous—there is no villain. Even Vigor, who is momentarily suspected of treachery, turns out to be as patriotic as his rival. The play might have been a melodrama, with absolute virtue pitted against absolute villainy (as in *Rosslav*); it is saved from this by the nobility of Riurik's personal character, which the drama emphasizes from beginning to end. In classical fashion the characters are "given," not developed; and being as they are, the outcome is inevitably tragic. Vadim is the fanatical champion of abstract "liberty," to whom the idea of monarchy in itself, regardless of the virtues of an individual monarch, is anathema; Riurik is a man of chivalric instincts and a high sense of honor, which forbid his taking the only possible way out of the dilemma— abdication. And Ramida is utterly dominated by the duty of unquestioning obedience to her father's will, regardless of the consequences to herself. There is, therefore, no "right" and no "wrong" in conflict here; the conflict is between the two "rights" which are irreconcilable.

Unquestionably the tragic power of the drama rests primarily on Kniazhnin's surprising portrayal of Riurik in attractive colors. What remains uncertain is the dramatist's intention in this portrayal; is this merely a dramatic device to save the piece from becoming a melodrama, and does Kniazhnin himself feel as Prenest does, that however virtuous Riurik may be, absolute power will inevitably corrupt him—"What hero in a crown has not been diverted from his path? Drunk with the poison of his own greatness, who among monarchs has not been corrupted in the purple? Autocracy ["Samoderzhavie"] is everywhere the creator of misfortune, ruins even the purest virtue, and by opening unhampered paths to the passions, gives kings freedom to be tyrants." This is of course the line which all Soviet critics take, and the magnificently rhetorical tirades which Vadim hurls at Riurik and at the servile Novgorodian people are always quoted as the play's high points. It may be wondered, however, whether this was indeed all of Kniazhnin's intention. Vadim is everywhere depicted as the utterly fanatical champion of the abstract principle of "liberty." To Riurik's reasonable description of the condition of Novgorod when he assumed the power, torn by factional strife and conflicting ambitions, Vadim has no answer, and one must assume that for him "liberty" is the one supreme value, even if accompanied by a political chaos that would poison all ordinary life. Perhaps it was Kniazhnin's purpose by thus driving his characterization to an inhuman extreme to underline the absolute transcendence of the idea of liberty; but if so, he would seem to have gone too far. To a sympathetic, but non-Marxist, observer it must inevitably appear that Riurik is a more admirable character than Vadim, just as it must appear to any modern reader of Corneille's *Horace* that that inflexible representative of Roman virtue, who is capable of murdering his sister because she mourned the death of her lover, is an inhuman monstrosity.

Concluding these remarks on Kniazhnin's tragedy in general, a few words must be said about his style. As indicated above, the majority of his tragedies belong in what may be called the "sentimentalist" direction, or at least exhibit a classicism that has been considerably contaminated by new influences. As regards his use of language, this is not so true. He writes in a quite standard Russian, without excessive Slavonicism. It is interesting to note that in *Vadim,* where the word "daughter" occurs quite frequently, this is usually the ordinary Russian "doch'," but that the Slavonic "dshcher'," which is of very frequent occurrence in older Russian tragedy, almost to the exclusion of its Russian synonym, appears occasionally, but always at the end of a line, where it is obviously used merely to furnish a rhyme. The understanding of Kniazhnin's tragic verse is almost never impeded by the use of an antiquated and non-Russian vocabulary; it is, however, rendered difficult very often by a contorted and unnatural word order. A relative pronoun, for instance, is very often placed at a considerable distance from the beginning of its clause; and hyperbaton is omnipresent, with words which belong grammatically together being arbitrarily separated, often with no metrical justification for this violence, but only in conformity with the poet's ill-conceived notion that this kind of perversion is a mark of "high style." In these respects, however, Kniazhnin is at one with his age; exactly the same sort of stylistic effects may be found in Derzhavin's dramas, at least in the dialogue, in marked contrast with the simplicity of the lyric passages. Not until Pushkin can a Russian tragedy be composed in a normal, undistorted language readily intelligible to every reader or listener, without losing the requisite tragic sublimity.

C. Late Classical Comedy

The great legislators of classicism, such as Boileau and La Harpe, decreed that like tragedy, the lesser breed of drama should have five acts, be in verse, and conform to the three unities. It should be designed not for the vulgar purpose of giving amusement for its own sake, but with the intent of correcting morals by showing vice in a ridiculous or disagreeable light. Thus the comedy would necessarily be peopled by two sharply differentiated sets of characters, the "positive" and the "negative," and the dénouement must show the positive character or characters triumphant, the negative brought to shame and grief. The language of comedy should be less pompous than that of tragedy, and might, as spoken by negative or minor characters, even be "low." In the practice of comedy, from Menander and his Latin imitators Plautus and Terence, the invariable basis of the plot was a love affair between two "positive" young people, temporarily threatened by some complication provided by the "negative" side.

For various reasons the prescriptions governing comedy were never as strictly observed as those laid down for tragedy. Molière himself, it may be noted, the acknowledged model of classical comedy, frequently trespasses against them; many of his comedies are written in prose; some of them have only one act; and at least one of them (Le Misanthrope) ends with the discomfiture of the principal "positive" character. In Russia Sumarokov, who aspired to be his country's Molière, never himself wrote a comedy in verse, nor in the traditional five acts. In fact, it was left to Kheraskov to compose the first Russian comedy in verse, with his Atheist (1761). Fonvizin, in his Korion (1764) has the honor of second place. Neither of these works, however, can be considered a "comedy" in any but the most formal sense. They

345

are tedious, lachrymose and devoid of humor, and were very properly ignored by a public which, as Lukin lamented, unaccountably preferred to be amused rather than edified by the stage. Fonvizin, as we have seen, returned to Sumarokov's practice of writing in prose with his comedies *The Brigadier* (c. 1768) and *The Minor* (1779).

The obstacle to composing a comedy in verse is of course the relatively realistic language which comic convention demanded. Generations of use had developed for the tragedy a lofty, conventional language, remote from the spoken word, which could be readily fitted to the requirements of the obligatory Alexandrine verse. Even rhymes in tragic verse are so often repeated as to become clichés; but the situation becomes vastly different when the "common" language, of a peasant servant, for example, or a bribe-taking *podiachii,* is to be represented. Most dramatists were unequal to the task; if they attempted it at all, their "verse" was wooden and halting, and dialogue was rendered painfully awkward, stultifying any kind of liveliness and naturalness. In *Korion,* it may be noted, Fonvizin attempted to use the "low" style with only one minor character, the peasant; his other characters, including the servant Andrei, speak a smooth, upper-class Russian, approximating to the language of tragedy, but with less of the artificial perversions of word order than the tragic poet would use. It took a considerable amount of practice before a degree of fluidity and naturalness could be achieved in the handling of verse in comedy. This required, among other things, a willingness to break the monotonous set speeches of characters in dialogue by interruptions that might divide an Alexandrine line, for example, into three or four fragments each given to a different speaker. One of the first dramatists who had an ear delicate enough to do this convincingly was Iakov Borisovich Kniazhnin. The perfect solution of the problem, however, never to be surpassed, belongs to the next century, to Griboedov's *Woe from Wit (Gore ot uma).*

1. Nikolai Petrovich Nikolev: The Self-Loving Poet

N.P. Nikolev (1758-1815) has been already encountered as the author of the comic opera *Rozana and Liubim* (1776) and the tragedy *Sorena and Zamir* (1784), as well as of numerous satires, epistles, and other non-dramatic verse. As a one-time pupil of Sumarokov Nikolev endeavored to show his mettle in all recognized classical genres. Besides his eight comic operas, he wrote three regular (that is, verse) comedies: *Nothing Ventured, Nothing Gained, or a Successful Attempt* (1774), in three acts; *The Self-Loving Poet* (1775), in five acts; and *Constancy Put to the Test* (1776), in three acts. Of these, the best is *The Self-Loving Poet.*[29]

Nikolev's relations with Sumarokov are rather ambiguous; in his early work he appears as an admiring and compliant pupil of the old classicist, and indeed throughout his career he never seriously deviated from the paths laid down by Sumarokov. Apparently, however, he found the master's personality both disagreeable and ridiculous, and in his comedy *The Self-Loving Poet* he makes merciless fun of Sumarokov's propensity to regard any other poet who ventured to write tragedy as a trespasser. The comedy was not produced until 1781, several years after Sumarokov's death in 1777, but was written while he was still alive, and when the young dramatist was only about eighteen years old. It is a remarkable piece for such an age.

Using the approved comic constructional technique, Nikolev derives both the complication and the solution of his comedy from character—in this instance, the absurd self-esteem of Nadmen (Sumarokov), a tragic poet who finds the efforts of all rival poets utterly worthless and despicable— even when he has not read them! The inevitable love affair which must be solved happily is between Nadmen's niece Milana and the young Chesnodum. The complicating factor is the fop Modstrikh, who is also in love with Milana and is an amateur versifier. Nadmen's character is exhibited first in his impatient encounter with Modstrikh and then, in a highly amusing scene in which Chesnodum, in spite of the frantic efforts of Milana and her servant Marina to prevent him, presents a tragedy of his composition to the old poet, who of course tears it to shreds and denounces the author as a presumptuous upstart, ignorant of the very elements of the poetic art. The conflict is resolved by the device of the two women, abetted by Chesnodum's clever servant Panfil, whereby Modstrikh is lured into presenting the unfortunate tragedy of Chesnodum to Nadmen as his own, thus bringing upon his head all the storm previously visited upon Chesnodum. The latter can then claim that he has only been acting as intermediary for an acquaintance; and Kruton, the young man's crusty and sensible father, can prevail upon Nadmen to bestow his niece in accord with her and Chesnodum's desires. As long as he is not a poet, the latter is an acceptable husband for Milana!

The comedy has a good deal of eighteenth century conventionality, especially in the characters of the two servants, who bear no resemblance whatever to any actual Russian servants, but have their ancestry in the *callidi servi* of Plautus and Terence. There is little lifelikeness in Chesnodum and his sweetheart, but they are a little more convincing than the usual young lovers of comedy. Nadmen himself, portrayed as he seems to have been, from life, is, in spite of the obvious exaggeration, a surprisingly multidimensional character. He is irascible and flies off the handle at the slightest provocation, and he is, of course, as his name indicates ("arrogance"), extremely conceited. But he also has a sardonic sense of humor, and in some of his utterances regarding the writing of verse makes remarkable sense. He is, for one thing, contemptuous of French affectation, as his first scene with Modstrikh displays. Nadmen has emerged from his study preoccupied with finding a rhyme for "rok" ("destiny"). He talks to himself first, then discovers Modstrikh, who greets him with the polite phrase "humble servant!"

Nad. *Rok? tok?*.... I've forgotten.... no rest for even a day. Surely the devil must have brought you here!

Mod. Me?

Nad. You, sir, you, stupidest of monsters. I've forgotten my verse because of your coming and because of your being my "humble servant." Don't ever set foot here again. Leave me, stupid!

Mod. *(in a foppish voice)* Wherefore this warmth?

Nad. Because you have jumped in, like a devil, from another world.

Mod. *(aside)* I would challenge him to a duel, I'd give him to understand... But unfortunately, my object—is his niece...

Nad. He's still here!

Mod. *(gently)* I'm here.... But do relax just a little!

Nad. *(with still greater anger)* I don't know on what account.... and what has undertaken.... What kind of being has undertaken to create you in the world? For what purpose give the world such a creation? The Furies, surely!.... Hell itself!.... But no, it was not savagery, but stupidity itself that produced you. You don't deserve to be compared even with an animal...

Mod. Not thus was I created... Monsieur is mistaken in this.

Nad. And moreover he calls me "monsieur," and entwines Russian words with French, as though I were just such an ass as he!

Mod. However, monseigneur! You are.... you are....

Nad. Will you get out! Will you leave me alone!

Mod. You are very rude, i' faith!

Nad. I'm rude, and you're a fool, I shall tell you two hundred times, if you've come with the object of driving me mad.

Mod. Fie! To attribute such rudenesses to me? What though I was formerly rude.... But, being in Paris....

Nad. In Paris you became still closer to an ass. There was a soul in you; now there's only vapor.

Mod. *(aside, growing angry)* Pfui! How his *façon* is old-fashioned for a *galant! (to Nadmen)*. Good-bye... But know, I don't forgive your insults.

Nad. And I, once rid of the twaddle, won't take vengeance on the twaddler. Are you satisfied with me? Go, sir... Good-bye.[30]

One further feature of the comedy deserves some mention, as an elementary bit of realism rather out of place amid the classical conventionality. In the fifth scene of Act II a drunken type-setter ("naborshchik") appears with a set of proofs for the poet. The scene has no connection whatever with the course of the plot, but seems only to have been introduced in order to clinch the identification of Nadmen with Sumarokov; in a correction which he makes on the proofs, Nadmen discourses on the proper spelling of "elegy," which was one of Sumarokov's pet obsessions. Nadmen tears up the proofs and dismisses the type-setter with orders for another set, properly corrected. Reluctantly he tips the type-setter, in spite of his avowed aversion to drunks, and then soliloquizes:

They're all spoiled.... Depravity is everywhere. They've no regard for anything, and there are no rules anywhere. Freedom is given to all tricks leading to destruction. There's rascality in the schools, there's rascality in the departments. The professors are rascals, and the judges are rascals. They all.... they all have serpents in their bosoms! They all

348

cherish weaknesses, they all fondle vices, and, in destroying usefulness, they have no pity for usefulness.... But enough of this.... Let's search out that verse the fool Modstrikh robbed me of.[30a]

2. Yakov Borisovich Kniazhnin: The Braggart; The Eccentrics

The tragedies of Kniazhnin (1740-1791) have already been discussed, as well as his comic opera *Misfortune from a Carriage*. This, his earliest in that genre, was produced in 1779. For several years, following its success, he continued to write comic operas: *The Soft-Drink Seller (Sbitenshchik)* (1783), with a plot similar to that of Beaumarchais' *Le Barbier de Seville; The Miser* (in collaboration), (1782); *Husbands, Suitors of Their Wives* (1784?); *Mourning, or the Widow Comforted* (1784) and *The Pretended Madman* (printed in 1787). Aside from *The Soft-Drink Seller,* which incorporates a good deal of the living Russian scene, these pieces have no great interest.[31]

Kniazhnin's first full-length verse comedy is *The Braggart (Khvastun),*[32] written in 1784 or 1785. It is a reworking, in Russian dress, of the French comedy *L'Important,* of David Augustin de Brueys (1640-1723). The plot of the comedy in brief is as follows. A minor nobleman, Verkholet, having squandered his small fortune, is plotting to marry Milena, the beautiful daughter of a well-to-do but stupid lady from the provinces, Chvankina. Milena, however, is in love with the honest young nobleman Zamir, and at the opening of the comedy has won over her mother to this marriage. The action begins with the arrival of Prostodum ("simple mind"), the old country-bred uncle of "the braggart" Verkholet. He first encounters Polist, Verkholet's rascally servant, who hoodwinks him into believing that Verkholet has become a very influential person in the capital, and that he, Polist, is now his secretary. Polist is in love with Marina, Milena's maid, but she has thoughts of making a match with a gentleman. When Verkholet appears and finds his uncle and Polist in conversation, he at once understands the situation and plays up to it; he assures the old man that he has just been made a count, and when an importunate tailor appears to demand his overdue bill, he is explained as a petitioner for a court position. Finally old Prostodum is induced to take on a position as "administrator" for his nephew (this position involves, among other things, paying his bills with a vague promise of future reimbursement), and to prented to be the uncle, not of the illustrious "count," but of his servant Polist. In this way, since Prostodum is a gentleman, his "nephew" also becomes one, and Marina agrees to marry him. The two servants then plot to dazzle Chvankina with the glamor of a count as son-in-law; the plot succeeds easily, for Chvankina (her name means something like "Mme Conceit") has always craved entrée into high society, and she at once promises her daughter to "the count." In order to get rid of Zamir, Marina puts on a dress of Milena's and arranges to have a conversation with Polist so that Zamir may overhear it, in which she alludes to her coming marriage with Verkholet. Zamir, a very irascible young man, is enraged at Milena's apparent infidelity. He has, however, already asked his father Cheston to come up from the country to make arrangements for his marriage. When Cheston arrives and learns the new developments, he counsels his son to give up such a fickle love and take active service as a soldier.

The crucial scene comes when Cheston encounters Verkholet; deferring to the wishes of his country neighbor, Cheston does not at first reveal his relationship to Zamir, "the count's" rival, and the braggart, hearing of Cheston's presence in the city, claims to know him and to have been instrumental, through his great influence at court, in procuring the elder man's present honorable position. When Cheston indignantly denounces this impudent falsification, Verkholet lamely admits that his protégé must have been another Cheston, and abruptly leaves with the excuse that he "is awaited at court." Of course Cheston, having been in this fashion apprised of Verkholet's real character, goes out at once and makes inquiries in town, and readily discovers the truth, that "the count" is an impostor who is desperately trying to marry Milena for her money. Cheston meets his simple-minded old neighbor Prostodum and learns that Verkholet has promised to obtain for him a position as "senator," and has even given him a self-signed patent to that effect! There is then an encounter between Milena and Zamir, and after the inevitable quarrel, the truth of Marina's deception is discovered, the lovers are reconciled, and all that remains is for Cheston to arrive on the scene, accompanied by Verkholet's creditors and the police, to unmask the fraud. Marina, discovering that Polist is after all not a gentleman, but a mere lackey, throws him over; Chvankina's eyes are opened to "the count's" intrigues and her consent readily won to the original betrothal of Milena to Zamir; and old Prostodum, realizing that he has lost his money as well as his senatorship, leaves the stage with the philosophical admission: "Well, I ate the mushroom!" i.e., "I asked for it!"

The plot follows the best comedy principle, of making everything depend on character, and not external circumstance. Actually, the vanity and gullibility of Chvankina contribute at least as much to the plot as the braggadoccio of Verkholet, and to this degree the name of the comedy is inappropriate; but all the complications arise from character—the simplicity of Prostodum, the irascibility of Zamir, the vanity and stupidity of Chvankina, the unscrupulous trickery of Polist, the empty-headed self-importance of Verkholet, and the honesty and good sense of Cheston. There is no *deus ex machina* who enters at the last moment to bring everything to a happy conclusion—Cheston is introduced early, and his intervention is very adequately motivated by anger at his son's misadventure with Milena and on his own part with the braggart's lies. The play has, of course, to end happily, in proper comedy fashion, but it might be suspected that in real life the forces of good would not have been so easily triumphant.

Unlike some of its predecessors (e.g., Kheraskov's *Atheist* or Fonvizin's *Korion*), *The Braggart* is a proper comedy, with amusing lines and situations, and with a good deal of incidental satire on the *mores* of Russian society—the traffic in government posts, the possibilities of money-making from selling recruits to the army, etc.—and of course, first and foremost, on the plague of "favorites" under Catherine's rule. That an empty-headed nobody like Verkholet might indeed become a count, or reach even higher status under an autocratic ruler who could, and did, raise many a nobody to nobility at the merest whim—and not only her lovers—becomes perfectly plausible, and must have given the comedy an immediacy which it would not possess in other times.

There is some didacticism in *The Braggart* of an overt sort, but nothing like the tedious moralizing of Starodum in *The Minor*. When Cheston lectures his son on forgetting his unfortunate love affair and assuming his duties as a gentleman in the service of his fatherland, he sounds momentarily like Starodum, and even like Menander in *Korion*. Cheston is as near as Kniazhnin gets to providing a raisonneur, as may be seen especially in his colloquy with Prostodum regarding that old simpleton's expected "senatorship." Cheston tries to make his old neighbor see that he hasn't the qualifications for such a post, but the latter, it appears, views a high government position only as affording the opportunity of appropriating his neighbors' property with impunity!

The characterization in *The Braggart* is, as indicated, the clue to the plot. This characterization, however, is flat, in the usual classical manner. Each person has certain given qualities, which are those that move the plot, but no others. Chvankina, for instance, is stupid and a social climber; if she has any other qualities, these are irrelevant to the plot, and accordingly ignored. We have noted that in *The Self-Loving Poet* Nadmen, being drawn from life, does have qualities—a glimmer of common sense where poetry is not concerned, a sardonic sense of humor, and the like—which do not contribute to the unfolding of the plot. There is nothing of the kind in Kniazhnin's comedy. Prostodum is doubtless the most convincing of the cast; he has been well described as an inferior reflection of Fonvizin's Skotinin, with the original's limited intelligence coupled with political ambition. He is, in any case, genuinely Russian. The same cannot be said for the two most active characters in the comedy, Marina and Polist. These "tricky servants" are straight out of Le Sage or Marivaux, and are not made any more Russian by occasional references to their village backgrounds, or the like.

As usual, the young lovers are the most pallid and unlifelike of all, despite Zamir's uncharacteristically hasty temper. He has, however, one curious trait that smacks a bit of sentimentalism, such as we shall see full blown in Kniazhnin's second comedy *The Eccentrics*. Zamir is, to be sure, given this trait not for the sake of verisimilitude, but as a device for solving the plot. In his conversation with Milena he reproaches her for playing him false while wearing the very dress which she wore when earlier she declared her love for him, and which he had for that reason begged her always to consider sacred! This is the gown, it appears, that Chvankina has given Marina for her expected wedding, and by this means the maid's masquerade is detected.

The naming of the characters is in the best tradition of the eighteenth century—that is, no one bears a name that might ever be encountered in real life—cf. Molière's Valère, Harpagon, Dorimène, Célimène, etc. These names are also, most often, "speaking names," such as are familiar also from English usage of the period, that is, they provide the audience with an instant clue to the bearer's character (cf. Sir Benjamin Backbite, Lady Sneerwell and Mrs. Candour, of *The School for Scandal*). Prostodum ("simple mind") and Chvankina ("Mme Conceit") have been mentioned; Cheston carries a suggestion of honesty ("chest'," "honor") and Milena of lovableness ("milyi," "beloved"). Polist probably carries a reference to the lackey's resplendent attire ("polistyi," "with broad coat-tails"). As for Verkholet, his name might be approximated as "high-flier" ("verkh," "the heights" and "letet'," "to fly"). Zamir is exceptional: his is the name of Nikolev's tragic Polovetsian hero, from *Sorena and Zamir,* which dates also from 1784.

The language of the comedy, even that of the lower-class characters and rustics, is standard Russian, spiced occasionally with slangy or popular expressions, such as Prostodum's "Well, I ate the mushroom!" already cited; or Cheston's reply to Chvankina (Act III, sc. vi) when she remonstrates with him over giving offense to Verkholet: "You don't know how powerful he is at court! You're sunk, forever!" to which Cheston simply says: "Ubila ty bobra," literally "You've killed a beaver!" i.e., "You've come a cropper!"

Kniazhnin's second (and last) five-act comedy in verse is *The Eccentrics (Chudaki),*[33] from 1790. Like its predecessor, and like most of the poet's tragedies, it has a western prototype, in this case *L'Homme singulier* of Destouches. The original is again thoroughly Russified.

The plot of the comedy is intricate, with some quite needless complications which are introduced purely "for laughs." The "chudaki" ("queer ones," "eccentrics") include the wealth Lentiagin, a smith's son, as he proudly avows, recently ennobled, who likes to consider himself a philosopher, and believes all men are equal; his nobly born and socially ambitious wife; their flighty and coquettish daughter Ulinka; and her mooning and sentimental lover Priiat, who lives in the dream world of eclogue and elegy. Vetromakh (his name means something like "windmill") is not so much eccentric as scheming; he proposes to marry the rich, though low-born, heiress Ulinka in order to pay off his large accumulation of debts. On the eccentric side, but entirely extraneous to the plot, are Trusim, whom the poet describes as "everybody's friend, deaf and lame; he delights in offering his services to everyone without their being requested." Such a gratuitous

352

service is his appearance with four absurd suitors for Ulinka, themselves certainly "queer"—a retired, but still litigious judge; a retired, but still bellicose Major; and two poets, Trompetin (from the word "trumpet"), a composer of bombastic odes, and Svirelkin (from "svirel'," "shepherd's pipe"), a writer of pastorals.

It appears at the outset of the comedy that each of the two principal suitors for Ulinka's hand has planted an advocate in the Lentiagin household: Vetromakh's former servant Vysonos ("nose-in-air") is now Mme Lentiagin's major-domo, while Prolaz (the name means something like "trickster") is Lentiagin's new lackey. These two servants, in addition to their masters' business, have concerns of their own with the Lentiagins: each is in love with the maid-servant Marina.

The action of the comedy begins with Lentiagin's "eccentric" behavior with his new lackey, whom he invites to sit down and "philosophize" with him, wearing a comfortable night-cap; Prolaz is even to address him as "ty" ("thou") instead of "vy" ("you"), and call him by his first name! The conflict is introduced when Mme Lentiagina discovers this appalling whim of her husband's, and upbraids him for his familiarity with a servant, but without the least result. Then Prolaz and Marina have a conversation, at the end of which the maid agrees to put in a good word for Priiat with her mistress.

This she does at the beginning of Act II, but finds that Ulinka rather favors the glamorous Vetromakh; it seems that Priiat is so shy that he has never even dared to approach her! Lentiagin's eccentricity is next displayed in a scene with his wife and Vetromakh, who is her choice for son-in-law. She has just informed the Frenchified fop that her own French is a little rusty, but her husband speaks it fluently; he is a little odd, however, and prefers Russian! He is, of course, of the highest nobility, with a lineage that goes back for a thousand years. Lentiagin indignantly gives the lie to both these allegations, and declares that his father was a smith! Vetromakh's aristocratic prejudice gets the better of his urgent need for cash, and he departs in disgust; Mme Lentiagina faints. After a futile scene with Trusim and his unasked "services," Prolaz puts in motion his intrigue whereby he hopes to bring the bashful Priiat and Ulinka together. He tells Lentiagin that he has a friend named Semen who has just the same egalitarian principles as his, and who would make a nice third for their philosophic discussions. Lentiagin tells him to bring his friend around, and retires to take a nap. It remains now to prepare Priiat for his part, which Prolaz attempts to do. The young sentimentalist exclaims: "So! I can already imagine the delight—how I shall always be sighing at her feet on the soft meadows, beside the brook and the flowers, as the innocent sheep browse not far away!" But there is one serious obstacle: Priiat is willing to assume disguise—but Semen! "A name how harsh to the ears! Wouldn't Philemon do better, or Tirsis, or Arsam—or what about Arkas?" Prolaz replies impatiently: "Gone off again into eclogue! Shall we have much more of this?" When he is informed that there are rivals for

Ulinka's love, Priiat, who has barely exchanged two words with his idol, says bitterly: "I see! Cruel Ulinka has been faithless!" Prolaz: "Once more the shepherd's pipe a-droning! I can't take it! Let's go to my quarters. Marina will be there. She and I are on your side—what have you got to fear?"

At the beginning of Act III the conflict, momentarily eliminated by Vetromakh's haughty refusal to consider a mésalliance with the grand-daughter of a smith, is renewed: Vysonos, who seems to be the manager of his master's almost non-existent finances, informs him that ruin is at hand if he doesn't marry an heiress—and besides, what about his contract for 8000 a year with his little French mistress Zhabot (from "jaboter," "to chatter")? Reluctantly Vetromakh accepts the inevitable. But his renewed decision to sue for Ulinka's hand comes to grief when Prolaz deliberately insults him with the object of getting himself beaten and thus bringing down Lentiagin's fury on the head of Vetromakh. The ruse succeeds, Lentiagin, who despises the Frenchified Vetromakh anyhow, is enraged at his effrontery in beating a favorite servant, and orders him out of the house. At this juncture the two sides in the conflict come into open collision: Mme Lentiagina appears and announces Vetromakh as their son-in-law to be, which her husband vehemently disputes. The plot then takes a completely unexpected turn, still motivated by Lentiagin's "eccentricity": he abruptly announces his lackey Prolaz as his chosen son-in-law! Thereupon ensues a scene in which the indefatigable "Mr. Fix-it," Trusim, fusses about as mediator to patch up the quarrel of husband and wife, which he apparently succeeds in doing until each party discovers that the other has not changed his mind in the least! The act ends with an irrelevant scene in which the two poets ingratiate themselves with Mme Lentiagina, in whose honor they promise to compose verses.

Act IV carries the plot toward its solution by some farce worthy of Molière. Prolaz introduces Priiat as "Semen" to Lentiagin, but the presence of his idol's father so overawes the young lover that he is utterly tongue-tied, and Prolaz has to answer Lentiagin's questions for him by ventriloquism! At last "Semen" bolts unceremoniously, and Prolaz hesitantly confides that he thinks his friend would be a better husband for Ulinka than he—he will be satisfied with Marina! Such philosophical self-abnegation overwhelms Lentiagin. Shortly after Prolaz, dragging after him the terrified Priiat, appears before Ulinka and Marina. Again the servant has to take the initiative in presenting his master's suit. Prolaz speaks for Priiat and Marina for Ulinka, until at length both bashful lovers can be brought to declare their feelings for one another in their own persons.

The device with which the conflict is finally resolved is one of Kniazh-nin's best inspirations. It arises quite naturally, it generates a delightfully humorous situation, and it affords a most reasonable and plausible means for unmasking the schemes of Vetromakh. That ardent suitor, in conference with his accomplice Vysonos, hits on an idea for getting rid of Prolaz, whom they both acknowledge as their really dangerous adversary. Vysonos will challenge Prolaz to a duel! He is not particularly happy over this prospect, but philosophizes to himself that if his opponent is as big a coward as he is, all may be well. Reluctantly he presents his challenge, and a farcical scene follows in which both parties alternately posture defiantly, and try to avoid the fight with the short swords which Vysonos has provided. After a good deal of verbal altercation they both decide that there has been enough duel; they can now "bind up their wounds"—and the best place to do this is in the tavern! Thither they adjourn: fighting has induced a great thirst in both. At the beginning of the last act Vysonos, very drunk and extremely talkative, encounters his mistress Mme Lentiagina, and inadvertently discloses all of Vetromakh's secrets to her—his debts, his desire to "marry money," and most of all, his French wench Zhabot, whom he is bound by contract to continue keeping, even if he marries Ulinka! After Vysonos has retired to sleep off his drunk, Mme Lentiagina meditates alone on her narrow escape from an adventurer. Her meditations are interrupted by the two ridiculous poets with their productions; they both begin with fulsome flattery of each other, which shortly develops into vituperation—a scene lifted almost bodily from Molière's *Les Femmes savantes.* Vetromakh then makes his appearance, accompanied by the Judge, whom Prolaz has induced to threaten him with suit from his creditors. Vetromakh turns confidently to Mme Lentiagina, as one who will stand as guarantor for his payment, but is stupefied to be angrily repudiated, with references to Zhabot! Accused of keeping a mistress, Vetromakh, unruffled, replies: "Why, Madame, is there any reason for getting into an argument over this? Can you be concerned with such a bagatelle? I made this contract—it's no great sin—so as not to forget the French language!"

The final scene of the comedy brings the whole cast together: Ulinka kneels before her mother, evidently expecting to be told that she must marry Vetromakh; the latter, despite the previous disclosures, evidently still expects to be the lucky bridegroom; Priiat, faint-hearted as usual, is in an agony of apprehension that Vetromakh may after all win Ulinka; and Lentiagin, appearing after his nap, is more than a little confused over his wife's sudden change of heart and over the transformation of "Semen" into Priiat. But Mme Lentiagina, united now with her husband, proclaims Priiat the lucky man, and Vetromakh retires, discomfited, muttering: "Why did I demean myself by pleading?" But in the "happy ending" it appears that even Vetromakh may come off better than he deserves—the Judge, who has just been threatening to prosecute him in behalf of his creditors, now undertakes—for a fee, naturally—to defend him against them! Prolaz ends the comedy with some "philosophical" remarks addressed to the audience: "You'll see, if you're not too much a fool, that everyone, great or small, is a queer one ["chudak"] , and folly, presiding over every man's birth, blesses us all to play the fool."

That this plot is improbable and absurd scarcely requires demonstration; such is the ordinary nature of eighteenth century comedy plots. Once this initial absurdity is accepted, everything falls neatly into place, and the situations are developed without forcing from the traits of the individual characters. The essential conflict, which is between the two Lentiagins, is an aspect of their completely different "philosophies of life": Mme Lentiagina's pride of birth and respect for aristocracy, and her husband's eccentric egalitarianism. It is, however, the intrigues of the servants Prolaz and Marina which keep the plot moving and bring about the dénouement. And each of these is in turn set in motion by the "queerness" of his or her master or mistress: Marina by the necessity of saving the flighty Ulinka from the folly of marriage with Vetromakh, and Prolaz by the simple inability of Priiat, in his romantic dream world, to do anything for himself.

By comparison with the quite flat characterizations in *The Braggart,* those in *The Eccentrics* are surprisingly multi-dimensional. Lentiagin's is the most subtly developed. One trait of his character is proclaimed by his name, which derives from "lentiai," "a lazy," or "easy-going fellow." Lentiagin likes to take naps, and to loll around the house in slippers, dressing-gown and night-cap; in fact he has such an aversion to putting on formal clothes that the first thing we hear of him is Prolaz's complaint that it takes him five hours to dress—more time than a coquette would need! Of course this trait of his is in no way connected with his quixotic notions of social equality, which are the source of the comedy's plot. No more is his rather contradictory behavior toward servant and daughter; Prolaz he spoils in the most eccentric fashion, and at the same time issues orders for his daughter to marry the man of *his* choice without a moment's consultation with her, in the tradition of the Russian "household tyrant" ("samodur"). Priiat is likewise given characteristics, not indeed contradictory, but only one of which contributes to the plot—extreme bashfulness, and romantic sentimentalism. Mme Lentiagina, too, is not merely the seedy aristocrat dazzled by the surface glitter of such a representative of high society as Vetromakh. She is also a generally submissive and loving wife, and a good mother, who is horrified at her daughter's narrow escape from the schemes of the adventurer.

Professor Lidia Kulakova has suggested very plausibly (in her introduction to the *Selected Works* of Kniazhnin in the "Poet's Library" edition[34]) that the dramatist had learned this unclassical technique of character elaboration from Carlo Goldoni, the great Italian comedy writer, three of whose plays Kniazhnin translated. The suggestion is very attractive, for no French dramatist of the eighteenth century comes even close to the extraordinarily well rounded and life-like characterizations of Goldoni.

Even, however, with his new technique of character depiction, Kniazhnin does not succeed in fixing his people unmistakably in place and time. The upper-class characters have a vaguely Russian appearance, to be sure, and Vetromakh is chided by Lentiagin for his habit of barbarizing his native language with French; but Gallomania has been an habitual object of ridicule and satire at least since Sumarokov, and there is nothing like the bit in this picture of it that Fonvizin provides in *The Brigadier*, precisely because in that play it is projected against a wholly Russian background. The Brigadier and his wife and the Councillor and his wife could not be imagined coming from any other milieu than the Russian provinces; but it would not be hard to imagine the Lentiagin family as non-Russians. This defect of national color is of course particularly glaring, as usual, in the lower-class characters, Prolaz and Marina, who are unimaginable as Russian servants.

One of Kniazhnin's quite extraordinary innovations in this comedy is the treatment of the pair of young lovers. Young lovers may often be, in real life, comic and ridiculous—but never in classical comedy! The young man's despairing utterances over parental opposition, his mistress's inconstancy, or whatever it is which momentarily stands in the way of his blissful union with his love are always taken seriously. But not here! The pastoral and elegiac clichés of which Priiat delivers himself are a spoof of these varieties of sentimental verse, and Priiat's sentimental attitudinizing is highly ridiculous. As if this were not enough, the one love scene which Priiat and Ulinka are allowed is pure farce—the lover is so bashful that he can't even declare himself, but must be helped out by his servant! This does not, however, mean, as Kulakova seems to imply, that the comedy lacks a sympathetic hero or heroine. To the contrary, an audience must surely react with particular indulgence toward a pair of lovers as helpless and ridiculous as these two.

Of the language of the comedy much the same may be said as of its predecessor. The Russian is the standard upper-class variety, even when spoken by the servants, and is varied only by the Frenchified jargon of the fashionable Vetromakh, the sentimental moonshine of Priiat, the Judge's legalese and the Major's military vocabulary. But even these varieties have the effect of printing each individual's speech with the mark of his character— artificially and conventionally, it is true, but still unmistakably.

A blemish in the comedy has been noted in passing—the totally needless group of characters headed by Trusim. They dash in and out of the action, occasionally with some slight effect on the course of events (e.g., the Judge's threat of bringing suit against Vetromakh) but for the most part only to provide comedy, which is crude enough (e.g., the Major's preparations to "storm" Ulinka as though she were a fortress!). Satire of the military, legal and literary professions is neither a novelty nor pertinent here.

3. Vasily Vasilievich Kapnist (1758-1823): Iabeda

Classical comedy is often provided with such subdivisions as "comedy of manners," "comedy of character," "comedy of intrigue," etc., according

357

to the prevailing emphasis in the piece, although obviously such subdivisions overlap and critics may disagree as to the proper placing of many comedies. Is Beaumarchais's *Le Barbier de Séville* a "comedy of character" (Figaro) or a "comedy of intrigue"? Is Molière's *Les Femmes savantes* a "comedy of manners" or a "comedy of character"? The classification is of course really unimportant, and most probably never consciously entered the mind of the author of the play. One category of comedy which seems to have become more prominent in the course of the eighteenth century than it had been in the seventeenth is the "satirical comedy." Such, for example, is Lesage's *Turcaret.* Comedy as satire is certainly not an innovation—one may think of Aristophanes's *Clouds!*—but more commonly the satire in the earlier classical period is incidental and not the main business of the drama. Thus, in Kniazhnin's *The Braggart* there is a great deal of satire on rustic gullibility, unscrupulous "nobility" and the like, but the play's principal emphasis is not on the unmasking of these vices. When we come to Kapnist's famous *Iabeda* (*Chicane* is the usual, not very satisfactory, translation) the case is entirely different. The character drawing is realistic, convincing, and thoroughly repellent; the construction of the plot is neat and, except for the implausible "happy ending," properly developed from the data of character without external intervention, etc.; but the comedy cannot be regarded as either a "comedy of character" or a "comedy of intrigue." Neither is it a "comedy of manners"; the savagery of the picture of judicial misdoing is entirely out of tone with the light, ironic handling of society's foibles in a proper *comédie des moeurs.* There is a grim seriousness about Kapnist's "comedy" that links it with Molière's great satiric masterpieces. The spectator of Tartuffe's hypocrisy or of Krivosudov's mishandling of justice is more likely to be frightened than amused.

Kapnist, whose principal literary production is lyric poetry, and who will be considered in detail in that connection, began his career with a *Satire— First (and Last)*, which won him great unpopularity from those satirized. He had some unpleasant experiences with the law and apparently learned involuntarily at first hand the numerous fashions in which a perfectly just case could be twisted by an unscrupulous litigant abetted by corrupt judges and assessors. The comedy *Iabeda*[35] was written in 1791 and published in 1798, under Emperor Paul. It could obviously have hoped for neither publication nor stage presentation under Catherine, who did not care to have the wholesale corruption of her "benevolent" reign so pitilessly exposed. Unlike Kniazhnin's and Nikolev's comedies, Kapnist's has no foreign model. The subject and the characters are Russian through and through; moreover, they are neither abstract nor conventional, as classical comedy demanded, but highly individualized and bound to a single time and place.

A fairly detailed résumé of the comedy is required. In externals it is entirely classical: it is in verse; there are five acts; the unities of time, place and action are duly observed; there is the requisite love affair to serve as the

358

conventional center of the action, even though this takes a secondary place in the development. The "decencies" are maintained, as virtue triumphs and vice is punished, artifical though this dénouement may seem.

Act I. The young hero of the comedy, Major Priamikov ("priamyi," "straight") comes to the house of Judge Krivosudov ("krivoi," "crooked" and "sud," "judgment") and meets there an old acquaintance and friend of his father's, Dobrov ("dobryi," "good"), who is the Clerk of the Civil Court ["povytchik"] . In a conversation between the two the exposition is skillfully given. Priamikov has a law-suit on his hands—Pravolov, a retired assessor and land-owner (his name comes from "pravo," "law" or "right" and "lovit'," "to seize") is suing him for possession of the estate left by the young soldier's father. Priamikov is sure of the rightness of his case and is at first inclined to treat the suit quite lightly—but Dobrov opens his eyes by describing Pravolov as a most notorious and unscrupulous artist in legal chicanery ["iabeda"] ; moreover, the Civil Court, where the case will be tried, is utterly corrupt— and he describes Krivosudov, the President, as a notorious bribe-taker, and then the members of his court: Bulbulkin, a drunk (his name comes from the gurgling sound of liquor being poured from a bottle), Atuev (from "atu," the hunter's "halloo!"), who is a passionate hunter, Radbyn (from the phrase "rad by"—"(I'd be) glad—"), a stupid stammerer who can never get out an intelligible sentence, and Parolkin (from the French *parole*, as used in cards), an inveterate gambler. The secretary Kokhtin (from "kogti," "claws") is a very skilled shyster who can turn the law inside out, and the Procurator, Khvataiko (from "khvatat'," "to grab") lives up to his name. In other words, Priamikov's case, however meritorious, has little chance of winning. This is the more so, as Pravolov is about to become Krivosudov's son-in-law! This brings up another side to the conflict: Priamikov has met Krivosudov's daughter Sofia at her aunt's in Moscow, and is in love with her. He intends to ask for her hand. He is surprised to find that the Court is actually in Krivosudov's house—the court building has burned down, and this is the temporary arrangement. He also learns that today is Krivosudov's name-day. By these clever and plausible devices the author contrives to keep all the action in one house (unity of place), and to give the opportunity of showing the drunken revel of the court members later on, as they celebrate Krivosudov's name-day with the liquor supplied by the plaintiff.

Anna, Sofia's maid, enters, is surprised and pleased to see Priamikov, and reassures him on the score of Sofia's affection. Sofia herself appears, and the lovers have a short scene in which Priamikov tells Sofia that he intends to ask for her hand, and she expresses hope that he will succeed. Krivosudov himself enters, and Priamikov explains how he met Sofia, and makes a formal offer of marriage. The Judge does not reject him outright, but promises an answer later, after he has consulted his wife. Priamikov leaves. Dobrov tries to put in a good word for Priamikov, and then presents a docket of cases that have been long pending, and which should be settled. From Krivosudov's replies it is apparent that they will not be, since the requisite palm-greasing has not been done. Finally the Judge drives out the importunate Dobrov, has a short soliloquy, and the scene is invaded by Krivosudov's wife Fekla, the shyster Naumych, who is a confidant and underling of Pravolov's, and Pravolov's servant Arkhip, who staggers in with baskets of food, drink, and other presents, ostensibly sent in honor of the Judge's name-day by his prospective son-in-law. After Naumych and Arkhip have left, Krivosudov tells his wife of Priamikov's offer of marriage. Fekla indignantly dismisses the idea: Pravolov, who has sent her some dress material, is her choice, and it is evident that Fekla rules the Krivosudov household.

Act II. Naumych is a shyster who is a trusted agent of Pravolov's. In the first scene of the second act the two discuss some arrangements in the making for the suit with Priamikov. Naumych, it appears, has, with Pravolov's money, bribed each of the assessors with various gifts; there remains only the President of the Court himself. In the course of the conversation reference is made to several other extremely shady doings of which Pravolov is party, including one murder. The matter of Pravolov's marriage to Sofia comes up, and Naumych asks him if he really intends to marry this little country simpleton. "Of course not," is the contemptuous response; Pravolov will wait only until the Priamikov suit is favorably decided, and then break off the engagement. Kokhtin, the Court Secretary, enters: his function is to collect the laws that the case will involve. He has combed the various codes and brought together all the pertinent laws and decrees (it must be remembered that at this date Russia had only the *Ulozhenie* of 1649 as legal basis, and a vast deal of subsequent, often contradictory, enactment). But Kokhtin has brought very good news that should decide the Priamikov case at once in Pravolov's favor. The will of the elder Priamikov states that the property is to go to his only son, whose given name is Fedot—but Priamikov's given name is Bogdan! Actually Fedot (Greek *Theo-dotos*) and Bogdan (Russian "Bog-dan," "God-given") mean exactly the same thing, and are interchangeable—but the law will not take this into account. Pravolov is overjoyed and gives Kokhtin a reward, which Anna, entering at this time with news that the dinner guests have arrived, sees. Fekla enters and effusively thanks Pravolov for the presents, then leaves to get dressed for the party. Pravolov then outlines his "case" to the Judge, and the reasons why it should be settled in his favor. Although Krivosudov keeps reiterating that the suit is "delo plokhovato," "a pretty bad business," he is finally convinced of the rightness of Pravolov's case when the latter generously offers to advance the Judge the 3000 rubles that he needs to buy a village he has his eye on! In the sixth scene of the act the name-day guests arrive: they are the four members and the secretary of the court, and the Procurator Khvataiko. Pravolov goes around individually to the members and asks if each is satisfied with the "present" he has received—some Tokay for Bulbulkin, some hunting dogs for Atuev, a carriage for Khvataiko and a repeating watch for Parolkin.

After some general conversation, all the guests march out to the dining room for the grand dinner.

Act III. Arkhip and Naumych open the scene, as the servant puffs in with huge baskets of wine for the party—another gift of Pravolov. He leaves, and Anna and Sofia enter and begin to set up card tables and distribute the bottles. Anna repulses some impudent attempts of Naumych to kiss her, but is reproved by Fekla, who enters at this time. She wants to do everything to conciliate her future son-in-law Pravolov. When Anna has left, Fekla confronts her daughter: she is certainly going to marry Pravolov. The girl falls on her knees and begs for any other fate, but is sternly rejected. The guests, pretty well in their cups, now enter from the dining room and begin to play cards, conversing briskly all the while. Pravolov starts to brief his partners on his suit, and at this moment Priamikov enters. He is coldly received—he has, of course, not been invited to the party, but he has come, out of politeness, to congratulate Krivosudov on his name-day. Fekla is very rude to him, and he gets into a noisy argument with Pravolov. Finally, losing patience, he takes his rival aside and threatens him with physical damage if Pravolov dares to marry Sofia—the suit doesn't so much matter. He leaves at the end of the scene, and the court members express their unanimous opinion that Pravolov is in the right and the rude boor Priamikov in the wrong. Sofia's father orders her to sing a song to entertain the guests, and she goes out and returns with a harp. Her song is a lyric of which the refrain reiterates that "happiest of all in the world is the man who lives with justice." These sentiments are not much appreciated, and when Sofia leaves, Khvataiko strikes up his song, which begins: "Take—there's no great art in this! Take whatever it's possible to take. Why else were hands hung on you, if it was not to take?" The card game, meanwhile, has been going on, and it appears that Naumych, with Pravolov's money, has been paying everyone' debts. By this time the guests are all immoderately drunk, and at last they all leave; Fekla and Anna, one on each side, help Krivosudov out and to bed.

Act IV. Anna and Sofia begin the scene; it is the morning after the name-day party, and Anna asks her mistress why she is up so early. Sofia replies that she hasn't been able to sleep all night, with the horrid thought of Pravolov in her mind. Anna tries to induce her to refuse her parents' choice point-blank, but she is a well brought-up girl, and can't bring herself to this. Anna ironically outlines to her the kind of life she will lead with Pravolov. Priamikov comes in, anxious to get an answer from Krivosudov. The latter enters, with Fekla, and Fekla with extraordinary coarseness and rudeness dismisses him and his suit, while Krivosudov tries to get a word in and is contemptuously shut up by his wife. Left alone with her, Krivosudov protests her behavior—after all, Priamikov had come with good intentions: he had announced that he had heard rumors that denunciations of Krivosudov's legal decisions had been received by the Senate, and he wanted to warn the Judge. Fekla is supremely contemptuous—as if anything could be pinned on them! And how could Priamikov have any such knowledge? It is an obvious ploy for favor in the decision of his suit. Krivosudov, however, is considerably alarmed and mentions several cases which might have got to the Senate and could cause trouble. Fekla dismisses them all and accuses him of being a coward. Kokhtin and Naumych enter; the latter brings a letter from Pravolov. When Krivosud opens it, bank notes fall out—they are payments of gambling debts, Naumych hastens to say. Kokhtin brings a legal document, already drawn up, which contains the court's decision that Pravolov has won the suit—although, of course, no "hearing" has yet been officially held. Krivosud confides to Kokhtin the rumor of the Senate's intervention, but is reassured: the news, brought by Priamikov, is certainly only a ruse for him to gain the case. Fekla calls her husband a fool and a coward for even thinking twice of the matter.

Act V. Anna and Dobrov come in to straighten up the "court room," which is littered with bottles. They hide these under the "red cloth" which covers the court table—a symbolic act, as their words indicate. The "court" assembles, all with hangovers. Dobrov, as clerk, proposes several cases, previously mentioned in Act I, which are all dismissed untried. He comes to the Priamikov case, and reads off the prosecutor's deposition. He then begins the defendant's deposition, which he reads intelligibly. Kokhtin grabs the paper from him, alleging that he is unable to read properly, and himself reads it out with all the pauses in the wrong places, so that the document is quite unintelligible. In the meanwhile, the assessors have discovered the bottles under the table, some of which are still full, and have begun drinking and carrying on conversation, paying no attention to the reading. Krivosud calls for a vote on the case—and it is, of course, in Krivolov's favor. The members of the court thereupon sign the already prepared document. The Procurator Khvataiko enters, and mentions that Pravolov is in the vestibule, waiting to know his fate. He is brought in and congratulated on his success. At this point Dobrov enters with a packet which he hands to Khvataiko; it has just been delivered from the capital. Khvataiko begins to read: it is an order for the immediate arrest of Pravolov, against whom many complaints have been made. He must be put in prison until the matter has been investigated. Pravolov falls on his knees and pleads for mercy, but Khvataiko, whose own security is involved, can offer him none. Pravolov runs out, followed by the Procurator in hot pursuit. In the ensuing confusion Krivosudov opens another packet addressed to him, and discovers that the Civil Court, against which complaints have also been made, is to undergo a strict investigation. While all the members react in horror, Fekla enters and tries to find out what the trouble is. Dobrov finally tells her, and she is very indignant: surely there are thieves in more places than just the Civil Court! And what business is it of the Senate? Krivosudov reproaches his wife: it is all her fault that he hadn't heeded Priamikov's warning. Priamikov himself now appears: he has heard the "bad news," and comes to offer his condolences—and to repeat his offer of marriage to Sofia; now that Pravolov is in prison, he is out of the running. Fekla, realizing at last that the game is up, humbly accepts the offer, and the play ends with Dobrov expressing some hope that perhaps, after all, the Judge and his associates may be able to slip through the Criminal Court—and in any case some general amnesty may rescue them!

It is perhaps significant of the anti-classical trend toward realism in this comedy that some, at least, of the names are genuine and such as might be borne by real people—Sofia (which, of course, has been used quite frequently before, e.g., in *The Minor*), Anna, Arkhip, Naumych, Fekla. Also marking a decided break with classical tradition, there is little or no overt didacticism in *Iabeda*, certainly nothing to compare with the tedious moralizing of Starodum in *The Minor*. The nefarious doings on stage certainly require no auctorial raisonneur to demonstrate or denounce them.

The characterization of the Judge, his wife, the assessors, the Procurator, and the rest of the "negative" portion of the cast of *Iabeda* is exaggerated, of course, but realistic and lifelike to a degree approached only by the Prostakov family of Fonvizin's *The Minor*, in all of Russian eighteenth century comedy. As usual, the "positive" characters are far less distinctive: but Priamikov is quite different from the usual namby-pamby young lover, when he grabs Pravolov and in a savage whisper assures him that he will cut off his nose and ears if he doesn't give up Sofia! Exceptionally there is really no intrigue (in the dramatic sense, that is—there is plenty of the legal kind!) in this comedy, and consequently the servants play no major part in the action; Anna acts only as her mistress's confidante, while Priamikov is not even provided with a man-servant to be Anna's husband in the happy finale! The peasant Arkhip is an entirely secondary figure, with no plot connection, yet very sharply portrayed, with a genuinely rustic speech, quite different from the conventional "peasant dialect" of most classical comedy, with its endless use of the *-sta* and *-ka* suffixes, supposed to be typical of country talk.

The verse is superbly well handled, with some really extraordinary *tours de force*, such as the general conversation during the card game. Here, in a perfectly natural fashion, bids are made, debts reckoned up, scandal recounted, Pravolov's case discussed, etc., with the Alexandrine line often broken into almost unrecognizable fragments. Nothing like this will be seen again until Griboedov's *Woe from Wit*.

Note has been made of the skillful way in which Kapnist contrives to observe the unities: all the action takes place in one room—the "court room" of Krivosudov's house, because the official court-house has burned down! And all the action takes place within the period of twenty-four hours, even though a night elapses between Acts III and IV. The third unity is absolute: there is only one action, the law-suit and the attendant chicanery, although from a formal point of view the love affair of Priamikov and Sofia is the

363

center, which is first threatened and finally resolved happily by the course of the law-suit. The one exceptionable feature of the play's construction is the ending. The intervention of the Senate has all the effect of a *deus ex machina*, unexpected and unmotivated; it is, moreover, at least as implausible as the abrupt appearance of the King's officer to arrest Tartuffe and restore Orgon's property to him at the end of Molière's play. Such forcing of events serves in both cases only the more sharply to focus audience attention on the grim reality.

Despite its very considerable merits, *Iabeda* fails of being an altogether satisfactory piece. The reasons for this are two-fold: in the first place, it is not very funny—the spectacle of a gentleman being legally defrauded of his father's estate by an unpalatable gang of rascals has little that is amusing. In this respect, incidentally, Gogol's *Inspector General,* which is often compared with *Iabeda* and evidently owes much to it, is greatly its superior; Gogol is funny, even when at his most caustically satirical. But in the second place, it is difficult for a modern reader or audience to comprehend all the nuances of the comedy because—fortunately—the background of the Russian eighteenth century legal system (or lack of system) is entirely unfamiliar, and has to be laboriously explained in foot-notes. The judicial system itself, the functions of the several officials, as well as the existence of an antiquated, disorganized and contradictory body of "law," in which diligent search would be sure to find justification for nearly anything, are beyond the grasp of a modern reader, whether Russian or western. The language too, which of course reflects the realities of the time, is often inaccessible, full of obsolete legalese, when not, as in Fekla's case, a doubtless faithful, but often unintelligible transcript of the vulgate of the urban merchant class, from which she and her husband appear to have only recently emerged to the verge of respectability. For these reasons a play that could very probably, with discreet modernization and cutting, be very effective on the stage, remains buried in little-read anthologies.

Probably discouraged by the impossibility of producing or even printing such a play as *Iabeda,* Kapnist did not try his hand again with a comedy. His later works, surprisingly different from his satire and the comedy, are melancholy and sentimental elegies, odes, and the like. Excellent as these are in their kind, they show no trace of his magnificent satirical talent. *Iabeda,* however, stands directly in the line of comic development between *The Minor* and *Woe from Wit,* with Gogol's *Inspector General* and some of Ostrovsky's merchant comedies at the nineteenth century end of the line.

4. Ivan Andreevich Krylov (1769-1844)[36]

Ivan Krylov belongs mostly to the nineteenth century, and of his quite voluminous literary heritage the precious, indeed immortal, portion is the collection of *Fables,* which belongs entirely to the nineteenth century. He did, however, have a literary apprenticeship in the age of Catherine the Great, and his comedies, while of quite uneven quality, merit at least consideration for their serious effort to replace classical abstractness with a genuine Russian background.

Krylov was the son of a poor army officer who had reached gentry rank by working up to a captaincy, but had no estates. Ivan was obliged at the tender age of nine to begin earning money to support his then widowed mother and his younger brothers and sisters. As a result of this necessity, he never had the opportunity to obtain any formal education; but by avid reading and making use of chance acquaintances as tutors, he was able to pick up a good deal on his own, in particular a reading knowledge of French and German, to which he later added Italian and possibly English. As he himself confesses in some autobiographical accounts, he had a mania for writing, and filled every available scrap of paper with his scribblings. His first attempt at comedy was written at the age of fifteen; he was twenty when, in 1789, he launched a periodical to which he was in all probability the sole contributor—the *Spirits' Post (Pochta dukhov)*—which we will consider in another connection. Two years before this he had given up his bureaucratic position in the Justice Department to take service in the Mining Department, the head of which, P.A. Soimonov, was also director of the court theater. A year later, in 1788, Krylov quarreled violently with Soimonov, and also with the leading dramatist of the day, Iakov Borisovich Kniazhnin, who became the butt subsequently of some of the young satirist's most vicious attacks. In the years 1788-1801 Krylov held no post in the government, but attempted, with very poor success, to make a living as a professional writer. After the first journalistic venture in 1789 he joined with three other men—the writer A.I. Klushin and the actors I.A. Dmitrievsky and P.I. Plavilshchikov—to form a publishing company, which in 1792 put out a regular periodical called *The Spectator (Zritel'),* and after its demise, *The St. Petersburg Mercury* (1793). Neither of these ventures proving a success, and entry into the theatrical world effectively shut for him as a result of his intemperate attacks on Soimonov and Kniazhnin, Krylov left the capital for private service, and for several years wandered widely through Russia, and by contacts with all classes of commoners, acquired the unsurpassed command of the spoken language which his *Fables* manifest. It was only after the publication of his first collection of *Basni* in 1809 and the relative success of his last two comedies, *The Fashion Shop* and *A Lesson for Daughters* (1807) that entrée into aristocratic literary circles was at last accorded Krylov; he was by birth a *raznochinets,* and always felt himself to some extent an outsider among the gentry, toward whom he harbored a hostility and resentment which found expression in some extremely sharp satire. The picture of Krylov often given in histories, as a genial, simple-hearted fellow, with a peasant's sly sense of humor and ingenuous affability is what one might describe as "a type characterization," attributed also—and also wrongly—to La Fontaine, and derived ultimately no doubt from legends about Aesop, the first fabulist! It is entirely false as applied to Krylov, who was pushing, self-assertive, thin-skinned, sarcastic, quarrelsome and a holder of grudges.

The earliest of Krylov's dramatic attempts is the *Kofeinitsa,*[37] written in 1783-84, when the author was fifteen! This is a three-act comic opera, centering around a conniving old woman who reads the future and discovers hidden secrets by means of coffee grounds (the *kofeinitsa*). The flimsy plot is the habitual eighteenth century comic opera cliché: the peasants Peter and Aniuta, who belong to an empty-headed noblewoman with the revealing name of Novomodova, are lovers, but a villainous bailiff ["prikazchik"] has marked Aniuta for his prey, and tries to rid himself of Peter by suborning the *kofeinitsa* to accuse him of the theft of a dozen of his mistress's new silver spoons, which the bailiff himself has actually taken. Mme Novomodova threatens to send Peter as a recruit to the army, but Aniuta's father and mother scratch together enough money to buy him off from this dire fate; the mistress accepts the money, but plans to sell Peter none the less to a recruiting trader. These rascally schemes all come to naught when the *kofeinitsa* demands six of the stolen spoons as her payment, the bailiff is forced to disgorge them, and Mme Novomodova walks in while the spoons are being handed over. The bailiff promptly takes Peter's place as a recruit, and the lovers are united.

There is a rudimentary bit of characterization in the completely heartless and cynical mistress, who has no scruples about enriching herself at the expense of her peasants, and of going back on her pledged word. She is a thoroughly nasty and unpleasant person, and since she, the fortune-teller and the bailiff—all "negative" characters—occupy most of the scenes most of the time, the effect of the little opera is anything but "comic." This would perhaps account for its fate. Krylov sold the script to a certain Breitkopf for 60 rubles worth of books; the buyer was supposedly going to write music for the interpolated verses, but nothing further came of the project, and the manuscript was returned to Krylov some thirty years later. One feature of *Kofeinitsa,* however, gives some hint of its author's future direction: conventional as the plot may be, it is thoroughly Russian, and the picture of the relations between landlord and serf are not glossed over or prettified as they are, for instance, in *Rozana and Liubim* or in Ablesimov's *Miller.*

In 1786, at the age of seventeen, Krylov made his only extant attempt with the tragedy (he had written, according to his own testimony, a *Cleopatra* which has not survived). *Philomela*[38] is a full five-act drama in verse, following all the classical conventions. It was never played, but was printed in 1793 in the collection of Russian plays which also contained Kniazhnin's *Vadim of Novgorod.* When the Kniazhnin tragedy was suppressed at Catherine's orders, most of the copies of Krylov's *Philomela* shared its fate—no great loss, as the author himself admitted in later years.

The plot was drawn from Ovid's *Metamorphoses,* and is the well-known tale of the lawless love of the Thracian king Tereus for Philomela, sister of his wife Progne, and his attempt to conceal his crime by cutting out Philomela's tongue. Needless to say, Krylov did not attempt to introduce the Ovidian dénouement—the transformation of Tereus into a hoopoe, Progne into a swallow and Philomela into a nightingale! The drama gets off to a good start in the first act, as Tereus returns from Athens to his solicitous wife and tells her a fabrication about how her sister, whom he has been escorting for a visit, has been swept off the ship's side by a great wave and lost; but it rapidly degenerates, and the final act is particularly bad. Worst of all is the wooden stylization of characters. Tereus, like Sumarokov's Dmitry, is an unredeemed and unredeemable villain, who freely discourses to his confidant on his own villainy, which he excuses by the absolutely irresisitible passion which has him in its grip. Progne within a few lines turns from a loving wife to a demon of vengeance, intent on punishing with the most inhuman barbarity the husband whom she has ostensibly doted on. A non-Ovidian turn is given to the plot by the device of a popular revolution which unseats the tyrant Tereus—an element in the play which would undoubtedly have condemned it in the eyes of the government in any case. Philomela, the title character, is extraordinarily pallid and uninteresting; even though she retains her tongue until the last act, she has nothing of consequence to say. Perhaps the most awkward element in the whole drama is Progne's vengeance. True to the antique plot, she is made to punish her faithless husband by killing their child Itys and serving up his flesh to his father in a ghastly banquet. Whatever effect this scene might have had is cancelled by Krylov's treatment: Itys, though listed among the *dramatis personae*, does not appear on the stage at all, and is never even mentioned by either parent until the time comes from him to be murdered; and the hypothetical audience can thus hardly be expected to feel a great deal of sympathy for his fate! Progne, moreover, apparently feels no compunction at all in killing her innocent child—she scarcely even refers to her relationshp to her victim. One could think of a Medea-like and harrowing vacillation over her act—but all opportunities for drama here are consistently missed.

Philomela has the distinction of being one of the very few classical dramas in any language on this rather unrewarding plot; and it has the distinction surely of being one of the very worst of Russian classical dramas. No wonder Krylov himself regarded its loss as a blessing!

Krylov succeeded a great deal better with comedy than with tragedy or opera; but even with the comedy his first efforts are disasters. The same year, 1786, as saw the composition of *Philomela* saw that of another comic opera: *A Crazy Family,*[39] in three acts. This effort has not even the merit of a Russian plot: it is a tedious farce held together by the preposterous device of having Mr. Sumburov's grandmother, mother, sister and daughter all madly in love with a young nobleman named Postan, who himself is in love with the sister, Priiata. The antics of the "crazy family" are assisted by the usual serving man and ladies' maid of comedy. No one in the entire mad company bears the slightest resemblance to a Russian, or indeed even to a living human being—they are comic-strip characters and nothing more.

Two years later the ambitious young author wrote his first five-act comedy, in prose, under the title *Prokazniki,*[40] which was published in the fortieth volume of *The Russian Theater.* Contemporary tradition held that several of the ridiculous persons whose antics carry the plot of this piece were intended as caricatures of real men and women: Rifmokrad ("Rhyme-stealer") is supposed to have been the dramatist Kniazhnin, his wife Taratora ("Jabberer") Mme Kniazhnina, who was Sumarokov's daughter, and herself wrote verses; the parasite Tianislov ("Word-puller'), perhaps Semen Bobrov, etc. The identities, however, are of little interest, for any similarity between the "characters" of this pitiful farce and genuine human beings is meager. The "plot" is feeble and long drawn out, and all the persons, with the possible exception of the serf Ivan, are synthetic absurdities.

The title of the comedy, *Prokazniki,* can perhaps best be rendered as *The Antics;* each of the principals is given some absurd characteristic which his or her name indicates, and which serves to keep the plot in motion—but not to solve it: this is done by an entirely external device. Rifmokrad is a dramatic poet (virtually his only visible connection with Kniazhnin); his wife Taratora is a giddy blue-stocking who writes verses and is carrying on a flirtation with Doctor Lancetin; their colorless daughter Priiata ("Charming") is in love with Milon ("Lover-boy"), and the object of suits also by the Doctor and the hanger-on and poetaster-seminarian Tianislov. Accessory characters are Milon's uncle Azbukin ("A-B-C") and his sister Princess Troikina (her name comes from the word *troika* as used in card-playing—the trey or "three-spot"). The plot, such as it is, is eventually resolved by the machinations of a remarkably talented and remarkably beautiful maid-servant of Milon's household, Plutana ("plut", "rascal"), who appears in male costume and makes love to the willing Taratora, while at the same time she reveals her real sex to Rifmokrad and is pursued by him! The piquant situation of having husband and wife rivals for the favors of the same person is at least fairly original. A farcical duel between Lancetin and Tianislov, fought in what is supposed to be total darkness, enlivens the last act.

Individual scenes in this hodge-podge are genuinely funny, and for the first time show Krylov's latent abilities; they are often also spiced with some outrageous *double-entendres.* One of the funniest scenes is that (III, vii) in which Rifmokrad and Tianislov discuss the plot of a tragedy which the latter is composing, and cold-bloodedly plan various scenic killings while the horrified Azbukin lurks under the table and hears the following dialogue:

Tia. Now no one will interefere with us... In such matters of course secrecy is always necessary. But with what sort of death do you advise me to kill them?

Rif. In my opinion, in order to increase the beauty of the action, the princess should be given a poisoned drink.... or poisoned food; and her brother, her brother....

Azb. (*aside*) Oh! Now it's my turn! They're going to kill me, the dogs, for a crow!

Tia. But for him, sir, I've devised a new manner of death; only will it be a good one?

Rif. Oh, splendid, sir! What is it?

Tia. I want to strangle him; surely this will strike the spectators.

Rif. Indeed, sir, this will be a divine *coup de théâtre!*

Azb. (*aside*) Oh, the accursed scoundrels! They are chuckling as though over a glass of vodka, without pity for innocent souls! I won't say anything about the princess— but what has my poor little soul been guilty of?

Unfortunately, such scenes contribute nothing to the plot, but are entirely inorganic; in this case, Azbukin's terrors are allayed and explained away between the acts, and nothing comes of the episode.

In the year 1800, according to its first editor, belongs the two-act parody tragedy called *Podshchipa,* or *Trumf.*[41] Krylov is said to have read this to a circle of friends, who "died with laughter" over it. The author's reading must have been particularly effective, for the text itself, while mildly amusing at times, is for the most part an egregious bore. It is supposed to have been intended both as a parody of the conventions of the classical tragedy—in which aspect it is fairly convincing—and also a bitter spoof of the German militarism of Tsar Pavel Petrovich. Of course *Podshchipa* was never printed until 1859, and then outside of Russia; copies of it were, however, possessed by several of the poet's friends, and it was known, for example, to Pushkin, who had a rather high opinion of it.

Both the parody aspect of the piece and its references of Emperor Paul's spit-and-polish militarism are dead issues to a present-day reader, and interest in them is somewhat hard to reconstruct. As it stands, most of the comic effect of *Podshchipa* is contributed by the use of distorted language— not a particularly subtle technique. The "villain," a German prince named Trumf, suitor for the hand of Princess Podshchipa, speaks a barbarously Teutonic Russian, while Podshchipa's true love, Prince Sliuniai (his name means "slobberer") mutilates his own native tongue by turning all "r's" and "l's" into "y's," and otherwise making himself ridiculous and offensive. Podshchipa's father, King Vakula, speaks the commonest sort of peasant language, interpolating "slysh' " ("y' hear!") into every other sentence. Podshchipa herself plays the high tragic heroine, determined to die rather than give up her beloved "slobberer" in favor of the German, who at the start of the play has the military advantage. Sliuniai, on the other hand, is a practical fellow with no such romantic notions; when Podshchipa proposes a suicidal leap from an upper-story window, he agrees, but only if it be from a lower level! When she proposes another method—jumping into a pond—he protests: "But I can't swim!"

The first of Krylov's comedies which is both really funny and also very well put together is the little one-acter, *The Pie (Pirog)*,[42] written some time between 1799 and 1801. Vanka, servant of the gentleman-adventurer Fatiuev, enters, bearing a large and succulent chicken pie, which his master has ordered sent to his prospective in-laws to be the *pièce de résistence* of an al fresco lunch. To Vanka's surprise, he meets his girl-friend Dasha, who is the maid at present, it seems, of Prelesta, his master's bride. Vanka is very hungry, and without much urging from Dasha, resolves to sample the pie. At Dasha's suggestion, they turn it upside down, open the bottom, and help themselves to the contents, until, to Vanka's utter dismay, he discovers the pie is practically empty. It now becomes necessary to try to conceal the crime; so when Fatiuiev appears for the lunch (his hosts are off on a woodland walk, fortunately), Vanka gets rid of him on the pretext that one of his most importunate creditors is with the bride and her parents. Fatiuiev decides to retire until this danger is past, and with Vanka's help composes a polite note to Mr. Vspyshkin to explain his unexpected absence and recommend the pie; Vanka is to deliver the note. Mr. Vspyshkin (his name implies an explosive temper), his sentimental wife Uzhima (related to "uzhimka," "an affected simper"), their daughter Prelesta ("charming") and her disconsolate lover Milon appear after their walk, and Vanka delivers the note and the pie. All sit down to start work on the pie—which they immediately find to be empty. Vspyshkin flies into a temper over what he believes to be a rude practical joke, and the note is produced. He begins to read:

Vsp. Give me the letter—What's this? It's not signed, not sealed! The boor! *(he unfolds it)*. And in pencil! Oh, fine, son-in-law! If while he's still only betrothed, he has no respect for me.... But where's the beginning?

Van. Here it is, sir!

Vsp. "Excuse me, that I cannot"... Was such a thing ever seen? You might begin so to your tailor or your shoemaker! "Excuse me, that I cannot!" Where is "Dear Sir," or "My Dear Sir"? Or maybe even just plain "Sir!" "Excuse me that I cannot!" How stupidly put! What a stupid style! Read, wife! What "cannot he" do?

Uzh. "Excuse me, that I cannot devour the pie with you"—Devour the pie! What low expressions! "I swear, I haven't time. You remember, I presume, that my family are urgently pressing me to marry Princess Snafidina. Finally my uncle has this moment sent for me on the matter of this betrothal. I fly to finish the business— and how? This pie will tell you for me."

The letter is handed from one to another of the family to be read, ending with Dasha, who invents a postscript of her own to clinch the matter:

"Let my pie tell you that my heart is just as full of love for Prelesta as it is full of stuffing.... Eat it and good health to you—there's something to feast on! I myself gave orders and made very effort that it should be as rich in good stuffing as my promised father-in-law is rich in intelligence... You will see in the stuffing as many good things as there are good and amiable qualities in my promised mother-in-law!... *(Dasha reads)*. "In a word, my pie will be the translator of my feelings for you. Farewell! I wish Prelesta all happiness, but I am not the bridegroom for her."

Seething with indigation, Prelesta's parents forthwith betroth her to her Milon, the pair are happily married in a church that happens to be near by, and when the giver of the fateful pie turns up at last, he finds himself entirely discomfited. Of course the truth comes out at last, but too late for the adventurer; Vanka and Dasha are forgiven, and Fatiuiev's only expressed regret is for his "poor creditors," whose only hope for payment has vanished with the pie.

The characters here, at last, are real people, with credible human qualities. Even the young lovers are endowed with considerable personality. Mr. Vspyshkin is the most natural; his somewhat affected wife is rather a stereotype of the sentimentalist—a palpable hit at Krylov's literary adversary, Karamzin and his school. Mme Uzhima replies to her daughter's despairing plea to reverse the parental decision about her marriage to Fatiuiev: "Oh, my God! You know my sensibility: I am torn, beholding the obstacles which fate is placing in the way of your tenderness. But my husband is of quite other sentiments; there's no way of bringing him around." One can hear the very words—"sensibility," "obstacles," "fate," "tenderness," etc. of a myriad elegies. Helpless as she is to "bring her husband around," Uzhima can still offer some consolation to the ill-starred lovers: "Oh, no, don't go away, sir—stay with us! After lunch we'll sit down somewhere in the shade of a spreading willow-tree and I'll sing you for consolation my favorite song: 'I would I were a little bird.' " Her attempt to sing this sentimental ditty is interrupted by her husband, who addresses her abruptly with: "Wife! I must have a word with you." This unsentimental directness is too much:

Uzh. My God! How this word hurts the ears! Won't you ever outgrow it, my soul?
Vsp.   A fine time to seize on this! It would seem that you've been hearing this from me for thirty years, and it's hard to break the habit in one's old age.
Uzh. If anyone has been doing a folly for thirty years, it would be commendable to stop it in the thirty-first.
Vsp.   Well, well, all right! What a trifle to get angry over! Listen, then, Malania Sysoevna!
Uzh. Oh, what barbarity! Call me simply Mélanie, sir! Look, I'll show you in all the novels!

Of all the characters in the little play, the servants Vanka and Dasha are perhaps the most convincing, chiefly because they are, for once, real Russians, and not merely "clever slaves" out of Plautus and Terence by way of Molière. But best of all, the action of the play is simple and completely unified, and in the very best technique of the classical comedy, everything is derived from a single source—in this case, the "pie." From this homely object proceed the entire complication and unravelling of the plot. Vanka's and Dasha's gluttony begins things; then Fatiuiev's ill-timed efforts to impress his bride's parents with flowery language and analogies regarding the pie's contents, which lead at once to Vspyshkin's explosion of wrath over the direct injury of frustrated appetite and the culminating insult of having his head compared with an empty pie shell!

Krylov's last two comedies, the one-act *A Lesson for Daughters (Urok dochkam)* and *The Fashion Shop (Modnaia lavka)* were written in 1807 and printed after their very successful stage presentations. *A Lesson for Daughters*[43] reverts, unfortunately, to the kind of unnatural caricature that marks *The Antics* and *A Crazy Family.* The plot has some points of contact with Molière's *Les Précieuses ridicules,* which was perhaps Krylov's point of departure; the theme is the extremely well-worn one of Gallomania, which Fonvizin had handled far more amusingly and convincingly in *The Brigadier.* The nobleman Velkarov, a widower, has let his two daughters Fekla and Lukeria be educated in the city by a French governess. To his dismay, he finds them so addicted to French—which he does not himself understand— and hostile to everything Russian that he devises a drastic plan for their cure: he carries them off to his country estate and strictly forbids them to speak French at all! To enforce this Draconian prohibition he employs the girls' old nurse Vasilissa to report them whenever one of them utters a word of French. All this exposition comes out in the first scenes of the comedy, when the servant Semen unexpectedly encounters his intended bride Dasha, who is the maid of the Frenchified daughters, in the country village to which their father has brought them. Semen himself is a free commoner, in the employ of a young officer "on his way to beat the Turks," who has just happened to stop momentarily in Velkarov's village. Both Semen and Dasha have been trying to find money enough to enable them to get married, but so far without success. Hearing Dasha's tale about the situation with the two French-mad daughters, Semen conceives a brilliant scheme for getting some fast money: he will pretend to be a French nobleman who has been robbed by highwaymen of all his money, and will try to negotiate a "loan" to enable him to reach his journey's end. His ignorance of French will be covered up by Velkarov's stern prohibition against the use of that language by his daughters. This scheme works out perfectly: Fekla and Lukeria are charmed by their visitor's refined "French" manners, to such an extent that they write curt notes of dismissal to their Russian suitors—the country gentlemen whom their father has picked out for them. The notes, however, are intercepted by Velkarov, who also presently discovers the "Frenchman's" real identity, and shames his daughters with the disclosure. He generously gives Semen the money he has been trying to obtain by his masquerade, and the comedy ends with the disconsolate daughters still in the watchful care of nurse Vasilissa:

Luk. (*going out*) Oh! Ma soeur!
Fek. (*going out*) Ah! Quelle leçon!
Nurse Vasilissa (*going out after them*) Young ladies, be pleased to do your mourning in Russian!

Here the characterization is far less natural than in *The Pie;* the daughters are improbable caricatures, and Semen and Dasha are not much more than the habitual stereotypes of conniving servants. Nurse Vasilissa has only a small part, but she is recognizably Russian. Velkarov has little individual color, and has too little to do or say in the play to make much impression.

Ivan Krylov's three-act prose comedy *The Fashion Shop*[44] is the best of all his completed pieces. The unities of classical drama are unobtrusively observed; all the action takes place in "the fashion shop," an establishment run by an emigrée Frenchwoman, Mme Carrée, with the help of an attractive and clever Russian girl, Masha, as her assistant. The first act takes place in the morning, the last act in the evening of the same day. "The fashion shop" is the source of the play's entire action: to it naturally gravitate Mme Sumburova, who is mad about French fashions, and her step-daughter Liza, who has to be outfitted for her coming marriage. Thither also Mr. Sumburov quite naturally makes his way, in his futile attempt to prevent his women from squandering his money on frivolities. The resolution of the plot contains an extraneous element, which however, also has its center in the "fashion shop." Establishments of this sort had in Krylov's time rather shady reputations as places for assignations and seduction—and also as centers of illicit foreign goods smuggled into the country without the payment of excise taxes. Krylov utilizes this aspect of his "fashion shop" first to motivate Sumburov's suspicions (well-founded, incidentally) of his daughter's and Lestov's behavior; and second, to bring about the dénouement through the vengefulness of Monsieur Trichet, who informs the police that his country-woman, Mme Carreé, is dealing in smuggled goods. In this ingenious fashion nearly everything that happens in the play can be directly traced to the "fashion shop" and its personnel.

The first act of *The Fashion Shop* takes place in the forenoon: a young gentleman, Lestov, is conversing with the attractive young Russian assistant of Mme Careé, Masha, who, it appears, is still a serf, belonging to the estate of Lestov' sister. Lestov, after many compliments to Masha, tells her of his infatuation with a girl whom he has chanced to meet in the provinces, Liza, daughter of Mr. Sumburov (his name connotes something like "rumpus"!) by his first marriage. Lestov characterizes the Sumburov's as follows:

Mr. Sumburov is an old man, good-hearted, to be sure, but hot-tempered and ardently attached to the Russian manners of our grandfathers; he is only happy on a day when he has the chance to rail at either the fashions, or foreigners; and he is such a queer sort that even a trifling bit of foolishness done in his family torments him as would a criminal act that brought shame to the whole clan.... [his wife] is a backwoods fashion-plate, who has been thirty for the past fifteen years; self-willed to boot, malicious, stingy, sly, and crazy.

Mr. Sumburov, who was acquainted with the young man's father, was at first agreeable to Lestov's marriage with Liza, but was finally persuaded against it by his wife, who wants her to marry her own nephew—an improvident young rake who does not appear in the play. Lestov had parted sorrowfully from his beloved, and has not heard from her for a year. By the usual providence that operates in comedies, at this moment Mme Sumburova comes into the shop; she and her family have come to the city to make preparations for the wedding, and she has naturally yielded to the temptation of visiting the modish French shop. She is accompanied by her servant Antrop, and she has left her step-daughter outside in the carriage in the coachman's protection. Lestov presents himself, but is rebuffed when he proposes to make a call on the Sumburovs. While Mme Sumburova is in the back room with the proprietress, being shown some exclusive French wares, Lestov enlists Masha's aid, with the promise that he will prevail upon his sister to give the girl her freedom so that she can set up her own "fashion shop." Lestov then tries desperately to make the stupid Antrop take a note to Liza, and when this fails, gives the serf a tip with which he and the coachman go off to the nearest tavern for drinks; during this while Lestov has the chance to have some unchaperoned conversation with his idol. Suddenly Mr. Sumburov storms into the shop; he is in a rage, of course, having seen his wife's carriage outside the establishment—he hates both the French and expensive fashions. Antrop returns, drunk, and Sumburov orders his wife home with the drunken lackey; Liza is to return with her father.

The first act contains all that is strictly necessary for the evolution of the plot, but a fine *coup de théatre* is worked out by the introduction in the second act of a shady Frenchman, Monsieur Trichet ("trickster"), who turns out later to have been a bailiff of Lestov's and to have absconded with some of his employer's property. This coincidence is improbable, but not really necessary for the plot. Trichet gets into an angry dispute over money matters with Mme Carrée, and to wreak his vengeance on her, informs the police that the "fashion shop" is largely stocked with contraband imports. This leads to a police raid on the place; Mme Carrée, however, has been tipped off. She and Masha hide all the contraband, leaving a large armoire virtually empty. A note sent by Masha to Mme Sumburova lures that lady back to the shop for some wonderful bargains. Lestov thus has the opportunity, while the step-mother is away, of seeing Liza and making arrangements with her; the girl even gets into his carriage and the servants believe she has eloped with him.

The last act takes place in the evening; the shop is ostensibly closed, but Mme Sumburova is there, looking at "bargains." Suddenly Mr. Sumburov once again appears, and pounds at the door, demanding to be let in. Masha hurriedly hides Mme Sumburova in the empty armoire, and opens for Sumburov. The old man is determined to have vengeance on this place, which is both French and a temptation to feminine extravagance—and has probably

374

had a hand in his daughter's "elopement." When the police raid takes place, Sumburov eggs on the officer to examine everything with great care—especially the armoire, which is locked. At this point Masha whispers to him that he had better not go too far—his wife is in the armoire! He has to climb up and peek through a hole in the top to be convinced—but then hastily changes his tone and prevails on the police to leave; Sumburov is nearly apoplectic with rage, mutters curses on all womankind and his wife in particular; M. Trichet is put to shame by the failure of his plot—and by the sudden confrontation with Lestov, who appears on the scene with Liza. Sumburov had been informed earlier that the pair had eloped, but it appears that they only had a pleasant ride together, and have returned to obtain his blessing. Mme Sumburova, thoroughly in disgrace with her husband because of the near-scandal she has caused, is informed that Liza will not, after all, be married to her scape-grace nephew, but to Lestov, and everything thus takes the turn appropriate to a comedy finale.

The intrigue of the piece is a little too complicated, and the Trichet-Mme Carrée feud an element not directly related to the rest; but the comedy excels, for once, in natural characterization. Mme Sumburova is a stupid, snobbish creature, in awe of her husband, but perfectly willing to disobey his orders when she thinks he will not know it; he is a quite plausibly complicated person: fond of his daughter, and of Lestov, but rather easily led by the nose by his wife; he is, however, very stingy and feminine extravagance enrages him; and he is almost pathologically anti-French. His temper, moreover, is very short, and he is subject to fits of violent rage. All these qualities, which are not just the usual comic clichés, but are perfectly credible in combination as individual traits, contribute to the outcome of the action, and are thus dramatically justified. As an exception to the usual comic treatment, the young lover Lestov is resourceful and enterprising, and also not an entirely one-sided character: even though entirely devoted to Liza, he has no hesitation in offering some conventional gallantry to Masha, serf though she is. Masha is a natural, level-headed, clever girl, with no illusions, and with a well-developed sense of humor; she treats Lestov's amorous sufferings with a deal of good-natured irony. She is perhaps a little too sophisticated and clever to be a Russian serf, but Krylov is careful to give her a rather unusual background. The lackey Antrop is very well drawn, and his scenes are among the funniest in the play. Filled with open-mouthed amazement at the wealth of goods in the shop, he is completely oblivious to Lestov's desperate attempts to get him to carry a message to Liza. When Lestov at last in vexation wishes him to the devil, he grumbles that "no one will let him so much as open his mouth." When Sumburov accuses him of being drunk, he explains: "I'm at fault, sir—your former friend [i.e., Lestov] was pleased to give Senka and me a tip ["na vodku"], and showed us a tavern—so, you know, it would be against our conscience not to have a drink."

The only other dramatic work of Krylov at all comparable to *The Fashion Shop* is the unfinished verse fragment called *The Sluggard (Lentiai).*[45] One act and portions of a second were composed, and the whole apparently planned, but never executed. It is customary to point out the similarity between the character of Lentul ("sluggard") and Goncharov's Oblomov; but actually all that we know of Lentul's character is inferential: he never appears on the stage in the portions of the play that Krylov completed, but is presumably sleeping. It is only through his servant Andrei, his father Pravdon, his friend Chesnov, and the father of his betrothed bride Sumbur (who is called Burnei in the second-act fragments) that we get a picture of the pathologically lazy man, who spends all his days in dressing-gown and slippers, never goes out, and gravitates from bed to sofa and back again. He is too lazy even to get out of bed to greet his bride, her father, or his own father, on their arrival at his country place. Sumbur, by contrast with his sluggish son-in-law-to-be is a violently energetic old fellow, intolerant of inactivity. Here is obviously the comic collision, and it would be interesting to know how Krylov would have worked out the plot. By the end of the finished portions a possible position has been found for Lentul, with Chesnov's uncle: but it will be necessary for the "hero" to get out of bed and take some action in order to obtain it, which at the point when the comedy breaks off seems an unlikely prospect, even with the prodding of all the interested parties.

A work of an entirely different sort may be mentioned to complete a picture of Krylov's dramatic output—*Ilya Bogatyr*, in four acts, qualified by the author as a "volshebnaia opera," or "opera of witchcraft."[46] It is in prose with interpolated verse songs—solos, duets, trios and choruses. The piece was performed in 1806 in the St. Petersburg theater. It would be interesting to know what the regisseur did with the enormously complicated sets specified by the dramatist, and the numerous transformations, magical effects, and the like. Thus, scene iv of Act II is described as follows: "The theater represents cliffs and waters plunging down from them, which finally, issuing from a cave, form a river; at the base of the mountains, on the other side of the theater, is visible a low cave, overgrown with a thicket; in front of it a small stone elevation.... Tarop and Vladisil appear above; the latter is in a magical sleep.... Their boat appears lower down; Tarop catches at the twigs of a tree growing out of the cliff.... the boat breaks away again.... Vladisil and Tarop are carried out of the cave on the boat, which stops at the bank."

The plot of the piece is rather remotely derived from the traditional popular songs about Ilya Muromets and his combat with "Nightingale the Bandit." But in spite of the title, this element of the plot is very minor: the young prince of Chernigov, Vladisil, is betrothed to the Bulgarian princess Vsemila, but his captive the Pecheneg princess Zlomeka, who is a witch, is in

376

love with him and by her enchantments attempts to thwart the course of true love. The "good witch" Dobrada and her daughter Lena befriend the couple and eventually conquer the spells of Zlomeka. The Jester ["shut"] of Vladisil, Tarop, and his beloved Rusida play a large part in solving the plot, through the arbitrary device which makes the cowardly and self-indulgent jester the only person who can obtain the key to the casket in which is the magical sword with which Ilya is fated to conquer the Pechenegs. Tarop withstands all the diabolical temptations put in his way by the witch, until he is finally corrupted by the enticements of wine; but of course the good triumphs in the end, Zlomeka and Dobrada have a climactic battle in which thunder and fire are the weapons, and Ilya, single-handed, routs the entire Pecheneg force that is besieging Chernigov.

In such a fantasy nothing like characterization can be expected, of course, and nothing is to be found. All the persons are improbable stereotypes. The combination of the invented plot with the popular ballad material is very clumsy, and the momentary defeat of Vladisil and his Russians in the last act is palpably contrived only to give Ilya the opportunity of coming to the rescue and ending the opera triumphantly. Whatever attraction the play may have had must have been contributed by the scenic effects, which would have taxed the resources of Wagner's Bayreuth! The nearest thing in genuine opera to this extravaganza would be *Die Zauberflote*—but Krylov had no Mozart to lend real enchantment to his tawdry piece.

Even here, however, the critic may discern, as in all Krylov's dramatic ventures from the *Kofeinitsa* on, an effort to overcome the usually abstract and conventional setting of eighteenth century comedy by the introduction of genuinely Russian elements. The effort in *Ilya Muromets* is awkward and blundering; in *The Pie, The Fashion Shop*, and the incomplete *Sluggard*, it is entirely successful. This is Krylov's principal contribution to the development of the comic genre.

Khemnitser

Krylov

N. Gnedich, V. Zhukovsky, A. Pushkin, I. Krylov.
Lithograph from a painting by G. Chernetsov.

Petrov

Kniazhnin

Dmitriev

Bogdanovich

Below: Plavilshchikov in a
woman's role

Top right: Levshin
Bottom right: Ablesimov

ТРУДОЛЮБИВАЯ ПЧЕЛА.

Генварь 1759 года.

ВТОРЫМЪ ТИСНЕНІЕМЪ.

ВЪ САНКТПЕТЕРБУРГѢ,
при Императорской Академіи НаукЪ
1780 года.

"The Labor-Loving Bee" for January 1759, second printing 1780.

БАСНИ и СКАЗКИ

И. И. Хемницера,

ВЪ трехЪ частяхЪ.

Came: — antiq.
G. M.

ВЪ природѣ, въ простотѣ онъ истинну искалъ:
КакЪ видѣлЪ, такъ ее списалъ.

Печатано вЪ Императорской Типографіи.
ВЪ Санктпетербургѣ, 1799.
СЪ дозволенія Ценсуры.

Khemnitser's "Fables & Tales,"
St. Petersburg, 1799.

ПОЧТА ДУХОВЪ,

ЕЖЕМѢСЯЧНОЕ ИЗДАНІЕ,

ИЛИ

Ученая, Нравственная, и Критическая переписка Арабскаго философа *Маликульмулька* сЪ водяными, воздушными и подземными Духами.

ЧАСТЬ I.

Печатано съ дозволенія указнаго

ВЪ САНКТПЕТЕРБУРГѢ 1789 ГОДА.

Krylov's "Spirits' Post,"
St. Petersburg, 1789.

ПУТЕШЕСТВІЕ.

изЪ

ПЕТЕРБУРГА ВЪ МОСКВУ.

„Чудище обло, озорно, огромно, стозѣвно, и лаяй„

Тилемахида, ТомЪ II. Кн: XVIII. сти:

1790.

ВЪ САНКТПЕТЕРБУРГѢ.

Radishchev's "Journey from Petersburg to Moscow," 1790. Unlike most of the other books, the legend "With the permission of the censorship" does not appear on the title-page.

M. D. Chulkov. A copper plate from his tomb
with verse written by Chulkov.

The Kremlin in Moscow, viewed from the Stone Bridge, by De la Barthe, c. 1790.

View of the Admiralty from Nevsky Prospect. Engraving by G. Kachalov from a drawing by M. Makhaev. 1753.

Pugachev, 1773. The unknown painter painted him over Catherine II.

Church of the Transfiguration in Kizhi, 1714.

Potemkin, Prince of Taurida

Paul I. Pencil drawing by N. I. Tonchi.

A barber cutting off the beard of an Old Believer, a "lubok" from 1710-20.

A tapestry from 1745-47, providing a Russian view of "America."

Fyodor Rokotov, 1763. Portrait by I. Orlov.

I. Argunov, 1754. Portrait by E. Lobanova-Rostovtseva

Fonvizin

Radishchev

Karamzin

Derzhavin

CHAPTER XIII

GAVRIIL ROMANOVICH DERZHAVIN
AND THE BEGINNINGS OF SENTIMENTALISM

A. The Beginnings of Sentimentalism in Russian Literature[1]

Toward the end of the eighteenth century the European literary world saw the beginnings of a phenomenon which can be explained largely as a reaction to the over-emphasis upon rationalism which marks the classical period. The tacit assumption that the human reason must dominate all life, and that the key to moral improvement lies in the perfecting of the intellect met with increasingly vigorous challenge, as champions of the emotions raised their heads and dared to propose that "a good heart" was more important for moral man than a disciplined intellect. The movement against the classical point of view grew up among members of a different social class from that which had been the mainstay of rationalism, and to this extent at least the anti-rationalist rebellion can be said to have a social and political coloring, although these aspects of the movement neither initiated nor determined it. Rationalism, eighteenth-century classicism, was a phenomenon of the aristocracy; "sentimentalism" began among the bourgeoisie, that is, the newly emerging class of townspeople, and was dominated everywhere in Europe by the values of this class. In Russia, where the urban bourgeoisie was too small and unimportant to count as a distinct class at this time, the new movement took the form of a rebellion from wiithin the ruling aristocracy, and was represented also by the small but intellectually very important group of rootless intelligentsia called in Russian "raznochintsy," that is, "of various castes." This group typically comprised impoverished noblemen, enfranchised serfs or their children, sons of priests, educated scions of the town merchant class, and the like. Devoid of consciousness as a class, and because of their diverse origins lacking any sense of tradition, this group tended toward radicalism both in political thought and in literary expression. Its chief importance, however, comes at a considerably later period than the end of the eighteenth century; only its beginnings date so far back.

The European movement of "sentimentalism" can be traced first to England. More than any other single source, Samuel Richardson's novel *Pamela* (1740) may be held to initiate the phenomenon. The two later novels of the same author, *Clarissa Harlowe* (1751) and *Sir Charles Grandison* (1754) contributed to the movement, but it was left to another Englishman, Laurence Sterne, to give the new trend its name. *Tristram Shandy* (1760) is so original and whimsical a piece of work, so entirely *sui generis*, that it could hardly by itself have exercised much influence; but *A Sentimental Journey Through France and Italy* (1767), with its lyrical outpourings of the heart, as the future parson Yorick encounters various human conditions in his French wanderings, served to crystallize the tendencies of the age in the form of vaguely humanitarian and egalitarian effusions which were calculated to reveal the narrator's "good heart." "Sentimentalism" became the vogue. Goldsmith's idyllic *Vicar of Wakefield* (1766) was another English component of the movement. In the realm of lyric poetry a parallel, but slightly different anti-classicist rebellion goes back to the so-called "Ossian" poems published by James Macpherson in 1762. The history of "Ossianism" in European literature, including Russian, is another matter, however, and belongs more definitely to the rise of romanticism, to which "sentimentalism" may be considered a prelude.

British sentimentalism was centered in the novel; and it was J.-J. Rousseau's novel *Julie, ou la nouvelle Héloise* (1765) which initiated the trend in France. But even in England the anti-classical rebellion had had an earlier start in the drama, which it was left to the French to carry further. George Lillo's tragedy *The London Merchant* (1731), for all its literary deficiencies, marks a most important turning point in the history of the drama. Here best of all can be observed the rise of the new urban class which was to dominate nineteenth century English letters. For the first time the protagonists of a serious and tragic work are members of the middle class, not kings or noblemen, and for the first time an author dares assume that members of this non-aristocratic caste are capable of having the same tragic experiences as their aristorcratic superiors. Although as far as the drama was concerned, this lesson failed to have any significant consequences in England, across the channel, in the hands of that restless and intensely original genius Denis Diderot it gave rise to a new form of theatrical creation—the *drame*. Diderot's *Fils naturel* (1757) initiated the type, which to the scandal of the French classicist, projected tragic motifs in prose against a middle-class background. Although Diderot's own dramatic efforts are singularly tame and unexciting, as well as tiresomely didactic, they provided the opening wedge for the later romantic drama and the demolition of the seventeenth century idol of classicism. German dramatists, less emotionally attached than their French compeers to the traditions of the age of literary absolutism, soon began writing in the new vein: the best productions of the sort are those of Ephraim Gotthold Lessing, beginning with *Miss Sara Sampson* (1755) and reaching a real dramatic height in *Emilia Galotti* (1772). At the same time the strictly drawn line between classical tragedy and classical comedy was broken through by the French experimenters of the *comédie larmoyante*, such as

379

La Chaussee, De Balbiare and Mercier. The spectator could now weep at a comedy (and indeed was expected to) and exhibit thus his noble sentiments.

Although from geographical contiguity one might expect German example to be more influential upon Russia than French, the contrary at this date is true. French prestige and the aristocratic Russian practice of employing French tutors for their children insured that literary movements in France should be almost immediately reflected in Russia. We have already seen how the "tearful comedy," decried as a monstrosity by the arch-classicist Sumarokov, made its Russian appearance in such works as Lukin's *The Prodigal Reformed by Love* and Fonvizin's *Korion.* It never, to be sure, supplanted genuine comedy, which the classicist Krylov most successfully defends, but kept a certain vogue among the élite class who felt that the stage must be primarily the corrector of morals, and that tears excelled laughter for this purpose. The importance of the Masonic movement in Russia, with its emphasis upon philanthropy, education and self-perfection, notably in the work of Mikhail Kheraskov, should not be under-emphasized as a promoter of sentimentalism.

More significant for Russia than its place in the drama, however, is the impact of sentimentalism in the realm of non-dramatic verse. "Ossian" has been mentioned: the sombre forests, rushing streams, misty seas—the gloomy bards, death-doomed heros, despairing maidens—the echoes of "old, unhappy, far-off things, and battles long ago"—these exercised a most powerful influence on Russian poets of the end of the century. Thomas Gray's Scandinavian imitations—*The Bard, The Descent of Odin,* etc.—acted in the same direction—in fact, as we shall see, Celtic and Norse cultures and mythologies were widely identified in Russia. Gray's famous *Elegy,* with its "graveyard" atmosphere, its melancholy reveries and its subjective picture of night joined with the even more famous *Night Thoughts* of Edward Young to produce hundreds of imitative Russian mood pictures, which were destined to become in time as much a literary cliché as the classical elegy, and as much ridiculed. Another English contribution to sentimentalist poetry was James Thomson's *The Seasons* (1726-30), which inaugurated the vogue of "nature poetry," with strong didactic overtones. Inspired in part by Thomson, two Swiss Germans, Johann Jacob Bodmer (1698-1783) and Salomon Gessner (1730-1786) fought to emancipate German verse from the stultifying pseudo-classicism of Gottsched. Gessner's "Idylls" represent an ingenious attempt to naturalize among the Swiss mountaineers the already artificial and sentimental pastoral genre. Albrecht von Haller (1708-1777), a German, introduced the descriptive poem into the literature of his people with his once famous *Die Alpen,* (1732), which cautiously explores the possibilities of the wilder, less "civilized" aspects of nature for poetry.

French pre-romantic verse, like French pre-romantic drama, is more immediately significant for Russian sentimentalism than the analogous German variety. Here, however, the picture is clouded by the virtual falsification of their national literature by French critics who contemptuously ignore the entire field of eighteenth century lyric verse as second-rate and literarily valueless. This indeed it probably is—but its immense importance for foreign literatures, especially Russian, cannot be ignored, and even in French literature the apparently sudden rise of romanticism in the second decade of the nineteenth century is explicable only when this despised material is taken into account. French "light verse," that is, verse of a private and unpretentious nature, as opposed to the pompous public ode and its kind, is a phenomenon of the utmost literary importance, even if little of it can be considered poetry of genius. We shall see the degree to which such poets as Kapnist, Muraviev, even Derzhavin, owed their inspiration to this kind of French verse. Without the contribution of such totally forgotten versifiers as Colardeau, Bernis, Dorat and other French Anacreontists, and of such German imitators as Friedrich von Hagedorn (1708-1754), the flourishing lyric poetry of the last two decades of Russia's eighteenth century would be an inexplicable phenomenon.

The final literary area to be invaded by sentimentalism in Russia is the prose narrative, and we shall defer consideration of this until we take up the prose of Karamzin, although that master's reform of Russian literary style is intelligible only in the light of his earlier verse, and this in the light of the practice of such predecessors as Lvov, Muraviev, and Dmitriev. Literary revolutions do not occur unheralded nor in a vacuum, though the connections may sometimes be found only among "secondary" figures and their works.

B. *Gavriil Romanovich Derzhavin* (1743-1816)[2]

The greatest poet of eighteenth century Russia was, by an irony of fate, a professional soldier and administrator and one of the great "magnates" ["vel'mozhi"] clustered around the throne of Catherine II and her successors, about whom he wrote so disparagingly. A brief account of his life will perhaps throw some light on the reasons why his poetic work marks such a decisive break with classical tradition. Derzhavin came to poetry as an outsider, almost without preparation of the usual kind, and at least until his retirement in 1803 poetry was an avocation, not his principal business.

He was born in 1743, the son of a poor army officer with a small estate in the Kazan region. His ancestors, he used later to boast, had been Tatar princes. The boy was from the first destined for a military career, which after a very desultory education, he entered at the age of eighteen as a private in the Preobrazhensky Guards Regiment. He reached ensign rank by 1772, and served as an intelligence officer in the Volga region in the campaign against Pugachev, first under General Bibikov and then under Peter Panin. In 1777 he was discharged from the army, transferred to the civilian service with the rank of Collegiate Councillor (equivalent to that of Colonel in the army) and rewarded for his services by the grant of a sizeable estate (300 peasants) in Belorussia. His civilian duties were in the Senate, where he was under the supervision of Prince Vyazemsky, an envious intriguer who hated him. Difficulties with Vyazemsky led him to resign from the service, but the favor with the Empress won by his famous ode "Felitsa" (1783) soon brought him reappointment. In 1784 he was made Actual State Councillor (equivalent to General in the army) and appointed to the governorship of Olonets province in north Russia. Quarrels with another official of the province led to his transfer, also as governor, to the Tambov province. Again trouble ensued with a superior, and Derzhavin was even brought to trial before the Senate for insubordination, but exonerated. The publication of his great ode "Portrait of Felitsa" (1789), designed to placate the Empress, had the desired effect, and the poet was made Catherine's own secretary of petitions. In this capacity he found himself in the immediate entourage of the Empress and one of the most powerful people in the realm—but of course also one of the most envied and hated. His relations with Catherine became strained and he was dismissed in 1793 with the rank of Privy Councillor. Catherine died in 1796, and despite some difficulties with Emperor Paul, Derzhavin occupied some high administrative posts during his short reign—Presidency of the Department of Commerce and a responsible position with the Treasury. After Paul's murder the poet became briefly Minister of Justice under Alexander I, but again his independence and inflexibility led to quarrels with other high officials, in this case Mikhail Speransky, and he was definitively retired in 1803. The last thirteen years of his life Derzhavin spent on his estate Zvanka on the Volkhov River near Novgorod. One incident of his final years is, from its symbolic significance, worth recounting. In the words of Professor G. A. Gukovsky:[3]

On January 8, 1815 Actual Privy Councillor Derzhavin, an important magnate, ex-minister and one of the last "pillars" of Catherine's times, the famous poet, generally recognized as the greatest lyric writer of Russian literature, arrived at the Lycée of Tsarskoe Selo for the public examination. The fifteen-year-old Pushkin read his verses before him [Pushkin's poem "Recollections of Tsarskoe Selo"]. "Derzhavin was in ecstasy: he asked for me, wanted to embrace me," wrote Pushkin 18 years later. On July 9, 1816, Derzhavin died.

Even such a brief sketch as this is enough to highlight Derzhavin's administrative—and military—abilities, and at the same time his very difficult character. Catherine the Great was not one to advance incompetents to the highest ranks in her empire (her behavior with her lovers is, of course, another matter—but Derzhavin was never one of those!). Despite a failure on one occasion to obey orders, which embroiled him with General Panin, Derzhavin's energy and initiative in the campaign against Pugachev and his contribution to the rebel's capture were sufficient to win him the rather extraordinary promotion from lieutenant to lieutenant colonel in one jump; and his administration of both the Olonets and the Tambov governorships was

outstandingly successful. He was a man of vision, energy, and intense patriotism—and of conscience, a rarity in Catherine's civil service. But the record
of his difficulties with other officers, both military and civilian, is impressive.
He was endowed with a very sharp tongue and a fearless disposition, and utterly lacked tact. Even allowing for the evident malice and back-biting of his
numerous enemies, intent on pulling down the successful upstart, it must be
said that Derzhavin's impetuosity, brusqueness, and lack of all social complaisance were responsible for a great many of his perennial quarrels with
superiors, subordinates and merely fellow noblemen.

The precise position which Derzhavin occupies in the history of Russian
literature is a matter of considerable concern to Russian critics, and one
seemingly quite impossible to define. Derzhavin cannot be pigeon-holed.
As Professor Berkov[4] points out ironically, he has been called a classicist,
a romantic, a pre-romantic, and even a representative of the Baroque! The last
mentioned classification, nonsensical though it is, has actually had some
quite reputable adherents. It is perfectly indefensible: the Baroque is a period
style, and to move it from the seventeenth to the end of the eighteenth
century deprives it of all meaning whatever. Neither can Derzhavin be put
down as a genuine and unalloyed classicist. Perhaps the pre-romantic label
comes a little closer to the truth than the others—but it is, after all, best to
eschew the attempt to label. Derzhavin is a transitional figure, both in
point of time and in poetical practice; there are elements in his work which
show unmistakably his close connection with the classical poetical system.
There are, however, other elements which link him just as certainly to the
beginnings of romanticism. The number and importance of the classical
norms which he repudiated, both theoretically and in practice, was impressive.
Other poets of his own age, and even of his own literary circle—Lvov, Kapnist, Khemnitser et al.—are far more traditional and conservative in this regard
than Derzhavin. Why is this so?
Two reasons can be advanced for Gavriil Derzhavin's cavalier treatment
of the revered norms of classical verse composition. The first is a fact of his
environment and early life; the second of his psychological make-up. Derzhavin had, for his time, a very deficient education: his earliest tutors were
country ignoramuses—a local sexton, a tyrannical German exile, and an army
artilleryman. He later had a few years of "high school" education in the
Kazan Gymnasium, where everything was taught by one, not universally
competent, teacher. He did not even finish the Gymnasium course, but was
called up for army duty at the age of eighteen, and spent the next fourteen
years in military uniform. As a result of this early background, Derzhavin
had no knowledge of the classical languages or of French; he had learned
conversational German from Herr Rose. He was, however, by ignorance of
the essential languages of classicism, cut off from the originals and obliged
to rely on such mediocre translations as were availabe. But he did not even

383

have any literary training at all, even in Russian, beyond the reading of the Slavonic Scriptures which his mother insisted on. In fact, literature did not at first attract him—he wanted to be a scientist! He came to literature as an outsider—a badly educated soldier, completely ignorant of everything that his contemporaries took for granted as the necessary preparation for a literary career. When he did, about 1777, at the beginning of his civilian career, come for the first time in contact with a genuinely cultured literary group, the circle that had formed around Nikolai Alexandrovich Lvov (1751-1803)— Lvov himself, Kapnist, Khemnitser, Muraviev and others—these men were already touched by the new literary currents that we associate with preromanticism. Thus, Lvov "translated" a typical, and popular, quasi-Scandinavian piece, "The Song of the Norseman Harald the Brave"; he translated the *Odes of Anacreon*; and he was strongly attracted to Russian popular song, under the influence of Herder, and made a collection of such songs together with the tunes. All this means that the literary influences which reached Derzhavin just at the time when, according to his own testimony, he was first beginning to find his own personal way (1770), were not the strictly classical ones which he would have felt had he been educated properly.

As for the second, psychological, factor in Derzhavin's literary non-conformity, it needs only a glance at his biography to convince one that he was by temperament a man who could never brook coercion or arbitrary dictation. Even in military service he was not willing to accept orders which he considered unreasonable, and suffered accordingly; and it would be difficult to point to a single superior in all his long and very successful administrative career, from the Empress on down, with whom he did not quarrel. That he should have tamely accepted the dictates of normative eighteenth century taste is as unthinkable as that he should carry out the arbitrary orders of Catherine II about planting trees in Olonets province! His attitude toward the "rules of taste" and their makers is revealed in his angry note protesting the rejection of a young playwright's effort by a pedantic director on the grounds of its "bad taste": "Who gave the right to this dictatorial tone?"

What has been said above does not of course mean that Derzhavin had no literary schooling whatever. He learned to read from his boorish tutors, and he did read, rather undiscriminatingly. Of course the poetic models that at once offered themselves to his eye were the poems of Lomonosov and Sumarokov. It was a fundamental dictum of classicism that a poet must *imitate:* and what should he imitate but the great masterworks of the past— primarily the Latin writers of the Augustan age, then the great French classics of the age of Louis XIV, and finally in Russia, the acknowledged Russian classics, who would, of course, be Lomonosov (died 1765) and Sumarokov (died 1777). Derzhavin began by imitating, and the first collection of his verse to see the light, published anonymously in 1774 while the author was still in the Volga country hunting Pugachev, is, as should be expected, im-

mature and imitative. Derzhavin himself spoke of the book very disparagingly, as the work of an aspiring poet who tried to soar with Lomonosov, but
lacked the genius. Actually, these *Odes, Translated and Composed at Chitalagay Hill* show a surprising amount of originality; for example, his very sincere
and quite moving "Ode on the Death of General-in-Chief Bibikov," though
written in the traditional ten-line strophe of iambic tetrameter, is unrhymed!
Derzhavin explained that he thought the embellishment of rhyme inappropriate to the expression of sorrow. So, incidentally, did Edward Young; but
whether Derzhavin had encountered the *Conjectures on Original Composition*
at this date is not certain. The influence of Lomonsov is, however, apparent everwhere in these odes. At the same time he was also writing songs,
which he did not publish separately, but incorporated over twenty years
later in his volume *Anacreontic Songs* of 1804. In this genre his model
was of course Sumarokov, and it must be said that he came closer to his
prototype here than he did to Lomonosov in his "odes." In accordance with
accepted eighteenth century practice he was following different models
for different genres, and himself employing two consciously different styles.

The classical poet of the eighteenth century followed unquestioningly
the principle that every poetical genre has its own appropriate style, and its
own appropriate poetic *persona*. The poet who writes an elegy, for example,
assumes the mask of an ardent lover facing separation from his mistress;
he may himself be a happily married man, no matter; the elegist must be a
melancholy bachelor. The writer of Anacreontic verse must put on the mask
of the old toper from Teos; the satirist must borrow Juvenal's indignation
and thunder against the depravity of the times. As Sumarokov's example
shows, the same poet can wear all these, and numerous other, masks—but
successively. What his own personality is like he will not have any occasion to
reveal. This is not to say that the classical poet is necessarily insincere; the
mask of the passionate patriot and inspired prophet which Lomonosov wears
in his great odes corresponds truly to his own personality, and doubtless
the same is true of the pungent satirist which his "Ode to the Beard" reveals.
The conventional faces which tradition accepted for the tragic poet, the
satirist, the writer of comedy, of ode, of elegy, and all the rest, were all
normal human varieties of personality and such as any individual might assume at different times. The patriot may also be a lover, the harsh critic of
society may in another mood be a tolerant wit. But for the classicist these
conventional masks may no more be combined and confused than the genres
of poetry themselves, which the usage of the ancients has once and for all
set apart in impermeable compartments.

Derzhavin repudiated all this. He rode rough-shod over the entire
eighteenth century genre system, and the personality which he exhibited,
though there are still differences between the solemn manner of such poems
as "The Waterfall" and the intimacy of "To Eugene. Life at Zvanka" or the
Epicureanism of "The Bath of Aristippus," is still recognizably the same,

and is not dictated by the kind of verse he is writing. The first intimation of this significant revolution may be found in a poem of 1779: "On the Birth in the North of a Porphyrogennete Child."[5]

In the notes which Derzhavin wrote many years later for an edition of his works which did not materialize, he makes this significant statement about this poem; he, it appears, like several other poets, wrote an ode to commemorate the birth of the prince who was to become Alexander I, "but in a style not in conformity with the author's gifts, but in that of Lomonosov, for which he felt himself unsuited; this ode accordingly has not been printed in his works, and the present one was written later."[6] The "ode in the style of Lomonosov" has apparently not survived; the existing verses were published in the *St. Petersburg Herald* in 1779, with a full title which explains the poetical device which the poet employs in constructing his piece: "Verses on the Birth in the North of a Porphyrogennete Child on the Twelfth Day of December, on Which the Sun Begins his Return from Winter to Summer." Alexander Pavlovich was born December 12, 1777 OS, equivalent to December 23 NS; the winter solstice is on December 22, so the 23rd is in fact the date "on which the sun begins his return from winter to summer." Whether the original ode utilized this device is unknown; in any case the inflated, pompous style of Lomonosov, "for which" Derzhavin "felt himself unsuited" was rejected, and a poem written in a style as different from it as possible. The meter is not the iambic tetrameter of the ode, but trochaic tetrameter, traditionally associated with songs and Anacreontics; there is no strophic division, and the rhyme scheme is a simple alternation: aBaB. Most significantly, the poetic mask of the author is almost playful rather than solemn and prophetic. The poem begins with a fairly realistic description of a northern winter, with, however, some oddly incongruous mythological elements in the classical style: thus the white-haired, gray-bearded Boreas makes all nature tremble:

The earth is turned to stone by his chill hand; the beasts have fled into holes, the fish have hidden themselves in the depths, the choirs of birds dared not sing, the bees have huddled in their hives; out of boredom the nymphs have fallen asleep amid caves and rushes, and the satyrs have gathered around fires to warm their hands.

At the moment of the birth of the "porphyrogennete child," however, "Boreas ceased to roar.... and the beautiful sun turned back toward spring." Around the child's cradle gathered various "genii" in classical style to confer their gifts—wealth, the glory of the purple, joys and delight, peace and repose, etc. Finally the last genius, Virtue, gives the crowning gift: "Be master of your passions, be a man ["chclovek"] upon the throne!"

The poem shows clearly the classical inheritance—the allegory of winter, the intrusive mythology, etc.; at the same time it flagrantly transgresses the classical canons of style by employing a light, dance-like meter for a "lofty" subject. Other poems of the same year 1779, which Derzhavin himself considered the turning-point in his search for a style of his own, show the same combination of classical and anti-classical elements.

Such a poem is "The Spring" ("Kliuch"),[7] with its three rather oddly assorted and not very harmonious elements. It begins with a neo-classical picture, which Professor I.Z. Serman,[8] certainly rightly, regards as suggested to Derzhavin by the writings of his friend N.A. Lvov on sculpture:

Seated, crowned with sedge, in the shade of branching trees, leaning with one hand on an urn, showing the face of the heavens—such is the beautiful spring which I see.

The pose of the figure and its attributes—the urn, the crown of sedge— are precisely those of the conventional classical allegory of the fountain. Then comes a description, beautifully realized of a *real*, not allegorical fountain:

When upon your silvery arcs the red dawn gleams, what fiery purples and flaming roses roll, burning, with the fall of your waters!

* * *

Your bank becomes purple when the sun is descending from the heavens; your crystal is set afire by his rays; in the valley the forest begins to turn blue, and a sea of mists spreads out.

Here we may see, incidentally, an early example of Derzhavin's wonderful sense of color and an anticipation of the gorgeous description of "The Waterfall." But by the eighth strophe of "The Spring" we become dimly aware that there is more to this fountain than meets the eye:

Burning with a poet's passion, I come to you, O rill; I envy the fortune of the bard who has tasted of your waters, [the poet] crowned with Parnassus's laurel.

Give me to drink, give me to drink of you, and I shall sing similarly, and my thought in songs shall be comparable with your pure stream, and [my] lyre's voice with your striving.

May your honor pass through all barriers, as echo from the mountains through the slumberous forest: sacred fountain of Grebenevo, you have given the creator of the immortal *Rossiad* [Mikhail Kheraskov] to drink of the water of poetry.

It is with some shock that we finally recognize that the prettily described fountain is no other than Castalia, in a Russian disguise! Awkwardly as the elements of sculptural emblem, realistic description and classical allegory are combined, they show clear evidence of Derzhavin's impatience with the classical prescriptions that would keep them isolated.

The greatest of the 1779 poems and one of Derzhavin's masterpieces is "Ode on the Death of Prince Meshchersky."[9] Here we are closer to the traditional form: the meter is iambic tetrameter, in eight-line strophes, rhyming *AbAbCddC.* The theme is one of the commonest of classical themes, although significantly, not one found in Lomonosov—the inevitability of death, which brings poor and great to the same end. Two famous poems of Horace (Odes I, 24 and II, 14) are almost the canonical examples of it, and Derzhavin's poem follows the Horatian construction so faithfully that one wonders if he had not been by this time introduced to the great Latin poet— the more so as "The Spring" has such an obvious similarity with Horace's *O fons Bandusiae* (III, 13). The Derzhavin ode, however, is powerfully original, even when it makes use of the trite allegory of Death as "the grim reaper"; Edward Young's *Night Thoughts,* especially his *First Night,* played a part in Derzhavin's development, but, as we shall see, a chiefly negative one.

O word of time![10] Metallic peal! Your dread voice confounds me; Your groan calls me, calls me, calls—and brings me nigh to the grave. Hardly have I seen this light, when Death gnashes his ["Death" in Russian is feminine, but it seems best in translating to follow the gender familiar in English] teeth; his scythe flashes like lightning, and cuts down my days as grass.
    None escapes from his fatal claws, no creature. Monarch and captive are food for the worm, the grave's malevolence devours the elements; time gapes to blot out glory; as swift waters pour into the sea, so days and years pour into eternity; greedy Death swallows kingdoms.

* * *

    Only the mortal thinks not to die, and fancies he is immortal; Death comes to him like a thief and of a sudden steals his life. Alas! where we fear it least, there may Death soonest appear; no more swiftly do the thunders fly down upon proud mountain peaks.

And so the great chant goes on, every stanza marked by the word "death" or a related idea. The words are solemn and the solemnity is heightened by the echoes of Scripture: "Cuts down my days *as grass";* Death comes to him *like a thief,* etc. Ideas are pounded home by constantly repeated words: *Zovet menia, zovet* tvoi ston, *zovet*—i k grobu priblizhaet (strophe 1), or I ves', *kak son,* proshel tvoi vek, *Kak son,* kak sladkaia mechta," etc. (strophes 8 and 9) ["And, *like a dream,* all your life has gone by, *Like a dream,* like a sweet vision"]. And then, suddenly, at the end, following immediately upon the superb line: "Ia v dveriakh vechnosti stoiu," "I stand at the door of eternity," comes a strophe that seems to clash most dissonantly with all that has preceded:

To die, today or tomorrow, Perfilev, is of course the destiny of us all. Why then torment yourself and mourn that your mortal friend did not live eternally? Life is heaven's momentary gift; arrange it for your own repose, and with your pure soul bless the blow of the fates.

Such an Epicurean admonition after the magnificent picture of all-conquering death is disconcerting, to say the least—but perhaps not more so than the last two lines of Horace's ode on the death of Quintilius (I, 24), which follow four strophes that reiterate with all manner of mythological examples the notion that Death is inexorable: "durum, sed levius fit patientia quidquid corrigere est nefas"—"It's hard; but patience makes easier whatever cannot be corrected." Horace's example was probably in Derzhavin's mind in ending his poem thus; almost certainly he was also in a way engaging in a polemic with Edward Young. The English poet's deep dejection at the omnipotence of death leads him to admonish his reader to think only of the inevitable end and abandon concern for the ephemeral pleasures of life that are so soon to be snatched away. For Derzhavin's lusty, life-affirming nature such an attitude was intolerable, and he adds his final strophe almost as an act of defiance.

The year 1779 marked a turning point in Derzhavin's verse; but the poems of that year, fine as they are, still show certain awkwardnesses and uncertainties. The poems of 1782, however, are fully and triumphantly mature, and usher in the series of odes on which Derzhavin's fame securely rests. The first of these is an example of a familiar eighteenth-century genre, the "paraphrase of a Psalm." In this case the Psalm is No. 81 (82 in our numeration).[11] Dissatisfied with his first version, he made two others: the final one was published in the *St. Petersburg Herald* in 1780. The issue in which it appeared, however, was ordered suppressed, and a new page substituted for that which contained the poem. Derzhavin was put to some trouble to convince the authorities that "King David was not a Jacobin," and that the paraphrase was perfectly innocent. It was not issued for the public until 1787. The paraphrase is headed: "To Potentates and Judges" ["Vlasteliam i sudiiam"] :

The Most High God has arisen to judge the gods of earth [i.e., kings] in their assembly: "How long," He says, "how long shall you continue to spare the unrighteous and wicked?

Your duty is to maintain the laws, to regard not the faces of the mighty, not to leave orphans and widows without aid, without defence.

Your duty is to save the innocent from tribulation, to give shelter to the unfortunate; from the powerful to protect the powerless, to snatch the poor from [their] chains."

They do not heed! They see, and do not realize! Their eyes are covered with lucre; evil-doers make the earth to tremble, unrighteousness rocks the heavens.

Kings! ["Tsari"] I deemed ye were mighty gods, no one a judge over you; but ye are moved by passion, even as I, and likewise mortal, even as I.

And even as I, ye fall, as the withered leaf falls from the tree! And ye die even as your lowliest slave dies!

Arise, O God! God of the just! And give ear to their prayer; come hither, pass judgment, chastise the crafty, and be sole king of the earth!

The paraphrase is in fact very close to the original, but Derzhavin has in a few places allowed himself to interpret a somewhat obscure text; thus the first verse of the original reads: "God arose in the assembly of gods; amid the gods he has pronounced judgment." The phrase "earthly gods" as a synonym for "kings" is an eighteenth-century commonplace, and comes very naturally here, whatever the Hebrew may have meant. The original of the third verse contains only an imperative; Derzhavin has added the phrase, doubtless offensive to Catherine: "your duty is." In the fifth verse "their eyes are covered with lucre ["mzdoiu," "reward," that is, "bribe"] corresponds to the original "they walk in darkness." Finally, in verse 6, the line "but you are moved by passions, even as I, and likewise mortal, even as I," is entirely a Derzhavin interpolation; the original reads: "I said: ye are gods, and sons of the Most High, all of you."

Whatever embarrassment his "Jacobin" version of the Psalm may have caused Derzhavin was erased by the signal success of his "Ode to Felitsa" of 1782, which found such favor with Catherine that the poet was presently promoted and most handsomely rewarded. Since this is Derzhavin's most famous poem, and shows with particular clarity the decisive break between his poetical system and the norms of classical usage, it will be well to consider it in some detail.

The background of the "Ode to Felitsa"[12] is the following. In 1782 there appeared, in a restricted edition, a didactic fairy-tale for children which Catherine II had written for her little grandson, Prince Alexander Pavlovich—the "Porphyrogennete child" of Derzhavin's earlier poem. "The Tale of Prince Khlor"[13] describes the mission of the Prince (Alexander) to discover "the rose without thorns." He accomplishes his task through the aid of Queen Felitsa of "the Kirghiz-Kaizak Horde" (the tale is laid in the East). Felitsa, in Catherine's allegory, represents "Reason," by whose assistance the young prince at last finds at the top of a mountain "the rose without thorns," i.e., Virtue. Doubtless Felitsa in Catherine's intention is also a disguise for herself: her flatterers habitually called her "Minerva." Derzhavin's bold and original idea was to utilize this tale of Catherine's own making in order to eulogize her in, as it were, an Oriental masquerade. His secondary, and even more revolutionary, idea was to compose his eulogy of the Empress—"Felitsa"—by the device of contrasting her virtues with the weaknesses of the great noblemen of her entourage, whom he calls "murzas," in accord with the assumed Oriental location of Queen Felitsa's realm. Thus, in the ode form most commonly used by Lomonosov and associated with solemn panegyric in exalted style, Derzhavin, assuming as his own poetic mask the person of one of Queen Felitsa's "murzas," describes the Queen's hard-working, beneficent, abstemious mode of life as a contrast to the idleness, luxury and parasitism of her courtiers. Not only is the device of an Oriental masquerade in an ode unheard-of, but by the admixture of the accusatory elements of satire in the picture of the "murzas" the inflexible classical prohibition against genre mixture is broken. Further to affront the classicist, the hierarchic distinctions of language levels is also broken: in the passages which concern "Felitsa," i.e., Catherine, Derzhavin's language belongs to the level classified as "middle" by Lomonosov, while in the "murza" passages it is decidedly "low," with the startling appearance of an everyday vocabularly undreamed of before in an ode—"tobacco," "coffee," "fools" (a card game), etc. Less obtrusive, but still a decided break with tradition is the intrusion of the poet's own personality, even though disguised under the mask of a "murza," and the half-playful, light tone of the whole. Derzhavin had indeed performed the perilous feat of "pouring new wine into old bottles," and with brilliant success. A few strophes of the long ode (260 lines) will illustrate the various novelties just discussed. The poem begins with a strophe that at once sets the tone:

Godlike queen of the Kirghiz-Kaizak Horde! Whose incomparable wisdom revealed the true path to young Prince Khlor, to ascend to that lofty mountain where grows the rose without thorns, where Virtue dwells—she captivates my mind and spirit: let me find her counsel.

Give [me], O Felitsa! instruction: how to live both splendidly and justly, how to tame the agitation of the passions, and be happy in the world! Your voice arouses me, your son [i.e., Khlor] leads me on; but I am [too] weak to follow him. Confused by life's vanity, today I am master of myself, but tomorrow I am a slave to caprice.

The contrast between Queen and courtiers is immediately drawn, and the language descends a level accordingly; the "common" words are underlined:

Not imitating your murzas, you often walk *on foot*, and the simplest food is usually on your *table*; not valuing your ease, you read, write at your *desk*, and from your pen pour out happiness for all mortals. You do not, like me, *play cards* from morning to morning.

Presently the satiric element takes over entirely, and strophes 5-10 take the form of confessions by the murza-poet of the frivolous ways in which "he" wastes his time. Actually, the descriptions of these several kinds of dissipation fitted individual magnates of Catherine's court so precisely—as they were meant to—that it is said that the Empress took pleasure in sending each of those described a marked copy of the poem! Potemkin, naturally, occupies first place, followed by Alexei Orlov, Peter Panin, Semen Naryshkin and Prince Vyazemsky. It scarcely needs to be said that the Empress' delight in the new ode was not shared by her courtiers, and Derzhavin's popularity with his fellow peers, never very great, disappeared in a wave of indignant outrage. A good example of the homely, "vulgar" but realistic pictures which the poet paints is strophe 6:

Or I am at a sumptuous banquet, where they are giving a feast for me, where the table glitters with silver and gold, [and] where there are thousands of different dishes: there is the famous Westphalian ham, there are the slices of Astrakhan fish [i.e., sturgeon], there stand pilau and pasties, I wash down waffles with champagne; and I forget everything on earth, amid the wines, the sweets and the perfumes.

The picture of imperial virtues which Derzhavin sketches hardly conforms to the notion of later generations about Catherine the Great, but was probably at this date in the poet's life quite sincere (he became disillusioned later):

To you alone, O Queen, it belongs to create light out of darkness: dividing Chaos harmoniously into spheres, to strengthen the entirety by union [supposed to refer to Catherine's creation of the administrative districts called "governments"] ; from discord, harmony, and from greedy passions you alone are able to create happiness. Thus the helmsman, sailing over the deep, catching the roaring wind in his sail, is skilled to guide his ship.

You alone do not offend, do no one an injury; you look through your fingers at foolishness—evil alone you do not tolerate. You correct faults with indulgence, you do not oppress people as a wolf does sheep, you truly know their worth. They are subject to the will of kings, but yet more to the just God who lives in their [i.e., the kings'] laws. (strophes 13-14).

As he nears the end of his ode, the poet, who has for some time forgotten his Oriental locale, returns suddenly to it, and asks (strophes 25-26):

But where in the world does your throne gleam? Where, O heavenly branch, do you bloom? In Baghdad, Smyrna, Kashmir? Hearken, wherever you live—in noting my praises of you, do not suppose that I wanted hats or jackets from you for them. To feel the charm of good, such is the wealth of the soul, the like of which even Croesus did not amass.

I pray the great prophet that I may touch the dust of your feet, and delight myself with the most sweet flow of your words and the sight of your face! I pray the heavenly powers that, spreading out their sapphire wings, they may invisibly keep you from all sickness, evils and sorrow; that the noise of your deeds in posterity may shine forth like the stars in the heavens.

The device of flattery which Derzhavin hit upon in "Felitsa" he made use of several times again, it seems not without Catherine's prompting. In 1783 he wrote his "Thanks to Felitsa"[14] for her munificent rewards, and in the same year or the next "The Murza's Vision,"[15] in which "Felitsa," now in the pose and costume of Levitsky's famous painting of Catherine II, appears to her faithful courtier in a dream of the night. In the same year, probably at a hint from Potemkin, he wrote "To Reshemysl,"[16] using the second of Catherine's children's stories, "Tale of Prince Fevei," in which Potemkin appears in the guise of the wise Reshemysl. In 1789 he wrote another long ode (464 lines), "Portrait of Felitsa."[17] Thereafter, however, as he notes in his autobiography, he was unable to find inspiration in the subject again, and dropped it, despite Catherine's hints that she would like it revived.

The "Verses on the Birth in the North of a Porphyrogennete Child" are, in form, a radically novel variation on a common classical genre, the congratulatory ode. The poem "To Potentates and Judges" is a Psalm paraphrase differing from others of its kind only in its boldly denunciatory language; "Felitsa" is in form a perfectly classical ode, but in content a completely unorthodox combination of eulogy and satire. In 1784 Derzhavin laid hands on another favorite eighteenth-century genre, the religious ode, with results hardly less innovative. The ode entitled "God"[18] utilizes, as did "Felitsa," the Lomonosov stanza—ten lines of iambic tetrameter, rhyming *aBaBccDeeD*. It begins, in quite orthodox fashion:

O thou, infinite in extension, living in the motion of substance, eternal by the flow of time, without person, in three persons of Godhead! Being spirit everywhere and unique, who has neither place nor cause, whom no one has been able to reach, who fills everything with himself, embraces, creates, preserves—whom we call God.

Then the poet proceeds through five further stanzas to emphasize the infinitude of God and the insignificance of all creation in comparison—a theme already familiar from Lomonosov's "Meditations." In strophe 6 comes the word which stands as a pivot in the whole composition—"nothing":

As a drop lost in the sea is all this firmament before Thee. But what is the universe that I behold? And what, before Thee, am I? In that aerial ocean worlds multiplying other worlds by the hundred million—and this, when I dare compare it with Thee, will be but a pin-prick; and I, before Thee—am nothing.

The next strophe begins with the same word—"Nothing!" But now the emphasis is shifted: man is God's image, and God lives in him—so he is not "nothing," but shares in the divine infinitude:

Nothing! But Thou shinest in me with the magnitude of Thy goodness; in me Thou dost reflect Thyself, as the sun in a tiny drop of water. Nothing! But I feel life, with a certain unsated soaring I am ever flying aloft; my soul trusts in Thy existence, probes, thinks, reasons; I am—and so Thou are too!

Thou art!—my heart knows the order of nature, proclaims this to me, my reason affirms, Thou art—and I am no longer nothing! I am a particle of the entire universe, set, it seems to me, in that honored center of existence where Thou didst end Thy bodily creation, and where begin the heavenly spirits, and with me Thou didst link the chain of all beings.

I am the connector of worlds everywhere existing, I am the utmost step of matter, I am the midpoint of living things, the initial stroke of Godhead; I moulder with my body in the dust, [but] in mind I give orders to the thunders. I am king, I am slave, I am worm, I am God! But being so wondrous, whence have I come? It is unknown; but of myself I could not exist.

Thy creation I am, O Creator! I am the creature of Thy wisdom, Thou source of life, giver of good, soul of my soul and king! Thy justice would needs have it so, that my immortal being should traverse the abyss of mortality; that my spirit should be clouded in mortality and that through death I should return, O Father!—into Thy deathlessness.

Inscrutable, unfathomable! I know that my soul's imaginings are powerless to sketch even Thy outlines; but if blessing be one's duty, then for weak mortals it is impossible to honor Thee by any other means than only for them to raise themselves to Thee, to lose themselves in [Thy] measureless diversity, and to shed tears of gratitude.

This ode represents just as drastic a departure from classicism as "Felitsa," but here the novelty is in the thought rather than the form. The theme of man's insignificance in comparison with the Infinite is a Biblical one (e.g., the Book of Job), and traditional to the religious ode. A good deal of the matter in Derzhavin's 8th and 9th stanzas on the human paradox was borrowed, as his contemporaries were quick to note, from Edward Young's *Night Thoughts*. Compare Young's "Night First," lines 68-82:[19]

> How poor, how rich, how abject, how august,
> How complicate, how wonderful is man!
> How passing wonder He who made him such!
> Who centered in our make such strange extremes!
> From different natures so marvelously mix'd,
> Connexion exquisite of distant worlds!
> Distinguish'd link in being's endless chain!
> Midway from nothing to the Deity!
> A beam ethereal, sullied and absorb'd!
> Though sullied and dishonor'd, still divine!
> Dim miniature of greatness absolute!
> An heir of glory! a frail child of dust!
> Helpless immortal! insect infinite!
> A worm! a god!—I tremble at myself,
> And in myself am lost! etc.

But there is nothing essentially unorthodox in the famous theme of "the great chain of being." The development, which would, I think, have startled the good English clergyman as much as it must have Derzhavin's countrymen, *is* unorthodox. I exist, therefore God exists! The traditional reasoning could hardly be more boldly violated. Where is "faith" in this meditation? Everything is subjected to reasoning—and reason declares that I—the human being—have only one duty: to raise myself to divinity! Presumption unheard-of! Where is the doctrine of original sin, of the essential imperfectability of man? Where is the redemption? Where is grace? Derzhavin is reasoning like a man of the enlightenment, not a Christian. Man is *perfectible,* and his purpose in life is to make himself divine. Deistic optimism is triumphant.

One of the eighteenth-century varieties of the lyric most frequently cultivated by Lomonosov and his imitators, such as V.P. Petrov, was the ode in commemoration of great military victories. Derzhavin wrote a few such odes, grandiose and inflated in style, such as the one "On the Capture of Izmail" (1790 or 1791).[20] They seem to be evidently concessions to popular taste, and show little of Derzhavin's originality, although in the Izmail ode there are traces already of Ossianic influence. Much more characteristic, indeed, one of his best poems, is the 1788 ode "Autumn During the Siege of Ochakov".[21] It was written while Derzhavin was governor of Tambov, in the neighborhood of which was the estate of Prince S.F. Golitsyn, who was actively engaged in the siege of Ochakov, a Turkish fortress west of the Crimea, guarding the approaches to the Dnieper River. The ode was composed early in November; Ochakov fell to the Russians in December. It is notable in this very unorthodox ode that it is neither General-in-Chief Potemkin, who was nominally in charge of operations in the Crimean campaign, nor Golitsyn, who was the actual commander at Ochakov, but the ordinary, anonymous Russian soldier who is glorified—and far less space is devoted to "the siege of Ochakov" than to attendant circumstances: the autumn at Tambov, where Derzhavin and Princess V.V. Golitsyna, the General's wife, were anxiously awaiting news from the front; and the domestic picture of the General's family. In this poem, as in so many of Derzhavin's, the eighteenth century conventional "description through mythology" stands in incongruous juxtaposition to actual, realistic genre scenes of Russian life, not entirely unlike the masterly sketches of autumn and winter in *Eugene Onegin*. Such a medley would have been unthinkable to Lomonosov or Sumarokov, or indeed to any of Derzhavin's own contemporaries. The ode begins:

> Gray-haired Aeolus has let Boreas loose from his iron chains out of the caverns; spreading wide his fearful pinions ["krile"—accusative dual number! an unexampled Slavonicism, said to have been suggested to Derzhavin by the poet I.I. Dmitriev], the doughty warrior ["bogatyr"] has flapped over the world; he has driven the blue air in herds, he has thickened the mists into clouds; he has pressed, and the clouds have settled, rain descended and drummed.
>
> Already ruddy Autumn is carrying the golden sheaves to the threshing-floor, and luxury with greedy hand is demanding the grapes for wine. Already the flocks of birds are crowding, the feather-grass is silver on the steppes; rustling red and yellow leaves are scattered everywhere on the paths.

The picture of the autumn rains is wholly mythological, but with the curiously unlikely identification of the Greek wind-god Boreas with a Russian *bogatyr!* The second strophe begins with a quite conventional personification and a *classical* description of autumn activities. The "golden sheaves" may answer to Russian realities, but most certainly the grapes do not; as Belinsky impatiently notes:[22] "Beautiful verses too—but where they take us, God knows!" The excuse that Derzhavin is describing the natural scene at Ochakov, where grapes might grow, is ingenious, but unconvincing. The rest of his description is obviously north Russian. The flocks of birds ready for migration, the feather-grass and the autumn leaves fallen on the paths belong to the real world of Russian experience. Noteworthy once again is Derzhavin's keen sense of color—he even creates the compound adjective "red-yellow" ["krasno-zheltyi"] to describe the leaves. The third strophe moves us entirely into Russian reality, with no classical conventions and with a homely vocabulary startling in a formal ode: "On the forest edge lies the swift-footed hare, having settled like the spoonbill; the hunting-horns resound, and the baying and clamor of hounds peals out. The peasant, having laid in his store of bread, eats good cabbage-soup ["shchi"] and drinks beer; enriched by generous heaven, he sings the happiness of his days." The next strophe once more brings in Boreas and personifications of Autumn and Winter; then another genre picture: "On the carpets of the green fields the white down lies scattered; deserts and dales mourn, and hungry wolves howl in them"; then another strophe (No. 6) which combines the two disparate elements: "The reindeer has gone out into the mossy tundras and the bear has lain down in his den; in the villages the loud-voiced nymphs [here obviously just the village girls] have stopped singing in round-dances; the houses smoke with gray smoke ["dymiatsia serym dymom"], the traveler hastens on his path; the Mars of the heavens [not war-god, but the Star] has laid aside his thunders, and lain down in the mists to rest." Mention of Mars is introduced in order to bring in, in strophe 7, "The Russian Mars, Potemkin," the Crimean campaign and the siege of Ochakov; but Potemkin has no great place in the ode (nor had in the siege); after this polite reference he disappears, and at Ochakov it is "the invincible Russian [soldier]" who "in the frost reaps green laurels, scorns the gray storms, flies against ice, against trenches, against thunder, [and] amid water and fire thinks: he will either die or win victory." Derzhavin then, in two strophes (9 and 10) addresses the Russian heroes directly: "Be men, you Russian Achilleses, sons of the northern goddess [i.e., Catherine] ; though you were not dipped in the Styx [as the Greek Achilles was] , yet by your deeds you are immortal." Then he turns to his friend General Golitsyn with the exhortation: "Bring back to your home the laurel with the olive." The mention of Golitsyn's home then at once introduces his anxious wife and family: "When with warmth you shall embrace your seven sons, you will cast tender glances at their mother and in your joy seek no words." The tender scene of husband and wife reunited is then elaborated with homely details extraordinary in a classical ode:

Hasten, husband, to your faithful wife, be joyful yourself and give her joy; she is thoughtful, sorrowful, in simple attire, her hair scattered over her brow in disarray, she sits on the sofa at a little table, and her light-blue ["sveto-golubye"] eyes are always shedding tears.

There are fifteen strophes in Derzhavin's ode "Autumn During the Siege of

Ochakov," and of these four are devoted to the siege and military exploits, while two others refer to the delights of listening to tales of prowess at the hero's home-coming—surely a quite extraordinary proportion for a "triumphal ode!"

Derzhavin's universally recognized masterpiece is the great ode entitled simply "The Waterfall,"[23] written during the years 1791-1794. The ode was occasioned by the sudden death in 1791 of the most spectacular magnate of Catherine's reign, Grigory Potemkin. Derzhavin of course knew Potemkin and had very ambivalent feelings about him. Unnamed, but identifiable by unmistakable allusions, he is the first of Catherine's "murzas" to be satirized in "Felitsa"; and he appears often enough elsewhere in the poems, but never with any great adulation. Even in "Reshemysl" the portrait of the ideal courtier is evidently not meant to be identified with Potemkin. The man was an enormous force in his time; a magnificent, magnetic, overpowering personality, devoured by ambition and obsessed with the most visionary and fantastic schemes, such as the recovery of Constantinople for Christianity and the reestablishment, under a Russian protectorate, of a Greek "Byzantine Empire." But he was capricious, vain, petty, and an intriguer; he was inordinately fond of luxury and extravagance, and in the last decade of his life, when he was dominant over even the Empress and perhaps actually her morganatic husband, he was a ruthless tyrant. And yet with all his negative qualities, Potemkin was such a titanic figure that the ordinary criteria of morality seemed hardly to apply to him—or so it appeared to Derzhavin.

The ode on Potemkin's death is dominated by the image of the "waterfall,"—a very real waterfall, in fact, which Derzhavin had encountered during his Olonets governorship; it is called Kivach and is on the Suna river, which flows into Lake Onega, northeast of St. Petersburg. The ode opens with a splendid, realistic description of the cataract itself, with Derzhavin's usual eye for color:

A mountain of diamonds pours down from the height in four cliffs [i.e., the waterfall makes four successive leaps] ; an abyss of pearl and silver boils below, and beats aloft in hillocks; a dark-blue hill of spray stands high, and the roar thunders afar through the forest.

The noise goes up, and then is lost in the depths amid the thick woods; the sun's ray glances quickly through the torrent; beneath the pliant vault of trees, as though roofed with a dream, the waves pour quietly, drawn together in a milky stream.

The stupendous power of the waterfall is then briefly noted, and the terror which it inspires in three symbolic animals that visit its bank—the wolf, fallow-deer and horse (malice, meekness and pride, Derzhavin tells us). Then comes an Ossianic vision: an old man, with spear and shield and helmet at his feet, sits under a low-hanging cedar tree, on the bank overlooking the waterfall, and meditates. An unmistakable allusion in a simile of the "red" ["rumianoi"] sunset identifies this spectator as General Peter Alexandrovich Rumiantsev (1725-1796), hero of the Seven Years War and of the first of Catherine's wars against Turkey. Rumiantsev, whom the envious Potemkin had intrigued to disgrace, was universally regarded at this time as the model of self-effacing, patriotic heroism. Watching the noisy waterfall the old man is moved to make it a symbol of human life: "Is it not thus that time pours down from heaven, the torrents of the passions seethe, fame spreads abroad, the fortune of our days flashes past, whose beauty and joy are darkened by griefs, sorrows, and old age." Again the theme of universal death emerges, with the same kind of development as in the "Verses on the Death of Prince Meshchersky":

Into this maw does not king fall from throne, and friend of kings? They fall— and, commander invincible, Caesar fell in the Senate House amid his praises, at the very moment when he desired the diadem—and covered his face with his cloak. [His] projects, hopes disappeared, and the eyes covetous for a throne were closed.

So far in the ode everything has been general and there has been nothing to hint at Potemkin's death—but the *exemplum* of Julius Caesar, followed by that of Belisarius, unmistakably points to another mortal of insatiable ambition, cut down at the moment of triumph by inexorable death. Then, after some melancholy reflections on his own vanished glory and present frustration: "[My] strength weakened, the tempest wrenched the spear from my hands, and hale though my spirit is still, fate has deprived me of victories," the old man falls asleep. His dream of his own glorious career is suddenly interrupted—and again the influence of the dark Ossianic poetry is very apparent—by natural signs that portend some ominous event:

He listens: the fir-tree is riven, the company of ravens awakes, the stony hill breaks in a terrible fissure, the mountain with its riches falls, echo rumbles through the mountains, like thunder rolling upon thunder ["kak grom gremiashchi po gromam"] .

Culminating the ominous dream comes a vision of a black-clad woman with a scythe—Death. Awakened from his vision, the old man proclaims: "Surely, some chieftain has died!" Then follows a strophe that could hardly have been interpreted as unqualified praise of the "chieftain" Potemkin: "Blessed is he if, in striving after glory, he has maintained the general good, been merciful in bloody war, and spared the lives of his very enemies; blessed among later ages be this friend of men!" The next strophe ends with the line "if.... he did not seek for false glory!" This leads to the comparison which is the central theme of the ode:

O glory, glory in the world of the mighty! You are exactly this waterfall. By the torrent of its abundant waters and the noise of the pouring coolness it is magnificent, bright, beautiful, wondrous, mighty, thunderous, clear;

It gathers people about it in crowds for constant admiration; but if with its water it does not give all to drink comfortably, if it bursts its banks and if there is no profit from its swiftness—ah! would it not be better to be less famous, but more useful? Like the charming little brooks to sprinkle fields, meadows, gardens, and from a distance with gentle murmur to attract the notice of posterity ["potomstvo":cf. Potemkin] ?

The old man's speech ends with another guarded benediction for the still unknown hero: "Oh! Be immortal, warlike knight, *if* you have maintained all your duty!"

Then again an Ossianic passage, as the poet, now in his own person, sees a great shade "hastening over the clouds to mansions aloft." "The wind is too slow to flow by his paths; he surveys the kingdoms round about, he clamors, and glitters like a star, and scatters sparks in his wake." A vision of the corpse on the steppe, and the poet cries:

Whose bier is the earth—whose baldequin the blue air, whose palace the sights of the desert about you—Are you not the son of Fortune, son of Glory, magnificent Prince of Tavrida? Was it not you who from the summit of honors fell suddenly amidst the steppes?

The last portion of the ode is largely a fairly conventional glorification of the dead hero, mourned by his army, by Catherine herself, by poets and preachers:

A single hour, a single moment are capable of smiting kingdoms, a single breath of the elements of converting giants to dust! Their places are sought, but not found, and the dust of heroes is trampled upon.

Of heroes? No! But their deeds gleam forth from the dusk and the centuries; [their] memory uncorrupted, their praises fly forth even from ruins; their tombs blossom like hills. Potemkin's labor shall be recorded.

At last, as though almost against his intention, Derzhavin, returning again to his key metaphor, sees in the noisy waterfall now only beauty:

Roar, roar, O waterfall! Touching the regions of the air, gladden hearing and sight by your torrent, bright, noisy, and in mankind's memory live hereafter only by your beauty.

Most of Derzhavin's poetical work from his debut in 1779 until about 1795 was public and monumental—great odes, commemorative poems, satires such as "The Magnate" (1794)[24] and the like. These poems, as we have noted, were for the most part highly innovative and stylistically quite far from the models created by Lomonosov and Sumarokov, but they nevertheless belonged to the same class of public document, the utterances of a Russian patriot speaking as the mouthpiece of the people. In the latter part of his life, however, Derzhavin came more and more to dissociate himself from such public themes and to speak increasingly in his own personal quality. It has been noted before that he was attracted to the so-called poems of Anacreon, especially after a translation of these had been published by his close friend Nikolai Alexandrovich Lvov (in 1794). Derzhavin of course had no knowledge of Greek, but using his friend's version (in unrhymed verse) as a point of departure, he "translated" quite successfully some of the Anacreontea. More significantly, he began to imitate "Anacreon," and in 1804 published a collection of translations and imitations which even contained some of his earliest songs, written long before he had even known of the Greek poet.[25] The concerns of this Anacreontic *persona* are entirely private, like those of his model—chiefly Epicurean delight in the innocent pleasures of eating, drinking and love-making. A healthy, life-affirming hedonist by temperament, Derzhavin felt a natural affinity for such themes.

Other private concerns, however, make their appearance in Derzhavin's later poetry. Mention has been made earlier of the evident influence of Horace on such a poem as "Verses on the Death of Prince Meshchersky." The Roman poet is almost the only writer from classical antiquity, except the spurious "Anacreon," who seems to have had a genuine influence on Derzhavin. One of Horace's most famous poems, the last of the first published collection of *Carmina* (III, 30) is the confident proclamation of his poetical immortality: "Exegi monumentum aere perennius"—"I have reared a monument more enduring than bronze." In 1795 Derzhavin wrote his imitation of this Latin ode; it is entitled simply "Monument";[26] it may be remembered that Lomonosov had translated the same poem.

I have reared me a monument wondrous, eternal; it is stronger than metal and higher than the pyramids. Neither tempest nor swift thunder shall break it, and the flight of time shall not destroy it.

Yes! I shall not wholly die, but a great part of me, escaping corruption, shall live after death, and my fame shall grow, unwithering, as long as the universe shall honor the race of the Slav.

* * *

For I first, in entertaining Russian style, dared to proclaim the virtues of Felitsa, in sincere simplicity to converse about God, and with a smile to tell the truth to kings.

The odes "Felitsa" and "God" evidently constitute the poet's chief claim to immortality in his own opinion, and whether we share this opinion or not, Derzhavin's contemporaries certainly did.

In 1794 Derzhavin's beloved first wife died. They had been married in 1778, and the poet and his "Plenyra," as he affectionately disguised her in his love poetry, had been a model couple. The little six-stanza poem which he wrote "On the Death of Katerina Iakovlevna [Bastidon], Occurring on the 15th Day of July, 1794"[27] he never published; it was evidently too personal a revelation. Professor G.A. Gukovsky published it in 1933, in his selection

400

of Derzhavin's verse. The poem has a strong flavor of Russian popular verse, with its lines of irregular metrical structure and frequent dactylic rhymes; the very fact of its lack of polish makes it more effective. The emblem of the swallow has a connection with a poem, published in 1792, called "The Swallow,"[28] to which, after his wife's death, Derzhavin added two wistful last lines. The unpublished poem "On the Death of Katerina Iakovlevna" reads as follows:

No longer the sweet-voiced swallow, the household [guest], from the eaves—oh! my dear one, my beautiful one, she has flown away—and my joy with her.

The moon's pale radiance does not shine from the cloud in the terrible darkness—oh! her body lies dead, like a bright angel in sound slumber.

The dogs are digging the ground, of a sudden they begin to howl, the wind howls, the house howls; they do not waken my dear one. The thunder shatters my heart!

O you, gray-winged swallow! You will return to my house in the spring; but you, my wife, my dear one, will be seen with me no more forever.

My loyal friend is no more, my good wife is no more, my priceless comrade is no more—oh! they are all buried with her.

Everything is desolate! How can I bear life? Great anguish has devoured me. Farewell, the half of my heart, the half of my soul! The coffin planks have hidden you.

Derzhavin's Epicurean outlook on life and at the same time his sharp break with eighteenth-century decorum that barred from poetry such vulgarly specific items as foods and drinks may be seen in his "Invitation to Dinner"[29] of 1795. It begins:

The golden sterlet of the Sheksna, clabbered cream ["kaimak"] and borsht are already standing [in preparation] ; in the carafes wine and punch allure, one sparkling with ice, the other with flame; from the censers pour perfumes; fruits are smiling in baskets, the servants do not dare even to breathe, as they await you around the table; the shapely young mistress [Derzhavin's second wife, Daria Alexeevna Diakova, whom he married early in 1795] is ready to stretch out her hand.

The banquet, like Horace's, is to be "a feast of reason and the flow of soul," not a vulgar drinking-bout; but the poet, again like Horace, is moved to admonish his guests to enjoy themselves while they can:

To my friends I dedicate this day, to my friends and to beauty; I know the value of merits, and I know this, that our life is a shadow; that scarcely have we passed our childhood when we have already arrived at old age, and death is peeping at us through the fence. Alack! Then why not become philosophers, garland ourselves, if but once, with flowers, and leave off our gloomy looks!

Even kings, it appears, are not always happy—"He that is eternally on duty is as pitiable as a poor sentryman!" The final strophe of the "Invitation" ends with the perfectly Horatian sentiment: "Happiness is not in the gleam of purple, nor in the savor of foods, nor in the delight of the ear; but in soundness and repose of spirit; moderation is the best banquet." It may be noted that the "Invitation to Dinner," in marked contrast of its form to the homely vocabulary and easy, unconstrained tone, is in the strictest ode form: Lomonosov's ten-line iambic tetrameter strophe, rhyming *aBaBcc-DeeD!*

One of Derzhavin's masterpieces, and the most complete example of his delight in the beauties of life and his consummate ability to enshrine them in vivid word pictures is the epistle: "To Eugene. Life at Zvanka."[30] The addressee was Derzhavin's close friend Bishop Eugene Bolkhovitinov (1767-1837), a learned historian, archaeologist and literary critic. Zvanka was Derzhavin's fine estate in Novgorod province on the Volkhov river, to which he retired in 1803. The epistle, written in 1807 and published in the same year, is quite long (252 lines), in four-line strophes which consist of three Alexandrines followed by a four-beat iambic line; the rhymes are alternate masculine and feminine: *AbAb*. The strophic division is irregular for an epistle, which is normally in straight Alexandrines.

The poem describes what presumably might be a typical day at Zvanka during the summer, from the moment of rising to the reveries of evening. All the pictures are sharp and clear:

> I hear close at hand the call of the shepherd's horn, and at a distance the dull drumming of grouse, "lambs in the air" [i.e., snipe, which have a bleating call like lambs], the whistling of nightingales in the bushes, the lowing of cows, the thundering of woodpeckers and the neighing of horses. I note how the swallow twitters on the roof—and from the house is wafted the vapor of Manchuria [tea] or the Levant [coffee]. I go to the round table: and there there is a chattering about dreams, the gossip of the city and of the peasants.

* * *

> From the cow-barns, bee-hives and ponds I look at gold covered with leaves— now of butter and now of honey-comb; at the purple of berries, the velvet down of mushrooms, and the silver of threshing bream.

* * *

> The hour of midday strikes, they run to serve at table; the mistress with a chorus of her guests goes to the dining-room. I inspect the table—and see a flower-garden of various dishes, set out in a pattern.
> Pink ham, green cabbage-soup with the yellow of egg, reddish-yellow pasty, white cheese, red crayfish, caviar like pitch or like amber—and there the varicolored pike with blue fin—beautiful!

* * *

> Or standing we note the sound of the green and black waves; how the plow

402

mounds up the turf; how the ripe heads of the hay fall under the scythe, the gold of the cornlands under the sickle—and how, full of aromas, the wind takes flight amidst the rows of nymphs [i.e., the reaping women] .

Or we watch how beneath a black cloud the shadow races over the ricks, over the sheaves, over the yellow-green carpets; and how the sun descends to its lowest step toward the blue-black hills and groves.

As usual, the precise color words, often compound adjectives put together as a painter might mix his paints on a palette, are prominent in these scenes; the still-life of the dining table is justly famous. But the other senses are not neglected; there are more precise words describing bird sounds—drumming, whistling, thundering, twittering—then are to be found in all Russian literature before Derzhavin; and indoors we hear "the thunder from the resonant harp, that penetrates the soul, the soothing, melting tones" that "flow from the strings of the piano-forte ["tikhogrom"] ."

The gentle, pastoral repose of "Life at Zvanka" is interrupted here and there by meditation; the poet retires in the forenoon to his study, and perusal of history shows him "nothing but the self-love and wrangling of men." " 'All is vanity of vanities,' think I, sighing; but casting my eyes on the radiance of the noon-day sun—O how beautiful is the world! Why should I burden my soul? The universe is in the Creator's keeping." As the day wanes, melancholy returns: "What is our worthless life? My fragile lyre? Alas! Even the dust of my bones Saturn will sweep away with his wings from this world of corruption. This house will be torn down, forest and garden will wither, nowhere will there be even a remembrance of the name of Zvanka; but the fire-green eyes of hoot-owls and barn-owls [will peer] from the hollows, and perhaps smoke will roll up from a mud hut." But at the last the poet reminds himself that his younger friend Eugene will not let his name pass into oblivion: "Waking with your pen our descendants from slumber, near to the capital of the north, you shall whisper in the wanderer's ear, like quiet thunder in the distance: 'Here lived the singer of God—and of Felitsa.' "

The peculiarities of Derzhavin's linguistic practice have been pointed out in nearly every poem discussed, and it need only be remarked, by way of summary, that he treated the hierarchies of language with as little respect as he did other eighteenth-century poetical conventions. Champagne, playing cards, tobacco, Westphalian ham in an ode, side by side with solemn Slavonicisms—a bewildering medley. Nor is his grammar always conventional, although it would be too difficult to document this for an English reader. Pushkin, much too harshly, remarks in a letter to his friend Anton Delvig:[31] "So help me, this genius thought in Tatar—he hadn't the time to be bothered with Russian grammar." Actually, Derzhavin's deviations are not so much grammatical solecisms as a tendency, seen also in vocabulary, to employ the language of the common people.[32]

Much has also been said about his use of meter. Most notable, probably, is the appearance in so many of his poems of a perfectly classical form, as for example the Lomonosov strophe, in a thoroughly uncanonical ode, such as "Felitsa" or "Invitation to Dinner." But he is also experimental in metrical matters: the use of a slightly irregular "popular" line in the poem on his wife's death has been noted. A much more determined—and published—effort in the popular direction is his "Maiden-Tsar" ["Tsar'-Devitsa"] [33] of 1812, written in the spirit of a popular ballad, and employing the quasi-popular four-line stanza of trochaic tetrameter rhyming *aBaB*. But perhaps his greatest metrical experiment, and an extremely successful one, is the famous "Gypsy Dance"[34] of 1805. This is written in six stanzas of six lines each, of which the last two lines in each stanza constitute an ever-repeated refrain: "Set souls aflame, hurl fire on hearts from [your] swarthy face." The first four lines are amphibrachic trimeters, with alternating feminine and masculine rhyme. Zhukovsky and the romantic poets came to use this triple measure quite extensively, but the amphibrach is a great rarity in Russian verse before this time. Derzhavin's metrical *tour de force* was intended to transfer to verse the curious syncopated beat of gypsy music. A metrical analysis of the first strophe will make this clearer:

Возьми, египтянка, гитару,	Take the guitar, Gypsy maiden,
Ударь по струнам, восклицай;	Strike on the strings, cry out;
Исполнясь сладострастна жару,	Filled with voluptuous fire,
Твоей всех пляской восхищай.	Entrance all with your dance.
Жги душу, огнь бросай в сердца	Set souls aflame, hurl fire on hearts,
от смуглого лица.	From [your] swarthy face.

Our discussion of Derzhavin's lyric poetry has emphasized throughout the simultaneous presence in it of elements characteristic of the classical system of verse composition, and of elements antithetical to that system. Let us now attempt to summarize these disparate elements in Derzhavin's style, beginning with the classical inheritance.

It hardly needs to be said that much of Derzhavin's verse is, as Belinsky quite unjustly said of it all, rhetoric. So, of course, is Lomonosov's or Sumarokov's. In an age when verse composition was regarded as a form of intellectual exercise, and reason its guide, all poetry, with rare exceptions, tends to take the form of rhetoric. Too often for modern tastes the best efforts of a poet become merely moral or philosophical discourse in metrical form. What else is there, indeed, in the verse of Pope, or of Voltaire? Derzhavin's verse is, however, in this as in most other respects, transitional—and his poetical theory, as we shall presently discover, equally vacillating. "The Waterfall," "God," "The Magnate," etc., are indeed rhetoric, versified reasoning, with little basis in or appeal to the emotions. "Life at Zvanka," "On the Death of Katerina Iakovlevna," "Gypsy Dance," and many other of the smaller lyrics are, however, no more rhetorical than, let us say, the lyrics of such pre-romantics as Batiushkov or Zhukovsky. But in the prevalence of rhetoric in his verse Derzhavin is truly a representative of his age.

In another regard too we may consider Derzhavin typically classical—his didacticism. Classical theories of poetry always assume that art must teach, must be aimed primarily at inculcating a lesson. Very typical of this side of Derzhavin's verse is the short piece called "The Peacock."[35] It begins with a minute and sharply observed description of the gorgeous bird, with Derzhavin's usual painterly eye for color:

> What proud creature, spreading his tail magnificently, displays, sparkling, the black-green feathers with loose fringe behind his scaly body, like some proud and wondrous shield?
> Azure-gray-turquoise shadowy circles on the end of each feather, new waves of undulating gold and silver; he bends—and emeralds glitter! He turns—and sapphires burn!

Then follow the ironically phrased expectations aroused by the peacock's beauty:

> Is not this the famous feathered king? Is not this the paradisal Fire-bird, whose so rich adornment inspires creation with wonderment? Where he steps, rainbows play! Where he stands, there is radiance around!
> Surely in his wings are the strength and soaring of eagles, in his sweet mouth the trumpet's voice, the song of the swan—and the pelican's virtue in his heart and soul!

The last strophe pounds home the, by now obvious, "message" of the poem, with all the insistence of a schoolmaster: "But what an extraordinary phenomenon! I hear a sort of strange screech! This Phoenix has suddenly lowered his plumes at sight of the ugliness of his feet. O magnificence! How you blind [people]! A witless nobleman ["baryn"] is a peacock."

There is a good deal of didacticism in Derzhavin, not often as obtrusive as this. Many also of the habitual classical procedures of verse description may be found in his poetry; they must have been almost automatic. Such is the mythological ornamentation: late autumn or winter is ushered in by Boreas, the god of the North-wind ("Verses on the Birth in the North of a Porphyrogennete Child"; "Autumn During the Siege of Ochakov"); nymphs and satyrs inhabit the woods; Mars presides over battles, Venus over scenes of love, etc. But this convention is so deep-rooted in European verse from the Renaissance on, that it is not even wholly accurate to call it merely classical. In this connection it is worth noting that some Russian eighteenth-century poets, uncomfortably aware of the incongruity of a Greek pantheon in the Slavic world, but still feeling the indispensability of mythology as a poetic instrument, tried to find a native substitute, and *faute de mieux,* to create one. Such is the love-god Lel', assumed to be identical with Cupid, whom Derzhavin sees in a vision in the poem "The Cupid of Falconet".[36]

The classical elements in Derzhavin's style are unobtrusive and omnipresent—but it would be a great mistake for this reason to regard him as a typically classical poet. Too many features of his verse are precisely anti-classical, as is his poetical theory, as we shall see. Two of these anti-classical elements have been frequently commented upon above—the naturalism of his descriptions and his disregard of genre distinctions. Classical theory required the elimination of all specific details in description: a group of trees is "a shady grove," not "a clump of birch and alders!"; a table is set "with savory viands and sparkling wine," not with "Westphalian ham and champagne," etc. The goal is to make everything universal. We have seen how antithetical to this is Derzhavin's practice. Especially, as has so often been pointed out, is this true of his use of color designations. Where the autumn leaves would perhaps be called "motley" or "varicolored" ["pestrye"] by a classical poet at his most specific, Derzhavin makes them "red-yellow." His peacock has "azure-gray-turquoise" circles on his tail feathers, etc. This specificity is equally noteworthy in words denoting sounds—the peacock's voice is "a strange screech," the bleating call of the snipe makes them "lambs in the air," etc. Derzhavin is a poet of the senses, and he refuses to blur the impressions which his senses bring him in order to create a universally intelligible picture.

The genre distinctions which form the corner-stone of classical poetics are an inheritance from Greek antiquity, although in their original environment they never were regarded with the veneration which they acquired in the eighteenth century. With the Greeks genre was simply a category of verse form, not a determinant of content. An elegy, for example, was a poem composed in the elegiac meter; its substance might vary all the way from an exhortation to bravery in battle to a description of a voluptuous erotic encounter to a narrative description of an old.woman's supper preparations. Derzhavin knew no Greek, and of course had no access to the meager remains of Greek lyric verse, which were still inaccessible to his age, with few exceptions. But he seems to have almost intuitively perceived the artificiality of the compartmentalization of poetic types which classical theory evolved from a misunderstanding of Greek and Latin usage, and reacted against it, both in practice and in theory. We have noted how "Felitsa," an ode in form, contains elements of satire, how another formal ode, "Invitation to Dinner," is a friendly epistle in content, and how "Life at Zvanka," a formal epistle has elements of both elegy and pastoral; and we have seen how, in all types of verse that he touches, it is not the prescribed classical *persona* of the genre who speaks, but Derzhavin himself. This is a radically anti-classical innovation.

I have labeled such features of Derzhavin's verse "anti-classical" without further definition, because they can better be appreciated as reactions against the prevailing style than as premonitions of the sentimentalist or pre-romantic styles which supplant classicism at the end of the century. But some specific pre-romantic characteristics are to be found in Derzhavin's verse, as previous discussions have indicated. Here the composite influence of Celtic and Scandinavian models is most prominent. The principal source for Russians of this material was the work of the Swiss savant Paul-Henri Mallet (1730-1807),[37] entitled: *Monuments de la Mythologie et la Poésie des Celtes et particulièrement des anciens Scandinaves pour servir de supplément et de preuve à L'Introduction de Danemarc* [i.e., the author's earlier work of 1755]. This was the source in which Derzhavin's friend Nikolai Lvov found the original for his Scandinavian "Song of Harald the Brave," and in its Russian translation of 1785 was accessible to Derzhavin himself. It is worth noting that neither Mallet nor other scholars for many years made any distinction between Celtic (i.e., Ossianic) and Scandinavian; both ancient cultures were regarded as a single "northern" entity. This one may see with particular clarity in Ozerov's tragedy *Fingal*. Celtic and Scandinavian color—wild and gloomy natural surroundings, mists and dark forests and ominous birds such as ravens and owls—marks Derzhavin's "Waterfall" particularly, but may be found in other poems also, such as "The Capture of Izmail." Another non-classical element characteristic of the pre-romantic style is the exploitation of native Russian, popular verse forms, styles and subjects. The most notable such piece in Derzhavin's work is the narrative poem "The Tsar-Maiden" (1812).[33] The subject is a Russian folk-story, and although the regular four-line stanza form is remote from popular usage, the poet attempts to convey a popular flavor by the occasional use of such expressions as "zhila-byla," "was once on a time," or "they swam like cheese in butter" ["plavali kak v masle syr"] , i.e., "lived a very pleasant life."

Like most true lyric poets Derzhavin did not theorize about his art until quite late. It was not until 1811 that he began work on his "Dissertation ["Rassuzhdenie"] on Lyric Poetry, or the Ode." A portion of this theoretical treatise was published by Grote in his "Complete Edition" of Derzhavin's works;[38] a good deal of it, however, remains still in manuscript in the Leningrad State Public Library. A few extracts from the unpublished portion have been made accessible in essays by L.I. Kulakova and others.

Apparently a good deal of the complete treatise is relatively valueless, being chiefly a rehash of esthetic theories already obsolete in Derzhavin's day. If one were to be guided by such entirely second-hand matter, Derzhavin's position as a classicist would be a certainty. But in his theories as in his practice, the poet held with no attempt at consistency to two quite different concepts of poetry. He had, as has been noted before, a knowledge of German which opened for him a good deal of pre-romantic theory that he might not have had access to readily in Russian. Herder is one of these theorists, and another is Edward Young, whose *Conjectures on Original Composition* (1759) were published in German as early as the 1770s. Another pre-romantic whose influence on Derzhavin is obvious is Johann Georg

Hamann (1730-1788); his famous dictum on primeval poetry: "Poetry is humanity's mother tongue, just as silviculture is older than agriculture, painting older than literature, singing older than declamation, the apologue older than the syllogism, barter older than commerce,"[38a] is echoed by Derzhavin early in his treatise:

Lyric poetry makes its appearance from the very cradle of the world. It is the most ancient [kind of poetry] with all peoples; it is the outpouring of the enflamed spirit, the echo of touched feelings, the ecstasy or effusion of the rapturous heart. Man, arisen from the dust and entranced by the wonders of the world, must first have uttered the voice of his joy, wonder and gratitude in lyrical exclamation. Everything surrounding him: sun, moon, stars, seas, mountains, forests and rivers filled [him] with lively feelings and wrung utterances from him. Here is the genuine and original source of the ode; and for this reason it is not, as some think, merely the imitation of nature, but inspiration by it, whereby it is distinguished from other poetry. It is not science, but fire, heat, feeling.[39]

Says Young: "An *Original* [that is, a work of inspiration] may be said to be of a *vegetable* nature; it rises spontaneously from the vital root of genius; it grows, and is not made; *imitations* are often a sort of manufacture wrought up by those *mechanics, art* and *labour*, out of pre-existent materials not their own."[40]

Classical theory held that the poet must *imitate:* the unapproachable models for all subsequent writers are the poets of Greece and Rome. The modern composer of odes must model himself on Pindar, Horace and Anacreon. Young's *Conjectures* decisively reject this notion: imitation leads to second-rate work; only "original composition" is first rate, and originality of composition springs from "genius." Direct inspiration by nature, not imitation of models, was the procedure of the ancients, and the modern poet must imitate, not the *work*, but the *method* of the ancients. This is precisely what Derzhavin says in his "Dissertation," and a more radical break with classicism can hardly be imagined.

Continuing on the subject of inspiration, the poet contemptuously jettisons the classicist's dictum that poetry is the creation of the all-powerful reason:

Inspiration is born by the contact of chance with the poet's passion, as a spark in ashes which is animated by the breath of the wind.... In genuine inspiration there is neither connection nor cold reason; it even shuns them, and in its lofty soaring seeks only lively, engaging presentations. From this it is that in superior lyric poets every word is a thought, every thought an image, every image a feeling, every feeling expression, now lofty, now fiery, now powerful, or possessing in itself its own peculiar color and attractiveness....

Loftiness [i.e., what English eighteenth-century theorists call "the sublime"] is of two kinds. One is *sensual* and consists in the lively presentation of *things;* the other intellectual, and consists in the display of the activity of a lofty spirit.... The first belongs to the lyre, the second to the drama.[41]

It is perhaps because Derzhavin's own inspiration is precisely what he calls "sensual," and hence, in his theory, essentially lyric, that he failed quite decisively in the drama, which requires, at least in its eighteenth-century versions, an "intellectual" inspiration.

Still on the subject of inspiration, he emphasizes its non-voluntary, almost divine character:

Inspiration is nothing else but a lively feeling, the gift of heaven, illumination from divinity. The poet in the full intoxication of his feelings, enflamed by that fire that comes from above, or to speak more simply, by imagination, goes into a rapture [Lomonosov's "vostorg"], seizes his lyre and sings what his heart commands him.[41]

Later in his essay, returning to the topic of what he has called the sensual "presentation of things," which as we have constantly noted, plays such a very large part in his poetical practice, he speaks of:

Brilliant, lively pictures, that is, views taken from nature, which instantly strike the imagination of tender or sensitive people and produce before their very eyes a fantasy (dream) or fanciful feelings. These pictures in lyric poetry (not to speak of epic) must be short, sketched with a fiery brush, or with a single stroke of terror or delight, magnificently.[42]

Part of the classical striving toward universality concerns the question of "taste." If every literary or artistic genre has its model marked out, one and unchangeable; and reason has laid down the rules by which this model is to be imitated, then esthetic appreciation ("taste") must be identical in all educated people. If "nature" and not humanly created models is followed, then it is not what we might call "raw" nature, which always is "imperfect," but "nature with its insufficiencies removed," "elegant nature,"—the formal garden and not the wilderness. In any case, reason decrees that there can be only one "true taste."

This position, of course, came under attack as soon as the unconditional veneration of classical precept and practice began to come into question, and the individual personality of the artist began to assert itself. The complete rejection of the classical notion of "taste" belongs to developed romanticism, but intimations of it are to be found considerably earlier. In her introduction to the "Poet's Library" edition of the poems of Mikhail Nikitich Muraviev (1757-1807), Professor L.I. Kulakova, using the unpublished archive of Muraviev now in the Leningrad State Public Library, writes as follows:[43]

"Letters" ["pis'mena"].... are called beautiful [i.e., "Belles lettres"] for this reason, that they pursue and represent beauty, which is different in all the creations of nature and the works of man" (3, 31)—of this Muraviev is firmly convinced, just as he is that "the true and tender feeling for beauty in nature and the arts is called *taste*" (3, 128). In further defining taste he contradicts himself. Now, in accordance with the dictates of classicism, he recognizes a certain unitary and unchangeable "model of taste," the legislators of which are Aristotle, Horace, Boileau; now, abandoning classicism, he shows that "the beauties of a poem or painting recoil from the rigor of proof" (3, 131), speaks of the "inexplicable attractiveness" of a poetical work, discusses "original compositions marked with the imprint of the popular mental outline" (3, 121), explains the difference in writers by time and national peculiarities (1, 178-179), rejects every kind of rationalism in poetry:

> Reflection does not create
> By its counted and measured course,
> But feeling by its all-powerful madness
>   Hastens the birth of miracles [State Public Library, No. 3]

and in the final analysis arrives at the romantic theory of genius.

Muraviev was a brilliant and highly cultured man, and associated in a literary way with the circle centered on Nikolai Lvov, Derzhavin's close friend. Although most of Muraviev's work remained unpublished, it no doubt circulated in manuscript among his friends, and was quite possibly known to Derzhavin. At any rate Derzhavin too rejects the classical definition of taste:

"True taste" is not the traditional following of "the rules," not the "rectification of nature's insufficiencies," not "the imitation of elegant nature," the obligatory character of which is still maintained even after Derzhavin. No, it is: "the observance of all the circumstances that relate to man—time, customs, religion et al."[44]

In both Muraviev and Derzhavin, in the passages quoted above, may be noted the beginnings of a historical view of art and literature, again totally at variance with the dictates of classicism, one of the basic principles of which is the universality of human experience. Differences of environment, cultural inheritance, etc., are irrelevant—human nature is always and everywhere the same. Derzhavin repudiates this position very sharply in one passage:

Climate, location, religion, custom, degree of education and even temperament have their influence on every poet. But it is observed in general that the more barbarous a people was, the more fiery was its imagination, the more abrupt and curt its style, the less connection, development and consecutiveness in ideas, but the more picturesque nature in images and the more imagination. On the contrary, with cultured societies, there is more diversity, development, charm, brilliance in thoughts and loftiness in language.[45]

What he has to say here about abruptness of style and lack of logical development of ideas applies precisely to the Scandinavian poetry and the verse of Ossian.

One of the classical pedantries which evidently annoyed Derzhavin particularly was the minute classification of lyric verse into subject categories, such as German theorists were fond of. In the unpublished portion of his

"Dissertation" quoted by Kulakova[46] he writes:

> But I shall say that [even] if the names do not lend things an importance without their real deserts, yet one must agree with me that they, that is, those designations, or particular divisions of songs, are rather an oversubtlety, or pedagogues showing off their knowledge of antiquity, than a genuine necessity; for while one speaks in them on one subject, he may with propriety also mention another.

Derzhavin submitted his "Dissertation" in manuscript to his friend Bishop Eugene Bolkhovitinov, a very learned literary historian, who was scandalized by this lack of respect for genre classifications which he declared in a letter to Derzhavin were by no means mere scholastic subtleties, but originated from nature. The classification which Derzhavin proposed as a substitute, by individual poets—odes would be "Pindaric" or "Sapphic" or "Horatian," etc.—he declared would simply not do. His friend bowed to the superior erudition of Bishop Eugene, but with reluctance: "I have no great respect for the pedantic divisions of lyric poetry, but in order not to bring the whole mob of the schools down on my head, I'll change [the text] merely touching on the matter a little."[47]

At the advice of Eugene Bolkhovitinov Derzhavin suppressed his dislike for "pedantic divisions," but he prepared the ground for their abolition by referring to the ode ballads and romances and *stanze* and songs, with the categorical assertion that eulogies must be accompanied "by an Attic power of moral instruction or satire," by the practical embodiment of this thesis in odes which destroyed the customary views on genres and the unity of style, obligatory for classicism. In the unpublished portion of the "Dissertation" was maintained also the theory of the "mixed ode," which completely justifies the system of Derzhavin's odes.[48]

From all that has been said it should be obvious that in theory, at least, Derzhavin was at so many points in direct opposition to classical poetics that there is nothing surprising in his being sometimes hailed as a pre-romantic, divorced altogether from classicism.

In his declining years the great lyric poet, to everyone's surprise, turned his talents to the writing of drama, a type of literature which by his own definitions required a completely different kind of inspiration from his own. Of the numerous pieces—tragedies and operas—which he composed between 1804 and 1816, only one, *Herod and Mariamne,* was ever staged, and this with no marked success. This is also the only one of his plays which has been published since the Grote edition of Derzhavin's *Complete Works.*[49]

Derzhavin was particularly intrigued by the lyrical and semi-operatic dramas of the Italian Metastasio (1698-1782), and in his first dramatic efforts attempted to follow the same direction: *Dobrynia,* an opera based on the famous folk-tale *bogatyr* (1804), and *Pozharsky, or the Liberation of Moscow* (1806). It is worth noting that Derzhavin, in treating historical themes, paid meticulous attention to the "facts" of history; he was highly critical, for instance, of such an anti-historical extravaganza as Ozerov's *Dmitry Donskoy.* Two later dramas—*Eupraxia* (1808) and *The Dark One* [i.e., Vasily II "the Dark," i.e., "Blind"] (1809), and an opera *The Terrible* [i.e., Ivan IV], *or the Subjugation of Kazan* employ subjects from Russian history. He also wrote a "children's comedy in one act, with choruses" (1806), and a couple of comic operas, of which the one called *Miners* has considerable interest from its realistic scenic presentation of a mine and its pioneering use in literature of an industrial theme. On the whole it appears that Derzhavin's success with the drama was slight, but until more of his work in this area is made generally available, a final verdict were better withheld.

The tragedy *Herod and Mariamne,* the only one of his dramatic works to be actually staged, is said to have been quite coldly received, although some authorities dispute this. A chilly reception seems not unlikely, in view of some features of the drama, which must have shocked the conservative theater-going public.

In the first place, the plot is drawn from a source doubtless not very familiar to a Russian audience. Sumarokov's tragedies, and those of most of his successors, including Kniazhnin, have plots based on either classical legend or Russian history. There are a few exceptions—Sumarokov's *Hamlet* or Ozerov's *Fingal*—but even these have relatively familiar plots, for Voltaire's detailed analysis of Shakespeare's *Hamlet,* which was Sumarokov's source, and Ossian's "epic" on the tale of Fingal were familiar to any literate audience of the time. But how many people were intimately acquainted with chapters xxii-xxxiii of Flavius Josephus's *Jewish War*? It was from this source that Derzhavin drew his material for *Herod and Mariamne,* and with him it was not merely a question of lending historical names to the conventionalized and abstract figures of classical tragedy—the jealous tyrant, the wronged and loving wife, the ambitious plotter, etc.—but of a genuine attempt to reconstruct, with some freedom, to be sure, the historical and complex facts of a historical action. It is quite safe to say that even with Derzhavin's abundant expository material no reader or listener would have been able to understand the play without a prior knowledge of Josephus's story. And the history of Herod the Great, his relations with the Hasmonaean house, with Mark Antony, with Cleopatra, with Julius Caesar and with Augustus, to say nothing of his own family, are exceedingly complicated and confusing even when one has the historical text before him. This feature of the play in itself would account for its want of success.

In this connection one may note another aspect of Derzhavin's non-classical feeling for history. His characters are given a savagery and violence that transgress all the bounds of classical propriety—because, as he explains in a note to the published text, the historical Jews of the first century were in fact barbarians! So, of course, were the Russians of such a remote period as the ninth century A.D., yet Kniazhnin's *Vadim of Novgorod* pictures a cultured and sophisticated society indistinguishable from the tragic portrayals of

412

Athens, Rome or Moscow! Derzhavin did not want his first-century Jews and Idumaeans to resemble French marquises!

But in developing the characters of his tragedy, Derzhavin goes even far beyond the indications given by Josephus—and in this respect he is certainly under the influence of the *Sturm und Drang* dramaturgy of the German pre-romantic movement. Family feuds, rivalries between brother and brother or father and son, murders of kin, and especially, incestuous relationships were favorite plot devices of the Sturmer und Dranger. Derzhavin knew German, and may have been acquainted with some of the dramatists of that group whose later lives were passed in Russia, such as J.M.R. Lenz and Maximilian von Klinger. In any case, in his tragedy Derzhavin makes Antipater, who was actually a son of Herod by his first wife Doris, whom he had divorced to make way for the Princess Mariamne, a man of very ambiguous birth indeed. In the *dramatis personae* he is called, quite properly, "Herod's son by his first wife Doris"; but Salome (Russian Solomiia) is called "Herod's sister, who is called Antipater's mother!" And the text of the play does nothing to clarify this ambiguity. Antipater clearly believes that he is Salome's son, and even when in the fourth act Salome proposes that he marry her, and he quite reasonably objects that public opinion would be shocked at a marriage between mother and son, she does not really disabuse him, although in pointing out that there is only a five-year difference in their ages, she would seem to be hinting either that she could not really be his mother— or else that she has had a remarkably precocious sex life! Derzhavin is obviously leaving this ambiguity with deliberate intent, so that uncertainty remains as to whether Antipater is really the child of a liaison between brother and sister, and in his assent to a marriage with Salome is actually about to compound incest by a union with his own mother! Russian audiences were not used to this kind of titillation.

In characterizing his persons, Derzhavin follows Josephus quite carefully, with one exception. Herod is made the insanely suspicious and jealous husband, passionately devoted to Mariamne, but ready to murder her at every hint, however unfounded, that she might be unfaithful to him. In developing this character, the poet shows him in several reversals of feeling, as Salome's plots seem to cast suspicion on Mariamne, and she succeeds in demonstrating her innocence—until the last occasion, when the cup-bearer accuses her of trying to poison him. Herod is thus shown constantly vacillating in his feelings toward Mariamne; and when, in the final act, she voluntarily drinks the poison and dies before the entire plot of Salome and Antipater is revealed, Herod is depicted in a frenzy of rage ordering his son and sister to be cut into little pieces and burned in a slow fire! The villains of the piece, Salome and Antipater, are depicted throughout as cold, scheming, hypocritical and devoid of all feeling for Herod, despite their close relationship to him.

The one major change in characterization from the original is that of

413

Mariamne. Josephus makes her hate Herod as passionately as he loves her, because of his murder of her brother Aristobulus and her grandfather Hyrcanus. With Derzhavin she is deeply in love with her husband, even though she fears him and fully recognizes the danger she runs from him. Falsely accused and reproached by Herod, she reacts with dignity and reasonableness; but seemingly at the last calumny she loses hope and patience, and resigns herself almost willingly to death in order to escape the constant uncertainty of her life. Both Herod and Mariamne are complex and credible characters.

According to Josephus Herod had five children by Mariamne; Derzhavin gives him two sons, Alexander and Aristobulus, 12 and 11 years old respectively. Actually these two sons survived their mother's murder by many years, lived to manhood and themselves had children, before they fell victim at last to their half-brother Antipater's plotting. Derzhavin condenses this, and makes their situation more pathetic by reducing their ages.But it cannot be said that his depiction of the children is lifelike in any degree. They weep and despair at their mother's misfortune, and claim that life holds nothing for them without her—but their language is that of all the rest of the characters, and there is no attempt to make them childlike, or to individualize them. They are as much alike as Rosencrantz and Guildenstern, and as little like children.

And in this connection one more remark may be made about Derzhavin's dramatic composition. We have seen how boldly he treated the linguistic conventions in his lyric verse, introducing "low" and even colloquial words into genres for which convention required the "high style." There is nothing of the kind in his dramatic verse. He employs the usual Alexandrine verse in the dialogue, and a style that, even if not hyper-Slavonic, is marked by such quantities of inversions, hyperbata, and such generally unnatural word order that comprehension is made exceedingly difficult. Very often nothing short of a complete rearrangement on paper of a period into its natural order will render his verbal puzzles intelligible. This is in the sharpest contrast to the "choruses" which appear from time to time to greet the returning Herod, enliven Mariamne's garden retreat, or lament her fate at the Sanhedrim. The language of the choric passages, which are in lyric meters, is perfectly natural, simple, free of bombast, essentially the same as that of all Derzhavin's non-dramatic lyrics. One is bound to wonder why the poet should have reverted in his dramatic verse to the pompous incomprehensibility of Trediakovsky!

It is a pity that Derzhavin's dramas proved so unsuccessful, for in much he was ahead of his age. Certainly his feeling for history in the drama cannot be paralleled before Pushkin's *Boris Godunov*. His characterization and the construction of his tragedy are dramatic, and should be effective on the stage. Even the sensationalism of the Antipater-Salome sub-plot would not detract from its effectiveness. The chief defects of *Herod and Mariamne* are

414

certainly the antiquated language and style, and the use of a plot requiring so much background knowledge to render it intelligible. It would be interesting to see if he overcame any of these defects in his later plays.

Gavriil Romanovich Derzhavin was certainly the greatest poet of the age of Catherine II. It was perhaps not entirely clear to contemporaries, nor indeed to Derzhavin himself, to what a degree his work was no longer in harmony with that age. Yet it is always evident in this enigmatic poet that the classicism in which he grew up has had its day and is about to be displaced by something new. What this "new wave" is to be cannot yet be clearly discerned in Derzhavin's works, but there are numerous hints: the rejection of dictatorial "rules"; the dethronement of "reason" as the fundamental ingredient in poetry; the repudiation of classical universality; the emergence of the individual; the first glimmerings of realism, and the rest. We know, looking back, that these elements were all to become parts of that complex movement inadequately called "romanticism." To a contemporary Derzhavin probably looked like a merely eccentric and self-willed genius who quarreled more cantankerously than most with the system of which he nevertheless remained a part. To us he looks like a premature herald of an entirely new system. Derzhavin must always remain uneasily poised between two ages, belonging wholly to neither one.

CHAPTER XIV

NIKOLAI ALEXANDROVICH LVOV AND THE "LVOV CIRCLE"

A. Nikolai Alexandrovich Lvov as a Poet

In the discussion of Derzhavin mention was made quite frequently of the influence upon the great poet during the early years of his literary activity of the so-called "Lvov Circle"—Nikolai Alexandrovich himself and his friends Mikhail Nikitich Muraviev, Ivan Khemnitser and Vasily Kapnist. Derzhavin was, of course, too original and powerful a figure to remain permanently under the tutelage of these highly cultured but less gifted friends, and although he continued for the rest of his life and theirs to solicit their criticism, he quite frequently ignored it. As for the group itself, all of them made a mark in eighteenth-century Russian literature, less indeed than Derzhavin's, but by no means to be disregarded.

Nikolai Alexandrovich Lvov (1751-1803),[1] a native of the Torzhok district north of Moscow, belonged to an old noble family, and at the age of sixteen entered military service as a cadet in the Izmailovsky Guards Regiment. One does not ordinarily associate such service with educational opportunities, but gentlemen officers in eighteenth-century Russia were given a very broad and liberal training. Lvov learned foreign languages and acquired a lifelong interest in French philosophy and the fine arts, particularly architecture. A young man of extraordinary brilliance and breadth of interest and capacity, Lvov exercised a personal attraction which quickly made him the center of a circle of friends, some of them also cadets, of similar interests. Among these was the young *raznochinets* Ivan Khemnitser, who fell into Lvov's orbit in the 1770s, and in 1774 dedicated to his friend his translation of Dorat's "Epistle of Barnwell to Truman from Prison" (a fictitious *herois* based on Lillo's drama *The London Merchant*).[2] By this time Lvov had left the military service, and was living with his kinsman M.F. Soimonov, then director of the "Mining Institute." In 1776-77 Soimonov, accompanied by Lvov and Khemnitser, made a journey to western Europe, where they visited Germany, France and the Low Countries. Khemnitser kept a journal of their pilgrimage, which records the many enthusiasms of the friends and their exposure to the drama, poetry and fine arts of the west.

Returned to Russia, Lvov entered the Foreign Office, where he quickly became the right-hand man of Chancellor Bezborodko, at whose house he lived for a time. It was at this period that he became friendly with P.V. Bakunin, then a councillor in the Foreign Office, and with his nephew, Alexander Mikhailovich Bakunin (1768-1854), father of the future anarchist, Mikhail Alexandrovich Bakunin.

Lvov had been from his earliest years attracted to the fine arts. He learned to sketch, as did so many of his contemporaries, and on his several trips to western Europe, especially Italy, on the affairs of the Foreign Office, he familiarized himself with the monuments of classical and Renaissance architecture, as well as with the theoretical writings on art, such as Winkelmann's *Geschichte der antiken Kunst.* He also studied attentively the contemporary esthetic writings of Denis Diderot devoted to the Paris exhibitions of paintings—the "Salons." As a result of these tastes and experiences, Lvov became Russia's foremost authority on architecture, and designed a considerable number of buildings, both public and private, including the Neva Gateway to the fortress of Saints Peter and Paul and the St. Petersburg Post Office.

In connection with his architectural interests Lvov studied the possibilities of using pounded earth as a material for constructing peasant houses; such a mode of construction would eliminate the omnipresent danger of fire. His ideas appealed greatly to the Emperor Paul, who commissioned him to attempt to teach his methods to a peasant village. Although the experiments were successful, and some of Lvov's "earthen houses" were built, and are indeed still standing, peasant conservatism and the death of Paul brought the project to an end. Paul was also interested in utilizing Russia's fossil fuel, and the polymath Lvov, who was among other things an amateur geologist, was sent to explore northern Russia for deposits of hard coal. In this too he was successful, but again the emperor's death brought an end to the project. Lvov in 1799 published anonymously a treatise entitled "On the Usefulness and Utilization of Russian Coal."

Poetry, architecture, geology, diplomacy—surely Lvov's interests were those of a genuine Renaissance *Universalmensch.* But the list is not yet exhausted. Acquaintance with the German preromantics of the *Sturm und Drang,* and especially with Herder's collection of European folk poetry ("Stimmen der Volker") led Lvov to attempt a similar collection for Russia. *Collection of Russian Popular Songs, with their Melodies,* issued anonymously by Lvov and the musician I. Prach in 1790, is the completest and most scholarly compilation of its kind in the century. It may be noted incidentally that in his comic opera *Coachmen at the Relay Station (Iamshchiki na podstave)* (1788) Lvov used some of the genuine popular coachmen's songs which he later incorporated in his collection.[3]

Nikolai Lvov was a person of such varied and dazzling talents that he made an indelible impression on his friends and contemporaries. The portraits of him by the great portraitist Dmitry Grigorievich Levitsky (1735-

1822) show an extremely handsome young man with a very sensitive face—
and reminiscences of Derzhavin and Kapnist, who were his long-time friends
and brothers-in-law (Lvov was married to Maria Alexeevna Diakova [1780],
Kapnist to her sister Alexandra [1781] and Derzhavin, after his first wife's
death, to the youngest sister Daria [1795]) show a man of the greatest
charm. Derzhavin writes:

This man belonged to the select few, because he was endowed with that decided sensitivity to the beautiful, which, with the rapidity of lightning filling the heart sweetly,
is often manifested by a tear, stealing away words. With this rare, and for many, incomprehensible feeling, he was filled with intelligence and knowledge; he loved sciences
and the arts and was distinguished by a fine and elevated taste, from which no fault
and no excellence in a work of art or literature could remain concealed.[4]

The conspicuous ease with which Lvov mastered the many diverse subjects of
his interest amazed and mystified Derzhavin: "He always possessed an easy
and pleasant gift, so that when he began anything, it seemed to be without
any labor, and as though the Muses themselves were producing it."[5]

Poetry was for Lvov, as one can readily see, never more than a minor
avocation, and although he wrote verse all his life, he published very little
of it. No complete collection of his works has ever been made, and apparently a considerable amount of manuscript material exists; the nearest
approach to a collected edition is the section devoted to him in the "Poet's
Library" volume *Poets of the Eighteenth Century*, edited by G. P. Makogonenko and I.Z. Serman (Volume II, pp. 191-257). Lvov evidently circulated manuscript copies of his verse among his immediate family and friends,
and apparently wrote most of it only for such an intimate audience. It bears
the marks accordingly of what is sometimes called "occasional verse," and is
probably more casual and off-hand than it would have been if intended for
the eyes of a wider and more critical public. In many respects it stands rather
closer to the poetry of Derzhavin than any other.

Of the published works which the "Poet's Library" editors have collected, the earliest appear to be two fables, "The Lion's Decree" and "The
Monkey Passed Over in Promotion," which Khemnitser included in his own
volume of *Fables and Stories of N.... N....* (1799). Neither of these shows
any particular distinguishing quality.[6] The first piece of any length or genuine
interest is the one entitled "The Russian Year 1791."[7] This was published
separately in the year 1791, and later, anonymously, in 1796 in the periodical
Muza. It is preceded by a dedication to the poet's wife, in "free iambics," of
which the following is the concluding portion:

My springtime verse would not so pride itself, were it not adorned with your praise.
That pursuer of wicked vices and zealot of the truth, that friend of simple nature, dear
Khemnitser, has dedicated his talent as a sacred pledge of friendship—he has consecrated
to you as protection the blazing candlestick of truth [Khemnitser's *Fables* were dedi-

cated to Maria Alexeevna Diakova (1779), who in 1780 became Lvov's wife].[8] But I, treading in his path, although not plucking the same flowers, nor inspired by the same zeal, yet encouraged by your affection, rapturously devote my toil. Not with temples nor altars nor aromatic herbs is the sacrifice great and glorious: it is with zeal it burns.

The body of the poem, 400 lines long, is entitled "Winter," and is a very interesting evocation of the beauties and interests of that season, done in the pseudo-popular style of a *skazka*. Exceptionally for light and semi-humorous verse, it employs the four-beat trochaic line, with a free and unpredictable rhyme scheme. The poem begins:

On ivory skis, over the spreading porcelain [i.e., the snow], all in silver attire and precious stones, his beard waving and his white hair gleaming, in boots of fine morocco, amid clouds of coral, in haste the brisk crier comes from the crystal chambers, and takes out of his wallet a proclamation from Queen Winter: "That all are to prepare themselves, dress themselves, deck themselves, for a masquerade in her [palace] ; but whoever refuses this, shall not be glad of his life: he shall lose either fingers or nose or heels." Here all meet the crier, one with laughter, one with tears; they harness their brisk trotters, dress themselves in fox-fur, dress up as wolves, or as a bear, or as beavers— Everyone in accordance with his purse.

The "tale" then continues with the appearance of Queen Winter herself and with the jollification attendant on her reign:

In the houses and on the streets the fires are already gleaming; all [the people] are riding around in fine attire; some are dancing in parlors, others on the street, without music—where some are beating golden mittens in honor of the winter days. Amid spicy confections the sweet aromatic wines exhibit through drunken eyes a blissful lot. In the midst of joys and pleasures the old [man] has made his peace with time and striven toward youth through the foggy fumes of wine; he even forgets the years, manifests new cheerfulness, covered over [as he is] with a warm fur coat, and with nimble step he hurries, blushing a little, after a red-faced young girl.

In the description Lvov shows an interest characteristic of the late eighteenth century in the superstitions and magical practices of the common people, which he describes in detail. The *skazka* ends with the inevitable retreat of Queen Winter and the end of her court. The poet, however, offers consolation:

Don't, however, suppose, my dear reader! that a single kind of happiness constituted the Golden Age. The brilliant before one's eyes allures with its beauty because it has various fires. And we do not regret the beauties of winter for the reason that other beauties have matured in Russia's joyful regions. The warm influence of [the sun's] rays has given us the promise that the bare look of diamonds is changing into emeralds. Their beneficent power promises us a new world, and teaches [us] by the change that everything is going for the best.

"Winter" exhibits several facets of Lvov's poetic originality: first of all, his light, ironic attitude of never taking himself or his subject very seriously. This is true not only of this, in itself humorous, poem; L.I. Kulakova, in her chapter on Lvov in Volume IV of the Academy of Science's *History of Russian Literature*, quotes a few lines[9] from the end of Lvov's "Triumphal Ode in the Taste of Archilochus on the Capture of Warsaw," which show, even in a serious poem, the same kind of self-irony—which is indeed "in the taste of Archilochus," the Greek satirist who was quite capable of making fun of himself:

> Here the poet would have raised his tone:
> Under the cedar the laurels are green,
> New Achilleses mature in it,
> Troy city has fallen. But I am not he.

Although Lvov lacks Derzhavin's marvelous color sense, and the description of winter scenes have nothing of the brightness of e.g., "Life at Zvanka," nevertheless they are not merely conventional and abstract—witness the street dancers' "drunken eyes," or the "golden mittens" of the cabbies—a badge of their trade under Catherine II. Of course, the fairy-tale character of the scene precludes much naturalism, but it intrudes, nonetheless. The poem is quite decidedly anti-classical, and a worthy forerunner of Pushkin's *skazki*.

In 1793 Lvov published anonymously a free translation of a supposedly original Scandinavian poem, from P.A. Mallet's *Histoire de Dannemarc* (1763). The Russian title of this poem almost eliminates the need for annotation: "Song of the Norwegian Hero Harald the Valiant, from the ancient Icelandic Manuscript of the Knitlinga Saga, copied by M. Mallet and placed in his 'Danish History'; paraphrased in Russian in the manner of ancient verse on the example of 'It is not a star that shines far off on the clear plain...' "[10] The poem purports to be the actual song of the eleventh-century Viking Harold the Brave, who loved and eventually married Elizabeth, daughter of Yaroslav the Wise, Prince of Novgorod. The text actually is a couple of centuries younger, and a rather inferior product of Old Norse literature, but it enjoyed a great vogue in eighteenth-century Russia, being "translated" (from the French, of course) by numerous poets besides Lvov. The case is instructive: the connection, in this case historical, between the world of the Scandinavian Vikings and Kievan Russia, reflecting the—probably unhistorical—legend of Riurik and his two brothers as founders of the principality of Kiev; and the great vogue in the last quarter of the century of "northern" atmosphere and mythology, an uncritical anti-historical amalgam of Scandinavian and Celtic (Ossianic) elements. Lvov, evidently believing in the "Norman" background of Russian civilization, and in the appropriateness of Russian popular verse forms to translate the kindred Scandinavian poetry, utilized the so-called "Russian line" as his metrical unit—a line of four or five unpredictably placed beats, without rhyme, but usually ending in a dactylic foot. Such a line is the first of the popular song specified in the poem's title: "ne zvezda blestit daleke vo chistom pole" ("It is not a star that shines far off on the clear plain"). The song, however, is rather arbitrarily divided into six-line strophes, each ending with the refrain line: "a menia ni vo chto stavit devka russkaia" ("But the Russian maiden counts me for naught"). It is an interesting, although incomplete attempt, to utilize a purely popular or "folk-lore" form for artistic purposes.

A similar, and much more ambitious, attempt of the kind is the fragment of an epic poem, "Dobrynia," composed in 1796 and published posthumously in 1806 in the periodical *Friend of Enlightenment*.[11] The fragment was to have been the first canto or chapter of an epic based on the popular ballad or *bylina* on the career of the *bogatyr* Dobrynia Nikitich. In a foreword to the published poem the editor of *Friend of Enlightenment* makes a very revealing comment on the origin of the piece:

Some ten years earlier he [i.e., Lvov], discoursing in a certain circle of his friends in general on the superiority of accentual over syllabic versification, asserted that Russian poetry also would have more harmony, diversity and expressive movement in a free accentual type of verse, than in servitude to trochees and iambs alone; and that it would even be possible to write a whole Russian epic in perfectly Russian taste.[12]

The fragment was evidently composed as an experiment to verify such an assertion; the lines are of irregular lengths, varying from two to five beats, without rhyme, and frequently ending in a dactylic foot. The language at times echoes the familiar formulas of bylina verse, e.g., "Okh ty goi esi, russkii tverdyi dukh ("Ho, you stout Russian spirit!"), but the poet is not at all averse to mixing styles; in a digression on Lomonosov he writes, in a manner that could hardly be more remote from the "popular": "To be sure, we had a son of might, and he overpowered difficulties with a supernatural gift. He made the impossible easy, by the power of Russian eulogy." There is a certain grotesque quality in some of the effects, as for example in the attempt to transpose into "popular" phraseology the boast of Horace (III, 30) to have brought "Aeolian song into Italian measures": "Svat Kvintinovich, metry grecheski Perestroivshi na latinskii lad Kak Kistrin budto, vzial bessmertie" ("Kinsman Quintinovich [i.e., *Quintus* (!) Horatius Flaccus], having transposed Greek meters into a Latin mode, captured immortality as if it had been Kustrin!"). There is also a touch of Lvov's habitual self-irony, in, for example, the description of the poet's fright as he wanders through the dark forest, and in the effects of his first attempt to play the "fiddle" ("gudok") left by the personified "Russian spirit": "I took the fiddle I know not how; it began to screech in a strange fashion, like an ungreased cart!" The content of what would apparently have been an introduction to the epic itself is largely polemical and whimsical: the poet, seeking a genuine Russian theme, rejects Bova Korolevich—"I don't want to sing him— no Russian he. He's from the town of Antona, son of a certain Gvidon, king of macaroni!" He imagines himself meeting with derision from his fellow poets: "No, give me such a hero as, in the wondrous age of Volodimir, was the lowly son of Strap-makers [i.e., Ivan Usmovich], as was Polkan or as was Lazarich [i.e., Eruslan Lazarevich] or Potania—But what's this, comrades! Why are you making faces? With what have you sealed up [your] sugary lips? [an expression from popular oral tales]. You have cast down your bright eyes; I suppose the *bogatyr* speech is too low for you? Or is the Russian word out of place for you?' You have clambered around on trochees; without a hexameter, it's as painful for you to step with your own tread as if you were barefoot. But friends! in our language it's impossible to place many necessary words in tight foreign frames."

The attempt to naturalize for artistic verse the accentual meter of popular Russian balladry, abandoning the syllabo-tonic versification which had been the sole mode of verse composition since Trediakovsky, was a bold experiment, not to be seriously tried until the twentieth century. Both Radishchev and Karamzin made partial and half-hearted experiments along this line a few years after Lvov's, and much less successfully. Lvov was probably not entirely serious in his effort; at least it is certain that he would either not have published his "epic" canto at all, had he lived, or would have freed it of many of the awkwardnesses that mar it in its present form.

Nikolai Lvov began his poetic career by following in the footsteps of Sumarokov in the area where that master was almost unrivaled—the song. Some of Lvov's "art songs" were printed in the *Collection of Popular Songs* which appeared, anonymously, in 1790. Many of the songs were written in perfectly conventional metrical form, with syllabic definition and rhyme; such is this,[13] in trochaic trimeter, in quatrains rhyming *aBaB:*

> The precious sun ["solnyshko"] is setting, the day grows dark, from the flowery mountains the shadow is cast on my heart.
> With flattering dream slumber beguiled me, with the morning's dew I freshened my path.
> Nina seemed to me only a flattering dream, as though she were waiting there beyond the brook.
> Through some sort of force, through mountains and forest, somehow beneath me my toilsome path disappeared.
> Shadow and rustle, movements I took for Nina; in every sensation I met with Nina.
> But if waiting is so sweet, is it possible to grieve? Only so there be someone to wait for!

But many also, like his epic attempts, are in "popular" metrical form, and with a phraseology modeled on that of the genuine popular songs. Such is No. 103;[14] it is divided into regular quatrains, which does not often happen with genuine popular songs, but employs the free accentual line without either rhyme or prosodic definition:

Now, it seems ["byvalo"] you, darling, beautiful sun, are running away from us in the dark autumn! We all grieve over you, we sorrow, we mourn over your rays.

But now run, beautiful sun, to all four quarters; we all without boredom are glad to wait for you until the very spring, the green one.

For another sun is rolling toward us, a beautiful sun, our own, our unchanging quiet, bright moon ["nash tikh svetel mesiats"] on wings of love is coming to visit us.

Hurry, hurry to us, our darling, our own beautiful sun, our unchanging, quiet, bright moon, descend to us, your children.

We have all been longing for you; let us gaze on your face; let us listen to your words, all of us, from young to old.

One of the characteristic features of the anti-classical revulsion of the end of the century usually known as sentimentalism, is the abandonment of the solemn ode (or its transformation, as with Derzhavin) and the substitution for it of a less pretentious and more intimate type of lyric. Theorists of the time usually call this "light verse," or sometimes, following the French nomenclature, "fugitive verse." Its models were French poems written by a host of minor versifiers—Dorat, Bernis, Leonard, Berquin, etc.— mostly ignored in French literary histories, which tend to leave in oblivion everything that cannot be properly regarded as a masterpiece. Mikhail Muraviev, one of Lvov's friends, was an early experimenter with such verse; one of his collections he called *Pièces fugitives.* For such "light verse" the classical archetype was of course Anacreon, or what passed for Anacreon in the eighteenth century. Horace's odes occupied a kind of middle ground: intimate and deceptively "light" and personal in subject matter, they were actually the most elegant and studied of all ancient verse in style. We have noted Derzhavin's fondness for Horace; Kapnist, another of the Lvov circle, translated (from prose versions, for he knew no Latin) many of the Horatian odes, and freely imitated and paraphrased others. As for Anacreon, he had been popular in Russia throughout the century. As we have seen, Kantemir translated some of the Anacreontea, Lomonosov made versions in his "Conversation with Anacreon," and imitations of Anacreon's meters, and sometimes of his themes, had been composed by Kheraskov, Bogdanovich, Dmitriev, and several others. Nikolai Lvov and his friend Mikhail Muraviev had learned Greek when they were still cadets in the Izmailovsky Guards Regiment, and although Lvov apparently distrusted his competence in the language (he used an interlinear Russian translation by a friend as his "pony"), he knew enough to sense the rhythm and word positioning of the poems. In 1794 Lvov's *Poems of Anacreon of Teos*[15] was issued, anonymously as usual. The sixty-odd pieces of the Anacreontea are faithfully rendered into unrhymed Russian verse, in the same meters as the originals. These versions of Lvov's were, as we have seen, the originals from which Derzhavin made his rhymed "translations" of the old Greek verses.

As we shall presently see, Lvov's friend Vasily Kapnist, besides his Horatian experiments, composed numerous pieces in perfectly conventional ode form, but on such highly unconventional subjects as "Slavery," "Hope," "Happiness," etc. Indeed, where Lomonosov and the other great ode writers of the first half of the century had employed the form almost exclusively for the celebration of military victories, anniversaries of monarchs, the signing of peace treaties and similar public events, Kapnist, Muraviev and other poets of the end of the century made it the vehicle for entirely personal utterances; thus Kapnist writes an "Ode on the Death of [My] Son." Such an ode is Lvov's "Music, or Septemtonia."[16] Such a theme is no great novelty in English verse—one may think of Dryden's "Ode on St. Cecilia's Day"—but the ode in Russian had a narrower province. The "sentimentalist" inspiration of Lvov's ode on music may be seen in the first strophe: "Mysterious word of heaven! Only the heart understands thee; the first of thy marvels the reason scarce dares to believe. Potent music! Pour out thy sweet and holy balsam upon my lonely days, upon my ardent friends!" One cannot but note the quite explicit dissociation of music from reason and the intellect—the sources of all esthetic pleasure for the rationalistic classicist. For the "sentimentalist," esthetic enjoyment is a matter of the emotions, not the reason—and of all the arts, music probably fits this definition most aptly. Lvov goes on (strophe 4) to denounce the unfeeling—and therefore essentially evil—men who are insensitive to music: "Unknown to me forever be that cruel, cold, ill-starred, morose, pitiable man, adversary of harmonious, sonorous might; bliss he will not know, he will not meet a friend with rapture, he will not honor with a heart-beat either the applause of happiness or the groan of grief."

One of the fullest expressions of Lvov's sentimentalist position is in a lengthy "Epistle to A.M. Bakunin from Pavlovsk, June 14, 1797."[17] The first portion of this epistle is headed "Fortune." In making the rather stereotyped contrast between the rich and famous "son of Fortune" and such a humble but contented person as himself, the poet writes:

I am truly convinced, my friend, that if Fortune's favorite (in whom the heart had not become completely hardened) should have a look at us in Nikolskoe [Lvov's estate], how, having finished our day's task with a song, we get ready to take a rest in the summer evening on the lawn under the lime tree, surrounded by the household life, by a healthy handful of children, a cheerful gang of people that love us, he would say: "How they are blessed, and their good luck doesn't turn [i.e., with Fortune's wheel]! Mine is always whirling, their happiness lies still. Over my happiness with my anxieties I always have to stand guard, like faithful Fido [Lyzha—a favorite dog's name] ; their happiness chases after them everywhere, it knows no weariness, it works and hums a song, and on a holiday dances as they order—it does not drowse even while they sleep! Why, if I dozed off, Fortune would fall asleep. No, it's evident, Lady Luck, you've deceived me, for I sought you, Madam, for happiness, but you deafened me with an empty alarm call, you fed me opium ["durmanom"] , you lit me with fox-fire, I haven't tasted happiness, but I've already grown gray and feeble. I've become with you like that soldier who earned his bread up to old age with that hard trade, war; but has come to eat it without teeth, without hands, and blind. I too acquired everything—acknowledged—with which to seem happy and content. But I've lost the feeling ["chuvstvo"] with which a man knows how to have pleasure even in poverty. What has my life been? A mist. What my happiness? A dream. What my office, the first of the important ones? Vanity. It has gripped my reason with fear and forbidden genuine joy access to my soul. The rapture of love has not watered me with the drop of a tear, and friendship has not warmed my blood with a spark. In changing everything for everything, I've worn out my heart, and I've lost even belief in virtue. Coldness has to such an extent enveloped my heart that I have done good deeds only by example and without satisfaction. But I was born good and I deserve to be happy. O Orthodox people! I adjure you by this holy virtue, whose sweet voice is surely not strange to you: take what you wish, but give me shelter in humanity and, opening feeling, unburden my heart, reconciling me with nature.

Perhaps, when spring shall return with love, I too shall acquire sensitivity ["chuvstvitel'nost' "] once more, my gloomy spirit shall come alive, and communicate to my heart the warmth of nature, whose charms I even now recall! I have not yet lost the impressions, how in rustic simplicity with love alone I was unable to embrace gladness. My voice, my look, my step expressed that in the heart, and not the mind, I nurture happiness. Now I desire to sigh; but on the contrary, I yawn amid honors, amusements, as though I had not slept for an age!

The sentimentalist poets often seem to suffer from a kind of *fin de siècle* world-weariness, and one of their pervasive themes is the horror of losing "sensitivity." Muraviev, in 1779 and 1780 was, to judge from both his verse and his letters, profoundly depressed by encroaching age (he was twenty-two or three at the time!). It was not physical infirmity which he feared, but rather the loss of his capacity to *feel* (see his "Regret for Youth," 1780).[18] In this high value placed on feeling, and the corresponding deprecation of intellect one may see the influence of Rousseau, whom Lvov and his circle idolized. It may be noted that the "Son of Fortune" pointedly complains: "And yet I was born good [that is, for a Rousseauist, "endowed with a sensitive soul"] and I deserve happiness." It is, of course, the abrasions from "the world," that is, the *haut monde* of society and the court, that destroy sensitivity; it is axiomatic that "nature," the simple country life, restores and fosters the all-important capacity to feel—to throb with pure love, unselfish friendship and dedication to humanity. All of this one may sense in the complaint of the "Son of Fortune."

"Nature poetry," best exemplified by James Thomson's *The Seasons*, enjoyed particular favor among the sentimentalist poets. Sensitivity to inanimate nature was considered a mark of refined feeling, and hence of a naturally good heart. Botanical excursions were especially in vogue; Jean-Jacques Rousseau's *Méditations d'un promeneur solitaire*, although in prose, undoubtedly contributed largely to this fashion. Lvov paid his tribute to this sentimentalist genre in a work entitled "Botanical Excursion to Dudorova Hill" ["Botanicheskoe puteshestvie na Dudorovu goru"]. This is not reprinted in the "Poet's Library" anthology and is therefore inaccessible; but the title indicates the general contents.

A final example of Lvov's verse is the extraordinary "Night in a Finnish Hut in the Open Plain."[19] The poem, first published in the *Literaturnoe*

Nasledstvo, 9-10, 1933, was generated by an experience which Lvov narrates in a letter to his wife:[20]

Now, my dear, when you had left, and the Sovereign [i.e., Paul I] had sent me to construct a pounded earth house in a Finnish village, I was living there all alone, in a hut in the midst of the open plain such that for all my short stature, it was never possible for me to stand upright. The weather, moreover, was hellish—the wind, and at night the unceasing howl of the wolves so stirred me with melancholy that I had the feeling that they were children. I couldn't last through a single night, but the wolves would always be howling. I imagined that they had devoured a young girl, and I should now write a funeral song for her. None of this would have happened, if you hadn't left—the night would have been left to itself, and we to ourselves. Now when I come to you at Nikolskoe, I'll give you notes for the wolves; let them sing as they may, it will seem to me a concert by Paisiello.

The poem (No. 96 in the Makogonenko collection) is in the unrhymed "Russian line," with four or five irregular beats to the line. L.I. Kulakova, in her chapter on Lvov in Volume IV of the Academy of Sciences *History of Russian Literature,*[21] calls the piece a ballad, "one of the first in Russia." This is certainly a mistaken classification: the poem narrates an experience in the first person, whereas a ballad is always, by definition, in the third person. The form, moreover, is entirely unlike that of a normal ballad, which is strophic; Lvov's poem has several natural divisions, but is not strophic. It is, in other words, one of those quite unclassifiable pieces which become increasingly common as the eighteenth century genre system begins to break down.

The poem begins with a description of the situation:

The wolves are howling—the autumn night, surrounding with a black darkness the shelter of my tumble-down hut amid the dead open field, multiplies horrors—and I am alone! Having passed in toil the day's foul weather, I hoped to find rest in my lonely bed; but rest flies from the hut, where gloom is broken only by the whistle of the stormy wind! I open the window, look out—isn't there a glimmer of dawn far off? Don't I hear a cheery bird, waking folk to their labors? Is not the herald of dawn crowing? The wolves are howling—the rainy night has enveloped the whole face of the earth with cold and horror—and I am alone!

Cold, horror and gloom, cruel children of solitude, have entwined me, like a cold snake, and in their tormenting embraces hold my breast tightly bound; sluggishly the blood flows in my veins; my heart beats, wants to jump out; it is seeking, it seems, a companion with whom to share the misery.

Then the poet, as in his letter, thinks how the presence of his wife would put an end to the gloom and terror of the night: "Storm, darkness, wilderness, hut—in ardent, close embraces, beneath the wing of tried love, would multiply our happiness." But his loved one is far away, and the dreadful night still oppresses him. He determines to go outside and "meet the night face to face." "The storm has torn an old oak tree up by the roots, the roof of my hut has tumbled in; the dark storm has saved my life; surely it was for this that it called me out, out from my cozy resting-place." Then the hallucination begins: the poet seems to hear a human voice calling out—a girl's voice, "dying, torn to pieces, the youthful victim of the ravening, malicious, howling pack!" Imagination pictures vividly the victim's father and mother, gathered around the supper table, waiting for their daughter who will never return. The father sees a white-sheeted wraith ascending to heaven, and cries: "My beloved daughter is dead, and sorrow has entered my bitter house." Then the girl's lover sets out to meet his "Nina," heedless of storm or darkness. The poet addresses him in spirit: "Far away is your heart's guest, and your hours of happiness are engulfed in the abyss of eternity." The piece ends with a quasi-popular lament for the dead girl and her hapless lover: "Do not rise, beautiful sun, continue, night of horror.... perhaps the wind's whistle in the cracks seemed to me in my wild solitude to be a girl's voice."

To whatever category one may assign this poem, there is no denying its pre-romantic characteristics: the somber, Ossianic vision of loneliness, night, storm, darkness, the terror of elemental nature; the echoes of the phraseology of the folklore dirge; and above all, the entirely personal, individual coloring of the episode. This is nothing that could be generalized into the experience of common mankind, in the classical manner; it is a unique, unrepeatable hallucination.

Nikolai Alexandrovich Lvov is a minor poet, to be sure; but very often minor poets are surer indicators of literary movement than their greater contemporaries. Lvov's verse has much in common with that of his friend Derzhavin; but in many respects both he, and, as we shall see, Mikhail Muraviev, go considerably beyond Derzhavin in their revulsion from the rigid canons of classicism. The way they point leads to the nineteenth century and such genuine romantics as Zhukovsky and Batiushkov.

B. Ivan Ivanovich Khemnitser (1745-1784)[22]

Russia's most significant fabulist before Krylov was the son of a German army doctor, Johann Chemnitser. Destined by his father for an uncongenial medical career, the boy at the age of thirteen enlisted in the Noteborg Infantry Regiment as a private soldier, by concealing his age. He continued his military service for twelve years, undergoing the hardships and dangers normal to that career. He retired in 1769 and took a civilian post with the "Mining Institute" ["Gornoe Uchilishche"], with whose director M.F. Soimonov he soon became friendly. At this time Khemnitser made the acquaintance of the brilliant young poet, artist and architect Nikolai A. Lvov. Lvov was the center oi a literary circle which included the

Ukrainian-born poet V.V. Kapnist and Gavriil Derzhavin, soon to be recognized as Russia's leading poet. Under the influence of Lvov and Kapnist the young man began to write—two satires, which he never tried to publish, and a series of fables and satirical short narratives which were published in 1779. During most of the year 1777 Khemnitser, together with his friend Lvov, accompanied Lvov's kinsman and Khemnitser's chief, M.F. Soimonov, on a grand tour of western Europe—Germany, France and Holland—which familiarized him with many aspects of the cultural life of his age which were missing from Russia. Khemnitser kept a diary of this pilgrimage, from which it appears that he and his friends were assiduous habitués of the theater in Paris, and of various museums, especially in Dresden. It was at this time that Khemnitser became an ardent admirer of Rousseau, and in his own thinking began to follow the enlightenment philosopher.

Upon his return to St. Petersburg Khemnitser continued for a few more years in close association and friendship with the Lvov circle. Unfortunately, however, his patron and friend Soimonov left the service in 1781, and Khemnitser was obliged to follow suit. Poor and with no powerful connections, he was obliged to accept a not very congenial post which Lvov and Kapnist were able to procure for him, the Russian consulship in the Turkish port of Smyrna. He took up this position in 1782; during this year also his second book of fables was published. He devoted himself energetically to his consular duties, and maintained an active correspondence with his friends, but soon succumbed to the unhealthy climate of Turkey and died in March, 1784.

Khemnitser's verse belongs almost entirely to what Chernyshevsky called "the satirical direction" of Russian literature—fable, satire, parody and epigram. Of other types of verse he left a few very feeble serious odes, and some occasional pieces addressed to his friends on anniversaries or the like. Besides a considerable number of epigrams in Russian, he composed others of exactly the same kind in German—sharp and caustic social and literary comment.[23]

His *Fables and Tales (Basni i Skazki)* were the only pieces published during his lifetime: Part I in 1779, Part II in 1782; a third edition, with some additions and alterations was issued in 1799 by his friend Kapnist.[24] The scholar Ia. K. Grote published in 1873 a complete edition, including much of the manuscript material, the diary of the 1777 travels, letters, etc.

Grote's edition of Khemnitser's complete works contained, among much previously unpublished material, a number of "Satires," both complete and fragmentary, from the poet's manuscripts.[25] The date of composition of these pieces is uncertain, but one, at least—"Epistle to Mr. K[apnist], Author of Satire I"—belongs certainly to 1780 or very shortly after, when Kapnist's "Satire First—and Last" was published and aroused much fierce criticism. Of Khemnitser's manuscript satires the one numbered "I" is headed: "On Bad Judges," number II has the rather wordy title: "On the Bad Condition of the Service, and that even Posts are Distributed for the Satisfaction of

Covetousness." Apparently Satire II was elaborated for a possible publication after another piece, originally given the same number, had been abandoned; this, possibly incomplete and rather short satire, is labeled: "Against Gain-Seeking Poets." There is also a short and probably incomplete "Satire Against Compliments" ["na poklony"—that is, the custom of making formal visits of congratulation on festivals, anniversaries, and the like, to all the influential persons of one's acquaintance]. Besides a few other very short satirical fragments, there is an "Epistle" written probably to N.A. Lvov on the eve of Khemnitser's departure for his post in Smyrna,[26] and a very vivacious and interesting parody ode (in one of the common ode-forms, the 8-line iambic tetrameter stanza, rhyming *aBaBccDD*) entitled "Na Pod'iachikh," which may be approximately rendered as "On Pettifoggers."[27]

In these satirical pieces Khemnitser follows the Sumarokov model: the verse form (except for the odes) is the approved Alexandrine, the language belongs to the "middle style," without either Slavonic or vulgar admixture to any great degree, and the subjects arc mainly social evils. The satire "On Bad Judges" describes quite realistically various types: there is the ignoramus whose knowledge of geography leads him to assert that "Taganrog is in France, and Peking in the neighborhood of Moscow," and who queries, when someone mentions the plague ["iazva morovaia"]: "What kind of beast is the *iazva morovaia*—a butterfly or a cricket or some other kind of creature?" The ignoramus is a bad judge largely because all he knows how to do is to say "good" to anything his secretary proposes, and the secretary actually makes the decisions. Then there is the rascal "who disgraces his office with his villainy and makes himself a scourge to the people." Everyone in his office, from the judge to the guard, takes and expects bribes: "Just walk into such an office: they all stand to attention and look only to fleece the petitioners.... you don't dare so much as put your hand in your pocket for a handkerchief without their thinking immediately that they're getting a tip." At this point a possible objection is raised—doesn't the government do anything about graft? Yes, but the government can't be everywhere, and even when it catches up with an offender, he can always say to himself: "Suppose someone else is to have this position, what I have in my pocket won't be lessened. I shan't have any reason to worry about the future; enough, it's time now to live for myself, it's time for me to live snugly in repose after my labors. I have, thank God, enough now to live on." Then the imaginary objector calls for proof—it's not enough to write satire— you must prove the man a thief. It's proof enough, the poet thinks, that from an estate of fifteen "souls" he has come to one of five hundred! After the ignoramus and the rascal comes the turn of the honest, well-intentioned judge, who doesn't know his way around, but leaves everything to his secretary, who for the gift of a gold watch will be glad to procure one a place that will bring in a thousand a year. The last examples which Khemnitser gives of "bad judges" are the lazy fellow who decides all cases, as we would say "by a flip of a coin"—in this case by a chance sneeze at an appropriate spot—and the   conscienceless judge, who makes up his mind firmly before hearing the evidence and is moved by no arguments. At the end of the satire, the poet realizes the futility of his invective: "No one, it seems, can touch them. Satires are written for fun, as it were, and not to correct manners."

Despite the apparent difference of subject—"bad judges" and "the bad condition of the service"—Satire II largely repeats the charges of venality made in Satire I, except that the bribe-takers are now officials of the "service" rather than judges. The poet, doubtless from bitter personal experience, describes the petitioner's futile efforts to gain the ear of an important personage, whose anteroom he has to frequent day after day, only to be told that the great man is busy or "not receiving." Like Kafka's petitioner who gets to know "the very fleas in the beard" of the Guardian of the Law, Khemnitser's *alter ego* says: "You'll get to know all the mice in his house, but yet not have the luck of seeing the master." and if, at long last, contact is made, all the great man will say is: "I shall try to help you," without even waiting to find out what is wanted! "If you don't have with you a letter from those who are his friends, your repetition will be in vain, though you have ten thousand merits." If you expect to get anywhere, have plenty of bribes ready, even if it means mortgaging your estate; and don't make the mistake of stopping with one bribe: when the recipient says: "I'll see—I'll try to help you," what he means is: "I'll see—whether you come through with some more cash."

Satire, the poet remarks to his friends, puts these things in an amusing light, "but if you enter upon these transactions with feeling, there's nothing to laugh at, but rather to shed tears over." Indignation overcoming him, the satirist turns to the Almighty Himself: "O God! How is it that your throne in heaven is not shaken, when justice is being sold for bribes! Shall your people long be oppressed by this evil, and shall not your thunder forthwith take vengeance for the righteous!"

"The service" apparently in Khemnitser's meaning embraces all of the civil bureaucracy—and it is all equally tainted. Rhetorically he asks his friend: "Do you think to find much good in it? Don't you also think that it is full of violence and underhandedness and trickery? Oh, you make no mistake if you think so, and judge the service, alas! to be such." "Know this: to serve with success, one must be a rogue, and not an honest man, and must try to find all underhanded means; but if you are not such, you won't escape the consequences." "All the thieves will be enraged at you because you aren't a thief, when all in the service thieve." To hope to bring any of these rascals to justice however, is the height of futility: if the culprit will share his ill-gotten gains with the judge, he will escape even the gallows. At the end of his pessimistic picture the poet reiterates his own determination: "No, no, I've said already and I repeat again, that I am abandoning search for a position—and the city."

The other satiric fragments are rather uninteresting, with the exception of the unnumbered "Satire on Compliments," which has some vividly realistic passages describing the absurd custom of dashing madly from house to house to pay one's compliments to the great on festal occasions, often only to find that the great man has gone himself to greet someone still higher in the social scale! The poet's conclusion to all this nonsense is a declaration of independence: "I live for myself and for my friends."

The "Ode on Pettifoggers" may be called "indirect satire": the despised and abominated tribe of *pod''iachie*, whom the eighteenth century frequently referred to as "nettle seed," are praised in this parody ode for all the good they do—for thieves and scoundrels. "If one goes to a horse-fair and buys a horse, the law decrees that he pay an excise-tax. But if the horse happens to be expensive, he will of course be ruined by the tax. Straightway the petti-fogger will give the advice: a hundred-ruble horse will go down as bought for a ruble." It should perhaps be explained that the *pod''iachii* is actually one of the petty government recording clerks found in every office; miserably paid, and having in his hands as recorder the opportunity for endless small changes, like this, in the record; it is not surprising that he took advantages of his chances to make a dishonest penny. But, of course, he never took bribes, as the poet is quick to point out: "The law prohibits bribes and sternly searches them out; and the *pod''iachie* punctually observe the strictness of these laws: it is impossible to take bribes as bribes (this is explicitly forbid-den), but to take presents given in friendship—they see no law against this." The poet ends his panegyric with the exhortation: "So, take refuge with the *pod''iachie*, you whom the knout threatens hereafter, and give them bribes as much as possible: they are your shield and salvation; they will be a pro-tection to you all your life, and will not forget your friendship, as long as life remains in them and their tribe endures."

It is not hard to see why Khemnitser should have made no effort to publish his "satires." Catherine II did not like to have the corruption of her regime exposed, and though doubtless the *pod''iachie* were hardly influential enough as a class to make trouble for a hostile satirist, the "bad judges" and bribe-taking department officials certainly were, as the experience of Khem-nitser's friend Kapnist showed: both his "First—and Last—Satire" and his terrifying "comedy" *Iabeda (Chicane)*, which attack exactly the same classes of people as Khemnitser's satires, brought their author into serious diffi-culties—and he was a "gentleman," and moderately wealthy; Khemnitser had neither rank nor fortune.

The model which Khemnitser took for his *Fables and Tales* was the similarly titled volume of the German poet Christian Fürchtegott Gellert, *Fabeln und Erzählungen* (1746-47).[28] Gellert was strongly imbued with the didactic ideal of classicism, and his "fables and tales" are narrated to serve as moral lessons. The "fables" are Aesopic allegories in which human foibles

431

are satirized in animal guise; the "tales" are short anecdotes about human beings, usually, in classical fashion, abstract and devoid of localization in either place or time. Khemnitser follows his model in these respects, and in some cases actually translates Gellert, although the majority of his pieces are original. Less than half of the *Fables and Tales* are what one would strictly call "fables," that is, animal stories masking human manners; these are usually fairly short. The "Tales," on the other hand, often run to two or three pages. Usually the "moral" is explicit and given either at the beginning or the end of the poem; sometimes too the author gives his own comments throughout. Least common is the case where Khemnitser lets his narrative speak for itself, without editorial comment.

The subjects of the *Fables and Tales* are scarcely classifiable—general human stupidity and ignorance, marital infidelity, oppression of the small by the great, the rascality of lawyers and tax-collectors, the arrogance and inhumanity of the aristocracy, and the like. Khemnitser's outlook on life is generally pessimistic: most of the pieces end with a wry twist and a cynical remark. A good example is the short tale "The Dying Father":[29]

There was a father, and he had two sons: one son was intelligent, the other son was stupid. The father's end approaches; and seeing his end, the father is distressed, and mourns because he is leaving his intelligent son in the world, and he does not know his future fate. He says to him: "Oh! my beloved son, with what anguish do I part from you, because I am leaving you in the world, intelligent! And how will you get along, I don't know. Listen!," he continued, "I am leaving you the sole heir of all my property, and your brother I am cutting off from the inheritance; he has no need of it." The son was in doubt and did not know what to think of his father's speech; but finally he puts his brother's case to his father: "But how is my brother to live, if I alone, to his hurt, am to receive the property as inheritance?" "There's no reason to worry about your brother," said the father. "A fool always finds means to be happy in this world."

As has been noted earlier, the Lvov circle was strongly imbued with the enlightenment ideals of citizenship and ideologically, although never actively, was opposed to the autocracy of Catherine II. Echoes of this opposition are audible in some of Khemnitser's animal fables, in which, as by tradition from Aesop's time, the lion figures as the monarch. Particularly caustic in its implied reference to the "vel'mozhi," "magnates," or leading aristocrats, is the fable entitled: "The Lion Who Created a Council":[30]

The Lion instituted a Council, of what sort is not known; and while seating in the Council elephants as members, added to them a large proportion of asses. Though for elephants to sit with asses is out of place, the Lion was unable to pick the number of elephants which should rightfully have sat in that Council. So what then? What though the whole number were insufficient, surely this would not prevent carrying on business. No—but what about its transgressing the decree? Though they might be fools, the judges, at least there would be the right number of them. But, moreover, when the Lion instituted this Council, this is how he reasoned and flattered himself: "Really now, won't the elephants' intelligence bring the asses to intelligence?" However, when the

Council opened, events turned out in a quite different way: the asses robbed the elephants of *their* intelligence.

The Lion himself is not a flattering picture of a monarch, even when he is better than the usual run of lions:

A certain lion once on a time resolved to inspect his whole realm, to see his people and how they live. This lion, you must know, was better than many lions—not that he spared the animals and didn't flay the hides from them. But he was considered good because, though he himself flayed hides, he permitted none besides himself to do any flaying. ("The Lion's Pilgrimage")[31]

The poet notes with particular distaste the proclivity of "lions" to make war:[32]

A certain dog chanced to come to live in lions' country; though he had heard about lions, he had never set eyes on any, and still less knew about their way of life. How he came to mingle with lions I am unable to say, without lying. Enough: the dog chanced on the lions and lived among lions. The dog sees how a life of craft obtains among the lions; there is no friendship among them, the lions know no justice; they flatter one another to their faces, and tear each other apart inwardly. Having been accustomed to live among dogs in mere simplicity, knowing neither craft nor any malice, he is amazed at such a life and reasons with himself: "Though dogs squabble together and even, maybe, fight, yet their life otherwise is without any guile and malicious thoughts, not like that of lions." Such a life annoys the dog, and he leaves the lions' abode. The dog, having run home, tells the [other] dogs: "No, it is a punishment to have to live with lions, where every moment each one is glad to kill another—and the whole reason for it, if you ask the lions, is that each lion wants to be the big lion."

The fable "The Two Neighbor Lions" [33] is even more explicit, with a pertinence that would be hard to miss in a land where the "lion" (or "lioness!") had systematically made war on every one of her neighbors:

Two lions, neighbors to each other, went to war with one another—for what reason, to what end, no one knows; this was their pleasure, it is said. Besides, when they merely take the notion—just as happens with human kings, as it chances—they can find more than one reason for waging war. These lions were different from them only in that, when they declared war on one another, they had no need of breaking a treaty of eternal peace, which sometimes doesn't serve for even a week, as is, they say, often the case with human kings—for the reason that lions don't ordinarily have such documents. So, one of the lions captured both the realm and the people of the other. Habit and prejudice have their own reasoning: although, as I heard it, the life of the animals under this lion, in comparison with the former one, was in no way worse (I don't know what the past was like!) yet every animal was a secret foe, and kept only this in mind, how he might go about it so as to be again under the old [lion]. As in the world everything goes by turns, the old lion, recovering, began to consider how to regain by war what he had lost by war. The animals were only looking for the chance to betray the new lion, and waited for no other occasion; the lambs, as the saying goes, even became wolves. And what advantage did that former lion gain, when he went to war against the other lion? In warring he lost his own animals and did not solidly conquer the others for

433

himself. That is what war is like: you lose what belongs to you, and what you have conquered you cannot call your own.

Another favorite theme of Khemnitser's "Fables," also common to the Lvov circle, as we have seen in Derzhavin, is the foolish pride of birth, backed by no personal merit. The classical expression of this is the fable "The Riding Horse":[34]

A proud riding horse, seeing a nag in the fields working with a plow, and not in the kind of luxury and not in the adornment and not in the kind of grooming which the proud horse had from his master, looked with disdain at the nag, capered in front of the peasant's nag, and boasted, put on airs and bragged of this and that. "What," says he to the nag, "Have you ever had on you such adornment as you see on me? And do you know how everyone respects me? Everyone who meets me, makes way for me. Everyone talks about me and everyone praises me. But who in the world knows you?" The horse's arrogance was unbearable to the nag. "Go on, braggart," he answers him. "Leave me in peace. Can you count yourself with me and make fun of me? You wouldn't be able to brag, if you didn't eat the oats of my labor."

But Khemnitser's themes are not always political: he is very prone to mock at love and marriage (it may be noted incidentally that he never experienced the latter, at least). Some of the little tales ("skazki") of his title are cynical jokes straight out of medieval fabliaux, such as "The Fortunate Husband"[35]—a young man who sells, not his soul, but only three years' labor, to the Devil in order to win a certain beauty for his bride. "Although the Devil ordinarily lies, in this case he kept his word," and the young man got the girl—only to plead urgently with the Devil in a few weeks to take her back again, for the price of no matter how many years of labor. "Though it's a hard thing to be the Devil's servant, yet it's still easier than living with a cursed wife." The *skazka* cynically entitled "A Happy Marriage" extols the idyllic bliss of a couple who lived their whole married life in complete love and unselfishness, and whose "last kiss, when they were dying, was as passionate as the one when they were first wedded." "And how many years did their life last?" "How many years? About a week and no more. But for this it would have been like a fairytale."[36] Both these pieces, incidentally, are versions of originals by Gellert.

Bad poets and critics also come in for some of Khemnitser's satire. The very first poem in his first collection, after the dedication, is entitled "The Writer"—again after a Gellert original ("Der Maler"—the Russian "pisat'," of course, is ambiguous, meaning both "to write" and "to paint," but the latter meaning, in spite of the German, seems excluded here).[37] The writer, doubting the merits of his own work, offers it to an ignoramus for criticism. The critical decree is: "See, here it is low! There ignoble! In this place the thought is dark! There there isn't any at all! This place is unlike the truth! Here there is no art!" and so forth. The writer's final comment to himself is: "Now I have hopes that my labor has not failed." "The Nightingale and the Crows"[38] reflects a literary dispute of the '70s, with the enemies of the Lvov circle in the guise of envious crows who try vainly to drown out the song-bird. "The House-Spirit" ["Domovoi"], again patterned on Gellert ("Das Gespenst"),[39] tells of a man who suffers from a *domovoi*, which in this case appears to be a sort of Poltergeist. The victim's brilliant solution is to invite in a literary friend on several successive evenings to read some of his "tearful comedies." The cure is effective: the *domovoi* leaves the house, never to return.

One pointed fable, "The Dancing Bear,"[40] is evidently directed at conservative and unappreciative audiences. A dancing bear escapes from captivity and returns to his native forest, where he is warmly greeted by all his old friends and relatives. When telling of his adventures, "Mishka" shows how he can dance. The audience is at first impressed, praises his art and tries to imitate him, but for all their efforts are unable even to stand on their hind legs. "Then they flew at Mishka, and envy and malice blackened all his art; they all raised an outcry against Mishka: 'Away! Away from here at once! What a beast is this who wants to be cleverer than we!' And they fell on Mishka, gave him nowhere to go, and began to chase Mishka until Mishka was compelled to flee."

Some of Khemnitser's last fables were not published in his lifetime, and were considerably softened or even omitted entirely when Kapnist edited his friend's work for the 1799 edition. One such is the bitter political satire "The Privilege":[41]

A certain lion thought to publish an edict that the animals might henceforth, without fear, throttle and flay anyone that any is able. What could be better than such a permission for those who flay even without it? This decree didn't need to be read twice for it to be known. Now what a festivity there was! And the hide, whoever could from anyone, he flayed without more ado, and praised the edict. What lives, what lives perished there, one may count, but never come to the end!

To the fox, however, it seemed strange that such permission should be given; by edict to give the animals freedom at will to flay the hides from one another! The fox found it very dubious in her own thinking, and that of all the beasts. "The lion should be warned!" said the fox, and asked His Leonine Highness, not directly, no—but as questions are put to lions, in fox-like fashion, weighing the significance of the words, craftily, all with circumlocutions, all in smooth courtly words: "Will it not be to His Highness's hurt for the animals to receive such power?" The lion, however, answered her neither yes nor no.

But when, according to the lion's calculations, the decree had had enough effect, then, at His Supreme Highness's pleasure, the lion ordered all the animals to appear before him.

All those which appeared fatter than the rest never found their way back again. "Here's what I meant," said the lion to the fox, "when I issued such a decree about freedom. Since it was trouble for me to collect fat from the animals in scraps, I may better let it accumulate. The Sultan, you know, also allows his pashas to flay the people privately, and himself later flays the pashas in piles; and so I resolved to take an example from the Sultan."

The fox would have liked here in reply to speak her own mind on the matter, and to explain to the lion the bad consequences—but imagined that she was talking to the lion.

But I would like here, I must confess, to say a little word about the excisemen, that they also belong to the number of the pashas; but I too think I'll keep quiet, in the fox's fashion.

The reference to the excisemen ["otkupshchiki"] is doubtless a hit at Catherine's edict of 1767 which allowed the liquor dealers to charge whatever they would for spirits—a decree which, as may be remembered, moved Maikov to compose his "Elisei, or Bacchus Enraged."

"The Privilege" illustrates very well one of the facets of Khemnitser's language—the popular element. Expressions such as "uzh to-to bylo pirshestvo ("now what a festivity there was!") or "dush, dush pogiblo tut, chto ikh schitaiut, ne sochtut" ("what lives, what lives perished there, one may count, but never come to an end!") are idiomatic popular expressions of the common people. This, however, is not to be taken as a particularly characteristic feature of Khemnitser's style—on the contrary. Whereas Sumarokov, it would seem, took delight in availing himself of the license which the "low style" of the fable sanctioned, to use the vulgate extensively, the coarser the better, Khemnitser's language belongs rather to the "middle style," and such excursions into common language as those in "The Privilege," or in the fable called "Freedom and Captivity"[42] (a version of La Fontaine's *Le Loup et le Chien*) are rather uncommon. Indeed, contemporary writers were somewhat shocked and puzzled by Khemnitser's abandonment of the Sumarokov tradition.

In spite of a somewhat heterodox use of language levels, however, Khemnitser remains a thorough classicist. His subjects for the most part are abstract and generalized, with no Russian color whatsoever. This is particularly the case when he is translating or adapting a tale of Gellert—but even when he is being original, Russian national features do not appear in his fables, as they do so strongly in Krylov's. Moreover, he makes no attempt to individualize his persons. Animals or humans, they all speak essentially the same language—a smooth, cultured, bookish Russian, with very rare Slavonicisms—an almost Karamzinian language. In the same connection, and again in sharp contrast with Krylov Khemnitser almost completely ignores the real characteristics, the "psychology" as it were, of the animals he writes about. It might indeed be expected that his lions would not be very lifelike—the lion is not a familiar animal in Russia. But except for very obvious clichés of fable characterization—e.g., the fox is cunning and the ass is stupid, etc.—there is no effort at individualization. Certain creatures are taken as symbols for human classes—the lion is a monarch, the wolf is a nobleman, the sheep is a peasant, etc.—and quite without regard for the actual relations of animals with one another, the symbols are given the characters of the humans they represent. This is all entirely in keeping with eighteenth-century tradition— indeed it is Krylov who is the iconoclast in this regard. The fable is by tradition an essentially didactic genre, and lifelikeness is decidedly a second-ary consideration. Not all fabulists are as careless of this as Dmitry Ivanovich Khvostov (1757-1835), who made himself a laughing-stock by providing his crows with teeth and his asses with claws, but the difference is only a matter of degree and not basic.

Structurally, Khemnitser's *Fables and Tales* are also conventional. He employs the "free iambic verse" which has been the vehicle for Russian fable since Sumarokov, with its unpatterned alternations of short and long lines. He habitually provides his pieces with an explicit moral comment, which may come either at the beginning or at the end. He is needlessly long-winded, although far less so than Maikov; he makes use of the exceedingly tiresome convention established by Sumarokov and faithfully followed by his succes-sors, of elaborate disclaimers of knowledge regarding trivial points in his narrative, as though his imagined audience were importuning him for exact information on places and times!

Khemnitser's position in the history of the Russian fable is an inter-mediate one, in style as in time. Inheriting much from Sumarokov and from the German classical fabulists, he nevertheless shows considerable indepen-dence and originality, and the line leads directly from him to Dmitriev and Krylov, whom he anticipates in many regards.

C. Mikhail Nikitich Muraviev (1757-1807)[42]

In the year 1774 Gavriil Derzhavin, at the age of 31, still an officer fighting the rebel Pugachev, published anonymously his first, extremely derivative and unimpressive volume of verse, *Poems Translated and Com-posed at Chitalagay Hill.* In the same year a boy of 17, a cadet in the Iz-mailovsky Guards Regiment, published his *fifth* book of verse; in the follow-ing year a collection of his *Odes* saw the light—the last volume that Mikhail Muraviev, then 18, was ever to publish. He had begun at the age of 14 with his *Fables: Book I* (1773).

This precocious youth was the son of a military engineer who, with his family, had lived in a number of provincial Russian towns. Young Mikhail had been enrolled as a cadet in 1772. His literary interests had led him to acquaintance with Vasily I. Maikov, who assumed the direction of the boy's poetical development, and with Mikhail Kheraskov. He naturally gravitated also into the circle of that other Izmailovsky cadet, Nikolai A. Lvov, who was six years his senior. Through Lvov he met Ivan Petrovich Turgenev, Ivan Khemnitser and other literary men. Lvov and he studied Greek together, and Muraviev translated one of Sappho's odes—using, however, a French transla-tion of Longinus's *Essay on the Sublime* in which the poem is quoted.[43] In association with the Mason Kheraskov he naturally met N.I. Novikov and others of the Masonic order, but did not himself join. Among his other literary associates may be mentioned the actor I.A. Dmitreevksy, Vasily Kapnist, Yakov B. Kniazhnin, the official ode-writer V.P. Petrov, and after about 1777, Gavriil Derzhavin, who was by then a poet of consequence.

Muraviev's association with the literary life of St. Petersburg lasted for about thirteen years—1772-1785. In the course of this time he had acquired a phenomenal education, mastered not only French, German and Latin, but also Spanish and English and a considerable amount of Greek. He also developed a great interest in mathematics and the physical sciences, and attended lectures at the Academy of Sciences. It may be noted that Mikhail Lomonosov was one of his idols.

In 1785 the Empress Catherine II, having learned of Muraviev's extraordinary attainments, appointed him to tutor the second of her grandsons; and soon the elder, Alexander (later Emperor) also came under his care. From this date Muraviev's time was too completely occupied with his educational duties to permit much literary activity. His tutorial career terminated in 1796. In 1800 he became a senator, and in 1803 curator of Moscow University, in which capacity he made strenuous efforts to improve the curriculum, with especial attention to the teaching of Latin and Greek. He died at the age of 50, on July 29, 1807. During his later years he had continued to write verse, which he published occasionally in periodicals, but did not collect into a volume. He wrote some prose stories, including a fantastic "historical" tale entitled *Oskold* on the career of the Varangian Askold, who, according to the Primary Chronicle, was the first prince of Kiev.

Muraviev's *Complete Works* were published in three parts in 1819-20;[44] but despite the title, the collection is far from complete. A very considerable amount of his verse remained in manuscript and was first published in the "Poet's Library" edition, edited by L.I. Kulakova, in 1967. Any estimate of the poetical quality and literary position of Muraviev made before this date is accordingly virtually valueless. It should be noted that the editor of the *Complete Works* was K.N. Batiushkov, who was a kinsman of Muraviev, lived for a time in his house, and was an admiring poetical disciple of his.

It is an ironical fact that Muraviev's six volumes of published verse, written, as we have noted, before the age of eighteen, are poetically insignificant; his only important verse is that which appeared occasionally after 1775 in periodicals such as Novikov's *Morning Light,* or Karamzin's *Aonides,* or sometimes failed altogether to see the light in his lifetime. In the juvenile published material he is a classicist *à contre-coeur;* in the later pieces he is a rebellious pre-romantic.

It was highly unfortunate for Muraviev's development that he fell early into the hands of Vasily Maikov. Maikov, as we have seen, was a servile imitator: in the ode, of Lomonosov; and in the fable, of Sumarokov. The only area in which he exhibited any originality was in the parody epic—and this area, apparently, had no appeal for his pupil. Neither did the "ode," as Lomonosov, Sumarokov and Maikov composed it. Perhaps least of all was the sensitive young man attracted to the kind of project which his poetical mentor foisted upon him—a didactic poem on "The Art of War!" He faithfully followed instructions, however, and wrote odes, e.g., "On the Victories Won by Russian Arms in the Course of the First Turkish War" (1773), and a "War Song" and a "Temple of Mars" (same year),[45] which are little more ·than tedious recountings of Russian military successes, from Oleg to Catherine II! Poetically, this material is worthless. Even more emphatically must this be said also of his *Fables*[46]—but the work of a fourteen-year-old is hardly likely to be of great poetical merit.

Muraviev's natural bent, fostered doubtless by assiduous reading of such German poets as Klopstock and Hagedorn, and such English pre-romantics as Thomson and Gray, was "sentimentalist." He throbbed with lofty ambitions to give his life to the good of mankind, and, in the sharpest contrast with Enlightenment notions, he saw his highest spiritual qualification not in the acuteness of his intellect, but in the sensitivity of his soul. In an entry in his journal following his promotion to the rank of Lieutenant in the Guards, he writes: "My greatness is in my soul, not in production, not in ranks, not in the opinions of my friends." "But to serve mankind, one's society, is one's real nobility."[47] It went against his grain to be associated in the society of the capital with frivolous, self-seeking wastrels, and he retreated so much the more eagerly into the narrow society of his serious literary and philosophical friends. The cult of friendship, which is such a marked feature of sentimentalist literature, makes an early appearance with Muraviev. From the year 1770 probably, when the poet was thirteen (!) comes a fragment in Alexandrines addressed to Ivan Petrovich Turgenev, then eighteen, entitled "Friendship."[48] In this piece Muraviev declares: "I sing not mighty war, not shepherds' contentions—I shall chant before you the feeling of hearts which holds us captive and will subsist forever, this sister of love, or rather [this] daughter of heaven: of friendshp before you I mean now to be the herald." A few lines later he announces his fitness for his subject in the words: "It [i.e., friendship] is familiar to me: I was born to feel."

Bound to his very affectionate and understanding father, and to a younger sister, Fedosia Nikitishna Muravieva (born 1760; later the wife of S.M. Lunin) by remarkably close ties, the poet seems not to have experienced any of the usual juvenile love affairs. The heroines of his so-called "love poetry" are conventional and shadowy abstractions, with names such as Nina, Aglaia, etc., borrowed from French "light verse."

Friendship, affection for family, the "simple life"—such are the themes dearest to the sentimentalist poet. The thirteen-year-old Muraviev pays his respects to the third of these themes in another fragment ambitiously entitled "Rustic Life,"[49] in which he disclaims any intention of writing epic ("the trumpet that calls the soldiery in the hour of battle") and declares: "The rustic life I sing, I sing the green of meadows and the pleasant declivity of the summits of cloudy mountains." As though he were a world-weary habitué of court festivities, the boy announces: "Already I am abandoning the city's sumptuous occasions, which the people esteem, but now I despise; for me everything which is desirable there—diversions, banquets—has become cold before the spectacle of all nature; I do not dwell in those spacious palaces where often I seek myself, but do not find.... the luminary of beautiful days does not fall straight within, winter is not winter there, nor summer summer; on the coldest days their dwelling is heated, and in their sumptuous houses, within those thick walls neither in autumn nor in spring have they any change." Apparently the youngster from Archangel did not care for central heating!

Exposure to the literary demands of classicism, as set forth by Maikov, forced the temporary replacement of Muraviev's sentimentalist themes by those public pieces—panegyrics, etc.—which classical standards demanded. Among the poems composed during this period are nine odes, quite classical in character, although not always in form: "Third Ode,"[50] for example, is composed in six-line trochaic strophes, and "Sixth Ode"[51] in six-line iambic strophes. The subjects are chiefly didactic and moralistic—the brevity of life, the vanity of human efforts, and the like. In 1775, however, Muraviev wrote three pieces—two sonnets and a "Tenth Ode"—in which he makes a decided break in his approach to poetry. Two of these pieces are addressed to his mentor Maikov; the third, a "Sonnet to the Muses," seems to indicate a briefly held resolution to abandon verse altogether in favor of a military career. It reads as follows:[52]

Disappear, O dreams that have held me captive! My mistresses, and now my foes! All your beauties turn dark before me; leave me forever, goddesses of Permessus!

It is impossible for me to celebrate with a single mouth both the wrath of the god of battles, and your benefactions, and it does not behoove me with the same fingers to touch the sword and your sanctuary.

And how should I now play upon the strings! Phoebus does not dwell in war-like encampments; here are no Permessian waters, nor the winged horse.

I do not touch the lyre with reeking hand; needful for verses are both time and quiet, while my torment is my only reward for my labors!

This pessimistic utterance, fortunately, does not represent the young poet's final word, nor probably even a very seriously held resolution. In his "Sonnet to Vasily Ivanovich Maikov" (1775)[53] he pays tribute to the elder bard, but hints at his own inability to follow his lead:

I am now, O Maikov, captivated by the harmony of your lyre, with which I learned to tune my own. The sonorous strings of this lyre no barren places hear, and Fate has decreed that Moscow shall take pleasure in their voice.

You are fortunate, O Moscow! Your Zephyrs, as they blow, will mingle their lovely song with the sound of the groves, [and] beneath the shadow of the monarch's purple the trees of Permessus [i.e., the laurel] will adorn your head.

But the god of the Neva is sorrowful: shall he not hear that trill which the pipes dear to him of a sudden put forth, and whose sweet song he so loved to listen to?

I thought: on these shores I sang with warlike trumpet, so I might now—but, Maikov, that song I sang with you. Without you I am afraid that I have given rude offense.

Maikov answered this rather ambiguous sonnet with one of his own, the final tercet of which quite pointedly warns his young protégé not to deviate from the classical canons, as he evidently showed signs of doing:

If you, Muraviev, are captivated by the voice of this lyre, with which you learned to tune your own, follow it, and sing: the places will not be barren, which you, after me, shall make rejoice.

Moscow beneath the shadow of the monarch's purple will here attend to a re-doubled song, if, blowing over her, the cool zephyrs shall, with our [i.e., my] tones make your tones too resound.

And the god of the Neva, though he will not, methinks, forget us [i.e., me], will yet not for a long while sorrow for song, if you shall use your zeal.

So that your style may be like the style of pleasing singers, as Sumarokov showed the way to this for all—then, believe it, you will not give rude offense with your songs.[54]

Fortunately for poetry, young Muraviev refused (politely) to follow Maikov's fatuous adivce. His "Tenth Ode,"[55] also from 1775, and also addressed "To Vasily Ivanovich Maikov," has the thoroughly unclassical title "Spring." The classical ode was, of couse, always devoted to grandiose public themes—military victories, peace treaties, royal name-days, anniversaries of succession, and the like. But "spring" can hardly be placed in such a category! And the development, moreover, is markedly unclassical—the natural background, although enlivened by the habitual population of the pseudo-classical Olympus, has startling marks of a northern, purely Russian, landscape. Thus, for example, in the second and third strophes, "Neptune with his trident strikes from out the Baltic waves against the thick ice," "the springs roar, the bays groan, and the mossy silt is full of their flow; full-fed, the banks sink in the fresh water in the inundation of their waves. Already on the fields the rivulets are winding; gurgling through the rushes, with hundred-fold bends, the streams are forcing their way. Coming out, the plowman digs ditches for them, and the water gives way to force, pouring into new channels." Here are no pallid echoes of Virgil or Theocritus—the landscape is unmistakably and unclassically Russian. The mixture of elements, however, is awkward, and sometimes almost grotesque. Thus (strophe 6):

The raindrops have watered the fields, hardly grown warm; the meadows at night have drunk up the dew and the earth has become enriched. But meanwhile, as the rain splashes, the maiden [daughter] of Thaumas [i.e., Iris, goddess of the rainbow] gleams, the rain's beautiful companion; and becoming a new dawn, shows us azure and gold and purple in her rainbow.

441

The mythological intrusion here is a bit startling, amid the realistic picture of the spring rains!

The poem's final strophe is, in some respects, Muraviev's "declaration of independence." He has learned the techniques of classical verse—but henceforth he will use them, not as Maikov would wish, but on entirely different themes:

I strike my lyre, O Maikov, which you tuned for me, and I repeat the resounding tones, as I sing the beauties of spring. Formerly I sang of clamorous battles, but now I have proclaimed succulent vegetation and the springs that well up in the fields. You admonished me to sing of battles—but for you I have composed this poem, as a sign of a sensitive soul.

There seems to be no record of Maikov's reaction to his pupil's rebellion, his bizarre decision to eschew "clamorous battles" in favor of the rustic beauties of nature. But the break was final. Only rarely in his verse written after 1775 does Muraviev deviate from the repertory appropriate to "a sensitive soul."

An interesting piece, composed a few years after the "Tenth Ode" is "The Grove" ["Roshcha"] of 1778.[56] For the first time in Russian literature since Trediakovsky's *Tilimakhida* this poem is composed in hexameters, rather heavily loaded with Slavonic forms. It is short and largely descriptive, the pictures, like those of "Spring," being specific and Russian, rather than conventionally classical. The sentimentalist concept of nature as the refuge of the virtuous, inaccessible to wicked men, is prominent in the beginning, followed by a realistic depiction of the sunrise:

> With gaze attentive I shall accompany the cultivator.
> The moon is setting, and, it seems, falling from the sky;
> Light is pouring into the atmosphere; the waves of the east have
> > become red....
> Oh! I have beheld the moment when the morning light has arisen.
> The charms of the young immortal [i.e., the goddess of the
> > dawn] have renewed my sensibilities,
> The quiet brightness embraces my touched soul
> Like the transparent cloud in which the sun is resting,
> Only washed in the waves....

The sun reaches the zenith, and the peasant's labor halts for a bit:

> The sun lords it over nature, and all nature without activity
> Is idle at that moment when the sun has reached
> The mid-point of the heavens' vault. End your toil, O plowman!
> You have succeeded in turning up a great deal of the corn-land
> > this morning.

442

See how, reflecting the sun's rays, the plow-share glistens.
Behold, the cultivator unfastens the yoke from the steaming horse
And himself turns aside to the quivering shade of the branching
                                                    oak.
With handkerchief he wipes from his brow the streams of sweat,
Throws aside his hat and lies face down, hugging the ground.
Meanwhile, while the plow is at rest, plunged into the soil,
The horse, freed from his bridle, rolls, transfigured,
Spreading his mane on the grass; the air, smitten
By the sound of his neighing, after a moment, gives an answer
                                                    back.
Now see, sated with playfulness, he raises his head briskly,
And braced with one knee on the ground, he exerts himself to
                                        place the other hoof
So as to move his whole weight with this,
And thence lifts himself up, if at once he jumps to his feet.
The hair from his neck falls on his back,
His nostrils are distended, and the steam spreads out in the air.

The description of the horse's movements, obviously the result of careful observation, is particularly notable; any such detailed realism might be found in a genuinely classical source, such as Hesiod or Virgil, but never in an eighteenth-century pseudo-classical work. The picture of the noonday siesta is finished by the arrival of the farmer's wife with his meal, and of the affection of the young pair, which the poet modestly refrains from describing, on the grounds that "Only that heavenly singer, only Milton can do this," as he did in describing the "innocent passions" of Adam and Eve.

"The Grove" is a concentrated epitome of sentimentalist themes—the feeling for external nature (the sunrise), the sympathetic depiction of the peasant and his labor-loving existence, and the glorification of family affection. We shall find exactly the same themes in that pre-romantic classic, Zhukovsky's translation of Gray's "Elegy in a Country Churchyard," where they belong with equal right to the original and his Russian translator.

Muraviev, as has been mentioned, fell into the Masonic orbit during the 1770s, and although he never himself became a Mason, he was attracted to the order's program of self-perfection and meditation. He undertook such a program with enthusiasm, and confided to what he called a "Sentimental Journal" many of his thoughts and meditations. Some of this journal he even published, in Novikov's Masonic vehicle *Morning Light*. Many of the same subjects became the themes of poems written during these same years, which often bear the designation "Odes." These were collected by the poet under the general heading of "New Lyrical Experiments," in 1776, apparently with the aim of publication; they were circulated among the poet's friends, but never published during his lifetime.

443

The term "ode," as Muraviev employs it in this collection, has lost all specific meaning, and signifies no more than "lyric poem." This is a symptom of the general breakdown of the classical genre system, for many of these poems could have been, and in an earlier period certainly would have been, classified as epistles, elegies, or the like. Such are "Sorrowful Verses to [N.A. Lvov]," 1776,[57] which, although composed in the ten-line strophe of the classical ode, is elegiac in content; "Longing for Winter" (1776),[58] which might be classified as a pastoral; "To Khemnitser,"[59] which is certainly an epistle, etc. The themes of these lyrics are almost all personal, and reflect the poet's inner life. Note, for example, the contemplative and moralistic content of the poem "Time" (1775):[60]

> Stop, my friends, and let us contemplate fleeing time:
> Not long since the sun's light sank, strengthless—
> And see, thrown on the corn-land, the seed has come into ears,
> And is calling for the reaper.
>
> Yesterday I followed the sun to the evening waters.
> "Rest! For you too it is pleasant to lie in the waves,"
> I exclaimed; but he, having circled the antipodes,
> Has just rekindled the day.
>
> However, thought I, the moment reposes.
> Already I have passed two years beyond the third lustrum [I am
> seventeen years old].
> O happy life! Alas! You have been thrown into oblivion.
> Is not one's whole lifetime a dream?
>
> In time we are able to capture only one point.
> The minute which one has lived is longer than a year of sleep.
> And the butterfly, whose life is bound to the leaf,
> Is still not closely confined.
>
> Every moment has its peculiar color, taken from the heart's
> condition.
> It is dark for him whose heart is heavy with evil;
> For the good it is golden.
>
> All the seasons of the year have delights;
> In every time of life there is a happiness of its own;
> But the height of wisdom is the art of maintaining
> Pleasures for life.

Repentance is a gall which spreads its repulsive grief
In the fair weather of time. But time at last
Wipes from the heart's tablet
    This alien rust.

If you have saved your heart amid the waves from shipwreck,
What though it should finally please Fate to darken
The brightness of your days—if much comfort
    Yet remains in you?

Not all, indeed, of the lyrics collected into his "New Experiments" are capable of classification at all on classical principles. One that completely eludes classification is "Journey" ["Puteshestvie"],[61] composed in the first half of the 1770s, which is a poetical record of an actual journey of Muraviev, from Vologda and the embraces of his "tenderest of fathers and his incomparable sister" to the capital city. The poem might be called, in fact, a "Sentimental Journey" in verse. Another unclassifiable piece is "Complaint to the Muses,"[62] which begins: "O you, who were my first passion, you, whose delightful voice I have grown accustomed to listen to—forgive me, O Muses, I have a complaint against you—Oh, no, I weep tears because you have forgotten me! It is hard to endure coldness from one's friend, but to see him [turned] away from you is the hardest of all."

Muraviev's early reading must have included a good deal of Horace, for the themes and even the wording of the Latin master appear with great frequency in the early poems. In his "Essay on Writing Poetry" ["Opyt o stikhotvorstve"][63] (1775; 1780), after paying tribute to an interesting assortment of classical models from Homer and Sophocles to Tasso and Lomonosov (!), he calls on his poet to "garland the wine with Horace, with the fragrant rose and the lily's whiteness, and with him also, laying aside amorous vanities, in epistles scatter for us the flowers of philosophy ["mudrosti"]." These lines, of course, allude specifically to Horace's "Odes," which celebrate, often enough, wine and love; and his later, moralizing "Epistles." On the model of the latter is, for example, Muraviev's "Epistle to N.R.R."[64] [i.e., Nikita Romanovich Rozheshnikov] (1776), which the nineteen-year-old moralist begins with the declaration:

Happiness, which is so alluring for us, dear friend! is incommensurable with this life. In vain do philosophers grasp at it with the mind: fools are just like them, as far as happiness is concerned. The prisoner, whom chains weigh down all his life long; the haughty fellow who in shame conceals his tears in vain—why hide from us? Such is man—and happiness? No, he does not know it forever. Let Seneca and Epictetus dispute on this subject with me—it's a rare man who is comforted by their counsel.

His conclusions are entirely in keeping with Horace's: "In a word, the man whose soul is in repose—he alone is wise, and always free, even in chains."

One of the 1776 "Odes"[65]—written, like Horace's, in a succession of identical quatrains, and in no way resembling the classical Russian ode either in theme or in form—begins with a line that almost verbally echoes Horace's "Eheu fugaces, Postume, Postume labuntur anni" (*Carmina* II, 14): "Fleeing, fleeing, O friends, is irrecoverable time [cf. Virgil's *irreparabile tempus*]; is it long since the zephyrs here softened the fierce frost? The seed only just came up, after being dug into the ground—and the hour of reaping has come." "Frustra cruente Marte carebimus Fractisque rauci fluctibus Hadriae, Frustra per autumnos nocentem Corporibus metuemus Austrum," sighs Horace in the fourth strophe of his ode ("*In vain* shall we shun bloody Mars and the hoarse Adriatic's broken waves; *in vain* through the autumns shall we be fearful of the South-wind that harms bodies"). Each line of Muraviev's fourth strophe begins with "votshche" ("in vain"); "In vain shall the sword rust and be returned into the scabbard; in vain shall we hide ourselves from the furious waves; in vain shall we be cautious of foul weather—we shall all descend into the dark grave." Muraviev's development, of course, departs from Horace's in many respects; he meditates on whether death is sleep or a waking into another life, and takes the Christian alternative. "Happy am I," he announces, "If gray hair shall cover my head, if it shall be my lot to guide my steps with a staff, and yours, my friends, to say [to me] amid quiet conversation, 'Farewell.' "

It is apparent that Muraviev's ideal of the "ode" was changing at this period from the pseudo-classical, basically "Pindaric" form, which Maikov and his revered model, Lomonosov, composed, to the lighter, more personal Horatian variety. His "Sixth Ode. To D[mitrievsky]" (1776)[66] contains some revealing lines:

The citizen ["grazhdanin"] of Lesbos walked in streams of blood, and sailed the waves; however, that man of war used to celebrate the pure Muses and, along with Bacchus, the mother of love.

The flooded river, with deep swiftness, tears away and whirls off the bank; just so Pindar, soaring out of eyesight, flies with magnificent speed.

But whoever, heedless, directs his audacious flight after him, that one plaits for himself wings of wax, and falls noisily into the sea.

I, a weak pupil of Glycera's lover, laboriously gather the honeycomb, and, concealing myself in the soft retreat of a cave, turn away from the heights.

The "citizen of Lesbos" is of course Horace's principal Greek model, Alcaeus, whose favorite poetic themes, as tradition has it, were war, love, and wine. The picture of Pindar as a swollen river, carrying away its banks, and the caution that any would-be imitator of the great master is a foolhardy Icarus, flying on waxen wings, comes from Horace (Odes IV, 2): "Pindarum quisquis studet aemulari"—"Whoever is zealous to rival Pindar, O Iulus, is relying on Daedalus's skill, on waxen wings—destined to give his name to the glassy sea. Like a river that rushes down from the mountain, which the rains have fed

446

above its familiar banks, Pindar seethes, unbounded, and rushes with deep mouth, destined to be rewarded with Apollo's laurel," etc. The last strophe quoted of Muraviev's ode (st. 6) quite pointedly announces the poet's resolution *not* to try to follow Pindar (and Maikov and Lomonosov) but rather "Glycera's lover," i.e., Horace.

Quintus Horatius Flaccus and Edward Young make a strange pair—the genial Roman Epicurean and the gloomy, death-haunted English divine; but Muraviev seems to have been oblivious of the incongruity. His poem "To Khemnitser"[59] (1776) begins with Horace's "Otium divos rogat in patenti" (Odes II, 16) and follows the themes faithfully through several strophes:

The mariner longs for repose, seeing a storm; and even the hero, coming to loathe war, longs to enter quiet. But their confused souls long for that in deception, which it is possible for them to purchase, O Khemnitser, with neither silver nor gold.

The torturer cannot escape from disquiet either into castles that rise to the clouds, or into the gardens of Alcinous; and the whole crowd of his confused slaves is unable to banish the cares that flit about his gilded ceilings [cf. Horace's "curas laqueata circum Tecta volantis"].

Horace ends his "hymn to repose" with the admission: "To me the Fate, free from deceit, has given small fields and the subtle spirit of the Greek Muse, and to scorn the malignant crowd." Muraviev pays his respects to the Muse, but suddenly at the end injects a discordant note—the "graveyard theme" of Young's *Night Thoughts:*

I shall sing to the pipe by this sacred wave, and you shall accompany the voice of my song on [your] gilded lyre; and let my day come; you shall lull me to rest here and, perhaps, hereafter come with tears to the ashes of your friend.

If you and Lvov shall come together, and begin to strew flowers above my grave, suddenly shaken, I shall adjure you: "Stay! Do not flee," and embracing one another in silent agitation, you will say: "Lo, here lies our friend!"

In 1780, for reasons concealed from a later age, Muraviev's verse suddenly introduces a theme not derived from Horace or any other literary source, but from personal experience. This is despondency over what the young poet feels as a progressive loss of "sensibility," of the ability to respond throbbingly to all the beauties of nature, human virtue, and the other stimuli of the "sensitive soul,"—and accordingly, as an encroaching poetical impotence. Other poets, e.g., Lvov, of Muraviev's circle, were troubled by the same concern, but it reduces Muraviev almost to despair. At the same time his journal and his letters, as well as his verse, reveal that at this period he was, for the only time in his life, feeling the attractions of the life of "society"; and it is evident that the loss of sensibility is in his mind connected with the artificial and "worldly" life he is leading, and the consequent feelings of shame and compunction over his disloyalty to the "Muse" exacerbate his gloom. The new theme is first introduced in a lengthy elegy entitled "Regrets for Youth" (1780).[67] After passing in review the significant spiritual events of his youth—enchantment with the beauties of Virgil's verse, the first impulse to create poetry of his own, the first excitement at the expanded horizons of life in St. Petersburg, initiation into the beauties of Italian verse, acquaintance with Maikov and Kheraskov and their poetry, etc., he comes at the end to the pessimistic view of his own capabilities:

But my spirit is unworthy of your [i.e., Kheraskov's] inspiration: in the shadow of your banners the last warrior, fearing to follow after you, I now remain in inglorious sloth. Oh, shall it be long, long, that I am thus to weary myself, wasting my days away in reprehensible idleness? O reason, come [to the aid of] my stagnant life!

Probably of the same year or the year before, is a short "Fragment,"[68] addressed to the poet's close friend V.V. Khalikov. This is worth quoting entire:

Ashamed of idleness, I break its chains; I long to feel that I have a soul. From this protracted non-being into the abyss of which my life is sinking, I long, trembling, to save myself to your embraces, and by your name to dispel the gloom of conception. Do you hear the wail of my heart in your own, and will you give my utterance the loan of [your] feeling? No, colors of such darkness do not exist, as might represent the appearance of my life. Confined in a meager circle of feelings and ideas, reduced to the enticements of animals, I look on my passing life without regret. Everything moves ennui, which alone is awake in my heart. But, in painting the sequence of my reproaches, I am using shadow more than light, and hence, because all confessions are cruel, I am striving to encircle all vices with [one] line. This gift, which I dare not name, the art of blowing the quiet pipes, has departed. And so it has become oppressed by vice. Oh! Of virtue scarce has so much been left me as to regret its loss! Oh, would that my brush might be found false!

Similar despairing cries are found in Muraviev's "Epistle to Feona"[69] (his sister) of 1781: "Now, my dear one, I amuse myself with the idea that I am thinking, if I put some [verse] feet together. Everything is eroded which I confided to memory, and, in losing everything, I have lost tears. But in this loss what most afflicts me—your beautiful image is disappearing from my heart. O guardian of my thoughts, inclinations and feelings, I have seen them fleeing from my heart. They dwell only with virtue. Together with virtue, even the Muses fly away!.... O Feona! I implore your return! Increase for me the depth and strength of feeling, and in my memory renew the features in which you appeared to me in better days."

A poet's spiritual biography is of course impossible to follow, and indeed it is dangerous even to take all such utterances as Muraviev's despondent laments as entirely personal—they may belong not to the man but to the poet, his *alter ego*. In any case, the themes of despair and self-flagellation disappear after a year or two. They are, of course, part and parcel of the sentimentalist glorification of sensibility, which appears in Muraviev's poetry in its quintessential form in "Letter to * * *" (1783):[70]

I recall the days spent with you, occupied with dreams and sweetened by them, as, believing that in vain thoughts we were listening to the heart's voice, we used to love the wisdom that fled from us. I recall those happy moments as, making to each other mutual revelations, with the fire of youth, with the sincerity of [our] years, we used to show one another the trace of good deeds. Quietly, mitigating the winter cold with a fire, we met with happiness, not expecting to find it. Now the man of Britain in his "Nights" [i.e., Edward Young] portrayed the world to us with a picture in which the gloom devours the feeble light, as he wept the funerals of his beloved children; now we read of Berenice [heroine of Racine's tragedy of that name] as she made reproaches to the hero [Titus] who was pitiless only to himself. We judged that Racine was superior to those dark traits of the poet who, for tears, left the banks of the Thames. We delighted in feeling the sighs of Heloise [Rousseau's heroine] ; we paid the tribute of esteem and tears to that place where Rousseau, who pierced the breast of mortals with mysterious gaze, sees spectacles of a better heaven and delights in the conversation of the wise.

These dreams, the voice of sensibility, will they come again and delight us? Have they not once and for all rolled by in our hearts, having dried up the spring of the saving thirst (!) to be moved, to sigh, to delight oneself in sympathies, to exist living? Those palpitations, which you feel at sixteen, will you find place for them in your heart when you have passed twenty? When already, thrown from dream to dream, you have seen the dark and measured the height of the waves and felt your soul slipping into the abyss of death; when you have given your heart's reality to be effaced by violent feelings and furious passions, those thieves of virtue and happiness? Without virtue, where shall the heart find rest? Without happiness, you destroy all that you think to build. And vulgar egoism, having taken possession of you, swallows up in its maw all the sentiments of love. You will look upon your best friend without rapture, and the lovely companion of your tender days will appear in your eyes a simple maiden. You have died—and why does the beating of your heart continue? The blood in your veins will not cease circulation—but farewell beauty, love and rapture! You will still have sight, but everything which you see is dead, and everywhere you will meet crude matter. Come, sensibility! And resurrect the unfortunate, thou giver of potent quickening; inflame life in him, return to him wakefulness, open the overgrown paths of feeling. Let the poor man sigh, recognizing nature once more, and weep for joy [at] having been reckoned with the race of mortals. He will be son, father, lover and husband—he will tell his children of the disease that has passed, his own alienation ["ottorzhenie"], the loss of sensibility, and will beg them, in payment for his love, that their young hearts may never be severed from feeling, by which alone man is happy. Blessed, my good friend, are you, if, true to yourself, severe only to yourself, kindly to all others, you freely pay the dues of life, the zealous guardian of your own sensibility.

With all allowances for a horrendous mixed metaphor, and some rather awkward phrasing, this is an eloquent and quite moving confession, a veritable "hymn to sensibility."

In 1783 Muraviev composed a lengthy "Epistle on Light Verse, to A.M. Br[ianchaninov]."[71] This is his most significant verse work on poetical theory. It would appear that as he matured, he became more and more attracted to a type of verse scarcely represented in Russian before him, the model for which he found in eighteenth-century French poetry. He calls this "light verse" (French *poésie légère*) or "fugitive verse" (French *poésie fugi-*

449

tive), or even sometimes "society verse" ["obshchestvennye stikhi"] (French *vers de société*). Unfortunately for historians of comparative literature, French literary history is habitually written as a history of masterpieces and masters; the forest giants alone appear, as in a European woodland, all the undergrowth having been assiduously cleared away. Such a picture is in the highest degree misleading; very often the literary masterpiece is entirely un-typical of an age, the real picture of which can be obtained only by study of precisely the "undergrowth" which has been eliminated. So it is with eighteenth-century French poetry. The writers of the "light verse" which Muraviev so admired are poets whom even the most detailed French literary history passes over with obliterating scorn. Their very names are ignored, and their works, having never been reprinted, are almost totally inaccessible. They are Charles-Pierre Colardeau (1732-1776), Claude-Joseph Dorat (1734-1780), François-Joachim de Bernis (1715-1794), Jacques-Charles-Louis de Malfilâtre (1732-1767), Stanislas-Jean de Bouflers (1737-1815) and others. The general verdict upon them all is that of Larousse on Dorat: "type de frivolité élégante et maniérée." This verdict is not undeserved: of itself their verse is indeed very "light weight" and insignificant, except that it marks the beginning of a revolt against serious, heavy, "civic" or philosophical verse—and this revolt *is* important, and when it does appear on the literary scene in most handbooks it is with unexplained suddenness, as though from one generation to the next the leading poets with remarkable unanimity aban-doned reason for sentiment as their guiding light.

It is probable that Muraviev, in his enthusiasm for Dorat, for example, saw in his cold and lifeless verse qualities which were not there—spontaneity and insouciance—with which he endeavored to invest his own "light verse." It is even possible, as A.N. Brukhansky claims,[72] that in translating the French phrase *pièces fugitives* with *ubegaiushchaia poeziia* (literally "fleeing poetry"), he was misunderstanding the French: his simile (in the poem "Society Verse"[73]) of the poet, "as the butterflies in the luxuriant summer fly suddenly aloft, alight on the flowers, but cannot stay on one object," makes it appear that he claimed the butterflies' license to flit inconsequently from one subject to another as the whim took him. In any case, the poetical ideal which replaced in young Muraviev's mind both Horatian moralizing and Youngian gloom, was that of an airy, elegant, musical, and quite unprofound verse, with a prevailingly amatory content. It was no bar to the writing of such verse that the poet in his personal life seems to have been singularly "fancy free"—he could always sigh on paper for some shadowy Algora or Zila or Aglaia. His "Epistle on Light Verse" begins with an address to his legal friend Brianchaninov which he would probably have regarded, with complaisance, as equally applicable to himself: "O chronicler of your own amorous playfulness." He questions his friend whether he still remains peri-lously balanced between blonde and brunette, and whether "in busying your-self still with literature, you exalt them in verse to the flattering rank of

450

Lesbia and Corinna," (Catullus' and Ovid's mistresses respectively).

Following his sportive introduction, Muraviev introduces his first serious theme: [74] "Listen to the interpretation of my heresy: the means with which I desire that the rhymester shall win the name of a writer of love. The two different titles—'lover' and 'poet'—are fused into one and cannot be separated." After proclaiming Colardeau, Dorat and Bernis his models, and indulging in a rhetorical query on why such poets are not to be found in Russian verse, he turns to a bit of autobiography: "I would at once have started on two different paths, that diverged far apart: I wanted to provide myself with qualities such as to be [both] a poet and a man of the world ["svetskim chelovekom"], and keep in a certain harmony philosophy and the taste for dissipation. With both I went wandering into impassable wildernesses. The ways of society are chains on the thinker, and he who in society has passed the test, yawns in the converse of the Muses."

Mention of Voltaire in this connection leads to a lengthy characterization of that "centenarian rascal," who was able to do what no imitators of his work should ever dare to try. "Voltaire could do all this. And he had a glorious old age, with envy at his feet, above praise, above reproach."

In the last but one section of his "Epistle" Muraviev turns to some, perhaps not entirely sincere, self-criticism. "But judgment is proper for all: it is a difficult art. Let us pass ourselves in judgment, knitting our brow. Alack! I have not gathered roses without thorns. My merit is to write prose in rhyme, without imagination, in defiance of the language, falling hourly under the critic's rod. Has comparison been left between me and the virtuoso who captivates the ear with the movement of his bow? His art is beautiful, noble; mine is handy to all and disagreeable to the ear. In order to rise, poetry must be compounded of painting and music. Ariosto deserves to walk with Paisiello—but the rustic buffoon has fallen to my lot, who having been obliged to scratch on the fiddle, hinders the peasants from singing in tune." The self-characterization is certainly unfair, but the insight that "poetry must be compounded of painting and music" is brilliant; and in his best "light verse," e.g., "To the Goddess of the Neva," Muraviev's own poetry fulfills this ideal.

The final section of the "Epistle on Light Verse" contains some of the poet's most mature observations on his art, and implicitly, some of the most telling criticism of the classical fashion of composition which he had outgrown:

For feeling, deeply rooted, for a style full of ideas, for a painterly eye, for charms of intellect and mastery of writing the honor of poets should not be extinguished forever; but not for having an abundance of rhymes and being able to clothe a worthless matter in them. In a lame verse a good idea falls—but a verse is no more than sound, if there is no idea in it. To write is something common to all—to write like a master is rare. It is for this reason that we see that the trifles of minds such as Horace was are the delight of the ages; while books in folio corrosive Time devours, or else lets live to the shame of their creators. Paint, you into whose hands nature has placed a brush, and given spirit to fly about the measureless circle of learning ["nauki"] —paint without fear that envy will gnaw—your transports are your warranties of success, the beauty of the universe is your gain.

It should be noted that the Russian verb "to write" ["pisat' "] means also "to paint," and Muraviev's use of the verb is purposely ambiguous. It is also significant that the first element for which he considers a poet's honor to deserve immortality is "feeling, deeply rooted"—an element which a classical theorist would probably have placed last or ignored altogether.

A typical example of the "fugitive verse" which Muraviev composed at about this time is the following four-stanza piece of uncertain date entitled "The Dear Child";[75] like most of its kind, it is in trochaic tetrameter— a light, dancing meter appropriate to the content:

> You give me greetings, you dance gaily with me, and in all the amusements of childhood I am always your comrade.
> You do not keep silent with me, you sing me your songs, you reproach me for my absence, and do embroidery with me.
> But when my bold tongue begins to express passion, at once you become grave— and I do not dare continue.
> Ah, Rozana, you're a rogue, you have already emerged from childhood. A cold appearance is one trick—and Cupid laughs at it.

The finest, and most admired, of all Muraviev's "light verse" is the poem "To the Goddess of the Neva."[76] This is familiar to Russian readers from the circumstance that Pushkin, in a stanza of *Eugene Onegin*, alludes to its last quatrain.[77] The pictorial and musical qualities of Muraviev's best verse are very apparent in this delightful piece, which might well, as the critics like to point out, have been composed by Muraviev's admiring pupil, the romantic Konstantin Batiushkov:

> Flow on quietly, evenly, proud Neva, past the famous buildings of sovereigns and shadowy islands!
> You connect with the seas the stormy Russian lakes, and flow around the ashes of Great Peter.
> In the heart of the Mediterranean Sea your nymphs are celebrated; as far as Paris and as Lemnos their streams have swept;
> Greek rivers are ashamed, recalling their lot, that now by their current are reflected *bostanii* and *kizlar-aga* [Turkish court ranks],
> While you repeat the image of sportive graces, casting the tributes of the nations before the feet of Beauty.
> From the Thames and from the Tagus sweeps a flock of ships, and your kindred water is spread beneath it [i.e., the flock].
> I love your bathing places, where Chloe's beauties are covered with the clothing of the modest bedroom, and the Loves stand guard.
> Your evening is full of coolness—your bank is in motion with the crowds, and as of a magical serenade the voice of your wave is wafted.
> You bid the mists gather—a thin haze covers your billows, and you yourself

lean favorably to the deceits of love.

At the hour when you dispatch mortals, weary with their happiness, you rise up like a fine vapor to the surface of your waters.

You do not weigh down the smooth waters with the running of a swift chariot, and the Sirens around their Queen hasten to a round-dance.

With waking eyes the enraptured poet beholds the favoring goddess, as he passes his night unsleeping, leaning against the granite. (1794)

Throughout his poetical career Mikhail Muraviev was an experimenter and innovator, always sensitive to new currents of fashion and ready to meet them in practice. Two of the newer fashions in verse, which by the last decade of the century had already become prominent in the West and had begun to reach Russia, were the Ossianic craze and the vogue of ballads. The ballad as a popular, folk-lore genre was earliest brought into the ken of literary poets by the famous collection of Bishop Percy, *Reliques of Ancient English Poetry* (1765). Gottfried Bürger's poem *Lenore* (1773), an adaptation of Percy's ballad "Sweet William's Ghost," made a European sensation, and popularized the ballad form in Germany. Karamzin's "Raisa—an Antique Ballad" (1791) is usually credited with being the first Russian example of the genre, but it is probable that Muraviev's "Boleslav, King of Poland,"[78] although published only in 1810, may antedate it. The subject, taken from the history of twelfth-century Poland Muraviev had utilized in the 1770s for a tragedy which he never completed. By the time the ballad was published, the form, so assiduously cultivated by Zhukovsky, was of course no longer a novelty to Russian readers, and Muraviev's poem passed unnoticed. The form is the simple octosyllabic quatrain with alternating rhymes *aBaB*, so common in genuinely popular ballads. Zhukovsky, of course, very often and very effectively employs a more elaborate and musical form. The ballad recounts how Boleslav "Wry-mouth," King of Poland (c. 1139) fell in love with the princess who was betrothed to his rebellious brother Zbigniew; how the King was victorious over Zbigniew and his Czech allies and captured their leader, whom he failed to recognize because the vizor of his helmet was drawn. Seeing the captive fallen suppliant at the feet of the princess whom both brothers loved, Boleslav plunged his sword into his unrecognized rival's heart, only to discover his brother when the vizor was raised. Appalled at his unintentional fratricide, Boleslav tried to kill himself, and when his courtiers prevented this, he became a monk and thought to atone for his crime by confessing it to everyone he met.

The Ossianic craze was begun by James Macpherson's publication (1760-63) of several poems purportedly translated from ancient Celtic epics composed by the bard Ossian. We have already seen how some of the features of this "northern" type of verse were assimilated by Derzhavin—notably in "The Waterfall" (1791-94), and by other contemporaries such as Lvov. The most notable example of Ossianism in Muraviev's verse is a late piece, composed in 1804, the year before his death, and read at a session of the Russian

Academy; the poem is entitled: "Romance, Paraphrased from the Caledonian Tongue."[79] According to a laconic note in Kulakova's edition of Muraviev's verse "Only the names are borrowed from Ossian." The "romance" is composed in the same octosyllabic quatrain as the ballad of "Boleslav"; it is an instructive example of Muraviev's ability to combine various heterogeneous elements into a harmonious whole:

The sacred wood motions from its lofty summits. It seems as though it were calling: "Ossian, Fingal's son!

Rise, bring [your] plumed helmet and golden armor. Standing here, your winged charger is dropping tears upon the grass."

You are calling—[but] Fingal's son does not heed your call. His hand will not tear aside the cold shroud of death.

Ah, unfortunate Malvina, here at the midnight hour you seek your beloved, but fate is not indulgent to beauty.

He has drooped; as the flower just now enlivened by the morning dew, is mown down by the scythe, so he has fallen in the flower of [his] years.

Here an invisible barrier holds your beloved. Tears—they are your comfort— tears will reach him.

Or, better, direct your tearful gaze to the circle on high. Behold, soaring with the cloud, behold his radiant spirit—

So, even as once, storming away from the northern shores, he thundered upon the eastern mountains amid his foes,

As the youthful hero gave counsels to wise old men, or accompanied with sweet voice the strings of [his] harmonious harp.

He has finished the course of his days—[but] the current of life agitates us. Sound, O strings, in negligence. Cruel destiny carries everything away.

Although it would be an exaggeration to claim that Muraviev is one of Russia's greatest eighteenth-century poets, he certainly does not deserve the virtual oblivion into which his name had fallen during the nineteenth and early twentieth centuries. His principal interest remains his restless, experimental spirit. At its worst his poetry is rough, pedestrian and ordinary; at its best, it is fresh and elegant, musical and with the kind of "plastic" quality which is so much admired in his greater pupil, Konstantin Batiushkov. Muraviev was a poet, one might say by avocation—his principal concerns being always in other areas of life. Yet he was certainly marked by a profound poetical culture almost unrivalled in his age—the English poets, from Shakespeare, Milton and Waller to Young and Macpherson, the Germans of the *Sturm und Drang*, the bevy of French creators of "light verse" as well as Voltaire and Beaumarchais, and the Renaissance and seventeenth-century Italians, from Petrarch to Ariosto, Tasso and Metastasio—to say nothing of all the Russian poets from Feofan Prokopovich to his own contemporaries— these were all his familiars. If his knowledge and use of Greek verse were small, he had a rare mastery of Latin, as his imitations of Horace, Lucan, and even Petronius (he translated the "Civil War" fragment from the *Satiricon*[80]) attest. Too restless and uneven to be truly great, he is by these very qualities

454

one of the most interesting poets of his age.

D. *Vasily Vasilievich Kapnist* (1758-1823)[81]

The fourth and longest-lived poet of the Lvov circle was Vasily Vasilievich Kapnist. The son of a valiant officer who lost his life in 1757 at the battle of Gross-Jägersdorf, before his youngest son was born, Vasily was brought up by his mother (or step-mother, for there is a family tradition that his own mother was, like Zhukovsky's, a captive Turkish woman[83]), on his father's Ukrainian estate. His grandfather, Peter Kapnisi, was a Greek from the island of Zakynthos, who had been forced to leave his native land in 1711.

Young Vasily Kapnist had a good private education at home, where he learned French and German, and studied later in St. Petersburg in the school of the Izmailovsky Guards Regiment, in which he had been enrolled in consequence of his father's services. Later he was transferred to the Preobrazhensky Regiment, where he met Gavriil Derzhavin, who in 1773 had hardly begun his poetical career. It was at this time that he also became acquainted with Nikolai Lvov and Ivan Khemnitser and the brilliant circle of literary men, actors, painters and musicians of which Lvov was the center. In 1781 he married Alexandra Alexeevna Diakova, whose sister Maria Lvov had married the year before. After his first wife's death, Derzhavin in 1795 was to marry the youngest of the Diakova sisters. The three poets were accordingly united by ties not only of friendship but of family.

In 1775 Kapnist left the uncongenial military service and began to devote himself to literature. His first sensational publication was (1780) "First Satire."[84] The storm of hostile criticism which this met with drove the poet into retirement to his estate of Obukhovka, and a poetical silence of several years. He served as an elected official in his native province and in 1783, on the occasion of Catherine's decree transforming the free Ukrainian peasants into serfs, wrote his famous "Ode to Slavery,"[85] which was of course not published, but nevertheless caused Kapnist some unpleasantness from the government.

The comedy *Iabeda* (the usual translation of this title is the French *Chicane*[86]—there is no single-word English equivalent) was written in 1791, and although neither published nor played in Catherine's lifetime, became known to her, to Kapnist's embarrassment. It was dedicated to Emperor Paul and published (and performed) in 1798. The legend that the author was as a result sentenced to exile in Siberia but recalled at once is baseless. Kapnist enjoyed the favor of Paul, and was appointed by him director of the imperial theaters of St. Petersburg. Upon Paul's assassination Kapnist retired again (1801) to Obukhovka, where he remained until his death in 1823.

Kapnist's position in Russian literature has been too frequently determined by what Marxist critics usually refer to as his "denunciatory" or "unmasking" style—the works, that is, in which he follows the eighteenth-century satirical tradition, either in the comedy *(Iabeda)*, the ode ("Ode to Slavery") or the satire itself ("First—and Last—Satire"). Unquestionably these three works are impressive productions and would, without anything else, make a poet's reputation. But to concentrate all attention upon them is to ignore an entirely different, and no less important, side of Kapnist's genius. His was a contradictory personality, and while the vehement indignation which characterizes his "denunciatory" pieces is the mark of one side of his literary heritage, the gentle, sorrowful pessimism and brooding melancholy of much of his lyric verse is no less a part of him, and by its close connections with Russian sentimentalism (e.g., Karamzin and Dmitriev) and early romanticism (Batiushkov and Zhukovsky) is even more significant in the history of literature.

Iabeda has already been considered in some detail, in the section of this work dealing with the late classical comedy. Of the other "denunciatory" pieces the first is the satire entitled in its first version (published 1780 in the *St. Petersburg Herald*) "First Satire, by Mr. K.*," and in its revised form (published 1783 in the *Sobesednik liubitelei rossiiskogo slova*) demonstratively designated "First—and Last—Satire."[84] The first version contained a couple of lines referring to contemporary poets by slightly disguised but easily identifiable names. Such a storm of angry protest was aroused against the poet that the republication, under his own full name, contained in its title the implicit promise that nothing further of the kind would follow. This promise was kept.

The "First—and Last—Satire" has as its ostensible theme the ignorance and stupidity of all conditions of men. Actually "ignorance and stupidity," which are presumably excusable faults, outside the control of the will, mask the less venial sins of avarice, pride, and general inhumanity. The poem opens with a paragraph which states the theme:

Whomever it may anger, I shall begin to rail: with rascality, with human stupidity I cannot live. Everywhere debauchery shows its impudent face; there's dishonor in honor, shame has gone out of fashion. Almost with whomever I meet, with whomever I begin conversation, I encounter either ignorance or vice. Wherever you turn, there's no help for it: that man is honest, and so is a fool; another is intelligent, and so a rascal, hypocrite, deceiver, flatterer; in a word, in this world Aristideses [the Athenian Aristides was nicknamed "the Just"] are as rare as smooth verses in the poet of the *Tilimakhida* [i.e., Trediakovsky].

This quotation is from the revised—and milder—version; there are several differences in the two texts, most notably in the presence in the earlier of unflattering and quite unmistakable references to contemporary poets, which the later version eliminates.

"The rascals and fools" whom the Satire pillories all seem to have one quality in common: they are ostensibly one thing, but actually quite another. They constitute a universal masquerade:

And all in this world, as in a free masquerade [see notes on Lukin's *Shchepetil'nik*], in costumes not the usual and not their own, hiding themselves with masks, show a false appearance, until all shame is finally obliterated in them. [lines 53-56]

They include the well-meaning but inept judge, the arrogant newly ennobled parvenu, the official contemptuous of lesser ranks, the respected but thieving judge, the self-righteous hypocrite, the gambler who pretends to be your bosom friend in order to lose your bank-roll at cards, the boastful know-it-all, the pompous rhymester, the smooth-talking hypocritical friend who will stab you in the back, the seemingly incorruptible judge, to whom you don't dare offer a bribe—and so lose your case to an opponent who has no such scruples, etc. The poet considers the reasons why hypocrisy and "false fronts" should so flourish, and concludes: "To be right in everything we have discovered two means: one is to put ourselves above what people say; the other is to melt every kind of evil into good talk." [lines 128-130]

Naturally, such a sweeping indictment of Russian society must cast considerable discredit on the autocrat whose influence should be all-powerful. Kapnist attempts to neutralize such an impression by a passage of admiring description of Catherine's noble efforts toward combatting the evils which he has enumerated—efforts ineffectual, because "Villainy is destroyed, but stupidity remains." "It would be easier to subdue the universe by force than to extirpate fools from the number of mankind." Catherine is an energetic patroness of the arts and sciences, but—"The sciences have matured, the arts flourish, authors are born—but stupidity is there just the same." The poet then refers to some of his own early, and unsuccessful, efforts to celebrate the greatness of Catherine's reign. "Would that I might have had a strict master," he sighs; "he would have saved me from the number of fools." If only the government could pass laws to make fools into men of sense— but, alas, even the law is powerless to cure stupidity—or bad poetry! Here the castigation of fools in general passes to the particular, and a famous couplet in the first version, dropped from the second, names with slight disguise a group of poetasters who "roil with their snouts the pure Castalian waters": Kozelsky, Nikolev, Vladykin, Frezinovsky, Ablesimov, Khvostov, Verevkin and Kantorovsky. Except for Nikolev, Ablesimov and Khvostov, these porcine poets are mere names to us. Indignantly the satirist exclaims: "Punishment threatens evil-doers, and the strictness of the judge; contempt and shame are curbs on scoundrels—but to commit stupidities everyone has license without obstacle." Satire, however, should be able to accomplish what the law cannot—it is a mirror held up to fools, which may shock them into changing their ways. They should not be angered at the satirist, who is only writing for their own good. He is not aiming at individuals—"My quarrel is

457

not with men, but with vices."

The "First—and Last—Satire" is in the tradition of Kantemir and Suma-rokov, and is quite as outspoken as any of its predecessors. Kapnist's descriptions are in many cases very realistic, and in two instances—his portrait of a judge who by peculation is able to buy himself an estate and become the friend of noblemen; and the vivid little account of the poet's discomfiture in a law-suit—there are notable similarities with the comedy *Iabeda.* The language of the satire is normal and readily intelligible—Lomonosov's "middle style."

On May 3, 1783, Catherine II issued a decree which declared that henceforth all the peasants in three Ukrainian provinces should be counted as the serfs of the landowners for whom they were working. The anomaly of a free peasantry in areas closely contiguous to the Russian provinces where serfdom was most firmly established and the peasants were most decidedly "slaves," was thus at one stroke removed. Kapnist, a Ukrainian landowner, in a mood of sorrowful indignation, forthwith composed his famous "Ode to Slavery."[85] It was of course impossible to publish the ode during the reign of Catherine and her son; it saw the light, somewhat altered and softened in expression, in the second edition (1806) of Kapnist's "Lyrical Poems," during the temporary relaxation of the censorship in the first years of the reign of Alexander I.

The "Ode to Slavery" is a good example of the change in the concept of the "ode" and the break-down of the classical system of genres in the last years of the eighteenth century. As we have seen, many of the poems of Muraviev which carry the designation of "ode" would be, in an earlier period, "elegies," "epistles," or other categories of lyric. Kapnist's ode is composed in the canonical ten-line strophe introduced by Lomonosov, but the content is in the highest degree irregular for a classical ode. This is apparent in the very title: "Ode to Slavery," beside such triumphal titles as "Ode on the Victory at Khotin," "Ode on the Capture of Ochakov," or even "Ode to Felitsa" or "Ode on Happiness," sounds bitterly ironical. "Slavery" is scarcely a subject for celebration! Moreover the tone of indignation which pervades the poem is appropriate rather for a satire than an ode. In addition, the scene depicted in strophe 4 (strophe 3 in the revised and printed version) is marked by an Ossianic coloring, such as we have remarked in, for example, the setting of Derzhavin's "Waterfall," and belongs to the atmosphere of sentimentalism.

The "Ode" begins with an allegorical allusion to Kapnist's poetical silence since the harsh reception of his "First Satire" of 1780, and the reasons which impel him now to break it:

Taking up the lyre that I had forgotten, I wipe away the dust that lies upon it; extending the hand that is weighted with the burden of iron chains, I tune [the lyre] for songs of lamentation; and, concordant with my grief, I pour forth a somber, weary sound from strings that are washed by a river of tears; I shall sing the enslavement of my beloved country.

[Orpheus! If thou didst sigh to the lyre for Eurydice lost, and drew after thee lifeless trees and savage beasts in sympathy, give ear to me: I call to thee. It is not to a wife that I call; I have greater right to bring even rocks to sympathy; I shall sing the enslavement of my dear native land.] [87]

But Thou, who dost alone possess all the realm beneath the sun, and dost incline to mercy the souls of kings beloved by Thee, and dost preserve them from malicious slander! Bring it about that the world's lords may heed my unflattering utterance; may they mildly give ear to the voice of truth, and against evil-doers alone raise up the sword Thou has entrusted to them.

Sunk in sorrowful thought I shall go, I shall withdraw myself from mankind to a hill shaded by trees; I shall turn aside into a thick grove; beneath a dark and mossy oak I shall sit down. There to my sorrowful gaze everything reveals a sorrowful aspect: the rivulet, roaring, digs into the hill; the wind howls gloomily among the pines; as it flies from the trees, the foliage makes a languid rustle.

Wherever I turn my eyes, bathed in a torrent of tears, everywhere I see my native land here, like a sorrowful widow; disappeared are the pastimes of the village, the playful sportiveness, the dances, the laughs; the voice of gay song is silent; the golden cornland is desolate; the fields, meadows, forests are empty; sorrow lies upon them like a cloud.

Throughout the poem the figure of "iron chains," which weigh down the despondent villagers just as they do the poet's own hand, serve as a vivid symbol of the "enslavement" of the land. Indignantly the poet turns to the Empress herself, whose fateful decree has brought about such desolation:

You see, Tsaritsa—here your people is keeping festival, groaning in bonds. See, it is rapturously celebrating your thunderous ascent to the throne. Its heavy yoke it wears mildly, and beseeches heaven for your good, wiping its misery from its thought; but you burden it: you put chains upon the hands that bless you!

The monarch is like a stern mother who disciplines her children and refuses to heed their pleadings. The poem ends with a fervent plea that Catherine realize the harm her decree has done and revoke it, and so bless the land of which she is "the mother."

Catherine, of course, did nothing of the sort; but she did, in a very typical act, attempt to give herself credit for doing something which she would have found impossible in reality. In 1786 she issued a decree abolishing a humiliating and vexatious item of court etiquette. Hitherto all petitions addressed to the throne had to be subscribed by the petitioner's name and the words "Your Majesty's slave" [rab]." Rightly considering this usage demeaning to the nobility, Catherine eliminated it. The act, of course, did nothing toward eliminating the actual condition of slavery in which most of the country's peasantry languished. Kapnist, however, chose to interpret it as the abolition of slavery, and greeted it with his "Ode on the Abolition in Russia of the Condition of Slave by Catherine the Second, on the 15th of February, 1786."[88] In his ode Kapnist, who was certainly not so naive as to believe for a moment in the reality of such an "abolition," spoke out forthrightly in deprecating the "condition of slave" which Catherine was supposedly ending for all time; and in this way he was enabled, under cover of a laudatory ode to the Empress, to which she could hardly take exception, actually to denounce the institution itself. Catherine is reported to have remarked, when she read his ode: "Why, you want [the abolition of slavery] in reality... the words are enough!"[89]

When Kapnist published his collections of *Works* in 1796 and *Lyric Works* in 1806, he divided them, in accordance with the fashion of the times, by categories of genre, and modern editions have quite reasonably followed this division, although it obscures to some extent the chronology of the poems and hence the author's literary development. Most of the "Solemn Odes" belong to Kapnist's earlier work; the "spiritual odes," which are all paraphrases of the Psalms, belong to the first years of the nineteenth century, and the "didactic and elegiac odes," with two exceptions, to the last years of the eighteenth century. The "spiritual odes" are of little poetical merit, but to the "didactic and elegiac odes" belong some of Kapnist's best work. It should be noted that the very title of this section of his *Works* is revolutionary: the ode and the elegy, by classical convention, are two entirely separate genres of verse, and the fusion implied in Kapnist's title is a breach of convention. A closer look at some of the "odes" in this group will reveal more clearly their unclassical character. Thus, the "Ode to Hope" (1780),[90] while in the canonical ten-line strophe of Lomonosov, is entirely personal and elegiac in content. The poetical *persona* of the piece, as of many others of the group, is a gloomy, pessimistic poet, persecuted by fate and looking for "repose" ["pokoi"] only in the grave—a common sentimentalist pose. Even contemporaries pointed out the curious anomaly—Kapnist's poetry was very often profoundly melancholy, while gaiety and good humor were notable qualities of the man himself. The "Ode to Hope" opens with a conventional contrast of nature with inner mood, and then turns, in the second strophe, to a characteristic apostrophe to fate:

O destiny! O cruel judge! Inexorable king of time! How long shall I continue to pour forth floods of tears, condemned by you? How long, hiding my sorrows in my heart, shall I continue to seek my former repose, groaning in misfortune? Either end the time of my woes, or else at once, gathering together the burden of all disasters, hurl them on me!

At the beginning of the fourth strophe the poet looks back over his past life and exclaims: "From [my] youngest years I already felt the burden of the cruel power, and began to feel misfortune from the moment when I began to feel [at all]."

The tenth strophe turns at last to the subject promised by the title: if everything in the world is changeable, why not a change for the better? "Perhaps the time is already hastening on when she [i.e., fate], tearing away from me the heavy burden of misfortunes, may in their stead with generous hand arrange my days for repose, turning sorrow into blessedness." The long-ing for "repose" ["pokoi": Latin "otium"] , it may be noted, is common to the verse of both Derzhavin and Kapnist. With the former it seems to have more biographical justification, in view of his really quite turbulent career; with Kapnist one may conjecture that it is rather a literary echo, from his beloved Horace.

In 1784 Kapnist's year-old son Alexei died, and the bereaved father began the composition of an "Ode on the Death of [my] Son,"[91] which was published in 1787. Again the subject is too personal to fit gracefully into the classical conception of an "ode," even though the form, like that of the "Ode to Hope" is the Lomonosovian ten-line strophe rhyming *aBaBccDeeD*. The tone of the poem is typically sentimentalist: one is re-minded quite forcibly of Gray's "Elegy" by, for instance, strophe six:

> Never again will you look at me, curving your lips with a tender smile, and stretch out your arms touchingly, begging for [your] mother's embrace; you will not, emulat-ing us in everything, as you play with her and kiss her, learn to repeat my name; you will not, as you sit between us, entwine our necks with your tender arms.

In its original version the "Ode" consisted of 26 strophes; the revision pub-lished in *Works* has only 17. Some of the omitted strophes are of interest as revealing Kapnist's complex personality. Thus, strophe fifteen and sixteen of the extended version seem directly inspired by the somber, "graveyard" atmosphere of Young's "Night Thoughts":

> I feel a sweet consolation in this common lament [i.e., in the autumn mood of nature]. Gazing up at the mass of dark clouds which cut down the grain with solid rain:—at the wind, that carries the leaves from the trees, at the frost, that kills the vege-tation, at the water-course that has dressed itself in a crust [i.e., of ice]. I am com-forted in my griefs, that I am not alone in bereavement, that my lot strikes all things.
> Yet their portion is not so dreadful. Though autumn today kills the flowers, yet soon the lovely spring will give them all their former beauties. The trees will once more dress themselves in leafage, the streams will break out of their shrouds, everything will suddenly come alive with spring. My unhappiness is irrevocable: death will not be able again to lead my son back to the light.

Strophes 18-21, which contain the father's consoling thoughts of all the sorrows which his dead son has been spared, have almost a "denunciatory" character reminiscent of the "Ode to Slavery." Strophes 20 and 21, for instance, read:

> Is it possible, seeing evil guile leading righteousness into a deadly net—vice seeking by detraction to wipe out ["sotret' "] upright merit—seeing conceit trampling upon shame, injustice holding the scepter, flattery crawling at the feet of magnates—is it possible, without loathing them, without shuddering away from the sight of them, to endure their vileness and malice?
> But if you had plainly arrayed yourself against their throng, you would have

461

dragged out a life of unhappiness; with the union of common forces their malice would have gnawed your days; from this not even the door of the tomb would have protected you. Envy, like a venomous snake, would not have ceased to stir even your ashes, hidden in the dark urn.

The "Ode on the Death of My Son" is a curious medley of elements: a touching, personal sorrow, a great deal of literary reminiscence, some rather cold and unconvincing reasoning, and an obsolete and pompous vocabulary and style. There is a significant number of Slavonicisms in the piece—even that particularly bizarre and flagrant bit of archaism, the dative absolute, makes its appearance. One gets the impression that as Kapnist grew older, he consciously turned away from the light, easily intelligible Russian which had begun to come into vogue at the end of the century, and is associated primarily with Karamzin and Dmitriev, in favor of something not far removed from Lomonosov's "high style." This may be seen, for example, in the "translations" of Horace, which were mostly written around 1814, in contrast with the far better, more fluent and melodious "paraphrases" of Horace, which were published for the most part in 1806, and written often ten years earlier. We will return to the Horatian poems shortly.

The "Ode on Happiness" (1792),[92] again in the canonical ode form, resembles in content a classical satire—its subject is that of Juvenal's Tenth (Johnson's *Vanity of Human Wishes*). Man "in the circle of empty hopes and dreams passes both night and day; estranged from simple, natural goods, wandering in a labyrinth of vanities, he grasps after the mere shadow of happiness." Instances: the military man, who "flatters himself, in reddening his hands, that the blood-sodden field of battle will grow for him an everlasting laurel"; the moneymaker; the pleasure-seeker. All quests for happiness seem poisoned by attendant miseries—where does real happiness dwell? Even the monarch on his throne is not happy. Yet God intended man to be happy; our fault is in pursuing what we really have always with us. True happiness is inner, and comes from faith. "Elected from death to eternity, crowned with a crown incorruptible, they live the heavenly life." "But here virtue alone is the source of inexhaustible goods, the creator for us of the purest delights."

Kapnist was, as has been frequently mentioned, a devoted friend of Derzhavin. His eldest son was even named Gavriil for the great poet. When in 1794 Derzhavin's beloved first wife died, many of the master's friends, including Dmitriev and Kapnist, wrote commemorative poems. Kapnist's "Ode on the Death of Plenira"[93] (Plenira was Derzhavin's pet name for Ekaterina Yakovlevna Bastidon), like his "Ode on the Death of My Son," was published (in *Works*, 1796) in a longer version of 25 strophes, which he reduced in his *Lyrical Works* of 1806 to 14. Again, the omitted strophes have a particular interest—in this instance for the light they shed on Kapnist's later reversion to a stricter classicism. In the original text of the ode, which consists largely of a sympathetic picture of the bereaved husband as he wanders through the desolate house where everything reminds him of his dead wife, there is a strophe (No. 8) in which the poet with more than usual realism refers—in very general terms, of course—to the window drapes which "Plenira" had sewed:

In that mansion, adorned by her skillful hand, in the chamber dedicated to friendship [i.e., the salon], where the gay swarm of attractions in her train provided delights; where amusements, gaiety, laughter turned night into day—there he in hateful sorrow, by the rays of the gloomy moon sees with terror his own shadow.

Evidently the picture thus drawn struck the poet of 1806 as too particular, wanting in that universality which classicism demanded; the strophe was accordingly dropped, as was also the next (No. 9), with its reminiscences· of Homer and Aeschylus:

If slumber closes his weary eyelids, he sees his beloved; he presses her in his enamored embrace, but she flees from it. He calls her, grasps after her; waking, he does not find her, and.... realizing then his dream, rolls back with terror on his couch. The cold sweat drops from him, and his hair stands on end.

Obviously such a realistic depiction of terror is unsuited to the atmosphere of classical calm which pervades the "consolation" of the final strophes. But despite the prospect of a reunion with Plenira in a blissful hereafter, which Kapnist holds out to his friend, his own view of life is blackly pessimistic:

But what is life? In childbirth, torture; in childhood, the oppression of servility; in youth, the turbulence of passions; in manhood, the toil of vanities. Old age is a return to childhood; death is the heritage of birth. This is life—behold, a harvest of ills! Death sows and reaps, turns the earth into a grave, and the grave into his own dark throne.

Kapnist's "Ode to Dejection" ["Oda na unynie"] is the classical example of "graveyard poetry" among his works, perhaps even in Russian literature as a whole, and deserves quoting in its entirety:[94]

Days of happiness! Where have your brightness and beauty hidden themselves? The bright hours of old have been overshadowed by the darkness of grief. Everything takes on in my eyes a hateful, weary look; sorrow in my dejected soul kills the feeling of joy.

How attractive bloomed the morning of bright, youthful days! At noontide a cloud overshadowed the horizon of my life. The dusk thickened around me, the storm-cloud with the thunderstorm moved in, the whirlwind rose in a pillar to the cloud, the thunder pealed above my head.

Life of mortals! O how terrible is the ebb and flow of evils! In happiness you go to sleep free from danger, but awake [to be] unfortunate.

Thus, amidst delights, amidst repose, the abyss of woes opencd up for me. Sorrow with keen scythe mowed down the flower of my days.

Adorning the springtime meadow, the flower bloomed in the dawn; breathing fragrance, it lures the lickerish bees; the butterfly alights on it, sporting with its beloved mate, and the wayfarer is gladdened by its early beauty.

But of a sudden the despised worm gnaws the little root beneath; the stem wilts and the green leaf, the flower bows its head, grows pale, dries up and dies. The wanderer stands in astonishment, wonders, pities: "Why did it fade so early?"

Thus I too languish in longing, heavy sorrow oppresses my soul, but wheresoever I look, there is none who sympathizes; and to whose breast soever I lay my love-thirsty heart, everywhere I find only cold feeling, or betrayal.

Oh, if only I might for a moment be transported to a wild region, where the deep and dusky forest had never beheld the trace of man, where the smoke of habitations had never spread, the cry of the hunter never been heard, where only the ravening beast wandered, and in caverns howled with the tempest.

There on a rocky crag, washed by the wave below, seated beneath a dark and mossy pine, I would unite my dejected voice, my wail, my comfortless groaning with the groan of the tempest, and would reproach no one with cold insensitivity.

But wheresoever I might strive to hide myself, sorrow will everywhere follow me. Where is it possible to defend oneself from the oppression of cruel woes? Where, but in the bowels of the earth? The world is a difficult, sorrowful journey; only in the confining and darksome grave shall we be able to have rest.

Hasten, O comforting death! Be touched by my sorrow; let your cold right hand quickly close my eyes. You, O damp earth! Be softened, permit my step into eternity. Bosom of darkness! Be parted, and hide my ashes from sorrow!

It is odd to associate the writer of such gloomy lines with the genial life-loving Horace or the sensualist "Anacreon"—but Kapnist is a thoroughly contradictory poet. One section of his published lyrics consists of "Anacreontic Odes," and another, very extensive one, of paraphrases and translations of Horace. The Anacreontics have little of their Greek model but the meters; they are "songs," but seldom indeed about wine or love. Some of them are translations of French light verse; one famous one ("The Siskin" ["Chizhik"] [95])—the paraphrase of a Ukrainian poem by the eighteenth-century mystic Skovoroda. A typical example of Kapnist's "Anacreontics," with its obvious and typically sentimentalist "moral" is the three-strophe poem "Butterfly" (1796): [96]

Upward the lark spirals, above his head the hawk soars, above the clouds and toward the sun is borne the daring eagle; but over the ground, from soft grass to flower flies the butterfly, laden with delicate golden dust.

So for me also has a lowly bound been eternally ordained by fate. In Destiny's urn, to be sure, my lot is heavy. Howsoever chance may shake the urn, there is never any success; however she may stir it with her wand, my lot always falls lowest.

So be it—let the proud oaks stand on the heights, the tempest's winds do not hurt the low vines in the valley. And if Destiny is malicious even there, what is left? Endurance! The fortunate one is more afraid than the unfortunate of dying.

The best known and certainly the best of Kapnist's "Anacreontic Odes" is typically remote from the traditions of Anacreon. It is a simple four-strophe elegy, which was actually to become accepted as a folk-song, entitled "On the

Death of Julia";[97] in its first, anonymous, publication it bore the title
"On the Death of a Daughter." Kapnist's daughter Julia died in 1788; the
poem was written between that date and 1792, and is thus one of his earlier
pieces:

Already with the gloom of night quiet has been spread abroad. From behind the
wood the sorrowful moon steps out. Wearily I tune my lyre to sing the sorrow that has
enfolded my spirit. Come hither to grieve with me, O moon, friend of the sorrowful!

By this cold tomb, under the shade of thick trees, you hear my mournful wail
and the groaning of my sighs. Here are buried the dear ashes of lovely Julia. I am condemned to pour over them forever a flood of tears.

Like a tender rose you bloomed, Julia! In this tumultuous life you were my
friend, my everything. Now, losing you, it is left me to end my life or, lacerating my
breast with sorrow, to keep dying every hour.

But I must break off the moan of this tearful song; wet with tears, the lyre's
sound is muted. With wordless longing the spirit is more strongly oppressed. Come and
grieve with me, O moon, friend of the sorrowful!

Kapnist's collection of *Lyrical Works* contained a section headed
"Horatian and Anacreontic Odes." In thus lumping together what may be
classified as "non-Pindaric" odes, Kapnist was apparently conscious of the
less solemn and grave character of the former, although, as we have seen,
lugubrious themes are not wanting even among the Anacreontics. In a rather
lengthy essay written to accompany the "Horatian" odes,[98] Kapnist discloses the peculiar method which he employs in writing them. They are
"paraphrases" or "imitations" of the Latin originals, often quite free, in
which the Russian poet makes an effort to render allusions, proper names,
and the like, which for a Russian of his age could have been intelligible only
with a commentary, by analogous and perfectly intelligible contemporary
replacements. He makes no attempt to render the Latin with literal exactitude; indeed, as he confesses, he does not even know the language, and has
to rely on a careful interlinear translation made by one of his friends. The
results of this odd system are surprisingly excellent. Horace in Russian dress
is an attractive figure, with no loss of the essential qualities of his verse. One
side of Kapnist's complex personality seems to have been genuinely attuned
to Horace's. It may be noted that the "Imitations," eighteen of them in the
1806 edition, are drawn from the lighter and less gravely didactic of Horace's
odes. A good example of Kapnist's method is the ode entitled "To my
Friend,"[99] which freely paraphrases Horace's Book I, ode ix. A comparison
of the two poems will show Kapnist's skill in replacing the Roman "local
color" with Russian. Horace's ode reads as follows ("Vides ut alta stet nive
candidum—"):

You see how [Mount] Soracte stands white with deep snow, while the toiling
forests no longer hold up the weight, and the streams have halted because of the sharp
frost.

Dispel the cold by generously piling logs on the hearth-fire; and pour our quite abundantly, O Thaliarchus, the four-year-old wine from the Sabine jar.

Leave [all] else to the gods; as soon as they have laid to rest the winds that battle with the seething sea, the cypresses and old ashtrees are tossed about no longer.

Shun seeking what is to be tomorrow, and whatsoever days Chance shall give you, set down as gain. Do not, while a boy, spurn sweet loves and dances,

So long as morose white hair is far from [your] green youth. Now there is the Campus [Martius] and exercise grounds, and let soft whispers at nightfall be repeated at the appointed hour,

And the pleasant laugh of the girl lurking in the deep of a corner, and the keepsake snatched from arm or finger that puts up but slight resistance.[100]

In its Russian version this becomes:

See how, covered with snow, the peaks of the high mountains shine; how the pines, bent with the frost, and the streams, burdened with ice, stand, benumbed, in their banks.

Now, sitting at the hearth, make us forget the frosts; according to seniority of years and rank bid the Hungarian wine be served, and leave all else to the gods.

Snowstorms, tempests and frosts when they [i.e., the gods] are minded to pacify, then neither lindens nor birches nor the supple year-old vines dare to rustle a leaf.

What you shall meet with tomorrow do not trouble yourself to learn; make use of the moment's time, and the day allotted by fate learn to count a gift.

In your unruffled youth do not lose an hour with dances and games, and taste the fruit of fortunate love as long as your hair has not been silvered by grumpy old age.

Now promenades call you, the theater, concerts, the masquerade, and those assignations where tender whispers at evening make secret assurances of love;

When the involuntary laugh discloses the beauty in a dark corner, who loses a ring as a pledge, and only feebly defends it on the hand that is tenderly pressed.

Note how "Hungarian wine" replaces the "wine from the Sabine jar," northern "lindens and birches" the "cypresses and old ash-trees," and "promenades, the theater, concerts, the masquerade" Horace's references to the youthful pleasures of the wrestling mat and the parade ground. The "moral"—enjoy youth while you still have it—remains the same, and even the vivid picture at the end, of the evening tryst and the ring snatched as a keepsake.

Kapnist's interest in and affection for Horace did not abate as he grew old, but his later versions, composed from 1814 to 1821, are verse translations, not paraphrases. As such they are good, but lacking in the freedom and spontaneity of the "Imitations." The satirical and "denunciatory" aspect of Kapnist's verse often comes to the fore in his choice of Horatian odes or epodes to be translated; particularly noteworthy are "On Sumptuous Habitations" (Horace II, xv); "The Nullity of Riches" (III, i); "On Depravity of Morals" (III, vi); and "Against Acquisitiveness" (III, xxiv). It often seems that in these later translations a portentous solemnity destroys the light self-irony of the Latin original, as in "The Poet-Swan" (II, xx), "To

Maecenas" (I, i), "To Pyrrha" (I, v), "The Lover's Revenge" (Epode xv) and "Curses on the Tree" (II, xiii).

The 1806 volume of *Lyrical Works of Vasily Kapnist* was the last collection of his verse to be published during his lifetime. Besides the translations of Horace, a number of other poems which were composed during the last years of the poet's life (1806-1823), and a few "non-lyric" poems which for this reason or another were not included in his published works, remained to be gathered together after his death. Of the latter class are three experiments, very reminiscent of pieces by Kapnist's friends N.A. Lvov and M.N. Muraviev—the lengthy paraphrase of portions of Macpherson's "Ossian," entitled by Kapnist "Karton,"[101] and composed between 1792 and 1816; and two short pieces imitating Russian popular verse—"Fragment of a Russian Popular Tale, Paraphrased in Verse," and "Fragment of a Tale of the Escape of a Slavic Warrior from Captivity."[102] The latter are composed, quite authentically, in the accentual verse characteristic of the *byliny*, and not "regularized" as are, for example, similar experiments of Karamzin. The "Karton" paraphrase, which narrates the fatal duel of father and son, in which the hero Fingal unwittingly kills his son Karton, is written in numerous sections of varying meters, alternating long and short lines. Since the metrical form of the original Gaelic, in so far as Macpherson's "Ossian" had an original, was not preserved in the English "translation," nor of course in any of the numerous versions in French, German and Russian, which had to serve Kapnist, he was free to invent his own form, which he seems to have done with some vague knowledge of the varying meters sometimes encountered in the Norse poems of the "Elder Edda."

Of other experimental compositions of Kapnist one of the most interesting is the "Vision of a Russian Lamenting Over Moscow, 28 October, 1812."[103] The date, of course, refers to the capture and subsequent burning of the old capital during the Napoleonic invasion. Kapnist's poem was written on his Ukrainian estate of Obukhovka, far from actual contact with the fallen city. Like "Karton," this is composed in an irregular, rhapsodic form, with lines of varying lengths employed presumably to harmonize with the content of the several sections. The "weeping Russian" laments the fate of old Moscow, and even reproaches the Almighty for letting the pagan triumph. He sees a vision in which God reveals to him that the calamity has happened because of Russia's sins and the breakdown of true religion.

The "Poet's Library" edition of *Selected Works* of Kapnist, edited by Ermakovna-Bitner and D.S. Babkin (Leningrad, 1973) contains (pp. 270-293) two previously unpublished collections of short verse aphorisms, some of them "cautionary verses" to children, such as: "If you go into a strange house, show affection for the children and old women—so you will be dear to all and a friend." Not all of these jottings are on quite so low a poetical level as this, but Kapnist was no Rochefoucauld. Typical of the "Random Thoughts from Experience of Life" is this gem: "I have seen many people who were able to bear easily the wrath of stern fate, but could not endure good fortune." It can hardly be said that the publication of these collections enhances Kapnist's poetical stature.

Several of the later poems are odes, either so defined in the manuscript, or identifiable as such by the ten-line strophe. The "Poet's Library" edition separates these on the basis of their form from other pieces of the same period.[104] This separation is justified by the greater solemnity of theme and style of the odes, which are often on subjects of more public than private concern. The language also, with its abundant Slavonicisms and unnatural word order, shows the same reversion to the standards of the first half of the eighteenth century. Here also Kapnist's prophetic and denunciatory tone predominates, as in the odes "On Poets' Flattery," "On the Death of Napoleon" (1822) and "Murder" (1822). Two odes of 1816 were occasioned by the death in that year of Kapnist's great brother-in-law: "Ode on the Death of Derzhavin" and "A Handful of Earth on the Tomb of Virtue." Both odes are expressions of personal as well as of public grief, but at the same time, composed as they are in the strictest eighteenth-century tradition, give an impression of coldness and impersonality. By far the most impassioned of the later odes is "A Call to the Aid of Greece,"[105] written early in 1822 at the outbreak of the Greek revolt against the Turks. Here the heavily archaistic style seems more in keeping with the theme than elsewhere. Note, for example, strophe 3, with its contorted period (all ten lines form a single sentence) and the Slavonic "dlan' " ("hand"), "spiry" ("companies"), "vesi" ("villages") and "prichet" ("clergy"):

But the foe, for three centuries drinking the blood of this by him oppressed victim, having gathered companies, bringing vengeance, has spread forth his wicked hand over her, defiles the consecrated temples, murders the innocent clergy and drags wives and maidens to shame; burns villages, destroys cities, and the corpses of all the citizens piles in masses mountain-high on the pavements.

In addition to the Slavonic vocabulary, it should be mentioned that the participles "bringing" ["nesushchi"] and "consecrated" ["sviashchenny"] appear in their un-Russian apocopated forms (instead of the Russian "nesushchii" and "sviashchennye").

The appeal is addressed first to all Christian nations—"You mighty realms that have sworn to serve the cross"; but then specifically to Alexander I, victor over the "tyrant" Napoleon:

And you ["ty"] whose thunders have long been ready to fall upon tempestuous pride, who are accustomed to break foreign chains and humble the tyrants' power! Hasten, and from your thunderous chariot, with the stroke of your mighty right hand smash the brow uplifted—strike, destroy the nest of evil-doers and shatter the Achaeans' heavy chains like brittle glass.

To you it has been ordained by fate to come, to see, to conquer [like Caesar!], and with the hand that saves thrones to restore the order of the east. God himself admonishes to the righteous path; He knows that not the lure of glory, not reward is the goal of your soul, that the peace of empires is your joy, the bliss of subjects your reward, the cross's victory your trophy.

In Kapnist's later poems, as everywhere in his work, one may see contradiction. The reedited "Ode on the Death of Plenira" eliminated, as we have seen, the modest amount of realistic detail which the original version contained. In the best of the pieces composed from 1816 to 1822, exclusive of the formal and archaistic "odes," there is more of this realistic detail than anywhere else in his lyrical work. Note, for example, the third strophe of the charming poem "An Old Man, Awaiting Spring,"[106] begun in 1814 and revised in 1821:

Whether in the house I drag out hours of boredom—the house smells already of desolation; here's the garden; as old age has done to my hair, so does the hoar-frost powder it. There the elm is bent on its fragile stump, as the years bend an old man; and as the blood in me is cold under a fur coat, so are the waters cold beneath the ice.

The old man notes regretfully that even when spring comes, it will not restore his lost youth as it does the flowers; but the mood of gloom passes, and at the poem's end he cries: "But no—come, spring! Scatter flowers on the green sward; though you cannot straighten my back, bent like a crook; although it is no longer possible for me to enjoy my own happiness in the world—then I will comfort myself with that of others, and remember the past."

Generally acknowledged as the crowning achievement of Kapnist's later lyric production is the poem "Obukhovka" of 1818.[107] In this delightful description of his beloved Ukrainian estate Kapnist almost rivals Derzhavin's "Life at Zvanka"; some even of the greater poet's famous color sense adorns the charming picture—and some certainly of Horace's placid delight in his peaceful "Sabine farm." The poem begins:

At peace with neighbors, with kinsmen, in harmony with my own conscience, in love with my lovable family, here with joys alone I measure out the course of my quiet days.

My comfortable house beneath its thatch in my eyes is neither low nor high; there's a corner in it for friendship, and to the door, unknown to the noble, laziness has forgotten to fasten the latch.

Protected from the north by a hill, it stands on a grassy knoll, and looks into the grove, into the distant meadow; and the Psel, winding like a snake before it, is noisy as it rushes toward the mills.

The woods that surround the house are then described, and the modest "temple of Moderation" that stands on an artificial hillock:

Moderation, O heavenly friend! Be forever my way-companion; you lead people to happiness, but your altar, not known to all, is hidden from the mob ["cherni"] of the wealthy.

From my youthful days you taught me not to seek honors and gold, not to fly aloft without wings, and not to point out to the world as a marvel, a luminary in a glow-worm!

The poet then takes his reader on a walk through the estate. He comes to the mill on the Psel:

There coolness reigns forever and freshens the feelings, the mind; and the quiet, never-ceasing sound of the tumbling waterfall brings slumber amid sweet meditations.

There twenty wheels are turning at once, circle hurries after circle, diamonds from the glittering arches, opals, sapphires rain down; and under them pearls spray in a mist.

From the lively, noisy mill the poet guides his reader to a place of repose:

Let us go, before evening falls, to the nearby island to rest. A covered path leads to it, where even the sun's rays do not dare to slip through amidst the dark leafage.

There I shall sit down under a mossy birch tree, leaning against the sturdy trunk. Alas! Not for long will its branching summit spread its hospitable shade for me.

Already it has bowed its forehead to the water that washes the foot of the steep bank, already it is looking into the dark depth; and soon, in a season of storm, it will be hurled uprooted to the bottom.

The fate of the old birch tree, as we shall presently see, is the subject of one of Kapnist's last and most personal poems.

At the end of the poetical tour of his estate, the old man reaches the family graveyard:

Afar I see a mingling of open glades and groves that have covered the crests of the hills. Before me the bushes of tender roses, and beneath the curtain of branching trees, crosses white as marble.

O Piety! Mute, the eloquent speech of objects says: "You behold your predecessors. Blessed is this corn-land of the Lord. You must yourself lie down on it!"

The poet greets the dear ones who lie in the little graveyard, and imagines a wayfarer who comes by in a few years and reads his own epitaph on the modest stone: "Kapnist lies hidden by these clods; he was a friend of the Muses, a friend of his native land. He found comfort only in this, that in serving [her] he labored all he could—and only here found rest."

"Obukhovka" was written in the summer of 1818; the birch tree that he loved so much fell into the Psel in the spring freshets of 1822, and had to be cut to pieces with the axe and removed. In the same meter as "Obukhovka" and repeating one entire strophe of the earlier poem (lines 41-45: his prediction of the tree's fate), Kapnist wrote his elegy "To the Memory of a Birch Tree."[108] He remembers the old tree's welcome shade:

> Ah! How many times in the sultry summer days, pursued by boredom or grief I came beneath its thick vault, seeking sweet repose—and sweet repose I found.
>
> From storm, from rain, from hail it was for me a reliable shelter; and softer than silken carpets in the shade, where coolness was spread beneath it was a carpet made ready for me.
>
> There, in the moment of sacred inspiration, I thought to hear the Muses' voice; there I often flattered myself with the dream that the benevolent genius of Horace hovered above my head.

The necessity of clearing the wrecked tree for the safety of boats on the river afflicts the poet: "Even your fate has come, O birch! At your root the axe is already lying! O grief! But how change [your fate]? Evil destiny has determined to wipe you out—you, innocent inhabitant of the world—and I must be your murderer!" The last strophe of the poem promises the birch tree: "You often granted me repose—in you shall my ashes rest." In her "Reminiscences" the poet's daughter S.V. Kapnist-Skalon writes:[109] "My father loved this tree so much that without our knowledge he ordered it to be hauled out of the river after its fall, sawn into boards and these kept for his own coffin, which was done."

Vasily Kapnist is one of the most engaging and sympathetic poets of the Russian eighteenth century. A curious and contradictory combination of indignant satirist and melancholy elegist, of old-fashioned classicist and pre-romantic, he mirrors in his poetry the confused and transitional condition of Russian literature at the end of the century. In some of his verse and in his comedy he harks back to Sumarokov and even Kantemir; but in his best lyrics he foreshadows Batiushkov and Zhukovsky—and even gives hints, here and there, of Alexander Pushkin.

CHAPTER XV

MINOR VERSE WRITERS OF THE SECOND HALF
OF THE REIGN OF CATHERINE II

A. Yury Alexandrovich Neledinsky-Meletsky (1752-1828)[1]

The vogue of "light verse" among the literary men of the final years of the eighteenth century has been commented on above. The pompous and elaborate ode, which may be designated as "heavy verse" *par excellence,* had retired more and more into the background, and continued to be cultivated by only a few arch-conservatives such as V.P. Petrov. The literary public of 1783 certainly agreed with the satirical jingle penned by the dramatist Kniazhnin in his "Epistle to Princess Dashkova":[2]

I know that bold odes, which have by now gone out of fashion, are extremely capable of causing irritation. In a senseless chase after a rhyme, they were always comparing Catherine [Ekaterinu] with a Paradisal lily ["raisku krinu"], and assuming the rank of prophets and hobnobbing with God as with a brother, and with no misgivings turning with their pen the universe topsy-turvy in their borrowed rapture ["vostorge"], they would loose their paper thunder from here to the gold-rich lands [of America].

Derzhavin's remarkable rehabilitation of the ode, initiated by his "Felitsa," with its bold mingling of the light and the serious, the "high style" and the "low," was too idiosyncratic to be readily copied. Most writers of lyric verse from the '80s on turned to such new "sentimental" genres as the elegy, or to Anacreontic verse (e.g., Derzhavin, Lvov et al.) or its French imitations (e.g., Muraviev). One of the minor poets of the age most successful in this genre is Yury Alexandrovich Neledinsky-Meletsky.

Neledinsky-Meletsky belonged to an ancient' aristocratic family (the second of his hyphenated surnames derived from a Polish ancestor who defected to Muscovy in 1425). He was brought up by a grandmother whose house was frequented by Catherine's son Pavel Petrovich, and he moved all his life in the highest social circles. His career was in the army, in which he attained the rank of colonel, and after his retirement in 1785 he was employed by both Catherine II and Paul I in the civil service, becoming in 1800 a senator. He was never at any period of his life primarily a man of letters, but turned out his charming songs and romances as a gentleman's avocation, often anonymously. He never published a collection of his verses, but in a "Pocket Songbook"[3] edited by I.I. Dmitriev in 1796 a considerable number of them was collected and given wide currency.

Nedelinsky's verse is fairly varied: in the selection published in Vol. II of the "Poet's Library" edition of *Poets of the Eighteenth Century* (Leningrad 1972) may be found an "Ode to Friendship"[4] in the canonical Lomonosovian form, an "Ode to His Excellency Prince Nikolai Vasilievich Repnin on the Victory Won by him over the Turkish Forces Beyond the Danube on June 28, 1791,"[5] a sportive "friendly epistle" in iambic "free verse" to A.V. Saltykov,[6] translations of several of La Fontaine's *Fables* and a few miscellaneous *vers d'occasion*. But the bulk of these pieces (16 out of 32) consists of songs or poems which may be described as "romances," too long to be actual songs, but purporting to be the utterances of lovers in various circumstances. Some of these, e.g., No. 128 ["vyidu ia na rechen'ku"] [7] are modeled on actual popular songs, but thoroughly regularized, with rhyme and the usual strophic division. Most however, are songs, of the usual classical variety, in which the background circumstances of the singer are left completely vague and abstract. These songs, however, many of which are addressed to a lady whom the poet calls Temira, of unknown, but real, identity, reveal a depth of personal feeling quite alien to such conventional pieces as Sumarokov's songs. The meter of all these pieces is simple and easy, usually trochaic tetrameter, and the language a perfectly normal and simple Russian, free of all the ornamentation expected of more pretentious poetry.

One of the earliest pieces, "To Temira" (1782)[8] is exceptional in form, being composed in Alexandrine verse, without strophic division. It would probably be classed as an elegy, in the original Graeco-Latin meaning of the term—a love poem. It begins:

I would wish that I might have the whole world in my power, in order to see you as the mistress of it, to melt together into one all crowns for your head, and receiving from your beloved mouth gentle laws, to be the instrument of your generosity to [your] subjects, and to see that through you the whole race of mortals might be happy.

The hyperbole of passion in the piece is altogether alien to the usually moderate conventions of eighteenth-century love lyric:

What though souls and bodies were captivated by your beauty, and every one of your slaves were my competitor—love for you would not sow enmity amongst us: we would all love you with harmonious hearts. It is your lot to attract all souls to you; with one smile you can confer happiness; one look, but one of yours, one only word of yours is each time a benediction for all. In your presence there is no room for grief; where you are, there the dark itself is converted into light; Temira, repose of the suffering soul, receive the heartfelt sacrifice of all my feelings. No—in you I see nothing mortal; in your form I behold my God. Whatever I might wish in Him, I find in you, and in my soul I do not separate you from Him.

This is a personal utterance, as very evidently some of the "songs" may be taken to be, of which No. 122[9] is a good example:

You bid me be indifferent, O beautiful one, to you; if you want to see me obedient, give me another heart. Give me a heart that may be able, though knowing you, to be free. Give me such a one as may be willing to live not by you alone.

That one, in which dwells your incomparable image, that heart that suffers through you, that one is also moved by you. In it there is no longer any other feeling, and in it no other life; in the gloom of evil torment you are life, comfort for me, and light!

Should I break faith with you? You received my first sigh! You gave me to feel that I possess a soul. You put the soul in me, and I offer your own gift to you; but [since] you have forbidden sacrifices, I shall not allow myself to offer them.

Only do not torture me by desiring that I should cease to be yours; with what, with what can I anger you by suffering in silence? Surely you cannot count it a transgression that I gaze on your heavenly aspect, am plunged into confusion, and in helplessness—endure?

Sometimes Neledinsky-Meletsky's love songs are very much like the quasi-artless Alexandrian epigrams of the Greek Anthology, though the similarity is almost certainly accidental. No. 124[10] is one such:

My love was sitting yesterday under a bush by the brookside; she was singing a little song, [and] I was listening from afar. A nightingale from the near-by grove chimed in with my love. My love's voice rang out, and was echoed in my soul.

The zephyrs from time to time brought me her words; from time to time the trees that rustled round about drowned out her words. Be silent, everything! Stop interfering, you envious nightingale! Let my love's voice alone resound in my soul. (1795)

Following the tried and true formula of the classical love-complaint, but with a delicacy of expression and an intensity of feeling seldom encountered is No. 125:[11]

The days of happiness have passed, the days of [my] pleasant dream, in which [my] feelings were delighted—when you loved me.

The remembrance of the days that are past has become a torment beyond [my] strength; the more unbearable is the suffering, the happier one has been.

You swore to be faithful to me; I heard this with rapture, and plunged fearlessly into sincere love.

I see now to no purpose, that I have let myself into a disaster. Fly away, O time of tears! Carry away my passion.

When you found delight in my loving you, you asserted to me: "My dear one, you shall be beloved by me until death.

Our world shall change before your beloved does; the sun shall darken his light, before I forget you!"

Everything in nature has remained constant, there is no change, the sun is still undarkened—but already I am forgotten by you!

Neledinsky-Meletsky is a minor poet, with basically only a single string to his lyre—but on that single string he is an incomparable player.

B. Ermil Ivanovich Kostrov (1755-1796)[12]

If Neledinsky-Meletsky's lyre can be said to have had but a single string, the same reproach cannot be levelled at his contemporary, Ermil Kostrov. Rather, if anything, the contrary: Gukovsky[13] recognizes in Kostrov's verses no less than four separate styles, adopted in rapid succession. The poet, it seems, could serve by himself as a kind of miniaturized history of eighteenth-century verse from about 1773 to 1795. He was a sort of stylistic chameleon, always taking on the color of his surroundings.

Ermil Ivanovich Kostrov[13] was a peasant by birth, from the remote northern area of Viatka. His father was an "economic" peasant—that is, attached originally to monastery land, which Catherine II secularized in 1764. Young Kostrov was educated for the priesthood in Viatka seminary, but never took orders, and in some fashion succeeded in being admitted to Moscow University, from which he was graduated in 1779. Henceforth he signed himself "Baccalaureate of Moscow University." His talents as a versifier led to recognition as a sort of official university poet, in which capacity he turned out a great many congratulatory odes to Catherine II and some of her magnates on such state occasions as birthdays, accession anniversaries and the like. He apparently never held a salaried position, but lived precariously as a dependent of various prominent people, including I.I. Shuvalov and M.M. Kheraskov, both curators of the University. He was evidently an "original," and numerous legends grew up around his name, to one of which Pushkin refers:[14] "When festal days came around, they used to hunt all over town for Kostrov to compose verses, and usually find him in a tavern or at the house of a deacon—a great drunkard—with whom he was on very friendly terms." One of Kostrov's idols was the great general Suvorov, and the general is said to have preferred Kostrov's verses on the capture of Izmail to Derzhavin's poem on that subject.[15]

Kostrov is decidedly a minor talent, but as in many such cases, a better literary barometer than many poets of greater gifts. He is first known for a poem published in 1773, addressed to Ioann Cherepanov, archimandrite of the Novospassky Monastery in Moscow. The eighteen-year-old poet represented himself as already plagued by misfortune: "Fortune has been playing with me for a long time; long since she harshly informed me: 'I am pursuing you, and I shall keep pursuing you forever. Who ever slips out of my hands, you despicable fellow? Who will defend you from me?' "[16]

The young poet's first model was, understandably, Lomonosov. Not only was Lomonosov in the 1770s still the acknowledged master of the ode, but in his career (he was, it will be recalled, also of peasant birth, and a northerner) an inspiring parallel for Kostrov to emulate. The earliest poem in the collection published in the "Poet's Library" anthology *Poets of the Eighteenth Century*[17] is decidedly Lomonosovian in style. This is addressed, in a pompous and prolix heading, to Ivan I. Shuvalov on the occasion of a visit of that magnate to Moscow. Shuvalov, it may be remembered, was one of the favorites of Empress Elizabeth, and had been a powerful protector of Lomonosov in the latter's skirmishes with the Holy Synod. Shuvalov had been instrumental in obtaining the Empress's approval of the project of establishing a university in the old capital, and was thus regarded as in a sense its "founding father." Kostrov's ode is irregular in form, showing perhaps the influence of Petrov, who, conservative in everything else, did introduce some metrical innovations in ode-writing. Kostrov's strophes (18 in number) are of ten lines each, but of these seven are Alexandrines, while lines 7-9 are of 8/9 syllables; the rhyme-scheme is *aaBBccDeeD*.

The opening strophe will show clearly enough the clichés of Lomonosov's style--the classical mythology, the customary allegory of the lyre, the exclamatory and interrogative sentences, the "rapture," and the rest:

What is the spirit of the enraptured Muse celebrating, or the new Phoebus [i.e., day], as it enlivens me, bringing into being? What radiance is being poured into my zealous breast, revealing the grassy path to bright Parnassus? And lo, I already behold its gates thrown open! Touch the lyre-strings, touch [them], my fingers! Whom shall I now sing? What shall be the object of [my] gladness? Who is this, whom before all the world, as I climb Parnassus, I shall proclaim with rapture?

The strophe ending the ode gives evidence of the derivation of Kostrov's inspiration:

Realize at last the fire of the zealous Muse, who has broken in your honor the bonds of her silence! Though I may not possess Pindar's wings, to fly aloft to the height of your praises; [though] I am powerless to thunder with Lomonosov's tone—he was inspired by the wondrous Apollo and sang the fame of your goodness—yet I am afire with zeal, and consecrate [to you] my feeble lyre: accept, great man, accept such verse as is in my power.

Kostrov had a good classical education, and had doubtless encountered such a familiar Pindaric ode as the Second Olympian, that begins: "Hymns, lords of the lyre, what god, what hero, what man shall we celebrate?" It is of course also Pindar's example ultimately that Lomonosov and most other ode-writers of the century are copying when they use the trite cliché of the lyre: "But take from its peg the Dorian lyre," Pindar exhorts himself (First Olympian) as he begins his ode to Hiero of Syracuse. Lomonosov had carried on the Pindaric convention, and hence Kostrov's pairing of his two great predecessors in the final strophe.

A personal idiosyncrasy of Kostrov's style may be noted in this ode, which persists in later poems even in quite different styles—a tendency to the emphatic repetition of words or phrases: e.g., here, "*touch* the lyre-strings, *touch* [them], my fingers," or "*accept*, great man, *accept*," etc. In strophe 2, line 3 comes the phrase: "*extend* to me, *extend* your gentle ear"; in strophe 11, line 7 Elizabeth is represented as saying to Shuvalov: "*give heed, give heed* to my words," etc.

Mikhail Kheraskov, as we have seen, was a great force in Moscow University almost from its foundation, and it is not surprising that an impressionable undergraduate should fall under the influence of such a man, who was always on the look-out for poetical talent and extremely generous when he found it. Kostrov's second poetical period, which can be said to extend through the later '70s up to 1783, the date of publication of Derzhavin's "Felitsa," is dominated by Kheraskov. The odes of this period are less pompous, less "thunderous," and contain some rudimentary attempts at the ethical didacticism so dear to Kheraskov. Kostrov is not a thinker, and such ethical or political philosophy as may be found in his verse is of the most obvious kind. He is, however, a facile and agreeable writer, who makes up in fluency what he lacks in originality. His "Birthday Ode" to Catherine II in 1780 may exemplify his "second style." This is an orthodox Lomonosovian ode in form—the 10-line iambic tetrameter strophe—but rather longer (310 lines) than is usual with Lomonosov. But the opening is quiet and low-keyed in the Kheraskov manner:[18]

> Tender lover of the spring days, sleepless singer, O nightingale, at the cool and tranquil hour before the rising dawn you strain your delightful voice, and with it greet her rising: captivated by the beauty of the sleeping nymphs, you kiss their breasts and hands, and pouring your sweetest sounds into their ears, bid them break their nightly repose.
>
> Your voice, carried aloft to the Muse's ear, has aroused her from sweet slumber; Morpheus's bonds are cast off; she rises, entranced, flies to the hills of Helicon, and is minded with the sound of the lyre's tone to sing, in a chorus of bright festivity, not the rising of the morning's dawn, but the day of the Tsaritsa's birth—of her who the mortal nature.

Catherine of course is a "goddess" ["boginia khladnykh stran polnochnykh"], whose possession of the Russian throne is the result of the Almighty's direct intervention: "To the good fortune of the Russian realm, in order to establish righteous judgment ["sudy pravy"], to fulfill the promise of the Most High, to tear out the root of greedy malice, and scatter the snares of the guileful— you were born on the earth this day." In the course of the ode Catherine is even summoned by God to Mt. Sinai—now, as the poet hastens to say, no longer covered (as in Moses' time) with thick darkness—and receives from the Creator new "tables of the law!" Then suddenly—Kostrov's sense of structure is less than perfect—the spotlight is shifted to Prince Paul, the object of Catherine's maternal solicitude (!), to his goddess-wife Maria, and their infant sons Alexander and Constantine! Again an abrupt shift, and beginning with strophe 21 it is the University of Moscow, twenty-five years old, and the Empress Elizabeth, its founder, that are celebrated. Kostrov gets back in the final two strophes to his original subject, and the poem ends with patriotic hurrahs for Catherine, Paul, Maria, Alexander, Constantine—and the victorious Russian army and navy!

477

One original element in all this rather derivative and awkwardly arranged material is the obtrusive Biblical coloring—doubtless the lingering traces of Kostrov's seminary training. Thus, in stanza 7, Catherine's Russia is a land where "meadows and riverbanks drink the sweet honey, the drops of milk" (cf. the "Promised Land" in Exodus II, 8); in strophe 8, in the turmoil of the First Turkish War "the hills are levelled with the valley" (cf. Isaiah XL, 3); and in strophe 19 the royal grandchildren are "a hundred times more lovely than the lily of the field" (cf. Matthew VI, 28). In this connection may be mentioned the even more striking example in strophe 4 of the ode written in the same year 1780 for the anniversary of Catherine's ascension to the throne:[19] "You [i.e., Catherine], having displayed the helmet of salvation, and protected by the shield of faith, and resplendent in the full armor of righteousness" (cf. Ephesians VI, 14-17). Kostrov's later verse shows much less of this element.

In 1783 Derzhavin's famous ode "Felitsa" shattered forever the conventions of ode-writing. Kostrov reacted immediately, and from Moscow dispatched to St. Petersburg an "Epistle" ["pis'mo"] of 120 lines, greeting rapturously the dawn of a new style. The "Epistle to the Creator of the Ode Composed in Praise of Felitsa, the Kirghiz-Kaisak Queen"[20] is composed in a style that apparently tries to emulate Derzhavin's. Kostrov's earlier verse is strongly Slavonic in vocabulary and morphology; Slavonic forms are not wanting in the "Epistle" (nor are they in "Felitsa"), but vocabulary of a quite "low" and common sort makes its appearance for the first time, and the word order is far more simple and direct. It should be noted that though an "epistle" by title, the poem employs Lomonosov's rhyme-scheme $aBaBccDeeD$, but with Alexandrines substituted for the iambic tetrameters in lines 1-4, 7 and 10; it is thus a "quasi-ode" in form.

After a general greeting from the Muscovite poet to the bard of "Petropolis," comes a particularly significant strophe (2):

Please say, how without lyre, without fiddle ["skripitsy"], and moreover without having saddled the Parnassian runner [i.e., Pegasus], you celebrated sweetly the doings of Felitsa, and the life-giving radiance of her crown? Evidently, on the summit of Pindus, and in the rich valley of the pure Muses, you have traversed all the little roads and byways ["ulitsy"] through and through; and in order to celebrate the Queen thus—to delight, rejoice and entertain her—you have discovered a new and untrodden path.

Divested of its conventional allegory, this would mean: "How, without all the trite clichés of classical style, did you come to write 'Felitsa'?" Kostrov continues:

You did discover [it], and on a run you rush successfully along it; neither stump nor stone has harmed your feet. Everything seemed to you just like a grassy field—nowhere did you catch your coat ["kaftanom"] on the thorns.

One may note in the "Epistle" thus far scarcely any specifically Slavonic words, and several decidedly "common" terms, such as "fiddle," "runner," "little roads," "by-ways," and particularly, "coat"—words that Derzhavin himself might have used. The tone changes with strophe 4, and in keeping with the subject, as often in "Felitsa," Slavonicisms become abundant and "common" words disappear:

> With hair ["vlasy"] adorned with corals, hair let down from the head ["glavy"] upon the shoulders ["ramenam"], fondling a red-and-white ["belo-rumianu"—a compound color adjective like Derzhavin's!] breast with their cheeks ["lanitimi"], choirs ["liki"] of lovely nymphs have emerged from the Neva. Rocking gently on top of the surges, they have hearkened to you attentively, praising the lovely novelty of your verse; and [then], as a sign of their zealous tribute, after clapping their hands ["dlani"] with rapture, they sink once more into the crystal depths.

This pretty mythological picture is followed by a quite prosaic account of the reception of "Felitsa" in Moscow:

> By light post ["pochta"] Felitsa's praise reached Moscow also, to the rapture of all hearts; she moved all who read to give you honor, and all who know what taste is have woven you a crown. All have read her a hundred times; but they keep listening eagerly, attentively, in case someone should again begin to read her in their presence; they cannot so delight their spirits, sate their ears so taken captive, as not once more to attend to the diverting toys in her [i.e., the poem].

In strophe 7 Kostrov confesses that "thunderous" odes have become tiresome and the public has welcomed a change:

> Our ears have been almost deafened from the thunderous lyric tones, and, it seems, there has been enough of flying beyond the clouds, only, in defiance of the laws of equilibrium, to fly [down] from the heights and break our arms and legs. However much we shall try to elevate ourselves in our flight, Felitsa's deeds are revealed to be higher than we. She is pleased with simplicity in style, so it were better for us to travel this path modestly and raise our voices to her.

Then, most significantly, the poet describes his own previous efforts to eulogize Catherine as failures (st. 8):

> Sojourning in company with the nymphs of Parnassus, I used to let my fingers run over the resounding harp, as I celebrated the Kirghiz-Kaisak Queen—but only obtained cold praises; everyone then glorified my verses, flattering me, and diverted himself thereby; but now they [i.e., my verses] have the honor of lying in oblivion. It must be acknowledged, evidently, that soaring odes have already gone out of fashion. You have been able, by simplicity, to elevate yourself amongst us.

It is worth noting that Kostrov here even employs the same rhyme ("ody"—"mody") as Kniazhnin in his well-known verses to Princess Dashkova.

The "Epistle" ends with encouragements to Derzhavin to keep on in his novel course, writing letters to his neighbors, invitations to dinner, praises of the Greben' fountain, and celebrating the incomparable Felitsa. "For him who has thus glorified Felitsa, and established a new taste in verses, there is honor and praise from sincere hearts."

From the only verse of Kostrov at present accessible—the selection in the *Poets of the Eighteenth Century* volume—it is impossible to judge how much Derzhavin's example actually profited him: the only ode of a date later than 1783 printed in this anthology is one of 1789 "To His Excellency Count Alexander Vasilievich Suvorov-Rymniksky."[21] This ode, however, does appear to be considerably less inflated and bombastic than those of his first two periods. It is unconventional in form: twelve eight-line strophes, each of six Alexandrines followed by a pair of short lines of 6/7 syllables. The rhyme-scheme is *AbAbCdCd*, and the final lines of strophes 1 and 12 have the refrain: "Great, great [is] Suvorov!" The language is moderately Slavonic, even when the poet introduces Suvorov's soldiers as speakers, and the usual classical conventions of allegory are observed—a "genius" hands the poet his lyre, with directions to celebrate the hero, etc. The eulogy is put first in the mouths of Suvorov's foes, the Turkes, who find even their prophet and his Koran of no help against the great general; and then in the mouths of his own soldiers, who say:

Where Suvorov is, there is the might of an all-powerful arm; there hearts have no fear, and fate itself can be stormed. In his right hand ["desnitsa"] the sword is our bright cloud by day, our pillar of fire by night (cf. Exodus XIII, 21), directing against the foe ["sopostaty"] the shadow of various deaths and winged thunderbolts.... (strophe 5)

What is the reason for these victories? Our hero sleeps little; he is filled with love for the fatherland and with faith in God. He is quick, tireless, he has foresight and fore-feeling. He accomplishes ["zizhdet"] everything quietly; he devises measures. He is loved by his subordinates, he is solicitous for their needs, he shows them toils as though they were some sort of amusement. He is alien to vulgar greed, and a zealot for Russians' glory. (strophe 7)

There is a combination here of the "simplicity" which Kostrov admires in Derzhavin's verse, and which his own older efforts conspicuously lack, and a moderately elevated style. The picture of Suvorov as his soldiers see him, incidentally, is perfectly true to life—an almost unique instance in the eighteenth century laudatory ode!

The final transformation of Kostrov's style belongs to that phase of the sentimentalist mode which is represented by "light verse." A number of the verses of the poet's final years are songs, often with a conventional pastoral coloring, elegant love poems addressed to "Aneta" or "Lizeta." From the end of "Verses to Aneta"[22] come these typically sentimentalist lines:

Hundred-fold happy is that rill, deserving of envy that stream, in which Aneta shall choose to look at her own face; and that grove will appear dressed in new greenery where the noonday heats bids her seek repose. O joy of hearts, return more speedily— ah, return, O month of May! I shall say to my heart: "be joyful"; I shall say: "Here is Aneta—my soul, begin to sport!"

As a final example of this trend, and one scarcely distinguishable from similar verses of Muraviev or Dmitriev, may be cited "To a Butterfly":[23]

Lovely butterfly, do not tarry, fly hither; the spring is calling you, beautiful May is calling. See, already the flowers are sprinkled with dew, and the zephyrs have made friends with them. The zephyrs caress them—do not you be modest, do not be bashful, shamefast. Be inconstant, do not be firm, faithful—and so you will be forever happy. Fly away, and kiss with tenderness the pinks, then leave [them] and triumph over the chastity of the rose and the lily. From them go down to the violet on your way, and forget not to embrace the forget-me-not. Always keep changing such lovely whims, lead your life in delightful betrayals, and know—just such counsel I myself would give myself, if I had not seen charming Lizeta.

One aspect of Kostrov's literary accomplishment deserves final mention—his translations. The first of these, published in 1779, was a short satirical poem of Voltaire's, entitled "Tactics."[24] In 1780-81 appeared what is said to be an excellent version of Apuleius' *Metamorphoses, or The Golden Ass*—the only one in Russian until the twentieth century. Two sentimentalist French works by Baculard d'Arnaud were translated in 1779—the poem *Elvire* and the prose tale *Zenothemis*. But the really significant, and highly successful, translation, dedicated to Catherine II in 1787, was a version of the first six books of the Homeric *Iliad*. It is possible that Kostrov did the whole first half of the poem, for books VII, VIII and part of IX were discovered in manuscript after his death and published in 1811. Until superseded by Gnedich's translation of the whole poem in accentual hexameters (1815), Kostrov's was the only Russian version of the *Iliad*, and it long continued to enjoy popularity, even beside the more accurate and complete translation of Gnedich.

Gukovsky[25] characterizes Kostrov's *Iliad* thus: "Kostrov's translation was carried out in strict conformity with the traditions of classicism. Kostrov interpreted the *Iliad* as an epic in the spirit not so much of the *Aeneid* as of the *Henriade* and even of Kheraskov's *Rossiad*. His translation was written not in hexameters, but in the rhymed Alexandrines traditional to the epic and dramatic verse of classicism. This alone would have given it the coloring of a poetical work of the eighteenth century. However, Kostrov evidently did not set himself at all the task of rendering the genuine ancient tonality of the Greek epic: his approach to the text was altogether devoid of historicism." Such strictures as this inevitably recall those levelled by nineteenth-century critics (e.g., Matthew Arnold) against another eighteenth-century translation of the *Iliad*, and Richard Bentley's famous quip: "It is a pretty poem, Mr. Pope, but you must not call it Homer." A close examination of Kostrov's Russian, however, beside the original Greek reveals far greater fidelity than Gukovsky's remarks would lead one to expect. For purposes of comparison, chosen more or less at random, note the speech of Priam to Helen in the *Teichoskopia* (Book III, 162-170); literally rendered, the Greek reads:

Come hither, dear child, sit before me, so as to see both [your] former husband and allies and friends—you are not at all to blame in my eyes; it is the gods who are to blame in my eyes, who have roused up against me the tearful war of the Achaians—so may you name for me this giant man, whoever he may be, this Achaian man goodly and great; others indeed are even taller by a head, but one so beautiful have I never beheld with my eyes, nor [one] so stately; for he has the look of a king.

This, again literally rendered, becomes in Kostrov's Russian the following:[26]

Dear daughter, come, sit down before me, to behold [your] former husband and friends. Not you, but the gods [are] for me the authors of all the misfortune; through them this grievous destiny weighs me down in war. Inform me, who is this man, this Greek so wondrous both in height of stature and strength of shoulders? I see many taller than he among these tribes, but one so stately, so beautiful has never been beheld by my eyes among mortal heroes; verily he is in everything like a king.

The principal inaccuracies in this version are: (1) a needless expansion and interpretation of "eus te megas te" as "wondrous both in height of stature and strength of shoulders"; and (2) the "padding" of "among these tribes" and "among mortal heroes." In this connection Pope's version may be cited— surely no closer to the Greek!

> Approach, my child, and grace thy father's side.
> See on the plain thy Grecian spouse appears,
> The friends and kindred of thy former years.
> No crime of thine our present suffering draws.
> Not thou, but Heaven's disposing will, the cause;
> The gods these armies and this force employ,
> The hostile gods conspire the fate of Troy.
> But lift thy eyes, and say, what Greek is he
> (Far as from hence these aged orbs can see)
> Around whose brow such martial graces shine,
> So tall, so awful, and almost divine!
> Though some of larger stature tread the green,
> None match his grandeur and exalted mien:
> He seems a monarch, and his country's pride.[27]

Pope has succeeded in spinning out *nine* Greek hexameters into *fourteen* iambic pentameters, including one (the parenthesis in the ninth line of the quotation) unwarranted by anything whatever in the original! Kostrov's translation, incidentally, is only one line longer (10 instead of 9) than the Greek.

A quite different kind of translation, not from the original, as was the Homer, but itself from another translation, is that of Macpherson's "Ossian." This was published in 1792 under the title: "Ossian, son of Fingal, a bard of the third century: Welsh (!) ["gal'skie"] verses." Apparently Kostrov was unaware of any distinction between Welsh and "Caledonian," as Scotch Gaelic was usually called at this time. The version was made from the French translation of LeTourneur (1776). Gukovsky remarks:[28] "His translation was made not from the original, but from the French translation of Le Tourneur; hence it is not altogether exact. But Kostrov succeeded in rendering the romantic color, the gloomy poetry, the emotional intensity of Ossian, its fierce energy. His translation was a major triumph of preromanticism in Russian literature." Since the "Ossian" of Kostrov is at present inaccessible, Gukovsky's appraisal must be accepted without further comment.

Certainly Ermil Ivanovich Kostrov can hardly be rated as an outstandingly original poet, but his verse, exactly because of its derivative character, shows better than that of almost any contemporary, the whole stylistic gamut which Russian poetry traversed during the last quarter of the eighteenth century.

C. Alexander Nikolaevich Radishchev (1749-1802)[29]

Among the minor versifiers of the end of the eighteenth century Alexander Radishchev is particularly interesting for the variety of the poetical experiments in the rather small body of his verse. Radishchev is of course primarily a writer of prose, and the importance of his famous *Journey from St. Petersburg to Moscow* will be considered presently; but his verse output, although small, cannot be ignored.

Because of his radical political views, Radishchev is usually given a place in Soviet Russian literary histories out of all proportion to his literary merits, and this disproportion in turn is likely to prejudice a non-Marxist critic in his disfavor. Political views of course are irrelevant to a writer's achievement as a writer, although they have to be considered along with the other themes that he treats; but there is enough of the innovative in Radishchev's technical approach to poetry to justify, if not a large place, at least more than a cursory mention in a literary history.

Alexander Nikolaevich Radishchev was a nobleman's son from the Saratov district; after enrollment in the Pages' Corps, he was sent abroad for education, and returned to Russia with a degree from the University of Leipzig in 1771. He took a position in the civil service, and became acquainted with Nikolai Novikov, for whose periodicals he translated some French articles. After a short time in military service, he retired, took another civil position with the Commerce Department, and busied himself with economic theory. In 1790 he printed, privately and without official authorization, his revolutionary *Journey from St. Petersburg to Moscow.* Arrested by Catherine and interrogated, he was sentenced to death for treason, but the sentence was later commuted to ten years exile in Siberia. Catherine's death in 1796 and the accession of Paul terminated his exile, and he even returned briefly to the civil service in 1801 with Alexander's accession, but unexpectedly took his own life in 1802.

In the years 1781-83, inspired by the success of the revolution of the American colonies against Great Britain, Radishchev composed his ode "Liberty,"[30] which was subsequently printed as an appendix to his *Journey.* This ode appears to be the earliest of his poetical efforts. It is extremely long—54 ten-line strophes—and written in the Lomonsovian form and language.

An analysis of the ode's content will indicate the course of the thought development: the first six strophes hail "Liberty" and, following Rousseau's theory of the social contract and the general will, describe an allegorical temple to "the Law." Then follows in strophes 7-12 an allegorical description of religious fanaticism; then a long development is devoted to a description of the coming revolution and the dethronement and punishment of "the king" (strophes 13-34). In the next section (34-38) he hails the American revolution and General Washington. The final strophes (49-54) rather pessimistically prophesy that tyranny will follow civil war once again and Liberty be laid low—but only to rise once more at the bidding of Nature and Nature's God.

Radishchev's political theory, as the ode reveals it, is Rousseauist: he sees the "people" as the ultimate source of authority, the "king" as a brazen usurper. But he also sees a dialectic in history: "liberty" will be eclipsed and extinguished by self-seeking and internecine strife, and then again returned through revolution, presumably in eternally recurring successions. He evidently fears for the fate of liberty even in America; Rousseau's belief that republican government can succeed only in a small state seems to be behind his remark (st. 49): "But the more distant the source of authority, the weaker the union of the members.... The ray that streams from the sun is accompanied by both radiance and strength; in space it loses its power."

In the content of Radishchev's ode there is novelty, even quite startling novelty. To poeticize abstract political theory is not easy, and in the effort Russian ode-writing shows no precedent. The execution, however, is another matter. Stylistically, the ode is a monstrosity, replete with all the faults of classicism in their most flagrant form. It is, to begin with, perversely abstract and allegorical. Beginning with the presentation of the temple of the Law (strophe 4)—"In the midst of the grain-rich valley, amid corn-fields heavy with the harvest, where tender lilies bloom, among peaceful olives beneath the shade, whiter than Parian marble, brighter than the rays of clearest day, stands a temple visible everywhere"—and ending with the Creator's final establishment of "Liberty" (strophe 54)—"the bright light has sent forth its ray, and having trodden under foot the false scepter of servitude, having chased away the thickened murk, it has brought to birth the radiant day from the clouds"—the poet clothes all his thought in cold and distant allegorical form. Every image involves some form of metaphor—and the inevitable result of this plethora is the wildest and most absurd mixing of metaphors, which reaches its climax in strophe 51: "From the recesses of the enormous ruin [i.e., of a government of liberty], amid fires, rivers of blood, dark festering, which the cruel spirit of authority has kindled, small luminaries shall rise up; they will adorn their unshakeable rudders with the garland of friendship, they will direct their boat to the profit of all, and will crush the ravening wolf which the blind one had deemed [to be] his father!"

Even when he avoids such enormities as this, Radishchev remains everywhere true to the outworn Lomonsov tradition of rhetorical utterance. He declaims, in the tones of an ancient prophet; thus (st. 25) he hails the coming revolution:

Tempests of a sudden have begun to sound, breaking the peace of quiet waters. Even so the voices of freedom have begun to thunder, [and] every people runs to the assembly ["veche"]. It [i.e., the people] destroys the iron throne as of old Samson shakes the temple filled with falsehoods, and builds with law the foundation of nature. Great, great art thou, spirit of freedom, creative as is God Himself!

And not only is his mode of utterance that of fifty years before his time, so also is his language. Scarcely even Vasily Petrov's odes can rival Radishchev's in the number and unintelligibility of his Slavonicisms; one can almost say that whenever a Slavonic word can be used, the Russian equivalent is scorned. Add to this a pervasively Biblical coloration, sometimes even directly echoing a Bible passage, e.g., in st. 22: "Behold, thine evil hath gone over ["prevzyde"—an archaic Slavonic aorist tense] thy head,"—and the result is a language which can frequently be understood only by the kind of minute textual analysis usually accorded to the most abstruse Latin or Greek. Moreover, the periods are exceedingly awkward and confusing: the poet's tendency is to construct each strophe as a single unit, and then fill the first three-quarters of it with gerunds or participles, presumably to be understood with the subject, which does not appear until nearly the end of the strophe; thus st. 26, which reads literally, line by line:

> Having smashed the resistance of spiritual authority,
> And with the hard hand of vengeance
> [he] rent despotism in pieces,
> which [had been] raised by sanctified falsehood;

> darkening the triple tiara
> and shattering the rod of sanctity,
> [he] quenched the lightnings of anathemas;
> mocking at the imaginary interdiction,
> Luther lifted up the ray of enlightenment,
> [and] reconciled heaven with earth.

Here the first colon (lines 1-4) is constructed with a past gerund and a past masculine indicative ["rastorg"], but with no subject; the second (lines 5-7) of two present gerunds and another subjectless masculine past indicative ["utushil"]; the last colon [8-10], after another present gerund, at last introduces the subject, "Luther," in line 8, with two more masculine past indicatives.

At times, to add to the bewilderment, the dependent participles change reference suddenly within a period, a change indicated only by their gender, but unaccompanied by a subject. Thus, in the idyllic picture of the free peasant's marriage, contrasted with that of the serf (st. 32):

> Having accomplished [past gerund] the cycle of the day's labor,
> The free man hastens home;
> [his] innocent heart, without worry
> sleeps in [his] wife's embraces.
> Not by the hand of an arrogant lord
> given [*feminine* past passive participle] to him for punishment,
> in order to multiply innocent victims [i.e., slave children];
> guided [*masculine* present passive participle] by tender love,
> he has taken up marriage hopeful to his heart,
> chosen a helper for himself

The ungrammatical nature of such a period, with two distinct, but implied subjects, is obvious.

In a laudable but misguided effort at compression the poet sometimes leaves lines that can scarcely be made to yield sense, or can yield more than one: thus (st. 34):

> Behold upon the boundless plain,
> Where stands the army that has wiped out savagery;
> Not cattle there driven against their will,
> Not the lot gives [them] valor;
> Not a host [that] presses forward by the rules—[i.e., a regular
> army]
>
> There every warrior sees himself a leader,
> He seeks a death of glory.
> O warrior unshakable,

> You are and have been unconquerable,
> Your leader—freedom, Washington!

The entire strophe clearly is intended to refer to the American colonial army, but ambiguity persists. Most texts of the poem contain an indefensible error in the second line—*sterta* (past *passive* participle) instead of *stersha* (past *active* participle, correctly restored in Zapadov's edition). This would make it necessary, in order to make sense of the line, to take "sterta zverstva" as a kind of genitive absolute, "where savagery [i.e., the British!] has been wiped out." But no emendation will remove the awkwardness of three negative clauses, each with a different subject, all loosely referring to "army" ["rat' "] : "not *cattle—*," "not the *lot—*," "not a *host—*." And finally there is the, perhaps intentional, ambiguity in the last three lines. Does the "voin" ("warrior") in line 8 whom the poet addresses refer to the colonial soldier, and the last line accordingly mean "your leader *is* freedom [and] Washington!" Or does "voin" refer to Washington himself, and is the last line to be construed as: "Your leader, O Washington, is freedom!" Either construction is grammtically admissible, since there is no clear indication of where the "ty" of line 9 is meant to refer.

The ode "Liberty" is decidedly not a poetical success, however noble its sentiments and however "progressive" Radishchev's political ideology. It shows the same kind of stylistic archaism in verse as the *Journey* exhibits in prose, but with far less justification.

Fortunately, some of Radishchev's later verse is both more experimental and intrinsically more poetic. Always quoted in anthologies is the small, almost epigrammatic, piece supposed to have been composed when the poet was asked his identity by someone while on his way to his Siberian exile:

> You want to know who I am? What I am? Whither I am going?
> I am the same as I have [always] been, and shall be all my life!
> Not cattle, not tree, not slave, but Man!
> To lay out a road where there was no trace [of one],
> For swift, bold spirits, both in prose and verse;
> To the terror of sensitive hearts and the truth
>   To Ilimsk prison I fare.[31]

According to Radishchev's son, Alexander Nikolaevich learned English in the early 1780s and soon came "to understand Shakespeare and Milton." The poem "The Creation of the World,"[32] which was included in one version of the *Journey* as "an example of how to write verse without using iambics alone," is strongly influenced by the seventh book of Milton's *Paradise Lost*. It is a kind of oratorio, composed in a combination of meters—dactyls, trochees, iambics and anapests.

During the 1790s, while in exile, Radishchev composed a fairly lengthy epic poem on the subject of the popular tale "Bova Korolevich."[33] Of what amounted to an original eleven cantos or "songs," only the introduction and first canto are extant, together with a long prose summary of the rest. The poem is of considerable interest from several points of view. It is, in the first place, an attempt to utilize for literary purposes a well known and much loved popular story; Karamzin's "Ilya Muromcts" (1795) is an experiment along the same lines. "Bova" is also strikingly different in tone from such serious pieces as "Liberty" or "The Creation of the World": it is ironical, satirical, and bawdy. In the third place, it is, like several of Radishchev's later poems, a metrical experiment. In the "Introduction" the poet pretends that he is about to present the story as he heard it from his old peasant "uncle" Peter Suma. He then, more seriously, refers to the two poets to whom his tale is most indebted:

Peter Suma, come to [my] assistance and with the sweet stream of your eloquence, enliven my tale. Without rhyme or reason, it will follow in the footsteps of the poet of the *Tavrida*—but can there be any comparison with him?

O Voltaire, O most famous man! If it were possible for Bova to be like in any respect to Jeanette, the valiant maiden whom you sang of; to be worth even so much as her little finger—if it were possible for [people] to say that Bova is only the thin shadow of her—enough! this would be a shadow of Voltaire, and my carved image would nest in the Pantheon!

Semen Bobrov's *Tavrida* (1798), to which we shall presently come, is a descriptive poem in unrhymed verse, largely modelled on James Thomson's *The Seasons*. Since there is no similarity of subject, it must be the verse form and language of Bobrov's poem which Radishchev has in mind. *Tavrida*, however, is composed in iambic tetrameter unrhymed, while "Bova" uses the so-called "Russian meter," an octosyllabic line of two strong beats and one or two weak ones, basically trochaic in rhythm. It is not, as N.D. Kochetkova asserts,[33a] the same meter as Karamzin's "Ilya Muromets," which almost always has a dactylic clausula, as "Bova" never has. The meter inevitably suggests to an American Longfellow's *Hiawatha*, which is trochaic tetrameter acatalectic, and very similar; and since Longfellow's use of the meter, and indeed some of the episodes in his poem, come, by his own admission, from the Finnish *Kalevala*, one may wonder if Radishchev had encountered Karelian or Estonian prototypes of the ballads which Dr. Lönnrot collected to put together the *Kalevala*. In any case, "Bova" is an excellent illustration of Radishchev's theory that verse can be composed "not in iambics alone," and without rhyme—a view which, as we shall see, was also held by his contemporary Karamzin.

The connection with Voltaire's *La Pucelle*, on the other hand, is evidently one of plot and characterization. The fortunes of "The Maid of Orleans," and hence of France, are, in Voltaire's ribald treatment, dependent on

Joan's virginity, against which most of the male characters of the poem are in constant combat. It may be that Radishchev envisaged a similar development for his Bova; in the extant fragment the naive youngster, fleeing from his malevolent mother, is befriended with more than maternal solicitude by an old woman, the cook of the ship on which he is making his escape. She takes him into her galley, they crawl up for warmth on the stove, and there Bova starts relating the story of his parents, which has not come even to a climax, when the first "Song," and with it the extant poem, comes to an end. At the point where the distraught Meletrisa is minded to hang herself on a stout, thick wooden peg on which her mother hangs her furs, the old woman breaks in, outraged, and evidently identifying this peg with a similar object of other uses, launches into a rhapsodic hymn to her god Phallus, "who gives beautiful life to the world! Through whom everything lives and is joyful.... because Phallus is that wondrous axis on which the world turns!" She exhibits to Bova a clay image of her deity, but—

He is astonished.... He does not know, has not read in history the ancient tale of peoples, to him our words are unintelligible. And Bova, although he sees, does not know what he sees. Thus in the eye the sensitive retina, when it has become weakened or injured, loses life and sensitivity, and that magnificent miracle, the beautiful sense of sight— is suddenly darkened, clouded, put out, and the objects of the bright world plunged in a mist of gloom.... In a word, blind is he who does not see! So, not knowing history, our Bova did not recognize Phallus, and was blind in his cognition.[34]

It is evident from passages such as this in "Bova" that, despite the markedly indecent nature of the treatment, there is intended an esoteric secondary meaning, the nature of which can hardly be made out certainly from the meager fragment we possess.

The style and language of "Bova" are, as might be expected, easier and more popular than in the serious poems. Slavonicisms are numerous, but not extreme, and the construction of the periods is far closer to the norms of ordinary speech. An attempt at conveying epic or popular color is evident in the use of "constant epithets," such as "sonorous guzla," "dark, slumbrous forests" ["lesa dremuchi, temny"], "burning tears," and the like. An almost burlesque tone is conveyed by the juxtaposition of pseudo-epic allegory and common-place detail, as when dawn is described in terms of the pseudo-Slavonic mythology which Popov invented to replace the Homeric, and Dawn's horses have a prosaic breakfast:

The rosy-fingered Zimtserla [Popov's Dawn-goddess, replacing Aurora] had not yet hitched her shining steeds to Znich's caleche [Znich was supposedly a god of fire, and thus here replaces Helios], and in Apollo's livery the fire-storming nags ["klachonki ogneburny"—a Lomonosovian epithet with a "low" substantive] were eating their ethereal oats, when, etc.[35]

This is, of course, the heavy-handed travesty familiar from Maikov's *Bacchus*

Enraged. Radishchev's sense of humor is rudimentary and anything but subtle—note the ponderous scatology of his digression on the Dalai Lama. "Bova" is, like most of his verse, an interesting, but only moderately successful experiment.

Radishchev exhibits in his small body of poetry a strong proclivity toward ternary meters, especially dactyls, and unrhymed verse. A good example is the "fable," as he calls it, entitled "Cranes" (1797-1801),[36] translated from an original of Ewald von Kleist. The German poem is unrhymed and in blank verse (iambic pentameter); Radishchev's uses dactylic tetrameter unrhymed, alternately acatalectic and catalectic; his first two lines are scanned: *osen' listy oshchipala s derev* ('x 'xx 'xx 'x); *inei sedoi na travu upadal* ('xx 'xx 'xx '). The poem is an allegory, which Radishchev undoubtedly understood of his own fate:

Autumn has plucked the leaves from the trees, the hoar-frost has fallen on the grass; a flock of cranes has gathered to fly away to a warm, distant land, to live beyond the sea. One poor crane, mute and despondent, sat in sadness; a hunter had broken his leg with an arrow. He does not augment the cranes' joyful crying, [and] his brisk brothers mocked at him. "I am not to blame that I have become lame; I aided our kingdom [even] as you. You ought not to laugh at me, or despise [me], seeing my misfortune. How can I fly? My grievous infirmity takes away the possiblity, [my] valor, [my] strength; the waves will be the grave of wretched me. Ah, why did not the fierce hunter cut short my life?" Meanwhile, the wind blows, the flock circled aloft and with swift flight hastens at once to fly away across the sea. The poor injured one remains behind. Often over the leaves that float on the waters he sighs, grieves and moans. Sorrow and sickness eat away all the heart in him. Having delayed long, flying little by little, he got sight of the land that his soul longed for, the clear sky and the quiet haven. There the Almighty healed his injuries, to live in happiness as reward for his toils; but many mockers fell into the water.

O you, who groan under the heavy hand of misfortune and woes! Filled with anguish, you curse life and the world; lovers of the good, is there no hope?

Another experiment with the dactylic meter, certainly inspired also by German models, is the poem "The Eighteenth Century,"[37] composed in 1801. It is an unfinished piece of 79 lines, ending abruptly with the first line of a couplet. The meter is an accentual version of the classical elegiac distich--that is, the odd-numbered lines are dactylic hexameters, the even-numbered are the so-called "pentameter"—actually, catalectic hexameters with a pause at the medial caesura. The scansion of lines 5-6 will help to clarify the meter:

Ne vozvyshalsia tam ostrov, ni dna tam lot ne nakhodit ['xx 'xx 'xx 'x 'xx 'x]
Veki v nego protekli, v nem ischezaet ikh sled. ['xx 'xx ': 'xx 'xx ']

The meter is seldom used in English, although naturalized in German (cf. Goethe's *Römische Elegien*); an English version (by Longfellow?) of a couplet of Schiller's is often used to illustrate its effect:

In the hexámeter ríses the foúntain's sílvery cólumn,
In the pentámeter áye fálling in mélody báck.

The flexibility of the classical quantitative dactylic verse, in which a spondee can be substituted for a dactyl anywhere in the hexameter except in the fifth foot, is lost in the accentual version, although occasionally, as in the fourth foot of the hexameter above, a trochee may take the place of a dactyl. Trediakovsky, in his treatise "On Russian Versification, Ancient, Middle and Modern" (1755) had given some painful examples of the meter, but it had not been used previously for an entire poem in Russian.

"The Eighteenth Century" was apparently intended to be a sort of official piece glorifying Alexander I; the fragmentary last line reads: "May Alexander be ever among us the guardian genius." The "century" is described as a contradictory period: "No, you will not be forgotten, century witless and wise; you will be cursed forever, forever an object of wonder to all." "Blood in your cradle, your lullabies the thunders of battle; ah, soaked in blood you are descending into the grave." Part of the century's contradiction is that, filled with wars and bloodshed as it has been, it was also a time of great advances in knowledge—and Radishchev exclaims:

O unforgettable century! You give to joyful mortals truth, liberty and light, a constellation bright forever; the pillars of mortal wisdom you, having demolished, created anew; kingdoms were ruined by you, like a ship that is wrecked; kingdoms you create; they will flourish and fall once more; whatsoever a mortal creates, all will be destroyed, all will be destroyed, all will be dust.

Then he reviews the discoveries of the age: "Out of the Ocean waves new peoples and lands" [the voyages of Cook, Bougainville and others]; "you count the stars, as a shepherd his gamboling lambs; you summon the Comet once more by the thread of motion; the ray of light was cut off by you; you called up new suns" [Halley's comet, eclipse, and Herschel's discovery of the planet Uranus]; "even flying vapors you imprisoned in a yoke; you enticed the lightning of heaven into iron bonds on the earth" [Franklin's feat of collecting electricity from lightning in a Leyden jar] and "bore mortals to the sky on aery wings" [Montgolfier's balloon]. In less specific terms he lauds the thinkers who have laid phantoms to rest and freed men's minds: "but your strength was insufficient to banish all the spirits of hell which have been spewing flaming poison through many thousands of years." "Shall peace not return forever, that gives the peoples happiness?" "But no—cast off despair! Hope, O mortal. God lives—suns in their rising flourish and they grow pale with their setting. Eternal is Providence only."

The poem is impressive, but uneven; the hexameters are awkward, sometimes unmetrical, and too much—too many ponderous words—are often crowded into a single line. Nonetheless it is the first experiment of its kind, and would undoubtedly have been revised and improved had the poet lived.

The only perfectly satisfactory metrical experiment of Radishchev, and a quite charming poem in its own right, with which we shall leave him, are the "Sapphic strophes" of 1801.[38] The Sapphic meter, so named from the great poetess who invented the form in the sixth century B.C., was known to the eighteenth century in two of her poems—the "Hymn to Aphrodite" and the untitled masterpiece that begins "phainetai moi kenos isos theoisin" ("That man seems to me like the gods—"), translated by Catullus as *Ille mi par esse deo videtur.* Horace also employed the Sapphic strophe in some of his finest odes. It was the only classical lyric meter to survive into the middle ages—some Latin hymns are composed in accentual Sapphics. Simeon Polotsky composed some heavy-handed accentual Sapphics, and Trediakovsky's metrical experiments include this meter, but the form was still unfamiliar in Russian. The Greek meter is logaoedic, that is, a combination of trochees and dactyls: the first three lines are scanned: 'x 'x 'xx 'x 'x—that is, a five-beat line, with a solitary dactyl midway between two pairs of trochees; the final line, sometimes grammatically "run on" with the third, is an adonic: 'xx 'x. Radishchev's experiment, put into an English attempt at the same meter, is the following:

> Cool the night was; bright in the sky above us
> Stars were shining; quietly flowed the fountain,
> Gentle winds were blowing, the poplars rustled
>   Leaves in the darkness.
>
> You made solemn oath to be ever faithful,
> Gave me night's own goddess herself as witness.
> Only once the north-wind has blown more strongly—
>   Vanished your pledged word.
>
> Ah, what need to perjure yourself? Much better
> Be forever cruel—the heart more lightly
> So will suffer. Luring me on with passion
>   Feigned, you've destroyed me.
>
> End my life, O Destiny, cruel, ruthless!
> Or inspire in her to be true to sworn oaths.
> But be happy, you, if you can be happy
>   Being without love.

D. Semen Sergeevich Bobrov (1763-1810)[39]

At first sight it may appear strange to associate together the poetry of Alexander Radishchev, born 1749, and that of Semen Bobrov, fourteen years his junior. Actually, however, the two poets, as poets, were more contemporary than their dates would indicate. Radishchev's "Liberty" dates from 1781-83, and most of his other verse from around 1797-1802; Bobrov's first considerable ode, "The Kingdom of Universal Love" was composed in 1785, and his poem *Tavrida,* considered his masterpiece, was published in 1798; his collected works appeared in 1804, only two years after Radishchev's death.

The two men are indeed worlds apart in philosophical and political outlook—Radishchev an eighteenth-century deist, a republican, and Russia's "first revolutionary"; Bobrov an apolitical, semi-mystical philosopher-poet, with a scientific bent. What brings them together is their common approach to the poet's art.

Bobrov was a priest's son—a *raznochinets* whose earliest education was in a seminary. He was thus from childhood immersed in the old-fashioned religious atmosphere and the language and literature that belong to it, as were none of the gentry writers of his time. Religious usages, beliefs and especially the Slavonic language were an organic part of the life of a priest's son; for a "gentleman," however sympathetic he may have been to these features of the indigenous, inherited, Russian tradition, they always remained external, something that had to be learned and appropriated. As Professor Gukovsky points out, even Sumarokov was unable to compose a Church Slavonic sentence grammatically, while Radishchev, whose literary theory relied heavily on retention in prose of a Slavonic vocabulary and syntax, knew the language itself so inaccurately that what he evidently regarded as authentic Slavonic expressions are often neologisms of his own invention! For Bobrov, the language and the religious ideas associated with it were an organic part of his life.

He entered Moscow University in 1780, was graduated in 1785, and entered the civil service. During his Moscow years he became closely associated with Nikolai Novikov and contributed to his Masonic journal *The Lover of Labor at Rest (Pokoiashchiisia trudoliubets).* In 1792 Bobrov, still in government service, left Moscow for the south, where he remained for about ten years; it was during this period that he became familiar with the newly acquired, wholly Oriental, region of the Crimea, which became the subject of his most successful poem. He returned to St. Petersburg in the early 1800s, but died in 1810 of tuberculosis, aggravated apparently by heavy drinking. His literary opponents frequently at this period referred to him as "Bibris," from the Latin "bibere," "to drink."

Bobrov's verse has a somewhat anomalous position in the literature of the late eighteenth century. Like Radishchev's, it is, in language, extremely traditional and even archaic. He employs a Lomonosovian "high style" that bristles with Slavonicisms, and in this regard he approaches the literary ideals of Admiral Shishkov and the famous *Beseda* group, whom the Karamzinists liked to label the "Old Believers" of literature. On the other hand, again like Radishchev, his literary direction is decidedly in the sentimentalist traditions, although where Radishchev is political and an activist, Bobrov is an introspective mystic with strongly Masonic leanings. Bobrov cannot be convincingly pigeon-holed with any other writer of his time, and for this reason has the misfortune of being misunderstood and derided by both sides. Only Radishchev appears to have appreciated him as the really original and significant poet that he is.

The only more or less complete edition of Bobrov's verse is that which he issued in 1804, under the paradoxical title of *Rassvet polnochi, The Midnight Dawn*—presumably meaning the "Aurora Borealis."[40] This has never been republished, and the only representative and accessible selection of his verse is that which Professor Lotman includes in his "Poet's Library" volume *Poets of the Years 1790-1810.*[41] In this selection are a number of odes, of traditional form, but, like those of Kapnist and other "sentimentalists," of a private and generally ethical content. The earliest in date of these (1785) is "The Kingdom of Universal Love,"[42] of a strongly Masonic color; the first two strophes set the tone:

The worlds were not yet turning about the sun in the regions on high; these hanging spheres were still concealed in chaos, when thou, O Love, didst receive the law and give life to their beginnings; as the spirit diffused in their sprouts, the might of thine empire has from antiquity until now maintained its laws in these worlds.

Issuing from the dreadful abyss the assemblage of these heavenly luminaries would have been once more a disharmonious confusion, if thou hadst been deprived of power; thou, rocking ["zyblia"] incandescent arrows didst shoot them into remote realms. The fire forges ["kuiet"] so many of them that thou doest penetrate all creation, when all-powerfully thou fliest through the great world and the little world.

The expression in the ode is strange and strained, as very often in Bobrov, but the mystical idea of love as the universal principle of harmony, operating both in the macrocosm ("the great world") and the microcosm, or "man" ("the little world") is impressively expressed. Bobrov's preoccupation with the generation of the cosmos appears here; he is especially fascinated, as we shall see, with its dissolution. Indeed "scientific" concerns, if ideas so strongly mystical can be called "scientific," mark a great deal of Bobrov's verse.

Another ode, from 1789, is entitled "The First Hour of the Year."[43] In an allegory reminiscent of some of Radishchev's in "Liberty," time becomes an immense and mysterious abyss, and the years animate beings ascending and descending there:

The hour has struck, the spacious grave has opened, where lies the sequence of sleeping ages; thither the year just past, summoned, flies on decrepit pinions. Mists accompany him, and wet his path with tears; the scythe does not glitter in the hand ["dlani"], but, sated with the blood of mortals, and blunted by their bones, hangs amid the cypresses.

The son of mysterious ["neiz"iasnimoi"] eternity [i.e., the new year], suddenly

494

breaking free from the abyss, furnished with the wings of youth, flies into the dim circle of mortals; the daughters of Themis [i.e., the Horae, or "Seasons"] revive and play before his face. Spring hastens to strew before him the beauties that had died, and is zealous to introduce hours of repose in January instead of storms.

The poem is dedicated to Bobrov's friend, the minor poet Pavel Pavlovich Ikosov (1760-1811) and ends with a strophe which, with its sentimentalist exaltation of friendship and its extraordinary but thoroughly classical mythologizing of Christianity (Jesus becomes Phoebus, Mary is Latona!), is typical of the mingling in Bobrov's verse of quite unharmonious elements:

> If indeed the Parcae respect the Muses whom you deify, and mollify their sharp scissors so as not to cut short our union—then I shall say, enraptured: "O Phoebus, born of Latona! Give us still more new years, that we may continue our days in tender friendship, until our untroubled life-span silvers the hair upon us!"

One of the most characteristic of Bobrov's poems, in its extraordinary and almost grotesque mingling of pagan and Christian elements, and in its grandiose pictures of universal destruction, is "The Fate of the Ancient World, or the Deluge" (1789).[44] The piece is composed in quatrains of iambic tetrameter. It begins as a vision: "I see a vision—[my] lyre trembles; I see, from the grave of nature the shade of the dead ["usopsha"] world arisen, [she] who has been overthrown by divinity." This shade is represented in a classical pose of mourning, "leaning with her elbow on an urn," and lamenting the fate of "the ancient world." Her lamentation begins: "Where is hidden the blasphemous host of giants that strove audaciously to stride through the clouds to the divine house?" This would naturally conjure up the legend of the Titans, who tried to overthrow Zeus and the Olympian gods; but presently the narrative takes on a more Biblical coloring and we remember (Genesis VI, 6): "And there were giants in those days." In any case, the "universal flood," which is a legend both Greek and Hebrew, is a punishment for human presumption:

> Alas! O stiff-necked generations! Forgetting Who hurls the hail in tempests, and the noisy rain with the threatening thunder ["groznym gromom"—Bobrov is fond of alliteration!], you went astray a hundred-fold in thoughts!
> Went astray—and at this moment He opened the heavens in wrath, and waking the cruel element, hid in the abyss mountains, valley, forests.

In a typical miscegenation of Christian and pagan, the flood is described: "The husband of silver-footed Thetis [Bobrov means "Ocean,"—but that deity was the husband not of Thetis, but of Tethys!], with a frown on his azure face, raised with stern right hand the realm of the waters higher than the mountains of Ararat!" Again, with a fusion of Hebrew and Greek myth, Noah's rainbow appears—but is called Iris! At this point utter confusion overtakes the mythology:

495

O Pyrrha [wife of Deucalion, the Greek Noah] ! Sing praise to Him who sits upon the slope of this arch of peace! Kiss the almighty hand which holds the elastic reins of the elements!

But, O blessed daughter of Iris! I fear for your sons! Their flesh shall die, consumed with fire, as formerly thy flesh in the waves.

From the context and from what follows it would appear that Pyrrha (i.e., the mother of post-diluvian mankind] is intended by the phrase "Iridy dshcher' blazhenna" ("blessed daughter of Iris"); but Iris, of course, as a Greek goddess, had no daughter, and Pyrrha was the daughter of Epimetheus and Pandora!

The second portion of the poem is a prophecy, with considerable borrowing from the Apocalypse, of the Last Day. In its bizarre power and originality it is one of Bobrov's most successful pieces, and is worth quoting entire:

When in the world on high the flame-streaming Ocean shall be thrown in turmoil, the spheres in the ether shall be thrown in turmoil, blazing with fire on every hand.

Pyrois, Phlegon [horses of the Sun], plying their wings, and darting amid the suffering planets, will breathe on them with fiery mouths, will burn the whole firmament—will burn the whole world.

There the mountains will melt like wax from the face of the ravening fire, there the darksome abysses will moan, there the brimstone will neigh, sighing [!] .

Changeless Cynthius [i.e., Apollo] will not boast of his youth, nor Pan of his seven-fold pipe, nor Flora of the brightness of spring days.

The winged daughters of Themis [i.e., the Seasons] shall fly up to the Father at the appointed hour, throw wide heaven's door—throw it wide for the last time.

Only the voice of the thunder-born ["gromo-rozhdennoi"] trumpet will sound from the north to the distant south: the astonished tongue will be silent, the world's glory will suddenly be silent.

The laurel of heroes, the crown of kings, and the palm flower of their singers, the lines of Homer and Maro [i.e., Virgil] —all their deathlessness will die.

As a hair in the stove flares up, crackling; as the powder of sulphur flashes in the fire and disappears, in smoke after the blaze—so their eternity flashes—and is not...

Only the inalterable Word will cast His triumphant glance abroad, and from the clouds pronounce unerringly the last sentence upon the world.

And while *earth-born* man is consumed in the flame, *heaven-born* man will take wing, soaring on subtle pinions forever.

The worlds will fall from their great axles, the spheres be shaken from their places; but He, amid the desolate ruins will tread on the smoking ashes of stars.

O world, in posterity renewed! Give heed to [this] ancestral shade, who speaks her own fate accomplished, and thy coming day of tears!

Having spoken, the world spirit disappeared; behind her sighs resound; from the hands falls the trembling lyre—and I pronounce in terror: "Holy is God!"

Bobrov's intense preoccupation with time is everywhere apparent; it was his fortune to witness the changing of the centuries, and there are several poems that deal with this occurrence—"To the New Nineteenth Century," "Century Song," "Interrogation of the New Age," and "Premonitory Response of the Age."[45] Of these the longest and most successful is the "Century Song" ["Stoletniaia pesn' "—Horace's "Carmen saeculare"], with the subtitle: "or, Triumph of Russia's Eighteenth Century." The poem seems to be a metrical experiment: the five-line strophes of iambic tetrameter have alternating rhymes in the first four (aBaB), but the fifth line is unrhymed, and ends with a down-beat.

The "Century Song" is not a greeting to the new age, but, like Radishchev's "Eighteenth Century," a look back at the old, and as the subtitle suggests, a glorification of the age in the poet's native land. After his usual allegorical description of a long, dimly illuminated hall, where the centuries are lying, the poet encounters the two-faced god Janus, who, looking backward, launches into a description of the past century in Russia. It begins with mention of Halley's comet, which appeared in 1682, and was widely believed to portend the end of the world; instead, it heralded an unheard-of blessing for Russia, for it was in that year that Peter I became Tsar. Of the poem's 67 strophes, 30 are devoted to a fervent exaltation of the great Tsar and his transformation of Russia—one of the greatest panegyrics since Lomonosov's.

Russia is his graven image ["vaianie"], his monument, the price of [his] labors; she is his immortal construction ["zdanie"]; she is half a planet, where he was her divinity.

Being everywhere present and glorious, he divided all of himself for all things; he, methinks, was many-natured ["mnogosostavlen"], as a giant of measureless strength, or as the great Prometheus. [46]

It is significant of Bobrov's political outlook that after the magnificent eulogy of Peter the Great, he devotes two strophes to Catherine I, Peter's loyal wife, skips Peter II and Anna Ivanovna without mention, gives another two strophes to Elizabeth, Peter's daughter, skips Peter III altogether, allows six strophes to Catherine II, whom he calls "the heaven-eyed Athena" ["nebookaia Afina"], skips Paul I altogether, and ends his survey of the Russian eighteenth century, as Radishchev does, with Catherine's grandson: "Thus the famous age among the Russians flew in the midst of glory and beauty; thus its stalwart end and the golden age of Petropolis is glorified in thunder by Alexander."[47]

Like so many of his contemporaries, Bobrov was familiar with, and strongly influenced by, eighteenth-century English poetry. The "graveyard school," and primarily Edward Young's Night Thoughts are readily seen behind such poems as "Walk in the Twilight" ["Progulka v sumerki"] (1785),[48] "Midnight" ["Polnoshch' "] (1804)[49] and "Night" ["Noch' "] (between 1801 and 1804).[50] The first of this group, "Walk in the Twilight," subtitled, "or Evening Instruction to Zoram," is pervaded by Bobrov's astronomical and cosmological interests: "Already in the other hemisphere, which has awakened, the flaming luminary is chasing away the dark of nocturnal clouds, while we from behind the forests see in the thickening vapor his dying evening ray."[48] As we gaze at the darkening sky, we see there "bright fires, like sparks": "Not sparks are they—but worlds are quietly revolving, which are just as great as the Earth. Ever since they issued harmoniously from the depths of chaos, they have been coursing across the fields of fire." (st. 4) But the universe will have an end, as it had a beginning—and once more we have Bobrov's obsessive picture of world cataclysm: "But the fates inform us that sometime the trembling Earth will sink in waves of flame, and frail creation, burning with fire, will groan, and will come out of its bark ["kory"], shaking off the dust." But this time the picture does not end with world destruction, but as in "Universal Love," envisions a new order, rising out of the ashes like a Phoenix, evoked by "universal love."

"Midnight" begins with a Youngian description, and an invocation:

O darksome Night! Where didst thou derive thy beginning? From what father or mother dost thou come? Art thou not the hoary daughter of that primal darkness which once issued forth over the hidden abyss, to rock the cradle of tender nature?[49]

The poet's meditations are interrupted by an ominous thunder-storm, which he imagines as the apocalyptic approach of the Heavenly Bridegroom to execute the Last Judgment. From heaven he hears the dread voice of the Judge, exhorting mankind in the terms of the gospel parable of the wise and foolish virgins:

"Tremble, if this Bridegroom shall realize that the oil in thy lamp is scanty, and heaven's lively fire dies within thee! Thou art disorderly, thou art not wise—awake! Come with me! I shall reveal where Providence builds its mansion; on these mossy graves, where the peace of heaven blows! Come! Learn!"
The storm has passed—the moon shines red...

The third of the trio, "Night,"[50] is quite different from the others in its dramatic setting. It begins with the customary atmospheric description:

The bronze sounds in the tower—it is the hour of night; the languid voice groans in the darkness. All are asleep—only the gaunt Parcae are weaving. Ah, the night of the grave has covered us! Everything is quiet around, only, trooping together, methinks, like quiet winds over the water, the Shades are whispering in the misty stillness.

Then, rather startlingly, "The golden cupolas of Petropolis waver, as it were, amid dreams; there moan ominous birds, sitting aloft on the crosses." The atmosphere of dread and foreboding is built up; the omens are compared with those that attended the death of Julius Caesar. The cock crows—it is midnight—and the Angel of Death descends from heaven: "Viking ["Variag"], awake!—Now is the cruel hour; thou sleepest, while there.... a long-drawn sound; dost thou not hear in these moments the bell's groan of death? How it shatters the air here! And thou dost not heed it! Again, again it strikes—

dost thou awake? Ah, he is no more!" It is by now evident enough that the "Varangian" whom the Angel of Death has taken, is Emperor Paul, murdered during the night of March 11-12, 1801. The dead emperor's career is reviewed briefly and without a trace of sympathy, and in the final strophe he is represented as saying: "Farewell, earth! The end has come! I see, there the supreme throne shines red!.... the Creator calls me, calls me!"

Among the poems of Bobrov which Lotman's anthology includes are two rather unclassifiable semi-dramatic pieces. The first, which the poet labels a "ballad," although it hardly fulfills that description, is entitled "The Tomb of Ovid, Glorious Favorite of the Muses" (written between 1792 and 1800).[51] As is well known, the poet Ovid (Publius Ovidius Naso: 43 B.C.– A.D. 17?) was exiled by Augustus to the remote town of Tomis on the Black Sea, the modern Rumanian Constanta in the Dobrudia. This region has never been part of Russian territory, but several Russian poets, including Pushkin in "The Gypsies," have been inspired by the region's nearness to the Russian south and the similarity of Ovid's fate to that of Russian exiles, to write sympathetically of the Roman's unhappy lot. V.G. Tepliakov's "Second Thracian Elegy" (1829) is entitled "Tomis," and, like Bobrov's poem, introduces the ghost of "Naso" telling his own story to the sympathetic Russian bard. Bobrov's "ballad" describes Ovid's unjust banishment, using some of that poet's own verses in the *Tristia* and *Epistulae ex Ponto* as a source, and then, in the 23rd stanza, begins a direct monologue of the Roman ghost to his interlocutor, in which he bids him: "Mourn not, singer of later eons! Amid the vales of heaven I behold neither the threatening looks of authority, nor the false accusations of favorites, nor shameful dependence on their ambiguous smile." The poet's fame is everlasting, but as for the emperor who exiled him—"What is Octavius, who swallowed up the whole world? The self-same worm and pestilence eat him as now crawl over me."

The second piece of a semi-dramatic nature is headed: "The Voice of the Resurrected Olga to Her Son Sviatoslav" (between 1801 and 1804).[52] Olga, Grand Duchess of Kiev, was, it may be recalled, a Christian, while her son Sviatoslav son of Igor remained a pagan. Bobrov utilizes this situation to construct an unhistorical parallel with a more recent dissension in a Russian royal family. In his poem Olga, who speaks from the tomb, represents Catherine II, her disloyal and hostile son Sviatoslav represents the Emperor Paul I, whose murder is figured by Sviatoslav's death in a Pecheneg ambush. Most of the poem consists of Olga's admonitions to her grandson Vladimir, who of course represents Catherine's grandson Alexander I. The framing portion of the poem, which introduces an "Old Man" and a "Young Man" as witnesses of Olga's resurrection, is composed in unrhymed iambic tetrameter, while Olga's admonition utilizes rhyme in an irregular fashion. The framing device is somewhat reminiscent of Dmitriev's "Ermak" (1794).

Bobrov was not a "gentleman," as were most poets of his age, and hence had no estates and serfs to supplement his scanty income from the government service. His precarious financial condition was apparently relieved from time to time by the generosity of his superior in the service, Admiral N.S. Mordvinov. Three interesting autobiographical pieces of a type not familiar in Russian are among those in the Lotman anthology, "A Tribute to Virtue," "Song of an Unfortunate Man on the New Year, to Virtue" (1795/1804), and "A Setting Forth of the Life of the Talentless Vorbab" (1801-1804).[53] "Vorbab" is of course an anagram for Bobrov. All three poems are addressed to Mordvinov and are appeals for financial assistance; the third contains some specific autobiographical information.

Quite unique also is the poem "Against Sugar" (1804).[54] After enumerating all the good qualities of sugar, its use in tea, etc., he suddenly turns to some of its bad effects: "But if the nerves in us weaken, and scurvy gets the upper hand, or our teeth blacken from you [i.e., sugar], and a repulsive stench breath issues from our mouth; after your heavenly sweetness, a hellish stench comes in its wake—what shall I say? O deceptive nectar! In you lies a hidden poison!" But these are not the worst features of sugar: to produce it, the unfortunate blacks of Africa are kidnapped, enslaved, and forced to toil to their death on American plantations; this revolting picture is probably drawn from Thomson's "Summer," which served Bobrov as the principal model for his poem *Tavrida.* If we would be less luxurious in our tastes, such inhumanity might cease. The poem ends: "How shameful for the golden age to glitter with an iron barbarity, and to the eternal reproach of the sciences, to tickle a capricious taste!"

The last Lotman selection is one of the earlier in point of time, a portion (the seventh canto) of a long ten-canto descriptive poem—the first of its kind in Russian—called in its 1798 version *Tavrida,* and in the revision included in the complete works (*Rassvet Polnochi,* Part IV), *Chersonida.*[55] Both names are of course classical designations of the Crimea. The 1798 publication is entitled in full: *Tavrida, or My Summer Day in the Taurian Chersonese.* An extended description follows the title in the 1804 version: "A lyrico-epical song composition ["pesnotvorenie"], newly corrected and augmented, with a sequel of certain small works of translation and imitation and composed in verse and prose, relating in content to objects in the Chersonese and other localities."

The model of *Tavrida* was Part II ("Summer") of James Thomson's *The Seasons.* Bobrov's poem, in part VII, describes "a thunderstorm over the Taurian mountains," and utilizes a number of Thomson's themes, e.g., the description of a person struck by lightning—in Thomson's poem the lovely Amanda, in Bobrov's the scientist Richman, killed in the course of an electrical experiment reproducing Franklin's. But Bobrov's poem has a good deal that is original and not borrowed from Thomson, especially in the "local color" of the Crimea. After the long description of the thunderstorm, the Tatar princess Tsulma is suddenly introduced, love-sick for her absent lover Selim, and trying to console herself with a luxurious bath and the songs

500

of her attendant maidens. Tsulma is not identified in Lotman's notes, but presumably her story must have been begun in an earlier portion of the poem.

Radishchev's citation of the *Tavrida* as one of the models for his "Bova" has been mentioned above; the Bobrov poem is in iambic tetrameter, and like "Bova," is unrhymed. There is otherwise no similarity between the heavy-handed burlesque of a popular tale and the magnificent descriptive richness of *Tavrida*. As an example of the poem's style, and at the same time of its meter, is offered this brief passage:

> But hark! There sounds about the village
> A noise of weather-boding birds—
> The goose's honking, raven's cawing!
> And hark! The cock is loudly crowing!
> This harbinger of woe most surely,
> His head turned toward the coming tempest,
> Is warning us of heaven's anger,
> The tearful hour of nature's suff'ring!
> And hark! The cock repeats his warning!
> Most surely have the powers of heaven
> Concluded now their dreadful counsel
> To send down storms with thunder rolling
> Beneath Jehovah's fire-red throne!
> All, all is helpless now, bewildered,
> Is mute and shudders, is a-tremble!
> But suddenly a blinding blaze
> Flashes, and cleaves the distant south,
> The brighter as the murk is thicker.
> Are such the flaming cherubim
> In their supernal realm of light?

Bobrov's style, in all his verse, is the veriest antithesis of the "light verse" of his contemporaries, such as Dmitriev, Karamzin, Lvov or Kapnist. It is archaic, heavy with a Slavonic vocabulary, sometimes awkward in sound or even at times unmetrical. It is also what Schiller termed *Gedankenlyrik*, almost the first of its kind in Russian, "thought poetry," not poetry of sentiment. In most of these respects it is closer to the verse of Radishchev than to that of any other contemporary. But Bobrov is a far greater poet than Radishchev, whose verse is mostly metrical oratory. Bobrov's bizarre but powerful and unexpected combinations of ideas are often reminiscent of the English metaphysical poets. To contemporaries, especially of the Karamzinist school, whose literary ideal was a smooth, mellifluous, crystal-clear utterance, in verse or prose, Bobrov was a scandal, and it is not surprising that Batiushkov picked him as one of his candidates for oblivion in "Vision on the Banks of Lethe." In this satire Bobrov is made to say:[56]

501

I am the vinous genius. I have written three poems and a hundred odes, where everywhere there was night, everywhere shades, "where the neighing grove of muskets neighs" ["gde roshcha rzhushcha ruzhii rzhet"—Batiushkov comments in a note: "This line is taken from the works of Bobrov: I have no desire to lay claim to it." The line actually reads:[57] "se ruzhei rzhushcha roshcha mchitsia."]

Neither Bobrov's difficult and archaic style nor his horror-haunted visions of universal cataclysm were congenial to Batiushkov and his Arzamas associates; but many of the later romantics admired him, and even Pushkin admits to having "purloined" a line from the *Tavrida* for his *Fountain of Bakhchisarai*. To a modern generation, more attuned to the metaphysical style, Bobrov seems a truer poet than many of his more acclaimed contemporaries. Even the cacophony that Batiushkov ridicules is not unacceptable to a modern poet—compare Andrei Bely's line "kak vzropshchut, ropshchut roshchi" ("How the groves begin to grumble, grumble!").[58]

E. *Vasily Lvovich Pushkin* (1770-1830)[59]

If Russia's greatest poet had never existed, his uncle's name would probably have a greater place in literary histories than it does at present. A luminary of the first magnitude tends to eclipse lesser lights. But Vasily Lvovich, brother of Alexander Pushkin's father, is an interesting and quite original poet, and was recognized as such by his more brilliant nephew. His verse spans the turn of the century, and belongs in most respects to the early romantic movement; but at least in the satires of the 1790s he appears as the faithful continuator of the eighteenth-century traditions of Kantemir, Sumarokov, Kapnist et al. We shall confine our discussion of his work at this time for the most part to this material.

V.L. Pushkin was the son of a wealthy landowner and received an exceptionally good education at home. After a term of service with the Izmailovsky Guards Regiment he retired, settled in Moscow, married, and began to lead the life of a gentleman of leisure. He made the extended tour of western Europe in 1803-04 which is recorded in his friend I.I. Dmitriev's "Epistle"[60] to be discussed later. He had begun to publish verse as early as 1793, but his most productive period came in 1810-11. The Napoleonic invasion of 1812 dislocated his life: he was obliged to flee from Moscow to Nizhnii Novgorod, his house and library were destroyed in the Moscow fire, and he was desolated. After his return in 1814 he became involved in the embittered literary controversy between the Karamzinist supporters who eventually formed the club which they named Arzamas, and the conservative group headed by Admiral A.S. Shishkov which is known under the abbreviated title of *Beseda*. The story of this controversy belongs to the history of Russian romanticism, and is irrelevant here. V.L. Pushkin's latest literary work of note is an unfinished narrative poem, semi-parodistic in intent, called

Captain Khrabrov, inspired in part by the success of his nephew's *Eugene Onegin.*

V.L. Pushkin's verse was published in his lifetime (1822), and a more complete collection in 1893, including the work of his last years. A great deal of the complete oeuvre consists of insignificant "light verse" such as songs, madrigals and epigrams. He followed Dmitriev in writing a number of fables and "tales" ["skazki"] of no particular merit.[61] The most significant work of his best period is a group of "friendly epistles" discussing literary matters; since these largely concern the Arzamas-Beseda dispute, they will not be considered here. Of the work that remains two satires, "To My Hearth" (1793) and "An Evening" (1798), the "Epistle to I.I. Dmitriev" (1796) and the ribald narrative poem "A Dangerous Neighbor" (written in 1811, but not published until 1855) are the most significant.

In 1804, after his return from his trip abroad, V.L. Pushkin wrote, and read at the home of M.M. Kheraskov at a meeting of a private literary club, a short poem called "To the Favorites of the Muses," which he designates as "an imitation of Horace."[62] The imitation is not very close, but presumably concerns Odes I, ix *(Vides ut alta stet nive candidum).* The poem is programmatic and deserves quotation in full:

> The summits of the enormous mountains are white with snows; everywhere are mist and darkness, the rivers are covered with ice; dejected are the groves and vales. Where is the golden goblet? Let us sit before the fire. Let Zeus govern the universe as he pleases! He has spoken and created. Everything is subject to him; he plays with the thunder, the lightning.
> The storms, the tempest are obedient to Zeus alone. The favorite of the Muses is happy at all seasons of the year; he makes use of what he sees before him. Friends, for us Nature
> Even in her terrors gleams with beauty! Where is the lyre? Let us begin to sing. Phoebus unites us; the Virgil of the Russian lands [i.e., Kheraskov] by his presence breeds [in us] a fire for learning.
> He who lives with the Muses, joys are always with him! Long since have the Graces adorned you with crowns—you must sing, friends! Both Dmitriev and Karamzin with beautiful verses
> Captivate, instruct us—and I alone am silent! No, no! I too desire, like you, to thunder on the lyre: I fly toward glory, your spirit is afire in me, and I too shall be famous in the world!
> O joy, O rapture! I too—I too am a poet!

This naive utterance, with its gentle Epicureanism, its adulation of the "progressive" poets Kheraskov, Dmitriev and Karamzin, and its childlike delight in the thought of belonging to such a company, is characteristic of the man.

The "Epistle to I.I. Dmitriev,"[63] written in iambic "free verse," contains more of V.L. Pushkin's literary ideals and animosities. It is largely a mockery of the overworked themes and attitudes of the sentimentalists. We tend, of course, to think of Karamzin and Dmitriev as the twin coryphaei of the sentimentalist fashion, but to a contemporary it was their

503

second-rate imitators whose names are now hardly known that represented the movement, and so consequently Vasily Lvovich feels no inconsistency in addressing his satrical epistle on sentimentalism to Dmitriev himself! He begins, as though directly replying to a previous epistle of his "correspondent":

You're right, my dear friend! All our verse-makers want to win glory with a lachrymose lyre! Always their doves are flying to their pretty mates [cf. Dmitriev's own famous—and lachrymose!—song about the doves] ; always swallows are hovering, and it's always the same fancies; they all snivel and bawl, and all their thought is the same: now the moon is suddenly introduced, in pale yellow porphyry; now *he* [i.e., the poet] *has been left all alone in the world*—his dear one, his precious one is no more: she is buried 'neath a gray and mossy stone; and now under the branching oak-tree the owl begins to hoot dismally; a violent wind begins to howl, the lover flees, and a little tear drops on his [lyre-] strings. Then a host of exclamations—and dots make their appearance. There's no use of this. He imagines he's clever and has been brought into the world to be a poet; that he can be compared with Derzhavin, with you; that out of envy for him even our Sterne [i.e., Karamzin] gnaws his fingers. O, the wretched snivellers! To me their lot is pitiable! They do not realize at all that where eagles soar, there beetles do not fly.

Then the poet, who has obviously been demolishing imitators, admits that of itself imitation is permissible:

We can imitate without spoiling the style of others: thus Gessner imitated Bion [the Greek pastoral poet] ; thus, you, our amiable singer, by following in the footsteps of Anacreon, received a crown from the Graces. Thus our bard [i.e., Derzhavin] sings a eulogy to Felitsa [and] to God; thus dear, tender Karamzin has laid the way to the temple of taste; and thus, a zealous, loyal son of the fatherland, twanging on his resounding lyre for us, Kheraskov has sung of battle [i.e., in the *Rossiad*] , imitating Homer.

Abruptly personal comment interrupts the literary criticism, as Pushkin sighs that he has not the talent of such great masters; then he consoles himself that anyhow his whole soul is so devoted to "Temira" (possibly his wife?) that literary glory doesn't matter.

The satire "My Hearth" ["Kamin'"] of 1793[64] is V.L. Pushkin's earliest known verse; it was published anonymously and at one time falsely attributed to Dmitriev. In the tradition of eighteenth-century classical satire it introduces a series of unflattering, "typical" portraits under the usual conventional "speaking names." The young poet addresses his own beloved hearth, where he can be at ease and do as he pleases without meeting the despicable crowd who make up the *beau monde*. There is Glupomotov ("stupid spendthrift"), who squanders all his patrimony—but what do I care? There is Bezmosglov ("brainless"), who is arrogant. "But what is he? A stupid beast ["skot"] who, despising his native tongue, finding his bliss in satin dressing-gowns, arrays himself like a doll, and admires himself, fancying that he is captivating hearts with a French head." But let him be a fool—it's no concern of mine. "There are plenty of fools here, have been, and will be." For example, Prygushkin ("hopper"—i.e., "dancer"), who prides himself on his dancing ability, on his fashionable clothes, and the number of society people who come to call on him. But neighbor Pustiakov ("empty") is still worse—he imagines that he has the qualifications to be an ambassador! And Zmeiad ("snake-poison"), who has piled up an estate by chicanery, wants respectability. Nizkopoklonov ("low bow"), though a graybeard, thinks it a great honor to kiss Katya's hand, even though Katya's father polishes floors! "A poor man, though intelligent, is despised, persecuted; a Skotinin [cf. Fonvizin's *The Minor*], a perfect blockhead, is respected by all—and is betrothed to Liza." Liza, poor girl, for all her repugnance to such a marriage, is forced into it by an avaricious mother. Then the satirist moralizes: "We are given intelligence neither by famous family, nor luxury, nor rank, nor store-houses—intelligence can't be bought with millions! But gold, perhaps, gilds vices, and dear Liza's mother reasons exactly thus." Plutov ("rascal") abruptly interrupts the poet: "Hold on! Is it for you to judge how we ought to conduct ourselves and live in this world?" Plutov is a person of note and wealth, the poet poor and unknown; consequently even if Plutov got all his wealth by wrongdoing, he is right. The poet ends with his own determination, despite all, "to be honorable, respect the laws, serve my fatherland, love my friends, and love solitude—my heart's real delight!" It may be noted, incidentally, that the *persona* which Pushkin here assumes is the one that conventionally belonged to the satirist since at least Juvenal— he is poor, hates worldly ostentation, and loves the solitary life. None of these qualities belong to Pushkin the man.

"My Hearth" is conventional and traditional, a simple parade of obnoxious types, and is not greatly different in character from many other classical satires—e.g., those of Nikolev. On the other hand, "An Evening" ["Vecher"],[65] written five years later, has a character of its own and is a Hogarthian sketch of a modish supper party. The theme is set by the first words: "I've no more strength to bear it! Wherever you stick your nose, there are disputes and gossip and deceit and stupidity and discords!" The poet has just been to an evening party; he describes his hosts: "The master talks about nothing but music; the mistress plumes herself that their daughter dances famously; and the daughter, wearing her sash just under her neck, cries that a fashionable count has just driven up in a caleche." The count arrives, supposedly a suitor of Grushenka, whom he ignores however to make polite conversation with her mother, Vetrana ("veter," "wind"). Another guest arrives, Stukodei ("noise-maker"), "an insufferable talker," who knows all the latest gossip and airs his views on literature. "In his opinion, Nadutov ("inflated") captivates everybody, while Dmitriev.... Karamzin composes trifles; Derzhavin, for example, would write exceptionally, but he also, except for his odes, is worth no praise." An unnamed old man, standing beside

505

the poet, comments about the speaker that fools are often amusing, and "ridiculous censure is a writer's crown, a poet's praise." The hostess then approaches with an invitation to make a fourth at bridge ("boston"): "the orchestra blares, the count minces, Stukodei yells, and Zmeiada ("snake-poison"—a female here!) abuses everyone, and curses over the game." Dancing has begun, and the hostess remarks on how well Grushenka and the count do the waltz. To the poet's grief, a certain fat Beliza ("white") comes and sits beside him and begins to gossip about the family:

"So help me God," she says, "here's a wonderful family! The host spends all his time with the flute, his wife is exceedingly stupid and bores everybody. And as for Gru-shenka, believe me, she'll never be any good. But no matter for that: you're an intelli-gent man; you're at Skopidonov's house every day—you know all his tricks and every-thing about him. Isn't it true that he finds an enemy in his wife, and that she puts horns on him? Nakhalov["insolent"] is often with her at the theater and pleasure-garden; yesterday he danced two polonaises with her at the ball, and afterward saw her to her carriage. But unfortunate Skopidonov bought his own sorrow: God rewarded him with a beautiful wife! Yes, enough, the fool himself is the cause of all [her] pranks."

She goes on to cite Buianov ("brawler"), who at forty married a little flirt; she forthwith ran away with a Frenchman. The poet escapes at last from the gossip, listens to a conversation on the merits of a certain Lizeta's cutlets vs. her waffles, and finally gets to the supper table—only to find himself seated next to Vraliev ("vral' "—"nonsense" or "lies"). The old man prattles on about his hopeless son: "The youngster is already twenty, but he does nothing but read books; he doesn't look for rank, or want happiness." The father picked out a rich bride for the boy, but the ungrateful wretch refused, saying:

"I'm not going to marry for money at all; I'll take a wife when I've come to love her!" "How it will end with him I don't know—but I feel this, that he'll be a poor man, and nothing more. This is what your damned learning has done! He has no use for gold! If I could get my hands on Jean-Jacques [Rousseau]!" But the terrible infection of scorn for money, it seems, has spread even to the old—and Vraliev is off on the story of Prince Milov ("dear, pleasant"), fifty and more, with a marriageable only daughter—and the old fool is determined to let her marry a mere major whom she happens to love, who has only his officer's rank and an honorable name, but no money! Milov claims that since he is rich, his son-in-law doesn't have to be, "that being honorable is worth a hundred times more than being famous." "And that, my dear friend," concludes the old man in disgust, "is how they reason nowadays! And nowadays these are called men of sense!" The poet reassures his interlocutor: there aren't very many like Prince Milov, and the love of lucre doesn't appear to be in danger of dying out. The supper ends, the poet flees and returns full of relief to his own hearth, unafflicted with knaves and fashionable fools.

506

From the lively and humorous realism of "An Evening" it is no far step to V.L. Pushkin's notorious sketch "A Dangerous Neighbor."[66] This piece, which had a wide underground circulation and was well known and much appreciated among the poet's friends, could not, of course, be published in his lifetime in Russia because of its risqué subject. It is supposed to have been first issued in lithograph form in Munich in 1815, but no copies of this first edition are known to survive. It is a narrative poem, in perfectly conventional Alexandrine verse and quite neutral language of what purports to be a personal experience of the poet.

The scenario, in brief, is as follows. Speaking as though to an assembled group of friends, the narrator relates his experiences of the previous evening. A neighbor, Buianov ("Brawler") called on him to show off his new horses, and then described with relish a particularly handsome new girl at a local brothel, and suggested a visit there. The narrator, who describes himself as a pushover in such matters, agreed, and Buianov and he drove to the locale in question. This is described in some detail—the exterior, the madam, the girls and the patrons. Buianov appropriated the new sixteen-year-old beauty and began drinking with the other patrons, while another girl lured the narrator upstairs. Suddenly a terrific brawl began below—Buianov and one of the other patrons were in mortal combat, which presently involved everyone below stairs. The noise attracted the police, who broke in and began interrogating the disturbers of the peace. The narrator, terrified, fled by a back door, leaving behind his purse and his watch. Pursued by stray dogs and floundering through mud and darkness, he finally reached home, resolved never again to have any dealings with his "dangerous neighbor."

The effectiveness of the piece depends on the piquant juxtaposition of a "low" subject with a conventionally proper presentation. The language, although colloquial, is not vulgar—the word "whore" ["bliad' "] does occasionally appear, modestly indicated by its first and last letters—and to add to the effect, the conversation of the madam and the other denizens of her place of business turns on literary subjects! This, of course, gives Vasily Lvovich an opportunity for a particularly murderous hit at his literary opponents of the conservative *Beseda*. If this kind of treatment were carried to an extreme, we would have of course such a parody epic as *The Rape of the Lock* or Boileau's *Le Lutrin* or Maikov's *Elisei*. The charm of "A Dangerous Neighbor" is precisely that it is *not* carried to the point of a parody. The general effect is rather like Henry Fielding's use of pseudo-Homeric language to describe the battle in the churchyard between Molly Seagrim and a crowd of envious villagers (*Tom Jones,* Book IV, ch. viii).

A good deal of the poem's popularity was probably due when it was written to the topicality of the incidental literary polemics, which now have to be laboriously explained. Thus, in describing his and Buianov's drive to the brothel, the narrator has occasion to mention the team, which he calls a "two-some" ["dvoitsa"]—a neologism formed from the Russian "two" ["dva"] ; he then exclaims:

Deign, O Varangian-Russ, our gloomy singer, the Slavophil's god-father [Admiral Shish-kov, of course], to take this word as a model. Hitherto, tongue-tied and wallowing in our ignorance, in calling a "two-some" a "pair" ["para"—a French borrowing] in Russian, we have been writing so as to be understood. Well, to the devil with intelligence and taste! Just write, in good time!

This is of course aimed at the *Beseda* group's hostility to the use of foreign borrowings and their attempt to replace them with native Russian or Slavonic coinages.

At this point the equipage—whether a "pair" of a "two-some"—reaches its destination, which is thus described:

A little house, shaking like a reed in the wind, with a wicket-gate fastened with hooks presented itself to our view. *Khers* and *Pokois* were coupled on the walls [another hit at the Besedists: *kher* and *pokoi* are the Church Slavonic names of the letters called in modern Russian *kha (kh)* and *pe (p)*, here undoubtedly standing for the words *khui* and *pizda;* the collocation of the solemn ecclesiastical alphabetic names and these un-printable obscenities is particularly startling].

"Who's there?" a rude, hoarse voice inquired of us. "Open up briskly, or else—" yelled Buianov, "my fists are ready for the rascal's teeth!" And he kicked the door; all the hooks flew apart. Stooping our heads, we entered a sort of closet. What now? A parish deacon was playing pitch with a merchant. Punch, beer and tobacco stood on the table. The madam was sitting there, with a broad behind, pimples on her forehead, and all stinking of garlic and vodka, and with her the famous beauty. Sultan Selim, Voltaire and Frederick II in their frames hung meekly over a sofa. Two burly patrons were laughing, conversing, and lauding "The New Sterne" as a marvel. Genuine talent finds defenders everywhere! [This barbed thrust concerns an anti-Karamzinist comedy by A.A. Shakhovskoy]. And here's a lackey serving coffee; there stands the noseless cook in a padded jacket; chamber-pot, samovar and cups on a little bench. "Here I am," announced bully-boy Buianov. Everybody shuddered—the deacon, the madam and the merchant—but they all, standing up, gave us a polite bow. "Don't anyone move," continued my imperious Neighbor. "Don't anyone move! All are equal in a bordello with the whores! We haven't come to offend any of the honorable people here. Pankratievna [the madam], sit down; give me a kiss, Variushka [the beauty]. Let's have some punch; drink, deacon." And the drinking party began.

The cause of the battle royal which presently ensues is recounted in a solemn, moralistic fashion:

Here is what was the cause of this dreadful combat. The deacon, the merchant and Neighbor were drinking punch over their game, wanting to display their knowledge of the world. Variushka was trying to pour for all the guests; nothing disturbed the decorum. But Bacchus has proved more than once to be the beginning of calamity. That foe of innocent diversions, that lover of malicious tricks, Satan, does not sleep on such occasions. The merchant felt a hankering for Variushka (and a whore, there's no disputing it, is common property). In sitting down beside Aspasia [the madam], he gave the deacon a shove. Scowling, the deacon shoved Buianov. Buianov, impatient of this greeting, let the deacon have it in the face, without a word; the deacon, summoning his courage, hit the merchant in the nose; the merchant seized from the table a bottle and tray, hurled them at his friends—and Satan was delighted! In this vale of tears, alas, mourning is always close to laughter! On swift pinions joy flies away, and sorrow is there—and how!

The solemn and quasi-epic tone of the narration is intensified in the narrator's account of his escape:

> Of shaggy Cerberi the most horrendous band,
> The spawn of hell at once arise before my face
> And bark and howl resound of hungry hounds in chase.
> Needs must my great-coat go, a sop for them to tear.
> Wet snow and piercing wind! O woe without compare!
> In anguish, in despair, and rain-soaked to the bone,
> As midnight tolled, at last, wounded and woe-begone,
> I dragged myself, my friends, to my poor cottage door.

The naturalism of "A Dangerous Neighbor" is somewhat surprising, so early in the nineteenth century, but it must be remembered that it is, in V.L. Pushkin's work, an isolated instance, and adopted for a very specific purpose, just as is the naturalism of parts of Radishchev's *Journey from St. Petersburg to Moscow*. Furthermore, of course, as a work of an unpublishable nature it is exempted from the canons that would otherwise apply. It belongs, however, to the eighteenth-century system of genres just as much as does the lachrymose elegiac pose that Vasily Lvovich ridicules. It is still a very long way from the genuine realism of the nineteenth century, of which A.S. Pushkin's *Eugene Onegin* is the first important example.

CHAPTER XVI

THE SENTIMENTALIST SCHOOL IN VERSE

A. Ivan Ivanovich Dmitriev and the Genres of Fable and Tale

Literary reputations have a way of quite suddenly evaporating with the passage of time, and a reader of a later age may wonder in utter perplexity what was seen in the work of a once famous poet to make him famous. Such is the case with Ivan Ivanovich Dmitriev (1760-1837),[1] whose renown as a poet completely eclipsed that of his friend Nikolai Karamzin, and indeed rivalled that of Derzhavin himself. To a twentieth-century reader his satires, especially "Other Folks' Chatter," and his verse tales, such as "The Fashionable Wife" still offer considerable interest; but his "Fables" which some nineteenth century critics seriously considered superior to those of Krylov, appear dull and tedious, and his songs, once so highly regarded as models of lightness and elegance, seem to our age cold and vapid, not to be compared with those of Neledinsky-Meletsky.

Dmitriev's career as a writer had a rather slow start. Educated in a rather desultory way, partly at home, he was enrolled by his father at fourteen in the Semenovsky Guards regiment. Here he remained for twenty-two years, in a service that he thoroughly disliked, rising slowly from rank to rank until his retirement as a colonel. With the accession of Emperor Paul he transferred to the civil service, becoming in 1797 Ober-Procuror of the Senate— a very high and responsible rank. After an interval (1799-1806) of retirement he reentered the Civil Service under Alexander I and was made a member of that monarch's State Council and Minister of Justice. His final retirement from service occurred in 1814, after which he left the capital for Moscow, where he resided until his death.

During the long years of his military service Dmitriev, by assiduous reading, gradually overcame the deficiencies of his early education, and through association with Nikolai Novikov and others turned his thoughts toward a literary career. In 1783 he became associated with young Nikolai Karamzin, six years his junior, who had already composed some verse. The two young men, both from the Simbirsk area, found a good deal in common, but Karamzin after a year in military service in St. Petersburg, resigned and retired first to the estate of his recently deceased father, and then to Moscow,

510

where he too became an intimate of Novikov. Dmitriev and Karamzin did not meet again until 1789, at the end of Karamzin's eighteen-month European pilgrimage (recounted in his *Letters of a Russian Traveler*), at which time the younger man had formed the project of founding a literary journal. The project was carried out by the issuance in 1791 of the first number of the *Moscow Journal*, to which Dmitriev became a constant contributor. By this time Dmitriev had published a number of poems in the journal *Morning Hours*, and had made the acquaintance of Russia's foremost poet of the day, Gavriil Derzhavin. When Karamzin in 1794 published the collection *Aglaia*, and in 1797-99 the annual "almanac" *Aonides*, both he and Dmitriev were extensively represented. In 1794 Karamzin's first volume of verse appeared under the rather affected title *My Trifles*. Not to be outdone, Dmitriev issued in the following year (1795) his collection *My Trifles, Too (I moi bezdelki)*. Six editions of Dmitriev's verse, counting this first, appeared during the poet's lifetime, from 1795 to 1823.

Dmitriev's first great literary idol, according to his own account, was Abbé Prevost, whose six-volume novel *Mémoires et aventures d'un homme de qualité* was his first independent reading in French. This is an early example of the psychological novel with a distinctly "sentimental" tone. A later French writer of considerable influence on Dmitriev is Louis-Sébastien Mercier (1740-1815), a writer of sentimental bourgeois dramas. Although Dmitriev did not himself seriously attempt drama, his verse is marked throughout by the sentimental stamp. In this, as in much else, he and his friend Karamzin were entirely in accord.

Of the pieces classified by the poet himself as "lyric verses," there are a few of some formal interest, such as "To the Volga,"[2] a nine-strophe poem in the classical ode form, but of content completely outside the pale of the classical ode. We have seen in Kapnist's work similar cases; they typify the break-down at the end of the century of the entire genre system of classicism. Dmitriev's "To the Volga" resembles a travelogue more than an ode. In two imitations of Horace he experiments with, first an entirely novel strophic form with which to reproduce Horace's Alcaics; and second, with a rendering in iambic "free verse" without strophic division (for Horace *Carmina* I, iii).[3] Neither piece is comparable to the Horatian versions of Muraviev and Kapnist. A much later "Imitation of Horace" (1810)[4] is absurdly labeled "from Ode vii of Book XIII"! Whether this is Dmitriev's attempt at a joke is uncertain; the poem is a paraphrase of *Carmina* II, xvi.

The classical ode, with its pomposity and straining for effect, lent itself very readily to parody, and we have seen how even Sumarokov indulged in writing "nonsense odes." Among Dmitriev's 1792 pieces is a "Hymn to Rapture,"[5] which is in its way a good parody of the ode style, although its form has nothing in common with that of the ode, being both monostrophic and only twenty-four lines long. It is worth quoting entire:

511

Rapture [Lomonosov's "vostorg"], rapture of the poet's soul! Thou rushest on daring pinions over all the bounds of his world! Through thee he is now on the waves, and blows up mountains of foam; through thee he has soared in a moment to Aurora's palace, like a swift fly—and in a moment he falls headlong into the dale, where there are no flowers save the lily ["krinu"—a reference, of course, to the hackneyed "Ekaterinu-krinu" rhyme of the ode-writers], wherein the Ganges flows together with the Neva. And at that same moment—I tremble and thrill!—betwixt ether and earth, from the crests of the Caucasus, the mountains of ice, to which the eye cannot reach, through the frozen clouds he prophesies—like the maw of Aetna, he neighs, he belches! The voice is no longer a mortal's, every word there is enormous ["golemo"—an obsolete Slavonic word], inscrutable, thunderous, novel—Pegasus himself is spraying him! The lyre's strings are heard no longer, but only blazing thunder-bolts, tempest, tumult, roaring, whistling, glitter, crashing, thunder, ringing ["vikhr', shum, rev, svist, blesk, tresk, grom, zvon"—a nonsense line made up of nothing but monosyllables!] and slumber [or dream] covers all [men] with its wings!

That he was aware of the absurdities of the classical ode did not, however, prevent Dmitriev from writing some himself. His poem "The Death of Prince Potemkin" (1791),[6] although not so titled, is a perfectly regular ode, somewhat shorter than most such effusions (it has only nine strophes) but not otherwise unusual. There are three other pieces, each titled "Verses on—," which are also regular odes, and among the worst of their kind: "Verses on the Joyous Birthday of Her Imperial Highness" (1795),[7] a most repulsive example of the congratulatory ode, replete with every variety of bad taste; "Verses on the Annexation of the Polish Province of Courland and Semigalia to the Russian Empire" (1795),[8] a servile glorification of the infamous Third Partition of Poland; and "Verse to His Imperial Highness Paul I on His Ascension of the Throne of All the Russias" (1796).[9] An extract from this murky monstrosity, full of Slavonicisms, sounds as much like a parody as the "Ode to Rapture":

Russia blooms like a garden ["vertogradom"], is radiant with the light of gladness! Village ["ves' "] vies with village, city ["grad"] with city in their plenty, in their primacy. All, all the treasures of nature that are within the earth, that the waters cover, I see risen up before Paul! And the mountains exhale gold, and the oceans spew forth Leviathans in tribute to the Tsar!

Dmitriev, it seems, was not comfortable with the ode, and did very badly with it. He never mastered Derzhavin's unique system of coupling the high style lightly with the low. His unpretentious "songs," however, are far better, and in some cases come close to those of his contemporary. Neledinsky-Meletsky. Certainly not much can be said for the most famous of these, the saccharine little ditty that begins: "The little gray dove is moaning" ["stonet sizyi golubochek"], with its pseudo-popular diminutives, which used to elicit the copious tears of sentimental maidens by its affecting picture of the death of the heart-broken bird: "He lays him down on the grass ["travke"]; he has tucked his little bill ["nosik"] in his feathers; he moans no more, sighs no more; the dove.... has fallen asleep forever."[10] Better is the three-stanza "peasant woman's song,"[11] which Dmitriev assures his readers in a note is "an exact imitation of an old song of the common folk":

Ah! If I had known before that love gives birth to woe, I would not with gay heart have met the midnight star! I would not have cast, unknown to all, a golden ring! I would not have looked in sweet hope upon the beloved flatterer!

For the warding off of the blow in my cruel, malevolent fate, I would have cast for myself light little wings of the heated wax, and taken wing to the birth-land of my beloved; tenderly, tenderly I would have looked at him, if but once only.

And then I would have flown away with tears and longing; brooding, head in hand, I would have sat down by the highroad; I would have sobbed, I would have wailed: "Good people! How can I live? I loved an unfaithful one..... Teach me not to love."

The vogue of "light verse" at the end of the century is closely associated with the popularity of "Anacreon," that is, of the Alexandrian and Byzantine Greek songs believed at that time to be the genuine works of the poet of Teos. How Kheraskov perverted the Anacreontic meter and form by making them the vehicle for didactic moralizing we have seen. A less violent but still quite considerable distortion of the genre appears in Dmitriev's "Stanzas to N.M. Karamzin" (1794).[12] Here the regular Anacreontic meter is employed as the medium for an elegy. The poem begins with two conventionally "Anacreontic" strophes: "Begone from me, Cato, Seneca, begone, gloomy Epictetus! Without joys, the world would be empty, unbearable for man. Youth doesn't come twice. Happy is he who, while young, strews his path with flowers, without a foresight of stormy days." These are then followed by the poet's remark that thus he used "to tune his lyre" in the days of his heedless youth; but now, as he listens to the mournful nightingale, he feels only despondency: "The morning of my days has become darkened, and will not bloom again; my heart has said farewell to happiness, and the dream of springtime years." The poet appears to be in exile, and speaks wistfully of once more casting his "filial gaze" on the Volga, and of reclining under the shade of the trees of his home. The poem ends: "There was a time when we played here under the thick shade. You [trees] are blooming.... we have faded! Give repose to old age."

Closer to the spirit of Anacreontic verse, although not in the traditional form, is a rousing drinking-song of 1795, which begins:[13] "Friends! Time is swiftly-moving, and you don't see how it flies! We shall not be young forever—old age will be on us in a moment. What's to do? Very well, we'll drink while waiting." The usual Epicurean "moral" is drawn—"the best means of living in friendly fashion is: talk less nonsense, and drink more." It is the melancholy autumn—what can we do to lighten our gloom? "Drink more often punch and brandy." "O brandy, wondrous brandy! You have restored the spring to us; you have warmed us, like lovely May, covered our cheeks with roses—in what way can we do you honor? By drinking twice, three times as much!"

Another song of 1795 begins "Having tuned my languid ["tomnu"] lyre—."[14] This can be profitably compared with Neledinsky-Meletsky's "My love was sitting yesterday—" ["Milaia vchera sidela"] ;[15] where the Neledsinky-Meletsky piece is artless and naive in its impatience with nightingale and rustling trees that interfere with the poet's enjoyment of his beloved's song, Dmitriev's relies for whatever point it has on the conventional mythological picture of the love-god with his enamoring arrows:

Having tuned my languid lyre I was singing a song, and delighting with my playing hand my beloved Elvira.

She was looking at me with a tender smile. The lovely one's angelic look! I was confused at heart.

Then she struck up a song—even the nightingale fell silent! My soul burned with passionate love for her.

Hiding beneath a little bush Love, sporting, made a noise; approaching us silently, he was minded to loose an arrow.

"In vain, god of the universe, are you minded to pierce my breast,"—said I, enchanted. "In vain you are minded to tear my heart!

It is subject to my beloved, subject to her alone; it burns for Elvira: it is not in your dominion."

Just as Dmitriev saw the ridiculous side of the classical ode and composed parodies, even while continuing to write odes seriously, so he did also with the sentimental song. His 1796 piece beginning with the delightful line: "I would be a pug-dog" is contemporary with his best serious songs:[16]

I would be a pug-dog, so as to snore forever; no matter if I should take to barking, and sing no longer.

In one warm dress-coat I would go the year around, and I would pay off the great Dane with contempt for his barking.

I would see no denial from an English puppy at receptions by Clymene, when I visited her house.

I would lick her little hands always on a par with him [i.e., the puppy], and all little bitches would be equally lovable to me.

If a pug-bitch should be unfaithful, I would attach myself to a toy poodle; I wouldn't waste ink or write elegies.

But to turn myself into a pug-dog is impossible for me forever, so why flatter myself to no purpose? Let me stay on being a man.

Although the elegy as a genre was recognized by the classical legislators (we have seen it employed by Sumarokov and by Rzhevsky, among others), it is more characteristic of the romantic poets of the nineteenth century, and of their sentimentalist predecessors. Dmitriev's 1803 elegy "Grief"[17] ["grust' "] sounds less artificial than most, and may well be genuinely personal:

Led on by despondency ["unyniem"—a typical sentimentalist and pre-romantic word, a favorite of Zhukovsky] of heart, I shall go with my lyre to those places where Nature bestows eternal slumber, where sleep both sorrow and vanity.

There over the dust of virtuous Elvira I shall shed tears, and with the quiet sound of my languid ["tomnoi"] lyre I shall sing to the unspeaking shades:

"Eternal peace be yours! Taste the sweetness of repose in a haven free from woe; now for you both grief and sadness are nothing any longer; for you they exist no more!

No longer terrible for you are the blows, the inflictions of the wicked; neither their secret snares are perilous, nor their open persecution.

No longer can anyone with dishonorable judgment poison your soul, make the pure, the righteous, guilty, and plunge a sharp sword in your heart.

No! The heart beats in you no longer, it is quiet for all time; it is no longer responsive even to the best-loved voice.

O sensitive one ["chuvstvitel'nyi"]! Taste comfort, having accomplished the course of stormy days; do not fear the sweet poison of bewitching eyes;

Fear no more contempt and cutting reproaches as a reward for your meekness, for the simplicity of a gentle heart.

Ah! Shall it be long for hapless me, a wanderer here, to drag out my journey? When shall I have passed the terrible plain? It is time, it is time to rest at last!"

When we pass from what may be lumped together as the subjective lyrical varieties--ode, song, elegy, etc.—and come to the objective kinds, we find ourselves more unmistakably in the classicist's realm. But even here there are differences, as we shall note especially in the fable. One of the quite unclassifiable pieces from this area is the semi-dramatic poem "Ermak" (1794),[18] one of Dmitriev's most frequently anthologized pieces. It is composed in iambic tetrameter, and consists, between the poet's own utterances at beginning and end, of a dialogue imagined between two Siberian shamans, an elder and a younger. The two are pictured as sitting beside the banks of the Irtysh and mourning antiphonally the defeat of their khan Kuchum and his forces at the hands of the Russian Cossack Ermak (A.D. 1581). The elder shaman prophesies the ultimate subjection of all Siberia to Ermak's compatriots, and tells of a voice he has heard from heaven, proclaiming: "Siberia, who hast rejected my law! Remain forever, groaning, weeping, the bondslave of a white tsar!" The elder shaman ends his prophecy with the words "Woe to us!" which his younger colleague echoes as the two rise and disappear in the mist. The poet then addresses the shade of the hero Ermak, for whom he in turn prophesies an eternal fame: "The radiance of your glory shall be eclipsed when the light of the sun is darkened, when the heavens fall in ruins with a crash, and time falls to the scythe!" The poem's gloomy atmosphere, and especially the description of the wild and savage landscape where the colloquy of the two shamans takes place are evidences of the Ossianic influence, much as these may be seen in Derzhavin's nearly contemporary "Waterfall."

By the beginning of the nineteenth century the "ballad," popularized by German pre-romantics, had become established in Russia. We have seen some examples among the late verses of Muraviev, and we shall presently note

Karamzin's "Raisa" (1791) as the supposedly first published Russian example. Dmitriev has one fairly late poem (1805) entitled "Old-Time Love."[19] Its quite conventional theme coincides with that of Zhukovsky's "Castle of Smalholm," though Dmitriev's setting purports to be medieval Russian. The beautiful daughter of a "great chieftain" in "white-stone Moscow" falls in love with a singer, is imprisoned by her outraged father, and dies of grief when she sees the body of her murdered lover. Breaking the tradition of a proper ballad, the poet introduces a good deal of subjective comment in introducing his subject, instead of letting the story speak for itself.

The fable is one of the most ancient of literary types: East Indian collections exist, and in Greece the "Fables of Aesop," a Phrygian slave of the sixth century B.C., to whom legend attributed a collection of prose *mythoi,* served as the origin for subsequent literary versions—the Latin verses of Phaedrus, of the first century B.C., and the Greek choliambics of Babrius, of the second century A.D. The medieval beast fable, e.g., the stories about "Reynard the Fox," contributed its part to the growth of the genre, which first acquired "classical" status in the hands of the great French master, Jean de la Fontaine. Fontaine's *Fables* are the model acknowledged and imitated by all Russian fabulists of the eighteenth century from Sumarokov to Krylov.

The characteristics of the fable as a classical genre are readily defined: brevity, simplicity, and didacticism. From the servile status associated with the genre's founder Aesop, the literary type in its beginnings is assigned to the "low" style—that is, words and expressions of the ordinary vernacular language, especially proverbs, are admissible in it, indeed almost obligatory. Sumarokov, the first Russian poet to publish a collection of fables, employed in it a far more colloquial style than, for example, in his comedies.

A word of explanation about the Russian names for the genre is required. The word *pritcha* is the oldest term: it is a Biblical word, serving to designate both the book which we call the "Proverbs of Solomon" in the Old Testament, and the "parables" of Jesus in theNew. What these quite different kinds of composition have in common is a strongly didactic purpose and a more or less popular tone. The Aesopic fables translated into Russian in the seventeenth century and Sumarokov's collection of literary verse versions of the eighteenth are both entitled *pritchi:* the designation marks them first and foremost as moral and edifying short narratives, in allegorical form. The word *basnia* more specifically denotes a story in which beasts play human parts; it has a slightly more derogatory tone and implies nothing of a moral nature. *Basnia* is the term used for their collections by Khemnitser and Dmitriev. The Greek "apologue" (Russian "apolog") sometimes rather loosely applied to any form of fable, properly denotes a very brief and epigrammatic form, in which neither narrative nor characterization has place, but merely a brief statement of situation and a moral: Dmitriev published a collection of apo-

516

logues in quatrains.[20]

From its inception the fable was essentially a didactic genre. The teaching, however, was not necessarily or originally ethical, but rather what might be termed "worldly wisdom." The narrative would serve to illustrate a supposedly normal and constant feature of human nature and conduct—and this feature would be underlined by an explicit and unmistakable statement, placed either at the beginning of the fable, or, more emphatically, at its end, following the illustrative narrative. This "moral" was the essential and indispensable portion—the "narration" illustrating it might be reduced, as in the apologue, to the very barest skeleton; neither narrative nor moral in the earliest history of the type admitted much elaboration or ornamentation; the moral, however, always tended to be given with a certain epigrammatic concision.

Sumarokov's *Fables* are strictly and uniquely classical—brief, unadorned, in a deliberately "low" and common language, and always didactic in purpose. Many of them are on themes from the traditional Aesopic collection, or from La Fontaine's *Fables;* some are of Sumarokov's own invention. As with Aesop, the personnel of Sumarokov's *Fables* are not always animals—human beings play their part as well.

Many other Russian writers between Sumarokov and Dmitriev produced fables (e.g., Kheraskov and Maikov), but only Khemnitser achieved much renown and made any essential changes in the type. As we have seen, Khemnitser's language, with rare exceptions, is elegant and upper-class Russian—more or less identical with Lomonosov's "middle" rather than his "low" style. Khemnitser's models are very frequently the German verses of Gellert—and, as we have noted, Gellert's collection bears the designation *Fables and Tales.* La Fontaine, too, had composed "tales ("contes"), but these were not combined with his fables in the same book, and are entirely independent creations, most emphatically non-didactic. Most of them are mere amusing anecdotes, many derived from Boccaccio's *Decameron.* Khemnitser, following Gellert, entitled his collection *Fables and Tales,* and many of the pieces contained in it belong to the latter category—that is, they are devoid of moral instruction, the emphasis is entirely on the narrative, which becomes quite extended, and the place of the "moral" is taken by a "punch line"; thus, the poem entitled "The Dying Father" (see above, p. 432). This is a mere narrative of how a father at the point of death left all his property to his intelligent son, disinheriting the fool altogether. The "punch line," spoken by the father when the intelligent son pleads for his stupid brother, is : "Don't be concerned about him: a fool will always get along in this world." There is obviously no "moral" in this, and the poem is a "tale" rather than a "fable." The combination of the two genres in the same collection, however, leads inevitably to ambiguity and confusion, and with some of the pieces the distinction is not easy to make. Khemnitser's practice with both types is to give greater prominence to the narrative and less to the "moral" or its equivalent than classical precedent sanctioned.

The final step in this direction was taken by Dmitriev. The fable by its nature as a genre primarily directed toward inculcating a lesson, whether of a strictly moral nature (as usually with Kheraskov) or of mere worldly wisdom, was always in its earlier examples satirical in its approach—that is, the narration tended to expose the follies or inequities of man's existence, either directly or in the traditional allegorical form of the "beast fable." Thus, for example, Khemnitser's fable of "The Dancing Bear" exposes in allegorical form the natural human tendency to feel impatience and irritation with anyone who shows an attainment superior to one's own. This satirical element in the fable is linked with its status as a "low" genre. But Khemnitser raised the fable from its "low" position in the stylistic hierarchy and approximated it to the "middle style." With Dmitriev, whose collection *Fables and Tales*[21] (*Basni i Skazki*) was published in 1798, the style is raised still further. According to the well-known critique of Merzliakov, "Sumarokov found [fables] among the simple, low folk; Khemnitser brought them into the city; Dmitriev opened the door for them into enlightened, cultivated societies, distinguished by taste and language."[22]

Khemnitser had also lessened to a great extent the traditional didacticism of the genre. Many of his fables are quite devoid of a "moral," while in some cases the place of a "moral" is taken by a wry personal comment, not intended to be universally applicable, as the moral of earlier fables had always implicitly been. Here too Dmitriev carried to its final point a trend that his predecessors had initiated. Dmitriev's fables are almost entirely non-didactic. Instead of the traditional moral he often appends, or intrudes into his narrative, a personal lyric note, more appropriate, perhaps, to the elegy; an example is the early fable (1792): "The Bee, the Bumble-bee and I,"[23] where the subjective comment even enters the title:

The Bumble-Bee, rummaging in the dung, remarked about the clever Bee, which had lighted far away on a rose: "Why is she so much praised, in such honor and so fashionable with all? I too puff and pant and pour my sweat, and also give people honey; but for all that I am as it were a zero in nature, known to none hitherto." "Mine is the same sort of fate, Bumble-Bee," said I to him, sighing. "It's ten years since a malign fate inflicted me with a passion for verse. I, following after the best singers, keep writing, writing, toiling, sweating, and setting down rhymes precisely. But all the same I'm not rich in readers, and I find no path to glory."

In the fable "The Two Doves," imitated from La Fontaine's "Les deux pigeons,"[24] the "moral" at the end is the following:

Love, believe me, will replace everything for you. I myself have been in love; then I would not have exchanged marble palaces or kingdoms in the sky or the solitary meadow that my darling's presence brightened!.... Will you return again, moments of gladness, moments of ecstasy? Or shall I live by remembrance alone? Has the time of such dear enchantments gone by, and have I had my all of loving?

The fable consists essentially of three elements: the narrative, the characterization, and the moral. Of these, as has been noted above, the moral is the *raison d'être* of the genre When thi is lost or devalued, the purpose of the genre disappears, and it becomes simply another variety of narrative poem, marked only by the allegorical element (the animal disguise, where this still subsists). The fact that collections, such as those of Gellert and Khemnitser, lumped together "fables and tales" made it easier for the two types to merge. Shorn of its moral, the fable developed the narrative, which often reached a length approximating that of the tale, and the poet expended a great deal of his ingenuity in presenting the "characters" of his narrative—human or animal—in psychologially plausible portraits. Taken together with the trend, from Khemnitser on, for the fabulist to drop the traditional "low style" of the genre in favor of the colorless "middle style," and it is evident that the fable as a distinctive literary type has had its day and is on the way to disappearance.

The effect of Dmitriev's changes in the fable may be appreciated from his imitation of La Fontaine's *Le chêne et le roseau* (*Dub i trost'*: 1795):[25]

An Oak once entered into conversation with a Reed: "I pity," said the Oak, bending his dignified gaze upon her [i.e., the reed], "little Reed, I pity your lot! I suppose, for you a sparrow is a burden. The lightest breeze, that scarce ruffles the water, is as terrible for you as the storm in bad weather, and it bends you to the ground, while I am tall and spreading, and not only cut off Phoebus's rays to a great distance, but even despise the tempest and the thunder. I stand and listen tranquilly to the cracking and groaning around me. Everything for me is a zephyr, everything for you is a northern gale. Happy would you be if you had grown up with me; beneath my thick shade you would not fear the storms. But Destiny decreed for you to grow, instead of upon the grain-rich plain, upon the swampy banks of Aeolus's empire. I' faith, your lot has inspired even me with sorrow." "You are very sympathetic," replied the Reed to the Oak. "But, in truth, I have never sighed about myself—indeed, there is nothing to sigh over. The winds are less dangerous for me than for you. Though their terrible blasts have not hitherto been able to shake you, yet let us await the end." With this word a storm of a sudden began to blow from the north, and the sky was darkened; a terrible wind struck; it destroys and sweeps away, the foliage flies and whirls. The Reed bends, the Oak stands. The wind, redoubling its efforts, struck with all its might—and he, t whose top the eye could hardly see, who almost reached to heaven and to hell—fell!

The poem is a very close imitation, almost a translation, of the French original; neither provides an explicit moral; in both cases the principal emphasis is on characterization—the condescending benevolence of the magnate (the Oak) and the sturdy independence of the commoner (the Reed). Dmitriev achieves a more epigrammatic effect in his conclusion than does La Fontaine, with the abrupt and startling single-word line: "Kto ada i nebes edva ne dostigal—Upal!"

Dmitriev's fables enjoyed a most enviable reputation in his own time, chiefly, it seems, because of his elegant style, so different from the deliberately coarse and "common" tone of Sumarokov. It was this style which led

Prince Peter Vyazemsky to declare Dmitriev's fables superior to those of Krylov—[26] a verdict totally incomprehensible to a modern reader, to whom they seem rather light and flimsy, vapid pieces, devoid of either satire or local color. They are, to be sure, sometimes short and simple enough to be almost epigrammatic, and hence effective. Such is "The Traveler" (1803):[27]

A traveler, finding a monastery on his way, asked the brothers for permission to go up into their bell-tower. He climbed and began to praise the various sights which the height revealed to him. "What enchanting places!" he exclaimed. "Around me I see mountains, forests, lakes and valleys! Is it not so?" he asked one of the brothers who stood with him. "Yes," the man of toil, sighing, answered him, "for a traveler."

One may note here, incidentally that belfries are not a feature of Russian monasteries, nor mountains of the Russian landscape.

The fable "Father and Son" (1805)[28] is a lively dialogue, with an epigrammatic point:

"Tell me, daddy, how to attain happiness," a son asked his father. The latter said to him: "There's no better road than to toil with body and mind, serving father-land, your fellow-citizens, and to be most often with pen and book, if we want to be good for something." "Oh, that's hard! Isn't there an easier way?" "By intrigue, to worm one's way like a toad or a snake toward one who will rise through Fortune at court...." "But that's low!" "Well, then, simply—be a fool. That's how many succeed!"

Although beast-fables of the traditional Aesopic kind constitute a substantial portion of Dmitriev's work in this genre, they are the least original and the least interesting. Many of his fables are translations or reworkings, usually from the French. One quite impressive example is "The Book of Reason" (1803),[29] from a minor French fabulist named Auber:

At the beginning of the world, when the council of the gods, without demanding either lambs or flowers [i.e., as sacrifices], forestalled the desires of all creatures—at that time, as report has come down to us in tradition, Jupiter at a merciful hour gave man a book, which could take the place of a library. Its title: "Reason"; and it had been composed by Minerva herself, with the end that in it all ages might recognize the road to virtue and become happier. However, in this heavenly gift little profit was found on earth. In reading the work childhood saw only the pictures in it, youth only errors, maturity, belated regret; and old age—tore up the pages.

The modifications which Dmitriev, following Khemnitser, had introduced into the fable, and principally the elimination of the didactic purpose of the genre, disturbed the literary conservatives. Dmitriev's position as one of the chief followers of Karamzin and foes of the classical system of rigid genres enhanced the indignation aroused by his cavalier abandonment of what had been traditionally the principal identifying mark of the fable—its "moral." The chief spokesman for the traditional point of view was Count Dmitry Ivanovich Khvostov (1757-1835). Khvostov was a quite prolific writer of what the Karamzinist group of literati ridiculed as extremely bad verse. Actually, the bulk of his verse is neither better nor worse than that of many of his contemporaries. His *Select Fables* (*Izbrannye pritchi:* 1802), however, contain some particularly grotesque absurdities which his adversaries made the most of. Thus, for example, the adventurous pigeon, in the first version of his fable "The Two Pigeons,"[30] subsequently modified, escapes from the net he has fallen into in a fashion quite surprising for a pigeon: "Somehow he gnawed through the cords with his teeth and gained his freedom." The shelter-seeking ass, in "The Ass and the Rowantree"[31] tries to climb into the tree like the birds, "and firmly grasps the tree with his paws ["lapami"]." Khvostov, however, quite simply had no concern about the details of natural history; his interest centered entirely on the moral implications of his fables. When the Arzamas crowd made fun of his ass with paws and pigeon with teeth he replied indignantly:[32] "It is possible to know natural history, to be a Buffon, and still offend against natural morality." In his verse epistle "About Parables" (i.e., "Fables"),[33] he writes: "See to it that from the parable a lesson to us emerges," and again, "Admonition is your prime business." In his 1819 essay: "Some Thoughts on the Nature of the Fable" he adverts to another of Dmitriev's innovations—detailed characterization of the persons of his fables. For Khvostov one of the principal merits of the genre is that the animals always represent the same qualities *and no others:* "unlimited extension of the rights of the allegorical genre may destroy it completely." The wolf in fable is "the powerful and wicked man." To elaborate the wolf's character by making him cunning or stupid is to nullify the moral lesson, fable's only purpose.[33]

Khvostov's fable "The Crow and the Cheese" ("Vorona i syr")[34] is a typical example of his own style as a fabulist; his notes declare that he took it from "Aesop, Phaedrus and La Fontaine." The subject is that of the French fabulist's *Le Corbeau et le renard,* but the simplicity of Khvostov's treatment belongs entirely to Aesop:

Once after a banquet a crow was carrying away a small piece of cheese. With her booty in her lips ["gubakh"—another of Khvostov's anatomical boners!] she settled without delay upon a walnut-tree bough.

A fox hurried to the cheese, and as usual, began to sing her flattery (it was impossible to take the cheese by force): "I presume your voice is charming and tender and lofty." The stupid crow in her joy dreamed that she had become a Catalani [a famous Italian soprano], and opened her maw ["past' "]—out fell the cheese, which seizing, the sly fox said forthwith: "Never believe praise, sister. The world praises the crow when she happens to have some cheese."

Needless to say, both the "lips" and the "maw" of the crow aroused the mirth of the Arzamas crowd. Apropos of the latter Khvostov in his notes remarks:[35] "I say 'opened her maw.' What though the student of natural history may say that a crow has a mouth or a bill [while] 'maw' is used only with animals. But I mean here in a transferred sense, a 'wide mouth,' and am picturing an incapacity for beautiful song. The common folk say of a person: 'See now, he's opened his maw!' "

There is no need at this point to pursue further the history of the fable as a genre, or the fortunes of the conservative and progressive literary circles represented by Khvostov and Dmitriev. The final resolution of the problem belongs to the nineteenth century, with A.E. Izmailov and Ivan Krylov as the chief figures. Suffice it to say that as with all attempts to turn history backwards, the effort to maintain the fable as a didactic vehicle failed, and the genre itself, having no further reason for existence, disappeared after the middle of the nineteenth century.

Among Dmitriev's *My Trifles, Too,* the most trifling are surely his numerous "apologues, inscriptions and epigrams."[36] Much admired in his day, they seem to a modern reader merely tedious and silly, when not wholly incomprehensible through our ignorance of the circumstances that generated them. His best epigram, entitled "Inscription for a Portrait of Mr.—"[37] is also the shortest and most pointed; it is in full, in Russian and English:

И это человек?	And this is a man?
О времени! О век!	Oh the times! Oh the age!

The verse "tale" ["skazka"] was, as we have seen, almost a Siamese twin of the fable.[38] The Russian term translates the French *conte* and the German *Erzählung,* and, like its European model, is a very ill-defined concept. As Izmailov commented, "there are more excellent examples of the genre than there are adequate definitions of it." For some theorists the distinction from the fable lies in the nature of the actors: the fable is allegorical, its "persons" being animals, birds, fish, flowers, trees, etc., while the "tale" introduces only human beings, gods or the like. This, however, would exclude from the fable such Aesopic examples as "Death and the Peasant." Other definitions of the "tale" stress the every-day, realistic character of the scene—but this again would exclude such a "tale" as Dmitriev's "Notional Girl" ["Prichudnitsa"],[39] in which a fairy godmother transplants the heroine into a land of magical riches and beauty. Certainly one of the most distinctive features of the "tale.. as opposed to the "fable" is the total absence of the didactic element in the former, which, as we have seen, constituted the real essence of the latter. Whatever the "tale" may be or do, its purpose is not to instruct, but to amuse. Of course, when the fable loses its distinctive didactic aspect, it becomes almost, if not quite, indistinguishable from the "tale." Even the writers of "tales" are often uncertain of the proper classification of this or that narrative poem: Dmitriev, for instance, shifts some of his poems from one to the other category in the different editions of his complete works. Under such conditions, the blanket designation "Fables *and Tales,*" employed by Khemnitser, Dmitriev and later (1818) A.E. Izmailov, is a very convenient one, saving the poet the embarrassment of having to pigeon-hole his work.

Jean de la Fontaine was the author, as is sometimes forgotten, not only of the immortal *Fables,* but of a series of short and entertaining, sometimes rather ribald "stories" ("contes") in verse. Some French eighteenth-century poets, including Voltaire, continued this minor genre. As composed by La Fontaine and his followers the *conte* has in common with the *fable* the verse form, known in French as *vers libre*—verse, that is, that is "free" in the sense of having no fixed length of line or rhyme scheme. In Russian this becomes the so-called "free iambic," utilized by all writers of fables and tales from Sumarokov on, and otherwise most conspicuously by Bogdanovich in his *Dushenka,* which may be classified as in some sort an over-grown "tale."

Dmitriev, who had translated and imitated La Fontaine's *Fables,* tried his hand at the "verse tale" ["skazka"] likewise, with remarkable success. His light, ironic, tongue-in-cheek style and elegant language lent themselves admirably to the telling of a racy anecdote in such a way as to be entertaining without shocking. Of his *skazki* the best is the 1791 tale, "The Fashionable Wife."[40] The original of this tale is novel VI of the First Day of the *Heptaméron* of Marguerite of Navarre, itself borrowed from one of the *Cent nouvelles nouvelles* (novel 16—*Le Borgne aveugle*). The subject is a "wandering plot" known even in the East Indian *Panchatantra* (Book I, fable vi).

Dmitriev's *skazka* recounts how an aging, one-eyed bureaucrat takes a young wife and suffers the supposedly inevitable consequence of his uxorious folly. The "hero" is thus described:

Prolaz [the name means "rascal"] through the course of half a century had always been crawling and crawling and humbly petitioning, and finally, by such innocent arts had crawled up to the rank of a person of note—that is, he had got a name for himself (I'm speaking, of course, as the world speaks), that is, he had begun to drive a carriage with six horses [since only the first four in the "table of ranks" had this privilege, it appears that Prolaz had attained the civil equivalent of a generalship!]

Prolaz took a wife who was "pretty, knew how to live, was clever, adroit, and wrapped the old fellow around her finger." "One day his wife was—here's my trouble! I can't find words to express it better—not quite ill, but not quite well, and so neither the one nor the other, not up to sorts, as it were. She says to her husband: 'Listen, dear heart, I need some new things for the holiday. Please, buy me a turban at Mme Bobrie's; and listen, darling: I would like a screen for my fireplace. You know, it's only a step from her place to the English shop—and if it's still there—but no, it's too expensive! But it's just *terribly [uzhast']* nice!' " This broad hint has, of course, the desired effect, and Prolaz is soon off on an errand to get his wife an expensive shawl that has captivated her. No sooner is he out of the house than a fashionable "ladies' man" ["ugodnik damskii"], Milovzor, makes his appearance, and a modish conversation ensues, full of *double entendres;* in this metrical *tour de force* Dmitriev's astonishing skill in handling the iambic free verse is fully displayed:

"Oh! I was just thinking—! How nice!" "Your humble servant." "But I'm alone." "Alone? So much the better! Where's he?" "Who? My husband?" "Your tender Cupid." "I' faith, what a railer you are!" "At the least, I'm an adorer of all *nice* persons. However, this is no lie, you know, that my friend is just a little like him." "That is, he's just as old, though not as handsome." "No! I'll prove it to you." "Oh! that's labor in vain." "No joking, listen. The one [i.e., Cupid] is blind, and he's one-eyed; then aren't they alike?" "Oh, what a wicked tongue you have!" "Forgive me, I'll stop.... Yes, do show me your divan [i.e., boudoir]. You know, I haven't seen it in its adornment; by now it certainly must be a temple! A temple of taste!" "You've guessed it." "Of course—and.... of love?" "Alas! I don't know yet. Would you like to look at it?" "Please, with all my soul!"

The poet then discreetly leaves his tale for a brief look at the unfortunate husband, who, having successfully made his purchases, is hurrying home to surprise his doting wife. The alarm is given by faithful Fido, Premila's "most reliable friend," and Milovzor has just time to hide behind the boudoir door. Prolaz finds his wife just waking from sleep, and a most beautiful dream, as she informs him, which she hates to give up for reality. She has dreamed, she tells her fatuous "Cupid," that his blind eye has regained its sight—and she hastens to see if the dream is true by putting her hand over his good eye, and saying: "Now, can you see, my light?" The husband answers: "No!" "Not even a little bit?" "Not at all; it's never been as dark as now." "You're joking!" "No, really; let me see again." "Beautiful dream!" Lucretia cried.... How I wished that your one eye were like the other!" In the interval of Prolaz's "total eclipse," of course, Milovzor has slipped out, and there is nothing left but for the innocent wife to be presented with her coveted shawl.

Satire, according to the left-wing nineteenth-century Russian critics, was Russia's native and unexcelled literary forte. Most eighteenth-century poets tried their hands at the genre, in one way or another; as we have seen, even such a melancholic sentimentalist as Kapnist began his career with a "First—and Last—Satire." Dmitriev's essays in this area are varied and rather disappointing. He published in 1798, when he was already in middle age and a distinguished senator, a translation of Alexander Pope's "Epistle to Dr. Arbuthnot."[41] Still later, in 1803, he published what the title announces as "An Abbreviated Translation of Juvenal's Satire on Noble Birth"[42] (that is, Juvenal, Satire VIII). Pope's epistle is largely directed against bad poets, and Juvenal's against puffed-up and parasitic noblemen; both subjects had Russian pertinence, but the reader had to "read between the lines" and mentally translate English and Roman originals into figures familiar to him—a rather laborious task. Much more successful as a piece of satire is the original poem, from 1794, called "Other Folks' Chatter" ["Chuzhoi tolk"].[43] Like

Pope's "Epistle," this too is aimed at bad poets—but, by a piquant and original device, is put in the mouths of one of them and of an anonymous critic of their kind of verse. This device is carefully clarified by the adjective of the title, "chuzhoi," "belonging to others." The poem begins abruptly, with only quotation marks to make it clear that it is "another" and not Dmitriev who is speaking: "What a strange thing! Twenty years have already passed, as we, straining our minds, knitting our brows, have been writing and writing odes with utter devotion—yet nowhere do we hear praises either for ourselves or them!" It is the classical ode, then, which the "certain old man of the time of our grandfathers," who is the speaker, sees as having undergone a strange and puzzling transformation; and it is the ode which the unnamed "Aristarchus," presently introduced, ridicules in its senescent form. The poet's notes assure the reader of his satire that not *all* odes are envisioned, and of course not those of Derzhavin, Kheraskov or Petrov! It is certain, however, that it is precisely Petrov whose inflated style *is* the chief object of the ridicule, with Nikolev a close second.

The naive descriptions put in the mouth of the "grandfatherly" scribbler of the first part of the satire point to the differences between the pseudo-classical "Pindaric" ode and the genuinely classical odes of Horace and the Greeks. The latter, by comparison with the "two-hundred-stanza" effusions of "our" poets are absurdly short: "there's nothing to read in them! A page, or maybe three." And then they are such easy reading "that you seem to be just flying along!" The poets of the Horatian kind seem to have merely tossed off their verses without labor—"But you know, when *our* poet begins to write, away goes all fooling! He'll sit a night long over a couple of verses; he sweats, meditates, scrawls—and burns up his paper; and sometimes he'll take on such spirit that he'll sit a whole year over one ode!" But the old man admits with perplexity, these enormous odes, written according to all the rules, describing a battle in all detail—"where it was, how, and when"—are a dreadful bore! "They're fine—but I yawn!" Then there are the solemn festival odes to royalty—and he quotes notorious tag-ends of pompous verse, all identifiable in the actual odes of Petrov: "There you'll find what an unstable mind would never think up in an age: 'dawn's purple fingers,' and 'Paradisal lily,' and 'Phoebus' and 'the heavens opened!' So sonorous, so lofty!.... But no, it doesn't give pleasure and it doesn't, so to speak, stir the heart at all!"

The author himself then injects a short comment, and immediately begins to quote another bit of "other folks' chatter"—the "frightful verdict" of "a certain Aristarchus" (i.e., a very severe critic). There are various reasons, he begins, for the inferiority of the contemporary ode-writers; for one thing, "the greater part of them are: a corporal of the Guards, an Assessor, an officer, some pettifogger or other, or an antique specimen from the Kunst-kammer [i.e., Peter I's museum of curiosities]," etc.—a seedy bunch! And then, they never have uninterrupted time to hammer out their verse—there are always social engagements to be met. or the theater, or the masquerade!

Then there is the very different purpose for which the ancients and the moderns composed their odes:

"Horace, for example, feeding his breast with rapture—what did he want? Oh! *He*— he didn't aim high: immortality through the ages, but in Rome only a crown of laurel or myrtle, so that Delia might say: 'He's famous and through him I too have become immortal!' But the goal of many of our poets is reward with a ring, and often a hundred rubles, or friendship with a princeling who never in all his life read anything but sometimes the Court Monthly, or a eulogy of his friends."

Then the critic tries to show by example how different are the aspects of those poets (i.e., the ancients) and "ours." Ours scorn training: they say: "Nature makes a singer, not learning; he is learned without being taught.... the resources needed are: boldness, rhymes and fire." " 'And here's how one of nature's poets would write an ode":

The cannon's thunder will have just given the people the joyous news that the Alcides (i.e., Hercules] of Rymnik [i.e., General Suvorov] has smashed the Poles, or Ferzen has captured their chief Kosciusko, when he's forthwith to his pen, and in a moment has indicted: "Ode." Then he'll append: "on such and such a day and year." Then what?— "I sing.... or no, that's old-fashioned. Wouldn't this be better: *'Give me, O Phoebus!'*... or like this: *'Not thou alone* hast fallen under the heel, O turbaned Porte!' But what can I rhyme with this, except 'Devil' ['chert']? No, no, it's no good; I'd better go for a stroll, and illuminate myself with the open air." So he would go out, and on his way conclude in his thoughts: "The beginning never affrights singers; grind out what you please! Here's a sticker, how should the hero be praised? I don't know whom to compare him with. With Rumiantsev, or with Greig, of with Orlov? What a pity that I never read the ancients! With moderns, it's all a bit awkward. Why, I'll simply write: 'Rejoice, O hero! Rejoice, thou Hero,' I'll exclaim. Capital! That's something like! Here's rapture for you! I'll say: *'Who has torn away for me the veil of eternity? I see the lightning's flash! I hear from the world's heights*—this and that.' And then? Of course: *many years!* Bravissimo! Both plan and thought, all here! Long live the poet!" It remains to sit down for a bit and just write it out, and then print it boldly!

After the Aristarchus has finished his devastating critique, the poet himself, as though the criticism touched him, too, exhorts his fellow poets: "Comrades! To your desks, to pens! Let's be avenged, let's inflate ourselves, press hard, strike, smite! Let's write against him a mighty long satire, and with this justify the thunderous Russian lyre!"

"Other Folks' Chatter" is a first-rate satire, and cleverly and novelly constructed; it is also most penetrating criticsim of the second-rate odes of the classical *epigoni*.

One other work of Dmitriev must be mentioned as representing a side of his talent not otherwise prominent—his ability to catch character in an almost dramatic fashion. In 1803 Dmitriev's literary friend Vasily Lvovich Pushkin (uncle of Alexander Sergeevich) left Russia on an extended journey to France and England. Dmitriev composed and printed privately in an edition of only 50 copies for his own and Pushkin's friends, an "epistle" ostensibly from Vasily Lvovich himself on his western tour.[44] Alexander Sergeevich Pushkin thus characterizes this gentle mockery of his uncle:[45] "The 'Journey' is a gay, good-humored spoof of one of the writer's friends; the late V.L. Pushkin set off for Paris, and his childlike rapture gave occasion for composing a little poem, in which with marvelous exactitude is portrayed the whole of Vasily Lvovich. It is a model of playful lightness and a light and harmless humor."

Dmitriev's "Journey of N.N. to Paris and London, written three days before his journey" begins:

Friends! Sisters! I'm in Paris! I've begun to live, not [just] breathe! Sit down closer to each other, to read my little journal. I've been in the Lycée, in the Panthéon, to make my bow to Bonaparte! I stood quite close to him, hardly believing my good fortune. Yesterday Prince Dolgorukov introduced me to the charming [Mme.] Récamier, etc.

The second part of the epistle shows the eager traveler watching out of the window of his lodgings at the traffic in the Paris streets, while "on the table, where the coffee stands, are scattered the 'Mercure' and the 'Moniteur,' and a whole bundle of play-bills is lying." Vasily Lvovich, who was famous for his witty epigrams—"couplets"—is made to remark:

I myself am ready, if you wish, to admit my weaknesses: I love, for example, to be always reading my couplets, whether they're listened to or not; and I love to play the swell with a strange costume, if it only be in style. But would I want to hurt anyone in word, in thought, even in look? I'm kind, really! And with all my soul ready to embrace and love the whole world!

The third part purports to come from London; Vasily Lvovich has had a stormy channel crossing, has visited Westminster Abbey to pay his respects to the tomb of Pope, and watched "through the windows a skirmish of Pitt with Sheridan." He is soon to return to his friends, however: "Today I'm sending to the ship all, all my acquisitions in two most notable countries! I'm beside myself with rapture! In what boots shall I appear to you! What frock-coats! What pantaloons! Fashions the newest to everyone! And what a beautiful selection of books!" (Vasily Lvovich was renowned for his magnificent library, which was destroyed in the Moscow fire of 1812). A list of his newly acquired books takes up five lines of the poem: "Buffon, Rousseau, Mably, Cornelius [Nepos], Homer, Plutarch, Tacitus, Virgil, all of Shakespeare, all of Pope and Hume, the journals of Addison and Steele.... and all of Didot and Baskerville" (two publishers, one French, one English).

We have met Vasily Pushkin among the minor poets of the period, and can see, from some of his own writings, how accurately his friend has hit him off in this delightful little picture, with his naive self-satisfaction and childlike delight in life.

The place of Nikolai Karamzin (1766-1826) in Russian literature is chiefly determined by his prose work, to which we shall shortly return. As a poet he is neither very original nor very inspired, but none the less by his contribution to the literature of sentimentalism deserves consideration. He is temperamentally a curious figure: the enthusiastic defender of "sensibility" as virtually a synonym for virtue, he is himself, for all his "outpourings of the heart," singularly cool, calculating and almost indifferent in his "moderation." His verse especially seems flat and tame to a modern reader, perhaps by the unfortunate contrast that involuntarily obtrudes itself with the genuinely moving verse of his contemporary Zhukovsky. We must remember, however, that even Zhukovsky, by his own admission, considered Karamzin his "gospel," and certainly learned a great deal from him—more, indeed, in the area of language and verse technique than in theme and sentiment.

Nikolai Karamzin was, like his friend Dmitriev, the son of a landowner in the Simbirsk district on the middle Volga. He lost his mother in infancy, and his father in adolescence, while he was briefly in military service in one of the Guards regiments in the capital. It was during the period of this service that he and Dmitriev first became acquainted. His father's death left the boy, at the age of eighteen, the master of the family estate, to which he promptly returned. The next year (1785) he took up residence in Moscow, where he gravitated into the orbit of Nikolai Novikov and the Masons. For some years he collaborated with Novikov as a translator (largely from the German, which Karamzin had learned early and very well) and writer for the journal *Reading for Children.* This apprenticeship, as we shall see, had a great influence on his innovative prose style. He departed in 1789 for an 18-month journey to western Europe—Germany, Switzerland, France and England— which he was later to describe for Russian readers in his *Letters of a Russian Traveler in the Years 1789-1790.* Upon his return to Moscow he began publication, with Dmitriev's collaboration, of the literary periodical *Moscow Journal* (1791-1792), and after a few more years, of the almanacs (that is, annual collections of poetry, his own and others'), *Aglaia* (1794-95) and *Aonides* (i.e., *The Muses*), annually from 1796 to 1799. In 1794 Karamzin's first collection of original poems appeared, under the title *My Trifles (Moi bezdelki).* As we have seen, his friend Dmitriev followed suit the next year with *My Trifles, Too!* The years of Paul's reign (1796-1801) were a period of literary inactivity for Karamzin, which the poet explained as follows: "Censorship, like a black bear, stands athwart the path and removes all desire to take up the pen." With the accession of Alexander I Karamzin resumed his journalistic activity with the publication of *The European Herald (Vestnik Evropy,* 1802-03), but soon abandoned the venture and thenceforth devoted himself until his death to his monumental prose work, *A History of the*

Russian State. Three editions of *Collected Works of N.M. Karamzin* (1803, 1814 and 1820) were issued during the author's lifetime, of which the verse in each case constitutes Volume I; with very few exceptions, however, Karamzin's poetry was all composed before 1804.

It is probably most reasonable to begin a consideration of this poetical work with a very early piece (1787) entitled "Poesy" ["poeziia"],[47] which is a program poem of Karamzin's earlier period. Typically, it is prefaced by an epigraph from Klopstock, one of the German pre-romantics whom the poet most admired: "Die Lieder der göttlichen Harfenspieler schallen mit Macht, wie beseelend." Like many of Klopstock's poems, "Poesy" is composed of unrhymed iambic lines—in this case, hexameters with alternating ultimate and penultimate accent—unrhymed Alexandrines, in effect. The first section begins with the creation of Man, "that proud lord of the world," whose first feeling is of the greatness of the Creator. This sentiment he at once pours forth in a "tender hymn, striving to fly to the Father." "Holy poesy!" exclaims the poet, "Behold, thou art in his mouth, in thy fountain-head, in lofty simplicity! Holy poesy! I bless thy birth!" Karamzin was probably indebted to Herder for his fancy that the earliest poetic utterance was a hymn of praise to the Creator. The fall of man brought with it the fall of poetry, but the tradition of song lingered even among Adam's descendants, and angels sometimes descended to teach men to sing, "with heavenly hand tuning their lyre—feelings were expressed in more lively fashion, songs resounded more sonorously, men soared more speedily to the Creator." With the passage of time "holy poesy" was degraded and poets "celebrated matter, the soulless planets!" One race, however, remained faithful: "Thus the royal poet, born a shepherd, but enlightened in soul, played praises to the Creator and charmed the peoples with his song. Thus in Solomon's temple the song of God resounded!"

Thus the first poet whom Karamzin recognizes is David; there follow in succession: Orpheus, Homer, Sophocles and Euripides, Theocritus, Bion and Moschus (Karamzin showed a great predilection for Gessner's pastoral verse, hence the prominent place accorded to the quite inconsequential bucolic poets Bion and Moschus). Next comes "Augustus's poet, the shepherd of Mantua," Virgil, who seems a reincarnated Homer and Theocritus; then Ovid—obviously regarded only as the poet of the *Metamorphoses.* Pointedly skipping France altogether in his "progress of poesy," Karamzin then proclaims:

Britain is the mother of the greatest poets. Her oldest son, Fingal's somber son, would mourn his friends, the heroes fallen in battle, and summon their shades from the grave. As the noise of the sea-waves, borne in the wildernesses far from the shore, engenders gloom in the hearts of those who hear—so the songs of Ossian, filling the weary spirit with tenderest longing, attune us to sorrowful imaginings; but this grief is precious and sweet to the soul. Great art thou, Ossian, great, incomparable!

Here must be pointed out a whole constellation of pre-romantic "mood words": "mrachnyi" ("somber"); "unynie" ("gloom"), "nezhneishaia" ("tenderest"), "tomnyi" ("weary"), "pechal'nyi" ("sorrowful").

Shakespeare, Nature's friend! Who better than you has understood the hearts of men? Whose brush portrayed them with such art? In the soul's depth you found the key to all the great mysteries of Fate, and with the light of your immortal mind, as with the sun, you gilded with morning the paths of night in life!

> The cloud-cap'd towers, the gorgeous palaces,
> The solemn temples, the great globe itselfe,
> Yea, all which it inherits, shall dissolve,
> And like the baseless fabric of a vision,
> Leave not a wrack behind,*

But you, great man, shall abide unforgotten. [* Karamzin translates Shakespeare's lines (Tempest, Act IV, sc. i, 152-6), but gives the original (rather freely) in a note, with the exclamation: "What holiest melancholy inspired these verses in him?"]

After Shakespeare, with shorter treatment, come Milton, Young—"friend of the unfortunate, comforter of the unfortunate!"—Thomson, poet of *The Seasons,* and then the scene shifts to Germany. First of Karamzin's Teutonic poets is "The Alpine Theocritus, sweetest singer!" (i.e., Salomon Gessner): "In rapture you sang to us of innocence, the ways ["nravy"] of shepherds, and with your pipe charmed tender hearts." Klopstock follows, glorified as the poet "instructed in that great mystery, how God became man,"—the poet, that is, of the epic *Messias.* Karamzin cites the words of an old man "departing to the life of bliss," who "pronounced in rapture: 'O incomparable Klopstock!',", and then goes on: "Still the great man adorns the world—still his great spirit has not left this earth! But no! He has long since been living in heaven—here we see [only] the shadow of this most holy poet." (Klopstock, who died in 1803, was of course still alive when Karamzin wrote "Poesy").

The poem ends with an address to Karamzin's countrymen; they have not yet, it seems, produced any poets (!), but their day will come—and it is quite apparent that the modest young author expects himself to be the bringer of light:

O Russians! The age will come, in which poesy with you too will begin to shine like the sun at midday. The dark of night has vanished—already Aurora's light is gleaming in [Moscow—the word is obvious, but replaced by asterisks in the printed version], and soon all peoples will hasten to the north to kindle the torch, even as in fables Prometheus went to fiery Phoebus to warm and illuminate the cold, dark world.

The significance of "Poesy" can hardly be mistaken. It ignores in the most contemptuous fashion all representatives of classicism. The dramatists recognized are precisely the genuine classical poets Sophocles and Euripides, not the "pseudo-classical" Corneille, Racine and Voltaire—and Shakespeare, whom Voltaire regarded as an uncouth barbarian, is glorified almost in the rank of Klopstock! The poets of sentiment, Ossian, Young and Thomson are given prominent place, but the great lyric poet of classicism, Horace, whom other Russian sentimentalist writers such as Muraviev and Kapnist so much admired, is accorded no mention. The very minor genre of pastoral verse, perhaps precisely because it enjoyed little classical esteem, is very highly ranked; all its genuinely classical representatives—the Greeks Theocritus, Bion and Moschus and the Roman Virgil—are recognized, and the Swiss Gessner brought in as the recreator of the genre in modern times. And finally, there is the typically sentimentalist penchant for religious verse—Milton and Klopstock, to say nothing of David!

Composed a year after "Poesy" is another program piece which deserves comment: "To D[mitriev] ."[48] Metrically it is an innovation, composed of unrhymed quatrains, of which the first and third lines are made up of two adonics ('xx 'x // 'xx 'x), the even lines of dactylic trimeters catalectic ('xx 'xx '). The lyrical persona of the piece is represented as passing in review several genres of non-dramatic verse, and mourning over the present lack of poets; he is suddenly comforted by apprehending the strains of a new singer from St. Petersburg—Ivan Dmitriev, to whom the epistle is addressed:

"Many bards, having tuned their lyres, play boldly [and] sing. The sounds of their lyres, the voices of their songs course through the groves and are loud.
Many bards, raising their tones, sing of terrible battles. In the sounds of their songs are heard the blows, the groaning of those smitten to death.
Many bards, lowering their tones, sing of rustic gladness—the ways ["nravy"] of innocent, humble shepherdesses, the sighs, the delights of love.
Many bards in noisy rapture sing to us the praises of wine, calling on all to extinguish with it tedium, worries and sorrow.
Do all their songs touch the heart, bring the soul to rapture? Are they all Homers, Gessners, Kleists? Where is there a second Anacreon?
Few great bards are left." Thus I sighed as I sang. Tears coursed gently from my heart, the lyre fell from my hands.
Swiftly the zephyrs from the Neva's banks, swiftly are borne to me—they are wafted, they pour forth sweet songs, tender songs in my ears....
I am enchanted! In heart-felt joy I call out, I sing: "The bards of old have poured forth their spirit into the Neva's new bard!"

The poets and the poetical genres which this piece specifies are all significant of the new trend: the first strophe probably refers to the rustic verse exemplified by Thomson's *The Seasons,* of which Ewald von Kleist's *Der Frühling* was a popular example; the second, of course, refers to Homer, more or less rediscovered through Heinrich Voss's translation of the *Iliad* and the *Odyssey* into German hexameters; the third obviously celebrates the pastoral poetry of Karamzin's favorite Gessner; and the fourth the convivial songs of "Anacreon"—significantly, there is no "second," i.e., modern, representative of his verse, as there is none of Homer. Implicitly, the epic of Homer is contrasted with and preferred to that of Virgil, the "classical" epic poet, as the lyric of Anacreon is to that of Pindar or Horace. It is perhaps worth noting that Karamzin makes no mention, in connection with the epic, of Kheraskov; the *Rossiada* was already, by 1787 (ten years after its publication) an old-fashioned curiosity.

As these two poems give evidence, Karamzin during the early period of his poetic activity experimented a good deal with metrical innovations. He preferred unrhymed to rhymed verse, and frequently made use of ternary meters, dactyls chiefly, often combining them with trochees, as in "To D[mitriev]." After 1793 or thereabouts such metrical experiments become much rarer in his works and rhymed verse almost entirely replaces unrhymed. But during his innovative period he introduced a significant number of metrical and thematic novelties, usually derived from German pre-romantic verse.

In a poem entitled "Anacreontic Verses to A.A. P[etrov]"[49] (1788?) Karamzin tries his hand at this popular form, using the genuine Anacreontic measure, unrhymed iambic trimeter with dissyllabic ending. As we have seen, N.A. Lvov's translations of Anacreon employed this meter. Unlike the "Anacreontic verses" of Kheraskov and some others, which are totally remote in spirit from the original, Karamzin here takes a theme from "Anacreon's" first ode—the poet's inability to carry out his poetical intentions—and enlivens it with a new twist: he determines, as he says, to be a Newton, but finds that "it is impossible for me to penetrate the wondrous make-up of the world"; he determines to be a philosopher, but "the spirit of these philosophers does not dwell in me"; he determines to be a Thomson, "but, ah! I had at once to admit to myself that I cannot have Thomson's voice at all." "Now I wander in the fields, mourn and weep bitterly, sensing how little talent I possess." We may be highly doubtful of the sincerity of this self-deprecation, but it does appear to be biographically true that Karamzin was at one time attracted to all the goals which his verses suggest.

In 1789, perhaps during his sojourn in Weimar, Karamzin encountered a collection of Spanish and Portuguese *romances* translated into German by Friedrich Justin Bertuch, the translator of Cervantes' *Don Quixote.* His attention was particularly drawn to an old *romance* which Cervantes quotes in his novel, about the captivity of Count Guarinos, and he proceeded to translate this into Russian, using Bertuch's German version, since he did not know Spanish. This translation is of considerable interest, since it antedates by a number of years the general European interest in medieval Spanish popular literature. Following, of course, the German version, Karamzin divides the poem into quatrains, which he leaves unrhymed, but with alternating paroxytone and oxytone line endings. The lines are regular trochaic tetrameter. This is, in fact, the standard German and English "ballad meter," and Bertuch had by his use of it implicitly assimilated the Spanish *romance* to the ballad genre. The original Spanish poem, *Romance del cautiverio de Guarinos,*[50] is in the usual *romance* meter, a three-beat unrhymed line with syllables varying from seven to nine. This original meter, which Bertuch's translation regularizes, was of course unknown to Karamzin, but might have impressed him by its similarity to the native Russian folklore meter of the *byliny,* which he later attempted to use in his unfinished poem "Ilya Muromets."

Another metrical experiment is the elegy "Autumn,"[51] written in 1789 in Geneva. Here the quatrains are again dactylic: the odd-numbered lines trimeter catalectic ('xx 'xx 'x), the even lines dimeter catalectic. The somber mood of the poem is reminiscent of Edward Young's "Night Thoughts:

The winds of autumn are blowing in the dark wood; rustling, the yellow leaves are heaped on the ground.

Field and garden are desolate; the hills are mourning; song in the groves is stilled— the little birds have disappeared.

Belated geese in a flock are hurrying south, borne with fluid flight in the regions aloft.

The gray mists whirl in the quiet valley; mingling with the smoke in the village they rise up to heaven.

The stranger, standing on the hill, looks with despondent gaze at the pale autumn, sighing wearily.

Mournful stranger, be comforted! Nature withers for only a little time; it will still be revived,

Still be renewed by the spring; with proud smile once more Nature will arise in bridal garments.

The mortal, ah! withers forever! The old man in the springtime feels the cold winter of his decaying life.

"Count Guarinos," in Bertuch's German and Karamzin's Russian, is assimilated to the ballad form, which the European world had quite recently become familiar with through Bishop Percy's *Reliques of Ancient English Poetry.* British and Scottish ballads are most commonly in quatrains, with alternating iambic three and four-beat lines (e.g., "Chevy Chase"), and some German imitations copy this meter, although Bürger's famous *Lenore* uses a longer strophe. The exact relationship of Karamzin's "Raisa: an Antique Ballad"[52] with German models is uncertain; it was first published in the *Moscow Journal* in 1791. The collection of *Balladen* by Goethe and Schiller, in which subjects from antiquity (e.g., Schiller's *Die Kraniche des Ibykus*) are prominent did not appear until 1797. Karamzin's "Antique Ballad" may have been suggested, however, by some earlier poems of Schiller, with whose work he was very familiar. Some scholars claim that Bürger's ballad *Des Pfarrers Tochter von Taubenhain,* which has a somewhat similar subject, may have been Karamzin's inspiration. "Raisa" is in any case one of the first examples in Russian of the ballad genre. The subject is typically romantic: the heroine of the title rushes through a savage Ossianic landscape to the top of a precipice overlooking the sea, where she hurls reproaches at her faithless lover Kronides, who, like Theseus with Ariadne, has abandoned her in a wilderness and sailed away while she slept. At the end of her narrative of his desertion, "Raisa... hurled herself into the sea. The thunder pealed: with this heaven announced the destruction of him who had destroyed her." In his ballad Karamzin employs the iambic quatrain of four beats, with alternating paroxytone and oxytone endings—but unrhymed.

Perhaps Karamzin's experiments with the ballad, in "Raisa" and "Count Guarinos," and his familiarity with Herder and his theories on folk poetry may have turned his attention to Russian folk literature. There had already been a considerable interest in eighteenth-century Russia in the popular tales of *bogatyrs,* and collections of prose retellings, such as Levshin's *Russkie skazki* had made these tales of "Slavonic chivalry" familiar, although the actual *byliny* themselves had not yet been collected and published. In 1795 Karamzin published in *Aglaia* what purported to be the "first part" (no other was ever composed) of a *bogatyrskaia skazka* entitled "Ilya Muromets."[53] It is written in an irregular unrhymed meter which approximates trochaic tetrameter with a usually dactylic clausula: thus, the first line *ne khochu s poetom Gretsii* is scanned as 'x 'x 'x 'xx. This meter was known chiefly from anonymous soldier songs, and was mistakenly believed to be that of the popular *byliny*. It was evidently Karamzin's intention with this to create a "native Russian" epic, but one ostentatiously remote from the canons of classicism. His models, except for the metrical form, were quite evidently the chivalric romances of the Renaissance, such as Pulci's *Morgante,* Boiardo's *Orlando Innamorato* and Ariosto's *Orlando Furioso*. Probably Wieland's *Oberon* (1780) furnished a more immediate example of the type. The integration of knightly prowess in battle with amorous episodes, which is the principal thematic characteristic of the Italian chivalric romances and of their German copy, is to be assumed for Karamzin's poem, although in the fragment which exists, the famous warrior Ilya Muromets appears only as a languishing lover, who encounters a sleeping maiden of incomparable beauty, whom he gazes at for a full week without daring to disturb her! It may be presumed that his warrior prowess would have been exhibited in later episodes. The chief stylistic feature of the chivalric romance is the light, ironic tone of the narrative, reinforced by the poet's frequent direct address to his reader, as though the story were being told in an intimate, oral fashion. This convention, too, Karamzin faithfully copies. Thus he writes:

Here, dear readers, it will be necessary for me to explain myself to you, to annihilate the imaginings of strict, pale-faced critics: "How could Ilya, even though a Muromets [i.e., a native of Murom], even though a knight ["vitiaz' "] of ancient Russia, sit for a whole week, without getting up, in one place...?"

The programmatic rejection of classical models for his "epic," with which the poem begins, is also part of the convention of the genre:

I do not intend with the poet of Greece [i.e., Homer], in the sonorous voice of Calliope [Muse of the epic] to sing the enmity of Agamemnon and the valiant grandson of Jupiter [i.e., Achilles]; or, following Virgil, to sail from Troy destroyed with the cunning son of Aphrodite [i.e., Aeneas] toward the grain-rich shores of Italy....

I do not intend to ascend Parnassus. No! Parnassus is a lofty mountain, and the path to it is not smooth. I have seen how our knights, our verse-and-rhyme makers, drunk with ode-singing, crawl to the summit of Pindus, stub their toes and fly downward, not with crowns and not with laurels, but—ah!—with asses' ears, to be the mockery of scoffers!

Finally, in his whimsical introduction, Karamzin invokes, instead of the Muse, another goddess:

Thou, who art visible and audible everywhere beneath the sun; thou, who, like the god Proteus, assumest every form, canst sing with every kind of voice, dost amaze and amuse us—dost proclaim everything, except—the truth;.... thou, who, along with Liudmila, said, with tender and trembling voice to me: "I love you!"—O goddess of this wide world ["sveta belogo"—a familiar phrase from popular verse], O Falsehood ["Lozh'"], Untruth ["Nepravda"], phantom of truth! Be now my goddess, etc.

Karamzin's "Ilya Muromets" was very favorably received, and it is surprising that he never returned to it. It is, however, very far from being an "ancient folk tale." Ilya has lost all his epic character and is a pink-and-white-faced youth from an eighteenth-century salon; on one occasion the poet interrupts his narrative to remark: "The knight did not read Gessner; but, having a tender heart, he admired the beauty of the day"—he is, it seems, endowed with a properly sentimentalist "sensitive soul." The "popular" character of the tale is supported by nothing but the meter and occasional tags such as the "sveta belogo," mentioned above, or such cliches as "solntse krasnoie" ("beautiful sun") or "kop'ie bulatoie" ("steel spear"). Nevertheless, such an experiment as Karamzin's has to be considered as one item in the genealogy of such a masterpiece as Pushkin's *Ruslan and Liudmila*.

Karamzin's familiarity with Schiller's early verse is evidenced by another poem of 1791, "A Song of Peace" ["Pesn' mira"],[54] the external occasion for which was the conclusion of peace in December 1791 between Russia and the Ottoman Empire. Karamzin at this period was an ardent pacifist, and an adherent of some of the notions about "eternal peace" which were in the air in the last years of the century (cf. Kant's *Von ewiger Friede*, 1795). "A Song of Peace" is a free reworking of Schiller's *An die Freude* (1785). It employs the identical form of the German poem—eight-line strophes of four-beat trochaic verse, alternating feminine and masculine rhymes, followed each by a "chorus" of four lines. The rhyme scheme of the "chorus" differs slightly from Schiller's: Karamzin follows a couplet with feminine rhyme by a couplet of masculine rhyme, where the German *encloses* a masculine-rhymed couplet between two lines with feminine rhyme. The thought development is of course quite different in the two poems—

Karamzin's is dedicated to "peace," Schiller's to "joy"—but occasional parallelisms appear even so. Thus, the "chorus" following the third strophe of the "Song of Peace" reads: "Let the millions exult! Let the millions triumph! Age of Astraea, revive! With the whole world we are in love!" The first two lines are forcibly reminiscent of *Seid umschlungen, Millionen! Diesen Kuss der ganzen Welt!* Karamzin's final strophe returns to Schiller's assertion: "Brüder—überm Sternenzelt Muss ein lieber Vater wohnen," which is a theme not earlier touched on:

Form a chain, ye millions, children of one Father! To you are given identical ["odni"] laws, to you are given identical hearts! Embrace in tender, brotherly fashion, and swear—to love! Swear in feeling ["chuvstvom"], in thought ["mysliiu"] : eternally, eternally to live in peace!

The chorus replies: "We swear, all with sincere hearts to live eternally in peace with our brothers! Father! Dost hear Thy children's oath? We repeat it a hundred-fold." "A Song of Peace" is not, by classical definition, an "ode," but it is notable that it stands out quite prominently for the number of its Slavonicisms, and its "high" vocabulary, amid the usually very direct and simple Russian of Karamzin's verse; thus "chado" ("child"), "klas" ("corn-ear"), "zlatyi" ("golden"), "otche" ("O Father!"), etc.

The "ode," in its cold, official form, celebrating great (or artificially puffed up) public events was deeply repugnant to Karamzin and the other "sentimentalists"; but, as we have seen, they could on occasion turn it to far more personal and universal subjects—even to such a subject as "slavery." Often juxtaposed with Kapnist's "Ode to Slavery" is Karamzin's "To Mercy"[55] (1792). Both pieces were bold and indignant protests to Catherine II occasioned by high-handed acts of hers, Karamzin's by the arrest and imprisonment of Nikolai Novikov in 1791. Karamzin, not himself a Mason, was sympathetic with the humanitarian ideals of the order, although not with its mystical tendencies. He had great respect and admiration for Novikov, and the ode is a veiled, but unmistakable outcry against the injustice done him. In "To Mercy" the form is an eight-line strophe, less common for the ode than Lomonosov's ten-liner. Boldly Catherine is herself identified with Mercy, and so addressed:

What can be holier than thou, O Mercy, daughter of the kindly heavens? What more beautiful in the world, what more dear? Who, without heartfelt tears, without joy and exultation, without a sweet agitation in the blood, can contemplate thy charms?

What night is not illumined by thy sun-like eyes? What rebellion is not quieted by thy smile alone? Thou speakest, and the thunders are mute; where thou steppest, there flowers are scarlet, and bliss pours from heaven.

Love caresses thy footsteps and calls thee tender Mother; love crowns thee upon the throne, and gives the scepter into thy right hand. They come, they come, the tribes of earth, as the swift waters from high mountains, beneath the shade of thine empire.

Happy, happy the people who live in thy spacious realm! Happy the singer who sings thee, in the heat, in the fire of his soul! As long as thou shalt be Mercy, as long as thou forgettest not the right with which man is born;

As long as the contented citizen ["grazhdanin"—an almost revolutionary word at this date!] can go to sleep withou fear, and [thy] subject-children are free to dispose of their lives according to [their] own ideas, everywhere to enjoy Nature, everywhere to adorn themselves with learning, and to celebrate thy charms;

As long as malice ["zloba"], daughter of Typhon, shall remain banished to the darkness, afar from thy gold-bright throne; as long as truth is not a thing to be feared, and the pure of heart is not affrighted to reveal himself in his desires to thee, the mistress of his soul;

As long as thou givest freedom to all, and dost not darken the light in [men's] minds; while trust in the people is evident in all thy deeds—so long shalt thou be esteemed sacred, deified by thy subjects and celebrated from generation to generation.

The quiet of thine empire nothing can disturb; for thy children there is no greater glory, than to preserve [their] loyalty to [their] Mother. There the throne is unshaken forever where it is guarded by love, and where upon its throne—thou art seated.

Karamzin was perfectly justified in the high regard which he had for this poem, which he placed first among the verse in his *Collected Works*. It is certainly, both in conception and execution, the highest point of his poetical composition—dignified, eloquent, and fearless. It is also consummately adroit: the Empress who is so flatteringly apostrophized as Mercy incarnate can scarcely take exception to the implicit menace that lies behind the several "as long as" clauses. The conjunction implies that *at the present* the "citizen" is able to go to sleep without fear, etc.—and *as long as* this happy condition continues, Catherine's throne will remain unshaken. Lurking unspoken behind the last three lines of the poem is the terrible example of France, where the throne had obviously not been "guarded by love."

Karamzin's verse seldom treats political matters or public events. A deplorable exception is the long, bombastic "Ode on the Occasion of the Oath of the Inhabitants of Moscow to His Imperial Highness Paul I, Autocrat of All the Russias."[56] He later also composed an official ode "On the solemn Coronation of His Imperial Highness Alexander I"[57] (1801). Most of his *Trifles* are of a personal nature. A good many of them reflect the poet's penchant for philosophizing, as for example the "Epistle to Dmitriev, in Answer to his Verses in Which He Laments the Shortness of Happy Youth"[58] (1794). Such philosophical or moralizing pieces, however, are almost never overtly didactic, as were, for example, those of Kheraskov. In fact, they are sometimes even light and jocular, as for example portions of the "Epistle to Alexander Alexeevich Pleshcheev"[59] (1794); the poem begins:

My friend! As you enter the noisy world with a lovable, sincere soul, in the springtime flower of your young years, you desire in a free hour to converse with my Muse about what men are looking for in the world; what is man's eternal object; about which the learned, the philosophers and the ignoramuses, the rich in golden garments and the poor in a wretched shirt—upon thrones surrounded by glory, and in humble rustic cottages—are permitted to pass judgment; that which in every earthly clime constitutes the hope of mortals, [which] is always seducing hearts, but, alas! is not to be seen in one!

"I am speaking of happiness," the poet sums up; and then adduces the commonplace that there are as many definitions of happiness as there are philosophers:

My friend! Will you believe me, that there have been ten thousand opinions, of learned philosophical debates in the archives of hoary antiquity, about the means of living happily in the world, about the means of finding repose? But that's just the way it is, my friend; there's no mistake in this figure. Thales, Chilon, Pittacus, Epimenides, Crito, the Bions, the Simmiases, the Stilpos, the Aeschineses, the Hermeiases, the Zenos, in the Lyceum, in temples and gardens, in tubs [like Diogenes!] and dark garrets have been talking about the highest good and pointing mortals to happiness with their beggar's staff, swearing by their sanctified beards that the fruit of earthly perfection grows in the garden of their philosophy.

A long discussion follows, and every way in which men have attempted to find lasting happiness is reviewed and found wanting. Finally come the poet's own conclusions:

He who is able to be content with a little, [who] is not fettered in his feelings, is free in spirit, is not a flatterer of rank or wealth; is as straight in soul as in carriage; does not seek goods beyond the ocean, does not wait for ships from the sea, does not quail before noisy winds, possesses his little house in the sunshine, lives this day for this day, and does not stretch his thoughts to a distance; he who looks all men straight in the eye; he in whose food the tear of the unfortunate does not pour poison; to whom work is not hard, a walk in the fields not boring, and rest in a sultry hour pleasant; he who is sometimes useful to his neighbor with hand or mind; who is able to be an agreeable friend, a beloved, fortunate husband and a good father of dear children; he who out of tedium invokes the Muses, and the tender Graces, their companions; who amuses himself, his household and strangers with verses and with prose; who laughs out of a pure heart (laughing, surely, is no sin!) at everything which seems laughable—that one will get along in peace with the world, and will not cut his days short with the keen steel or poison; for that man the world will not be a hell; that one will make his path bloom with roses amid life's pricking thorns, and will find comfort in sorrows, will meet the evening hour with a smile, and at midnight fall asleep in quiet slumber.

This is unquestionably a portrait of the poet himself as he sees himself—rather idealized, no doubt. Karamzin is not a metaphysician, and his philosophy is eclectic, with the ethical element always dominant. When we come to the *Letters of a Russian Traveler*, we shall find him enthusiastically seeking out during his European pilgrimage philosophers as various as Kant, Lavater and Bonnet, and shedding sentimental tears over the grave of Rousseau.

In common with most eighteenth-century thinkers, Karamzin identifies human happiness with the "life according to Nature." Nature—either *Priroda* or *Natura*, but usually with a significant capital letter—plays a prominent part in his verse. His "Song to the Deity"[60] (1793) begins with the quatrain: "Lord of Nature, infinite, creator of unnumbered worlds, eternal source of being, father of sensitive hearts"; his impassioned "Prayer for Rain"[61] (1793) is addressed: "Lovable Mother, Nature!" In his "To a Poor

Poet"[62] (1796) he adjures the addressee: "Gaze at the thick, green forest and hearken to the song of the nightingale. Poet! Nature is all yours. In her lap, dear to the heart, you are a king on a magnificent throne!" Nature is so often personified and endowed with human attitudes that one Russian critic[63] finds elements of pantheism in his thought. In any case, although he vehemently rejects atheism (his "Song to the Deity" has the note: "Composed on that occasion when the madman Dumont in the French Convention said: 'There is no God!' "), he also is no Orthodox believer—at least at the period when his poetical work was done.

Philosophical meditations, even in as light a key as some of Karamzin's, may seem to be scarcely "my trifles." Much closer to the spirit of his title are the genuine "trifles" which occupy a considerable place in his book, and exactly parallel a similar group in Dmitriev's verse. Such are the ephemeral *vers d'occasion* sometimes called "album pieces," that is, more or less *ex tempore* effusions which could be inscribed by their author on the virgin pages of a young lady's "album"—many of them metrical *tours de force* of French or Italian derivation, such as madrigals, rondeaux, triolets, and the like. Very similar are the numerous epigrams, whose "point," if any, has been woefully blunted by time; and the "inscriptions," a once popular form of "trifle" composed, like many Greek epideictic epigrams, ostensibly to adorn a portrait or statue of a famous person. In these poetical games the object is, of course, to say something with memorable, "lapidary" wit and incisiveness. Karamzin's "Chloe"[64] (1795) is quite comparable in point, though not in brevity, to some epigrams of the Greek Anthology or of Martial:

What though the malicious world assert that there is no constancy in Chloe; that every day Chloe changes the object of her love! It isn't true; Chloe always adores one object, prefers it to everything. "Whom? Surely not you?" Oh, no... Herself!

Sometimes, as Lotman astutely points out in his preface to the "Poet's Library" edition of Karamzin's complete poetical works,[65] the poet's urge toward classical brevity can be followed in several versions, and leads to a truly impressive result; thus, in writing an epitaph for a "tender mother" whose two-year-old daughter had died, Karamzin composed five different versions, the first a quatrain, the next three distichs, and the last—and best— a single line. The first reads:

> A heavenly soul has returned to heaven,
> To the source of all, into the Father's embraces.
> She had not yet been sullied here by vice;
> She captivated all hearts with her innocence.

The final version is: "Rest, beloved dust, until the joyful morning!"

"Album verses" and their ilk form one branch of the "light poetry" which poets of the sentimentalist fashion opposed to the classical ode. A much more poetically significant branch is the "song," as we have seen it cultivated by such poets as Muraviev, Neledinsky-Meletsky and Dmitriev. Karamzin paid his tribute to this branch also; most of his songs are, as tradition demanded, amorous in content. The first of "Two Songs," from 1794[66] begins: "We wished it—and it has been accomplished.... Liza! Heaven loves us. Constancy has been rewarded: You are mine!—O blessed hour." The lover of another "Song" of 1795[67] is less fortunate; in the chorus, five times repeated, he vigorously "swears off" profitless love: "No, enough, enough! Henceforth I shall not continue to flatter myself with empty hope, and I shall forget you, [my] beauties. No, no! What profit is there in loving?" In the verses the *persona* of this song recounts his numerous misadventures with fickle and mercenary maidens, and concludes in the final one: "Ah! better to wander in the forests, to wallow in the snow with the Laplander, and to sail the seas in a little boat, than to be a snivelling Celadon, to keep repeating 'alack!' in mournful tones, and serve as your amusement forever!"

One of the best of Karamzin's "light verses," and an excellent example of the kind, is "Retirement" ["Otstavka"] of 1796:[68]

"So, you're released for retirement!... What's to do, tender shepherd?" Take hat and crook in hand, say "thank you, I've had enough!" Go, and not shed tears.

I go, wishing dear Chloe a happy time with her new lover. Freedom's a golden thing, freedom in thought and in love. A minute inflames the feelings, a minute puts out the fire in the blood. The hearts of lovers are attached not with a chain, but with a fine hair; if there should sigh a sportive breeze, if a butterfly should dart between them—all's at an end, and there's no bond! Why torment one another with empty reproaches? The wide world goes on with its own order forever. All love, Chloe, and fall out of love; they swear, and transgress their oaths; where is there judgment for flightiness of hearts? What is now dear to the sight, to the feelings, that will be hateful to them tomorrow. Now it's a philosopher you like, in an hour you'll be liking a fool, and often the god Apollo (antiquity is the witness of this) was replaced in love by a woodland satyr. Under the scepter of the murderer Kronos what constancy could there be? Where time's the king, there all has an end, and it will scarcely be necessary for you in eternity to love one eternally!

So, look me boldly in the eye; I'm not angry, Chloe, truly. To make a fuss is the act of unbearable men. The lover sees—and is silent; he'll be shown the door—and, with a bow, he'll close it behind him. Without quarreling with the new Celadon, he'll go home—and write verses.

I lived with you in Arcadia, not for an hour, but a whole forty days! It's enough—the finest nightingale sings no more than in the spring!.... I also, Chloe, sang of you!.... And you in rapture listened to me; with your hand you wrote on the sand: "I love—I love—I'll die loving!"

But your old friend will not forget that he who will keep remembering what is old, loses his eyes, like the Cyclops;* what though my broad brow, Chloe, shall sometimes be adorned with horns:—so that I have at least my eyes. [*Karamzin explains this point by citing in a note the Russian proverb: "He who recalls what is old, loses his eyes" ["Kto staroie pomianet, tomu glaz von"]

Hardly a trifle in scale—it occupies eleven pages in Lotman's edition—and quite original in conception is Karamzin's "Epistle to Women"[69] of 1795. In this extended "free verse" epistle are combined many varieties of verse—the personal autobiography, the philosophical meditation, literary criticism, the "art of love," and much else. The poet recalls his callow youth when he dreamed of military glory, with a kiss instead of the laurel as his hoped-for reward. Thereafter, he confides: "Having come to hate rank among proud men of rank, I put my sword in its scabbard. ('Russia, be triumphant,' said I—'without me!').... and instead of the keen blade, I took in hand sheets of paper, ink-well and pen, in order to be a writer, a creator, agreeable for you, O beauties!" The reward which he imagines is a chorus of women, saying: "He's really nice, and faithfully translates everything dark in hearts into a language clear to us; he finds words for subtle feelings!" Amid the light self-irony of the poem, this is certainly a serious, and quite accurate, evaluation of his own literary contribution. We shall see how his modernized and Frenchified prose style was conceived as a language such as ladies might use and understand in conversation with each other—the "salon style."

Passing from the literary to the philosophical, Karamzin propounds his doctrine: "Three passions rule the world: one has honor as its object, the second *gold*, and by the third we live for your bright eyes." The first produces Sullas and Attilas, bloodshed and horror. The man who pursues gold "is always crawling like a worm in the dust, and is always living in a terrible fright.... he hides, like an owl, in the shadow of dismal night.... this madman passes all his days with anguish, on the watch!" Naturally, it is the third passion which brings men happiness. Typical of the sentimentalist elevation of the emotions as contributing to happiness more than does the reason is this passage:

Let that stern man Zeno [the Stoic] in his moroseness cry that we must live in the world without passions, have only the name of men, but have a stone for a heart—this doctrine should be left in the archives, and not enter hearts forever; Nature and truth have not sanctified it with their zeal. This reason, which the kindly fates have bestowed on us, about which philosophers are all the time talking to us, is it not a vain gift without the heart's inclinations?

Why, even the baby is animated by love of a woman—his mother; and the poet digresses to tell of his own early bereavement and his re-creation of his dead mother as a kindly shade watching over his later life. Returning to his subject, he enumerates some of the goods that women are responsible for, but gives up in despair—"But he who would recount everything in which you are profitable to the world and to the heart, would have to be a second Euler [the great mathematician] in the science of counting." Surprisingly, at the end of the poem, the twenty-nine-year-old poet cries: "Bloom on, O tender sex! And heap your flowers on us! For me alluring dreams have vanished. No longer can I captivate you with beauty, nor with my youth:

my spring has passed—I see autumn before me, and autumn, they say, is tiresome and not nice." But none the less, "your glance remains my comfort and sweet reward." In the final lines the poet queries: "What shall truth with her own hand write on my tomb? *'He loved: he was the tenderest friend of tender women!'* "

Letters of a Russian Traveler were published in 1791-92, and most of Karamzin's prose stories by 1803. In 1804 he began the immense project which was to occupy him for the rest of his life, the monumental *History of the Russian State*. After the publication of the first edition of his *Works,* in eight volumes, Karamzin wrote little more verse, and this little is mostly official and of very slight interest.

Among Karamzin's prose, which will be considered later, are a number of pieces of considerable importance as statements of literary theory. Here it may be said as a general comment that his actual poetical practice lagged considerably behind his theories. Karamzin seems to have developed more and more conservative tendencies in all regards from about 1793, and his poetical practice shows this as well as his political theory. He began with a strong predilection for unrhymed verse, even in places, such as the Alexandrine, where it was quite startling. This was of course not a discovery of his own—other poets, such as Radishchev, were experimenting with unrhymed verse at the same time; but after 1795 most of Karamzin's poems are conventionally rhymed. The same may be said of his metrical innovations: most of the pieces composed in dactylic or dactylo-trochaic meters were written before 1793. His one experiment with amphibrachs, "To Lila,"[70] which begins: "ty plachesh', Lileta" (x 'x x'x), belongs to 1796, and is quite isolated. In 1789 Karamzin could write[71] in his *Letters of a Russian Traveler* (Weimar, July 20):

Herder, Goethe, and their like, having appropriated to themselves the spirit of the ancient Greeks, have been able to approximate their own language to that of the Greeks, and make it the richest language and most suitable for poetry; and for this reason neither the French nor the English have such fine translations from the Greek as those with which the Germans have now enriched their literature. Homer with them is Homer; the same artless, noble simplicity in language, which was the soul of antiquity, when queens went to fetch water and kings knew the count of their own sheep.

Yet when in 1795 he undertook to put into Russian one of the noblest pasages of the *Iliad,* "The Parting of Hector and Andromache," from Book VI,[72] he translated, not Heinrich Voss's German version, which is in unrhymed accentual hexameters, and is certainly closer to the original than any other translation then existing in any European language, but chose the French perversion of Mme. André Dacier, in mincing Alexandrines, and padded with non-Homeric lines of his own invention. Karamzin, to be sure, did not know Greek; but his *Letters* show that he did, at least in 1789, understand and appreciate the Homeric spirit. His "translation" shows a most regrettable lapse in the direction of literary conservatism.

Consideration of Karamzin's language may be postponed, for at its best his poetical usage differs little from that of his prose—indeed, contemporaries complained that his verse sounded prosy. It is, to be sure, the work rather of a "versifier" ["stikhotvorets"] than of a genuine poet ["piit"] — a distinction he always maintained; but it has a significant place in the history of Russian poetry, none the less.

CHAPTER XVII

RUSSIAN PROSE OF THE LAST QUARTER
OF THE EIGHTEENTH CENTURY

A. Generalities

The eighteenth century in France and England is preeminently the age of prose; in Russia it is the age of verse. Until the last decade of the century the only significant prose writer, amid a multitude of poets, is Fonvizin. The balance begins to be redressed with the appearance of Radishchev and Karamzin. And prose, as a literary and not merely expository medium, means primarily narrative prose with a plot—the novel, the short story and related genres.

The novel, as a genre, has had a very late recognition. Classical literary theory ignored it. The only varieties of artistic prose admitted on an equality with verse were history and oratory. The prose narrative with an invented plot had at first to masquerade as the former in order to be acceptable—a state of affairs reflected in the English word "story," an abbreviation of "history." The narrator was always at pains to represent his work as an authentic happening, to himself or another. If to another, the details of the narrator's acquaintance with the facts must authenticate the story's truthfulness.

In the classical and neo-classical theories of literature, oratory and history, as recognized prose genres, were assigned appropriate styles. Seventeenth-century prose oratory (e.g., Bourdaloue, Bossuet), being entirely religious and usually addressed to royalty, employed the most lofty of prose styles; history (e.g., Bossuet's *Essai sur l'histoire universelle* or Voltaire's *Essai sur les moeurs*) made use of a style neither colloquial nor excessively elevated; and it was this "middle style" which was deemed appropriate for the varieties of novel derived from history.

One variety of the novel with a very venerable background (perhaps the earliest extant example of it is Xenophon's *Cyropaedeia*) is the pseudo-historical didactic narrative. Its most prestigious European representative in the eighteenth century was Fénelon's *Télémaque*. Dealing as this does with characters and events from the legendary past of the Trojan War it was assimilated to the epic. This association and the fact that the didactic novel deals habitually with kings, princes, and the most serious political and philosophical concepts, made it requisite that it be written in a lofty style approximating that of epic verse.

Another variety of the novel with an almost equally remote ancestry is the picaresque. Although its earliest representative in modern European literatures dates from the sixteenth century, the *Satiricon* of Petronius Arbiter (first century A.D.) is its antique prototype. The picaresque novel by definition ("picaro" is usually translated "rogue") deals with low life, and is always narrated in the first person. It is therefore usually couched in a style at the opposite extreme from that of the pseudo-historical didactic novel—either in the vernacular or in a somewhat conventionalized modification of it.

There was thus in classical theory no generally accepted single style, nor indeed even a generally accepted single name, for the literary varieties which we classify as "novel" or "short story." Any style, from the highest to the lowest, might be employed, according to the content or narrative convention of the story.

The first, rather hesitant and awkward, beginnings of Russian narrative prose have been discussed earlier. Fedor Emin, it may be remembered, must be considered, for all his serious literary limitations, as one of the founders of the Russian novel; he composed works in the genres of the pseudo-historical didactic novel ("The Adventures of Themistocles"), the pseudo-historical adventure story ("Inconstant Fortune, or the Voyage of Miramond"), and even of the new sentimental epistolary novel (*The Letters of Ernest and Doravra).* Chulkov, a better writer than Emin, created in *The Comely Cook* Russia's first example of the *picaresca.* But both Emin and Chulkov, as has been pointed out before, represent not the gentry class, dominant in literature as in social life, but the newly literate middle class. Emin's attempt at a "high style" in "The Adventures of Themistocles" is so bad as to be almost parodistic; it is left to Mikhail Kheraskov (in "Numa Pompilius," "Cadmus and Harmonia," etc.) to endow Russia with didactic novels in genuine (gentry) versions of the "high style."

In western Europe the eighteenth century saw born a new variety of the novel, distinguished not by criteria of form but of auctorial attitude. This is what we usually designate as the "sentimental novel." Its prototype is Samuel Richardson's *Pamela, or Virtue Rewarded* (1740). Following on the heels of *Pamela* came *Clarissa Harlowe* (1751) and *Sir Charles Grandison* (1754). The new fashion reached France with the publication in 1761 of Rousseau's *Julie, ou la nouvelle Héloise.* England contributed several other landmarks to the sentimentalist trend in Laurence Sterne's *Tristram Shandy* (1760) and *A Sentimental Journey Through France and Italy* (1767), and in Oliver Goldsmith's *The Vicar of Wakefield* (1766). Germany's chief monument of sentimentalism in the novel is Goethe's *Die Leiden des jungen Werthers* (1774). Of all these works it can be said that, however different

545

in details they may be, their authors show in common certain traits which serve as criteria for the sentimental fashion in general, and the sentimental novel in particular: first, emotion and sentiment take precedence over reason as the characterizing element in human nature, and as the chief guarantor of virtue; the analysis of sentiment, accordingly, becomes the novelist's chief device. Secondly, the abstract and generalized figures of classical fiction are replaced by living, actual, flesh-and-blood men and women located in a perfectly concrete place and time—in other words, sentimentalist fiction introduces a degree of realism unknown before. Thirdly, the actors and actresses in most of these novels are men and women of the middle class, to which most of their authors belong by birth, and exhibit the ways of thinking of the middle class and particularly its suspicions and prejudices against the gentry. Fourthly, with the exception perhaps of Sterne, all the novelists cited attempt in one way or another to convey a moral lesson—a distinct reaction against the sceptical amoralism of the "age of reason." A final characteristic, shared by them all but most prominent in Sterne, is the veritable flaunting of the author's own individuality, which tends to eclipse all other concerns in *Tristram Shandy*.

Emin's *Letters of Ernest and Doravra* (1766) is, as has been remarked, Russia's first attempt at a sentimentalist novel—in this case awkwardly modeled on Rousseau's *La nouvelle Héloise*. This pioneering effort remained, however, isolated for over two decades, although some works translated from the French (e.g., Fonvizin's *Sydney and Silli*) can be cited. The reasons for this time lag require explanation.

Themes, construction, fictional devices—such things are readily enough appropriated by one literature from another; thus Emin can construct his novel as a series of letters, on the models of both Rousseau and Richardson, and present his hero and heroine as analyzing their sentiments in these letters. What cannot be readily appropriated from one language to another is style— and this is precisely where Emin fails most miserably. The Russian which he used, even if he had had a more native command of it, would have been inadequate to his task because of several deficiencies in it, unknown to the languages of western Europe.

From the very beginnings of Russian literacy a situation had evolved without parallel elsewhere in Europe: the literary language which the church employed (and nearly all literate Russians in the early ages were churchmen) was not vernacular Russian, but a South Slavic dialect nearly related to Russian. The result of this was that literature was from its genesis separated by a wide gulf from the vast majority of the Russian population. In the course of time, as we have seen, secular learning grew more prevalent, and with it the proportion of Church Slavonic admixture in the literary language decreased in relation to the native element. With Lomonosov's literary and linguistic reforms at the beginning of the eighteenth century a kind of *modus operandi* was imposed, which remained in force unchallenged until the last quarter of the century. By it the use of a more or less slavonicized Russian was linked up with the type of literature being composed: for matter considered of a lofty nature, such as epic poetry, the solemn ode or the tragedy, a poetic vocabulary of words supposedly intelligible to all Russians of the educated classes, but never used in anything except church writings or secular literature of the "high" genres, was obligatory; for matter of a comic or satirical nature, on the other hand, it was appropriate to use a language almost entirely devoid of Slavonic elements, and approximating at times even to the common vernacular. Between these extremes lay a middle style, which might utilize Slavonic elements where these were identical with Russian.

This theory of the "three styles," formulated by Lomonosov, took very little account of prose, and none at all of prose as a medium for imaginative narrative. It was natural therefore that Russian varieties of narrative prose should gravitate into the channels defined for such varieties by western European usage; thus Kheraskov's philosophical and didactic novels assumed the "high style," Chulkov's the "low," and such a piece as the junior Emin's *Play of Destiny* (1789) the "middle." The equivalent of the Lomonosovian "three styles," however, in western literature involved no such extraneous element as the Church Slavonic component of the Russian high style; to any literate Frenchman, for example, Malherbe's odes or Bossuet's funeral orations, in the highest of high styles, were perfectly intelligible. Not so to a Russian the highly slavonicized productions in prose or verse in the equivalent style. The well educated Russian of the upper class, for whom they were written, would have little difficulty, but the man of the middle classes would find them beyond him. And the novel and the short story were precisely the literary fare which the Russian middle classes, in so far as they were literate, preferred. Certain varieties of imaginative prose were accordingly almost or entirely inaccessible to a growing segment of the reading public.

For a Russian writer still another linguistic factor, unknown to the writers of western Europe, complicated the situation. From Kantemir on throughout the eighteenth century nearly every Russian satirist or writer of comedy inveighs against fashionable gentlemen and women who use French so exclusively that they can either not communicate at all in their native tongue, or else use it awkwardly and inaccurately, larding it with a half-digested French vocabulary and translating French idioms literally into Russian. There is doubtless considerable exaggeration in such pictures, but we must remember that when Lev Tolstoy was endeavoring to draw an accurate picture in *War and Peace* of gentry society in the period 1806-12, he at first felt bound to write about half of his dialogue in French! It can be readily understood that such a situation must have severely inhibited the full development of the Russian language for literary purposes. If resort must be had to a foreign language to express certain ideas, and this language is always available and universally understood, there will be no incentive to augment the resources of one's own language. The turning point comes when the foreign language is *not* universally understood—and this is increasingly the case at the end of the eighteenth century.

From at least the age of Peter the Great Russian literature, especially verse literature, was created by and for men of the gentry class. In the course of the eighteenth century literacy began to spread more and more widely among two other groups of the population—the urban bourgeoisie of merchants, craftsmen, and the non-noble officials in the lower ranks of the bureaucracy; and women. Even women of the gentry class were seldom as well educated as their male counterparts, and seldom had the opportunity, as the men did, of making lengthy pilgrimages to western Europe to learn French, German or English at first hand; and if this applied to the women of the gentry class, so much the more to the wives and daughters of the bourgeoisie. It was for the benefit of these two groups primarily, to whom neither Church Slavonic nor French were readily intelligible, that the revolution in Russian linguistic and literary usage was carried out in the last years of the eighteenth century.

Tolstoy's Anna Pavlovna Scherer speaks for many of the gentry class at the beginning of the nineteenth century when she complains that, unpatriotic athough it may be, there are some things she can say only in French—Russian simply doesn't have the words for them. This embarrassment of course was felt only by the gentry class, whose ideas themselves were largely derived from a western education. The Russian peasantry and the lower strata of the bourgeoisie, who were usually second generation peasants, felt no difficulty in expressing anything which they needed to say in the Russian language. The question may arise: why could not the Russian vernacular be as well employed by the gentry as by the peasantry? And why could not this vernacular be discreetly enriched by new coinages and the like to the point of equality with the western literary languages? Two factors chiefly militated against such a solution. In the first place, speakers of a language usually take the course of least resistance, and confronted with an idea not expressible at once in their own language, borrow a foreign term outright instead of laboring to create a native substitute; thus in English such terms as *fin de siècle* or *Lebensraum* or *Zeitgeist* have acquired full currency although English equivalents could be devised with no great difficulty. The Russian spoken language since Peter's time had been crammed with foreign borrowings; and when attempts were made to coin native equivalents, they usually involved the use of Slavonic, which was no less a foreign language. But the principal hindrance to the general use for literary purposes of the Russian vernacular was social. When the cultivators of the soil, who constituted some nine-tenths of Russia's population, were degraded during the eighteenth-century to a position not greatly differing from slavery, their language was degraded too in the eyes of the upper classes of society, and could be utilized in literature only patronizingly, in comic or deliberately vulgar material. Even as late as the first quarter of the nineteenth century critics could exclaim in horror at Pushkin's use of certain "peasant words" in *Ruslan and Liudmila*—inconceivable in a serious work of literature. Here again, the situation in Russia had no parallel in west European countries, because the Russian social structure itself had no western parallel.

For all the reasons mentioned: the want of a firm classical prescription of a medium proper to narrative prose; the serious inadequacies of all the three Lomonosovian styles for this purpose; the stultifying dominance of the French language among the upper classes; the social stigma attached to the Russian peasant vernacular; and above all, the existence of a growing class of readers for whom Church Slavonic and French were equally incomprehensible—when at the end of the eighteenth century western models of imaginative narrative prose began to be seriously imitated in Russia, the first order of business had to be the development of a native prose style as a vehicle. Two men, Alexander Radishchev and Nikolai Karamzin, met this challenge at about the same time with two completely different and contradictory solutions, to which we must now turn.

B. Alexander Radishchev (1749-1802)[1]

Alexander Radishchev has already been twice encountered in this survey, once as a journalist and once as a poet. It is unnecessary to recapitulate the facts of his biography. It will be recalled that he collaborated with Nikolai Novikov in some of the latter's journalistic ventures, and that there is extremely good reason to believe that the two articles published in issues 5 and 14 (1772) of the *Portrait-Painter* under the title: "Fragment of a Journey of I— T— to —" is the work of Radishchev. According to the headings of the two sections in the journal, the "Fragment" constituted part or whole of Chapter XIV; if this is not merely a literary device, and the pieces were actually portions of a much larger whole, the "Journey" must have been a very extensive work, comparable in scope to the *Journey from St. Petersburg to Moscow* of almost twenty years later. At the beginning of the first extract the author (Mr. I— T—, according to the editor), informs us that his purpose in making the journey is precisely to study the condition of the peasantry:[2]

On my departure from this city I stopped at almost every village and hamlet, because all these alike attracted my curiosity; but in the three days of this journey I have found nothing worthy of praise. *Poverty* and *slavery* have met me everywhere in the image of the peasants.... I did not pass up a single settlement without inquiring about the reasons for the poverty of the peasants. I listened to their answers, and to my great sorrow, always found that their landlords themselves were reponsible for this.

It is evident from the fragment that we have even here, in 1772, a piece modeled on Sterne's *Sentimental Journey* of 1767:

O humanity! They know you not in these settlements. O sovereignty! You tyrannize over men of your own likeness. O blessed virtue, love of neighbor, you are employed for ill: the stupid landlords of these poor slaves exhibit you rather to horses and dogs than to men! With a great quivering of a sensitive heart I begin to describe certain hamlets and villages and their landlords. Begone from me, flattery and partiality, the low qualities of base souls: truth guides my pen!

The fragments belong to the literature of exposure, like most of the articles in Novikov's journals—that is, their primary purpose is not literary, but propagandistic. They are directed toward the immediate aim of opening the eyes of readers possessed, like the author, of "sensitive hearts," to the evils of serfdom and of effecting some reform. They are, however, interesting, quite apart from the politico-social aspect, for two literary qualities. Earlier, in the discussion of Novikov and the journals, the portions of Mr. I— T—'s journey were cited which describe the hamlet which he calls "Ruination" ["Razorennaia"] . The description of the filth and squalor of a peasant hut, and of the three abandoned babies, tormented by hunger, heat, flies, and uncomfortable bedding, is a realistic masterpiece, not unparalleled, but certainly not common in literature of the classical period. Furthermore, the language of the fragment, while not entirely free of Slavonic vocabulary, and occasionally employing a word order that violates that of the spoken language, is for the most part remarkably simple and straight-forward. Both these characteristics must be explained by the purpose of the piece: if the author's intent is to expose most effectively the horrors of a serf's existence, the usual classical abstraction and generalization will not do; he must present a picture as specific and detailed as possible. And if he is to make his point to the largest possible circle of readers, he must employ the simplest and most normal kind of language, free of extraneous rhetorical embellishment. This is exactly what Mr. I— T— does. The strange thing is that Radishchev's masterpiece, the *Journey* of 1790, which had exactly the same purpose, follows its earlier prototype in only the first of these respects: linguistically it reverts to a style that must have made it widely incomprehensible, or at the least repellent to the ordinary reader.

Presumably to the middle 1770s belongs an extraordinary piece of writing by Radishchev which was discovered and published after his death. It is entitled "Diary of a Week" ["Dnevnik odnoi nedeli"] .[3] It would be hard to find its like in any literature, Russian or foreign—but nothing can better illustrate what is meant by that treasured sentimentalist quality "sensibility." It purports to be the entries made from one Saturday to the second following Tuesday, a period of eleven days, and is a record of the emotional ups and downs of the writer (not to be unconditionally identified, of course, with Radishchev himself—this is a work of fiction) during the absence of the "friends of his soul." In a fashion most typical of the classical elegy, all concrete details in the piece are avoided: the causes of the diarist's torment are never referred to except as "my friends"—how many of them there are,

of what sex, what their relation is to him, he never reveals. He is equally in-
definite about his "duty" and "business"—he merely reminds himself once
that on it "depends the well-being or detriment of your fellow-citizens." The
reasons for his friends' departure and return are never hinted at. All these
background matters the author evidently considers irrelevant, possibly even
damaging, to his main purpose, which is to depict the agonies and contradictions in his own soul caused by loneliness and longing.

The ordeal begins with the entry of the first Saturday:

They have left, the friends of my soul have left, at eleven o'clock in the morning....
In the wake of their departing carriage I strained my eyes, that kept involuntarily dropping to the ground [the Russian of the last phrase reads literally: "strained the falling
against my will to the ground gaze"—a good example of the unnatural word order,
based on Latin or German, which is a prominent feature of Radishchev's prose style].
The swiftly turning wheels dragged me with their whirling behind them—why, why did
I not go with them?....

According to my habit, I went for the peformance of my duty. In vanity and preoccupation I did not think about myself. I remained in forgetfulness, and the absence of
my friends was unfelt. Two o'clock already; I return home; my heart beats with gladness;
I kiss my beloved ones. The door opens—no one comes to meet me. O my beloved ones!
You have left me. Everywhere empty—O delightful silence! Longed-for solitude! With
you I once sought refuge; in grief and dejection you were my fellow-travelers, when
reason sought to pursue truth; now you are unbearable to me!

I could not endure to be alone, I ran headlong out of the house and, wandering
for a long while through the town without any goal, I returned home at last in sweat
and weariness. Hurriedly I lay down on the bed and—blessed insensibility! Hardly had
sleep closed my eyes, than my friends presented themselves to my gaze, and, although
asleep, I was happy all night long; for I was conversing with you.

In the succeeding days the diarist's sufferings only increase; he is tormented
that his friends' departure may be a sign that their affection for him is only
slight. He tries to apply reason to his despair—but "is man such a slave to
his sensibility that even his reason scarce speaks when it is urgently required?
O proud insect! Touch yourself, and acknowledge that you are able to
reason only because you *feel*, that your reason has its beginnings in your
fingers and your bare skin." He tries to find distraction in going to the
theater and sees a performance of *Béverlei* (a lachrymose drama of Saurin:
1706-1781): "Beverley is in prison—ah! How hard to be deceived by those
in whom we place all our hope!—He drinks poison—what is it to you? But
he is himself the cause of his misfortune—and who is my surety that I too
shall not be my own evil-doer?" By Tuesday he is so completely prostrated
that he is unable even to get out of bed. There is an abrupt change on
Wednesday: one of the most remarkable and unclassical things about this
essay in self-analysis is its contradictoriness. Here is no monolithic classical
personality, "given" and unchangeable:

The agitation in my blood has lessened—I spent the whole morning sitting at home. I
was cheerful, I read—what an unexpected change! What is the reason for it? O my

beloved ones! I read the lively representation [presumably in earlier pages of his own diary] of what went on each hour, each moment, when you were with me. O revery! O bewitchment! Why are you not lasting? I am called to dinner—me to dinner? With whom? Alone! No! Leave me to feel all the weight of separation—leave me. I want to fast. I shall offer to them as a sacrifice.... Why are you lying to yourself? There is no merit in this. Your stomach has grown weak along with your strength and does not require nourishment.

On Thursday he goes, in proper sentimentalist fashion, to a graveyard and contemplates the possibility of his own end—but he is not ready for it—his friends may be returning. He hurries home, but no one is there. His Friday meditations begin in utter despair—but he suddenly reminds himself—and startles his reader!—that his friends are to return on Sunday! But at once he upbraids himself for the thought: "O you, who can measure your separation from the friends of your heart by time! O you villain, barbarian, cruel serpent! Away with such cold-bloodedness—the heart feels within me, and you reason!" This, it seems, is a particularly revealing entry: "sensibility" deliberately rejects reason in order to wallow in its own emotions.

The week's record works towards its climax: Saturday is full of joyful anticipation. Sunday comes—and the joyful reunion does not take place. The friends do not appear, and, disappointed and hurt by their failure, he concludes: "They have forgotten me. Let them forget! I shall forget them...." They have still not arrived on Monday, and he resolves to leave town so that they may wait for *him.* The last entry is Tuesday's:

Good-bye, promise-breakers, good-bye, heartless ones, good-bye. Where are you [singular "ty," addressed to himself] going, unfortunate? Where can there be happiness, if you do not find it in your own home? But I'm abandoned, but I'm alone—alone—alone!
    A carriage has stopped—they're getting out—O joy, O bliss! My beloved friends! It is they, it is they!

To an unsympathetic modern reader such untrammeled effusion of feeling can hardly be taken seriously, even when he reminds himself of the paramount position of friendship in sentimentalist and romantic literature. But exaggerated and ridiculous though the "dairy" must seem to a less "sensible" generation, there is no denying that it is an extraordinary feat of self-analysis, a psychological study almost without contemporary parallel. It is, of course, something else too—a bold and unsparing revelation of self, for the analysis is obviously intended not merely for the writer's eyes. It is these qualities which make "Diary of a Week" a most important document in the history of Russian sentimentalist prose; we shall see the same kind of self-analysis and self-revelation a decade and a half later in Karamzin's *Letters of a Russian Traveler.*

In 1789 Radishchev published a short biographical sketch entitled "Life of Fedor Vasilievich Ushakov."[4] The subject of the biography was a talented young man who had been one of Radishchev's companions and

552

closest friends during his student years in Leipzig; he died in 1770. The biography, which purports to be, and is, chiefly reminiscences of the Leipzig years, and dedicated to another former student, A.M. Kutuzov, is largely concerned with a "student revolt" which the author and Ushakov had large part in. It has some interest as an indication that Radishchev's political radicialism may date even from the 1760s, when he was in Germany, but it is not unlikely that, writing twenty years later, he may be retroactively attributing to himself and his fellows in their student days ideas which he did not in fact adopt until much later. In any case, Radishchev's political ideas are of minor literary concern. More significant is the fact that in the "Life," which was published at the time when he was in the midst of writing his *Journey from St. Petersburg to Moscow,* his style is, not surprisingly, the same archaic and unwieldy instrument as in the *Journey.*

In May 1790 there appeared in St. Petersburg an anonymous publication entitled *Journey [Puteshestvie] from St. Petersburg to Moscow.*[5] It was accompanied by the usual declaration that it was printed "with the permission of the Department of Public Morals." The work was dedicated, like the "Life of Fedor Vasilievich Ushakov," to A. M. Kutuzov, and this fact and a few references in the text made it easy for Catherine's police to track down the author. Radishchev readily admitted that the work was his; the imprimatur was falsified—only a portion of the *Journey* had been seen by a censor, and Radishchev had printed it himself on a private press of his own. He was promptly arrested and condemned to death for circulating subversive literature. In August the celebration of Russia's peace treaty with Sweden (Treaty of Verelä) gave occasion for a general amnesty, and Radishchev's sentence was commuted to a ten-year banishment to Ilimsk in eastern Siberia. His powerful and devoted friend, Count Alexander Romanovich Vorontsov, by a series of judiciously placed bribes, procured relatively good treatment for the exile, and permission for his sister-in-law with his two younger children (his wife had died in 1783) to join him. She later married him and they had three children born in Siberia.

The harsh treatment which the *Journey* brought on the author should have been no surprise to him. The entire purpose of the work was very clearly to protest the institution of serfdom and the autocratic despotism which supported it. In this purpose the *Journey from St. Petersburg to Moscow* was identical with the "Extract from the Journey of I— T— to —" of eighteen years earlier. That the later *Journey* brought a stronger reaction from Catherine than its predecessor may be explained by two factors: the extracts published in 1772 in the *Portrait-Painter,* caustic and outspoken as they were in their criticism of the inhumanity of gentry landlords, were short and relatively inconspicuous; the later *Journey* was an entire book, and the cumulative effect of the various devices marshalled to demonstrate the author's point was overwhelming. And secondly, the timing was singularly inopportune. Rebellion had flared up in the British colonies across the

Atlantic, and been successful; and the contagion had spread to France, where Louis XVI, "king by the grace of God," had been dethroned by the "people" and was soon to be executed. These developments filled Catherine II with consternation and horror, and Radishchev's open admiration for Washington (parts of the ode "Liberty" were incorporated into the Tver' episode of the *Journey*), Mirabeau and other revolutionaries led her to believe that he contemplated a similar revolution in Russia. He was, as Cathcrine's secretary heard her exclaim, "a worse rebel than Pugachev." Actually, it is doubtful if Radishchev was a true revolutionary, although any Soviet critic would vehemently dispute such a conclusion. He envisaged the abolition of serfdom most certainly, and a government guaranteed against despotism by some kind of constitution; but these reforms in his view were to come about pacifically, without armed violence. To Catherine, however, the thought of any limitation on her powers was intolerable.

Radishchev's actual political views are the concern of a social or intellectual history of his times. The devices which he employs in the *Journey* to inculcate these are the business of a literary historian. In this instance the principal device is the "sentimental journey," a new genre of narrative prose introduced by Laurence Sterne and hitherto unrepresented in Russian literature. Sterne's *A Sentimental Journey Through France and Italy* (1767), which is the archetype of the genre, sets the form: it is ostensibly a travel journal, written in the first person, recording the writer's impressions and experiences as he moves over a concrete geographical course during a concrete period of time. Sterne's *Journey* starts with its author debarking at Calais, and ends abruptly with him somewhere in Savoy, after some rather haphazard touring of the Ile de France and Brittany. He never does get to Italy, despite the title's promise. In general the stops which Sterne makes serve as a mere framework for recording his encounters with people and the impressions which they make on him; he is little concerned about the history, economic aspect or other concrete features of the country he traverses. The *Sentimental Journey* could be almost anywhere geographically; it can be said without exaggeration to be really a psychological journey through Sterne's own sensibilities.

Radishchev's *Journey* does not lack this introspective character, but is a great deal more concrete, and is motivated by a compelling purpose—the exposure of serfdom—which Sterne's lacks. It has a definite geographical beginning and end, noted in the title, and its course can be plotted on a map. It is a journey by post-carriage over a well-known stretch of the Great Russian countryside, and its chapters are each headed by one of the twenty-four "stations," or post stops, on the route. But this concreteness is really quite illusory; like Sterne's, this *Journey* is not recorded in the manner of a travelogue, but is a hodge-podge of material of every sort loosely held together by the fictional thread of an actual journey. Most of the incidents recorded could be localized as well in one as in another of the "stations"; only perhaps at Novgorod is there any pertinent connection between the place and the traveler's account of his stop there. The material is of every possible kind—visual impressions, conversations with peasants along the way, stories told to the traveler by acquaintances whom he meets on his journey, meditations on means of bettering the grievous lot of the population, a detailed and symbolic dream in which the traveler is a tsar, whom Truth in person enlightens—all united by two factors: the traveler's "sensitive heart," as with Sterne; and the paramount object of exposing serfdom as a malignant evil, politically, morally and even economically inexcusable. He describes encounters with all sorts of peasant types—care-worn and hopeless old people; brisk, still optimistic youngsters; families being torn apart by the iniquitous separate sale of serfs; peasant girls being forcibly married to husbands picked by their masters; only sons being sold to the army for the usual twenty-five year term of service, etc. He meets friends along the way, men of his own kind, who relate their own experiences to him, e.g., of a heartless governor whom his servant dares not wake from his nap even to save a boatload of drowning countrymen, or of an idealistic young judge thwarted in his sincere efforts to dispense justice by a senior colleague who decides cases on the basis of bribes. He inveighs against the bigotry and intolerance of the clergy, who connive with the gentry to oppress the peasants, in defiance of the Gospel injunctions to love one's neighbor; he criticizes the Russian school system, which to him is based on the methods of the medieval scholasticism outgrown by the West for centuries. The chapter "Torzhok," the longest in the book, is devoted to a well-documented and bitter attack on Russian censorship, some of the material form which he may have derived from Milton's *Areopagitica*. The chapter "Tver' " quotes substantial portions of the author's own "Liberty," and the final chapter *Chernaya Gryaz'* is largely taken up with a long eulogy of Mikhail Vasilievich Lomonosov, who was, it may be remembered, peasant-born, although not a serf.

The material is disparate enough, but chosen primarily in every instance to reinforce the one leading idea of the whole work: serfdom is an intolerable evil, a cancer in Russian society, and the autocracy which maintains it by putting unlimited power into the hands of a debased and irresponsible gentry must be abolished. It is the leading idea which gives inner unity to what would otherwise be but a congeries of unrelated impressions.

Even in the construction of the individual chapters there is no formal unity, and subjects appear in the most haphazard order. Roderick Page Thaler, in the introduction to his edition of Wiener's English translation of the *Journey*[6] notes as an example: "From Zaytsovo to Tver' he takes up, in order, the Service, the abuse of peasants by landlords, calling on great personages, the Service, education, calling on great personages, venereal disease, an admirable peasant girl, the emancipation of the serfs, the abolition of the Court Service, censorship, an auction sale of serfs, and prosody." This arbitrary and whimsical illogicality is evidently an attempt to copy the same qualities in Sterne's work, where they are justified by the entirely subjective character of the work: Sterne's only overriding idea is the revelation of his own personality in all its contradictoriness.

Radishchev is certainly not as "sentimental" in his work as his model, and the seriousness of his social concern saves him from some of the excesses of Sterne's "outpourings of the heart." But he too is prone to interrupt his sober exposition with sudden emotional outbursts, usually apostrophes. Typical is this, from the chapter "Vyshnyi Volochok"; he has been busy watching the barges plying the canal, loaded with grain bound for the capital, and at first the sight has delighted him—but then he remembered under what conditions this grain has been raised:[7]

And you, O inhabitants of St. Petersburg, who nourish yourselves with the surplus of the fertile regions of your fatherland, at sumptuous banquets or at a friendly dinner, or alone, when your hand raises the first morsel of bread that is destined for the satisfaction of your hunger, stop and think. Can I not say to you the same about it as my friend said to me about the products of America? Have not the fields on which it grew been fattened with sweat, tears and groans? Blessed you are, if the morsel of bread you hunger for was drawn from ears that were born on a field that is called crown-land ["kazennoiu"], or at least on a field that pays its landlord quit-rent. But woe to you if its dough was composed of grain that has lain in a nobleman's granary. Upon it have lain sorrow and despair; upon it is branded the curse of the Most High, when in His wrath He spake: "Accursed be the earth in her works."

At an opposite extreme from such solemn eloquence are the occasional passages, e.g., in the chapter "Edrovo," where the narrator engages in a more or less natural conversation with a peasant. In this chapter his carriage overtakes a peasant girl who is carrying a load of newly washed clothes home from the river on a yoke over her shoulders. He accosts her and the conversation runs as follows:[8]

"Isn't it hard for you to carry such a heavy load, my dear—I don't know your name? "My name is Anna, and my load isn't heavy. And even if it were heavy, I wouldn't ask you, sir, to help me." "Why such severity, Annushka, darling ["dusha moia"]? I wish you no harm." "Thank you, thank you. We often see such big-mouths ["shchelkunov"] as you. Please be on your way." "Really, Annushka, I'm not such as I seem to you, I'm not such as those you're talking about. They, I suppose, don't begin a conversation with peasant girls except with a kiss. But I, if I had kissed you, it would certainly have been just as though it were my own sister." "Don't come near me, please. I've heard such stories. If you aren't thinking any evil, what *do* you want of me?" "Annushka, darling, I wanted to know whether you have a father and mother, how you live, rich or poor, whether you're cheerful, whether you have a bridegroom?" "And what's that to you, sir? This is the first time in my life that I've heard such talk." "From this you can judge, Aniuta, that I'm not a good-for-nothing. I don't want to insult or dishonor you. I love women because they have a make-up that corresponds to my tenderness. But I love country women or peasants girls even more, because they are still ignorant of pretense, they do not put on the masks of pretended love, and if they love, they love with their whole heart, and sincerely..."

556

The reader would doubtless share Annushka's suspicions if the traveler had not elsewhere revealed himself so entirely above frivolous thoughts; and he can certainly sympathize with her bewilderment at these tender sentiments, borrowed with some awkwardness from Sterne's Yorick, and scarcely likely to be intelligible to a Russian peasant girl.

The *Journey from St. Petersburg to Moscow* is a profoundly humanitarian document that reveals a most noble soul; it is also one of the earliest and most significant monuments of sentimentalist prose in Russia, and the earliest example in the language of the genre of the "sentimental journey." However, as Mr. Thaler remarks with considerable understatement, "Radishchev's style is not the best thing about the *Journey*." It would be hard, in fact, to imagine a style less suited to the subject matter and the sentimentalist ethos than that which Radishchev deliberately and purposefully sets out to create. If one were to try to translate Laurence Sterne's *Sentimental Journey* into the language of Sir Thomas Browne's *Hydriotaphia,* he might get an approximate notion of the effect.

In the literary hierarchy of the "three styles," such a work as Radishchev's would probably have been bracketed with the private letter and assigned to the "low style"; Lomonosov says that this style should be used "in comedies, humorous epigrams, songs, and in prose letters to friends and descriptions of everyday doings."[9] The vocabulary of the "low style" is to be drawn from words that are common to both the Church Slavonic and Russian dialects, and words which are in good Russian usage but never found in Church Slavonic. It would exclude "mean words, which it is not appropriate to use in any style." The "low style," however, carries with it an informal atmosphere which Radishchev judged to be inappropriate to the seriousness of his subject. Instead, however, of settling for the "middle style," which is in effect what his contemporary Karamzin did, in his *Letters of a Russian Traveler,* he vaulted directly into the "high style," which Lomonosov restricts in prose to "orations on important matters." The lexical marks of the "high style" are: words in Church Slavonic which are never used in Russian, but still intelligible; and words which exist in both dialects. The category of words which are in good Russian usage but not found in Church Slavonic is excluded altogether. Along with the use of an unfamiliar vocabulary never employed in actual speech went the use of Church Slavonic inflectional forms and syntactical usages. Thus, for example, verb forms which in Russian have developed into gerunds, that is, sentence modifiers without inflectional endings, such as "nosia," "carrying" or "mysliv," "having thought," are provided with endings in Church Slavonic and function as present and past active participles respectively, alongside the ordinary participles of these tenses, thus "nosiaia" or "myslivyi." Radishchev often uses these remotely archaic forms, utterly unintelligible to any but a highly educated reader. But perhaps the most prominent characteristic of the Lomonosovian "high style," of which Radishchev is very fond, is a stylistic distortion of the normal word-order of

557

the language. Russian is of course a highly inflected language, with endings in noun and adjective and pronoun for gender, case, and number. If an adjective, for example, is separated from its noun, it can be mentally brought into its intended relationship by the identity of its ending with that of the noun; if an object precedes a subject, its case will still identify it as an object, etc. But the fact remains that the language has a logical, normal, sequential order, which is the same as that of English: modifier—subject—modifier—predicate—modifier—object. If, for purely stylistic purposes, this natural order is violated, comprehension of the sentence is impeded. The violation may be justified by the special emphasis conveyed, or by a particularly harmonious collocation of sounds, or the like; but in extreme cases, as in some of Trediakovsky's verse, it may be necessary for the reader to proceed to a complete rearrangment of the words before any sense can be made of it at all. Yet an early nineteenth-century (1805) stylistic treatise quoted by Professor Vinogradov[10] actually recommends such a distortion in specific terms: "Just like the Greeks and Romans we are able to enliven our discourse by separating adjectives from substantives and pronouns from their nouns, and by placing the verb at will at the beginning or the middle or end of a sentence, depending on the movement of emotion and on the propriety of style." That such violence done to language in the name of "propriety of style" had come to be regarded as objectionable by the end of the eighteenth century may be gathered from a remark which I.I. Dmitriev makes in his autobiography:[11] "Elagin, I recall, begins the third book of his 'Russian History' thus: *'Neizmerimoi vechnosti v puchinu otshedshii Kniazia Vladimira dukh....'* [literally: "Of eternity into the gulf the departing of Prince Vladimir spirit..."] . Maintaining the natural order in the placing of words, this should have been: 'The spirit of Prince Vladimir, departing into the gulf of eternity fathomless...' Although arranged in this fashion part of the period would be inflated and intolerable to an educated taste." A nineteenth-century writer, N.I. Grech, quoted by Professor V.V. Vinogradov[12] writes of Lomonosov's *Rhetoric:* "Lomonosov does not speak of the proper Russian construction, i.e., the order and placing of words proper to the Russian language. From this omission has arisen the strange and absurd rule of later writers on grammar: 'place your words wherever you please.' " There is no historical warrant for this so-called "free order" of words in early Russian; it is an "ornament" entirely derived from foreign models, chiefly Latin and German. To this same source may be traced Lomonosov's penchant for placing the verb at the end of a periodic sentence, which his imitators also copy.

This, then, is the kind of style which Radishchev consciously adopts a as the vehicle for his pioneering *Journey from St. Petersburg to Moscow.* As Professor Lotman has pointed out, however, Radishchev as a nobleman never had what one might call a "native command" of the Church Slavonic language, which nevertheless forms such a large part of his vocabulary; he actually created numerous back-formations on the basis of Russian which had never existed in Slavonic, and a large number of quasi-Slavonic compounds. Of such a category would be a word which he uses in the sense of "warmth"— "the warmth ["sogreniie"] of my friendship." Both "sogrevanie" and "sogretie" in the literal sense of "warming" exist, but he presumably felt the awkwardness of using one of these in a transferred sense, and so resorted to a coinage.

Russian prose in general is rather chary of conjunctions, but Radishchev loads his long sentences with Slavonic connectives such as "ibo" ("because"), "iako" ("as"), "daby" ("in order that"), "neby" ("if not"), "amo" ("where"), "dondezhde" ("until"), and the like. He even occasionally uses a notoriously antique Slavonic construction, the dative absolute, e.g., "veshchavshu sie startsu," "when the old man had said this"; although of native origin, this usage is certainly an imitation here of the Latin ablative absolute.

In another rather conspicuous way also Radishchev deviates from the language of his time, following Church Slavonic usage—the use of the verb "to be." The present tense of the copula does not exist in modern Russian; occasionally the third person singular may still be found, usually as a substantive verb: "est'," "exists." In the ancient language, however, the verb had all six forms: "esm' " ("I am"), "esi" ("thou art"), "est' " ("he, she, it is"), "esmia" ("we are"), "este" ("you are"), "sut' " ("they are"). Radishchev uses them all, although they are made unnecessary by the development in the modern language of a specialized form of the predicate adjective.

But the "high style" which Radishchev affects is by no means pure, and one of the most disconcerting things about it is the incongruous juxtaposition of Slavonicisms with elements of the ordinary, colloquial language; thus, the narrator's friend, telling his story about the governor who considered drowning people none of his business, ends thus: "okonchati ne mog moeia rechi, pliunul pochti emu v rozhu i vyshel von." The first clause is perfectly formal, even to the non-Russian form "moeia" (Russ. "moei"); the second is almost vulgar: "I could not finish my discourse, *I almost spit in his mug,* and got out." "Rozha" is a demeaning peasant word for "face." Sometimes the contrast between style and subject is quite certainly intentional, but none the less grotesque. At the end of his chapter "Podberez'e," for no very obvious reason, he tells a story for which he gives Pierre Bayle's *Dictionnaire*[13] as his source:

Said [Slav. "veshchal"] Akiba [a Jewish Talmudist] : "Having gone behind ["po steze": Russ. "vosled"] Rabbi Joshua into a hidden place [i.e., a privy], I came to know a three-fold thing. I came to know, firstly: not to the east and not to the west, but to the north and the south it behooveth thee to turn ["obrashchatisia dovleet"]. I came to know, secondly: not while standing on thy feet, but sitting it befits thee to defecate. I learned, thirdly: not with thy right hand, but with thy left hand ["desnitseiu, shuitseiu"—obsolete Church Slavonic words of the most poetical sort] is it proper to wipe thy behind ["zadniaia"—a Slavonic use of the plural] ." To this retorted Ben' Hazas: "Hast thou ["esi"—Slavonic second singular of "to be"] to such a degree ["dotole"—

Slavonic] emboldened thy brow toward thy teacher, so as ["da"] to observe him defecating?" He replied: "These be [Slav. "sut'," third plural of "to be"] mysteries of the law, and it was necessary that ["da"] I do what was done and come to know them."

Finally, Radishchev's style is sometimes absolutely ungrammatical; he is guilty time and again of the fault which in English grammar goes under the name of "dangling participle." This in Russian would have to be augmented by a "dangling gerund," as in these absurdities: "*Lying in the kibitka*, my thoughts turned to the infinity of the world"; "*having lived quietly* to 62 years, the Devil inspired her to get married"; of course, since the gerund is uninflected, the effect is somewhat moderated; but Radishchev does not scorn even the participial construction, which *does* have inflection: e.g., "borne by the waves" ["nosimye," nom. plu., referring to "we"], suddenly our boat [neut. sing.] remained motionless"; or "converted [nom. plur. masc., referring to "soldiers"] by the punctiliousness of military discipline into puppets, even the will [fem. nom. sing.] to move is taken from them."

Radishchev's style was consciously devised, and its purpose was without question to dignify and elevate the prose narrative to a literary level equivalent to that of the solemn ode. We have already seen that in his ode "Liberty" he was also deliberately rejecting the sentimentalist innovations in that genre, and attempting to revive a style somewhat more antiquated than even Lomonosov's. His intentions were reasonable, and the means he resorted to were in perfect accord with this purpose. Unfortunately, however, the results of his experiment were, from a literary point of view, deplorable. What he achieved was a startlingly incongruous combination: a radical, almost revolutionary and intensely serious content; a literary vehicle borrowed from Sterne, and characterized in the latter's use of it by the most capricious kind of subjectivism, entirely alien to Radishchev's literary approach; and a linguistic medium that is archaic, poetical, and altogether remote, with a few glaring exceptions, from the everyday language of any class of Russian. A well-developed sense of humor, which is also a sense of the fitness of things, might have kept him from some of these extravagances—but as we have seen before, Radishchev lacked this saving grace. His experiment with Russian prose went exactly counter to the natural direction of the language. In the early nineteenth century Admiral Shishkov and his followers of the *Beseda* made a similar attempt to reverse the course of linguistic history. Neither effort achieved any lasting results, although in modified form the archaism of the *Beseda* made considerable contribution to the language and style of certain romantic poets. Radishchev's experiment was, quite fortunately for Russian prose, still-born.

C. *Ivan Krylov and the Parody Encomium*[14]

Ivan Krylov's comedies have been considered earlier in this study, and his greatest literary contribution, the *Fables,* belongs not to the eighteenth but the nineteenth century. His prose sketches, which belong in the tradition of Nikolai Novikov and the journalism of the first half of Catherine's reign, are important in the history of Russian satire, and in particular his exploitation of the device of the "parody encomium" marks a new departure in that history and the appearance of a new genre in Russian prose.

As was pointed out earlier, Ivan Krylov's first literary essays were in the dramatic genres—comic opera, tragedy, and comedy. Lack of success in this area—partly due, no doubt, to Krylov's plebeian origin and the snobbery of the aristocratic guardians of the drama—led to his temporary abandonment of this line of endeavor and the attempt to revive the satirical journal as this had been current during the period 1769-1772. The first of his journalistic ventures, the *Spirits' Post (Pochta dukhov)* of 1789, had its name and its satirical device from a short-lived earlier periodical of Fedor Emin, called *Hell's Post,* the contributors to which were devils. Krylov's correspondents are "spirits," of the four Rosicrucian orders familiar to English readers from *The Rape of the Lock*— gnomes, sylphs, salamanders and undines. These observant immortals post letters to the human "master," the magician Malik-ul-Mulk (Arabic: "King of kings"), whose secretary the journal's "editor" becomes after finding him in a run-down and abandoned house which magic transforms into a luxurious palace for those who live in it. It is usually said that Krylov got his hint for this device from a prose work of René Le Sage, *Le Diable boiteux,* itself reworked from the Spanish—but there are actually few resemblances. Le Sage's "Lame Devil" exhibits to the Spanish student who has liberated him from incarceration in a magician's bottle the stupidities and rascalities of mankind by the simple expedient of flying to some high observation point and unroofing the houses of the city without the knowledge of their inhabitants, and then explaining to his companion what is going on. Several fairly lengthy and independent novellas form part of the contents of this mélange. Of the forty-eight letters that Krylov published in the year's issue of his *Spirits' Post,* a few contain rudimentary stories of the Lesage sort, but for the most part they are simple prose satires, moralistic discourses on particular human weaknesses. Typical is letter XX,[15] headed "From the sylph Dalnovid ["Far-Seeing"]. Discourse on Certain Sovereigns, who by their behavior have caused great harm to man." Dalnovid, incidentally, is the most long-winded and tiresome of Malik-ul-Mulk's correspondents. A good deal of the substance of these letters appears to have been lifted from the proletarian French writer Sébastien Mercier and his *Songes philosophiques* (1768) and *Mon bonnet de nuit* (1784-86), which Krylov probably knew from a translation made by his associate I.G. Rakhmaninov.[16] As works of art, the spirits' letters cannot be accorded very high rank. Soviet critics are fond of dwelling on them, but for reasons unrelated to literary values: they "unmask" such social evils as conspicuous consumption, parasitism, Gallomania and contempt for things Russian—and above all, of course, that evil of all evils, serfdom. The *Spirits' Post* sketches, however, are so inferior in an artistic regard to the pieces of a few years later which Krylov printed in *The Spectator* and *The St. Petersburg Mercury* that they may be passed over in favor of the latter.

The forty-eight letters which make up the *Spirits' Post* were all, so far as we know, written by Krylov himself. The case is different with *The Spectator (Zritel')* (1792) and *The St. Petersburg Mercury* (1793), which were published by the company of which Krylov was only one of the four partners. He still did a great deal of the writing, but the other owners and contributors from outside the partnership assisted. To the first of these perodicals belong some of Krylov's most pungent and effective satire, of which the unfinished tale "Nights" ["Nochi"] [17] is the earliest.

"Nights" opens with some satirical meditations of Krylov's narrator, a young poet of the capital, as he ponders the manner in which various frauds and hypocrisies are unmasked by the coming of night. His reveries are interrupted by a visit of the goddess of night herself, who explains her coming by a long-winded story of a dispute arising among the gods at a dinner-party given by Momus, god of folly, the up-shot of which is that Night must compete with Phoebus, god of day, in a scientific effort to find out whether men commit more follies by day or night. She drafts the narrator into her service, and he sets out on his quest. Probably Krylov's intention was to use this framing device to introduce a series of unrelated stories, each illustrating some human foolishness. As it is, only two "nights" were published, and these both develop the plot of one story. The narrator, wandering through the dark streets of the city, stumbles upon an "abduction" in process: a young nobleman and his servant are getting ready to carry off a certain Jeannette, the assistant in a French fashion-shop. The narrator (Mirobrod) decides to intervene, and succeeds in a manoeuvre whereby he takes the abductor's place and drives off in a hired carriage with the girl—only to find that the supposed French beauty is a certain charming Masha whom he has known before! Explanation of past relations with Masha is never made, because the coachman whom Mirobrod has hired for his purposes, and who has evidently been employed earlier by another party, abruptly drops the narrator into the hands of a murderous thug and races off with Masha—who does not reappear in the story. Mirobrod is conducted by his abductors to a mysterious house, and ushered by a lady's maid into a woman's dressing-room, where in the dark an enamored and presumably beautiful unknown visits him. It is evident that he is being taken for the young nobleman who was originally plotting elopement with Masha, and whose name appears to be Vertushkin. The beautiful unknown, still supposing the narrator to be her faithless lover, explains that her husband is asleep in the next room, so that love-making is out of the question, but makes an assignation with him at the masquerade next evening, explaining the signs by which he will recognize her in her disguise. At the appointed hour and place (Night II) Mirobrod, in domino, is waiting for his charmer when he is unexpectedly addressed by a dancer dressed as a devil, who has recognized him—it is his old friend Tratosil. The presence of this friend is embarrassing, but the impatient lover fobs him off and tells him to call at his house next day. When Mirobrod and the unknown lady, who is dressed as a soldier, finally get together, they hurry at once to Mirobrod's apartment—only to find Tratosil already there, asleep on the sofa. What is more, he is the lady's husband! She is appalled to find that her companion is not Vertushkin at all, but an unknown man—but explanations are impossible, because Tratosil awakes from his drunken sleep, and thinks that he recognizes his wife—only to be assured by that imperturbable lady in her officer's costume that she is actually Obmana's young officer brother Khvatov! The husband is delighted to make the acquaintance of this charming brother-in-law, and proposes an all-night drinking bout to celebrate. The last Mirobrod sees of the pair, they are headed in a coach for Tratosil's house— and the narrator has no idea how the imbroglio is likely to turn out!

There are elements of satire in "Nights," but they are incidental—the French proprietress of the fashion shop seems to be a "madame" on the side (her name is "Plut-en-ville," "plut" being the Russian word for rascal): she knows all about the "abduction" of her assistant, and indeed is abetting it (the theme is reminiscent of the plot of Krylov's comedy *The Fashion Shop*); the masquerade is described as being a prime hunting ground for seducers, etc. For the most part, however, Krylov seems to have been carried away by the possibilities of his story, to the neglect of the satire. It is a pity that he never finished the piece.

Of all satirical devices, the one which Krylov employs with the greatest skill and effect is parody. We have seen an example of this in his *Podshchipa*, which is a moderately amusing spoof of the classical tragedy. Early in the career of *The Spectator* he hit upon a mechanism for parody which he found so successful that he tried it several times, until he quite ran it into the ground. This was the parody encomium. It was not by any means an original notion, but it is doubtful if Krylov was acquainted with Lucian's "Praise of the Fly," or perhaps even with Erasmus's *Encomium Moriae*. The technique, however, is simple and scarcely calls for a model: the orator, with a straight face, "praises" the qualities in his subject which to any right-thinking person are most reprehensible. Krylov's first essay in this genre is: "Speech Pronounced by a Scape-grace in an Assembly of Fools."[18] "Speech in Praise of the Science of Killing Time"[19] and "Speech in Praise of Ermalafid,"[20] which we will consider later, are only moderately successful. The best of the group is "Eulogy to the Memory of My Grandfather." This is, indeed, one of the highest points of eighteenth century satire.

The full title of the piece is: "Eulogy to the Memory of My Grandfather, Pronounced by His Friend in the Presence of His Associates over a Bowl of Punch."[21] The speech begins:

Dear Listeners!
Exactly a year has passed since the dogs of all the world lost their best friend, and this district its most intelligent landowner. It is a year ago, to the day, that while intrepidly coursing a hare, he tumbled into a ditch and shared the mortal cup wit his dappled horse in right brotherly fashion. Fate, respecting their mutual attachment, was unwilling that one of them should survive the other, and the world thereby lost the best of noblemen and the finest of horses. Which of them should we mourn the more? Which praise the more? Neither of them yielded to the other in merits; both were equally useful to society; both led lives of equal worth, and at the last died an uniquely glorious death.

The orator hastens to point out to his listeners that the late Zvenigolov's merits were not solely those of a hunter:

Besides this he had a thousand other capital gifts, essential to us noblemen: he showed us how a man of noble birth should spend in a week what two thousand commoners subject to him earn in a year; he furnished notable examples of how these two thousand people can be flogged with profit two or three times a year; he had the gift of dining on his estates sumptuously and luxuriously, when it looked as though on these estates Lent were being observed, and with such an art he used to afford his guests pleasant surprises. Thus, gentlemen, it often used to happen that when we would be riding to his village, to have dinner, as we saw all his peasants pale and dying of hunger, we would be afraid of dying ourselves of starvation at his table; looking at each one of them, we would conclude that for a hundred versts around his estates there wasn't a crust of bread or a consumptive chicken. But what a pleasant surprise! Sitting at his table we would find a wealth that seemingly was unknown there, and an abundance, not the shadow of which existed in his possessions. The most skilful of us could not comprehend that he was still able to squeeze anything out of his peasants, and we were compelled to think that it was out of nothing that he created his magnificent banquets.[22]

The eulogy proper begins with due account of the nobility of the subject's birth; the speaker indignantly rejects the notion that noblemen and peasants can both be descended from Adam. If such is indeed the case, it is a grave mistake of Nature! The nobleman should have had at least an extra finger to distinguish him—as it is, he has to wear a sword for this purpose.

The young hero of the eulogy showed his superior merits early, by scratching and biting his peasant nurses. He grew quite adept also at administering cuffs and boxes on the ear. His enraptured father decided to give him a companion—not a peasant, naturally, but a dog, more suitable for a nobleman's associate. Accustomed to bite, scratch and beat his human servants, the child tried this on his dog—and Zadorka bit him! Stunned and resentful, he complained to his father, and got this answer:

"My boy," said his unexampled parent, "aren't there enough slaves around for you to pinch? Why must you touch Zadorka? The dog isn't a servant, you know; you must behave more circumspectly with her, if you don't want to be bitten. She is unintelligent: you can't take her and force her to endure without opening her mouth, as you can a rational being."[23]

The young Zvenigolov starts his education:

In five months the pupil was better than his teacher and could rattle off with him the civil alphabet. Such success frightened his father. He was afraid his son might learn to read fluently and with understanding, and might get the idea of making himself sometime into an academician; and so with the last page of his primer he finished his course in literature. "This is literacy enough for you," he told him, "you should be ashamed to know more. I intend you to be a noble lord, so it is unseemly for you to read books."[24]

Following this fatherly admonition, our hero banishes all books from his establishment—with one exception: Rousseau's work "on the damage from learning" ("The First Discourse," presumably!). He does not read it, of course, but it is on his table to be recommended to visitors.

Zvenigolov's career in the "service" is the usual stereotype: he buys on credit and reneges on payment; he gambles away his property; he haunts low taverns, and shuns intellectual society. A penurious uncle leaves him a fortune, and he retires to his estates, where he declares a relentless war against all the hares in the neighborhood. Of course the constant trampling of dogs and horses over their fields ruins the peasants—but what of that? In a few years he would have left nothing for the hares (or the peasants!) to eat. "What an intellect, gentlemen!" exclaims the orator. "Did anyone ever have such a great and audacious enterprise? Nero burned magnificent Rome to extirpate a small band of Christians.... Caesar.... Alexander.... they killed people in order to win glory, he killed them in order to extirpate hares. But Fate, envious of great deeds, did not permit him to finish his undertaking." At the end of his peroration, the orator observes his audience all asleep around the punch-bowl, and concludes that this is the final tribute to his hero.

This masterpiece needs little comment. The sarcasm is absolutely devastating, and infinitely more telling than either indignant diatribe or moral preachment. But other attempts along the same lines are far less successful. One of these, "Eulogy of Ermalafid, Pronounced in an Assembly of Young Writers"[20] has a purely literary subject, and is usually taken to be directed against Karamzin. Ermalafid (the word means something like "great talker," "wind-bag"), however, is a composite picture, and by no means to be identified with Karamzin. He is the sentimentalist writer in general, and some of the characteristics attributed to him in the "eulogy" are contradictory and entirely inapplicable to Karamzin, who, for example, never wrote either tragedies or comedies, which are among Ermalafid's successes. He is praised for the overwhelming quantity of his work, in all categories—even though

565

his books gather dust on the bookseller's shelves until they are demoted to become wrapping paper! He is disdainful of "rules"; he refuses to read others' writings before composing his own:

Accustomed as we are to writing without thinking, such an enslavement of literature will be, of course, dreadful for us. And where do these inexorable critics put the freedom of the literary sceicnes, if they imagine that the writer must follow rules or read authors in order to imitate their beauties? No, my dear listeners, thc great intellect never follows anything. He has no use for either the rules of the ancients or their works.[25]

Ermalafid's declaration of independence, however iconoclastic it may have sounded to Krylov's contemporaries, has today an almost matter-of-fact sound:

If I am going to write, then when shall I have time for writing [i.e., if I have to study past writers?] No, it is my intention to teach, not to be taught. For me it is a low thing to acquaint myself with what others are thinking; I would rather have the whole world, in reading me, try to guess what I am thinking. The republic of letters has suffered too long under the oppression of rules. I was born to destroy them, and for this purpose I want to unshackle young minds; I want to write without rules, and demonstrate in very fact that literature is a free science, possessing no laws save liberty and imagination.[26]

The romantic would say "amen!" to this without a cavil. Perhaps, to a modern reader, the sarcasm of such passages falls rather flat, accustomed as we have been since the romantic era to accepting exactly such dicta as perfectly valid.

His repudiation of "rules" of course leads Ermalafid to the literary enormities that Sumarokov used to inveigh against—the "tearful comedy" and the bourgeois tragedy. Indeed, in writing even non-dramatic verse, Ermalafid "often, after writing up to half of his composition, still did not know whether it would be an ode or a satire; but the most amazing thing was that both the one and the other designation was appropriate; and perhaps, with time, all his compositions will rouse warfare among academicians on the question of the genre to which they belong." Could Krylov have been thinking here of Derzhavin? Certainly there are many who would consider "Felitsa" at least as much a satire as an ode!

Of a similar inspiration to the "parody eulogies" and of the same period is Krylov's "Thoughts of a Philosopher à la Mode, or a Method for Seeming Intelligent, Without Having a Drop of Intelligence."[27] The "philosopher" explains his purpose in his first paragraph:

Dear Brothers!... In respect for your noble zeal for appearing intelligent in society, while at the same time preserving your hereditary adherence to ignorance, I have undertaken to be of assistance to you, and to give you a method, flattering for present-day education, an enviable method—for seeming intelligent, without having a drop of intelligence.

Krylov's misogynistic bias is at once apparent in this piece: "Let us make women our exemplars, and learn from them: they have no science for being beautiful, but for seeming beautiful—this is the one art at which many of them labor up to seventy—and often with success." To have a healthy, naturally ruddy complexion, is of course fit only for a peasant wench:

Leanness, pallor, languor—these are her [i.e., the woman of fashion's] merits. In the present enlightened age taste in everything is approaching its apogee, and the woman of the world is like a Holland cheese, which is good only when it is spoiled... The same can be concluded also about our learning: genuine learning is suitable only for low persons. Learning, to the satisfaction of fashionable little gentlemen, is brought to the level of the other crafts, and here Newton and Euler are of course less respected than Bräutigam and Heck [presumably modish St. Petersburg tailors or cobblers!] ; but the art of pretending to be learned—here is one merit appropriate to the nobly born person, and which makes him a favorite in the eyes of society! Women themselves, open haters of books, love to hear their discussions, because these do not lower their own self-esteem. For a woman it is very pleasant to see, when a man of some forty years discourses as entertainingly as a fifteen-year-old girl, and with such beautiful adroitness conceals twenty years of his age. Tell me, my friends, isn't a man's first duty to be pleasing to a woman? But what, for her fastidious and calculating taste can be more delightful than a young man, with clean-swept mind, who, without insisting on anything, tries to talk about everything; who, with his discussions of important matters, is as entertaining and well-grounded as a little girl with her dolls."[28]

Concluding his preliminary remarks, the philosopher's statement of his intentions gives Krylov an opportunity to hit at another of his favorite dislikes—the Frenchman:

By now it is clear how great are your advantages, the prime importance of which consists in dazzling with your wit. The dandy who doesn't know how to pretend to be intelligent is unable to play a brilliant part in high society; but for this purpose certain rules are necessary, which bring things into order.... This is the object of my labor! I devote it to you, my friends, and I shall be content if one of those Frenchmen, who prepare us for the world and teach us the difficult science of thinking nothing—if one of those Frenchmen, I say, in reading my rules, shall say that they are in agreement with the model by which he has been educating our nobly born youth.[29]

The philosopher's rules follow—seven of them. They can be briefly summarized: (1) always remember that you are a gentleman, born to eat the bread that the labor of others provides you, and be a happy drone; (2) learn to make fun of whatever your elders have considered sacred; (3) to be entertaining in high society you must learn to kill time, and the best way is to play cards—no one is acceptable in society who doesn't play! (4) Laugh as much as possible, but not at obviously ridiculous people and things; "the wit of the present age must shun such a fault, and sharpen his tongue at the expense of important and respected people." (5) Pick an author, learn his name and his works, and defend him against all others, although of course you have never read a word of any of them! "Nothing is more delightful than to see two young fops disputing about their authors, without having read them; I have often been witness of how Rousseau's epigrams had the victory over Young's 'Night Thoughts'—a victory that always remained on the side of the defender with the healthier throat." (6) "Learn to talk without thinking; thinking is suitable to the man of learning, but learning is not for the dandy, and you must beware of saying anything intelligent." (7) "Beware of being modest, or you will make people think that you have nothing to say—and that is a great defect." Returning at the end to his "Frenchman," the satirist winds up his discourse with:

Make use of [my rules] ; I know that many Frenchmen will be envious that others have written what they have been teaching orally; but I am not ambitious, and I readily acknowledge that these admirable rules are not inventions of mine, and that we are obliged for them to those condescending Frenchmen, who, after finishing on the galleys their course in philosophy, have migrated hither to mold our manners.[29]

Of a quite different genre is Krylov's only other important prose piece: "Kaib, an Eastern Tale."[30] The "eastern tale" enjoyed great European vogue after Montesquieu's *Lettres persanes,* and Voltaire's *Zadig;* under the palpable disguise of Oriental names of persons and places the initiated reader would have no difficulty in detecting a reality much closer to his own place and time. Krylov had, indeed, sketched something of the sort in Letter XLV of the *Spirits' Post,* in which the court of the Great Mogul bears a remarkable resemblance to a certain Russian court. "Kaib," however, utilizes the Oriental masquerade not for satirical purposes, but simply as a means of distancing and abstracting the moral substance.

Kaib (the name is said to be Arabic for "the hidden one") is an Oriental caliph of fabulous wealth and legendary happiness. The splendors of his palace, the beauties of his harem are glowingly described; all the court poets reiterate to him that he is the happiest of monarchs—but Kaib is bored. He tries to find satisfaction with a few new wives, and then with a career of military conquest, but to no avail. At last one night, alone in his bedroom, he observes his favorite cat playing with a mouse. The mouse jumps on to his bed, he protects it—and it turns into a beautiful fairy, who at once offers him his heart's desire as a reward—only Kaib doesn't know what he desires! The fairy understands, gives him a magic ring and a book of odes which are a sure cure for his insomnia, and advises him to take a journey.

The chief satirical episode of the tale is the account of Kaib's "divan," or advisory council: one of his councillors owes his high place to the length of his beard; a second, directly descended from Mohammed, was born wearing a white turban; the third is a cobbler's son, who has wormed his way by bribery and flattery to his present eminence. Kaib presents to his council the problem: how can he go on the recommended journey without his absence being noticed? The councillors suggest various absurd and inhuman methods, all of which he rejects. He solves the problem himself by simply walking out in disguise one early morning. His first encounter is with an impoverished poet who gives him a night's lodging and discusses the technique of writing laudatory odes for those whose lives offer no grounds for praise. Next morning Kaib continues his way into the country, where the sight of a flock of sheep excites his intense interest. Here is the opportunity he has always wanted, of seeing the pastoral golden age in its glorious reality!

The caliph looked for a little brook, knowing that a clear spring of water is as dear to a shepherd as the antechambers of the noble are to the intriguer of fortune; and indeed, having gone a little further, he caught sight on the bank of a little stream of a tattered creature, burned by the sun, and covered with dirt. The caliph had some doubt whether this was a human being; but, by his bare feet and beard he was soon convinced that he was. His looks were as stupid as his outfit was poor.

"Tell me, friend," the caliph asked him, "Whereabouts here is the happy shepherd of this flock?" "That's me," replied the creature, and at the same time wet in the brook a hard crust of bread so as to chew it more easily. "You the shepherd!" exclaimed Kaib with astonishment. "Oh! You must play beautifully on the pipe." "May be; but, being hungry, I haven't much liking for songs." "At least, you have a shepherdess; love consoles you in your poor condition. But I marvel, why your shepherdess isn't with you?" "She's gone to town with a load of wood and our last chicken, so that, by selling them, we may have something to clothe ourselves with, and not freeze in the winter from the cold morning frosts." "But for this reason is your life not very enviable?" "Oh! anyone who is eager to die of hunger and freeze with cold might burst with envy, looking at us!"[31]

Disillusioned, the caliph resolves never again to believe poets' descriptions.

After this pointed jibe at pastoral poetry (and it should be emphasized that the conventions ridiculed are *not* any more those of the sentimentalist school than those of the strictest classicist, e.g., Sumarokov), Krylov carries his hero further on his journey until one evening, overtaken by twilight at a distance from any habitation, Kaib has to spend the night in a graveyard, perched on an elaborate tombstone, for protection against wild animals. During the night the wanderer is aroused by a ghostly apparition: it is the owner of the tombstone, a mighty conqueror of 20,000 years ago, whose cruelties, as he explains, were so great that he must undergo punishment in the after-world until such time as he performs one good deed! After all this time, he has at last redeemed himself by saving Kaib from being eaten by bears, and by giving him a salutary warning for his own royal conduct.

In the morning Kaib continues his journey, and comes on a solitary hut, near which an enchantingly beautiful fourteen-year-old girl is distractedly searching in the grass for something lost. This turns out to be a locket with her mother's portrait. Kaib finds it, is rewarded with a kiss, and urged to stay the night with the girl, Roxana, and her old father. Then begins a happy idyll for the caliph, who becomes more and more infatuated, until one day Roxana confides to him that she loves him as much as she hates Kaib. The caliph, it seems, listening to calumny from his viziers, has disgraced her innocent father, an upright judge, and threatened him with death, from which

569

he has escaped into the present solitude. This is the signal which the wanderer has been waiting for: the fairy had promised him that he would find what his heart desired when he should find one who loved and hated him at the same time. Kaib suddenly disappears from the rustic abode; but soon a sumptuous procession wends its way thither, with a decree from the caliph restoring Roxana's father to all his estates and dignities, and summoning father and daughter to the capital. There, to Roxana's bewildered delight, she recognizes in caliph Kaib her lover Hasan. "The caliph lifted Roxana to the throne, and those two, husband and wife, were so faithful and loved each other so much that in the present age they would have been considered mad, and people would have pointed at them with their fingers."

As with "Nights," Krylov in "Kaib" became so engrossed in telling a story, with didactic overtones, to be sure, that he dropped the satirical element almost entirely. What there is is fairly conventional—against the hypocrisy and sham of court life, against such literary "sitting ducks" as eulogistic odes and saccharine pastorals, against economic inequalities. But nowhere does this good-tempered, whimsical story with its fairy-tale "happy ending," approach the savage, bludgeoning sarcasm of "Eulogy of My Grandfather," which indeed stands out as one of the most powerful pieces of eighteenth-century prose satire.

It is a somewhat difficult matter to assess the importance of Krylov's contribution to Russian prose style. Unquestionably the language and style of the *Fables,* which lie outside the purview of this survey, had a tremendous and salutary impact on the verse style of Griboedov, Alexander Pushkin and Wilhelm Küchelbecker, as the latter noted. "Last night I dreamed about Krylov and Pushkin," writes Küchelbecker in his *Diary.*[32] "I told Krylov that he was Russia's first poet, and by no means aware of it. Then, very seriously, I proposed the same theme to Pushkin. I called Griboedov, Pushkin himself, and myself pupils of Krylov." Krylov's style in the *Fables,* however, is at no great remove from that of the best of his prose—in the comedies "The Pie," "The Fashion-Shop" and "A Lesson for Daughters," and in "Eulogy of My Grandfather," "Nights" and "Kaib." It is an un-self-conscious style, pungent, flexible and close to ordinary speech, at equal distances, it seems, from the stilted and archaic prose of Radishchev and the mincing and mannered Karamzinian medium. Krylov was a commoner by birth, and was never quite fully accepted into the charmed circle of gentry writers. Karamzin's triumphant reform of Russian prose, as we shall see presently, was based on the usage of the gentry, especially of noble ladies, in everyday conversation. Inevitably, of course, such a class dialect was too narrow to serve the needs of Russian literature indefinitely. As Küchelbecker expresses it in his article "On the Direction of Our Poetry":[33] "From the Russian word, rich and powerful, they [i.e., the Karamzinists] are striving to extract a tiny,

decorous, saccharine, artificially attentuated tongue, adapted to the few—
un petit jargon de coterie." Krylov doubtless did not speak this *petit jargon*—
he certainly did not write it—and his prose and his *Fables* are closer to the
common speech of the Russian people than the prose of Karamzin and the
other sentimentalists. As long, however, as literature remained the prero-
gative of the gentry class—that is, until about the middle of the nineteenth
century—it was the "salon style" of Karamzin that more directly answered
the needs of the Russian writer than the more broadly based idiom of Krylov.
Krylov's influence lies quite far in the future; Karamzin's is immediate.

D. *Nikolai Mikhailovich Karamzin* (1766-1826)[34]

At almost the same time as the publication of Radishchev's *Journey*
another Russian writer was making an epoch-making "journey" abroad.
This was Nikolai Mikhailovich Karamzin, who traveled in 1789-1790 through
Germany, Switzerland, France and England. Karamzin was a nobleman, with
a good education, and rather unusually for his time, one that was concentrated on German and English rather than French culture. He was not very
much interested in real philosophy, but had a dilettante's avidity for mystical
and pseudo-philosophical moonshine. As we have seen from his early poem
"Poesy," he had acquired a taste for most of the pre-romantic English writers,
including, of course, Laurence Sterne, and he had translated into prose parts
of James Thomson's then famous *The Seasons.* Perhaps by way of his German
reading he had come to Shakespeare, whose *Julius Caesar* he had also translated. This taste for the "romantic" drama of England almost inevitably implied a distaste for French classicism and its paler reflections in other literatures, and we have noted that in "Poesy" he contemptuously leaves seventeenth-century French drama out of account altogether. Above all Karamzin
had an observant eye and an ostentatiously sensitive and palpitating heart.
With this miscellaneous equipment he set out on his pilgrimage, intent on
piling up as many "agreeable" impressions as possible. These impressions
he recorded in a journal which he published in part, doubtless considerably
reworked, upon his return to St. Petersburg. It made an instantaneous
success.

The content of the *Letters of a Russian Traveler in the Years 1789-
1790*[35] follows the model for all such writings, Laurence Sterne's *A Sentimental Journey Through France and Italy,* but is considerably less capricious and whimsical than the original. Karamzin wanders overland from
St. Petersburg, through the Baltic provinces, into Prussia and Saxony, thence
to Switzerland, then across the border into France, and finally to England,
from which he returns to St. Petersburg by sea. His impressions he transmits
in the form of letters to unnamed friends in the homeland, rather than as
entries in a fictitious "journal," in the manner of Radishchev. He visits

571

celebrities along the way, particularly his favorite Swiss "philosophers," the physiognomist Lavater and the "divine" and "incomparable" Bonnet, whose pseudo-philosophical mysticism held the greatest attraction for the rather emotional young traveler. He stopped off at Königsberg to visit Immanuel Kant, a celebrity whose works he admittedly had not read; he met Herder and Wieland in Weimar, but missed meeting Goethe, whose noble Grecian figure he admired from the street in front of his house. When he arrived in France, he discovered himself in the midst of the Revolution; the *bonne compagnie* of French intellectuals and society leaders, as a French nobleman sadly informed him, had been dispersed to the winds, and all he could find in Paris was chaos and relics of the glorious past. In England, on the contrary, he found a society and political system which in its moderately aristocratic character greatly appealed to him, and a literature with which he was already familiar and which he greatly admired.

Naturally he visited along the way all the places rendered significant by historical connections and literary associations; he carried his favorite reading material along with him, and read selections in appropriate places— Ossian, Haller, La Harpe, etc. When near Vevey he visited the scenes immortalized by Rousseau's *La nouvelle Héloise:*[36]

You can understand the sensations which these objects awakened in me, knowing how much I love Rousseau and with what pleasure I read his *Héloise* with you! Although Héloise contains much that is artificial and exaggerated—in a word, much that is *romantic*—yet no one else has portrayed love in the French language with such brilliant, vivid colors as *Héloise—Héloise*, without which there would be no German *Werther*!

Naturally he also visited the Ile de St. Pierre and indulged in melancholy meditations over the tomb of Rousseau.

His taste for the English "romantic" theater already formed before his journey began, he looked with a very critical eye on the classical French productions which he attended in Paris, and in connection with them wrote a very important pronouncement on the nature of the theatrical art of France,[37] which was to influence the course of Russian romantic criticism. In another letter[38] he compares the French classical theater with Shakespeare and his German imitators, whom he finds—Schiller preeminently—incomparably superior to the French:

Even now I have not changed my opinion about the French Melpomene [i.e., Muse of tragedy]. She is noble, majestic and beautiful, but she will never move and trouble my heart as does the Muse of Shakespeare and some (only a few, to be sure) Germans. The French poets have a fine and sensitive taste, and in the art of writing they may serve us as models. But as regards the gift of invention, fire, and a deep feeling for nature, they must—forgive me, you hallowed shades of Corneille, Racine and Voltaire!— take second place to the English and Germans. Their [i.e., the French] tragedies are filled with elegant pictures, on which colors are very artfully matched to colors, shadows to shadows, but I admire them for the most part with a cold heart. Everywhere is the mingling of the natural with the romantic; everywhere *mes feux, ma foi;* everywhere Greeks and Romans *à la Françoise,* who melt in the raptures of love, sometimes philosophize, express a single thought with various selected words, and losing themselves in the labyrinth of eloquence, forget to act. The public here [i.e., in Paris] requires from the author fine verses, *des vers à retenir;* these give a play fame, and for this reason poets endeavor in every way to increase their number, and are concerned more with this than with the significance of incidents, than with novel, extraordinary but natural situations, forgetting that character is revealed above all in those unusual chances from which even the words borrow their force.

It is worth noting that the points in which Karamzin sees the superiority of the English and German dramatists—fantasy (the "gift of invention"), fire, and a deep feeling for nature—are precisely the aspects of emotional expressiveness which the new movement of sentimentalism was bringing into prominence. The French drama is too intellectual, too rigorously controlled by tradition and convention; the drama of Shakespeare appears to be "freer" and more natural. This was to be the line of the romantic school everywhere, first in Germany, then in Russia, and finally even in France itself, the stronghold of classicism, when Victor Hugo, De Vigny and De Musset begin defiantly to imitate (as they imagine) Shakespeare on the Parisian stage. Much of what Karamzin has to say on the subject will be repeated some thirty years later by Stendhal in *Racine et Shakespeare.*

The *Letters of a Russian Traveler,* as has been mentioned, became at once a great literary success. The reason for this lay not entirely in the novelty—for Russians—of the literary form and in the pleasant, dreamy, slightly melancholy *persona* of the traveler; it lay also in the revolutionary innovation of his style. Radishchev, writing a document not dissimilar in outward form, had transferred to prose the stilted and extremely old-fashioned style of the Lomonosov ode; Karamzin wrote as society spoke, particularly, as he was later to admit, as ladies of good society spoke—when they spoke Russian at all. This "salon style," as it was somewhat contemptuously dubbed by the adherents of the Lomonosov conventions, eschewed all Slavonic words in so far as these were not naturalized in actual Russian speech; it attempted to enrich the Russian vocabulary with the introduction of new compound words intended to translate concepts familiar in French or German, or to employ existing words in novel meanings—thus, for example, in the extract quoted above he uses the word *polozheniia* and follows it by the French *situations* in parentheses; and it made use, to a very limited extent, of Russian of a colloquial character. Notably, however, Karamzin was at great pains to avoid anything that might sound "low" or common. Actually, while Radishchev employed Lomonosov's "high style" (that is, an exclusively bookish idiom, absolutely alien to the spoken language), Karamzin composed his prose in the "middle" or literary colloquial style, avoiding the "low" or vulgate. He did not, therefore, as has sometimes been erroneously asserted, demolish the whole system of the three styles. But it should be noted that the peasant speech, which was perhaps the real living Russian language of the time, remained untapped. Critics of Karamzin's style point to many Gallicisms in it; despite his general orientation toward German and English, it was French from which he tried to enrich his native language. Many turns of phrase or novel uses of words may be traced directly to French models. It is not surprising that such "unpatriotic" usage should arouse the wrath of the ultra-nationalists, who came to associate together in a rather extraordinary mélange of ideas the old Church Slavonic vocabulary and syntax; Orthodoxy; Russian national pride; and social and political conservatism, while the contrary notions of a modern colloquial idiom, French atheism, and political radicalism formed a complex which they attributed *in toto* to their opponents. Needless to say such associations were most arbitrary; Karamzin, who in his youth and before personal exposure to the French Revolution, had been mildly progressive politically, was after 1793 a staunch conservative; and as we have seen, Radishchev, whose political ideas were the most advanced of his time, set these forth in a prose medium of the most exemplary conservatism. The ultimate effect of the new Karamzinian style was greatly to lighten the specific gravity of Russian prose. A comparison between the almost contemporaneous "journeys" of Radishchev and Karamzin reveals what seems like a century-long time gap; the *Letters* read like European writing of the same, or even a later, age; the *Journey* sounds like something from the age of Tsar Alexei.

The style of Karamzin's *Letters* immediately came under heavy criticism from certain arch-conservatives—Admiral Shishkov and his group, whom the literary progressives were later to dub "the Old Believers." Although they had no significant prose writer to put forward as an alternative (Radishchev was out of the question, as a political radical and in penal exile), they inveighed against the abandonment of Slavonic, which Shishkov erroneously believed to be an older form of Russian, and the introduction of new-fangled French words and turns of phrase. One of Karamzin's earliest defenders was P.I. Makarov, editor of the journal *The Moscow Mercury*, who wrote an article in 1803 in which he acutely hit on the crucial points of the new style: it was an attempt to bring written usage into conformity with the spoken language, and thus accessible to all classes of the people; the "high style" was entirely bookish, and the exclusive possession of a small élite class:

Fox and Mirabeau spoke as representatives of the people and before the people or their deputies in such a language as everyone, if he knows the language, can speak in society; but we cannot speak in the language of Lomonosov, and should not even if we could. Words which have passed out of use will appear strange, and no one will have patience to listen to a period to its end . . . [bookish language] has become a sort of consecrated mystery, and everywhere that it has existed, the writing of literature has remained in the hands of a small number of people.[39]

It might be remarked that certainly even Lomonosov did not speak as he wrote; the very concept of a "literary language" implies that it differs from the spoken one—but the differences need not be so extreme. Karamzin's reform of Russian prose reduced them by a great deal, but still left much to do.

As was noted at the beginning of this chapter, there was, at the end of the eighteenth century, neither a well-defined form for the Russian novel, nor an accepted linguistic idiom in which it might be composed. Some degree of order began to be achieved, however, when the English novel, which had crystallized as a literary genre during the century, began to be translated. Fielding's *Tom Jones,* itself an offshoot of the picaresque form, *Joseph Andrews* and *Jonathan Wild* made their appearance in Russian dress; Smollett was translated; *The Vicar of Wakefield* appeared in 1786 and was followed shortly by *Pamela*(1787) and a spate of imitations of Richardson. In an attempt to prove that his country also had virtuous maidens of Pamela's ilk, Pavel Lvov (1770-1825) wrote *A Russian Pamela* (1789). In the meanwhile some of the continental European sentimental literature of Richardsonian inspiration had made its way to Russia: Rousseau's *La nouvelle Héloise* had inspired Fedor Emin's *Letters of Ernest and Doravra* as early as 1766; Elagin translated Abbé Prévost's *Mémoires et aventures d'un homme de qualité,* including the famous *Manon Lescaut;* and Goethe's *Werther* here as elsewhere established a veritable cult. But it remained for Karamzin to give the novel a viable linguistic medium by utilizing his newly evolved "salon style" for this purpose.

When Karamzin returned to Russia after his European jaunt, he at once obtained permission to publish a literary periodical, *The Moscow Journal.* This ran for a year (1791-92), and again a few years later from 1801-1803. In it was published the first partial version of *Letters of a Russian Traveler in the Years 1789-90.* Several of Karamzin's short narrative pieces, written during these productive years, saw the light in the same periodical: "Poor Liza" (1791), "Frol Silin" (1791), "Natalia a Boyar's Daughter" (1792); two of them, "The Island of Bornholm" (1794) and "Sierra Morena" (1795) were published in his "almanac" *Aglaia.* These represent a variety of narrative types. "Poor Liza" is told by the author in the first person as a real event, knowledge of which he has gained by later association with one of the chief actors. "Natalia" has a most unusual origin, according to the author's foreword:[40]

It is my purpose to communicate to my dear readers a piece of life ["byl"] or history which I heard in the region of shades, in the kingdom of the imagination, from my grandfather's grandmother, who in her time was considered extremely eloquent and almost every evening used to tell stories to Tsaritsa NN.

"The Island of Bornholm" purports to be an actual experience of the author during his return trip by sea from England to St. Petersburg, while "Sierra Morena," written in the first person in the form of a confession, is unconnected with Karamzin's fictional personality altogether. The life which forms the background in "Poor Liza," "Frol Silin" and "The Island of Bornholm" is contemporary and presumably realistic, however idealized and romanticized; that of "Sierra Morena" is contemporary, but spatially remote—the scene of the story is Spanish Andalusia; while "Natalia," although Russian, is laid in a remote past. In these several fashions Karamzin experimented in techniques of setting forth his narrative. It may be noted that although earlier Russian fiction had utilized pseudo-historical backgrounds in novels of the didactic and philosophical sort, such as Emin's *Adventures of Themistocles* or Kheraskov's *Numa Pompilius,* Karamzin seems to have been the first to delve into the romantic past of his own country for such a background. The use of Russian history for the plots of tragedy, e.g. by Sumarokov or Kniazhnin, may have furnished the suggestion. He was to do this again somewhat later with his tale of old Novgorod, "Martha the Burgomaster's Wife" ["Marfa Posadnitsa"].

The earliest of Karamzin's tales is "Poor Liza,"[41] and it remains the most famous. The theme is one of the commonest in contemporary western literature (one may think of *Faust Part I*)—the seduction of a girl of the lower classes by a young nobleman. Poor Liza, however, is the first Russian maiden of literary fame to have suffered this fate. She is represented as a peasant girl, although Karamzin studiously avoids using the "low" word "krestianka"; she is apparently not a serf. Her home is in the environs of Moscow, on the banks of the Moskva River. Like Margarete, she lives alone with a widowed mother. The peasant life is portrayed in the most idyllic fashion, with little relevance to actuality. Liza does needle-work and knitting, and in the spring sells wild lilies-of-the-valley in the city. It is there that the young nobleman Erast (note the conventional eighteenty-century name) sees her and is captivated. Erast is described by the kindly author as having a good heart, but weak. He does not intentionally set out to seduce Liza, but in a thoroughly sentimental atmosphere deludes himself into thinking that he and his "shepherdess" can recreate the age of gold without descending to carnal love. The event proves him wrong, and after a fateful evening "under the old oak tree," where most of the meetings between the two occur, Erast rapidly loses interest in Liza. He leaves her at last on the pretext of having to join the army. Later, on a visit to the city, Liza sees him on the street, follows him to his house, and is told that he has been forced to marry another woman and that she must leave him and attempt to be happy without him. Liza returns to her home and commits suicide by drowning herself in a deep pond near the fateful oak. It should be noted that Liza's despair at losing Erast is the only cause of her suicide; she does not, like Margarete, have a child to expose her "loss of innocence."

Liza's character is attractively portrayed, as that of complete unsophistication. She is as simple and pure as though she did indeed belong to the age of gold. One wonders how a "peasant maiden," brought up amid rather crude surroundings, could have retained such a virginal innocence, but the author makes no attempt to explain. He is intent on rendering his tale "agreeable," and of course the rustic background is perfectly ornamental. On only one occasion does Karamzin betray the least "social consciousness"—when he exclaims: "even a peasant girl can love!"

The impressionable reading public of Moscow took "poor Liza" to their hearts, and many a tear was shed over her innocent sufferings. The pond near the Simonov Monastery, which was the fictional scene of her death, became a place of pilgrimage for the sentimental. The tale, even more than the *Letters,* triumphantly established Karamzin as the leading figure of the new sentimentalist fashion.

"Natalia a Boyar's Daughter"[42] is, by contrast, a happy idyll, written with the maximum of "agreeableness." Although mention is made of some "evil-doers," everyone in the tale itself is noble and virtuous. Natalia, only daughter of the widowed boyar Matvei, a trusted friend and counsellor of an unnamed Tsar, sees a strange youth in a blue caftan while at mass one day, and loses her heart immediately. The youth returns two days later, and the two exchange tender and meaningful glances. Shortly the young man, whose name is Alexei, suborns Natalia's old nurse to let him visit the girl at her home while Matvei is out; the two lovers exchange vows of eternal fidelity, and Alexei persuades Natalia to elope with him that evening. This she does; the pair are promptly and properly married by an old priest in a remote church, and go to live in Alexei's home, a rude cottage in the midst of an impenetrable forest, where he resides with a group of rough-looking retainers. He is the son of one Liuboslavsky, a boyar who has been exiled through the unjust machinations of his enemies, and has since died. Matvei, though desolated by his daughter's disappearance, is certain that she could not have eloped with any but a good man, and is ready to forgive her; in the meanwhile he continues his philanthropic activities with the Moscow poor. The city is attacked by an army of Lithuanians, and at the news Alexei determines to join the defense forces in order to prove to the Tsar that he is loyal and should be returned to his father's position. Natalia, unwilling to let her beloved face war alone, puts on male disguise and accompanies him as his younger brother. A messenger returns to Moscow and reports to the anxious Tsar that the Lithuanians have been routed, the victory being largely the result of the valor of an unknown youth and his young brother; they are brought back to receive the Tsar's gratitude, and of course everything ends with the past forgiven and forgotten, Alexei restored and Natalia returned to her doting father, who is delighted now to have a son as well as a daughter.

The background of this piece, carefully sketched in attractive colors, purports to be historical, but there is as little authenticity about it as there is in Liza's peasant existence. Karamzin, although evidently attracted to the

577

picturesque features of the Russian past, did not know as much about it at this time as he was to do thirty years later. The preface to the tale, however, is significant of an almost nationalistic attitude on the author's part—Karamzin, whom his literary foes accused of abandoning his Russian birthright for a lot of western fripperies!

Who among us docs not love those times when Russians were Russians, when they attired themselves in their own proper clothing, walked their own gait, lived in their own fashion, talked their own language, and in accordance with their own hearts—that is, talked as they thought? I, at least, love those times; I love on the swift wings of imagination to fly into their remote obscurity.[40]

There is here an evident, though tacit, criticism of the author's own times and their customs—an attitude that would somewhat later be called "Slavophil."

"The Island of Bornholm"[43] purports to be the experience of the author himself during his return by sea from England to Russia. While his ship is momentarily becalmed at Gravesend, he goes ashore and as he gazes out to sea becomes aware of a pale, emaciated young man with wild eyes, apparently mad, who presently sings a ballad in the Danish language (which the narrator conveniently knows) recounting his hapless love for a maiden named Lila. There are hints in this ballad which become meaningful only in the light of events in the later part of the story; the young man sings:

The laws condemn the object of my love; but who, O heart! is able to oppose you?
What law is more sacred than the feelings inborn in you? What power is more mighty than love and beauty?
I love—I shall love forever. Curse my passion, you pitiless souls, cruel hearts!
Holy Nature! Thy tender friend and son is guiltless before thee. Thou gavest me a heart;
Thy kindly gifts made her beautiful—Nature! Thou didst intend that I should love Lila!

It is apparent that the young man's love for Lila was in some manner contrary to the human law—but guiltless by natural law; still addressing Nature, he continues: "Thy thunder thundered over us, but did not strike us, when we were enjoying the embraces of love."

The sad song has enthralled the listener—but the wind rises, he has to return to his ship, and sails on, the haunting song still in his memory. Later, while sailing through the Baltic, the ship puts in on the Danish island of Bornholm, and there the author, curious to see something of the island, goes ashore and finds a night's lodging in an old castle. His host is an elderly man, broken by grief, with an evidently mysterious and terrible past. During the night the narrator is awakened by a terrifying dream, and wanders about, unable to sleep. In the moonlight he comes upon an underground chamber, fitted with an iron grating, in which he discovers incarcerated a young woman. He addresses her thus:

What barbarous hand has deprived you of the light of day? Surely not for any grievous transgression? But your beautiful face, but the quiet heaving of your breast, but my own heart convince me of your innocence.[44]

The young woman answers his sympathetic question with the words:

"Whoever you may be, by whatever chance you may have come here, stranger, I can ask of you nothing but compassion. It is not in your power to change my lot. I kiss the hand that is punishing me." "But your heart is innocent?" "My heart may have been deluded. God forgives the weak. I hope that my life will soon end. Leave me, unknown stranger."[44]

The narrator retires, but his host finds out that the prisoner has been discovered, and takes him back into the castle to tell him his "terrible story," "a story which you shall not now hear, my friends; it shall remain for another time."

All this is the familiar apparatus of the "Gothic novel," a variety of pre-romantic prose originating in England with Horace Walpole, and represented in Karamzin's own time by Ann Radcliffe, Clara Reeve and Matthew Gregory ("Monk") Lewis. The "Gothic castle," located in a gloomy natural setting and seen in the ominous glow of sunset is a commonplace of the type; Karamzin describes his "castle":

The crimson sunset had not yet been extinguished in the clear sky, its glow was spread over the white granite and in the distance, on a high hill, illuminated the sharp towers of an old castle. The boy could not tell me to whom this castle belonged. "We don't go there," he said, "and God knows what goes on there!" I redoubled my pace and soon drew near a large Gothic building, surrounded by a deep moat and a high wall. Everywhere silence reigned, in the distance was the roar of the sea, the last ray of evening light was going out on the bronze tips of the towers.[45]

The castle's interior is again very like the interiors of "The Castle of Otranto" and many another Gothic locale:

The gate clanged behind them, the draw-bridge thundered and was raised. Through a spacious court, overgrown with bushes, nettles and wormwood we came to an enormous building in which a fire was burning. A high arcade in the old style led to an iron porch, the steps of which rang under our feet. Everywhere it was dark and empty. In the first hall, surrounded on all sides by a Gothic colonnade, hung a lamp that scantily shed its pallid light on the rows of gilded columns, which were beginning to fall apart from age; in one place lay portions of a cornice, in another fragments of pilasters, in a third a whole fallen pillar. My guide looked at me for some time with penetrating gaze, but said not a word.[46]

579

The natural expectation of a reader of the English "Gothic novel" would be to find the master of this castle an unnatural ogre, certain to threaten with horrid death anyone attempting to penetrate his "terrible secret." Karamzin's mysterious old man deceives this expectation—he voluntarily recounts his story, and it is the narrator who withholds it. The reader, however, can readily surmise what it is. Incest is a fairly common theme in the German *Sturm und Drang*, and the English writers of Gothic novels employed it at times (e.g. Horace Walpole in *The Castle of Otranto:* 1764) to contribute an added "shudder" to their horror tales. In Lewis' *The Monk* (1796) the incest is unwitting and is presented as merely part of the horrendous criminal fate of the monster Ambrosio. Sometimes, however, as in Sébastien Mercier's *L'Homme sauvage* (1767) the theme is given another twist by being seen at first as an act sanctioned by nature, though later condemned by man's law. This appears to be Karamzin's approach, which becomes apparent when the ballad of the young man of Gravesend is put beside the utterances of the young woman in the underground prison. It may be presumed that the two are brother and sister, children of the old man of the castle, and that they both felt that their love was "intended by nature," as the young man sings in his ballad. His punishment by exile has apparently not brought him to repentance; "Lila," however, "kisses the hand that punishes her," and admits that her heart "may have been deluded." Artistically, leaving the story to be guessed by the reader is a very effective device.

"The Island of Bornholm," although it never enjoyed the same fame as "Poor Liza," is certainly the best of Karamzin's stories. It is well written, with an interesting contrast between the almost reportorial style of the framing account—the narrator's life on shipboard—and the romantic central tale. It is also one of the first examples in Russian of the Gothic tale. The genre presently became very familiar to Russian readers through a spate of translations of English and French examples (e.g. of Charles Nodier), and Karamzin's pioneering effort was forgotten.[47]

In all the stories so far considered ("Frol Silin" is a mere sketch, ostensibly from life, of a benevolent old peasant) love, and mostly unhappy love, forms the basis. This contrasts sharply with the quite varied thematic material of the earlier Russian prose narrative, which included military adventure, tricks and rascality, education in statecraft, and a great deal else, with a fairly minor part given to love. In his treatment of his subject, moreover, Karamzin shows considerably more sophistication than his predecessors. The typical hero of the older narrative—"Unfortunate Nicanor," for example—is a mere plaything of fate. He is tossed from pillar to post by events which he neither brings about nor controls. He is far indeed from being the engineer of his own destiny or "the captain of his soul." Indeed he is as passive as the hero of a Greek romance, from whom in fact he probably descends. The heroes and heroines of Karamzin, on the other hand, are the agents of their fates: Liza and Erast suffer their misfortunes directly as the result of their conduct, whether this is to be interpreted as "the punishment of heaven" or not; Natalia and Alexei take active steps to achieve their happiness; Elvira and her nameless lover in "Sierra Morena" bring about the tragic dénouement; and although the story in "The Island of Bornholm" is only hinted at, there can be no doubt that the tragedy is not the result of blind chance. But Karamzin's philosophy is pessimistic; the unhappiness which results from the actions of his characters seems to be out of proportion to their misdeeds. It should be observed that he passes no moral judgment on Liza's fall: when on the fateful night a frightful thunder-storm breaks over the lovers, the compassionate author is at pains to preclude the inference that this is the manifestation of heaven's wrath: "It seemed," he says, "as if all nature were *lamenting* Liza's lost innocence." In somewhat the same way the young Dane in his ballad emphasizes that he is guiltless before Nature: "Holy Nature! Thy tender friend and son is innocent before thee"; and although a thunderstorm, as with Liza and Erast, attended the consummation of his and Lila's love, "the thunder did not strike us." At the end of the same story the old man announces to the narrator: "You shall know [my story], you shall know, young man, and your heart will be torn. Then you will ask yourself: Wherefore did Heaven pour out the whole cup of its wrath upon this weak, gray old man—an old man who loved virtue, and honored its sacred laws?" The tragic outcome of "Sierra Morena"[48] even less than in the other tales seems explicable in terms of the misdeeds of its characters. Elvira, believing her first lover Alonzo the victim of a shipwreck, gives her heart to the narrator; on their wedding day Alonzo suddenly appears at the church, safe and sound, but finding that his sweetheart is faithless, kills himself. Elvira takes the veil and the narrator remains inconsolable. Karamzin thus appears to see tragedy as the working of a malign destiny; his characters, like Oedipus, bring their fate upon themselves, but it is a fate wholly disproportionate to their deserts.

Karamzin's early narratives are written in the same smooth, pleasantly readable style as the *Letters*. This mode of writing, as we have seen, was consciously adopted by the author in the expectation of making his work attractive and accessible to a largely female audience. He had had earlier experience which facilitated this: from about 1786 to the time of his departure on his European *Wanderjahr* he had been employed by the eminent philanthropist and publisher Nikolai I. Novikov, for whom he had edited a journal for children entitled *Children's Reading*.[49] Karamzin, in writing for a juvenile audience, had quite properly learned to avoid the stilted and obsolete Slavonic vocabulary, and to write in short, crisp sentences. What he learned from this experience he readily turned to advantage in addressing himself to the ladies. But it should not be supposed that his style remains uniform for all his tales, even though he makes no apparent effort to differentiate character by level of speech in recording dialogue—Liza, the peasant girl, speaks the same elegant Russian as her upper-class lover. In this respect

Radishchev, curiously, is far in advance of Karamzin; his peasants speak quite colloquially, even when the enclosing narrative is composed in an archaic and bookish Russian. But in Karamzin's tales there is, for example, a great deal more subjective and emotional coloring in "Sierra Morena" than elsewhere; and "Natalia" is not free from a certain amount of innocent archaizing, although the author admits in a note that lovers in olden times did not use the kind of language, which, to be intelligible to his modern audience, he attributes to them. The "salon style," though reasonably uniform in general, is capable of variations within limits.

Karamzin's early work—the *Letters,* the first *Tales,* and the poetry of *My Trifles*—is thoroughly in the tradition of European sentimentalism. But Karamzin was gradually becoming aware of some of the weak points of this literary mode, and in the productions around the turn of the century it is possible to find cautious experiments in a more realistic method.[50] Particularly is this true in the author's attempts at a more full-bodied psychological development of character. Typical of this trend is the sketch entitled "The Sensitive and the Cold Man"[51] (1803), in which he endeavors to portray two persons, Erast and Leonid, as representatives of the two temperaments. The temperaments are described statically, as something "given," the traits of which are exhibited fully, although of course in different manifestations, from childhood to maturity. He carefully defines his psychological terminology: "The basic capacity for receiving impressions is temperament; the form which these impressions give to the moral being is character."[52] In more modern terms, the "temperament" seems to be the inherited component, the "character" the environmental component of personality. The method is not unlike that of La Bruyère, and relies on an outmoded psychology, but the sketch reveals a remarkable power of observation. It is particularly noticeable that Karamzin is now beginning to treat the sentimental temperament—Erast, in this case—with a good deal of irony. Neither the "sensitive" Erast nor his "cold" friend Leonid emerges from the sketch as a very attractive figure. Erast's "sensitive" feelings seem rather superficial; confronted with the infidelity of his first wife with his best friend, Erast "wept for two weeks, moped alone for two weeks in the outskirts of the city, and then, anxious to be busy with something, conceived the notion of becoming an author."[53] As an author he attracted attention "because he was born a tender friend of humanity and portrayed in his works a soul passionate for the good of man." In the first ardor of his success as a writer Erast meditates thus:

O fame! Once I sought thee in the smoke of battle and on the bloody field; now, in a quiet study, I see thy shining image before me and dedicate to thee the remnant of my days. I have not been able to be happy, but I may be the object of admiration; myrtle wreaths fade with youth; a laurel wreath is green even to the grave![54]

When his dreams of fame are shattered by malignant critics, as his dreams of marital bliss had been by his wife's fickleness, Erast flees to his friend's wedding, and shortly falls in love with the bride, Kallista. After the discovery of this liaison, and Erast's humiliation and repentance, he falls into a melancholy from which he is carried to an early grave. As for Leonid, the man of the "cold" temperament, his conduct at his friend's death is characteristic: "Leonid did not go to see the invalid, because the doctors informed him that the disease was infectious; and he was not at the funeral, saying: 'The lifeless body is no longer my friend!' "[55]

In the same year (1803-04) in which this psychological sketch appeared, Karamzin published in the *European Herald* thirteen chapters of what was evidently intended to be a full-length novel, with a promise, never fulfilled, of a conclusion to follow. This fragment is entitled *A Knight ["rytsar' "] of Our Time.* [56] It is on several counts one of the author's most interesting prose works. The rest of his narrative prose ("Poor Liza," "Natalia," "The Island of Bornholm," "Martha the Burgomaster's Wife," etc.) belong in that genre, the "tale," which flourished in the eighteenth and early nineteenth centuries in English as in continental literatures (e.g., Scott's *Tales of My Landlord,* or Irving's *Tales of a Traveler*), and which falls somewhere between the modern genres of "short story" and "novel." *A Knight of Our Time* is Karamzin's only experiment with the novel—that is, with a work extensive enough to trace the development of character over a period of many years. At the same time the piece shows very evidently the influence of two important foreign writers, both favorites of Karamzin, but in works which up to this point have affected him but little—Sterne in *Tristram Shandy* and Rousseau in *Les Confessions.*

A Knight of Our Time, the author informs his reader, is to be not a historical novel (of the type of Kheraskov's *Numa Pompilius*—Scott's work was still in the future), but the life story of a contemporary, a friend of Karamzin's, who is, in fact, still alive. Whether he was fully aware of the fact or not, Karamzin was herewith inaugurating the "psychological novel" in his native land, for it is not incident, which plays a rather small part in the extant chapters, but character depiction with which he is concerned. The early chapters are full of Sterne-inspired illusion-breaking whimsy, as the author turns from his story to address the reader directly. Thus, one chapter is headed: "Chapter IV, Which Is Written Only for Chapter Five," and reads in full:[57]

Gentlemen! You are reading not a novel, but a piece of life ["byl' "]: consequently the author is not obligated to give you an accounting of events. *This is exactly how it was* .... and I'll not say a word more. Is it pertinent? Is it in place? That's not my affair. I am only following fate with my pen, and describing what she does in her omnipotence—what for? Ask her; but I'll tell you in advance, you won't get any answer. For seven thousand years (if we can believe the chroniclers) she has been performing her wonders in the world, and has never explained them to anyone. Whether we look at history, or observe what is going on around us: everywhere the riddles of the Sphinx, which even Oedipus himself can't unravel .... The rose withers, the thorn remains;

583

the century-old oak tree, benefactor of wayfarers, falls to the ground from a stroke of lightning; a poisonous tree stands uninjured on its own root. Peter the Great, in the midst of ideas beneficent for his fatherland, grows cold in the embraces of death; a non-entity not infrequently passes twice from age to age. A lucky young fellow, whose life could be called a smile of fate and nature, is extinguished in a minute like a meteor; an ill-starred wretch, useless to the world, a burden to himself, lives on, and can hardly wait for his end— What can we do? Weep, anyone who has tears, and console himself sometimes at least with the thought that this world is only the prologue of the drama!

This is, of course, the author's apologia for the death of Leon's mother in the following chapter.

The only portions of the novel which Karamzin finished deal with the childhood of his hero Leon, who is eleven years old when the novel breaks off. Karamzin's tale is the first example in Russian literature of an attempt to portray the psychology of a child. Part of his picture is certainly autobiographical: like Leon, he lost his own mother early and attempted to find a substitute in a beautiful and sympathetic older woman. But a great deal of the episode, which constitutes the bulk of the description of Leon's childhood, is drawn from Rousseau's glamorized and idealized account of his relationship with Mme de Warens. The last chapter written, significantly entitled "A New Actaeon," relates how the eleven-year-old lad, who has been caressed and pampered by the virtuous and childless Emilia, wife of a wealthy neighbor, and taught French and other worldly accomplishments by her, goes bathing in a secluded stream where he knows Emilia is also accustomed to bathe in the early morning; is surprised by her arrival and has to hide himself in the bushes, at some distance from his clothes. Emilia disrobes, the boy watches, until her two hunting dogs smell him out and pursue him until she calls them off. The titillating undertone throughout the chapter, of awakening sensual instinct on the boy's part and of the beginning of a change in Emilia's feelings toward him from the purely maternal, is entirely in the tone of Rousseau's highly ambivalent son-lover relationship with Mme de Warens. It is a great pity that this most promising beginning of a novel never had a continuation; Karamzin, of course, was too preoccupied after 1804 with his historical project to return to it.

One of the most interesting auctorial digressions in *A Knight of Our Time* shows that Karamzin, although as we have seen from "The Sensitive and the Cold Man" he had apparently become somewhat disillusioned in his idealization of the "sensitive temperament," nevertheless is still loyal to it in the main. His motherless young hero, Leon, learns to read with precocious ease, and thenceforward devours the library of his dead mother, which consists largely of novels, mostly translated from the French, but including Fedor Emin's *Miramond*. Karamzin, probably here from personal experience, describes the boy's sentimental day-dreams induced by this reading. He notes, among other bits of psychological observation, that at this age (Leon is now about ten years old) the love element in the novels he reads does not interest him—it is action and adventure that he is enthralled with, and it is in the role of a hero that he casts himself in his fantasies:[58]

Despite my own slight weakness for novels, I admit that they may be called a hot-house for the young soul, which from this reading comes to maturity before its time; and this, if philosophical medicoes are to be trusted, is injurious—at least to the health .... Leon in the tenth year from his birth could already, for a couple of hours at a time, play with his imagination and construct castles in the air. "Danger" and "heroic friendship" were his favorite dream. It is commentary enough to say that in dangers he always imagined himself the saviour, not the person being saved—a sign of a proud, glory-loving heart! Our hero would fly in thought in the darkness of night to the cry of the traveler assaulted to the death by bandits; or he would take by storm a lofty tower, in which his friend was languishing in chains. Such Don Quixotish behavior quite early defined the moral character of Leon's life. You, my quiet phlegmatics, doubtless have never dreamed thus in your childhood—you who are not alive, but drowse out your days in the world and weep only from boredom! And you, rational egoists, who do not attach yourselves to people, or hold fast to them only from motives of self-interest, as long as the tie is useful to you, and readily remove your hand the moment they might ask something of you! My hero takes his little hat from his head, bows low to you, and says politely: "Honored sirs! You shall never see *me* under your banners of egoism."

At about the same time as the two psychological pieces just discussed, Karamzin wrote his last tale, "Martha the Burgomaster's Wife" ["Marfa Posadnitsa"].[59] Marfa Borctskaia was a real person, widow of a famous *posadnik* or burgomaster of the free city of Novgorod in the fifteenth century. She and her sons headed the opposition of the wealthy commercial nobility of the town to the encroachments of the tyrannical Tsar of Muscovy, Ivan III. In her attempts to maintain the republican freedom of Novgorod, Marfa and her family even flirted with the King of Poland. The city, however, was forced to surrender when its rather ineffective volunteer levy was defeated by the Muscovite force, and the ancient free constitution abrogated; as a sign of this, the bell which used to summon the citizens to meetings of the *veche*, or town council, was transferred to Moscow. Marfa's son Dimitry, the *posadnik*, was executed; she and her grandson were deported to Muscovite territory. This historical background—and little more—is preserved by Karamzin. His tale begins dramatically: "The tolling of the *veche* bell rang out, and hearts in Novgorod began to beat fast. Fathers of families tore themselves from the embraces of wives and children to hurry whither their fatherland was calling them."[59] The author from the beginning shows a certain ambivalence of attitude toward the contending forces; it would naturally be impolitic to portray Ivan III, the real founder of Russian autocracy, as a consummate villain; on the other hand, Karamzin's sympathies are quite evidently with the freedom-loving people of Novgorod, a city which he seems to envision as a sort of Slavic Republic of Rome. Marfa's machinations with the King of Poland are unhistorically denied: the emissary of King Casimir is proudly told that Novgorod needs no assistance from him. Marfa's sons disappear from the narrative; instead she is given a beautiful daughter, Xenia, for whom she provides a husband in the glamorous (and also unhistorical) young Miroslav. On the advice of her ancient grandfather, the hermit Feodosii, Marfa, who seems, while occupying no official position, to be the Republic's real ruler, puts Miroslav in charge of the city's armies. Miroslav is killed in battle, the Novgorodians are obliged to surrender, Marfa is executed on the scaffold, Xenia dies of grief, and old Feodosii returns to his wilderness. Needless to say, the whole tale is in the highest degree unhistorical; with the exception of Marfa herself, none of the protagonists has any historical existence. Nevertheless the colorful and exciting picture of the restless old republic, and the passionate patriotism and loyalty to the ideal of freedom which the people exhibit redeem Karamzin's story from the banal. It shows the influence of the historical novels and poems of Sir Walter Scott, which were just beginning to become familiar to the Russian reading public, and perhaps does not much greater violence to fact than does *Ivanhoe*. The individual characters of the story, however, with the exception of the Posadnitsa herself, are singularly pallid; the tragic figures of Xenia and Miroslav are no more than lifeless puppets; only the mass effect produces a convincing sense of reality. One may wonder how it was possible for Karamzin, after his genuine success in psychological portraiture in *A Knight of Our Time* and "The Sensitive and the Cold Man" to revert to such unconvincing stereotypes. Indeed, the characterization even of "Natalia a Boyar's Daughter," several years earlier, is on a higher level than that of "Marfa Posadnitsa."

"Martha the Burgomaster's Wife" is the last important prose tale of Karamzin. After 1802 he began more and more to be preoccupied with other interests. He began in 1804 his twenty-one-year labor on the monumental *History of the Russian State.*[60] In the years 1797-99 he put out three annual collections of poetry ("almanacs") under the title *Aonides* (i.e., *Muses*), and during 1802-03 he edited the journal *European Herald (Vestnik Evropy)*. In connection with all these activities he published from time to time essays on political and esthetic subjects and reviews of books, which had considerable influence in molding liberal opinion in his own and subsequent times. Of great interest is his preface to the second collection (1798) of the *Aonides* for its revision of some of his earlier theories on the nature of poetry. In "Poesy," for example, it is evident that young Karamzin conceives of the art as first and foremost a means of escape from the real world into a realm of dreams, of the "ideal." Such also seems to be the tenor of his prose tales, in spite of the irony with which Erast and *A Knight of Our Time* are treated. In 1793, still in the heyday of his sentimental period, Karamzin published in the almanac *Aglaia* a short piece entitled: "What Does an Author Need?" He seems to need just about what the "sensitive" Erast possessed when he sought auctorial glory:[61]

They say that an author needs talents and learning, a keen penetrating intelligence, a lively imagination, etc. This is correct—but it is not enough. He must possess also a good, tender heart . . . . Vainly does the hypocrite think to deceive his readers and beneath the golden cloak of sumptuous words conceal a heart of iron; vainly does he speak to us of kindness, sympathy, virtue! All his exclamations are cold, without soul, without life; and never will the nourishing, ethereal flame pour forth from his creations into the tender soul of a reader. . . You desire to be an author: read the history of the misfortunes of the human race—and if your heart does not bleed, abandon the pen—or it will only portray for us the cold darkness of your own soul. . . . In a word, I am convinced that a bad man cannot be a good author.

This naive equation of the "sensitive" with the "good" soul is no longer so convincing to the Karamzin of only a few years later. In the preface to the second collection of the almanac *Aonides* (1798), turning as editor to the general consideration of the merits and demerits of the contemporary poetry included in it, he writes:[62]

Poetry consists not in an inflated description of terrible scenes in nature [one may think of Bobrov!], but in liveliness of thought and feeling. If the poet does not write about what really preoccupies his soul; if he is not the slave, but the tyrant of his imagination, forcing it to chase after strange, remote ideas which are not his own; if he describes not those objects which are close to him and attract the imagination to themselves by their proper force. . . . then in his productions there will never be any liveliness, any truth. . . . It is not necessary to imagine that only great objects can excite the poet and serve for the exemplification of his gifts; on the contrary, the real poet finds a poetical side in the most ordinary things; it is his business to apply lively colors to everything, to attach keen thought to everything, to reveal subtle shades which are hidden from the eyes of other people, to discover imperceptible analogies and likenesses, to play with ideas, and, like Jupiter in Aesop's fable, sometimes "make great what is small," and sometimes "make small what is great."

Not grandiose dreams of an ideal humanity, therefore, but close observation of real life is what makes a poet; it will not be enough to have a "good, tender heart"—the poet must also have an acutely observant eye, capable of discovering hidden analogies. It is a pity that Karamzin did not succeed in practice in breaking away from his earlier esthetic manner as thoroughly as he did in theory.

Although not strictly relevant to literature, the political thinking of Karamzin and its development need a few words of explanation. In the *Letters,* as we have seen, he reveals a rather cautious and neutral attitude toward the French Revolution; but from unpublished letters and other evidences not made public until much later it is apparent that at the beginning he was quite sympathetic with the aims of the revolutionaries. It was only after the bloody events of 1793 and the Jacobin period that he became thoroughly alienated from it. His political philosophy was largely derived from Montesquieu, with partial rectifications from Rousseau. Following the author of *L'Esprit des lois* he came to the conclusion that the nature of a large state, such as that of France, required a monarchy, and that accordingly the attempt to alter the form of government to that of a republic was a historical mistake, destined to failure; his conclusions were of course borne out by the career of Napoleon. Transferring the same thesis to his own country, larger in extent even than France, he was forced to concede the same results: Russia must remain an autocracy, and any attempt to impose republicanism on the country would be wrong and foolish. When he saw, as he imagined, the Russian autocrat himself toying with dangerous republican experiments (Alexander's liberalism was of course confined entirely to words), Karamzin was moved to compose his major political document, the "Memoir on Ancient and Modern Russia,"[63] written in 1811 and submitted through the Emperor's sister to Alexander I. This document has usually been interpreted as the utterance of the most ultra-conservative of reactionaries. In it the historian traces the history of Russian autocracy down to the years of Alexander's own reign, and points out the mistakes of the earlier tsars. He is, of course, the firm opponent of any form of liberal thinking, and even champions the existence of serfdom as necessary for the stability of the autocratic government. He bitterly criticizes Alexander's alliance with Napoleon and adherence to the disastrous "continental system"; but his chief object of attack is the reformation of the Petrine system of governmental "colleges," which had been the major success of the liberal Speransky. The replacement of the older bureaucratic order by a series of expensive Europeanized "Ministries" Karamzin views as only a paper reform, achieving no real reformation of the evils of red tape and detachment from the interests of the governed, and only augmenting the possibilities of graft and corruption. He accuses Alexander and Speransky of "throwing dust in the eyes" of the Russian people by this measure. The criticism was entirely justified; Speransky was notoriously blind to realities and dogmatically obstinate in believing that a change of names must effect a lasting improvement in affairs. Yet Karamzin, for all his bitterness against this aspect of Speransky's work, was not unaware of the importance of the one lasting achievement of the man, his great codification of the Russian law, a work with which Karamzin himself was briefly associated at the outset. The "Memoir" brought down upon Karamzin the wrath of Alexander, who was extremely cold to the historian from 1811 until the publication in 1818 of the first eight volumes of the *History of the Russian State,* upon which he became reconciled. Even then, however, the fearless critic was not minded to hold his peace, and in 1819 he again addressed the Emperor in a document entitled "Creed of a Russian Citizen,"[64] which he read personally to his one-man audience. Again it was a strong and eloquent criticism of many aspects of Alexander's later reign, especially his obsession with the "military colony" plan of the notorious Arakcheev. A heated argument followed the reading, and in a note appended to his copy of the "Creed," Karamzin declares that he told the Emperor: "Sire! You have a great deal of self-love. I am not afraid of anything. We are all equal before God. What I am saying to you I would have said to your father. Sire! I despise the present-day liberals, I love only that freedom which no tyrant can deprive me of. I am no longer pleading for your favor; I am speaking to you for perhaps the last time."[64] Evidently Karamzin expected serious repercussions from his vigorous intervention; they were not, however, forthcoming, and for the rest of Alexander's life Karamzin continued to enjoy the Emperor's respect, although, as Karamzin's notes show, his advice was never followed by the monarch whom he had undertaken to educate in the duties of an autocrat—not that Alexander's deviations were in any sense in a democratic direction!

Karamzin's final work was the huge *History of the Russian State,* on which he labored for the whole of twenty-one years, from 1804 until a few months before his death in 1826. Earlier, in an essay entitled "On Events and Characters in Russian History Which May be Artistically Utilized"[66] (1802) Karamzin had given evidence of the bias which he would have as an historian. He was animated by the patriotic notion that Russian history, as dramatically as the history of classical antiquity, could afford examples of great actions and heroic characters. His *History,* accordingly, is by no means a monument of scientific method; the earlier portions may be compared to the *Histories* of the Roman Livy, with their accent on patriotism, moral instruction, and the picturesque. The *History* is an artistic work, and should be judged as a work of literature just as much as should "Marfa Posadnitsa," although the fictional element in the *History* is of course far less prominent. The final two volumes of Karamzin's *History* reveal a slightly different attitude on the author's part; while the earlier volumes may be compared with Livy's moralizing and patriotic account of Roman history, volumes nine and ten, which deal with the picturesque and tumultuous reigns of Ivan the Terrible and the usurper Boris Godunov, show more of Tacitus than of Livy, and are bitterly critical of the misdeeds of these "tyrants." Unquestionably Ivan IV deserves much condemnation; but the uncritical rejection of his whole reign as an unrelieved and bloody madness is thoroughly misleading. Ivan IV was a capable and intelligent monarch, and his "terribleness" was not the result of madness or sadism merely—it had political purposes, which the "terrible" Tsar achieved. As for Boris, the whole picture which Pushkin so convincingly presents in his magnificent tragedy, of a criminal, however well-intentioned, who perishes of a weakness brought on by the pangs of conscience, is drawn directly from Karamzin's pages. Boris is assumed by Karamzin to have been the murderer of the child Dimitry; he may have been in fact, but there is no infallible proof of this, and his brief reign was, for the most part, a beneficial one, not a "tyranny." Karamzin, with the instincts proper to a novelist but rather suspect in a historian, chooses the most colorful and dramatic interpretations, which also at the same time serve to bolster his political conviction that the autocracy must have the assistance of an enlightened aristocracy in its rule. Obviously the *oprichnina* could not find favor with a thinker of this stamp, and in a contest between the representa-

589

tive of the old aristocracy, Vasily Shuisky, and the upstart "Tatar" Boris Godunov, the historian's sympathy must evidently be with the former. Much of Karamzin's highly colored picture of these two reigns persists, and the less dramatic "scientific" presentations by Soloviev or Kliuchevsky fail to catch the popular imagination.

As an example of Karamzin's style as a historian, which differs considerably from his prose in the *Tales*, the following extract from the account of Boris Godunov's encounter with the Pretender (the "First False Dmitry") may serve:[67]

These rapid successes of seduction [that is, of the Pretender in winning away adherents of Boris] dismayed Godunov and all Russia. The Tsar apparently saw his mistake—and made another; he saw that he should not have deceived people with signs of a feigned contempt for the renegade, but should have beaten him back from our border with a prepared and powerful army, and not let him into the [Novgorod-] Seversk region, where the old Lithuanian spirit was still alive and where an accumulation of criminals, runaways and disgraced [government] service people naturally awaited the insurgent as a good fortune; where the common people and the military men themselves, astonished by the Pretender's unhindered entry into Russia, might, believing the insinuations of his [i.e., the Pretender's] scouts, suppose that Godunov actually did not dare to oppose the genuine son of Ivan [i.e., Dmitry, son of Ivan the Terrible]. A new demonstration of how delusive is intelligence in a contest with conscience, and how craftiness, foreign to virtue, gets entangled in its own nets! Boris might still have rectified this mistake; have mounted his war-horse and led the Russians in person against the criminal. The presence of the wearer of the crown, his great-souled bravery and confidence would without doubt have had their effect. Though not born a hero, Godunov had nevertheless been from youth familiar with war; he had been able by the strength of his spirit to instill valor in men's hearts and to save Moscow from the Khan [of the Crimea], when he was only a commander. In his favor was the sanctity of the crown and the oath of allegiance, the habit of obedience, the recollection of many benefactions of his government—and Russia on the field of honor would not have betrayed the Tsar to the renegade. But confused by terror, Boris did not dare to go to meet the shade of Dmitry; he was suspicious of the boyars, and entrusted his fate to them, naming as commander-in-chief Mstislavsky, a conscientious, personally manful officer, but of greater renown than skill; he gave strict orders to the military, all without exception to hasten to Briansk—and as for himself, he hid, as it were, in the capital! In a word, God's judgment was thundering over the imperial criminal.

The historian will observe in this account the unabashed partisanship, the unsupported implication of motives, and the tone of moral judgment—all characteristics which "scientific" history rejects in principle. An observer of style will note the relatively long and balanced sentences. These are not "periods" in the Lomonosovian manner, with an artificial word order, the verb at the end in the Latin way; but at the same time they are far from the short, easy cola that characterize the style of the *Tales*, of which the following, from "Natalia," is a good specimen:[68]

The Boyar Matvei returned home late, and supposing that his daughter was already asleep, did not go to her *terem*. Midnight was approaching. Natalia did not think of

sleep, but of her beloved, to whom she had given her heart forever and whom she awaited with impatience. The moon was still shining in the sky—the moon, in which formerly
her eyes had always delighted, had now become hateful to her. Now our beauty thought:
"How slowly you are moving over the round sky! Set more quickly, bright moon! He,
he is coming for me, when you have hidden yourself!" The moon descended—already
part of it had gone below the horizon—darkness thickened in the atmosphere—the cocks
began to crow—the moon disappeared—and there was a tinkling of the silver ring at the
boyar's gate.

There is as little admixture of Slavonic vocabulary and syntax in the *History*
as in "Natalia" and the other tales, but the elegant, musical, slightly mannered language of the latter gives place in the former to a more complicated,
more sonorous, more dignified speech, as befits its more elevated subject
matter.

Before taking leave of Karamzin, we must consider once more briefly the
significance of the prose style which he evolved and which was enthusiastically adopted by other writers of the sentimentalist school and the early romantics. This style was, as has been remarked, a drastic departure from the
literary styles of the past. For perhaps the first time in Russian history, a
writer was making a conscious effort to write as people spoke. That the
people on whose speech Karamzin's style was based were not "the Russian
people" as a whole, but only that highly educated and westernized segment
of the population that nearly monopolized literature—the gentry of the
capitals—imposed a serious limitation on the Karamzinian reform. Karamzin's
style suffered also from a defect which exposed it very properly to the sneers
and jibes of the conservatives—a fatal fondness for an unnatural, mannered
indirection of language, which was supposed to be more "agreeable" than a
simple statement. Perhaps upper-class Russian ladies did in fact speak such a
language—we have the parallel example of the French *précieuses* to convince us—but certainly no one else did so, and the fashion was, very fortunately, short-lived. Karamzin's adoption of this periphrastic mode, however, tended in considerable measure to nullify the merits of his use of the
spoken Russian idiom; and as the periphrastic mode went rapidly out of
fashion, Karamzin's salon style went with it. An indication of what this
style could be may be gathered from a passage in Admiral Alexander Shishkov's "Dissertation ["Rassuzhdenie"] on the Old and the New Style of
the Russian Language"[69]—a hostile witness, to be sure, but not seriously
exaggerated:

We fancy we are being Ossians and Sternes when, in discoursing about a child at play,
instead of saying: "How pleasant to look upon your youth!" we say: "How edifying
to gaze upon you in your burgeoning spring-tide!" Instead of: "The moon is shining,"
"Pallid Hecate is casting wan reflections" . . . instead of: "Gypsy girls are coming to
meet the village maidens" [we say] "The motley throng of rustic oreads are encountering the swarthy bevies of Pharaoh's fawning daughters."

591

The simple, straight-forward Russian of Ivan Krylov's prose came far closer than Karamzin's to the ideal of a written language identical with normal speech. But Krylov was not a "westernizer"; Karamzin was, and one of the greatest merits of the new style was that it consciously and effectively, by the coinage of new words, the appropriation of western idioms, and the like, facilitated the Russian expression of ideas which were the common basis of European intellectual life. If the archaic and cumbersome style devised by Radishchev and later propagandized by the Beseda group had prevailed; or if at this date the Krylov style, relatively untouched by western influence, had prevailed, Russia might have continued to be isolated by an intellectual barrier from western Europe. It was Karamzin's great accomplishment to have effected a workable compromise. The "salon style" was based on spoken Russian, not on a dead and artificial Slavonic, and was thus far more widely intelligible than the old bookish tongue had ever been; and it was hospitable to western vocabulary, syntax and idiom, without losing its Russian character, and therefore reduced the dangers inherent in Russian dependence on French as a medium of communication. Like all compromises, it came under attack on both counts: by the conservatives who idealized the ancient Russo-Slavonic bookish language, and by the "Slavophil" element who idealized the Russian peasant and deplored the intrusion of western influence. But Karamzin's compromise worked, and for a couple of generations Russian literature, both verse and prose, is dominated by it.

While not a writer of the highest rank in Russian literature, Karamzin is one of the most important of mediators. He created a new and enduring style, and gave the death blow to the stilted archaism of the past; he introduced the attitudes of sentimentalism in artistically dignified new prose forms; and he gave Russia its first coherent political philosophy and its first artistic history. These are no mean contributions, which should not be lost to sight merely because Karamzin, to his misfortune, was so soon to be followed by Alexander Sergeevich Pushkin.

RETROSPECT

THE EIGHTEENTH CENTURY IN RUSSIAN LITERATURE

Like Radishchev, Bobrov and others who, as they entered a new century, turned to look back at the old, let us cast a glance backward and try briefly to summarize the literary developments of Russia's eighteenth century.

It began with a glaring contradiction between an inherited, basically ecclesiastical and Byzantium-derived medieval culture having few points of contact with the culture of western Europe, and the alien, secular, Latin-derived culture which Peter I attempted to impose on it from above. For nearly two generations this contradiction subsisted, rendering difficult, if not impossible, any genuine literary achievement. With Peter the Great the ecclesiastical domination of literature disappeared, never to be resumed, but the Russian language remained dominated by the Church Slavonic element, and was at the same time infiltrated by an influx of unassimilated western borrowings. The most striking single indication of changed orientation in literature, and the genuine beginning of modern Russian literary achievement was Lomonosov's codification of linguistic usage in the dogma of the "three styles," and the rapid and complete replacement of the cumbrous old syllabic versification by the syllabo-tonic system which he and Trediakovsky inaugurated. With increasing political and cultural contacts between Russia and the West, the Baroque elements in Russian art and literature, still very evident in the poetry of Lomonosov and Trediakovsky, gave way to the classical mode of contemporary Europe, primarily of France.

Classicism, of which Sumarokov became the principal spokesman and champion, dominated the entire period from about 1730 to 1775. The influence of France during this era remained the paramount one, and the Russian classicists prided themselves on being "the Russian Racine," "the Russian Molière," or "the Russian La Fontaine." Nevertheless, with all the imitativeness which this attitude presupposes, Russian classicism began to show increasing divergencies from France. This was particularly noticeable in the genres of fable and satire, where the abstract and universalized ideal of classicism failed from the beginning (e.g. Kantemir) to oust the concrete and specifically Russian element; and toward the end of the undisputed sway of classicism a concretely Russian background had made its appearance even in comedy (Fonvizin).

593

During the period when French-inspired classical ideals dominated Russian literature, the system of closed genres, each with its own ethos and its own linguistic medium, was its self-evident concomitant. Tragedy and comedy were strictly differentiated; the fable, the elegy, the epistle, the satire, the pastoral, et al., each with an accepted classical (usually Latin) model divided the field of literature. Chief of the hierarchy were the epic ·(represented by Kheraskov), the tragedy (represented by Sumarokov) and the ode (represented by Lomonosov, despite his Baroque tendencies). Toward the 1770s, this system of closed genres began to break down; the "tearful comedy," a hybrid of tragedy and comedy, made its appearance; the ode began to take on a more subjective and personal character, and with Derzhavin even to incorporate entirely disparate elements, such as satire. The strictness of the linguistic divisions between the "three styles" began to disappear and the "middle style" in effect to displace both others.

Artistic prose, from very crude beginnings, had by the 1770s achieved an accepted place in literature. As a medium which classical theory had never fully accepted or legislated for, prose was from the beginning less restricted and regularized than verse. A wide variety of narrative prose types had arisen, only two of which (the pseudo-historical and philosophical novel, and the picaresque) had genuinely classical prototypes. In this area, earlier than elsewhere, the new wave of sentimentalism made itself felt in Russian literature (Fedor Emin).

The break-down of the classical system, which began in western Europe even before the middle of the century, set in around 1775 in Russia. Classical acceptance of the reason as the dominant component of human character and the guide to virtue gave way, after Rousseau, to the exaltation of the emotions, or "sentiments," in the same role. The individual began to replace the generalized, abstract "man," and preoccupation with individual feelings and concerns led more and more to a kind of embryonic quasi-realism in literature. At this period prose narrative (tale and novel, e.g. Karamzin) came for the first time to take an important place in Russian literature, although verse remained still the dominant literary medium.

Although Rousseau may be considered as the prime mover in the sentimentalist development, his own impetus came from England, and his immediate influence was greater in Germany than on his own country. Accordingly during the last quarter of the eighteenth century in Russia the influence of English and German models came to displace to a large extent that of French, with the exception of Rousseau himself. The English novel (Richardson, Sterne), the English "graveyard school" (Young), English "descriptive poetry" (Thomson) and English "popular verse" (Percy's ballads, the poetry of "Ossian"); and parallel German preromantic developments (the *Sturm und Drang* drama, itself strongly influenced by Shakespeare and Lillo); the odes and religious epics of Klopstock; the pastorals of Gessner, etc.) took the place which French classical models had once occupied. At the same time a significant linguistic development in Russia went hand in hand with the new "sentimentalism": the old "high style," replete with non-Russian and scarcely intelligible vocabulary, succumbed to the attractions of a new, easy, flexible style, modeled more closely than its predecessor on the norms of speech—a development parallel in time and similar in effect to Wordsworth's reform of English poetic diction.

With the triumph of the sentimentalist fashion (Dmitriev, Karamzin) we cross the boundaries between the eighteenth and nineteenth centuries. The old fashion—classicism—which had dominated most of the eighteenth century did not of course die abruptly with the advent of the new, but it had already been rendered an árchaic anachronism. But sentimentalism itself was only a transitional phenomenon, and was destined soon to give way to the new trend of romanticism, many elements of which it anticipates. Like all transitional movements, sentimentalism looks both ways, and in many of its aspects could as satisfactorily be associated with the nineteenth as with the eighteenth century. There are no clean breaks in cultural history.

The eighteenth century in Russia has suffered principally from the stigma of imitativeness. From an age which sets a very high, and probably excessive, value on originality, little sympathy can be expected for an imitative age. But imitation characterizes Russian eighteenth-century literature not, as often used to be asserted, because it was juvenile, but because imitation of recognized classical models was one of the fundamental prescriptions of eighteenth-century literary theory—of French and German no less than of English and Russian. And even in genres where the existence of classical models of great authority, such as the epic and the drama, made imitation almost inevitable, a discerning eye will discover in Russian literature of the age a quite disconcerting degree of originality. Doubtless the *Rossiad* is unimaginable without *Jerusalem Delivered* as its model; but where is the model for the *Bakhariana*—or for that matter, for *Vladimir Reborn*? And yet Kheraskov is rated as one of the most derivative of eighteenth-century poets. Sumarokov's comedies often seem pallid reflections of Molière or Holberg, but the old people of *The Imaginary Cuckold* owe nothing to any literary model, and even the form and language of the comedy is unclassically original. Bogdanovich's *Dushenka* is wholly *sui generis*. The imitativeness of eighteenth-century Russian literature has been much exaggerated.

Probably the most serious obstacle for a modern reader toward enjoyment of Russian eighteenth-century literature is the language. The century begins with the motley, archaic, Latinate Russian of Feofan Prokopovich. Even with the drastic changes initiated by Lomonosov in the linguistic field, it remains a heavy and cumbersome language. To the end of the century the Russian that is written, by poets and prose writers alike, is a different language from that which is spoken, and of which only tantalizing glimpses are afforded by occasional scenes in comedy or dialogue in satire. With the Karamzinian reforms at the end of the century a greater degree of conformity is achieved between spoken and written language, but the dominant element is still only a class dialect—the self-conscious, affected idiom of the aristocratic salon. The Russian of the eighteenth century is in a very real sense not a single language at all, but a congeries of dialects, all somewhat artificial and remote from living speech. To this linguistic obstacle may be added a stylistic one: the prevailingly rhetorical character of the written language, of whatever stratum. Only rarely does one catch the intonations of normal speech amid the artificial embellishments imposed by the textbooks of rhetoric. An obtrusive and irritating example is the omnipresent mythological allusion: eighteenth-century Russian writers of all classes, from the plebeian to the highest aristocrat, seem to be far more at home with the Olympian pantheon and all the minor creatures of Hellenic folklore than any genuine Greek writer, except perhaps Callimachus! A modern reader is likely to be quite put off by all this paraphernalia of dead and irrelevant learning.

But the modern reader, if he is honest, will have to confess that the eighteenth-century literature of his own language is no more congenial to him than that of Elizabeth's or Catherine's Russia. Where is the German who can read with patience the tragedies of Gottsched or the epics of Klopstock? Are the pastorals of Haller and Gessner or the "novels" of Wieland any more accessible to the twentieth-century reader than the sentimental effusions of Kapnist and Karamzin? French readers, by the assiduous efforts of their own pedagogues, are spared the tedium of reading Delille and Parny, Saint-Lambert and J.-B. Rousseau, Ducis and Gresset, whom they are likely to know only by name, if at all. But even with the English reader, how congenial are the novels of Richardson, the tragedy of Addison, Thomson's *The Seasons* or Young's *Night Thoughts*—even, indeed, Johnson's *Rasselas* or Pope's *Dunciad*—and yet these are the acknowledged masterpieces of the age. It is not the immaturity or unoriginality of Russian eighteenth-century literature, which have been greatly exaggerated, that make it hard for the modern reader to approach it—it is, quite simply, the general character of the age itself, which all European literatures share in common, and which requires a deal of adjustment of one entering it. Such adjustment, however, is possible, and once made will reveal a period of great diversity, brilliance and beauty, well worth the pains of making it.

Esthetic fashions come and go, perhaps not as rapidly as fashions in dress, but just as inexorably; and if any sort of general law governs their succession, it has yet to be discovered. The Russian seventeenth century is dominated by the Baroque fashion, with some elements, it would seem, of the Renaissance which Russian culture in general by-passed. The earliest phases of the eighteenth century are still Baroque; but the classical mode, dominant in western Europe, soon establishes itself in Russia also and remains authoritative even into the nineteenth century. The first half of the nineteenth century—until about 1848—is the domain of the romantic fashion, to which the transitional vogue of sentimentalism forms a prelude. From 1848 to about 1893 "realism" governs all aspects of Russian culture; after the turn of the century, chaos ensues, as realism (whether "critical" or "Socialist") battles with various splinter factions of a neo-romantic character. In these successive fashions one may detect a quite indefinable similarity between Renaissance, classicism and realism on the one hand; Baroque, romanticism and "symbolism" and its congeners on the other. It must be emphasized, however, that such a similarity does not permit the critic to use without qualification, for example, the term "realism" for such an eighteenth-century phenomenon as Fonvizin's *Minor* or Smollett's *Humphrey Clinker;* or the term "romanticism" for Bogdanovich's *Dushenka* or Klopstock's *Messias.* Similarity is not identity, and both "realism" and "romanticism" are phenomena conditioned by specifically nineteenth-century features; they do not exist for the eighteenth century except by analogy.

With this we may terminate this study, with the hope that it has served in some degree to illuminate a period and a literature that have for various reasons suffered neglect in the past. If eighteenth-century Russian literature is not as exciting as nineteenth, and has no giants of the stature of Pushkin, Dostoevsky and Tolstoy to show, it can still show a Lomonosov, a Derzhavin and a Fonvizin—and these and their age deserve a sympathetic hearing, which we hope this study has made easier for the unprejudiced reader.

NOTES / BIBLIOGRAPHY / INDEX

FREQUENTLY CITED WORKS – WITH ABBREVIATIONS

GENERAL WORKS ON EIGHTEENTH CENTURY LITERATURE

Blagoi, D.D. ISTORIIA RUSSKOI LITERATURY XVIII VEKA. M. Gosudarstvennoe Uchebno-pedagogicheskoe izdatel'stvo Narkomprosa RSFSR, 1945. [Blagoi]

XVIII BEK. Sborniki 1-10. M-L. Izdatel'stvo Akademii Nauk SSSR. [XVIII vek]

Gukovskii, G.A. RUSSKAIA LITERATURA XVIII BEKA. M. Gosudarstvennoe Ucheb-no-pedagogicheskoe Izdatel'stvo Narkomprosa RSFSR, 1939. [Gukovskii]

ISTORIIA RUSSKOI LITERATURY. T. III. M. Izdatel'stvo Akademii Nauk, 1941. T. IV, 1947. [IRL]

ISTORIIA RUSSKOI POEZII. T. I. L. Isdatel'stvo "Nauka," 1968. [IRP]

ISTORIIA RUSSKOGO ROMANA. I. M-L. Izdatel'stvo Akademii Nauk SSSR, 1962. [IRR]

PROBLEMY RUSSKOGO PROSVESHCHENIIA V LITERATURE XVIII VEKA. M-L. Izdatel'stvo Akademii Nauk SSSR, 1961. [Problemy]

Serman, I.Z. RUSSKII KLASSITSIZM. POEZIIA, DRAMA, SATIRA. L. Izdatel'stvo "Nauka," 1973. [Serman]

Sokolov, A.A. OCHERKI PO ISTORII RUSSKOI POEMY XVIII I PERVOI POLOVINY XIX VEKA. M. Izdatel'stvo Moskovskogo universiteta, 1955. [Sokolov]

Stender-Petersen, Adolf. GESCHICHTE DER RUSSISCHEN LITERATUR IN ZWEI BÄNDEN. München: C.H. Beck'sche Verlagsbuchhandlung, 1957. [St.-P.]

ANTHOLOGIES

RUSSKAIA KOMEDIIA I KOMICHESKAIA OPERA XVIII VEKA. Redaktsiia teksta i vstupitel'naia stat'ia P.N. Berkova. M-L. Gosudarstvennoe Izdatel'stvo "Iskus-stvo," 1950. [Berkov]

KHRESTOMATIIA PO RUSSKOI LITERATURE XVIII VEKA. Sost. A.V. Kokorev. M. Gosudarstvennoe Uchebno-pedagogicheskoe izdatel'stvo ministerstva pros-vesshcheniia RSFSR, 1961. [Kokorev]

STIKHOTVORNAIA KOMEDIIA KONTSA XVIII–NACHALA XIX V. Vstupitel'naia stat'ia, podgotovka teksta i premechaniia M.O. Iankovskogo. M-L.Sovetskii Pi-satel', 1964. Biblioteka poeta. Bol'shaia seriia. [Komediia]

RUSSKAIA LITERATURA XVIII VEKA. Sost. G.P. Makogonenko. L. Izdatel'stvo pros-veshchenie, Leningradskoe otdelenie, 1970. [Makogonenko]

Manning, Clarence A. ANTHOLOGY OF EIGHTEENTH CENTURY RUSSIAN LIT-ERATURE. Volumes I and II. New York: King's Crown Press, 1951. [Manning]

RUSSKAIA POEZIIA XVIII VEKA. Vstupitel'naia stat'ia i sostavlenie G. Makogonenko. M. Izdatel'stvo "Khudozhestvennaia Literatura," 1972. [Poeziia]

POETY XVIII VEKA V DVUKH TOMAKH. Vstupitel'naia stat'ia G.P. Makogonenko. Biograficheskie spravki I.Z. Sermana. Sostavlenie G.P. Makogonenko i I.Z. Ser-mana. Podgotovka teksta i premechaniia N.D. Kochetkovoi. L. Sovetskii Pisatel', 1972. Biblioteka poeta. Bol'shaia seriia. [Poety XVIII v.]

POETY 1790-1810-KH GODOV. Vstupitel'naia stat'ia i sostavlenie Iu.M. Lotmana. Podgotovka teksta M.G. Al'tshullera. Vstupitel'nie zametki, biograficheskie sprav-ki i primechaniia M.G. Al'tshullera i Iu.M. Lotmana. L. Sovetskii pisatel', 1971. Biblioteka poeta. Bol'shaia seriia. [Poety 1790-1810 gg.]

RUSSKAIA PROZA XVIII VEKA. Vstupitel'naia stat'ia, sostavlenie i primechaniia G. Makogonenko. M. Izdatel'stvo "Khudozhestvennaia literatura," 1971. [Proza]

POETY-SATIRIKI KONTSA XVIII-NACHALA XIX V. Vstupitel'naia stat'ia, podgotov-ka teksta i primechaniia G.V. Ermakovoi-Bitner. L. Sovetskii Pisatel', 1959. Biblioteka poeta. Bol'shaia seriia. [Satira]

STIKHOTVORNAIA SKAZKA (NOVELLA) XVIII-NACHALA XIX VEKA. Vstupitel'-
naia stat'ia i sostavlenie A.N. Sokolova. Podgotovka Teksta i primechaniia N.M.
Gaidenkova i V.P. Stepanova. L. Sovetskii Pisatel', 1969. Biblioteka poeta. Bol'-
shaia seriia. [Skazka]

STIKHOTVORNAIA TRAGEDIIA KONTSA XVIII-NACHALA XIX V. Vstupitel'naia
stat'ia, podgotovka teksta i primechaniia V.A. Bochakareva. M-L. Sovetskii Pisatel', 1964. Biblioteka poeta. Bol'shaia seriia. [Tragediia]

CHAPTER TWO
1. G. A. Gukovskii, RUSSKAIA LITERATURA XVIII VEKA (M. 1939), pp. 5-8 and V. V. Vinogradov, OCHERKI PO ISTORII RUSSKOGO LITERATURNOGO IAZYKA XIX VEKOV (Leiden, 1950), pp. 48-92.
2. Feofan Prokopovich, SOCHINENIIA. Ed. I. Eremin (M.-L. 1961), pp. 3-146.
3. Ibid., 103-12.
4. Ibid., 116.
5. Ibid., 72.
6. Gukovskii, pp. 23-24. Also see V. N. Tatishchev, ISTORIIA ROSSIISKAIA V SEMI TOMAKH (M.-L. 1962-68).
7. Gukovskii, pp. 22-23.
8. D. D. Blagoi, ISTORIIA RUSSKOI LITERATURY XVIII VEKA (M. 1945), pp. 25-32. Gukovskii, pp. 37-44.
9. G. N. Moiseeva, RUSSKIE POVESTI PERVOI TRETI XVIII VEKA (M. 1965). Pp. 191-210.
10. Ibid., 211-294.
11. Gukovskii, p. 27.
12. Prokopovich, pp. 209-226.
13. Ibid., 209-14.
14. Ibid., p. 214.
15. Ibid., p. 216.
16. RANNIAIA RUSSKAIA DRAMATURGIIA (M. "Nauka," Vols. 1-2, 1972, Vol. 3, 1974, Vol. 4, 1975). Also see Blagoi, pp. 39-50.
17. Blagoi, pp. 43-44.
18. Ibid., 46.

CHAPTER THREE
1. Antiokh Kantemir, SOBRANIE STIKHOTVORENII (L. "Sovetskii pisatel'," 1956), Introduction by F. Priima. Also see Blagoi, pp. 79-98 and Gukovskii, pp. 46-60.
2. Prokopovich, pp. 216-17.
3. Kantemir, p. 280.
4. Ibid., 241-47. A. N. Sokolov, OCHERKI PO ISTORII RUSSKOI POEMY XVIII I PERVOI POLOVINY XIX VEKA (M. 1955), pp. 84-95.
5. Kantemir, pp. 57-67 (2nd version), 361-67 (1st version).
6. Kantemir, pp. 66-88 (2nd version), 368-77 (1st version).
7. Kantemir, pp. 89-108 (2nd version), 378-87 (1st version).
8. Kantemir, pp. 109-118 (2nd version), 388-392 (1st version).
9. Kantemir, pp. 119-46 (2nd version), 393-406 (1st version).
10. Ibid., 190-92.
11. Ibid., 147-56.
12. Ibid, 157-72.
13. Ibid., 173-80.
14. V. G. Belinskii, SOBRANIE SOCHINENII V TREKH TOMAKH (M. 1948), II, 732.
15. Kantemir, pp. 407-28.

CHAPTER FOUR
1. V. K. Trediakovskii, IZBRANNYE PROIZVEDENIIA (M.-L. "Sovetskii pisatel'," 1963). Blagoi, pp. 98-118. Gukovskii, pp. 61-81.
2. Trediakovskii, pp. 101-104.
3. Ibid., 129-34.
4. Ibid., 453-58.
5. Ibid., 365-420.
6. A. M. Panchenko, RUSSKAIA STIKHOTVORNAIA KUL'TURA XVII VEKA (L. 1973).
7. Trediakovskii, p. 75.
8. Adolf Stender-Petersen, GESCHICHTE DER RUSSISCHEN LITERATUR IN ZWEI BÄNDEN (Munich, 1957), I, 345.
9. Trediakovskii, p. 383.
10. Ibid., 425-450.
11. Ibid., 442.
12. Ibid., 494.

13. Stender-Petersen, I, 340.
14. Trediakovskii, p. 6 (quoting Mitropolit Evgenii, SLOVAR' SVETSKIKH PISATELEI, Moscow, 1845, II, 221).
15. Trediakovskii, pp. 158-63.
16. Ibid., 164-75.
17. Ibid., 196-322.
18. POETY XVIII VEKA V DVUKH TOMAKH. Ed. G. Makogonenko & I. Serman (L. "Sovetskii pisatel'," 1972), I, 79-97.
19. Gukovskii, p. 71.
20. Ibid.
21. Trediakovskii, p. 390.
22. Gukovskii, p. 73.
23. Trediakovskii, pp. 352-53.

CHAPTER FIVE
1. M. V. Lomonosov, SOCHINENIIA, ed. A. Morozov (M.-L., 1961). See also Blagoi, pp. 119-55; Gukovskii, pp. 82-120; Stender-Petersen, pp. 349-58.
2. François Salignac de la Mothe Fénelon, OEUVRES DE FÉNELON... (Paris, 1826). XII vols. Vol. XI, pp. 273-278. M. V. Lomonosov, IZBRANNYE SOCHINENIIA V STIKHAKH I PROZE (St.-P., 1882). pp. 312-15.
3. Lomonosov, SOCHINENIIA, p. 47.
4. Ibid., 261.
5. Trediakovskii, p. 425.
6. Lomonosov, p. 270.
7. I. Z. Serman, POETICHESKII STIL' LOMONOSOVA (M.-L., 1956), p. 111.
8. G. A. Gukovskii, OCHERKI PO ISTORII RUSSKOI LITERATURY I OB-SHCHESTVENNOI MYSLI XVIII VEKA (L. 1938). pp. 238-39.
9. The theory is formulated, for instance, in the anonymous Latin treatise known as the *Rhetorica ad Herennium* (1st century B. C.): *Ad C. Herennium Libri IV de ratione dicendi,* English translation by Harry Caplan (Cambridge, Mass.: Harvard University Press, 1954). Book IV, chap. VIII.
10. Serman, POETICHESKII STIL', p. 206.
11. Quoted in Blagoi, p. 139.
12. Quoted in Blagoi, p. 137.
13. Lomonosov, p. 120 ("Oda Elizavete Petrovne na prazdnik vosshestviia na prestol, noiabria 25 dnia 1761 goda").
14. Lomonosov, p. 441.
15. Ibid., 444.
16. Ibid., 445.
17. Ibid., 41.
18. Ibid., 109-114.
19. Ibid., 68-73.
20. Ibid., 80-86.
21. Ibid., 94-100.
22. Ibid., 139-42.
23. Ibid., 145-46.
24. *Oeuvres poétiques de Malherbe... Nouvelle édition avec une préface par M. Louis Moland.* (Paris, 1874), p. 195.
25. *Oeuvres de Boileau... Précédées d'une notice par M. Amar* (Paris, 1864), pp. 264-69.
26. Arthur Graves Canfield, *French Lyrics* (New York, 1899), pp. 26-28 (Jean-Baptiste Rousseau, "Ode à la Fortune"); MASTERA RUSSKOGO STIKHOTVORNOGO PEREVODA, ed. E. G. Etkind (L., "Sovetskii pisatel'," 1968), I, 83-87 (Sumarokov, "Zhan-Batist Russo, ODA"). Also Lomonosov, SOCHINENIIA, pp. 147-51.
27. *Oevres de Boileau,* p. 263.
28. J. C. Günther, *Gedichte,* in DEUTSCHE NATIONAL-LITERATUR, B. XXXVIII (Stuttgart, 1883).
29. Lomonosov, SOCHINENIIA, p. 69.
30. Ibid., 48.
31. Ibid., 47 and 94 and 74.
32. Ibid., 87.
33. Boileau, p. 196.
34. Lomonosov, SOCHINENIIA, p. 109.

35. Lomonosov, p. 120.
36. Ibid., 56.
37. Ibid., 275-439 ("Kratkoe rukovodstvo k krasnorechiiu").
38. Lomonosov, p. 70.
39. Ibid., 61.
40. Ibid., 89.
41. Ibid., 98.
42. Ibid., 59.
43. Gukovskii, p. 111.
44. A. P. Sumarokov, IZBRANNYE PROIZVEDENIIA, ed. P. N. Berkov (L. "Sovetskii pisatel'," 1957), pp. 288-89.
45. Lomonosov, SOCHINENIIA, p. 247.
46. Boileau, p. 262.
47. Malherbe, p. 177.
48. G. P. Derzhavin, STIKHOTVORENIIA, ed. D. Blagoi (L. "Sovetskii pisatel'," 1957), p. 92.
49. Lomonosov, SOCHINENIIA, pp. 130-31.
50. Ibid., 133-35.
51. PSALTIR'. Psalom rg, vi.
52. Lomonosov, SOCHINENIIA, p. 145.
53. Ibid., 541.
54. Ibid., 544.
55. Trediakovskii, p. 499.
56. Lomonosov, SOCHINENIIA, pp. 161-207.
57. Lomonosov, p. 253.
58. Ibid., 237.
59. Ibid., 242-43 (lines 231-76).
60. For a much more enthusiastic evaluation of Lomonosov's "Peter the Great" (1760-61), see Sokolov, pp. 95-128.

CHAPTER SIX

1. Sumarokov, IZBRANNYE PROIZVEDENIIA. Blagoi, pp. 155-78. Gukovskii pp. 121-69. Stender-Petersen, I, 363-70.
2. Gukovskii, p. 122.
3. N. I. NOVIKOV I EGO SOVREMENNIKI. IZBRANNYE SOCHINENIIA. Ed. I. V. Malishev (M. "Akademiia nauk," 1961), p. 358.
4. Ibid., 350-51.
5. Gukovskii, p. 133.
6. Novikov, pp. 365-66.
7. Sumarokov, pp. 49-51, pp. 58-63.
8. Ibid., 112-25.
9. Ibid., 68-71.
10. Ibid., 74-77.
11. Ibid., 66.
12. Ibid., 134-39.
13. Ibid., 112-115.
14. Ibid., 115-25.
15. Ibid., 173.
16. Ibid., 319-64.
17. A. P. Sumarokov, POLNOE SOBRANIE VSEKH SOCHINENII (M. 1781), III, 60-119. English translations of Khorev, Semira, Hamlet, Dmitrii the Pretender may be found in SELECTED TRAGEDIES OF A. P. SUMAROKOV, trans. Richard and Raymond Fortune (Evanston, Ill., 1970).
18. Sumarokov did not know English, and his knowledge of Shakespeare's Hamlet appears to have been derived from a prose version in French by P.-A. de la Place, in the 2nd volume of his Le théâtre anglois (London, 1746). Academician Alexeev [Shekspir i russkaia kul'tura. M.-L., 1965, Chapter One.] disproves the usually accepted theory that Sumarokov utilized Voltaire's prose excerpts from Shakespeare in the eighteenth of his Lettres anglaises. Alexeev quotes Sumarokov's indignant reply to Trediakovsky's charge of plagiarism: "My Hamlet, he [i.e., Trediakovsky] says, having heard this from I know not whom, was translated from a French prose version, in which he is completely mistaken. My Hamlet, except for the soliloquy at the end of Act III [the "to be or not to be" speech], and Claudius on his knees, has hardly any similarity with the Shakespearean tragedy" [Shekspir i russkaia kul'tura, p. 23.]

19. Sumarokov, pp. 425-70.
20. Act III, Sc. 5.
21. Sumarokov, p. 121.
22. P. N. Berkov (ed.), RUSSKAIA KOMEDIIA I KOMICHESKAIA OPERA XVIII VEKA (M.-L. 1950), pp. 67-84.
23. Ibid., 16.
24. A. V. Kokorev, KHRESTOMATIIA PO RUSSKOI LITERATURE XVIII VEKA (M. 1961), pp. 192-206; p. 195.
25. Ibid., 206-212.
26. Sumarokov, pp. 108-109.
27. Ibid., 99-102.
28. Ibid., 165-69.
29. Ibid., 278-280.
30. Ibid., 247-48.
31. Ibid., 140-49.
32. Ibid., 150-55.
33. Ibid., 156-64.
34. Ibid., 158-60.
35. Ibid., 183-86.
36. Ibid., 186-89.
37. Ibid., 189-91.
38. Ibid., 192-93.
39. Ibid., 193-95.
40. Ibid., 195-96.
41. Ibid., 196-99.
42. Ibid., 199-202.
43. Ibid., 203-46.
44. Ibid., 203.
45. Ibid., 217.
46. Ibid., 213.
47. Ibid., 227.
48. Ibid., 231.
49. Ibid., 224.
50. Ibid., 228.
51. Ibid., 205.
52. Ibid., 261-75.
53. Ibid., 264.
54. Ibid., 266.
55. Ibid., 270.
56. Ibid., 272.

CHAPTER SEVEN

1. ISTORIIA RUSSKOI LITERATURY (M. "Akademiia Nauk," Vol. 4, 1947). Vol. IV, Chapter III — N.K. Piksanov, "Masonskaia literatura," pp. 51-84.
2. Ibid., 73.
3. Quoted in Blagoi, p. 188.
4. Blagoi, p. 189.
5. Catherine's journalistic efforts are discussed in ISTORIIA RUSSKOI LITERATURY, IV, 368-71 (by Gukovsky).
6. Novikov's satirical journals are discussed in ISTORIIA RUSSKOI LITERATURY, IV, 123-51 (by Serman and Makogonenko). Copious extracts are given in N. I. NOVIKOV I EGO SOVREMENNIKI.
7. SATIRICHESKIE ZHURNALY N. I. NOVIKOVA (M.-L. 1951), p. 165.
8. NOVIKOV I EGO SOVREMENNIKI, p. 23.
9. Ibid., 52-53.
10. G. P. Makogonenko (ed.), RUSSKAIA LITERATURA XVIII VEKA (L. 1970), p. 254.
11. Ibid., 254.
12. Ibid., 254-55.
13. Ibid., 255-56.
14. Ibid., 256-57.
15. NOVIKOV I EGO SOVREMENNIKI, pp. 74-75.
16. ISTORIIA RUSSKOI LITERATURY, IV, 130.

17. NOVIKOV I EGO SOVREMENNIKI, pp. 89-90.

18. Ibid., 100-03; 113-14.

19. Ibid., 114-18.

20. Ibid., 123-28.

21. Blagoi, pp. 256-62; Gukovskii, pp. 205-12; IRL, IV, 256-264 (A.V. Zapadov); IRR, I, 50-52; 60-61; Serman, pp. 226-67.

22. Gukovskii, p. 206.

23. Kokorev, p. 578.

24. Blagoi, pp. 262-71; Gukovskii, pp. 222-35; IRL, IV, 270-77 (A.V. Zapadov); IRR, I, 58-60.

25. Proza, pp. 41-80.

26. Ibid., 55-56.

27. Ibid., 63.

28. Makogonenko, pp. 41-80.

29. Blagoi, pp. 271-72.

30. Ibid., 272.

CHAPTER EIGHT

1. Blagoi, pp. 219-22; Berkov, pp. 23-30; IRL, IV, 284-95 (A.V. Zapadov).

2. Rousseau, J.-J. LE DEVIN DU VILLAGE.... Opera in One Act (Angel Records).

3. Blagoi, pp. 219-20; Gukovskii, pp. 235-37.

4. POETY XVIII VEKA, I, 520, 62.

5. Ibid., 524.

6. Makogonenko, pp. 209-17; Vsevolodskii-Gerngross, V.N. RUSSKII TEATR VTOROI POLOVINY XVIII VEKA (M. 1960), pp. 119-22.

7. Ibid., 122.

8. Berkov, pp. 169-216; Kokorev, pp. 429-36; Vsevolodskii-Gerngross, pp. 122-28.

9. Kokorev, p. 429.

10. Ibid., 458-63.

11. Blagoi, p. 220; Gukovskii, p. 236; Vsevolodskii-Gerngross, pp. 194-200; POETY XVIII VEKA, II, 7-17.

12. Berkov, pp. 217-46; Kokorev, pp. 327-99.

13. Berkov, pp. 263-308; Kokorev, pp. 400-08; Vsevolodskii-Gerngross, pp. 184-90.

14. Blagoi, pp. 214-17; Gukovskii, pp. 212-13; IRL, IV, 265-69 (A.V. Zapadov); Vsevolodskii-Gerngross, passim.

15. Berkov, pp. 85-122; Kokorev, pp. 265-94 (SHCHEPETIL'NIK); Makogonenko, pp. 145-77 (MOT, LIUBOVIIU ISPRAVLENNY).

16. IRL, IV, 364-80 (Gukovskii); Stender-Petersen, I, 416-24. Extracts from Catherine's writings are given in Manning, I, 82-90.

CHAPTER NINE

1. Fonvizin, D.I. SOBRANIE SOCHINENII V DVUKH TOMAKH. Ed. Makogonenko (M.-L. 1959); Blagoi, pp. 231-43; Gukovskii, pp. 322-54; Vsevolodskii-Gerngross, pp. 57-74 (KORION, BRIGADIR); 209-26 (NEDOROSL'); Stender-Petersen, I, 407-16.

2. The preface to this work is given in Fonvizin, I, 221-22.

3. Fonvizin, I, 443-608.

4. Ibid., 417-42.

5. Ibid., II, 117-86.

6. Ibid., II, 109-16.

7. Ibid., I, 207-08.

8. Ibid., 209-12.

9. Ibid., I, 3-43.

10. Ibid., I, xiii.

11. Ibid., II, 583-608. A complete description of the two notebooks containing this version, the paper, the corrections, the handwriting, etc., is given in the appendix to the Vsevolodskii-Gerngross volume, pp. 366-73. A.P. Mogilianskii,"K voprosu o tak naz.

'rannem' 'Nedorosle' " XVIII VEK, SBORNIK 4 (M-L. 1959) controverts the attribution to Fonvizin.

12. Fonvizin, I, 45-103.
13. Ibid., II, 187-93.
14. Ibid., II, 279-89.
15. Ibid., II, 412-580.
16. Ibid., I, 412-580.
17. Ibid., II, 194-230.
18. See above, pp. 176-81.
19. Fonvizin, II, 254-67.
20. Ibid., I, 105-77.
21. Ibid., II, 81-105.
22. RUSSKAIA KHRESTOMATIIA S PRIMECHANIIAMI SOSTAVIL' ANDREI FILONOV. Chast' Treti'ia: Dramaticheskaia Poeziia (SPB. 1869), p. 572.
23. Fonvizin, I, 187-203.
24. Ibid., II, 40-78.
25. Ibid., II, 24-27.
26. Ibid., II, 271-75.
27. Ibid., II, 28-39.

CHAPTER TEN

1. Kheraskov, M.M IZBRANNYE PROIZVEDENIIA (M-L. Sovetskii Pisatel'. Biblioteka Poeta. Bol'shaia seriia. 1961). Blagoi, pp. 276-86; Gukovskii, pp. 183-200; IRL, IV, 320-41 (L.I. Kulakova); Stender-Petersen, I, 376-83; 396-98.
2. Gukovskii, p. 185.
3. Kheraskov, p. 9.
4. Ibid., pp. 297-373.
5. TVORENIIA M. KHERASKOVA VNOV' ISPRAVLENNYE I DOPOLNENNYE. Chast' V (M. 1810), pp. 167-292.
6. Ibid., 293-400.
7. Ibid., 398.
8. Kheraskov, p. 76; Makogonenko, p. 137.
9. Kheraskov, p. 74.
10. Kheraskov, p. 83; Makogonenko, p. 138.
11. Kheraskov, p. 122.
12. POETY XVIII VEKA, I, 189-305.
13. Kheraskov, p. 92.
14. Kheraskov, p. 91; Makogonenko, p. 139.
15. Kheraskov, pp. 24-25; IRR, I, 56.
16. Ibid.
17. Kheraskov, p. 26.
18. Ibid., 26-27.
19. Sokolov, pp. 153-87.
20. See Tvoreniia M. Kheraskova (M. 1796-1803).
21. Kheraskov, 143-74.
22. Ibid., 158.
23. Ibid., 163.
24. Ibid., 157.
25. Kheraskov, M.M. ROSSIADA. POEMA V XII-ti PESNIAKH (SPb: Russkaia klassnaia biblioteka, No. 20, 1895). Kheraskov, IZBRANNYE SOCHINENIIA, pp. 177-237 (Pesni I, X, XII); Kokorev, pp. 569-73 (Pesn' I); Canto II and part of XII are printed in Manning, II, 80-91. Kokorev prints in full Kheraskov's summaries of the twelve cantos, pp. 564-69.
26. Kheraskov, IZBRANNYE SOCHINENIIA, p. 34.
27. Ibid., 37-38; Sokolov, pp. 180-83.
28. Kheraskov, p. 40.
29. Kheraskov, pp. 239-45.
30. Ibid., 30.
31. Tvoreniia, chast' I, 288.

CHAPTER ELEVEN
1. POETY XVIII VEKA, I, 75-130.
2. Ibid., 98.
2a. Ibid., 28-31. Introduction by G.P. Makogonenko.
3. POETY XVIII VEKA, I, 319-425; Gukovskii, pp. 282-87; IRL, IV, 353-63 (Gukovskii).
4. POETY XVIII VEKA, I, 326-32.
5. Ibid., 36.
6. Ibid., 321.
7. Ibid., 355.
8. Ibid., 409.
9. Maikov, Vasilii. IZBRANNYE PROIZVEDENIIA (M-L., Biblioteka poeta. Bol'shaia seriia 1966). Blagoi, pp. 243-51; Gukovskii, pp. 170-83; IRL, IV, 201-26 (A. M. Kukilevich).
10. Ibid., 185.
11. Ibid., 190.
12. Ibid., 229-33.
13. Ibid., 202.
14. Khemnitser, I.I. POLNOE SOBRANIE STIKHOTVORENII (M-L. Biblioteka poeta. Bol'shaia seriia, 1963), p. 220.
15. Maikov, pp. 253-54.
16. Sumarokov, A.P. IZBRANNYE PROIZVEDENIIA, pp. 311-12.
17. Maikov, p. 145.
18. Ibid., 331-82.
19. Ibid., 383-433.
20. Ibid., 49.
21. Ibid., 311-15.
22. OEUVRES DE BOILEAU (Paris, 1864), p. 190 (L'Art poétique, Chant I).
23. Ibid., 224.
24. Sumarokov, pp. 122-23.
25. Maikov, pp. 55-71.
26. Ibid., 57.
27. Ibid., 73-134.
28. Ibid., 77.
29. Makogonenko's views are cited with approval by A.V. Zapadov in his introductory article to the Maikov edition: Maikov, pp. 37-38; Makogonenko, RUSSKAIA LITERATURA (1964), No. 4, pp. 145-47.
30. POETY XVIII VEKA, I, 189-305.
31. A rather superficial history of the Russian elegy is: Frizman, L.G. ZHIZN' LIRICHESKOGO ZHANRA: RUSSKAIA ELEGIIA... (M., "Nauka," 1973).
32. Boileau, OEUVRES (Paris, 1864), p. 196 (L'Art poetique, Chant II).
33. Sumarokov, IZBRANNYE PROIZVEDENIIA, p. 125.
34. POETY XVIII VEKA, I, 227.
35. Ibid., 276.
36. Ibid., 296.
37. Ibid., 262.
38. Ibid., 223.
39. Ibid., 196-97.
40. Ibid., 584.
41. Blagoi, pp. 251-55; Gukovskii, pp. 310-17; IRL, IV, 342-52 (L.I. Kulakova); SPb, I, 372-75.
42. Bogdanovich, I.F. STIKHOTVORENIIA I POEMY (L. Biblioteka poeta. Bol'shaia seriia, 1957).
43. Ibid., 207-12.
44. Ibid., 187-94.
45. Quoted in IRL, p. 354 (Kulakova).
46. Bogdanovich, pp. 21-22.
47. Sokrashchenie sdelannoe Zhan-Zhakom Russo, zhenevskim grazhdaninom, iz proekta o vechnom mire, sochinennogo Adamom de Sen-P'erom. Per. s Frants (SPb, 1771).

48. Bogdanovich, I.F. DUSHEN'KINY POKHOZHDENIIA (M. 1778). (Kniga pervaia).

49. Bogdanovich, I.F. DUSHEN'KA, DREVNIAIA POVEST' V VOL'NYKH STIKHAKH (SPb, 1783).

50. Quoted in Bogdanovich, STIKHOTVORENIIA I POEMY, p. 225.

51. Bogdanovich, I.F. DUSHEN'KA... (SPb, 1794).

52. La Fontaine. OEUVRES COMPLETES (Paris, "L'Intégrale," 1965), p. 403.

53. Lafonten. ZHALOVY PSISHI I KUPIDONA. Per. M.A. Dmitrieva-Mamonova (SPb, 1769).

54. Bogdanovich, STIKHOTVORENIIA I POEMY, p. 63.

55. Ibid., 76.

56. Ibid., 106.

57. Ibid., 60.

58. Ibid., 65.

59. Ibid., 107-08.

60. Karamzin, N.M. IZBRANNYE SOCHINENIIA (M-L., "Khudozhestvennaia literatura," 1964) II, 198-226.

61. POETY XVIII VEKA, I, 161-88.

62. Ibid., 38-41.

63. Ibid., 164-72.

CHAPTER TWELVE

1. Blagoi, pp. 320-23; Gukovskii, 374-80; IRL., IV, 250-55 (Motol'skaia); Stender-Petersen, I, 401.

2. Komediia, pp. 70-174.

3. Selections from Nikolev's verse are published in POETY XVIII VEKA, II, 18-111.

4. Ibid., 36-40.

5. Ibid., 41-43.

6. Ibid., 43-52.

7. Ibid., 52-54.

8. TRAGEDIIA, pp. 63-128.

9. OEUVRES COMPLETES DE VOLTAIRE (Paris, 1823), II, 231-305. ALZIRE, OU LES AMERICAINS.

10. Kniazhnin, Ia.B. IZBRANNYE PROIZVEDENIIA (L. Biblioteka poeta. Bol'shaia seriia. 1961); Blagoi, pp. 333-35; Gukovskii, pp. 357-69; Stender-Petersen, I, 398-401.

11. Kniazhnin, pp. 9-10.

12. Pushkin, A.S. SOBRANIE SOCHINENII, VII, 194 ("O russkoi istorii XVIII veka"): "Radishchev was exiled to Siberia; Knyazhnin died under the rod—and Fonvizin, whom she feared, would not have escaped the same fate had it not been for the fact that he was extremely well known."

13. Kniazhnin, pp. 615-26.

14. SKAZKA, pp. 198-202.

14a. Kniazhnin, p. 25.

15. SKAZKA, pp. 219-30.

16. Kniazhnin, p. 24.

17. Ibid., 61-115.

18. Ibid., 86.

19. Ibid., 89.

20. Ibid., 115.

21. Ibid., 117-81.

22. OEUVRES DE VOLTAIRE. Théatre, III, 27-91.

23. Kniazhnin, Ia. B. SOCHINENIIA V 5 TOMAKH. Izd. 3 (SPb. 1817-1818), II.

24. Kniazhnin, IZBRANNYE SOCHINENIIA, pp. 42-44; Kniazhnin, SOCHINENIIA, I.

25. Kniazhnin, IZBRANNYE SOCHINENIIA, pp. 183-247.

26. Kniazhnin, SOCHINENIIA, II.

27. Ibid.

28. Kniazhnin, IZBRANNYE SOCHINENIIA, pp. 249-303.
29. Komediia, pp. 70-174.
30. Ibid., 87-89.
30a. Ibid., 112.
31. All Kniazhnin's comedies and comic operas are to be found in Kniazhnin, Ia.
B. SOCHINENIIA, III, IV. Kniazhnin, IZBRANNYE PROIZVEDENIIA, pp. 305-602
(KHVASTUN, CHUDAKI, NESCHASTIE OT KARETY, SKUPOI, SBITENSHCHIK).
32. Kniazhnin, SOCHINENIIA, III; Kniazhnin, IZBRANNYE PROIZVEDENIIA,
pp. 305-427; Makogonenko, 385-428.
33. Kniazhnin, IZBRANNYE PROIZVEDENIIA, pp. 429-561.
34. Ibid., 34.
35. Kapnist, V.V. SOBRANIE SOCHINENII V DVUKH TOMAKH (M-L. "Akademiia Nauk," 1960), I, 285-402. Kapnist, V.V. IZBRANNYE PROIZVEDENIIA (L.
Biblioteka poeta. Bol'shaia seriia, 1973), pp. 331-462.
36. Krylov, I.A. SOCHINENIIA V TREKH TOMAKH (M. GIKhL, 1945). Blagoi,
pp. 374-76; Gukovskii, pp. 471-75; IRL, V, 235-38; 249-50 (A.V. Zapadov).
37. Krylov, II, 7-61.
38. Ibid., 63-116.
39. Ibid., 117-68.
40. Ibid., 221-338.
41. Ibid., 339-75; Berkov, pp. 645-77.
42. Ibid., 377-416.
43. Ibid., 555-600.
44. Ibid., 417-88.
45. Ibid., 603-30.
46. Ibid., 489-554.

CHAPTER THIRTEEN
1. IRL, IV, 430-45 (Pumpianskii).
2. Derzhavin, G.R. STIKHOTVORENIIA (L. Biblioteka poeta. Bol'shaia seriia.
1957). Blagoi, pp. 286-315; Gukovskii, pp. 389-424; IRL, IV, 383-429 (Blagoi); Stender-
Petersen, I, 383-95.
3. Gukovskii, p. 398.
4. Berkov, P.N. "Problemy Izucheniia russkogo klassitsizma," XVIII VEK, Sbornik VI (1964), p. 29.
5. Derzhavin, P. 398.
6. Ibid., 369.
7. Ibid., 83-85.
8. IRP, p. 130 (I.Z. Serman).
9. Derzhavin, pp. 85-87.
10. Young uses the metaphor of the bell as the tongue of time: "The bell strikes
one! We take no note of time, But from its loss: to give it then a tongue, Is wise in man."
Edward Young, The Complaint and the Consolation, or Night Thoughts. (London,
1797), p. 3.
11. Derzhavin, p. 92.
12. Ibid., 97-104.
13. This tale is printed in Manning, I, 85-90.
14. Derzhavin, pp. 104-05.
15. Ibid., 109-13.
16. Ibid., 106-09.
17. Ibid., 133-47.
18. Ibid., 114-16.
19. Young, pp. 3-4.
20. Derzhavin, pp. 156-66.
21. Ibid., 121-24.
22. Belinskii, V.G. SOBRANIE SOCHINENII V TREKH TOMAKH (M. 1948), II,
504.
23. Derzhavin, pp. 178-90.
24. Ibid., 211-16.

25. Some of Derzhavin's anacreontics may be found in the STIKHOTVORENIIA volume on pp. 79, 97, 171, 226, 233, 245, 255, 259, 268.

26. Derzhavin, p. 233.

27. Ibid., 207.

28. Ibid., 207-08.

29. Ibid., 223-25.

30. Ibid., 326-34.

31. Pushkin, A.S. POLNOE SOBRANIE SOCHINENII (M. 1962), 10, 162.

32. Vinogradov, V.V. OCHERKI PO ISTORII RUSSKOGO LITERATURNOGO IAZYKA XVII-XIX VV (Leiden: Brill, 1950), pp. 139-43.

33. Derzhavin, pp. 352-58.

34. Ibid., 306-08.

35. Ibid., 232.

36. Ibid., 305.

37. Sharypkin, D.M. "Skandinavskaia tema v russkoi romanticheskoi literature," RANNIE ROMANTICHESKIE VEIANIIA (L. 1972), pp. 96-167.

38. SOCHINENIIA DERZHAVINA S OB"IASNITEL'NYMI PRIMECHANIIA-MI Ia. GROTA. 2e Akademicheskoe izdanie (1878), VII, pp. 530-618.

38a. The first words of Georg Hamann's treatise "Aesthetica in nuce" (1761).

39. Derzhavin (Grot), VII, 531-32.

40. Young, Edward: "Conjectures on Original Composition."

41. Derzhavin (Grot), VII, 536, 550.

42. Ibid., 561.

43. Murav'ev, M.N. STIKHOTVORENIIA (L. Biblioteka poeta. Bol'shaia seriia. 1967), p. 16.

44. Kulakova, L.I. "O spornykh voprosakh Derzhavina," XVIII VEK, sbornik 8 (L. 1969), p. 37.

45. Derzhavin (Grot), VII, 535.

46. Kulakova, p. 34.

47. Derzhavin (Grot), VI, 340.

48. Kulakova, p. 36.

49. TRAGEDIIA, pp. 290-364 (G.R. Derzhavin, IROD I MARIAMNA. Tragediia v piati deistviiakh).

CHAPTER FOURTEEN.

1. POETY XVIII VEKA, II, 191-257. IRL, IV, 446-50 (L.I. Kulakova).

2. Khemnitser, I.I. POLNOE SOBRANIE STIKHOTVORENII (M-L. Biblioteka poeta. Bol'shaia seriia. 1963), pp. 201-13.

3. POETY XVIII VEKA, II, 512.

4. Ibid., 192.

5. Ibid., 195.

6. Ibid., 196-98.

7. Ibid., 199-210.

8. Khemnitser, pp. 53-56.

9. IRL, IV, 448.

10. POETY XVIII VEKA, II, 211-12. D.M. Sharyshkin, "Skandinavskaia tema v russkoi romanticheskoi literature," RANNIE ROMANTICHESKIE VEIANIIA (L. 1972), pp. 102-03.

11. POETY XVIII VEKA, II, 226-36.

12. Ibid., 519.

13. Ibid., 250.

14. Ibid., 251-52.

15. Ibid., 212-23.

16. Ibid., 223-24.

17. Ibid., 236-42.

18. Murav'ev. M.N. STIKHOTVORENIIA (L. Biblioteka poeta. Bol'shaia seriia. 1967), pp. 203-07.

19. POETY XVIII VEKA, II, 242-46.

20. Ibid., 521.

21. IRL, IV, 448.
22. Khemnitser, I.I. POLNOE SOBRANIE STIKHOTVORENII. Blagoi, pp. 316-19. Gukovskii, pp. 317-21; IRL, IV, 473-84 (G.V. Bitner).
23. Khemnitser's verses in German and French are printed in POLNOE SOBRANIE, pp. 239-62.
24. Chast' I, POLNOE SOBRANIE, pp. 53-115; Chast' II, PP. 116-55.
25. For satires, see Khemnitser, pp. 159-77.
26. Ibid., 179-80.
27. Ibid., 180-82.
28. Gellerts Dichtungen, herausgegeben von A. Schullerus (Leipzig und Wien, 1891).
29. Khemnitser, pp. 57-58; Gellert, pp. 82-83, "Der sterbende Vater."
30. Khemnitser, pp. 79-80.
31. Ibid., 146-48.
32. "Pes i l'vy," Khemnitser, pp. 149-50.
33. Ibid., 150-51.
34. Ibid., 81; Gellert, p. 88, "Das Kutschpferd."
35. Ibid., 82-83; Gellert, pp. 52-53, "Der glücklich gewordene Ehemann."
36. Ibid., 102-03; Gellert, pp. 86-87, "Die glückliche Ehe."
37. Ibid., 56-57; Gellert, 77-78, "Der Maler."
38. Ibid., 90-91.
39. Ibid., 92-94; Gellert, pp. 19-20, "Das Gespenst."
40. Ibid., 74-75; Gellert, pp. 5-6, "Der Tanzbär."
41. Ibid., 126-29.
42. Ibid., 110-11.
42a. Murav'ev, M.N. STIKHOTVORENIIA. IRL, IV, 454-61 (L.I. Kulakova); IRP, pp. 167-69 (N.D. Kochetkova).
43. Murav'ev, p. 250.
44. POLNOE SOBRANIE SOCHINENII MIKHAILA NIKITICHA MURAV'EVA (SPb. chch. 1-2, 1819, ch. 3, 1820).
45. Murav'ev, STIKHOTVORENIIA, pp. 94-105.
46. Ibid., 53-80.
47. Ibid., 7.
48. Ibid., 83-84.
49. Ibid., 84-85.
50. Ibid., 119-20.
51. Ibid., 121-22.
52. Ibid., 129-30.
53. Ibid., 129.
54. Maikov, Vasilii. IZBRANNYE PROIZVEDENIIA (M-L. Biblioteka poeta. Bol'shaia seriia. 1966), pp. 305-06.
55. Murav'ev, STIKHOTVORENIIA, pp. 125-28.
56. Ibid., 169-71.
57. Ibid., 156-57.
58. Ibid., 158-59.
59. Ibid., 153-55.
60. Ibid., 137.
61. Ibid., 143-45.
62. Ibid., 145-46.
63. Ibid., 131-36.
64. Ibid., 146-48.
65. Ibid., 152-53.
66. Ibid., 155-56.
67. Ibid., 203-07.
68. Ibid., 207-08.
69. Ibid., 208-09.
70. Ibid., 216-17.
71. Ibid., 217-23.
72. Brukhanskii, A.N. "Murav'ev i 'legkoe stikhotvorstvo'," XVIII VEK, sbornik

4 (M-L. 1959), pp. 164-65.
    73. Murav'ev, pp. 212-13.
    74. Ibid., 218.
    75. Ibid., 223-24.
    76. Ibid., 234-36.
    77. Pushkin, A.S. SOBRANIE SOCHINENII V DESIATI TOMAKH (M. 1960), IV, 30 (EVGENII ONEGIN, I, 48): "S dushoiu, polnoi sozhalenii,/ Stoial zadumchivo Evgenii/ Kak opisal sebia piit." p. 180 (Pushkin's note).
    78. Murav'ev, pp. 238-41.
    79. Ibid., 241-42.
    80. Ibid., 269-77.
    81. Kapnist, V.V. SOBRANIE SOCHINENII V DVUKH TOMAKH (M-L., AN, 1960). Kapnist, V.V. IZBRANNYE PROIZVEDENIIA (L. Biblioteka poeta. Bol'shaia seriia. 1973). Blagoi, pp. 335-36; Gukovskii, pp. 380-83; IRL, IV, 485-500 (G.V. Bitner); IRP, pp. 169-71 (N.D. Kochetkova). Berkov, P.N. "Kapnist kak iavlenie russkoi kul'tury XVIII veka," XVIII VEK, sbornik 4 (M-L. 1959), pp. 257-68; Serman, I.Z. "V.V. Kapnist i russkaia poëziia nachala XIX veka," ibid., 289-303.
    83. Kapnist, IZBRANNYE PROIZVEDENIIA, p. 8, note 2.
    84. Ibid., 51-58; 538-41.
    85. Ibid., 59-63.
    86. Ibid., 331-462.
    87. The stanzas which Kapnist omitted from the published version are printed in IZBRANNYE PROIZVEDENIIA, pp. 519-20.
    88. Ibid., 63-67.
    89. Babkin, D.S. "V.V. Kapnist i A.N. Radishchev," XVIII VEK, sbornik 4 (M-L. 1959), p. 272.
    90. Kapnist, IZBRANNYE PROIZVEDENIIA, pp. 84-87.
    91. Ibid., 87-92; 520-23.
    92. Ibid., 92-99.
    93. Ibid., 99-103; 523-25.
    94. Ibid., 105-07.
    95. Ibid., 120.
    96. Ibid., 121-22.
    97. Ibid., 118-19.
    98. Kapnist, SOBRANIE SOCHINENII, II, 38-48.
    99. Kapnist, IZBRANNYE PROIZVEDENIIA, pp. 153-54.
    100. Horatius. CARMINA, recensuit Fridericus Vollmer. Editio maior... (Lipsiae,, 1912), pp. 19-20.
    101. Kapnist, IZBRANNYE PROIZVEDENIIA, pp. 216-34.
    102. Ibid., 252-53.
    103. Ibid., 237-45.
    104. Ibid., 301-28.
    105. Ibid., 318-22.
    106. Ibid., 248-49.
    107. Ibid., 261-65.
    108. Ibid., 296-97.
    109. Ibid., 576.

CHAPTER FIFTEEN
    1. POETY XVIII VEKA, II, 258-96. IRL, IV, 451-53 (L.I. Kulakova).
    2. POETY XVIII VEKA, I, 45.
    3. Karmanny Pesennik, Ili Sobranie luchshikh svetskikhi prostonarodnykh pesen, chch 1-3. M. 1796.
    4. POETY XVIII VEKA, II, 261-64.
    5. Ibid., 270-75.
    6. Ibid., 264-66.
    7. Ibid., 283-84.
    8. Ibid., 261.

9. Ibid., 278.
10. Ibid., 280.
11. Ibid., 280-81.
12. POETY XVIII VEKA, II, 112-90. IRL, IV, 462-72 (G.A. Gukovskii).
13. IRL, IV, 462.
14. Pushkin, A.S. POLNOE SOBRANIE SOCHINENII (M. 1958), VIII, 106.
15. POETY XVIII VEKA, II, 117.
16. IRL, IV, 463.
17. POETY XVIII VEKA, II, 119-24.
18. Ibid., 129-37.
19. Ibid., 138-39.
20. Ibid., 151-54.
21. Ibid., 173-75.
22. Ibid., 186-87.
23. Ibid., 188.
24. Ibid., 124-29.
25. IRL., IV, 470.
26. POETY XVIII VEKA, II, 163.
27. THE COMPLETE POETICAL WORKS OF POPE (Boston, 1903), p. 290.
28. IRL, IV, 471.
29. Radishchev, A.N. STIKHOTVORENIIA (L. Biblioteka poeta. Bol'shaia seria. 1975). Blagoi, pp. 369-73; Gukovskii, pp. 425-69; IRL, IV, 507-70 (Gukovskii); IRP, pp. 152-62 (N.D. Kochetkova).
30. Radishchev, pp. 56-75. The ode "Liberty" exists in several versions with widely differing texts and numbers of strophes. The full text, printed in Zapadov's edition, has 54 strophes. Radishchev himself used an abbreviated version in 50 strophes for partial citation and prose paraphrase in the Tver chapter of A JOURNEY FROM ST. PETERSBURG TO MOSCOW, printed in 1790. A still more truncated version in 28 strophes was inserted in full in some copies of the JOURNEY. A full conspectus of the variants is given by Zapadov in Radishchev, STIKHOTVORENIIA, p. 239.
31. Radishchev, p. 76.
32. Ibid., 52-55.
33. Ibid., 130-61.
33a. IRP, 156.
34. Radishchev, pp. 160-61, ll. 945-69.
35. Ibid., 156, ll. 751-56.
36. Ibid., 125-26.
37. Ibid., 180-82.
38. Ibid., 162.
39. POETY 1790-1810-kh GODOV. Vstupitel'naia stat'ia Iu. M. Lotmana (L. Biblioteka poeta. Bol'shaia seriia. 1971), pp. 68-160. Al'tshuller, M.G. "S.S. Bobrov i russkaia poeziia XVIII-nachala XIX v.," XVIII VEK, sbornik 6 (M-L. 1964), pp. 224-46.
40. RASSVET POLNOCHI Semena Bobrova, chch. 1-4. SPb. 1804.
41. POETY 1790-1810-kh GODOV, pp. 68-160.
42. Ibid., 71-74.
43. Ibid., 77-79.
44. Ibid., 79-83.
45. Ibid., 91-108.
46. Ibid., 95.
47. Ibid., 100.
48. Ibid., 75-76.
49. Ibid., 115-17.
50. Ibid., 126-30.
51. Ibid., 85-91.
52. Ibid., 121-26.
53. Ibid., 109; 119-21; 130-32.
54. Ibid., 117-19.
55. Ibid., 132-58.
56. Batiushkov, K.N. POLNOE SOBRANIE STIKHOTVORENII (M-L. Biblioteka

poeta. Bol'shaia seriia. 1964), p. 99.

57. Batiushkov's citation is inexact: the line, which is from the poem "Konets voiny pri Dunae" (Rassvet polnochi II, 23), actually reads: "Se ruzhei rzhushcha roshcha mchitsia."

58. Belyi, Andrei. STIKHOTVORENIIA I POEMY (M-L. Biblioteka poeta. Bol'-shaia seriia. 1966), p. 302 ("Prosti," 4).

59. POETY 1790-1810-kh GODOV, pp. 651-702; SATIRA, pp. 261-92; SKAZ-KA, pp. 420-30.

60. See below, pp. 526-27.

61. Some of the fables are printed in SATIRA, pp. 276-87; seven *skazki* are to be found in SKAZKA, pp. 420-30.

62. POETY 1790-1810-kh GODOV, p. 663.

63. Ibid., 658-59.

64. Ibid., 654-56.

65. Ibid., 659-63.

66. Ibid., 668-72. See also RLT 14 (1976), pp. 314-20, for an English translation.

CHAPTER SIXTEEN

1. Dmitriev, I.I. POLNOE SOBRANIE STIKHOTVORENII (L. Biblioteka poeta. Bol'shaia seriia. 1967). Blagoi, pp. 410-13; IRL, IV, 121-43 (E.N. Kupreianova); IRP, pp. 176-85 (N.D. Kochetkova); Stender-Petersen, II, 50.

2. Dmitriev, pp. 87-89.

3. Ibid., 90-92.

4. Ibid., 364-65.

5. Ibid., 282-83.

6. Ibid., 272-75.

7. Ibid., 305-06.

8. Ibid., 313-14.

9. Ibid., 322-25.

10. Ibid., 128-29.

11. Ibid., 132.

12. Ibid., 123-25.

13. Ibid., 299-300.

14. Ibid., 312.

15. POETY XVIII VEKA, II, 280; see above, 474.

16. Dmitriev, p. 322.

17. Ibid., 345-46.

18. Ibid., 78-82.

19. Ibid., 139-41.

20. Ibid., 243-46.

21. Ibid., 186-214.

22. Cited in Stepanov, V.P. IVAN ANDREEVICH KRYLOV (L. 1975), pp. 212-13.

23. Dmitriev, p. 374.

24. Ibid., 197.

25. Ibid., 186.

26. Letter of A.S. Pushkin to P.A. Viazemsky, November 4, 1823: "About Dmitriev I shall not argue with you, although all his fables aren't worth a single good fable of Krylov, all his satires not worth one of your epistles, and all the rest of his stuff not worth the first poem of Zhukovsky. 'Ermak' is unbearable rot, his 'tales' are written in a bad style, cold and long-winded. In my opinion, Dmitriev ranks below Neledinsky and a hundred times below Karamzin as a poet. I'm curious to see his 'Life' not for his sake, but for yours." [Viazemsky had written a "Life of Dmitriev"]. A.S.P. IX, 385.

27. Dmitriev, p. 205.

28. Ibid., 211.

29. Ibid., 380.

30. POETY 1790-1810-kh GODOV, pp. 433-34.

31. Ibid., 432-33.

32. Quoted by Stepanov, p. 208.

33. Stepanov, p. 207.
34. POETY 1790-1810-kh GODOV, pp. 430-31.
35. Ibid., 844.
36. Dmitriev: Apologi, pp. 233-46; Madrigali, Nadpisi i Epitafii, pp. 134-38.
37. Ibid., 136.
38. SKAZKA, vsupitel'naia stat'ia, pp. 5-42.
39. Dmitriev, pp. 176-85.
40. Ibid., 172-76.
41. Ibid., 101-13.
42. Ibid., 95-101.
43. Ibid., 113-16.
44. Ibid., 348-51.
45. Ibid., 458.
46. Karamzin, N.M. POLNOE SOBRANIE STIKHOTVORENII (M-L. Biblioteka poeta. Bol'shaia seriia. 1966). Blagoi, pp. 405-09; Gukovskii, pp. 517-24; IRL, IV, 55-105 (Gukovskii); IRP, pp. 163-87 (N.D. Kochetkova). Stender-Petersen, II, 29-35.
47. Karamzin, pp. 58-63.
48. Ibid., 64-65.
49. Ibid., 68-70.
50. Menendez-Pidal, Ramón. FLOR NUEVA DE ROMANCES VIEJOS (Madrid, 1928), pp. 112-14.
51. Karamzin, p. 79.
52. Ibid., 101-04.
53. Ibid., 149-61.
54. Ibid., 106-08.
55. Ibid., 110-11.
56. Ibid., 185-90.
57. Ibid., 265-70.
58. Ibid., 136-40.
59. Ibid., 140-45.
60. Ibid., 121-22.
61. Ibid., 123-24.
62. Ibid., 192-95.
63. IRP, p. 177.
64. Karamzin, p. 165.
65. Ibid., 38-40; 112.
66. Ibid., 146.
57. Ibid., 163-64.
68. Ibid., 195-97.
69. Ibid., 169-79.
70. Ibid., 227-30.
71. Karamzin, IZBRANNYE SOCHINENIIA V DVUKH TOMAKH (M-L. 1964), I, 174-75.
72. Karamzin, POLNOE SOBRANIE STIKHOTVORENII, pp. 165-69.

CHAPTER SEVENTEEN

1. Blagoi, pp. 341-74; Gukovskii, pp. 425-69; IRL, IV, 507-70 (Gukovskii); Stender Petersen, II, 12-20.
2. N.I. NOVIKOV I EGO SOVREMENNIKI. Ed. I.V. Malyshev (M. 1961), p. 100.
3. Makogonenko, pp. 634-36.
4. Ibid., 638-52.
5. Radishchev, A.N. PUTESHESTVIE IZ PETERBURGA V MOSKVU (L. GIKhL, 1938).
6. Radishchev, A.N. A JOURNEY FROM ST. PETERSBURG TO MOSCOW, translation by Leo Wiener, edited. with an introduction and notes by Roderick Page Thaler (Cambridge, Mass., 1959), p. 27.
7. Radishchev, PUTESHESTVIE, p. 223.
8. Ibid., 187-88.
9. See above, p. 112.

10. Vinogradov, V.V. OCHERKI PO ISTORII RUSSKOGO LITERATURNOGO IAZYKA XVII-XIX VV. (Leiden, 1950), pp. 111-12.

11. Dmitriev, I.I. VZGIAD' NA MOIU ZHIZN', cited by Vinogradov, p. 112.

12. Ibid., 112.

13. Radishchev, PUTESHESTVIE, p. 113.

14. Krylov, I.A. SOCHINENIIA. I: Proza (M. GIKhL, 1945). Blagoi, pp. 377-82; Gukovskii, pp. 471-89; IRL, V, 229-45 (A.V. Zapadov). Kochetkova, N.D. "Satiricheskaia proza Krylova," IVAN ANDREEVICH KRYLOV: PROBLEMY TVORCHEST-VA (L. 1975), pp. 53-112.

15. Krylov, pp. 120-23.

16. Kochetkova, pp. 57-58.

17. Krylov, pp. 283-315.

18. Ibid., 316-23.

19. Ibid., 375-83.

20. Ibid., 384-92.

21. Ibid., 337-45.

22. Ibid., 338.

23. Ibid., 340.

24. Ibid., 340-41.

25. Ibid., 385.

26. Ibid., 389.

27. Ibid., 329-36.

28. Ibid., 330.

29. Ibid., 332.

30. Ibid., 336.

30a. Ibid., 346-74.

31. Ibid., 367.

32. IRL, V, 263.

33. DEKABRISTY, II: Proza, Literaturnaia kritika (L. 1975), p. 361.

34. Karamzin, N.M. IZBRANNYE SOCHINENIIA V DVUKH TOMAKH (M-L. 1964). Blagoi, pp. 383-413; Gukovskii, pp. 494-524;IRL, V, 55-120 (G.A. Gukovskii; A. Ia Kucherov); IRR, pp. 67-83 (E.N. Kupreianova); Stender-Petersen, II, 20-49.

35. Karamzin, I, 79-601.

36. Ibid., 279.

37. Ibid., 463-67.

38. Ibid., 389.

39. The development of the "salon style" and of Karamzin's connection with it are the subjects of Chapter IV (pp. 148-88) of Professor Vinogradov's OCHERKI PO ISTORII RUSSKOGO LITERATURNOGO IAZYKA XVII-XIX VV. Vinogradov quotes Makarov's article, p. 179.

40. Karamzin, I, 623.

41. Ibid., 605-21.

42. Ibid., 622-60.

43. Ibid., 661-73.

44. Ibid., 670-71.

45. Ibid., 666.

46. Ibid., 666-67.

47. For a discussion of Karamzin and the Gothic novel, see Vatsuro, V.E, "Literaturno-filosofskaia problematika povesti Karamzina 'Ostrov Borngolm'," XVIII VEK, Sbornik 8 (L. 1969), pp. 190-209.

48. Karamzin, pp. 674-79.

49. See Privalova, E.M. "O sotrudnikakh zurnala 'Detskoe chtenie dlia serdtsa i razuma'," XVIII VEK, sbornik 6 (L. 1964), pp. 258-68.

50. See the article of Kulakova, E.M., "Esteticheskie vzgliady N.M. Karamzina," XVIII VEK, sbornik 6 (L. 1964), pp. 146-75.

51. Karamzin, I, 740-54.

52. Ibid., 283.

53. Ibid., 749.

54. Ibid., 749.

55. Ibid., 754.

56. Ibid., 755-82.

57. Ibid., 751.

58. Ibid., 772.

59. Ibid., 680-728.

60. Karamzin, N.M. ISTORIIA GOSUDARSTVA ROSSIISKOGO. I-VIII, 1818; IX, 1821; X-XI, 1824. SPb.

61. Karamzin, IZBRANNYE SOCHINENIIA, II, 120-22.

62. Ibid., 143-44.

63. This document has been edited by Richard Pipes: A MEMOIR ON ANCIENT AND MODERN RUSSIA: THE RUSSIAN TEXT (Cambridge, Mass., 1959) and MEM-OIR ON ANCIENT AND MODERN RUSSIA: A TRANSLATION AND ANALYSIS (Cambridge, Mass., 1959).

64. Karamzin, IZBRANNYE SOCHINENIIA, I, 65-66.

66. Ibid., 188-98. Karamzin's essay singles out pathetic and picturesque episodes in chronicle history which could serve as subjects for painters or sculptors, with emphasis on their psychological and emotional possibilities.

67. Ibid., II, 502-03.

68. Ibid., I, 641.

69. Cited by Tynianov, Iu. N., PUSHKIN I EGO SOVREMENNIKI (M. AN., 1969), p. 30.

ABBREVIATIONS

(These are the standard abbreviations listed in the latest MLA International
    Bibliography)

Aatseel	American Association of Teachers of Slavic and East European Languages
AR	Antioch Review
AUMLA	Journal of Australasian Universities Language and Literature Association
BNYPL	Bulletin of the New York Public Library
CASS	Canadian-American Slavic Studies [Formerly *CSS*]
CL	Comparative Literature
CLS	Comparative Literature Studies (U. of Ill.)
CSP	Canadian Slavonic Papers
CSS	Canadian Slavic Studies [Now *CASS*]
DA	Dissertation Abstracts
DAI	Dissertation Abstracts International [Supersedes *DA*]
ECLife	Eighteenth-Century Life
ECS	Eighteenth-Century Studies (U. of Calif. Davis)
ESl	Etudes slaves et est-Européennes
FI	Forum Italicum
FMLS	Forum for Modern Language Studies (U. of St. Andrews, Scotland)
GR	Germanic Review
GSlav	Germano-Slavica
HSS	Harvard Slavic Studies
IJSLP	International Journal of Slavic Linguistics and Poetics
ISS	Indiana Slavic Studies
JES	Journal of European Studies
JHI	Journal of the History of Ideas
M&L	Music and Letters (London)
MelbSS	Melbourne Slavonic Studies
MLR	Modern Language Review
MusQ	Musical Quarterly
NZSJ	New Zealand Slavonic Journal
OL	Orbis Litterarum
OPLLL	Occasional Papers in Language, Literature, and Linguistics

	(Ohio U.)
OSP	Oxford Slavonic Papers
PMLA	Publications of the Modern Language Association of America
PPNCFL	Proceedings of the Pacific Northwest Conference on Foreign Languages
RLC	Revue de Litterature Comparée
RLT	Russian Literature Triquarterly
RusL	Russian Literature
RusR	Russian Review
SB	Studies in Bibliography: Papers of the Bibliographical Society of the University of Virginia
SCB	South Central Bulletin
SEEJ	Slavic and East European Journal
SEER	Slavic and East European Review
SGECRN	Study Group of Eighteenth-Century Russia Newsletter
SlavR	Slavic Review (Seattle)
SPR	Slavistic Printings and Reprintings
SR	Sewanee Review
SSl	Scando-Slavica (Copenhagen)
SVEC	Studies on Voltaire and the Eighteenth Century
Thr	Theatre Research/Recherches Théâtrales
YWMLS	Year's Work in Modern Language Studies

BIBLIOGRAPHY

RUSSIAN LITERATURE OF THE EIGHTEENTH CENTURY

A. *Anthologies*

1. *The Bakchesarian Fountain and Other Poems by Various Authors.* Tr. W.D. Lewis. Philadelphia: Sherman, 1849. 72 pp.

2. Bates, Alfred. *The Drama: Its History, Literature, and Influence on Civilisation.* London: Athenian Society, 1903. Vol. 18: Russian Drama.

3. Bowra, Cecil Maurice. *A Second Book of Russian Verse.....* London: Macmillan, 1948. 153 pp. Reprinted: Westport, Conn.: Greenwood Press, 1971.

4. Bowring, John. *Specimens of the Russian Poets with Preliminary Remarks and Biographical Notices.* 2nd ed. London: Hunter, 1821. 239 pp.

5. Bowring, John. *Specimens of the Russian Poets.* Part two. London, Whittaker, 1823. 271 pp.

6. Coxwell, Charles Fillingham. *Russian Poems.* Intro. by D. Mirsky. London: Daniel, 1929. 306 pp.

7. Creekmore, Hubert. *A Little Treasury of World Poetry.* New York: Scribner, 1952. 904 pp.

8. Deacon, Olga. *Before the Iron Curtain. A Selection of Russian Verse.* Elms Court, Ilfracombe, Devon: Stockwell, 1951. 63 pp.

9. Gangulee, Nagendranath. *The Russian Horizon. An Anthology.* Foreword by H.G. Wells. London: Allen-Unwin, 1943. 278 pp.

10. Guerney, Bernard Guilbert. *The Portable Russian Reader.* New York: Viking, 1947. 658 pp.

11. Guerney, Bernard Guilbert. *A Treasury of Russian Literature.* New York: Vanguard, 1943. 1048 pp.

12. Noyes, George Rapall. *Masterpieces of the Russian Drama.* New York-London: Appleton, 1933. 902 pp.

13. Parr, Margaret S. Linn. *God and Other Poems.* Tr. J. Bowring. Boston: Badger, 1912. 96 pp.

14. Pollen, John. *Rhymes from Russian.* London: Kegan Paul, 1891. 118 pp.

15. Pollen, John. *Russian Songs and Lyrics.* London: East and West, 1917.

181 pp.

16. Pritchard, Francis Henry. *Great Essays of All Nations.* London: Harrap, 1929. 1017 pp.

17. Pritchard, Francis Henry. *The World's Best Essays: from Confucius to Mencken.* New York: Halcyon House, 1939. 1012 pp.

18. Reeve, Franklin D. *Anthology of Russian Plays.* Vol. I:1790-1890. New York. Reprinted as: *Nineteenth Century Russian Plays.* New York: Norton, 1973.

19. Roberts, Carl Eric Bechhofer, tr. *Five Russian Plays with One from Ukrainian.* London: Paul-Trench-Trübner, 1916. 173 pp.

20. Roberts, Carl Eric Bechhofer. *A Russian Anthology in English.....* London: Paul-Trench-Trübner, 1917. 288 pp.

21. Rudzinski, B.A. and Stella Gardiner. *Selections of Russian Poetry.* Introd. by Donald MacAlister. Glasgow: Blackie, 1918. 102 pp.

22. Segel, Harold B., comp. *The Literature of Eighteenth-Century Russia. An Anthology of Russian Literary Materials of the Age of Classicism and the Enlightenment from the Reign of Peter the Great (1689-1725) to the Reign of Alexander I (1801-1825).* Ed., tr., and with Introd. and Notes. 2 vols. New York: Dutton, 1967. 472; 448 pp. Review: Edgerton, W.B. "Recent Anthologies of Eighteenth-Century Russian Literature: A Review Article." *SEEJ* 12(1968):59-78.

23. Spector, Ivar. *The Golden Age of Russian Literature....* Caldwell, Idaho: Caxton Printers, 1943. 258 pp. (1st ed. 1939).

24. Spofford, Ainsworth Rand and Charles Gibbon. *The Library of Choice Literature.* Philadelphia: Gebbie, 1894. 10 vols. Vols. 5, 8.

25. Turner, Charles Edward. *Studies in Russian Literature.* London: Low-Marston-Searle-Rivington, 1882. 389 pp.

26. Underwood, Edna [Worthley]. *The Slav Anthology: Russian, Polish, Bohemian, Serbian, Croatian.* Portland, Me.: Mosher Press, 1931. 346 pp.

27. *The Warner Library. The World's Best Literature.* New York: Knickerbocker Press, 1917. 30 vols. Vol. 4.

28. Wells, Carolyn. *The World's Best Humor.* New York: Boni, 1931. 872 pp.

29. Wiener, Leo. *An Anthology of Russian Literature.* New York: Putnam, 1902-03. Vol. I. 447 pp. Vol. II. 500 pp. Reprinted: New York, Blom, Benjamin, 1967.

30. Wilson, Charles Thomas. *Russian Lyrics in English Verse.* London: Truebner, 1887. 244 pp.

31. Yarmolinsky, Avrahm. *A Treasury of Russian Verse.....* New York: Macmillan, 1949. 314 pp.

B.   *Bibliographical Materials*
American Bibliography of Russian and East European Studies. Bloomington,

Ind.: U. of Indiana Press, 1956———

Johnson, C.A. "Russian Studies: The Eighteenth Century." *YWMLS* 1964

Lewanski, Richard C. *The Literatures of the World in English Translation: A Bibliography.* Vol. II. Slavic Literatures. New York: Ungar, 1967. 630 pp.

Line, M.A. *A Bibliography of Russian Literature in English Translation, to 1900.* London: The Library Association, 1963. Reprinted: Totowa, N.J.: Rowman and Littlefield, 1972.

Nerhood, H.W. *To Russia and Return: An Annotated Bibliography of Travelers' Accounts of Russia from the Ninth Century to the Present.* Columbus: U. of Ohio Press, 1968. 367 pp.

Smith, G.S. "A Select Bibliography of Works on Eighteenth-Century Versification Published Outside the Soviet Union." *SGECRN* 1(1973):43-8.

C. *Collective Works*

1. *American Contributions to the Fifth International Congress of Slavists, Sofia, September 1963.* Vol. 2: Literary Contributions. The Hague: Mouton, 1963.

2. *American Contributions to the Fourth International Congress of Slavists.* The Hague: Mouton, 1958.

3. Auty, R., L.R. Lewitter, and A.P. Vlasto, eds. *Gorski vijenac: A Garland of Essays Offered to Professor Elizabeth Mary Hill.* Cambridge: Modern Humanities Research Assn., 1970. 321 pp.

4. Baer, J.T. and N.W. Ingham, eds. *Mnemozina. Studia litteraria russica in honorem Vsevolod Setchkarev.* München: Fink, 1974. 345 pp.

5. Black, J.L., ed. *Essays on Karamzin: Russian Man-of-Letters, Political Thinker, Historian, 1766-1826.* (SPR 309). The Hague: Mouton, 1975. 232 pp.

6. Bond, W.H., ed. *Eighteenth-Century Studies in Honor of Donald F. Hyde.* New York: Grolier Club, 1970. 424 pp.

7. Braun, Maximilian, Erwin Koschmieder, and Irmgard Mahnken, eds. *Slawistische Studien zum V. Internationalen Slawistenkongress in Sofia 1963.* (Opera Slavica 4). Göttingen: Wandenhoeck & Ruprecht, 1963.

8. Cross, Anthony Glenn, ed. *Russian Literature in the Age of Catherine the Great. A Collection of Essays.* Oxford: Meeuws, 1976. 229 pp.

9. Curtiss, J.S., ed. *Essays in Russian and Soviet History in Honor of Geroid Tanquery Robinson.* New York: Columbia U.P., 1963.

10. *Dutch Contributions to the Fourth International Congress of Slavists.* The Hague: Mouton, 1958.

11. Folejewski, Zbigniew, Edmund Heier, George Luckyj et al., eds. *Canadian Contributions to the Seventh International Congress of Slavists, Warsaw, August 21-27, 1973.* (SPR 285). The Hague: Mouton, 1973. 254 pp.

12. Garrard, J.G., ed. *The Eighteenth Century in Russia.* Oxford: Clarendon, 1973. 256 pp.

13. Gesemann, Wolfgang, Johannes Holthusen, Erwin Koschmieder, Ilse Kunert, Peter Rehder, and Erwin Wedel, eds. *Serta Slavica in memoriam Aloisii Schmaus.* München: R. Trofenik, 1971. 764 pp.

14. Harkins, William E., Olexa Horbatsch, and Jacob P. Hursky, eds. *Symbolae in Honorem Georgii Y Shevelov.* München: Logos, 1971. 506 pp.

15. Legters, L.H., ed. *Russia: Essays in History and Literature.* Leiden: Brill, 1972. 165 pp.

16. Pagliaro, Harold E., ed. *Racism in the Eighteenth Century.* (SEEC). Cleveland: Press of Case Western Reserve U., 1973. 468 pp.

17. Raeff, Marc, ed. *Catherine the Great: A Profile.* New York: Hill and Wang, 1972. 331 pp.

18. Terras, Victor, ed. *American Contributions to the Seventh International Congress of Slavists, Warsaw, August 21-27, 1973. Vol. 2: Literature and Folklore.* (SPR 296). The Hague: Mouton, 1973. 597 pp.

D. General Works

Alston, P.L. *Education and the State in Tsarist Russia.* Stanford: University Press, 1969. 322 pp.

Anderson, Matthew Smith. *Britain's Discovery of Russia 1553-1815.* New York: St. Martins, 1958. 243 pp.

Anderson, Matthew Smith. "Some British Influences on Russian Intellectual Life in the 18th Century." *SEER* 39(1960):148-63.

Arinshtein, Leonid M. "Pope in Russian Translations of the Eighteenth Century." *SB* 24:166-75.

Baehr, Stephen L. "The Masonic Component in Eighteenth-Century Russian Literature." In C-8: pp. 121-139.

Baehr, Stephen L. "The Utopian Mode in Eighteenth Century Russian Panegyric Poetry." (Ph.D., Columbia, 1972). *DAI* 36:2887A.

Barratt, G.R. "The Melancholy and the Wild: a note on Macpherson's Russian Success." In C-16, pp. 125-35.

Berkov, Pavel Naumovich. "English Plays in St. Petersburg in the 1760s and 1770s." *OSP* 8(1958):90-97.

Berman, M.H. (Heim, M.H.). "Trediakovskij, Sumarokov and Lomonosov as Translators of West European Literature." (Ph.D., Harvard, 1971).

Bida, C. "Shakespeare in Polish and Russian Classicism and Romanticism." *ESl* 6(1961):188-95.

Bischoff, I. "Madame Vigée Le Brun at the Court of Catherine the Great." *RusR* 24:(1965):30-45.

Brewster, Dorothy. *East-West Passage: A Study in Literary Relationships.* London: Allen, 1954. 328 pp. [pp. 20-33].

Bryner, C. "Moscow University, 1755-1955." *RusR* 14(1955):201-13.

Bucsela, J. "The Birth of Russian Syllabo-Tonic Versification." *SEEJ* 9

(1965):281-94.

Bucsela, John. "The Problems of Baroque in Russian Literature." *RusR* 31:260-71.

Burgess, M.A.S. "Fairs and Entertainers in 18th-Century Russia." *SEER* 38(1959):95-113.

Burgess, M.A.S. "The First Russian Actor-Manager and the Rise of Repertory in Russia during the Reign of the Empress Elizabeth Petrovna." In C-3; pp. 57-84.

Burgess, M.A.S. "Russian Public Theatre Audiences of the 18th and Early 19th Centuries." *SEER* 37(1958):160-83.

Burgess, M.A.S. "A Survey of the Stage in Russia from 1741 to 1783 with Special Reference to the Development of the Russian Theatre." (Ph.D., Cambridge, 1953).

Burgi, R. *A History of the Russian Hexameter.* Hamden, Conn.: Shoe String, 1954. 208 pp.

Čiževskij, D. *Comparative History of Slavic Literatures.* Vanderbilt: U.P., 1971. 225 pp.

Čiževskij, D. *History of Russian Literature: from the Eleventh Century to the End of the Baroque.* The Hague: Mouton, 1962. 451 pp.

Coleman, A.P. *Humor in the Russian Comedy from Catherine to Gogol.* New York: Columbia U.P., 1925. 94 pp.

Coleman, A.P. "Kotzebue and Russia." *GR* 5(1930):323-44.

Coleman, A.P. "The Siberian Exile of Kotzebue." *GR* 6(1931):244-55.

Cooper, B.F. "The History and Development of the Ode in Russia." (Ph.D., Cambridge, 1973).

Craven, K. "Laurence Sterne and Russia: Four Case Studies." (Ph.D., Columbia, 1967).

Cross, Anthony Glenn. "The English Garden and Russia: An Anonymous Identified." *SGECRN* 2(1974):25-29.

Cross, Anthony Glenn. "An Oxford Don in Catherine the Great's Russia." *JES* 1(1971):166-74.

Cross, Anthony Glenn. "Arcticus and *The Bee*." *OSP*, NS 2(1969):62-76.

Cross, Anthony Glenn. "British Freemasons in Russia during the Reign of Catherine the Great." *OSP*, NS 4(1971):43-72.

Cross, Anthony Glenn. "The British in Catherine's Russia." In C-12: 233-63.

Cross, Anthony Glenn. "Early English Specimens of the Russian Poets." *CASS* 9:449-62. [Disc. of the 1st tr. of Rus. poetry of the 18th and 19th cent. into English].

Cross, Anthony Glenn. *Russia under Western Eyes, 1517-1825.* New York: St. Martins, 1971. 400 pp.

Cross, Anthony Glenn. "The Russian Literary Scene in the Reign of Paul I." *CSS* 7(1973):39-51.

Dabars, Z.D. "The Simile in the Poetry of Sumarokov, Karamzin, and Derzhavin." (Ph.D., Indiana, 1971).

Dabars, Z.D. "The Simile in the Poetry of Sumarokov, Karamzin, and Derzhavin." *RLT* 7(1974):387-406.

Day, H.R. "Voltaire's Portrayal of Peter the Great." (Ph.D., Boston, 1971).

Drage, C.L. "The *Anacreontea* and 18th-Century Russian Poetry." *SEER* 41(1962):110-34.

Drage, C.L. "The Rhythmic Development of the Trochaic Tetrameter in Early Russian Syllabo-Tonic Poetry." *SEER* 39(1961):346-68.

Drage, C.L. "Trochaic Meters in Early Russian Syllabo-Tonic Poetry." *SEER* 38(1960):361-79.

Drage, C.L. "Trochaic Metres in Russian Syllabo-Tonic Poetry from Trediakovsky to Krylov." (M.A., London, 1959).

Duda, S.T. "The Theme of the Caucasus in Russian Literature of the XVIII-XIX Centuries." (Ph.D., Vanderbilt, 1971).

Eekman, Tom. *The Realm of Rime: A Study of Rime in the Poetry of the Slavs.* Hakkert (Amsterdam), 1974. 364 pp.

Findeizen, N. "The Earliest Russian Operas." *MusQ* July, 1933: 331-40.

Gesemann, Wolfgang. "Herder's Russia." *JHI* 26(1965):137-50.

Gibian, George J. "Shakespeare in Russia." (Ph.D., Harvard, 1951).

Gleason, Walter. "Political Ideals and Loyalties of Some Russian Writers of the Early 1760s." *SlavR* 34:560-75.

Glowacki-Prus, X. "A Brief Survey of Memoirs Written in Russian from Peter the Great to S.T. Aksakov." *NZSJ* 12(1974):10-26.

Goodliffe, J.D. "Some Comments on Narrative Prose Fiction in Eighteenth-Century Russian Literature, with Special Reference to Čulkov." *MelbSS* 5-6(1971):124-36. Abstract in C-14:447-49.

Gronicka, André von. "Early Russian Reaction to Goethe and His Work." *GR* 37(1963):137-50.

Gronicka, André von. *The Russian Image of Goethe: Goethe in Russian Literature of the First Half of the Nineteenth Century.* Philadelphia: U. of Penna. Press, 1966. 304 pp.

Hammond, K.G. "The Metrical and Rhythmical Development of the Russian Fable in the Eighteenth Century." (Ph.D., London, 1970).

Hans, N.A. "Dumaresq, Brown, and Some Early Educational Projects of Catherine II." *SEER* 40(1961):229-35.

Hans, N.A. "François Pierre Pictet: Secretary to Catherine II." *SEER* 36 (1958):481-91.

Hans, N.A. "The Moscow School of Mathematics and Navigation (1701)." *SEER* 29(1951):532-6.

Hans, N.A. "Polish Schools in Russia, 1772-1831." *SEER* 38(1960):391-414.

Hans, N.A. "Russian Students at Leyden in the Eighteenth Century." *SEER* 35(1957):551-62.

Hans, N.A. *The Russian Tradition in Education.* London: Routledge, 1963. 196 pp.

Harkins, William Edward. *Dictionary of Russian Literature.* New York:

Philosophical Library, 1956.

Hart, Pierre R. "Continuity and Change in the Russian Ode." In C-8, pp. 17-43.

Heim, M.H. "Two Approaches to Translation: Sumarokov vs Trediakovskij." In C-4:185-92.

Hollingsworth, B. "The Friendly Literary Society." *NZSJ*, NS 1(1974):12-41.

Houldsworth, H.F. "A Comparative Study of the Fable in France, Germany and Russia, with Special Reference to Krylov and La Fontaine." (M.A., Nottingham, 1955).

Jensen, K.B. and P.U. Møller. "Paraphrase and Style: A Stylistic Analysis of Trediakovskij's, Lomonosov's and Sumarokov's Paraphrases of the 143rd Psalm." *Scando-Slavica* 16(1970):57-73.

Jones, W. Gareth. "A Trojan Horse within the Walls of Classicism: Russian Classicism and the National Specific." In C-8:95-120.

Karlinsky, S. "Tallemant and the Beginning of the Novel in Russia." *CL* 3(1963):226-33.

Katz, M. "Russian Literary Ballads of the 1790s," *The Literary Ballad in Early 19th-Century Russian Literature* (Oxford, 1976), pp. 18-36.

Laserson, M.M. *The American Impact, Diplomatic and Ideological, on Russia 1784-1917.* New York: Macmillan, 1950. 441 pp.

Lavrin, Janko. *Russian Writers. Their Lives and Literature.* New York, 1954.

Lentin, A. "Introduction," in Bil'basov, V.A. *Didro v Peterburge.* Cambridge: U.P.; 1-27.

Lentin, A. "Voltaire and Peter the Great." *History Today* 18(1968):683-9.

Lewitter, L.R. "A Study of the Academic Drama in Russia and the Ukraine in the Seventeenth and Eighteenth Centuries, with Special Reference to its Polish Origins." (Ph.D., Cambridge, 1950).

Lincoln, W.B. "Western Culture Comes to Russia." *History Today* 20(1970): 677-85.

Loewenson, Leo. "E.G. von Berge, Translator of Milton and Russian Interpreter (1649-1722)." *SEER* 34:487-9.

Lojkine, A.K. "Molière in Russia in the XVIIIth Century." *AUMLA* 39 (1973):85-93.

McConnell, A. "Helvétius' Russian Pupils." *JHI* 34(1963):373-86.

McConnell, A. "The Origins of the Russian Intelligentsia." *SEER* 8:1-16.

McMillin, A. and C.L. Drage. "*Kuranty:* An Unpublished Russian Songbook of 1733." *OSP* 3(1970):1-31.

Maggs, Barbara Widenor. "China in the Literature of Eighteenth-Century Russia." *DAI* 34:5918A-20A (Illinois).

Maggs, Barbara Widenor. " 'The Jesuits in China': Views of an Eighteenth-Century Russian Observer." *ECS* 8:137-52.

Maggs, Barbara Widenor. "The Poetry of Eighteenth-Century Fireworks Display." *ECLife* 1:68-71.

Malnick, B. "David Garrick and the Russian Theatre." *MLR* 50(1955):173-5.

627

Malnick, B. "The Origin and Early History of the Theatre in Russia." *SEER* 19(1940):203-27.

Malnick, B. "The Theory and Practice of Russian Drama in the Early 19th Century." *SEER* 34(1955):10-33.

Manning, Clarence A. "A Russian Translation of *Paradise Lost.*" *Slavonic Review* 13:173-6.

Marcell, Noah. "Impact and Influence of Russian Literature upon German Writers in the Eighteenth and Beginning of the Nineteenth Centuries." *DAI* 31(1970):2392A (Illinois).

Markov, V. "Russian Poetry." In Preminger, A. *Encyclopedia of Poetry and Poetics.* Princeton: U.P., 1965. Pp. 728-9.

Marsden, Christopher. *Palmyra of the North: The First Days of St. Petersburg.* London: Faber, 1942. 280 pp.

Martynov, I.F. "English Literature and Eighteenth-Century Russian Reviewers." *OSP*, NS 4(1971):30-42.

Matthews, W.K. "English Influences in Russian Literature 1700-1830." (M.A., Manchester, 1923).

Menut, Albert D. "Russian Courtesy Literature in the Eighteenth Century." *Symposium* 3(1949):76-90.

Mirsky, Dmitrii S. *A History of Russian Literature. From the Earliest Times to the Death of Dostoevsky* (1881). Reprinted as: *A History of Russian Literature,* edited and abridged by Francis J. Whitfield. New York: Knopf, 1949. 518 pp.

Mohrenschildt, D. von. *Russia in the Life of Eighteenth-Century France.* New York: Columbia U.P., 1936. 325 pp.

Neuenschwander, D.B. "Themes in Russian Utopian Fiction: A Study in the Utopian Works of M.M. Shcherbatov, A. Ulybyshev, F.V. Bulgarin, and V.F. Odoevskij." (Ph.D., Syracuse, 1974).

Neuhäuser, Rudolf. "Periodization and Classification of Sentimental and Preromantic Trends in Russian Literature between 1750 and 1815." In C-11:11-39.

Neuhäuser, Rudolf. *Towards the Romantic Age: Essays on Sentimental and Romantic Literature in Russia.* The Hague: Nijhoff, 1974. 250 pp.

Okenfuss, M.J. "Education in Russia in the First Half of the Eighteenth Century." (Ph.D., Harvard, 1971).

Papmehl, K.A. *Freedom of Expression in Eighteenth-Century Russia.* The Hague: Nijhoff, 1971. 166 pp.

Papmehl, K.A. "Matthew Guthrie—The Forgotten Student of 18th Century Russia." *CSP* 11(1969):167-81.

Pitcher, H. "A Scottish View of Catherine's Russia: William Richardson's *Anecdotes of the Russian Empire* (1784)." *FMLS* 3(1967):236-51.

Putnam, Peter. *Seven Britons in Imperial Russia (1689-1812).* Princeton: U.P., 1952. 424 pp.

Raeff, Marc. "The Enlightenment in Russia and Russian Thought in the

Enlightenment." In C-12:25-47.

Raeff, Marc. "Filling the Gap between Radishchev and the Decembrists." *SlavR* 25:395-413.

Raeff, Marc. *Imperial Russia 1682-1825. The Coming of Age of Modern Russia.* New York: Knopf, 1971. 176 pp.

Raeff, Marc. *The Origins of the Russian Intelligentsia: The Eighteenth-Century Nobility.* New York: Harcourt, 1966. 248 pp.

Rogger, Hans. *National Consciousness in Eighteenth-Century Russia.* Cambridge, Mass.: Harvard U.P., 1960. 319 pp.

Rogger, Hans. "The Russian National Character: Some Eighteenth-Century Views." HSS 4(1957):17-34.

Ryu, In-Ho L. "Freemasonry under Catherine the Great: A Reinterpretation." (Ph.D., Harvard, 1967).

Ryu, In-Ho L. "Moscow Freemasons and the Rosicrucian Order. A Study in Organisation and Control." In C-12:198-232.

Seaman, G.R. "Folk-Song in Russian Opera of the 18th Century." *SEER* 41(1962):144-57.

Seaman, G.R. "The Influence of Folk-Song on Russian Opera up to the Time of Glinka." (Ph.D., Oxford, 1962).

Seaman, G.R. "The National Element in Early Russian Opera, 1779-1800." *M&L* 44(1961):252-62.

Seaman, G.R. "Russian Folk-Song in the Eighteenth Century." *M&L* 40 (1959):253-60.

Seaman, G.R. "Russian Opera before Glinka." In C-15:56-78.

Segel, Harold B. "Baroque and Rococo in Eighteenth-Century Russian Literature." *CSP* 15:556-65.

Segel, Harold B. "Classicism and Classical Antiquity in Eighteenth and Early Nineteenth-Century Russian Literature." In C-12:48-71.

Seidl, G. "History of Russian Journalism, 18th Century." (Ph.D., California, 1956).

Shatz, M.S. "The Noble Landowner in Russian Comic Operas of the Time of Catherine the Great: the Patriarchal Image." *CSS* 3(1969):22-38.

Silbajoris, Rimvydas. *Russian Versification: The Theories of Trediakovskij, Lomonosov, and Kantemir.* New York: Columbia U.P., 1968.

Simmons, Ernest James. *English Literature and Culture in Russia (1553-1840).* Cambridge, Mass.: Harvard U.P., 1935. 357 pp.

Simmons, J.S.G. "Samuel Johnson 'On the Banks of the Wolga.' " *OSP* 11 (1964):28-37.

Simmons, R.W. Jr. "Some Notes on Comparative Drama in the Seventeenth and Eighteenth Centuries: Russian, Polish, and German." *ThR* 2 (1964):13-17.

Slonim, Marc L'vovich. *The Epic of Russian Literature. From its Origins through Tolstoy.* New York: Oxford U.P., 1950. 367 pp.

Slonim, Marc L'vovich. *Russian Theatre from the Empire to the Soviets.*

New York: World, 1961. 354 pp.

Smith, G.S. "The Contribution of Glück and Paus to the Development of Russian Versification: The Evidence of Rhyme and Stanza Forms." *SEER* 51(1973):22-35.

Smith, G.S. "Sentimentalism and Pre-Romanticism as Terms and Concepts." In C-8:173-84.

Smith, I.H. "An English View of Russia in the Early Eighteenth Century." *CSS* 1(1967):276-83.

Steele, Eugene and David Welsh. "The *Commedia dell' arte* in Eighteenth-Century Poland and Russia." *FI:*409-17.

Stenbock-Fermor, E. "The Story of Van'ka Kain and its Ties with Russian Folklore." (Ph.D., Radcliffe, 1955).

Struve, Gleb. "Russian Eighteenth-Century Literature through Party-Colored Spectacles." *SEEJ* 15(1957):22-33.

Sullivan, J. and C.L. Drage. "Poems in an Unpublished Manuscript of the *Vinograd rossiiskii.*" *OSP*, NS 1(1968):27-48.

Tompkins, D.R. *The Russian Mind:* Vol. 1. *From Peter the Great through the Enlightenment.* Norman, Okla.: U. of Oklahoma Press, 1953. 302 pp.

Treadgold, D.W. *The West in Russia and China: Religious and Secular Thought in Modern Times.* 2 vols. Cambridge: U.P., 1973.

Tumins, V.A. "Enlightenment and Mysticism in Eighteenth-Century Russia." SVEC 58(1967):1671-88.

Tumins, V.A. "Voltaire and the Rise of Russian Drama." SVEC 27(1963): 1689-1701.

Turkevich, L.B. *Cervantes in Russia.* Princeton: U.P., 1950. 255 pp.

Unbegaun, Boris O. *Russian Versification.* Oxford: Clarendon, 1956. 164 pp.

Varneke, B.V. *History of the Russian Theatre (Seventeenth through Nineteenth Century).* New York: Macmillan, 1951. 459 pp.

Vickery, Walter N. " 'Mednyj vsadnik' and the Eighteenth-Century Heroic Ode." *ISS* 3(1963):140-62.

Vickery, Walter N. "On the Question of Emergence of the Dactylic Caesura in the Russian Eighteenth-Century Six-Foot Iamb." *IJSLP* 16(1973): 147-56.

Vorobiov, Nikolai S. "G.R. Derzhavin and His Age-Group." *Aatseel Bull.* 10: 72-73.

Waliszewski, K. *A History of Russian Literature.* New York & London: Appleton, 1900. 451 pp. Reprinted: New York: Kennikat, 1969.

Warner, E.A. "The Russian Folk-Theatre." (Ph.D., Edinburgh, 1970).

Welsh, D.J. "Metastasio's Reception in 18th Century Poland and Russia." *Italica* 41(1964):41-6.

Welsh, D.J. " 'Philosophers' and 'Alchemists' in Some Eighteenth-Century Russian Comedies." *SEER* 42(1964):149-58.

Welsh, D.J. "Satirical Themes in 18th-Century Russian Comedies." *SEER* 42(1964):403-14.

Whaples, M.K. "Eighteenth-Century Russian Opera in the Light of Soviet Scholarship." *ISS* 2(1958):113-34.

White, R.S. "The Development of Russian Prose in the Early Eighteenth Century." (Ph.D., Michigan, 1971).

Wilberger, Carolyn U. "Comrade Philosophe: Russia and the West in the Eighteenth Century." *PPNCFL* 26:65-8.

Wilberger, Carolyn Y. "Voltaire, Russia, and the Party of Civilization." *DAI* 33:1748A-49A (Cornell).

Wilson, Arthur. "Diderot in Russia, 1773-1774." In C-12:166-97.

Wilson, Francesca,M. *Russia through Foreign Eyes. 1553-1900.* London and New York: Longmans Green, 1955. 289 pp.

Wilson, Reuel K. *The Literary Travelogue: A Comparative Study with Special Relevance to Russian Literature from Fonvizin to Pushkin.* The Hague: Nijhoff, 1973. 136 pp.

Worth, Dean S. "On Eighteenth-Century Russian Rhyme." *RusL* 3(1972): 47-74.

Worth, G.H. "Thoughts on the Turning Point in the History of Literary Russian: The Eighteenth Century." *IJSLP* 13(1970):125-35.

Zenkovsky, Serge A. "Anthologies of Eighteenth-Century Russian Literature." *Aatseel Journ.* 13:79-82.

Zenkovsky, Serge A. *A History of Russian Philosophy.* Vol. I. New York: Columbia U.P., 1953. 465 pp.

E.   *Individual Authors*

ABLESIMOV

Translations in A 29.

BARKOV

Cross, Anthony Glenn. " 'The Notorious Barkov': An Annotated Bibliography." *SGECRN* 2(1974):41-52.

BOBROV

Translations in A 4, 13, 27.

BOGDANOVICH

Translations in A 3, 4, 13, 22, 24, 27, 29.

CATHERINE II

Cross, Anthony Glenn. "A Royal Blue-Stocking: Catherine the Great's Early Reputation in England as an Authoress." In C-3:85-99.

Gukovskii, G.A. "The Empress as Writer." In C-17:64-89.

Hilles, F.W. "Sir Joshua and the Empress Catherine." In C-6: 267-77.

Hyde, Harford Montgomery. *The Empress Catherine and Princess Dashkov.* London: Chapman and Hill, 1935. 282 pp.

Lentin, A. "Catherine the Great and Denis Diderot." *History Today* 22(1972):313-20.

Lentin, A. "Introduction," in *Voltaire and Catherine the Great: Selected Correspondence.* Cambridge: U.P., 1974. Pp. 4-32.

McConnell, A. "The Empress and Her Protégé: Catherine II and Radishchev." *Journal of Modern History* 36(1964):14-27.

Permenter, H.R. "The Personality and Cultural Interests of the Empress Catherine II as Revealed in Her Correspondence with Friedrich Melchior Grimm." (Ph.D., Texas, 1969).

Petschauer, P. "The Education and Development of an Enlightened Absolutist: the Youth of Catherine the Great, 1729-1762." (Ph.D., New York, 1969).

Schmurlo, E. "Catherine II and Radishchev." *SEER* 17(1939):618-22.

Simmons, Ernest J. "Catherine the Great and Shakespeare." *PMLA* 47(1932):790-806.

Translations in A 2, 10, 22, 25, 29.

CHULKOV

Garrard, John G. "Narrative Technique in Chulkov's *Prigozhaia povarikha.*" *SlavR* 27(1968):554-63.

Garrard, John G. "The Portrayal of Reality in the Prose Fiction of M.D. Chulkov." *SEER* 48(1970):16-26.

Garrard, John G. *Mikhail Chulkov: An Introduction to His Prose and His Verse.* The Hague: Mouton (SPR 116), 1970. Review: Rice, J.L. *SEEJ* 15(1971):495-501.

Titunik, I.R. "Mikhail Chulkov's 'Double-Talk' Narrative (*Skazka o rozhdenii taftianoi mushki*—The Tale of the Origin of the Taffeta Beauty Patch)." *CASS* 9:30-42.

Translation in A 22.

DASHKOVA

Babenko, Vickie. "Princess Dashkova's Nationalist Mission." OPLLL A 22 (May).

Lentin, A. "The Princess Dashkova." *History Today* 18(1968):823-26; 19(1969):18-24.

Longmire, R.A. "Princess Dashkova and the Cultural Life of 18th-Century Russia." (M.A., London, 1955).

Translation in A 29.

DERZHAVIN

Bailey, Leslie Francis. "Consonant Variance in Deržavin's Rhymes: A Preliminary Study." *DAI* 36:446A.

Clardy, J.V. *G.R. Derzhavin: A Political Biography.* The Hague/Paris: Mouton, 1967. Review: Cross, A.G. *SEER* 46(1968):498-500.

Harris, J.G. "The Creative Imagination in Evolution: A Stylistic Analysis of G.R. Derzhavin's Panegyric and Meditative Odes (1774-1794)." (Ph.D., Columbia, 1969).

Hart, Pierre R. "Derzavin's Ode *God* and the Great Chain of Being." *SEEJ* 14(1970):1-10.

Hart, Pierre R. "Life against Death in Deržavin's Odes." *CSS* 5(1971): 22-34.

Hart, Pierre R. "Aspects of the *Anacreontea* in Deržavin's Verse." *SEEJ* 17(1973):375-89.

Hart, Pierre R. "Mirza and Mistress in Derzhavin's 'Felitsa' Poetry." *SlavR* 31(1972):583-91.

Hart, Pierre R. "Frederick II's *Poesies diverses* as a Source for Gavriil Derzhavin's Early Odes." *GSlav* 2(1973):19-27.

Harris, J.A. "In Defence of Deržavin's Plays." *NZSJ* 2:1-15.

Harvie, J.A. "The River of Time." *NZSJ* 1969:54-66.

Hedrick, H.R. "The Poetry of Deržavin." (Ph.D., Princeton, 1966). *DA* 27:2132A.

Shaw, Sandra. "The Quest for 'pokoj' in Derzhavin's Poetry, with Some Reference to Horace." *NZSJ* 11(Win.):133-44.

Springer, A.R. "The Public Career and Political Views of G.R. Derzhavin." (Ph.D., California, 1971).

Wortman, R. "Gavrila Romanovich Derzhavin and His *Zapiski.*" In G.R. Derzhavin, *Zapiski.* Cambridge: U.P., 1973. Pp. 1-8.

Translations in A 1, 4, 5, 6, 8, 11, 13, 14, 15, 22, 24, 28, 31 and *One Hundred Choice Selections.* Ed. Phineas Garrett. Philadelphia: Penn Publishing Co., 1913. No 4, 65-68.

DMITRIEV, I.I.

Cross, Anthony Glenn. "Dmitriev and Gessner." *SGECRN* 2(1974): 22-9.

Cross, Anthony Glenn. "The Reluctant Memoirist," in I.I. Dmitriev. *Vzgliad na moiu zhizn'.* Cambridge: U.P., 1974. Pp. i-xii.

Swidzinska, Halina. "I.I. Dmitriev: A Classicist and a Sentimentalist in the Context of the World and Russian Fable." (Ph.D., Pittsburgh, 1972). *DAI* 33:1150A.

Translations in A-1, 4, 5, 11, 13, 27, 29, 30.

EMIN, F.A.

Budgen, David E. "Fedor Emin and the Beginnings of the Russian Novel." In C-8:67-94.

Garretson, Deborah Anne. "Compound Words in the Prose of F.A. Emin: An Historical Study." *DAI* 36:2176A.

Translation in A-22.

FONVIZIN, D.I.

Bryner, C. "Denis Fon Vizin, Patriot." *Slavia* 14(1939):11-18.

Kantor, Marvin. "Fonvizin and Holberg: A Comparison of *The Brigadier* and *Jean de France.*" *CASS* 7:475-84.

Translations in A-2, 10, 12, 18, 20, 23, 25, 29.

KANTEMIR

Boss, V.J. "Kantemir and Rolli-Milton's 'Il Paradiso Perduto.'" *SlavR* 22(1962):441-55.

633

Evans, R.J.M. "Antiokh Kantemir and His First Biographer and Translator." *SEER* 37(1958):184-95.

Evans, R.J.M. "Antiokh Kantemir and His German Translators." *SEER* 36(1957):150-8.

Evans, R.J.M. "Antiokh Kantemir: A Study of His Literary, Political and Social Life in England, 1732-8." (Ph.D., London, 1960).

Evans, R.J.M. "Kantemir as a Westerniser in Russian Eighteenth-Century Literature." (M.A., London, 1956).

Redson, David B. "Kantemir and His Translations." (Ph.D., Vanderbilt, 1973). *DAI* 34:1931A.

Schroeder, Hildegard. "Impossibilia." In C-7:359-78.

Silbajoris, Rimvydas. "Rhythm and Meaning in Kantemir's 'Letter to Prince Nikita Jur'evič Trubeckoj.'" *SEEJ* 16:163-72.

Translations in A-6, 22, 25, 29; in *Slavonic Review* xxi 56(1942-43): 1-5.

KAPNIST

Edgerton, William B. "Laying a Legend to Rest: The Poet Kapnist and Ukraino-German Intrigue." *SlavR* 30:551-59.

Edgerton, William B. "A Textological Puzzle in Kapnist's 'Ode on Slavery.'" In C-13:435-44.

Swoboda, A. "Review of Ohlobyn, O. *Lyudy staroyi Ukrayiny.* München, 1959. In *SEER* 61(1962):271-4.

Translations in A-3, 5, 26, 29.

KARAMZIN

Anderson, Roger B. "Evolving Narrative in the Prose of N.M. Karamzin." *DA* 28:5042A (Michigan).

Anderson, Roger B. "Karamzin's *Bornholm Island:* Its Narrator and Its Meaning." *OL* 28:204-15.

Anderson, Roger B. "Karamzin's Concept of Linguistic 'Cosmopolitanism' in Russian Literature." Studies by Members of *SCMLA* 31(1971):168-70.

Anderson, Roger B. " Karamzin's *Letters of a Russian Traveler:* An Education in Western Sentimentalism." In C-5:22-39.

Anderson, Roger B. *N.M. Karamzin's Prose. The Teller in the Tale: A Study in Narrative Technique.* Houston, Tex.: 1974.

Anderson, Roger B. "The 'Split Personality' of the Narrator in N.M. Karamzin's *Pis'ma russkogo puteshestvennika:* A Textual Analysis." *ESl* 13(1968):20-31.

Barratt, Glynn, R. "James Thomson in Russia: The Changing of *The Seasons.*" CLS 12:367-73.

Black, J.L. "History in Politics: Karamzin's *Istoriia* as an Ideological Catalyst in Russian Society." *Laurentian University Review:* 1,2 (1968):106-13.

Black, J.L. "Nicholas Karamzin's Scheme for Russian History." In

Eastern Europe: Historical Essays. Toronto, 1969: pp. 18-33.

Black, J.L. "N.M. Karamzin, Napoleon, and the Notion of Defensive War in Russian History." *CSP* 12(1970):30-46.

Black, J.L. "The *Primečanija:* Karamzin as a 'Scientific' Historian of Russia." In C-5:127-47.

Black, J.L. "The Soviets and the Anniversary of N.M. Karamzin." *The New Review: A Journal of East-European History* 8, 3(1968): 139-47.

Cross, Anthony Glenn. "Karamzin and England." *SEER* 43(1964):91-114.

Cross, Anthony Glenn. "Karamzin in English: A Review Article." *CASS* 3(1969):716-27.

Cross, Anthony Glenn. "Karamzin's First Short Story?" In C-15:38-55.

Cross, Anthony Glenn. "Karamzin Studies." *SEER* 45(1967):1-11.

Cross, Anthony Glenn. "Karamzin's Versions of the Idyll." In C-5:75-90.

Cross, Anthony Glenn. "N.M. Karamzin and Barthélemy's *Voyage du jeune Anacharsis.*" *MLR* 61(1966):467-72.

Cross, Anthony Glenn. *N.M. Karamzin: A Study of His Literary Career 1783-1803.* Carbondale, Ill.: 1971.

Cross, Anthony Glenn. "N.M. Karamzin's *Messenger of Europe (Vestnik Yevropy),* 1802-3." *FMLS* 5(1969):1-25.

Cross, Anthony Glenn. "Problems of Form and Literary Influence in the Poetry of Karamzin." *SlavR* 27(1968):32-48.

Davidson, D.E. "N.M. Karamzin and German Literature: Antecedents of Russian Romanticism." (Ph.D., Harvard, 1972).

Davidson, D.E. "N.M. Karamzin and the New Critical Vocabulary: Toward a Semantic History of the Term Romantic in Russia." In C-4:88-94.

Dewey, H.W. "Sentimentalism in the Historical Writings of N.M. Karamzin." In C-2:41-50.

Garrard, J.G. "Karamzin in Recent Soviet Criticism: A Review Article." *SEEJ* 11(1967):464-72.

Garrard, J.G. "Karamzin, Mme de Staël, and the Russian Romantics." In C-18:221-47.

Garrard, John G. "Poor Erast, or Point of View in Karamzin." In C-5:40-55.

Karamzin, N.M. *Letters of a Russian Traveler.* Translated and abridged by Florence Jonas. Introduction by Leon Stilman. New York: Columbia U.P., 1957.

Karamzin, N.M. *A Memoir on Ancient and Modern Russia.* Trans. Richard Pipes. Cambridge, Mass.: Harvard U.P., 1959. 266 pp.

Karamzin, N.M. *Russian Tales.* Trans. J. Elrington. London: Sidney, 1803. 262 pp.

Karamzin, N.M. *The Selected Prose of N.M. Karamzin*. Tr. Henry M. Nebel. Evanston: U. of Ill. Press, 1969. Review: Rice, J.L. *SEEJ* 14(1970):384-8.

Karamzin, N.M. *Travels from Moscow through Germany, Switzerland, France, and England*. Trans. A. Feldborg. London: Badcock, 1803.

Kisljagina, L.G. "The Question of the Development of N.M. Karamzin's Social Political Views in the Nineties of the Eighteenth Century: N.M. Karamzin and the Great French Bourgeois Revolution." In C-5:91-104.

McGrew, R.E. "Notes on the Princely Role in Karamzin's *Istorija Gosudarstva Rossijskago*." *SlavR* 18(1959):12-24.

Mocha, F. "The Karamzin-Lelewel Controversy." *SlavR* 31(1972): 592-610.

Nebel, Henry M., Jr. *Karamzin: A Russian Sentimentalist*. The Hague: Mouton, 1967.

Neuhäuser, Rudolf. "Karamzin's Spiritual Crisis of 1793 and 1794." In C-5:56-74.

Pipes, Richard. "Karamzin's Conception of the Monarchy." HSS 4 (1957):35-58; in C-5:105-26.

Rothe, Hans. "Karamzin and His Heritage: History of a Legend." In C-5:148-90.

Translations in A-3, 4, 5, 6, 20, 21, 22, 24, 26, 29.

KHEMNITSER

Translations in A-4, 22, 26, 28, 29; in *Slavonic Review* xx(1941): 85-87.

KHERASKOV

Green, Michael A. "Mixail Xeraskov and His Contribution to the Eighteenth-Century Russian Theater." (Ph.D., U.C.L.A., 1973). *DAI* 34:771A-72A.

Vlasto, A.P. "M.M. Kheraskov: A Study in the Intellectual Life of the Age of Catherine the Great." (Ph.D., Cambridge, 1952).

Vlasto, A.P. "A Noble Failure—Kheraskov's *Vladimir Vozrozhdyonny*." In C-3:276-89.

Translations in A-22, 29.

KNIAZHNIN

Translations in A-22, 29.

KOMAROV

Titunik, I.R. "Matvej Komarov's *Van'ka Kain* and Eighteenth-Century Russian Prose Fiction." *SEEJ* 18:351-66.

KOSTROV

Worth, Dean S. "Remarks on Eighteenth-Century Russian Rhyme (Kostrov's translation of the *Iliad*)." In Jakobsen, Roman et al. *Slavic Poetics*. The Hague and Paris, 1973. Pp. 525-30.

Translations in A-4, 29.

KRYLOV

Reve, Karel van het. "The Silence of Krylov." In C-10:131-7.

Stepanov, Nikolay. *Ivan Krylov.* New York: Twayne, 1973. 174 pp.

LOMONOSOV

Bucsela, John. "Lomonosov's Literary Debut." *SEEJ* 11(1967):405-22.

Bucsela, John. "The Role of Lomonosov in the Development of Russian Literary Style." (Ph.D., Wisconsin, 1963). *DA* 24:2458-59.

Huntington, W.C. "Michael Lomonosov and Benjamin Franklin: Two Self-Made Men of the Eighteenth Century." *RusR* 18(1959):294-306.

Johnson, C.A. "Lomonosov's Dedication to His *Russian Grammar.*" *SlavR* 23(1964):328-32.

Johnston, Robert. " 'An Original Champion of Enlightenment': M.V. Lomonosov and Russian Education in the 18th Century." In C-14:373-94.

Jones, D.N. "M.V. Lomonosov: The Formative Years, 1711-1742." (Ph.D., North Carolina, 1969).

Kudryavtsev, B.B. *The Life and Work of Mikhail Vasilyevich Lomonosov.* Moscow: Foreign Language Publishing House, 1954.

Lomonosov, M.V. *A Chronological Abridgement of Russian History.* Trans. J.G.A.F. London: Snelling, 1767.

Martin, Amanda. "Lomonosov's Rhetoric." (Ph.D., New York, 1974). *DAI* 35:4438A.

Menshutkin, B.N. *Russia's Lomonosov: Chemist, Courtier, Physicist, Poet.* Princeton: U.P. 1952.

Smith, M.N. "Old Russian Literature—Michael Vasilievich Lomonosov (1711-1765)." *SCB* 28(1968):126-28.

Vasetsky, G. *Lomonosov's Philosophy.* Moscow: Foreign Language Publishing House, 1968.

Translations in A-3, 4, 5, 6, 10, 13, 22, 24, 25, 26, 29.

LOPUKHIN

Lipski, A. "A Russian Mystic Faces the Age of Rationalism and Revolution: Thought and Activity of Ivan Vladimirovich Lopukhin." *Church History* 36(1967):1-19.

LUKIN

McCormick, P. Andrew. "The Critical Ideas of Vladimir Lukin." (Ph.D., Georgetown, 1973). *DAI* 34(1973):2572A.

McLean, H. "The Adventures of an English Comedy in Eighteenth-Century Russia: Dodsley's *Toy Shop* and Lukin's *Scepetil'nik.*" In C-1:201-12.

MAIKOV, V.I.

Curtis, J.M. "Vasilij Majkov, An Eighteenth-Century Russian Poet." (Ph.D., Columbia, 1968). *DA* 29:3130A-31A.

637

Unbegaun, Boris O. "Metre and Language: Vasilij Majkov's *Arkas.*" In Jakobsen, Roman et al. *Slavic Poetics.* The Hague and Paris, 1973. Pp. 477-80.

Translations in A-22, 29.

NELEDINSKY-MELETSKY

Translations in A-1, 4, 26, 29.

NIKITIN, V.N.

Barratt, G.R.V. "Vasily Nikitin: A Note on an Eighteenth-Century Oxonian." *ECS* 8(1974):75-99.

NOVIKOV

Jones, W. Gareth. "The Closure of Novikov's *Truten'.*" *SEER* 50 (1972):107-11.

Jones, W. Gareth. "Novikov's Naturalized *Spectator.*" In C-12:249-65.

Jones, W, Gareth. "The Year of Novikov's Birth." *SGECRN* 2(1974): 30-32.

McArthur, G.H. "The Novikov Circle in Moscow, 1779-1792." (Ph.D., Rochester, 1968).

Translations in A-10, 16, 22.

PETROV, V.P.

Translations in A-5, 29.

POSOSHKOV

Lewitter, L.R. "Ivan Tikhomirovich Pososhkov (1652-1726) and 'The Spirit of Capitalism.' " *SEER* 51(1973):524-53.

O'Brien, B. "Ivan Pososhkov: Russian Critic of Mercantilist Principles." *SlavR* 14(1955):503-11.

Papmehl, K.A. "Pososhkov as a Thinker." *ESl* 6(1961):80-7.

Translation in A-29.

PROKOPOVICH

Cracraft, J. "Feofan Prokopovich." In C-12:75-105.

Translations in A-22, 29.

RADISHCHEV

Barratt, G.R. "A Note on Radishchev and Pugačovščina." *ESl* 18(1973):66-78.

Beck, L.N. "Pennsylvania and an Early Russian Radical." *Pennsylvania Magazine of History and Biography* 75(1951):193-6.

Clardy, Jesse V. *The Philosophical Ideas of Alexander Radishchev.* New York: Astra Books, 1964.

Clardy, Jesse V. "Radishchev's Notes on the Geography of Siberia." *RusR* 21(1962):362-9.

Evgeniev, Boris Sergcevich. *Alexander Radishchev. A Russian Humanist of the 18th Century.* London & New York: Hutchinson & Co., 1946. 52 pp.

Harvie, J.A. "A Russian View of Immortality." *Religious Studies* 10 (1974):479-85.

Hecht, D. "Alexander Radishchev: Pioneer Russian Abolitionist." *American Review on the Soviet Union* 7(1946):45-50.

Kochan, L. "Alexander Radishchev, the First of the Repentant Nobles." *History Today* 14 (1964): 489-96.

Lang, David M. "Alexander Nikolaevich Radishchev and His Contacts with French and German Thinkers." (Ph.D., Cambridge, 1950).

Lang, David M. *The First Russian Radical. Alexander Radishchev 1749-1802.* London: Allen and Unwin, 1959.

Lang, David M. "Radishchev and Catherine II: New Gleanings from Old Archives." In C-9:20-33.

Lang, David M. "Radishchev and the Legislative Commission of Alexander I." *SlavR* 6(1947):11-24.

Lang, David M. "Radishchev and Sterne. An Episode in Russian Sentimentalism." *RLC* 21(1947):254-60.

Lang, David M. "Some Western Sources of Radishchev's Thought." *Revue des études slaves* 25(1949):73-86.

Laserson, M.M. "Alexander Radishchev—An Early Admirer of America." *RusR* 9(1950):179-86.

McConnell, A. "Abbé Raynal and a Russian Philosophe." *Jahrbücher für Geschichte Osteuropas* 12(1964):499-512.

McConnell, A. "Pushkin's Literary Gamble." *SlavR* 6(1960):577-93.

McConnell, A. "Radishchev's Political Thought." *SlavR* 4(1958):439-53.

McConnell, A. "Rousseau and Radishchev." *SEEJ* 8(1964):253-72.

McConnell, Allen. *A Russian Philosophe: Alexander Radishchev, 1749-1802.* The Hague: Nijhoff, 1964.

McConnell, A. "Soviet Images of Radishchev's *Journey from St. Petersburg to Moscow.*" *SEEJ* 7(1963):9-17.

McGrew, R. "The Russian Intelligentsia from Radishchev to Pasternak." *AR* 23(1963):425-37.

Page, Tanya. "Radishchev's Polemic against Sentimentalism in the Cause of Eighteenth-Century Utilitarianism." In C-8:141-172.

Page, Tanya. "The Spiritual Conflict of A.N. Radiscev (1749-1802)." (Ph.D., Columbia, 1973). *DAI* 35:4448A.

"Alexander Radishchev," *The Critical Prose of Alexander Pushkin,* trans. C. Proffer (Bloomington, 1969): 173-82.

Radishchev, A.N. *A Journey from St. Petersburg to Moscow.* Trans. Leo Weiner. Ed. R.P. Thaler. Cambridge: Harvard, 1958. 286 pp.

Thaler, R.P. "Catherine II's Reaction to Radishchev." *ESl* 2(1957): 154-60.

Thaler, R.P. "The French Tutor in Radishchev and Pushkin." *RusR* 13(1954):210-12.

Thaler, R.P. "Radishchev, Britain, and America." HSS 4(1957):59-75.

Translations in A-3, 7, 22, 29.

SHCHERBATOV

Afferica, J.M. "The Political and Social Thought of Prince M.M. Shcherbatov (1733-1790)." (Ph.D., Harvard, 1967).

Lentin, A. "Introduction," in M.M. Shcherbatov. *On the Corruption of Morals in Russia.* Cambridge: U.P., 1969. Pp. 1-102.

Neuenschwander, Dennis Bramwell. "Themes in Russian Utopian Fiction: A Study of the Utopian Works of M.M. Shcherbatov, A. Ulybyshev, F.V. Bulgarin, and V.F. Odoevskij." *DAI* 36: 263-67.

Raeff, Marc. "State and Nobility in the Ideology of M.M. Shcherbatov." *SlavR* 19(1960):363-79.

Translation in A-29.

SUMAROKOV

Dabars, Zita D. "The Simile in the Poetry of Sumarokov, Karamzin, and Derzhavin." *RLT* 7(1973):389-406.

Lang, David M. "Sumarokov's 'Hamlet.' A Misjudged Russian Tragedy of the 18th Century." *MLR* 43(1948):67-72.

Lang, David M. "Boileau and Sumarokov. The Manifesto of Russian Classicists." *MLR* 43(1948):500-6.

Sumarokov, A.P. *Selected Tragedies of A.P. Sumarokov.* Trans. Richard and Raymond Fortune, intro. J. Fizer. Evanston: U. of Illinois Press, 1970.

Translations in A-2, 6, 9, 22, 25, 29.

TATISHCHEV

Daniels, R.L. "V.N. Tatishchev and the Succession Crisis of 1730." *SEER* 49(1971):550-9.

Daniels, R.L. *V.N. Tatishchev, Guardian of the Petrine Revolution.* Philadelphia, 1973.

Feinstein, S.C. "V.N. Tatishchev and the Development of the Concept of State Service in Petrine Russia and Post-Petrine Russia." (Ph.D., New York, 1971).

Znayenko, M.T. "Tatiščev's Treatment of Slavic Mythology." (Ph.D., Columbia, 1973).

Translation in A-29.

TREDIAKOVSKY

Jensen, Kjeld B. and Peter U. Møller. "Paraphrase and Style: A Stylistic Analysis of Trediakovskij's, Lomonosov's, and Sumarokov's Paraphrases of the 143rd Psalm." *SSl* 16(1970):57-73.

Rice, J.L. "Trediakovsky and the Russian Poetic Genres 1730-1760: Studies in the History of Eighteenth-Century Russian Literature." (Ph.D., Chicago, 1965).

Translations in A-22, 29.

643

649

654

655

656

658